ROLLING WITH THE STONES

ROLLING
WITH THE
STONES

Bill Wyman

with Richard Havers

DK Publishing

**LONDON, NEW YORK, MUNICH,
MELBOURNE, AND DELHI**

*For Brian, Charlie, Keith, Mick, Mick T, Stu, Woody and
the millions of fans who made it all so memorable*

Art Director Richard Evans
Senior Designer Thomas Keenes
Design Victoria Clark, Phil Gamble
DTP/Design Steven Laurie, Pamela Shiels, Sophie Young
Design Assistant Rachael Smith

Managing Editor Jake Woodward
Senior Editor and Project Manager Victoria Heyworth-Dunne
Senior Editor and Additional Research Lucian Randall
Editorial Consultant Kingsley Abbott

Picture Research Maria Gibbs
Photography Trish Gant
Production Manager Sarah Coltman
Production Controller Wendy Penn
Project Assistant Michelle Crane
Jacket Design Neal Cobourne
Jacket Editor Beth Apple
Index Janet Smy

Editorial Direction Andrew Heritage

First American Edition, 2002
02 03 04 05 10 9 8 7 6 5 4 3 2 1

Published in the United States by
DK Publishing, Inc.
375 Hudson Street
New York, New York 10014

Library of Congress Cataloging-in-Publication Data
Wyman, Bill
 Rolling with the Stones / Bill Wyman, Richard Havers
  p. cm.
 Includes discography (p.) and index.
ISBN 0-7894-8967-8
 1. Rolling Stones. 2. Rock musicians–England–Biography.
 I. Havers, Richard. II. Title

ML421.R64 W95 2002
782.4166'092'2–dc21
[B]
                                    2002073311

Color reproduction by GRB Editrice s.r.l., Italy
Printed and bound in Italy by Graphicom
See our complete product line at www.dk.com

Contents

Passages or pages marked with an ❛❜ or ❛commentary❜ represent additional information providing the reader with a fuller understanding of the context of the narrative.

Foreword

Photograph by Mary McCartney Donald

'IF YOU KNOW FROM WHENCE YOU CAME, THERE IS REALLY NO LIMIT TO WHERE YOU CAN GO.'

JAMES BALDWIN

I met the black American novelist James Baldwin when I moved to France in the 1970s. He lived in St Paul de Vence and we often had dinner together and talked of many things, especially music. His words are fundamental to what this book is about – history. I have always understood where I came from and am proud of what I achieved. I wanted to explain more fully where the Rolling Stones came from, how we got together and how we developed through some of the most changing times in history.

In 1966, Brian Jones described me in an interview as 'rather matter of fact', and I have to say that the facts have always mattered to me. I wanted to tell the band's story from an historical viewpoint, because so much that has been written about the Stones skirts the truth, embellishes half-truths or, in some cases, tells total untruths.

Being a member of the Rolling Stones has defined the greater part of my adult life. I have been privileged and fortunate enough to count Brian, Charlie, Keith, Mick, Mick Taylor, Stu and Woody as friends and colleagues. The Stones have always been like a family, one in which there is both strife and great times. As a band, I have always felt that we were greater than the sum of our parts. But it is also true that at times individuals have contributed more than others.

Mick has shouldered the responsibilities of taking care of business very effectively and at the same time he is, without doubt, the greatest front man in rock. On a personal level, Mick has been very caring and supportive; when times got rough he came through. Keith has been the epitome of guitar rock. He has defined the image and he has been one of the great innovators. While I have seen less of Keith than any of the others in recent years – as he lives in America – he will always have a special place in my heart. Charlie, for over thirty years, was my 'other half'. He has been a brilliant guy to play with and he has also been the very best kind of friend. Woody is a one-off, a wonderful guy, and I miss his sense of humour both on and off the road. Although Mick Taylor was in the band for less time than anyone else, he is a fantastic guitar player who, in recent years, has played on some of my solo albums. My memories of Brian and Stu remain with me and I have said how much they both meant to me in this book. All in all, it was our differences that made us. It was the chemistry within the band that created the magic that made the music, which in the end is what the Stones are all about.

The Stones have an extended family made up of hundreds of people who have worked for the organisation over the years; some have contributed over a short period, others over a long time. All, in their own way, have provided great help. One person whom I want to thank and offer my own tribute to is Andrew Oldham. Without Andrew we would have been a different band, and things would not have worked out the way they did. In those early years Andrew helped to define us, he had the insight to carve out our niche.

Being in the Stones is like living in a goldfish bowl, everyone is looking in on you and it is sometimes a little difficult to see the big picture. I asked Richard to write some commentary of his own to add perspective and objectivity to the book. In particular, his outside take on our recordings and tours provides a more balanced view than I would probably be able to give.

I am very proud of having been in the Rolling Stones and I wanted to share with you, not just my memories, but also some of what I have collected over the years. When I started to collect things, it was to show my little boy Stephen, who is now bigger than I am, that his father had spent a couple of years in a pop group; this 'couple', of course, turned into thirty one. I hope this book will let you share in some of what made them so memorable.

Thank you

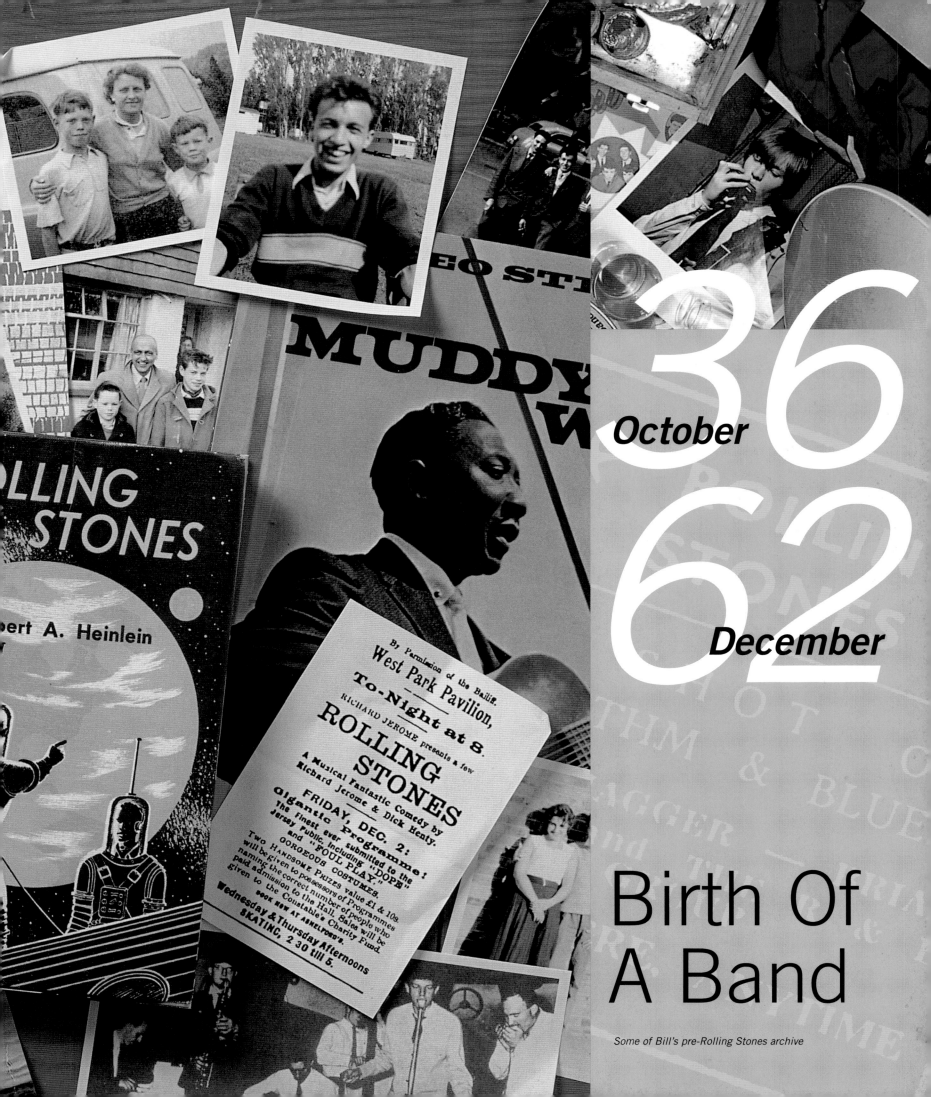

Birth Of A Band

Some of Bill's pre-Rolling Stones archive

Birth Of A Band

Where to begin? Well, I could start with myself, as I'm the oldest, or possibly Keith, the youngest of the original Rolling Stones. But I think it should be Brian, because we were his brainchild and it was Brian who named us. He was the driving force behind the band in the early days. Brian was the original Rolling Stone.

Our parents were born around the time of the Great War (1914–1918). We came from very different backgrounds, which was unusual for a band that emerged during the beat boom of the early 1960s. But, then again, we were always different from other groups.

LEWIS BRIAN HOPKIN JONES was born at the Park Nursing Home in Cheltenham, Gloucestershire, into a middle-class family on Saturday 28 February, 1942. He was of Welsh descent. His father, Lewis Blount Jones, was born to two teachers from Pencoed near Bridgend and studied at Leeds University, where he got a BSc in Engineering.

In Wales in 1938, he married Louisa Beatrice Simmonds, whose father was a master builder and organist at a church near Cardiff. The couple moved to Rosemead, Eldorado Road, in Cheltenham the following year, where they lived when their son was born. Louisa taught piano and Jones senior was an aeronautical engineer with the Dowty Group, but he shared his wife's interest in music. He dabbled with the piano, played the organ and led the choir at their local church. Brian's sister Pamela died in 1943, aged two, from leukaemia. A second sister, Barbara, was born in 1946.

Ian Stewart aged five

'Stu'

But for Andrew Oldham, our manager, there would have been one more Rolling Stone, because originally there were six of us. The second person to join Brian was Ian AR Stewart. His mother was Annie Black, whose family owned a farm called Kirk Latch in Pittenweem, East Neuk, Fife. Annie

Brian aged three

married an architect named John Stewart and moved to Sutton in Surrey, which was where Ian was conceived. She was at the farm when Stu was born on 18 July, 1938 and then the family returned to Sutton. Kirk Latch Farm was eventually taken over by Annie's sister and husband.

John Stewart spent his war years in the army, using his architectual skills to design barracks. It wasn't until well after the war ended, some 12 years after Ian's birth, that the couple went on to have their second son, Roy.

Michael Philip Jagger

Next to join the band were Mick and Keith. Their togetherness was evident even at birth, born in the same hospital, just five months apart. Michael Philip Jagger was born on Monday 26 July, 1943, at Livingstone Hospital in Dartford, Kent, and his brother, Christopher Edward, followed in 1947. Their mother, Eva Ensley Mary Scutts, was Australian, born 6 April, 1913, but she preferred to be thought of as English. Her family moved to England when she was four years old, eventually settling in Northfleet, Kent. A week younger than Eva, her future husband, Basil Fanshawe Jagger, was born in Greenfield in Lancashire. Basil (everyone called him Joe) came from a strict non-drinking Baptist family. He attended Oldham Hulme Grammar School and was an outstanding sportsman. Joe Jagger, who was an assistant schoolmaster, and Eva, then working as a hairdresser, were married at Holy

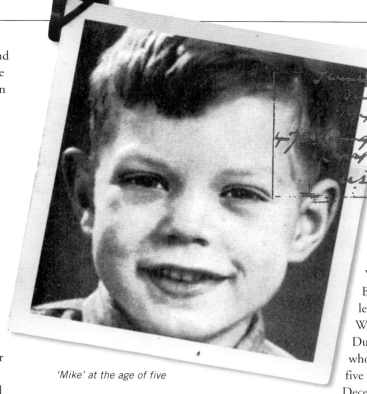

'Mike' at the age of five

Trinity Church, Dartford, on December 7, 1940. They lived at 3 Brentlands House, Brent Lane in Dartford.

Keith from Kent

Keith Richards, born on Saturday 18 December, 1943, was another Stone with Welsh roots. His father, Herbert William Richards, came from a large, working-class family that moved from Wales in the 1800s to live in Walthamstow, East

London. Bert, born on 25 January, 1915, was brought up in a puritanical household by a mother who served as Mayoress of Walthamstow during the Second World War. Bert's wife was one of seven sisters. The family left the Channel Islands and was living in Wales when she was born Doris Maud Lydia Dupree on 4 December, 1915. She and Bert, who worked for General Electric, went out for five years before marrying on Saturday 17 December, 1938. At the time of Keith's birth, when Doris was living at 1 Morland Avenue in Dartford, Bert was in the army in Bedfordshire.

'I didn't want to work and I fell pregnant. I was frightened,' said Doris. 'It was the most precarious of times to bring a child into the world.' The couple had no other children. The year after his son's birth, Bert was wounded in the leg and sent to an orthopaedic hospital at Mansfield in Nottinghamshire. Doris and Keith followed to stay for the rest of the war.

'It was great being an only child. That way I didn't have to share my toys with anyone.' KEITH

Monte Carlo Jagger

Joseph Hobson Jagger achieved legendary status and got himself into song long before his distant relative, Michael Philip. Discovering a bias in the way roulette wheels spin, Joseph watched the game in Monte Carlo for several days. Noticing that four numbers came up more than any others, he bet on these until the casino closed. It didn't open the next day, inspiring the famous music hall song 'The Man That Broke The Bank At Monte Carlo'.

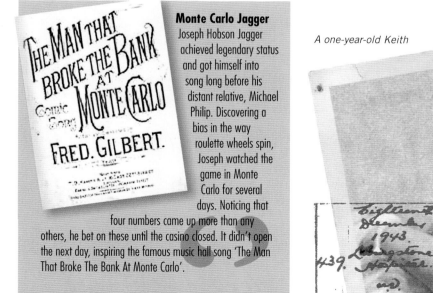

A one-year-old Keith

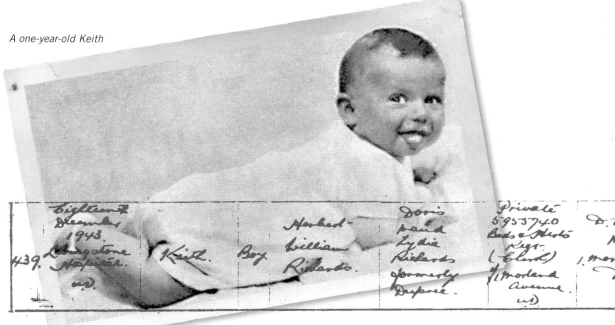

1936	BIRTH in the Sub-district of			
Columns:—	1	2	3	4
No.	When and where born	Name, if any	Sex	Name and surname of father

CERTIFIED to be a true copy of an entry in the certified copy of a Register
Given at the GENERAL REGISTER OFFICE, LONDON, under the Seal of the said Office

Perks of Penge

It was many years before I changed my name to
Wyman. I was given the same name as my father
when I arrived on Saturday 24 October, 1936, at
Lewisham Hospital in southeast London. My dad,
William George Perks, was born on 16 January,
1914, in Lower Sydenham. He was one of 10
children. My mother, Kathleen May Jeffery, was
born on 2 September, 1917, at 42 Blenheim Road
in Penge, London, the fourth of six children.

My father left school at 14 to be an apprentice
bricklayer, his trade for all his working life. As a
teenager, he taught himself the piano and bought
a piano accordion. My mum, always known as
Molly, left school in 1932 and went into service.
She and dad married at 9am on Christmas Day,
1935, in Christ Church, Penge. In April 1936,
they moved to 38 Miall Road, Lower Sydenham.

A day trip to Margate in July 1935 for Bill's mum and dad, before they were married.

Just before his sixth birthday, Bill at Blenheim Road, Penge, in September 1942.

Bill (far right), his brother and sisters play in the sandpit in the back garden, July 1945.

Birthday maths

In 1963, as the Rolling Stones were getting well-known, Bill's
year of birth was given as 1941 rather than 1936. In fact, he
was the oldest Stone and Keith was the youngest. Brian became
two years younger when his birth was brought forward to 1944.
Mick's was given as the same, when it was actually 1943.

It was an ordinary terraced house, with gas
lighting, no bathroom or hot water, and a toilet in
the back garden; a typical working-class home.

I had five siblings. Brian John, known as John,
was born in 1938, Anne Rosemary in 1939,
Judith Cecelia, known as Judy, in 1942 and Paul
Edgar in 1945. David Raymond was born in 1947
with jaundice and died four months later.

Like father, like son

The last to join the band was Charles Robert
Watts. He entered the world in University College

Hospital, London on Monday 2 June,
1941. Charlie's family was working class,
similar to my own and, like Brian and
me, Charlie was named after his father.
Charlie senior married Lillian Charlotte
Eaves in 1939 and lived in Kingsbury,
in Wembley, London, where he served in
the RAF, as ground crew and an officer's
driver. Baby Charlie lived with both
grandmothers, one of whom had her home
in King's Cross. His sister Linda (Lydia)
was born in 1944.

By September 1945, his demobbed
father was a driver with British Railways
and was still there when Charlie and
the rest of us were together as the
Rolling Stones.

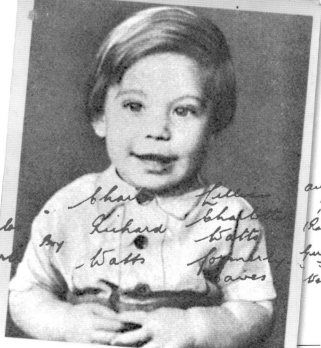

Charlie, three years old

BIRTHPLACES

Born into a world so different from today, the six boys who would grow up to become the original Rolling Stones could not have begun to dream of their futures. Unlike many bands that found fame in the 'Beat Boom' era their backgrounds were very different, as were their geographical locations.

Name: Lewis Brian Hopkin Jones
Born: 28 February, 1942
Park Nursing Home, Cheltenham
Address: Rosemead, Eldorado Avenue, Cheltenham

Name: Ian AR Stewart
Born: 18 July, 1938
Pittenweem, East Fife, Scotland
Address: Cheam, Surrey

Above: *People queuing to get into an air-raid shelter and,* right, *a postcard promoting Cheltenham Spa issued by GWR & LMS railways in the early 1950s.*

CHELTENHAM SPA
A BEAUTIFUL RESORT IN THE HEART OF THE
COTSWOLDS
GWR · LMS
Illustrated Guide free from Dept. D.R. Town Hall, Cheltenham

Wartime Britain

☐ Major city
• Other place of interest
☀ Subject to extensive wartime bombing
☐ Principal evacuation area

Left: *Building wartime camps for servicemen and,* below, *children evacuated from London find their own amusement.*

Name: Charles Robert Watts
Born: 2 June, 1941
University College Hospital, London
Address: 34 Girton Avenue Kingsbury, London NW9

Name: Keith Richards
Born: 18 December, 1943
Livingstone Hospital, Dartford, Kent
Address: 1 Morland Avenue, Dartford, Kent

Name: Michael Philip Jagger
Born: 26 July, 1943
Livingstone Hospital, Dartford, Kent
Address: 3 Brentlands House, Brent Lane, Dartford, Kent

Name: William George Perks
Born: 24 October, 1936
Lewisham Hospital London SE13
Address: 38 Miall Road, Sydenham, London SE26

War Stories

An Anderson air-raid shelter

Sometimes I would stay with my grandparents, often sleeping in the air-raid shelter in their back garden. Just before my fifth birthday in 1941, my father went to Nottingham to build hangars on airfields. A month later, my mother and I, along with my brother and sister, were evacuated to be close to my father. I was unhappy and returned to London to live with my grandmother in late 1942 and went to school at Melvin Infants in Penge. I remember being taught fire and air-raid drills in those early days at school. Around this time my father was called up to join the army and served in to the Royal Electrical Mechanical Engineers (REME).

One of my most vivid wartime memories was of Wednesday 20 January, 1943. I was on my way home from school when the air-raid sirens sounded. My friend and I got to the top of our road as a German fighter-bomber appeared at the other end. It roared towards us, seeming to fly between the rooftops, machine-gunning the length of the road. We ran past the houses and the small coping walls as it blasted over. I reached my grandmother's flat, where she hurried me down the back staircase to the air-raid shelter in the garden. Later that day we heard it was one of the planes that bombed a school in nearby Lewisham, killing six teachers and 38 children aged between five and seven.

'I lived close to the school that was bombed: the children are buried in Hither Green Cemetery close to where I live now. I remember the day vividly. We were just coming out of school at lunchtime when the air-raid sirens went. The policeman, seeing us across the road, told us to run home for our lives and as I got to our front door, my mum had the front and back doors open. We literally fell into the air-raid shelter until the raid was over.
A neighbour who had been walking along Rushey Green, Catford, had her legs injured from machine gun bullets. It was a black day for southeast London.' DOROTHY LEVETT, *A war-time neighbour who wrote to Bill in November 2001*

Not long after this, my mum, brother and sisters came back to live in London and I rejoined them. There were still air raids but things seemed somewhat safer. Then, in March 1944, there was a night-time air raid that gave the family no time to get to the shelter. Bombs started falling, so mum didn't hesitate to throw herself over us children in the bed; it was a good job we were all small.

Back from the forces
Bill's father was home on leave when this family photo was taken on Wednesday 15 November, 1944. Bill is on the far right.

As children we were all affected in one way or another by the Second World War, but in reality, wartime meant little to the other Stones: they were all too young to take it in. My family was evacuated to Pembrokeshire in Wales during 1940; we only stayed for two weeks, as we didn't like it. Back in London, I started infant school that September – around the same time as the Battle of Britain began. I vividly remember standing in the street with lots of our neighbours; we were all looking up at a sky that was filled with German bombers. Everyone cheered as we watched the white trails of our fighter planes diving in and out of the German formations.

Penge High Street, very close to
Bill's home, wrecked by a bomb on Friday 21 July, 1944.

Doodlebugs and jitterbug

German bomber raids began to be replaced by unmanned flying bombs, V1s, known in Britain as doodlebugs. During an attack in the spring of 1944, we were in our shelter listening to them drone overhead when we heard one cut out. When the sound stopped, that's when you knew it was going to fall.

A few seconds later, there was a tremendous explosion that made the ground shake; dust, dirt, leaves and branches all got blown into the shelter, making a real mess. When the All-Clear sounded, we came out to a very different garden. There was debris everywhere: even our large French windows were lying in the garden. The flying bomb had exploded just two streets away, flattening about 20 houses. Every stick of furniture in our flat had been flung against the walls nearest to the explosion. In July 1944, another flying bomb hit just around the corner. When I went to school the next day, I learned that two girls in my class had been killed.

Not long after that, we all lined Maple Road in Penge for a visit by Winston Churchill. He was in a large black open-top car, smoking his usual cigar while he stood waving and making the victory sign.

In September 1944, my friend Russell and his family moved out of 60 Blenheim Road in Penge. My grandmother managed to secure the house for our family. Mum and the other children, who had gone back to Mansfield while I stayed with my grandmother, came home and we all moved in together. On 8 May,

LEAVE THIS TO US
SONNY — <u>YOU</u> OUGHT
TO BE OUT OF LONDON

MINISTRY OF HEALTH EVACUATION SCHEME

1945, the war ended in Europe and we celebrated with a street party and an enormous bonfire in the middle of the road. There was another one just three months later, when the Japanese surrendered.

Around the time the war ended, Keith and his parents moved back to Dartford from Nottingham. They had to move as their old home had been demolished by a flying bomb. Charlie and Stu had vague memories of the war. Charlie recalled: 'I heard bombs exploding in the neighbourhood. I remember the mad rush from the house into the air-raid shelters. I was very young. War was something of a game to me – I don't think I ever really and truly got frightened.' Stu remembered the air-raid shelter at his home in Sutton, but he also spent some time in Scotland. As a steam enthusiast, he liked the train journeys. Mick, Brian and Keith were too young to remember anything.

Jitterbugging

Around the end of wartime, Bill's aunt, Dorothy, went out with an American serviceman. She would go to dances in Purley or Croydon; they took Bill a couple of times. Bill: 'I would watch them jitterbug, but I liked to hear the bands play best. I remember thinking that one day I would like to play in a band and then thinking I never would as it would take a lot of training.'

Up In The Morning… School Day

As the war came to an end, all of us were at school. Apart from Brian, we were all living in and around London. Music was beginning to play a part in our lives. The post-war years in Britain were a tough time. The war was not a distant memory – it was still a reality. Even sweets were rationed…

CHARLIE STARTED HIS school days at Fryant Way Infant School in Kingsbury and progressed to junior school in Wembley, in September 1948. He always liked to be neat and tidy: the following month he went to his uncle Albert's wedding in Holloway dressed in a satin suit.

Charlie said: 'My dad bought me suits and I wore them as smartly as I could, a kind of Little Lord Fauntleroy, I suppose. But I do remember that I didn't like jeans and sweaters in those days. I thought they looked untidy and I didn't feel somehow as good as I did in my little suits with the baggy trousers.' Charlie has continued to love his suits.

In 1952, he went to Tylers Croft Secondary Modern School: 'We had 40 kids in our class,' he said. 'I specialised in art. If I hadn't, I'd have played football and cricket all day long. We had a choir, but nobody liked singing in it much. We didn't have a band. Music was a guy lecturing us; nobody understood what he was saying.' Charlie was a speedy right-winger and he also loved cricket. He had a trial for Middlesex. Lillian Watts, his mother, said: 'He was a big boy with strong legs. We often thought he would become a footballer.'

Brian's school days

Four months after Charlie started school, it was Brian's turn. Around the same time, he got croup. According to his father, 'It left him with asthma; he had terrible attacks. It was always bad when he went to the beach on holiday.' In 1948, Brian's mother started teaching him the piano, which he continued until he was 14.

'Musically, I was guided by my parents. Later, there were several piano teachers in Cheltenham. I struggled to get the notes right early on, but eventually I found I had a feel for music. I guess I knew that I was going to be interested only in music from very early on.' BRIAN

In September 1949, Brian went to the fee-paying Dean Close Junior School in Cheltenham. He did well in music and English. Pretty soon there were signs of Brian's rebellious streak – he hated having his hair cut, and screamed the place down when he was taken to the barber. Brian passed his

Keith (fourth from left) *and Mick* (far right, front) *at school*

11-plus exam in July 1953 and went to Cheltenham Grammar School in September.

Mick at the Maypole

While I was starting grammar school in 1947, Mick was going to Maypole Primary Infant School. In September 1950, he attended Wentworth Junior County Primary School, Dartford. His brother was a few years behind. 'Chris was only about two at the time,' said Mick, 'and as far as I was concerned he was nothing more than a punch bag. I used to beat him up regularly.' Mick's father was Director of Physical Education at a large college. He worked with the British Sports Council, where he was a pioneer of the British Basketball movement. The family moved to a pleasant, white-pebbled, detached house, in the village of Wilmington, Kent, surrounded by old, twisted apple trees. In January 1951, Keith went to Wentworth Juniors. Being at the same school meant that it was not long before they met. Mick passed his 11-plus exam in July

1954, when he and Keith temporarily lost touch. At this time, the Richards family also moved to another part of Dartford.

Infant Keith

Keith Richards started at Westhill Infants School in January 1948. 'When Keith first went to school, I went to meet the teacher. She told me he'd been in a terrible state all day,' said his mother, Doris. 'I had to carry him home. He was frightened that maybe I wasn't coming to get him. With six aunts, he was a bit spoiled.

'Bert would take Keith to Dartford Heath; they'd play football together. Keith also liked going camping with us on the Isle of Wight.' Keith also started to go to Saturday morning cinema to watch his favourite cowboy, Roy Rogers, and he began to borrow books about America from the school library.

'America had all the things England had, only lots more. I loved the cinema. Just looking at American westerns... You didn't come across mountains like that where I lived. It all seemed so exotic. The wildest countryside I ever saw was the marshes across the river Thames.' KEITH

Even his mother said Keith was a dreamer. 'He was a funny kid. He never seemed to want to go out like other kids. He was always a bit of a mother's boy. He was a cry-baby, often in tears. A timid, introvert boy, he didn't like football. If a ball came near him, he'd run away. He hated being tackled and didn't like to be hurt. He didn't want to be on the rough side of life.' Keith also hated school; he only did well in English, history, drawing and painting.

Get a haircut
Even back in the early 1950s, the length of men's hair was an issue worthy of comment. On 10 April, 1950, the head of the National Hairdressers' Federation in Britain was quoted as saying that many men had longer hair than their wives.

Schoolboy Stu
Ian Stewart attended Glaisdale Preparatory School in Cheam, Surrey, and then Tiffin's Grammar School in Kingston-upon-Thames. He was a bright pupil, doing well at maths, and was also good at sports. He played rugby, lifted weights and was a keen golfer, like his mum. But he was also very shy and had an inferiority complex about the prominence of his jaw. His dad also had a big jaw and it was thought that Stu's grew following a childhood bout of measles. At around 16, he had a revolutionary operation to try to reduce his jaw size, which meant he was clamped for about six months. His speech was not confident and he tended to be a bit introverted. Nevertheless he was popular at school and not afraid to speak his mind. He gained several O-levels from Tiffin's.

Roy Rogers, King of the Cowboys

'Keith wanted to be like Roy Rogers and play guitar. I wasn't too impressed with the Roy Rogers bit, but the part about guitar did interest me.' MICK

Clacton-on-Sea, where Bill
almost drowned in 1946.

Bill aged 13

Grammar boy!

Much of my early education was disrupted by the war. In the spring of 1946, my dad was discharged from the army and in June we went on our first family holiday, to Clacton-on-Sea. We had a great time there, other than the fact that I almost drowned in the sea. I've hated water ever since and still cannot swim.

The winter of early 1947 was one of the worst on record. In January, the temperature fell to 16 degrees fahrenheit; 14-foot snowdrifts paralysed the country. It was very cold in our house, as the only heating was a stove in the kitchen. Our bedrooms were like fridges and we piled every coat we had on top of the blankets.

Three of us out of a class of 52 at my junior school passed the 11-plus exam that summer. I was accepted at Beckenham and Penge Grammar School for Boys, a very different environment. I was one of the only kids with a working-class accent, but even worse, we were not allowed to play football, just rugby. Even my parents disliked it. I had to wear an expensive school uniform and they were short of money.

With times hard and five kids to look after, my parents once again sent me to live with my grandmother, Florence, in Garden Road, Anerley. She had an early TV set with a tiny 6-inch screen, with a curved water-filled screen to make the picture bigger. I started piano lessons, joined the choir and, in my second year at grammar school, I took up the clarinet. I never really enjoyed it and it only lasted two years. I was doing pretty well at piano; my grandmother took me to the Royal College of Music, in London, where I passed the primary and preliminary examinations.

Fitting in

I went back to my parents' house in the summer of 1950. School was not going well; I had lost interest in learning. I was teased about my cockney accent in the day, then when I got home the kids in our street mocked me too. They thought my accent had become posh from mixing with kids at grammar school. It was a struggle to fit in. By February 1953, things had gone from bad to worse. My parents seemed resentful of everything I did; life was one long row. I had to be home by 10pm at night, where I shared a bed with my brothers. My father insisted I leave school so I could pay my own way. He wrote to my headmaster to say I would be leaving at Easter, two months before my GCE examinations. The headmaster tried to get my dad to change his mind, but he went ahead and found me a job – working for a bookmaker. I hated the idea. I started work at the City Tote offices as a junior clerk earning £3 10s per week, I was 16 years old.

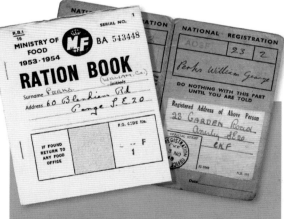

Post-war hardship

Despite the Allied victory, Britain had been impoverished by the war and would remain poor for many years. The Labour government introduced the Welfare State, with its notions of care from cradle to grave. But at the same time the Cold War with Russia worsened, food rationing continued and everyone had to carry identity cards (these were only abolished in 1952).

As well as the terrible floods of 1947 that killed livestock, there was a record number of divorces — up to 50,000 a year. The newspapers reported the new figures in March 1947 and the Lord Chancellor commented: 'Sometimes, the sooner the girl is rid of the man, the better.'

Bill was not allowed
to stay on at school, despite
the pleas of his headmaster.

Musical Discovery

Music began to play an increasingly important part in all our lives. We were trying different instruments and, spurred on by skiffle, there were thoughts of forming a group. For many young people in Britain, it was a time of musical discovery and the music we were most interested in came from America.

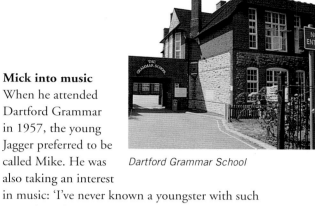

Mick into music
When he attended Dartford Grammar in 1957, the young Jagger preferred to be called Mike. He was also taking an interest

Dartford Grammar School

SOON AFTER HIS 14th birthday in 1956, Brian – known at school as Buster – became first clarinet in the school orchestra. He didn't show natural skill at sport, though he enjoyed diving and badminton. He was in trouble regularly and was often caned. None of this stopped him from getting seven O-levels when he was 15 and entering the sixth form.

'I encouraged him to take science subjects at A-level when his heart wasn't really in it,' said his father. 'Perhaps if he'd taken other subjects, he would have followed a more orthodox career.' Further education was a revelation to Brian: 'When I made the sixth form I found myself accepted by the older boys; suddenly I was in.' He became a ringleader and was twice suspended from school, once for not wearing his mortarboard.

'He was a rebel without a cause, but when examinations came he was brilliant.'
DICK HATTRELL, *Cheltenham friend*

Brian passed two more O-levels in his lower sixth year and then A-level physics and chemistry, but he failed biology. It was his IQ of 135 that got him through the exams; hard work had very little to do with his success.

Boogie and beat
Starting the piano early, somewhere between the ages of five and seven, music remained a real love for Stu. Sutton had a number of amateur bands and he played piano and banjo in various outfits.

Charlie first showed an interest in music when he was 13: 'I can't claim that I came from a musical family. The only instrument anyone could play at home was a gramophone.'

His mother remembered: 'Charlie always wanted a drum set, and used

to rap out tunes on the table with pieces of wood or a knife and fork.' Buying himself a second-hand banjo, Charlie was frustrated: 'I couldn't get the dots on the frets right. It drove me up the wall. I got pissed off with it and took the thing apart, made a stand for it out of wood and played on the round skin part with brushes.' For Christmas in 1955, Charlie received a £12 drum kit: 'He took to it straight away,' said his mother, 'and often used to play jazz records and join in on his drums.'

'It was just a collection of bits and pieces,' according to Charlie, 'but I got a lot of fun out of it. Any sort of jazz interested me, so I taught myself by listening to other people's records and watching drummers.' While Charlie was musically talented, he left school at 16 with just one O-level pass, in art, but he did receive two cups for running and three prizes for art, which he went on to study further.

'We wanted Charlie to go in to graphic art or draughtsmanship and were very pleased when he went on to Harrow Art School,' said his mother.

in music: 'I've never known a youngster with such an analytical approach to things. If he copied a song, he was able to capture the sound exactly,' said his father, Joe.

'He hated the name Mick, and I only used it when I was teasing him.'
CHRIS JAGGER, *Mick's brother*

Mick took basketball seriously. His father coached the Dartford Grammar School basketball society and Mick was honorary secretary. Mick got a pair of real American basketball boots to ensure that he looked the part, along with the rest of his teammates. His father said: 'He could have been a great athlete. He was excellent at basketball and cricket, but he didn't want to be tied down with the practice.'

Jagger on TV
In September 1957, Mick made his first TV appearance. With his father, he was featured rock climbing in Tunbridge Wells on BBC TV's *Seeing Sport*. Mick also demonstrated how to put up a tent and cook a meal over a campfire. For their holidays, the Jaggers travelled across the Channel: 'In the summer, we toured the

Mick Jagger (top row, far right) *with his school basketball team*

ATTENTION!

While the others were still enjoying school, I had more pressing problems on my mind. We celebrated my 18th birthday on Sunday 24 October, 1954, with a big party at home. All young men at this time were eligible for National Service once they reached this age. So, after the festivities, the waiting. When would I get my call-up papers? It didn't take long – they arrived just two months later.

There was one good thing about my call-up. I was chosen for the RAF and not the army. On 20 January, 1955, I reported for duty at RAF Cardington and four days later I was posted to RAF Padgate, near Warrington in Lancashire, for eight weeks of basic training. In late March, I reported to RAF Credenhill near Hereford for additional training, as a clerk. My pay was 28 shillings a week. In our hut we had a radio speaker, so we were able to listen to some pop music. We liked Eartha Kitt and the Crewcuts, Tennessee Ernie Ford's 'Rain' and Perez Prado's 'Cherry Pink', which was at No 1 in the UK and US.

In May 1955, I decided to sign up for an extra year's service, with the benefits of higher pay, a better uniform and more leave. In July, I left RAF Credenhill with the rank of AC1 and was posted to RAF Oldenburg in West Germany. I shared a room with four other boys and worked in the motor transport section. We were on a permanent four-hour alert as we were only 80 miles from the Russian border and in the middle of the Cold War. Here I had a mate called Gordon Lee Whyman – I liked his last name.

In early 1956, our room clubbed together to buy a radio and started listening to the BFN (British Forces Network). They played the English Top 10; it was

very dull. We then changed over to the American Forces Network, which was altogether different. We would wake up to country music on *The Stick Buddy Jamboree*; it was wonderful.

Young Elvis

We also heard the beginnings of rock'n'roll, Fats Domino and Little Richard records, and the first Elvis Presley releases, long before they were popular in Britain. We would go to a German bar and dancehall called Zum grünen Wald, and listen to the jukebox, hearing more of the latest American rock'n'roll records.

I really loved Elvis Presley's 'That's All Right'. I drew Elvis on the back of my sleeveless leather jerkin; soon they called me Elvis around the camp. I really enjoyed my time in the air force:

Pyjama-clad Bill emulating his hero Elvis in 1957.

The motor transport (MT) football team: Lee Whyman second from right front row, Bill second from left.

there was great camaraderie and the opportunity to play sport; I was in the camp's football team. I was lucky enough to be home on leave for my 21st birthday in 1957 and three months later I was demobbed. It was back to civvy street and a return to Blenheim Road to live with my family.

Ian Stewart was also called up to do his National Service. Like me, he went to RAF Cardington in Cambridgeshire, but he was discharged after only one week.

Zum grünen Wald, 1955

St Tropez area and camped on the famed Tahiti Beach. Mike acted as my interpreter,' said Eva, Mick's mother.

In 1956, Mick met the son of a plumber from Bexleyheath who went to the same school, Dick Taylor. The two boys went to see Buddy Holly at the Granada Cinema in Woolwich in March 1958. During the blistering early summer the following year, Mick passed seven O-levels, in history, English language, English literature, French, Latin, geography and mathematics. He went on to study A-level English, history and

French and became a school prefect.

Mick's earliest attempt at singing was at the house of Dartford school friend David Soames. David was trying to form a group with Mike Turner. They decided that Mick sang too strangely. While at Dartford Grammar, Mick, Dick Taylor with his second-hand drum kit, Bob Beckwith and Alan Etherington began practising together. Over two years, they never played publicly. 'We never thought of playing to other people,' said Dick. 'We thought we were the only people in England who'd heard of R&B.'

Teacher's pet?
'You couldn't help being aware of Mike [Mick] because he seemed alive where the other kids would just sink down in their chairs. He questioned authority – he'd ask why, which was unusual then.'
MR HARRIS, *maths teacher*

'I never got to have a raving adolescence, because I was concentrating on my studies. I don't think I was a popular kid, but then I wasn't particularly unpopular. I was just an ordinary rebellious, studious, hard-working kid.' MICK

'There was one occasion when I spoke to Mick about his attitude very severely. He was so deliberately insulting that I simply knocked him down.' DR BENNETT, *language teacher*

'Back in the early 1960s, I got to know Mick Jagger as we lived quite close and I turned him on to black American music. We would go around to each other's houses and play records... Some came from HMV on Oxford Street – they had a policy of buying at least one copy of everything – things by Bobby Bland, Jimmy Reed, Chuck Berry and Howlin' Wolf. Once when I was at his house, his mum said, "I can't stand all this darkie music". Mick was suitably embarrassed!' DAVE GODIN, *friend and founder UK Tamla Motown Appreciation Society, 2002*

In the summer of 1960, Mick played at Dartford Church Hall with friends. He sang Buddy Holly's 'It Doesn't Matter Anymore' and died a death. For work, he sold ice creams part-time from a tricycle outside Dartford public library. Keith bought one, their first meeting in a long time.

Keith and the First Lady
Doris Richards liked Billy Eckstine and Ella Fitzgerald and influenced her son's musical interests: 'Keith always sang to the radio or a record and he knew all the words. He tried the Boy Scouts, but that didn't last. Nor did he enjoy school, neither the work, nor the sport. I caught him smoking once; it made him ill.'

'We always went away in the summer, quite often it was a holiday camp. We'd dress Keith up in fancy dress.' DORIS RICHARDS

Keith soon grew to like cigarettes, as he later recalled, 'In cross-country, I would start off with the main bunch and as the others raced off into the distance, I would hide myself behind a bush or tree. A quick fag made me feel right as rain.'

Academia failed to involve Keith; he was made to retake his third year studies at Dartford Technical College in September 1957. Doris

Left: *Buddy Holly onstage at the Kilburn Gaumont State Theatre, Sunday 2 March, 1958.* Above: *Woolwich Granada, where Mick and Dick Taylor saw Buddy Holly.*

'The first guitar I picked up was Gus's. For years I couldn't play it, and I just used to pick it up and plonk on it.' KEITH

wondered what was to become of her son: 'Keith wanted a record player so we got one from the Dartford Co-op.' Keith said: 'It was murder winding up the arm. The first record I bought was a bad Woolworth's imitation on their budget Embassy label of a Ricky Nelson song.'

Keith would visit his grandfather, Gus Dupree, who ran a dance band in the 1930s and played a variety of instruments, including guitar, fiddle, piano and saxophone. By the 1950s, Gus was playing fiddle and his wife piano in a country and western band that toured US Air Force bases in England.

Doris: 'Gus had this guitar standing in the corner, and he was always afraid Keith would break it when he touched it.' But what Keith really wanted was his own guitar.

'I told him I'd buy him one if he actually played it,' said his mother, 'but no mucking about. I bought him a cheap acoustic guitar on hire purchase for £7 for his 15th birthday. My father taught him a few chords, but the rest he taught himself.'

By 1959, Keith was frequently playing truant from school and he became a bit of a teddy boy, sporting pink socks and drainpipe trousers. He would hang out at the snooker hall in Dartford. Keith's musical tastes were also changing: 'I was into Little Richard; I was rocking away.' In April 1960, he was asked to leave his college because of truancy. Luckily for Keith, the headmaster enrolled him into Sidcup Art School,

Saturday Club
On 4 October, 1958, *Saturday Club*, introduced by Brian Matthew, started on BBC radio. Initially billed as 'the best of today's pop entertainment', it broadcast from 10am until midday and the first show featured Terry Dene and Gary Miller. It became BBC Radio's flagship pop show in an era when it was difficult for teenagers to hear pop music elsewhere. *Saturday Club* was essential listening and its success continued right through the beat boom years.

to study advertising. It was here that he met Mick's friend and fellow band member Dick Taylor:

'When I was at art school, Keith, then known as Ricky, always wore a purple shirt, jeans, pointed shoes and a jean jacket and was always untidy.' DICK TAYLOR

Keith said: 'Dick Taylor was the first guy I played with. We played together on acoustic guitars. Then I got an amplifier like a little beat-up radio. Along with another guy at school called Michael Ross, we formed a country and western band. The first time I got onstage was a sports dance at Eltham, near Sidcup.' In an effort to earn some money, Keith briefly did a bread round.

No sax please
Sometime around the end of 1957, Brian first heard a Charlie Parker recording. As a result, he persuaded his parents to buy him a saxophone. He became obsessed with the instrument and practised endlessly, but it was a passing fad. Two months after Keith got his guitar, Brian's parents bought him an acoustic for his 17th birthday. However, it was not long before music and sex went hand in hand, something of a recurring theme for Brian.

In 1959, Brian's first illegitimate child was born to a 14-year-old Cheltenham schoolgirl named Valerie. Brian wanted her to have an abortion but she refused. She would have nothing to do with Brian and had the baby boy adopted. Brian also quit education, which was a major disappointment for his parents, who envisaged him attending a university and following a profession. Brian knew it wasn't for him.

'I quite honestly didn't feel much of an urge to do anything else except

HMV, Oxford Street: 'They had a policy of buying at least one copy of every release,' said Dave Godin.

play music. I thought about different jobs and rejected them: I knew I'd be bored stiff.'

Demobbed and hitched
Home from the air force in January 1958, I needed a job. I unsuccessfully tried the bookmakers where I had worked before. After several interviews, I got a job at a meat importers in the Royal Victoria Docks in East Ham. I travelled to and from work by train and bus and later by bike. I started going to the Royston Ballroom in Penge with friends.

'I met a 17-year-old named Diane Cory from Sydenham and pretty soon we were courting – well, that's what we called it back then.' BILL

In September, I became a storekeeper and clerk at John A Sparks, diesel engineers, in Streatham Hill and in March 1959, I bought my first car for £30, although I didn't take my test. Diane moved in with our family. We would go jiving at the Royston Ballroom – we'd often win the competition and get free tickets for the next week. Another haunt was Beckenham Ballroom. My mum remembers it well. 'He was turned away because his trousers were too tight,' she said. 'The next week Bill went along wearing a wide pair of trousers. Once he got in, he went into the toilets and took them off. Underneath were the drainpipes he wore the week before.'

On my 23rd birthday, Diane and I got married at Christ Church in Penge. Our honeymoon was just one weekend in Birmingham – we were skint! We moved to Woodbine Grove, Penge, soon after the wedding.

Skiffle...

Frankie Vaughan: his was a bland era

With blurred hindsight we recall Britain in the 1950s as the era of rock'n'roll, teddy boys and drainpipe trousers. It was also a time when Britain had a home-made musical genre, a music steeped in the blues, one that was essential to the British beat boom of the early 1960s. Skiffle, and its pioneer Lonnie Donegan, was a huge influence on just about every band that made it big in the 1960s, including the Rolling Stones. But for the most part it was an era of musical blandness: Dickie Valentine, Ruby Murray, Jimmy Young (the Housewife's Choice), Winifred Atwell, Ronnie Hilton, Guy Mitchell and Frankie Vaughan all topped the UK charts in the middle of the 1950s.

'I wanted to buy a record player, but I was short of money. So one Saturday in July 1953, I sold my stamp collection for £3 10s and went to a record shop in Anerley. I bought a second-hand, wind-up gramophone and a box of needles for £2 10s and my first 78 rpm records: Les Paul and Mary Ford's 'The World Is Waiting For The Sunrise', featuring Les Paul's wonderful multi-tracked guitar playing, and one by Johnny Ray.' BILL

Rock'n'roll represented all that was exciting about America to post-war British teenagers. Bill Haley's 'Rock Around The Clock' entered the UK singles chart, for the first time, on the January day in 1955 that Bill received his military call-up. At No 1 in Britain that week was 25-year-old Dickie Valentine's 'Finger Of Suspicion'. These two records neatly represent the ends of a musical spectrum that played itself out over the course of the decade.

We tend to think now that rock'n'roll happened simultaneously in Britain and America – a trick of memory. It started in America, some time before Bill Haley made it big. He was, as is often the case in pop music, the acceptable face of a form with much deeper and far hipper roots. Ask any music fan to name the first rock'n'roll record and you will get nearly as many answers as people you ask. Some say it was Jackie Brenston's 1951 hit,

'Rocket 88', with Ike Turner on piano or 'Lawdy Miss Clawdy' by Lloyd Price from 1952. Others have made a credible case for 1954's 'Shake Rattle'n'Roll' by Big Joe Turner (Haley took his version to US No 7 in August of the same year) or any number of brilliant records by Louis Jordan. Whatever they answer, it is almost certain that the choice will be a recording made by a black artist.

Haley stakes his claim

To the casual observer, though, Haley's 'Rock Around The Clock' is the record that signifies the birth of rock'n'roll. It was recorded in New York City on 12 April, 1954, and released the following month, but it failed to chart. The song finally topped the US chart in the summer of 1955, after featuring in the film *The Blackboard Jungle*. It made UK No 1 in January 1956. Cuddly Bill was 29, but looked a lot older, when it hit the top. This anthem to sexual gymnastics – for rock was black slang for sex – was clearly misinterpreted by the nice people at the British Broadcasting Corporation. Not that there were too many opportunities for 'Rock Around The Clock' to be heard on the wireless – the BBC radio's 'popular music' channel, the *Light Programme*, was just that. It featured light entertainment and even Dickie Valentine was considered racy.

'The rowdy element was represented by "Rock Around The Clock", theme song of the controversial film The Blackboard Jungle. *The rock'n'roll school in general concentrated on a minimum of melodic line and a maximum of rhythmic noise, deliberately competing with the artistic ideals of the jungle itself.'* ENCYCLOPAEDIA BRITANNICA, *1955*

By the end of 1955, record sales overtook those of sheet music.

Decca on 45
In October 1954, Decca, the label that would later sign the Rolling Stones, issued its first 45 rpm singles in Britain.

... And Good Old Rock'n'Roll

The coming of the King

On Monday 5 July, 1954, almost three months after the recording of 'Rock Around The Clock', Elvis Presley, Scotty Moore and Bill Black cut 'That's All Right' at Sun Studios in Memphis. While the track didn't reach the national charts, this one minute and 55 seconds of magic set Presley on his way.

'I made a decision to not make him another Eddie Fisher or Dean Martin. He'd have been another good singer, good-looking, an entertaining guy, but the worst thing I could have ever done is to come out and cut a conventional ballad.'
SAM PHILLIPS, *2000*

Elvis had his first transatlantic hit two years later, when 'Heartbreak Hotel' made UK No 2 in June 1956.

Above: *Elvis Presley, 1956 model*
Left: *Crowds wait to catch a glimpse of Bill Haley and the Comets.*
Below: *A teddy boy waits outside a cinema showing Haley's* Rock Around The Clock.

Transatlantic crossing

Chuck Berry first made the US Hot 100 in late summer 1955, almost two years before he found minor success in Britain with 'School Day', in June 1957. Nearly a year separated Little Richard's first US and British hit and Fats Domino's 'Ain't It A Shame' (everyone thinks it's called 'Ain't That A Shame' but 'It' is on the record) took almost 18 months to cross the water. This slow Atlantic crossing was a similar story for many artists from this era. Mass appeal was not what it was all about for men like the young pre-Stones. It was their love of American music, both black and white, that inspired their musical ambitions.

'In February 1957, I went to the Regal Cinema, Beckenham. Chuck Berry sang "You Can't Catch Me" in Rock, Rock, Rock. As he started doing his leg movements, everyone started laughing, thinking it was a comedy number. The hair stood up on the back of my neck, I got shivers all over. I'd never been affected like that. This was it! I became a dedicated fan. I wrote to a record shop in Chicago and ordered Chuck Berry's album **One Dozen Berrys***. It took three months to arrive.'* BILL

CHUCK BERRY
one dozen berrys

We'll be back after the break

On Thursday 22 September, 1955, commercial television began in Britain with the first ITV programmes. Three days later, the first *Sunday Night At The London Palladium* was broadcast. The show became an institution, one on which the Stones would later cause uproar.

Jerry Lee Lewis's 'Whole Lotta Shakin' Goin' On' took just three months to cross the Atlantic. It hit the UK charts in September 1957 and reached No 8. Rock'n'roll had well and truly arrived.

'On Saturday 24 May, 1958, Jerry Lee Lewis began his tour at the Edmonton Regal, London. Next day the papers broke the story of Jerry Lee's marriage to his 13-year-old cousin Myra Brown, two months earlier. On Monday 26, I went to see Jerry Lee at the Granada in Tooting, his last show before the tour was prematurely cancelled. His career went into free-fall, but he was and always will be one of the greats. He could have been bigger than Elvis.' BILL

Jerry Lee Lewis and his 13-year-old wife Myra, in London, 1958.

3620281

Skiffle or piffle?

In 1956, a *Melody Maker* article about the British skiffle craze, written by Alexis Korner, was headlined 'Skiffle Or Piffle?'. For many young men in the Britain of the late 1950s, skiffle was a musical passport to rebellion. Then, as today, parental disapproval of teenage music was guaranteed… it was all too raucous. The success of skiffle's superstar, Lonnie Donegan, was amazing. Between 1956 and 1962, Lonnie had 30 British hit singles, topping the charts three times. He had 14 other Top 10 singles. His first hit, 'Rock Island Line', made the US Top 10 in 1956, a rare achievement for a British record; he also toured the USA backed by the Johnny Burnette Trio.

'I saw Lonnie Donegan in concert in 1958. I got so excited, I danced in the aisles for the first and only time in my life.' BILL

This do-it-yourself musical craze may have had a short shelf life, but it was an inspiration. Skiffle made it possible for thousands of young Brits to dream of emulating their heroes. Anyone could be a pop star.

'In June 1957 at RAF Oldenburg, I got a skiffle group together with Casey Jones from Liverpool. Eric Clapton later played with Casey Jones and the Engineers for two weeks, in October 1963, before joining the Yardbirds. Tom McGuinness (Manfred Mann) also played with Casey. Everybody in a 1960s' rock band started with skiffle.' BILL

One day in late spring or early summer 1958, five young men cut a 78 rpm record at an electrical shop in Liverpool. This skiffle group called themselves the Quarrymen; three of the group were John Lennon, George Harrison and Paul McCartney. Around the same time, Brian Jones played washboard in a local skiffle group. Chris Rowe was often the group's singer and remembers Brian frequently losing the vital thimble. She later said: 'We were just kids messing about. There was no long-term planning. We did things on the spur of the moment.'

Russell Quaye's Skiffle Cellar, Greek Street, Soho

'Before any group is started up, there should be someone who can sing really well and a couple of guitarists who can play good strong chords.' MICK, *aged 15, in an essay on how to form a skiffle group*

Bill, partially obscured, plays a bass made from a broom handle, tea chest and string, with his room-mates at RAF Oldenburg.

John Lennon, centre-stage, with the Quarrymen in 1955

As American rock'n'roll took hold in the UK, a counter-offensive by home-grown British talent began. Tommy Steele was the first UK rocker (of sorts!) to top the UK chart in January 1957, with his cover version of Guy Mitchell's 'Singing The Blues' (Mitchell also topped the UK chart with the same song). Tommy was something of a lone British contender for a while, that is until Harry Webb, better known as Cliff Richard, came along in September 1958 with what is arguably the greatest British rock'n'roll record of all, 'Move It'.

'I would watch my lovely boys sitting so neat and clean watching that dreadful Cliff Richard, that awful hair and that sexy dancing.' EVA JAGGER

'English rock'n'roll started with skiffle groups.' MICK

Over the course of the next year, others joined the fray. Liverpool's Billy Fury first struck with 'Maybe Tomorrow' in February 1959, while Adam Faith got to UK No 1 that November with 'What Do You Want'. Marty Wilde, Johnny Kidd and the Pirates, Wee Willie Harris, Dickie Pride and Cuddly Dudley all played their part.

Trad fad

Besides skiffle there was the trad fad. Trad, short for traditional jazz, was more serious than rock'n'roll and was accepted by jazz fans. It did, however, make the charts. Its relationship with skiffle was through the likes of Chris Barber, in whose band Lonnie Donegan first performed his skiffle segment. Trad jazz was popular before skiffle, but only among a small group of enthusiasts. Its popular appeal came on the heels of the skiffle boom. Acker Bilk, Kenny Ball and the Temperance Seven had chart successes in 1959 and in the early 1960s.

Brian Jones drifted in and out of

It's Trad, Dad
Kenny Ball was in the film and Brian saw him live at the Cheltenham Rotunda. As is often true of music films, it came out in 1962, as the genre was waning.

the trad scene. In March 1960, he was playing local dances with John Keen's Trad Band and Jock Henderson's Dixielanders. He also sat in with Bill Nile's Delta Jazzmen.

Trad musicians were also into the blues and Brian saw the Chris Barber Band in Cheltenham with American harmonica player Sonny Boy Williamson. Brian fell in love with the blues and was soon searching for records by Sonny Boy and Muddy Waters. Barber's importance in championing the blues in Britain should not be underestimated and he therefore had a hand in creating the Rolling Stones.

Eva Jagger was not alone in condemning Cliff Richard – to an older generation, Cliff represented all that was corrupting in pop music.

Why should the devil have all the best songs?
The American Catholic Youth Center's newspaper, *Contacts*, demanded of all God-fearing Catholics in 1958: 'Smash the records you possess which present a pagan culture and a pagan concept of life. Check beforehand the records, which will be played at a house party or a school record dance. Switch your radio dial when you hear a suggestive song.'

Chris Barber with Sonny Boy Williamson on stage in England

To Work Or Not To Work

Most people in the late 1950s and early 1960s needed to find a job after leaving school. Few had the option of, or chose, further education. Mick and Keith did continue their studies, probably for somewhat different reasons, and were about to get together for the first time in years. Music was very much part of our lives, but none of us thought we might be able to earn a living from it… Money was the priority.

Tram 21 returns
In 1961, Brian helped to restore this Cheltenham tram to its former glory (*above*). Fred Lloyd, on the ladder, drove the bus on which Brian was the conductor.

Brian's love of buses came from this brief stint working for Cheltenham buses (*below*).

I N AUGUST 1959, Brian went to London. Lewis Jones takes up the story: 'He decided to go to work in London for an opthalmic firm, and I took him for the interview. He put on quite a good show and then we left. I said we should take the five o'clock train home. He said, "No, dad, I want to go to some jazz clubs. Would you like to come along?" I told him "No". He said he'd come home on a later train. He'd been to London more often than I'd known, hitchhiking, going to these clubs. He got home at 6am.' Brian started working for the optician, but music was still his passion. Eventually he quit the job and went back to Cheltenham.

his parents about work. He much preferred hanging around Cheltenham's coffee bars. On the second Sunday in January 1960, Pat Andrews and two girlfriends went to the cinema. Brian was there, too. During the intermission they chatted and arranged to meet. Pat learned that he was living in Hatherley Road with his parents. On their first date, Brian took her to the rehearsals of a local trad jazz band, Jock Henderson's Dixielanders.

Dirty work
Brian started working at a factory in Brockworth, about seven miles southwest of Cheltenham. This ended abruptly when he got a lift to work in a mate's van and it overturned. Brian's leg was injured and he had a front tooth knocked out. He then worked in a record shop until it went bankrupt. He also befriended John Appleby, 10

'Those months were the most free and happy of my life.' BRIAN, *on travelling*

Brian began playing in bands. He became a member of the 66 Club, a jazz event held at the Wheatsheaf Inn in Leckhampton. In September he went hitchhiking in Scandinavia with friends, to avoid the problems with Valerie's parents. He took his guitar, and busked for a while, but eventually ran short of money.

Wooden Bridge by the water
In November 1959, Brian went to the Wooden Bridge Hotel in Guildford (the Stones would play there four years later) to see a band. He met a young married woman named Angeline and they had a one-night stand. She later found out that she was pregnant. Angeline and her husband went ahead with the birth; the second of Brian's children. The following month, Brian was at one of his regular Cheltenham haunts, the Aztec coffee bar, when he was spotted by 15-year-old Pat Andrews. With his shaggy blond hair, she thought he was the scruffiest person she had ever seen, but he intrigued her.

Brian was continually at odds with

Brian's parents' house in Hatherley Road, Cheltenham

years his senior, who encouraged him to become a bus conductor. It lasted just three weeks, but Brian loved buses from then on.

Brian and his friend Dick Hattrell moved into a large bedsit in Parabola Road, Cheltenham with two art students: Brian and his parents had finally found each other too difficult to live with. The following month Pat Andrews found she was pregnant. Brian asked her to have an abortion, but Pat wanted the baby. He was nearly 19 and very worried. He didn't want to give up his new-found independence and refused to marry.

Days later he started work as a junior architect for Gloucester County Council, helping to design schools. This didn't last either. Brian applied for a scholarship to Cheltenham Art College. Overjoyed when he was accepted, his hopes were dashed two days later when the offer was withdrawn. Somebody had written to the college saying Brian was irresponsible and a drifter. Brian, still practising on his old acoustic guitar that was so difficult to play, started working behind the record counter at Curry's in Cheltenham High Street. This, too, only lasted a few months, and a job as a coalman lasted just three days...

A Squire or a Clifton

In October 1960, Diane and I found a scruffy flat in Birkbeck Road, Beckenham. It was so damp, the wallpaper peeled off by itself. A few weeks after my 24th birthday, I started working as a storekeeper at Duponts' department store in Penge High Street. I bought my first electric guitar, a Burns, for £52, on hire purchase. A workmate, Steve Carroll, also played guitar and I introduced him to Chuck Berry records. We decided to form a group, recruiting Dennis and Keith Squires (neither of whom stayed with us for long), and my brother-in-law Cliff Starkey. We practised at my flat using my tape recorder, recording songs such as 'It's Now Or Never', 'Frankie And Johnny', 'Dreaming', 'Summertime' and 'Blue Moon' (no, I haven't got the tape!). We thought of calling ourselves the Squires, but settled on the Cliftons.

Bill's parents' Blenheim Road house in 1959 – a world away from the home of Brian Jones

The Cliftons, from top: Brian Cade, Tony Chapman, Steve Carroll, Bill, Cliff Starkey and Dave Harvey

We auditioned at the Starlight Ballroom, Penge, and were given a booking, so we rehearsed 'Great Balls of Fire', 'Footloose' and 'Hooley Jump'. On Saturday 21 January, 1961, I made my first public appearance at the Starlight Ballroom. I broke a string and my guitar pick, the last time I failed to carry spares. Over the next few months, we played sporadic gigs and I bought a set of bass strings for my six-string guitar, but they didn't give me the sound I wanted. In April, drummer Tony Chapman joined. Tony would literally change the course of my life.

In retrospect, July 1961 was a very important time for me. Diane and I went to stay with my sister Anne and her husband in Aylesbury. At a dance in an old converted cinema we saw the Barron Knights. I was staggered by the sound of their electric bass: I realised what was missing in our band. Just a few weeks later I found out that Diane was pregnant.

Tuxedo bass

In the meantime, Tony Chapman had found me an old bass guitar, called a Tuxedo. I scraped the £8 together to buy it. With the help of a neighbour's fretwork machine, I reshaped the guitar body and then took all the frets out. I intended replacing them with new ones, but it sounded so good that I left it as it was – the first fretless bass. I needed an amplifier and speaker. We clubbed together and bought a Goodmans 18-inch bass speaker along with a Linear-Concorde 30-watt build-it-yourself amplifier. We built a cabinet and put concrete in the bottom, as we'd heard that it improved sound. It did, but made it almost too heavy to lift. I had to take the lid off the amp as it overheated. I also got a shock whenever I plugged in – the whole thing was live!

Advertising Charlie

Back in July 1960, Charlie left art school and became a tea boy at an advertising agency, earning £2 a week, and then a visualiser, designing posters.

'I worked next to Charlie in the studio. He was just about the smartest turned-out artist in the department. He used to help all of us with our drawing if we were in trouble. But you should have heard him talk about jazz. He was like a walking encyclopedia.'
ANDY WICKHAM, *showbiz publicist*

Alexis Korner

arm was a collection of imported R&B records from Chicago and New York, including Chuck Berry's *One Dozen Berrys*. They got a train and talked about Chuck Berry and music in general for 20 minutes, until Keith got off at Sidcup. They arranged to meet again to listen to each other's records, of which Mick had many more.

Within a couple of days Mick dropped by Keith's and found they had a mutual friend in Dick Taylor, who said: 'Keith asked me if I knew a guy named Mick Jagger. Keith knew me and Mick knew me and we thought why not join forces.' They rehearsed with Bob Beckwith and Allen Etherington in an upstairs room at Mick's house, with Keith playing a Hofner cutaway electric guitar. According to Mick's brother, Chris Jagger, 'When Keith and Dick came round to practise at our house, Mike [Mick] gave up the guitar and thought more about playing harmonica and singing.'

Eva Jagger said: 'Mike was a bit sensitive about his singing in those days. He didn't like being watched or overheard. We loaned them the money for their early equipment, although money was tight. We had to, to keep Mike quiet.' Mick sang, Dick played drums (inherited from his grandfather), Keith and Bob played guitars through a primitive six-watt amp, no larger than a portable radio, while Allen played maracas.

In 1961, he wrote a book on Charlie Parker, *Ode To A High Flying Bird*, eventually published in 1965. He played drums twice a week in a coffee bar and by September was performing at the Troubadour Club in Chelsea. Alexis Korner, a pioneer of the blues in Britain, invited him to join his band, but Charlie was going to work in Denmark and didn't come back to London until February 1962. When he did, he briefly played with pianist and comedian Dudley Moore's trio.

Political Mick

In July 1961, Mick passed three A-Levels and won a scholarship to the London School of Economics (LSE), signing a declaration to complete his economics and political science course.

A month or so after starting at LSE, Mick met Keith at Dartford Railway Station; Keith was on his way to the art school at Sidcup. Under Mick's

'When I went to the LSE, I thought of going into politics.' MICK

Dick recalled, 'Mick and Keith were always the ones. Mick always liked Keith's playing. As various people dropped out or were ousted, it was Mick and Keith that lasted. We were getting Jimmy Reed and Chuck Berry records, and listening to them and copying them.'

Meanwhile, at LSE, the ever-sporting Mick was playing football for the 2nd XI. By autumn 1961, he, Keith, Dick and their friends had begun calling themselves Little Boy Blue and the Blue Boys.

'I liked the sound of it. It tells people we're playing the blues.' MICK

According to Dick, their repertoire was mainly Chuck Berry songs along with a very long pseudo-Spanish version of 'La Bamba'. Mick's passion for Chuck and Bo Diddley prompted him to write frequent letters to Pye Records demanding they release their records in Britain. But all Pye did was to send catalogues and make suitably sympathetic noises.

Blues men or boys?

On Monday 23 October, 1961, Brian's third child, a baby boy, was born to Pat Andrews. They called him

'We were getting Jimmy Reed and Chuck Berry records, and listening to them and copying them.' DICK TAYLOR

Degrees of separation

It was not until October 1962 that Pye International issued their first Bo Diddley single in the UK, 'You Can't Judge A Book By The Cover'. Pye had released Chuck Berry's 'I'm Talking About You' in September 1961 and then did not release another until July 1963, when 'Go, Go, Go' backed by 'Come On' came out.

Julian Mark, after Julian Cannonball Adderley – Brian's favourite musician. Brian moved into a bedsit with another guy and Pat visited regularly. Soon afterwards, Brian and Dick Hattrell went to see the Chris Barber band perform at Cheltenham Town Hall. The group's set included a blues segment with Alexis Korner and Brian went wild. Afterwards, Alexis gave the two enthusiasists his address and phone number.

'I met Brian in Cheltenham. Brian came into the dressing room to talk, not about the band set, but the blues set.' ALEXIS KORNER

Within a few months of Pat Andrews having their baby, Brian was back to his old ways. He went out with

Elmore James

a 14-year-old schoolgirl and sometime around Christmas they went to London and stayed with Alexis Korner. It was at this time that Brian heard his first Elmore James recording. Brian was so excited that he bought an electric guitar, a Harmony Stratatone, with one pick-up, as soon as he got home. He used a converted tape recorder as an amplifier, until he could afford to buy one.

Brian became obsessed with the blues. He constantly practised playing slide guitar listening to any Elmore James, Robert Johnson and

Chuck Berry

Howlin' Wolf records he could get hold of.

Pond Mann

Around January 1962 Brian met Paul Pond, who lived in Oxford. He led a blues group called Thunder Odin's Big Secret. In search of pop stardom, Paul would later change his surname – with good reason – and as Paul Jones he would front Manfred Mann.

'My guitarist got married and moved, so I asked Brian if he wanted to join us because he was pretty good. The only way he wanted to join a band was on the understanding that he was leader. I said my band already had a leader.' PAUL JONES

Brian sat in with them and they made a tape together, as Elmo and Paul. On his way to and from London, Brian often passed through Oxford, sleeping on Paul's couch. 'I woke up one morning to hear this awful wheezing and snorting coming from the next room,' said Paul. 'Brian was lying on the couch, hardly able to breathe. He gasped out that he'd got asthma and had left his inhaler at the party we'd been at the night before. I jumped on my bike and went dashing off to get it.'

Expensive boys

A tape of Little Boy Blue and the Blue Boys sold at Christie's on 25 May, 1995. It includes: 'Around And Around', 'Little Queenie', 'Beautiful Delilah', 'La Bamba', 'On Your Way To School', 'I Ain't Got You', 'You're Right, I'm Left, She's Gone', 'Down The Road Apiece', 'Don't Want No Woman', 'I Ain't Got You (take 2)', 'Johnny B Goode', 'Little Queenie (take 2)' and 'Beautiful Delilah (take 2)'. It sold for £52,250.

'I discovered Elmore James, and the earth seemed to shudder on its axis.' BRIAN

THE EALING CLUB

Cyril Davies and Alexis Korner in 1962, with Charlie Watts behind them

Ealing as the birthplace of British rhythm and blues is as incongruous as it gets. It couldn't be further from the Delta and Chicago homes to the blues that so fascinated Brian. But in early 1962, Alexis Korner persuaded the Ealing Jazz Club to take a gamble and open its doors to rhythm and blues. In its own small way, the Ealing Club allowed British people to discover this exciting and very different style of music.

From The Barrel to Ealing
In the wake of the skiffle boom, Alexis Korner and Cyril Davies started the London Blues and Barrelhouse Club, in a pub. Korner played guitar and Davies harmonica, performing their own brand of country blues. Korner continued to play with Chris Barber's Band, playing a blues segment with Ottilie Patterson (Barber and Patterson were married in 1959). In 1961, Cyril Davies and Korner, who was half-Greek and half-Austrian, formed Blues Incorporated. With its harder-edged blues, the band established a residency at the Ealing Club.

Brian and Dick Hattrell hitch-hiked from Cheltenham to Ealing to see Alexis and Blues Incorporated play their first show. The band was Alexis (electric guitar), Cyril Davies (harp), Dave Stevens (piano), Dick Heckstall-Smith (tenor sax), Andy Hoogenboom (bass) and Charlie Watts (drums) who had finally decided to play with Alexis. Brian gave Alexis the tape that he and Paul Pond had made; he also asked for the chance to play at Ealing.

'The hours of hitch-hiking we did were well worth it. We would get so wound up, it was incredible. We were literally spaced out with the music. It excited us so much. Brian was dying to play. He was a really good guitar player, even on that homemade amplifier of his. You could tell the sounds were there. He played slide guitar before the average British guitarist had heard of it.' DICK HATTRELL

At a push, the club held 200 people and on that first Saturday night around 100 showed up, but within four weeks it was packed. Membership reached 800, with people even travelling from Scotland. For the second week, playing his new Hofner Committee with its green Elpico pick-up, Brian sat in with Blues Incorporated. It was also the first time that Brian spoke with Charlie Watts. The drummer was also moved by the Ealing Experience: 'When I first played with Cyril Davies, I thought "What the fuck is happening here?" because I'd only ever heard harmonica played by Larry Adler, but Cyril was such a character, I loved him,' he later recalled. 'It was an amazing band, but a total cacophony of sound. On a good night it was amazing, but it was like a cross between R&B and Charlie Mingus, which was what Alexis wanted.'

In *Disc* dated Saturday 24 March, 1962, Jack Good wrote: 'One small box ad was taken out in a jazz journal (*Jazz News*) and that was the extent of the advertising to announce this significant event. Alexis Korner, the man whose idea it was, had he been a realist, would never have got as far

ALEXIS KORNER'S BLUES INCORPORATE
THE MOST EXCITING EVENT OF THIS YEA

RHYTHM AND BLUES CLUBS
No. 1: THE EALING CLUB, EALING BROADWAY, (immediately Opposite Tube Station)
"To the many people who MADE the opening, A Thank You"
This week's Guests: DICK HECKSTALL-SMITH and LISTER (Saturday, March 24th at 7.30 p.m.)
"We're sorry we couldn't make the opening, but we' to wish the first R. and B. Club in this country every p success". CHRIS BARBER and OTTILIE PATTERS

Advert for the second week at Ealing, Saturday, 24 March, 1962

THE opening of an R&B club in London, the first in a proposed series, is causing great interest on the scene. A parallel to the increasing interest in R&B is the increasing use of the guitar in jazz (at a recent Jazz Band contest I attended, only one of the trad. entries used a banjo. The rest used guitar). When "Blues Incorporated" led by Alexis Korner opened in Ealing last Saturday, the session was well attended and the music exciting, bluesy and danceable. Perhaps R&B will now get the recognition it deserves.

*Jazz News
21 March, 1962*

A blues fan of Cheltenham writes…
Brian's response to Jack Good's column, was published in *Disc* dated 31 March, 1962. He had strong ideas about R&B.

Brian enthuses in a letter about appearing at the Ealing Club

THIS IS IT

"RHYTHM and blues" seems to be a term which needs defining, judging by Jack Good's column (DISC, 17-3-62).

It is a genuine blues style, evolved directly from the earlier, less sophisticated country blues. R and B in turn gave birth to a commercial offspring, universally known as rock 'n' roll. Billy Fury is a rock 'n' roll singer—not an R and B vocalist.

I listened to all the records quoted by Jack Good in his article, and all except one were rock 'n' roll records. The one exception was the Barbara George disc "I Know."

Please will somebody play Jack Good a Muddy Waters or a Howlin' Wolf disc so that he can hear what R and B really is?—**BRIAN JONES, 23, Christchurch Road, Cheltenham, Gloucestershire.**

as actually risking this venture. As it was, before the opening night he must have had moments of doubt. He could never have foreseen what actually happened. By word of mouth the news had spread and people flocked to it from all parts of London – some came from as far afield as Sevenoaks and Cheltenham. People had to be turned away. The place was jam-packed. The band played exclusively rhythm and blues – the Muddy Waters variety. The patrons danced and were knocked out. You see, the demand is there.' Jack Good's views aired regularly in the magazine and got a strong response from Brian, who wrote in to Jack two weeks later. That third week in Ealing, Long John Baldry joined Cyril Davies on vocals.

Brian's weekends were beginning to revolve around the club. Alexis Korner remarked, 'Brian didn't like Cheltenham because he found it very boring at weekends. He'd appear late Friday night, and Saturday and Sunday he spent sleeping on our floor. Then he'd catch the last train back to Cheltenham on Sunday night, and go back to work on Monday morning.'

Having read about the club in *Jazz News*, Mick and friends went along on the fourth week, Saturday 7 April, 1962. They saw Brian once again sit in with Blues Incorporated playing slide guitar on Elmore James' 'Dust My Broom'.

'Alexis said, "We got a guest to play some guitar. He's come all the way from Cheltenham just to play for you." Suddenly, it was Brian. He was sitting bent over, playing slide on his Hofner Committee, and calling himself Elmo Lewis. He was the first person I ever heard playing slide electric guitar. Mick and I both thought he was incredible.' KEITH

After the show Mick spoke to Brian for the first time. Brian mentioned he was forming a band.

Mick sent Alexis a tape of some of Little Boy Blue and the Blue Boys' sessions. Mick and Keith were invited to meet Alexis Korner. In the middle of May, *Disc* published an article stating 'Singer Joins Korner'. The story ran:

'A 19-year-old Dartford rhythm and blues singer, Mick Jagger, has joined the Alexis Korner group, Blues Incorporated, and will sing with them regularly on their Saturday dates at Ealing and their Thursday sessions at the Marquee Jazz Club, London.'

Mick remembered the venue: 'The Ealing Club was so wet that Cyril had to put a horrible sheet, revoltingly dirty, over the bandstand, so that the condensation didn't drip directly on you. It just dripped through the sheet.'

'A thin boy from Ripley named Eric Clapton came up to me at the Marquee Jazz Club and talked about guitar strings. He also used to come down to the Ealing Jazz Club and sing rock'n'roll songs, like "Roll Over Beethoven". He would simply stand there looking at his shoes, because he hadn't got used to looking at people he was singing to. He was learning guitar, but he couldn't play then.' ALEXIS KORNER

Cyril Davies' R&B All-Stars at the Ealing Club in 1962: Dave Stevens, Dick Heckstall-Smith, Alexis Korner, Jack Bruce, Mick Jagger and Cyril Davies

'It boils down to the fact that the first band in the field produces all the leaders.' **CHARLIE WATTS**, *on Blues Incorporated*

Let It Roll

In southeast London, playing with the Cliftons, I was oblivious to the Ealing Blues Club. Our guitarist Steve Carroll was becoming really good; he could copy a Chuck Berry solo note for note after only a few hearings. It was also a happy time for me as my son Stephen Paul was born on 29 March, 1962.

BRIAN'S IDEAS FOR FORMING a band revolved around talking to anyone who was a musician. One such was Gordon Harper, five years older; he and his friend Alan Carter came from Gloucester and played together.

'Brian was always the young learner,' said Gordon. 'He was never considered to be in the class of Alan Carter. One day, Brian came to my home and played a Muddy Waters record. He said he was going to form a group to play that type of music and asked me to join. I told him the group could never be successful and although he asked me a number of times, I turned down his offer.'

Brian decided to move to London and took a flat in Weech Road, Hampstead, where his 14-year-old girlfriend would sometimes stay. On Easter Sunday, 1962, Pat and the baby travelled up to London by bus. When she arrived at Brian's door he almost fainted. Pat and the baby moved in and they found a new flat in Powis Square, Notting Hill. Brian worked in the sports department at the Whiteley's store in Kingsway, while Pat worked in a laundry. Soon, he moved on to the Civil Service Store in the Strand.

'When I was living in West Hampstead,' said Long John Baldry, 'Jonesy [Brian] came round with a girlfriend of his and borrowed some singles of mine, which at that particular time were irreplaceable. They were American things like BB King, on the RPM Label. He never ever returned them. I think, in actual fact, he lost them. I wouldn't speak to him for two years after that.'

Blues still inc

Charlie returned from Denmark in February but was very unsettled. Playing with Blues Incorporated was just what he needed. They got the chance of a residency at the Marquee, playing the interval for the Chris Barber Band. Mick sat in on some numbers.

'In April, Harold Pendleton offered us a Thursday night residency at the Marquee Jazz Club,' said Alexis. 'We took it. At our first appearance, 127 loyal fans journeyed from Ealing to give us support.' In that same month, Charlie and Jack Bruce, who later played with Cream, moved to Primrose Hill, London. Charlie also started seeing Shirley Shepherd, who would later become his wife. She was born in London on Sunday 11 September, 1938, and met Charlie when she was studying sculpture at the Royal College of Art.

'I visited the Marquee on the regular Thursday night stints,' said singer Sylvia McNeill. 'I remember once when Keith was with us, Alexis said, "It would be a good idea if you got a group of your own together".'

In early May 1962, Bill and the rest of the Cliftons went to the coast for the day.

Page 18

JAZZ NEWS — Wednesday, May 2nd 1962

R & B AT THE MARqUEE

opening on MAY 3rd is the new R & B band **BLUES INCORPORATED**, formed by ALEXIS KORNER featuring **CYRIL DAVIS** on HOHNER HARMONICA.

The harmonica Cyril plays is one of a wide range. There is a leaflet describing them all.
HOHNER 11/13 FARRINGDON ROAD LONDON EC1

Blues Incorporated: Cyril Davies (harmonica), Alexis Korner (guitar), Jack Bruce (bass), Keith Scott (piano) and Charlie Watts (drums)

'Brian could have easily joined another group, but he wanted to form his own. The Rollin' Stones were Brian's baby.' **KEITH**

RHYTHM AND BLUES

Guitarist and Vocalist forming R. & B. Band, require Harmonica and/or Tenor Sax, Piano, Bass, and Drums. Must be keen to rehearse. Plenty of interesting work available.
BOX No. 1277

Brian's original advert, in Jazz News of 2 May, 1962

Mick and I used to stand on the side, hoping to be asked to get up and sing. One night we got up on stage and squawked out, "What'd I Say".'

The Killer

In May, Brian Cade joined my band as second lead guitarist. We played at a youth club at St Michael's Hall in Lower Sydenham and further afield, in Essex, Kent and South London, Musically, we covered the likes of the Coasters, Sam Cooke, Jerry Lee Lewis, Chuck Berry, Fats Domino, Ray Charles and Little Richard. On Monday 14 May, all the Cliftons went to the Majestic Cinema in Mitcham to see Jerry Lee Lewis play live.

Brian put an advert in *Jazz News* for R&B musicians. Piano player Ian Stewart was the first to respond. Stu loved R&B, boogie and blues, but

The Bricklayers Arms today, now called West Central, in Lisle Street, Soho

The Cliftons

Bill: 'We bought matching jeans and black mohair jumpers for stage and painted a sign with the band's name. We were a real group – we even played weddings!'

also liked Duke Ellington, Ella Fitzgerald and the big bands.

'On the spur of the moment I thought, I'll try and get hold of this guy,' said Stu. 'He was a strange character, but very knowledgeable. He was deadly serious about the whole thing. He wanted to play Muddy Waters, Blind Boy Fuller and Jimmy Reed stuff, who I'd never heard of. He couldn't find the people he wanted, because not many people had heard that Chess and Vee-Jay stuff. Then Howlin' Wolf's record "You Can't Be Beat" came out in London. That was the style he was really trying to achieve.'

Getting it together

Brian held rehearsals at the White Bear pub in Leicester Square. 'The first consisted of a friend of Charlie's called Andy Wren [Screaming Lord Sutch's piano player], who wanted to sing, another piano player who was playing like Count Basie – he wasn't what Brian wanted – and Brian on regular and slide guitar,' recalls Stu. 'Brian was living in an unbelievably awful state, drinking spaghetti out of a cup.' Thrown out of the White Bear because Brian stole cigarettes, they moved to the Bricklayers Arms in Soho's Lisle Street.

While Brian and Stu remained the nucleus, Alexis put Brian in touch with other musicians. Stu remembered an intense guitarist, Geoff Bradford: 'He'd worked with Cyril Davies and was into ethnic blues and Muddy Waters, John Lee Hooker and Elmore James. Geoff was a good guitar player and serious. He'd draw very distinct lines between what he'd play and what he wouldn't.'

'I formed a band called Blues By Six. We played the Marquee Jazz Club. This fellow came up to me and said, "My name's Brian Jones and I'm thinking of forming a band. Do you want to be in it?" I said that I'd have a go. There was Ian Stewart, Brian Knight (vocalist for Blues By Six) and a drummer. Ian Stewart used to turn up on a bike and park it outside.'
GEOFF BRADFORD

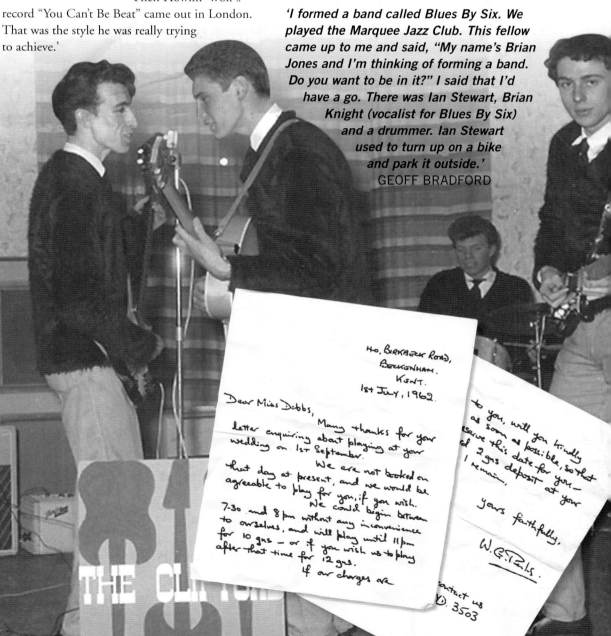

40, Birkbeck Road,
Beckenham.
Kent.
1st July, 1962

Dear Miss Dobbs,

Many thanks for your letter enquiring about playing at your wedding on 1st September.

We are not booked on that day at present, and we would be agreeable to play for you, if you wish.

We could begin between 7-30 and 8 pm without any inconvenience to ourselves, and will play until 11pm for 10 gns – or if you wish us to play after that time for 12 gns.

If our charges are ... to you, will you kindly ... as soon as possible, so that ... reserve this date for you – ... 2 gns deposit at your ...

I remain,

Yours faithfully,

W. Gills.

... contact us
...D. 3503

Top: By May 1962, Mick (front) and Keith (left) were regularly practising together and (above) Dick Taylor (left) and Keith duck-walk

Brian tried to persuade Paul Pond to come and join them, but he had decided to stick with his university studies – that is until he could no longer resist the lure of Manfred Mann. Paul did perform with Blues Incorporated at the Marquee, usually sharing the stage with Mick and Long John Baldry. Among others, Mick would sing Muddy Waters' 'Ride 'Em On Down' and Billy Boy Arnold's 'Bad Boy' and 'Don't Stay Out All Night', getting paid between 10 shillings and £1.

'I said it was a terrible name. It sounded like the name of an Irish show band or something that ought to be playing at the Savoy.' STU, *talking about the Stones*

'*I remember John Baldry and Paul Pond singing "Got My Mojo Working" with me. They were much taller than me, I used to feel very small. Paul was very cool in those days. He used to go up there with shades on, trying to be ever so cool, with his donkey jacket and sing quite nice. He was older than me and much spottier.*' MICK

In June, Mick went to one of Brian's rehearsals. Before long, Mick, Keith and Dick were rehearsing every Wednesday and Friday with Brian, Stu and Geoff Bradford. Keith remembered: 'When we rehearsed, Stu would always be looking out the window to make sure his bike was still there. He'd keep one eye on the bike and one eye on the piano; he'd always hit the right notes.'

Bradford, the purist, soon departed, unable to bring himself to play Chuck Berry and Bo Diddley.

Keeping it together
There were also early signs of Brian's erratic behaviour. According to Stu: 'Occasionally Brian would vanish, because he had a very complicated life. He set out to be a rebel and to upset people, and there was no need for it, because he was really quite a nice guy.'

Soon after Brian met Mick and Keith, Pat and the baby went back to Cheltenham. Brian later moved to a basement flat in Brackley Road in Beckenham. He and a girlfriend nearly burned the place down while cooking a meal. He simply put a piece of canvas over the hole in the ceiling to disguise their handiwork. Having got a job in a London record shop, Brian was caught stealing from the till and sacked. He worked briefly at WH Smith in Kingsway, until he was again fired for stealing.

Meanwhile rehearsals continued in and around the Dartford area. Joe Jagger, Mick's dad, was surprised: 'I didn't realise

Playing with Earl
Brian wrote to *Jazz News* informing them of the line-up for the Rollin' Stones. With no regular drummer, Brian used Earl Philips' name. Earl was an American session drummer who worked with the likes of Howlin' Wolf and Jimmy Reed. It was Brian's little joke to include him. Mick Avory eventually played the gig.

how well Mike was getting on until he started using the phone a great deal. It was only when they grew their hair long that a change came about. At first he and his group were just the sort of youngsters any parent could be proud of.'

In his final term at Sidcup Art School, Keith took Brian home to meet his mum. She recalled: 'Brian seemed all right, but a bit cagey. Like Keith, he didn't enjoy the rougher side of life. I had to put some carpet down and asked for help. Brian said "You've got to get a man to put this down".'

In early July 1962, Blues Incorporated were offered a spot on BBC Radio's *Jazz Club*. The Marquee's promoter, Harold Pendleton, issued an ultimatum: 'If you leave this Thursday to do the broadcast, I will not guarantee your gig the Thursday after.' The band met at the Marquee and agreed that Alexis and Blues Incorporated should play the BBC show, while Mick, Stu, Keith, Brian and whoever else would hold down the Marquee gig.

Disc reported the Marquee cancellation

'Mrs Richards, Keith should have a decent guitar now because we're gonna play in the big time.' BRIAN

The Rollin' Stones

Brian decided to perform under the name the Rollin' Stones and the day before the gig *Jazz News* reported: 'Mick Jagger, R&B vocalist, is taking an R&B group into the Marquee tomorrow night. Called the Rollin' Stones, the line-up is: Mick Jagger (vocals), Keith Richards and Elmo Lewis (guitars), Dick Taylor (bass), Ian Stewart (piano) and Mick Avory (drums).'

'I was there when they decided on the name, and there is no way that it came from the Muddy Waters 78 "Rolling Stone Blues". No one would be seen dead with 78s; we exclusively had 45s and 7" EPs. Nobody had that 78. I had the Muddy Waters Mississippi Blues EP on London from 1956. It includes "Mannish Boy", which has the interjection, "Ooh, I'm a rollin' stone".'
DAVE GODIN, *Mick's friend*

Brian was filled with optimism and called his parents, whom he had not spoken to for months; a few days later he went home to see them.

'He appeared to have found what he was looking for, a chance to become a competent jazz musician,' said his father. 'It was on this occasion that he first mentioned a group of people he called the Rollin' Stones.'

'I was 14 in the summer of 1962 and had a penfriend in London who was 16. My parents allowed me to go and stay with him that summer. My penfriend Chris and his 18-year-old friend took me to the Marquee for a sensation. Suddenly a band called the Rolling Stones appeared and it was a shock for the little Swedish boy. The band consisted of Mick, Keith, Brian, Dick Taylor, Ian Stewart and Mick Avory on drums. I remember them playing "Kansas City"; I was sold on them.'
ULF KJELLSTROM, *a fan*

'I hope they don't think we're a rock'n'roll outfit.' MICK, *on Marquee fans*

After the Marquee, the band later played Ealing Blues Club. Stu knew the traditional jazz scene and it was left to him to find a drummer – a tall order – as gigs were uncertain.

Drum shift

For the Cliftons, there was a change of direction: we became more of a white rock'n'roll band. Dave Harvey, our singer, wanted to leave so Steve Carroll and I shared the vocals. We added a saxophone player and started playing larger gigs. We even did a riverboat show up the Thames and a gig at LSE (Mick might have seen us!).

'I first met Bill in July 1962 when I was in the Paramounts and we were both on the same bill,' said Gary Brooker. 'The Cliftons, four other bands and ourselves played a gig at Greenwich Town Hall. It was an old trick by the promoter, a band contest with a small prize. With six bands, loads of people came to the dance and he didn't have to pay.' Gary went on to be in Procul Harum.

Keith had finished at Sidcup Art School but was in no rush to find a job. 'Brian and I had decided that this R&B thing was an absolute flop. We were gonna do an Everly Brothers thing. Then we decided to write a song. It sounded like a 1920s' Broadway musical – just the weirdest kind

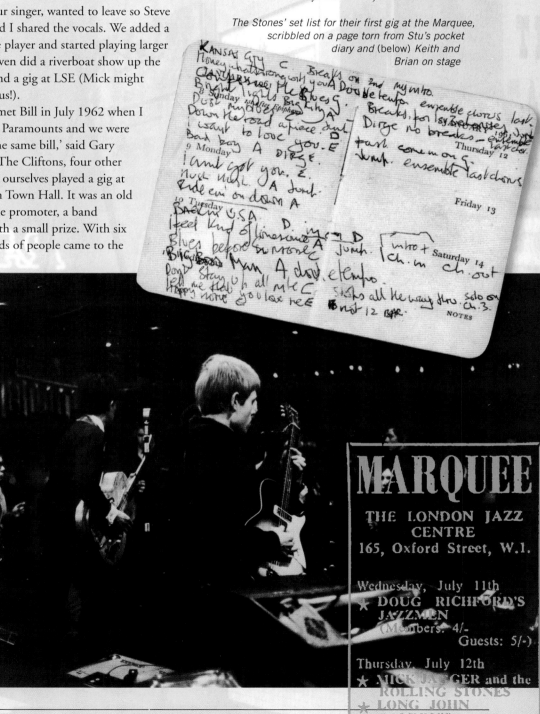

The Stones' set list for their first gig at the Marquee, scribbled on a page torn from Stu's pocket diary and (below) Keith and Brian on stage

Bill had no idea that his drummer, Tony Chapman, answered an ad placed in Melody Maker *on 18 August, 1962.*

Young hopefuls
Brian, Mick, Graham Ackers, Keith and Harry Simmonds in September 1962. Mick and Keith hold pictures of their heroes, Chuck Berry and Bo Diddley. Harry later managed Savoy Brown, the blues band led by his brother Kim.

Rhythm and Blues is getting bigger. Now that Alexis Korner is established at the Marquee with a regular audience of 700, new groups are springing up at the drop of a harmonica.

Keith Scott's recently formed BLUES PLUS SIX open a regular session at the Colyer Club on Sunday (30th) between 4 p.m. and 6.30 p.m.

The ROLLING STONES, yet another one, take over from Alexis at the Ealing Club now that Alex is so busy that he can't do the residency any more.

Jazz News, *Wednesday 26 September, 1962*

Stu in Cheam and Brian in Brackley Road, Beckenham. Dick Taylor played a big acoustic bass. They liked me because I was the first drummer who liked to play the shuffle, which I learned in the Cliftons, doing Chuck Berry songs. A day or so later, we all met at Mick's house in Dartford and played the album *Jimmy Reed At Carnegie Hall.* They asked me what I thought of it. I liked it and they said, "Fine, because that's the sort of music we want to play".'

Shady Grove
In late August 1962, Mick moved with Brian to 102 Edith Grove in Chelsea. Their rent was £16 per week. Pat and the baby moved in from Cheltenham and she cooked for them. Brian's money went on guitar strings and equipment, and Pat's money helped support them. It was a scruffy flat, lit by a single bulb in the living room. Soon, Keith moved in.

'I never consciously thought about leaving Dartford, but the minute I got out, I had pretty strong instincts that I'd never go back.' KEITH

Brian, Mick and Keith played records, more often than not Muddy Waters. Brian said: 'We wondered if we were doing the right thing, by not getting into worthwhile jobs. Suppose we went on not doing much, just soaking up music for a whole year. That would be the limit, we reckoned.

If we flopped, would it matter? At least we'd have tried.' Brian again badgered Charlie Watts about joining their group, but he was happy with his job and his semi-pro work with other bands. Rehearsing was the Stones' forte, much more than performing. The Wetherby Arms – around the corner from the flat – was their practice ground.

Brian often visited Cyril Davies, who taught him how to flatten the notes on the harmonica and create a bluesy sound. Keith half-heartedly tried to find a job in advertising, taking his portfolio to several agencies.

'I knew they were often desperate for money. I sent Keith cash whenever I could and food parcels too, because I knew money would just go on cigarettes instead of on a good, solid meal. It cost me about £1 a day to keep Keith going.' DORIS RICHARDS

Mick passed his first year exams at LSE and Brian continued to drift. By September, Pat decided her role as mother, cook and the worrier for all of them was too much. She left a note and returned to Cheltenham, affecting Brian greatly: he lost his job and had something of a breakdown.

Dick Hattrell moved into Edith Grove, which unbalanced the situation. Brian was awful to his old friend; he took Dick's money, his overcoat and even threatened to electrocute him. Brian was not nice to know: 'It was snowing and he sent me out for some fags, then locked me out for the rest of the night,' said Dick. 'He always wanted something new to happen.'

The outsiders
Sporadic gigs did little to enhance their reputation or the confidence of Tony Chapman: 'The bulk of

of song. Brian was utterly impossible to write with: he would dominate everything. Mick had to sing it, which he couldn't, because at that time he could only sing 12-bar blues.'

Before long they were back rehearsing, still in search of a drummer. The son of comedian Charlie Chester tried out, but he was a jazz man. Unbeknownst to me, our drummer in the Cliftons, Tony Chapman, decided to follow up an ad he'd seen in *Melody Maker*. He tried out with the Stones, although Stu was less than impressed: 'Tony wasn't very good: he would get onto the on-beat and slow down. He'd finish the number in the middle of a chorus.'

Tony had a different take on how things had gone: 'Mick and Keith were living in Dartford,

In residence at Edith Grove, SW10
Mick, Keith and Brian lived on the first floor at 102 Edith Grove, along with James Phelge. Visitors knocked twice on the door to get them to answer. Another resident, Ian Gilchrist, went up to meet his neighbours not long after moving in. He asked if they'd seen the landlord. 'Mick appeared, naked and looking very angry,' said Ian. 'He stood there looking at my feet and slowly moved his gaze upwards until it was level with my face. Then he spoke: "Fuck off!" and slammed the door in my face.' Ian was abused and had tricks played on him on many other occasions, and moved out.

the time I played with them, I was getting roasted for being a lousy drummer, but I didn't have a bass player. I thought it mildly unfair.' The lack of gigs was, according to Stu, not really to do with their ability. 'We had a job getting gigs, because there was this sort of Mafia thing. Trad had died and left a vacuum. Harold Pendleton, a guy called Bill Carey and Alexis tried to take over the R&B scene, and keep it very much a jazz thing. I was the only one working at this time. When I went off to work for ICI as a clerk, the Stones sat around all day rehearsing and trying to get bookings. We looked like a rock'n'roll band, so they played games, offering us gigs and cancelling them at the last minute. We'd find that Blues By Six or the

Mann-Hugg Blues Band had done them. We thought about starting a club in a pub.'

Charlie Watts heard bad reports about the boys from among the jazz fraternity. 'They were complete outsiders. Nobody wanted to know about the great sounds they were making; they were all too busy looking on them as a gang of long-haired freaks.'

'I was waiting for the Stones outside the Ealing Club, when a man started talking to me about the Stones, saying it was a disgrace that a group who looked so untidy should be making money out of the jazz world. He said they were just a bunch of animals, wild lunatics who didn't even look like musicians.' A FEMALE FAN

The shifting nature of the band's rhythm section was far from helpful. Carlo Little, from Screaming Lord Sutch's band, sometimes played drums along with a bass player called Ricky Fensen. Another problem was their inability to keep up with hire purchase payment on their equipment. They kept their money in an old tin, which mysteriously disappeared; Brian was the likely culprit. Stu helped them eat: 'The boys frequented the Earls Court Wimpy Bar using luncheon vouchers I fiddled from work.'

Stones play Woodstock
By October, Cyril Davies had decided to leave what was now Alexis Korner's Blues Incorporated. Cyril formed his own band that, for a short while, included Long John Baldry. The Mann-Hugg Blues Band took over their Monday night residency, before evolving into Manfred Mann. In the same month, the Stones played their first gig away from Ealing and the Marquee at the Woodstock Hotel in Cheam. The band comprised Mick, Keith, Brian, Stu and Dick Taylor. There were no drums at the gig. The following day they played Ealing – two gigs in two days should have been a success.

Love Me Do
Six days after the fledgling Stones played the Woodstock Hotel in Cheam, the Beatles entered the charts for the first time, on 11 October. 'Love Me Do' climbed to UK No 17, not that the Stones would have taken much notice.

IT appears there exists in this country a growing confusion as to exactly what form of music the term 'Rhythm & Blues' applies to.

There further appears to be a movement here to promote what would be better termed 'Soul Jazz' as Rhythm & Blues.

Surely we must accept that R & B is the American city Negro's 'pop' music — nothing more, nothing less. Rhythm & Blues can hardly be considered a form of jazz. It is not based on improvisation as is the latter. The impact is, and can only be, emotional. It would be ludicrous if the same type of psuedo-intellectual snobbery that one unfortunately finds contaminating the jazz scene were to be applied to anything as basic and vital as Rhythm & Blues.

It must be apparent that Rock 'n' Roll has a far greater affinity for R & B, than the latter has for jazz, insofar as Rock is a direct corruption of Rhythm & Blues, whereas jazz is Negro music on a different plane, intellectually higher, though emotionally less intense.

BRIAN JONES
London, SW 10
(Brian Jones plays guitar with The Rollin' Stones)

Brian's letter to Jazz News *of 31 October, 1962, shows how seriously he took his music.*

However, according to Dick, only two people paid to get into Cheam, while four others stood outside. By the end of the month Dick Taylor had left the band. 'I was a student at the Royal College of Art,' he explained shortly afterwards. 'I had to start concentrating on my exams... I parted company with the Stones. We didn't have a row or anything. I don't regret the break one little bit. I'm now lead guitarist with the Pretty Things. We're doing pretty well, so why should I complain?'

Fame and fortune
Life in Edith Grove went on much the same. Money and food were both in short supply, but the boys were long on dreams. Dick Hattrell had a burst appendix and moved back to Cheltenham, probably saving him from a worse fate. A girl named Judy Credland lived in the flat below; both

'Bill brought electricity to the Stones.' TONY JASPER,

The Cyril Davies All-Stars

When Blues Incorporated broke up, Alexis and Cyril went their separate ways. Cyril formed his own band, which for a short while included Long John Baldry. By November 1962, the Cyril Davies All-Stars had formed. Bernie Watson (lead guitar), Ricky Brown (Fensen) (bass guitar), who attended the Royal College of Music in 1970, Nicky Hopkins (piano) and Carlo Little (drums) had been in a group called the Savages and backed Screaming Lord Sutch. Cyril Davies himself was on vocals and harmonica.

Mick and Brian had a keen interest in her. She supplied food, some freely given and some not. They crept down to her kitchen at 3am and left scribbled IOUs on the draining board. Judy's hobby was palm reading and she examined Mick's hand. As he opened his fingers, she gasped, 'You've got the star of fame, it's all there.'

Flamingo and lions

An opportunity came up to audition at the Flamingo club, a jazz haunt. It went well enough, but neither the Flamingo's audience nor the band were ever comfortable with each other.

At their first Sunday afternoon Flamingo residency, the Graham Bond Trio also played (Graham Bond, Jack Bruce and Ginger Baker). It was their first gig. Shortly afterwards, Stu called Tony Chapman and said that in order to get a residency, they would have to use Carlo Little on drums. It was the beginning of Tony's end.

Sometime in November, the boys played the Red Lion pub in Sutton, Surrey for the first time. Colin Folwell, a friend of Stu's, says he was paid £3 to play this gig. According to later newspaper reports, jazz drummer Folwell thought they played too loud, leaving him deaf for an hour afterwards. Well, they must have had different equipment from when I joined a few weeks later; their amps were not capable of deafening anyone!

'We were beginning to sense that more and more people were getting sick of traditional jazz and they were looking around for something different. We all knew that something was us. We didn't like being hard up, but we put up with it because it was the price we had to pay.' BRIAN

Brian and the others desperately wanted to get on. Keith became ill and went home to his mother, but refused to miss a gig. Doris said 'I put him straight to bed, but he wouldn't stay there. He was really ill, but the next night he insisted on dragging himself off to play in London. He said, "We've got a date at the Flamingo. We've been booked, mum, and I've just got to go." I think that he was half afraid that he might lose his place with the group.'

They even had had a crack at running their own club. They chose South Oxhey, near Watford, for this sporadic venture.

Electric man

Tony Chapman was back on drums when the band next played the Piccadilly Jazz Club on 30 November. He played me tapes of what the Rollin' Stones were doing, mostly Jimmy Reed songs. The Stones needed a regular bass player and in early December Tony suggested I go to the Red Lion in Sutton to meet one of the members. We saw a reasonable crowd listening to Glyn Johns and the Presidents when we got there. In the interval, I was introduced to Ian Stewart, who suggested that we go to the band's next rehearsal.

That Friday, I went with Tony Chapman to the Wetherby Arms pub in Chelsea. We entered through a side door into the back room. I met Stu

Let's make a record

On Saturday 26 October, the Rollin' Stones went to jazz guitarist Curly Clayton's Studio near Arsenal football ground in North London.

Mick, Brian, Keith, Stu and Tony Chapman recorded three songs, from three of their principal inspirations, Bo Diddley's 'You Can't Judge A Book By The Cover', Muddy Waters' 'Soon Forgotten' and Jimmy Reed's 'Close Together'.

'I met everyone at the studio, near Highbury Corner tube station,' said Tony Chapman. 'There was one microphone in the middle of a small room. To balance the sound we moved the instruments around, all except the piano, which was nailed to the wall. There was no bass on the record. We actually did it to see what it sounded like. We all clubbed together and paid for it.'

A few days later the Stones sent the recordings to Neville Skrimshire at EMI Records and someone at Decca told Tony: 'You'll never get anywhere with that singer.' A well-worn acetate of this session, originally belonging to Tony Chapman, was sold at a Phillips rock'n'roll memorabilia sale in London on 6 April, 1988, for £6,000.

again and Mick, who was quite friendly. I was then introduced to Brian and Keith, who were at the bar. They all had hair well over their ears and looked very scruffy, all bohemian and arty. They were very cool and distant, showing little interest in knowing me. We brought my equipment in and set it up. Suddenly *everyone* was interested. I had my old homemade bass, my wardrobe-size bass cabinet, a Watkins Westminster, and a Vox AC30 amp that I'd bought on hire purchase in August. I was wearing a suit and tie, as I thought a band should dress smartly. It did not impress them, but my equipment did.

'There's a certain amount of truth in the old story about Bill being taken on because he had a few amplifiers,' admitted Stu, 'but he was very good. He was in quite a successful band. Actually, he was very strange and didn't know a lot about the blues, but he liked the idea of it.'

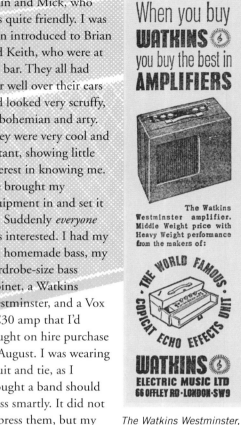

When you buy **WATKINS** you buy the best in **AMPLIFIERS**

The Watkins Westminster amplifier. Middle Weight price with Heavy Weight performance from the makers of:

THE WORLD FAMOUS COPICAT ECHO EFFECTS UNIT

WATKINS ELECTRIC MUSIC LTD 66 OFFLEY RD · LONDON · SW9

The Watkins Westminster, one of the amps Bill took to the Wetherby Arms, and Bill's spare Vox AC30 amp

'You can't play fucking 12-bar blues all night!' BILL, *on first night of rehearsal with the Stones*

I bought a round of drinks for everyone and offered them cigarettes, which they grabbed, but still, Brian and Keith hardly talked to me. Mick asked if I knew the music of many black blues artists. The only people I'd really heard of were Fats Domino and Chuck Berry. I talked about the Coasters, Jerry Lee Lewis, Eddie Cochran, Johnny Burnette, Lloyd Price and Sam Cooke, but the looks I got showed their distaste. Keith particularly hated Jerry Lee Lewis. Interestingly, 15 years later, he suddenly discovered Jerry Lee and started playing his records constantly – and still does. We rehearsed some slow Jimmy

The site of the Wetherby Arms on the King's Road as it looks today

Reed songs and other blues numbers. Brian and Keith chatted a little, but made it clear to me that I wasn't really in favour. The general opinion seemed to be that I was nothing special but they liked my equipment. They asked me to rehearsals again. Tony and I went to Edith Grove to leave my equipment in the front room… It was a disaster area.

Bill on board

Early in December, Charlie left Blues Incorporated: 'I really wasn't good enough. They were such fantastic musicians; I couldn't keep up the pace. When I left Ginger Baker took over.' Charlie started playing with other bands, including Blues By Six with Brian Knight and Geoff Bradford.

Early in December, Keith returned to Sidcup Art College with the Stones to play the Christmas dance. There was also a brief return to the fold for Dick Taylor. The following day Tony and I went to Edith Grove. It was bitterly cold and on our way we picked up fish and chips for everyone to share. They also shared my cigarettes (I was almost as popular for them as for my gear) and borrowed some shilling pieces for the electric meter to run their single-bar fire. The flat was a

'It was hard to concentrate on music when you were almost too hungry to think.'

BRIAN

tip. One chair had just three legs and it was so cold we had to keep our coats on. After we ate, it was down to the Wetherby Arms for my second rehearsal, when everyone was much friendlier.

I decided to throw in my lot with the Rollin' Stones. My son, Stephen, was eight months old. It meant the end of the Cliftons but something told me that the Stones were a better bet. The next day, 14 December, I played my first gig as a Rollin' Stone, at the Ricky Tick Club in the Star and Garter Hotel, Windsor. It was a large, square room, with a small triangular stage in one corner and a bar on one side. On the walls were posters of other groups that had played the club, including the Mann-Hugg Blues Band and Hogsnort Rupert's Band. The crowd was a mix of students and a smattering of American servicemen who knew Chicago R&B. They were impressed.

'The Stones, then all unmarried, were sympathetic to Bill. We agreed that he would only play with us if the money was good. If it was bad, then he stayed at home.' STU

…ROLLIN' STONES (wanted one BASSIST-must be Rhythm & Blues slanted) are heavily booked over the season

Jazz News, 27 December, 1962 – maybe Bill's equipment and cigarettes weren't enough?

On Saturday, we played Sandover Hall in Richmond, and Brain, Keith, Mick and I took the bus. The conductor was reluctant to let us on with all our equipment; he relented somewhat grudgingly. On the following Tuesday and Wednesday the boys played at Ealing and South Oxhey, but I skipped it – with work it was too difficult. At some of the early gigs, there weren't many people: they were more like rehearsals. We practised songs like 'Tiger In Your Tank', 'Blues Before Sunrise' and 'Hoochie Coochie Man'.'

Christmas day for Mick, Keith and Brian was low-key. They celebrated with lunch in a working man's cafe on the Kings Road. Four days later we were back at Ealing, our last gig of 1962. We had hopes but no inkling of how dramatically our lives would change during the next 12 months.

The Rollin' Stones 1962 gigs

'As I wasn't there for many of these, it has taken me endless hours of research to piece it all together. If anyone can fill in any gaps, they're welcome.' BILL

EALING CLUB R & B ROLLIN' STONES — BAR

12 July, 1962 Marquee Jazz Club, Oxford Street, London
4 August Ealing Jazz Club, Ealing, London
11 August Ealing Jazz Club
18 August Ealing Jazz Club
25 August Ealing Jazz Club
1 September Ealing Jazz Club
15 September Ealing Jazz Club
22 September Ealing Jazz Club
29 September Ealing Jazz Club
5 October Woodstock Hotel, North Cheam, Surrey
6 October Ealing Jazz Club
13 October Ealing Jazz Club
20 October Ealing Jazz Club
27 October Ealing Jazz Club
November Red Lion Pub, Sutton, Surrey
3 November Ealing Jazz Club
10 November Ealing Jazz Club
11 November Flamingo Jazz Club, Soho, London
14 November William Morris Hall, South Oxhey, Herts
17 November Ealing Jazz Club
18 November Flamingo Jazz Club
20 November Ealing Jazz Club
21 November William Morris Hall
24 November Ealing Jazz Club
28 November William Morris Hall
29 November Marquee Jazz Club
30 November Piccadilly Jazz Club, Soho, London
1 December Ealing Jazz Club
4 December Ealing Jazz Club
7 December Red Lion Pub
December Christmas dance, Sidcup Art College, Sidcup, Kent
11 December Ealing Jazz Club
14 December Ricky Tick Club, Star and Garter Hotel, Windsor (Bill's first gig with the band)
15 December Sandover Hall, Richmond, Surrey
18 December Ealing Jazz Club (No Bill)
19 December William Morris Hall (No Bill)
22 December Sandover Hall
29 December Ealing Jazz Club

TWIST, TWIST, SANDOVER HALL, Richmond, near L'Auberge coffee bar and hear The **ROLLING STONES,** Dec. 22nd, 7.30 to 10.30.

63

**January
September**

We Are
The
Rolling
Stones

Photographed in Edith Grove on 4 May, a few hours before playing in Battersea Park.

Are We Rolling Stones?

We began 1963 as we ended 1962, with a gig at the Ealing Club. It would prove to be one of the few things that were the same about these two years. On that first Saturday in January, I took the train to Ealing and met the others in the ABC Cafe, which was next door to the club. As I walked in they all jumped up and cheered. Gone was my quiff, I had combed my hair forward… I was a Rolling Stone.

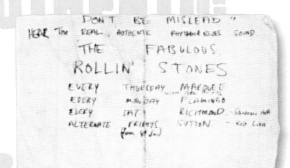

The band's handwritten draft of the advert for their regular shows in January 1963.

TO BEGIN WITH it was a little strange playing with the Stones, as I was still learning their material. I remember that Saturday at Ealing very well. I was concentrating on playing 'Put A Tiger In Your Tank' and looked over at Stu who was hammering out the song on his piano. About a minute from the end of the song, I looked over again and Stu was gone – he was standing at the bar with some friends having a drink!

Melody Maker *article on 5 January, 1963, one of Mick's first press quotes*

Enter the Phelge

While gigs were getting a little more regular, life at Edith Grove went on in the same old way. Tony, Stu and me were working; Mick was at LSE; Brian and Keith were both unemployed.

'We wouldn't bother to get out of bed some days, as there was no heating in the flat,' Brian commented, 'I didn't see the point in getting out of bed just to get cold. We put all our clothes into a communal kitty, so we couldn't all go out at the same time, especially if it was raining. A special food treat was the addition of a fried egg to the mashed potatoes. It sort of gave the spuds a colourful look'. A guy named Jimmy Phelge

moved into the flat, adding his own brand of dubious personal habits to the squalor. Jimmy worked in printing. His domestic hygiene left a lot to be desired and, unfortunately, it got progressively worse. Jimmy became part of Stones mythology.

'You'd walk in and he would be standing at the top of the stairs, completely nude, with his filthy underpants on top of his head. He'd spit at you.' KEITH, *on Jimmy Phelge*

We played the Red Lion in Sutton and met up with musician Glyn Johns. We went to a Chinese restaurant and spent all we earned, probably the only decent meal Keith and Brian had eaten all week. Next day we played the Marquee, supporting Cyril Davies, who had taken over the residency from Alexis after he moved to the Flamingo. We got £10 for supporting Cyril's All-Stars, featuring Nicky Hopkins on piano, Carlo Little on drums and guitarist Bernie Watson, a strange man who sat behind his amp with his back to the audience and a handkerchief over his head. Bernie played great licks. Cyril's bass player, Ricky Brown, was then my main influence.

Charlie Watts on drums

Despite helping me become a member of the Stones, I could

see that Tony Chapman's days were numbered. He didn't fit: we needed Charlie Watts.

As Stu remembered, 'We said to Charlie, "Look, you're in this band, that's it, end of story," and Charlie said, "Yeah, alright then, but I don't know what my dad's gonna say."' Charlie was still living with his parents in a prefab in Neasden. As an outsider, Charlie's view of the Stones was interesting and in truth about right: 'I thought they were mad. They were working a lot of dates

On 2 January, 1963, Brian wrote to the BBC's Jazz Club, asking for an audition.

Prefab street
There was a shortage of housing following the Second World War in Britain. A solution was to put up temporary — prefabricated — houses (such as the one Charlie's family lived in), gaining them the name 'prefabs'.

JAZZ AT THE MARQUEE
165 OXFORD STREET W1 (Nr OXFORD CIRCUS)

Friday, January 11th
★ **BILL NILE'S DELTA JAZZMEN**
★ **KANSAS CITY JAZZMEN**
(Members 4/-   Guests 5/-)
Saturday, January 12th
★ **JOE HARRIOTT QUINTET**
★ **DON RENDELL QUINTET**
(Members 6/-   Guests 7/6)
Sunday, January 13th
★ Big Band Night
★ **JOHN WILLIAMS BIG BAND**
★ **PETE SHADE QUARTET**
(Members 4/-   Guests 5/-)
Monday, January 14th
★ Rhythm and Blues Night
★ **BLUES BY SIX**
★ Pete Deuchar's
★ **COUNTRY BLUES**
(Members 4/-   Guests 5/-)
Wednesday, January 16th
★ **HUMPHREY LYTTELTON BAND**
★ GORDON BAKER OCTET
(Members 5/-   Guests 6/-)
Thursday, January 17th
★ Rhythm and Blues Night
★ **CYRIL DAVIES' ALL-STARS**
plus the fabulous
★ **VELVETS**
★ ROLLIN' STONES
(Members 4/-   Guests 5/-)

without getting paid or worrying about it. I was earning a pretty comfortable living, which obviously was going to nosedive. But I got to thinking about it. I liked their spirit and I was getting very involved with R&B. So I said okay.'

I used the name 'Wyman' for the first time on stage that January. Taken from my old mate in the Royal Air Force, I thought it sounded much better. I'd never be Perks again.

We played the Ricky Tick in Windsor on 11 January. After the show, as we packed up our equipment, Tony was told that his services were no longer required. He was furious and said, 'Come on, Bill, let's go and start a new band'. I told him I was staying with the Stones and Tony just upped and left.

Share ware
Charlie's first gig was the next night, appropriately enough at Ealing. It was 12 January and we were a

'Lots of my friends thought I'd gone raving mad.' CHARLIE

six-piece: Brian, Mick, Keith, Charlie, Stu and me.

While gigs were more plentiful, money was not. Another significant problem was the lack of transport. We wanted to play more, which meant getting bookings out of London around the country, but how were we going to get there? We struck lucky when Stu was given some shares in ICI, under a scheme to encourage workers to become shareholders. Good old Stu promptly sold them and used the profits to buy a van to carry us and all of our equipment to gigs. It was not the only part that ICI – based in Victoria – played in the success of the Rolling Stones.

Graham Bond
Graham Bond's Organisation started life as a trio and featured (*left to right behind him*) Ginger Baker, Dick Heckstall-Smith and Jack Bruce.

'None of the Stones were on the phone, and my desk at ICI was the headquarters of the Stones organisation. My number was advertised in Jazz News *and I handled the Stones' bookings at work. When the boss found out, I was called into the office and threatened with the sack.'* STU

GERRY LOUGHRAN AND ROYD RIVERS...a fine blues duo from Malcolm Nixon's 'folk' office (MAY 1735) ...other numbers...... KORNER (KNI 5935) HUNT (GER 0702), CYRIL DAVIES (EAL 1572) BLUES PLUS SIX (SOU 4003) ROLLIN' STONES (VIC 4444). WESTMINSTER (RAV 0141).

After about a week of Charlie being in the band, I already found him much easier to play with than Tony, or anyone else for that matter. It helped because I liked Charlie; I thought we had the makings of a pretty good rhythm section.

While I realised that we had to build a reputation in order to get better paying shows, we needed to be sure of not losing money. I made my feelings known after one particular gig at Ealing. I was paid five shillings and pointed out that it cost me more than that to get there.

Brian's creative band accounts had a list of deductions for flat expenses, guitar strings, harmonicas and all sorts of other things.

An indication of our growing appeal came when a girl asked for our autographs after a gig. I think Charlie summed it up for all of us. 'I felt quite embarrassed about it, but I did sign. We took our music seriously, but not ourselves and to have this girl wanting us to write our names shook me.' Brian was wrestling with his own problems. He would sit writing and rewriting letters to his parents. He desperately wanted their approval.

'Brian was a lot more conscious of his background and what his family thought of him than the rest of us.' KEITH

Name game: Bill: 'Sometimes we were billed as "Rollin'" and other times "Rolling". There was no mystery behind this; we just hadn't decided definitively which we were.'

At the end of January, Cyril Davies fired us from the Marquee. Crowds at the club were reaching 600 a night and we asked for a little more money. Even back then, £16 a show was not a lot between six of us. Harold Pendleton said later: 'I came out of the Marquee with Cyril Davies as they were loading their stuff into a van. I shouted,

"Goodnight" and they shouted back something unprintable. I said to Cyril, "What's the matter with them?" Cyril said, "I just fired them, they are not very authentic and not very good."' This was typical of the snobbishness associated with the jazz end of the blues fraternity. As Chris Barber explained: 'To me it was down to being authentic. We were all a bit highbrow at that time, and the Stones' attitude to R&B was to us rather poppy. We were a bit snooty about it.'

The jazz mafia

While our Ealing residency was secure, losing our regular Marquee and Flamingo gigs meant we needed to look elsewhere for work. The jazz mafia gave us a bad name and probably blocked us in some venues. To make up for our loss of dates, we started playing Ealing on a Tuesday night as well. At another of our regular gigs, the Ricky Tick, we increasingly found ourselves the centre of attention offstage as well as on. Girls started to hang around the group and chat to us between sets, which was an altogether new and not unpleasant experience. But I must say they all looked very plain to me. Most of them tended to wear no make-up and have long straight hair; this was the latest fashion. One of them was a 16-year-old called Linda Lawrence. Brian lost no time in inviting her to Edith Grove.

Linda Anne Lawrence was living in Windsor at the time, where her father was a building contractor. Both Stuart Lawrence and his wife Violet were Catholics.

'After I started working down at the Flamingo, me and the bass player used to live in the Cromwell Road district of London. In Earls Court was one of the only late-night diners in London. On our way back from the Flamingo, around five or six o'clock in the morning, I went to this diner and Bill was there with Mick and Keith. A few weeks later, they played the Flamingo and nobody came. I was there with John McLaughlin and a couple of other guys.' GEORGIE FAME

'What I liked in him at first, was that he treated me like a lady. He was just so nice and polite, and he looked after me. He was my first real relationship after leaving school.' LINDA LAWRENCE

We were still rehearsing at the Wetherby Arms and even tried incorporating two girl backing singers. Cyril Davies had three black female singers, which is what probably gave us the idea. Cleo Sylvester and a friend of hers called Jean, who, incidentally, couldn't sing a note, came along. We thought of calling them the Honeybees, but soon gave up the idea as they were forever giggling. Afterwards, Cleo occasionally visited Edith Grove to discuss her interest in singing with Mick.

At the end of January, Brian received a reply from the BBC about the *Jazz Club* audition. They asked him to fill out an application form. Two weeks later, we got another letter offering us an audition on 23 April, which seemed an awfully

'They didn't call themselves R&B; they just played it. They played blues the way I hear the blues.' ALEXIS KORNER

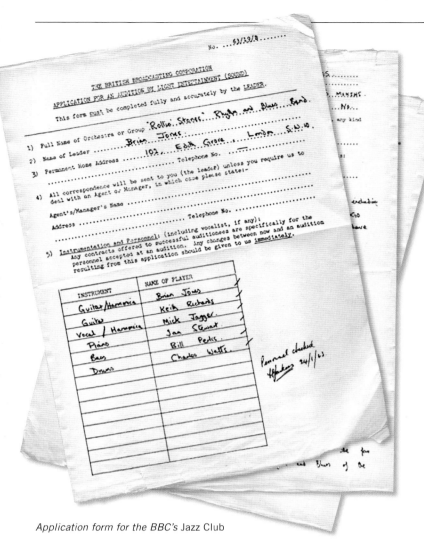

Application form for the BBC's Jazz Club

long way off. More importantly for our immediate future, Brian met the wonderfully named Giorgio Gomelsky at the Marquee and invited him to our Red Lion gig in Sutton.

Clubbing

We also got another new gig, the Harringay Jazz Club, at a pub called the Manor House, supporting Blues By Six, featuring Brian Knight. They didn't have a drummer, so Charlie Watts played with both bands. The club DJ was Long John Baldry and on that night he played the first John Lee Hooker track I ever heard. I went overboard for his music and started searching for his records. The next night, at the Ricky Tick, a couple of guys started asking us questions about guitars, amps, chords and all sorts of things. One of them was Paul Samwell-Smith, who would be a founding member of the Yardbirds early that summer. Managed by Giorgio, they went on to replace us at many of our club gigs when we began touring the ballrooms and clubs around the country.

The Red Lion, Sutton
On 6 February, 1963, Giorgio saw the Stones here. 'I liked what they were doing. I said, "Listen, I promised Dave Hunt a job, but the first time he goofs, you're in."'

International man of blues
Giorgio Gomelsky's mother was a French milliner from Monte Carlo and his father was a Russian surgeon, born in Soviet Georgia, who had to flee Stalin's repression of the professional classes. Giorgio hitch-hiked around the world, organised the first Italian jazz festival and became a passionate blues fan while living in Chicago. He settled in England in 1955 and worked as an experimental filmmaker. In August 1961, he produced a film about the first Richmond Jazz Festival, featuring the Chris Barber Band.

By early 1963, he was running his own club in the rear room at the Station Hotel, Richmond. The Johnny Dankworth Band featured on a Monday night. He decided to open on Sunday nights as well and booked the Dave Hunt Blues Band, with Ray Davies (later with the Kinks) on guitar.

'My favourite songs we were doing on stage at this time were Bo Diddley's "Cops And Robbers" and Chuck Berry's "The Jaguar And The Thunderbird".' BILL

Giorgio invited Brian and the boys down to the Station Hotel, where he ran the Richmond Jazz Club on Sunday nights; family commitments kept me at home. The Dave Hunt Band were turning out to be unreliable, so Brian said, 'Look, Giorgio, you can't run a club without knowing whether your band's going to turn up. Give us a break. We'll do it for nothing.' Typical Brian – he was so passionate and completely certain that we could do it. We all got together with Giorgio at Edith Grove and asked his advice on getting gigs. The opposition from the jazz-promoting mafia was an ever-present curse. Our Tuesday night gigs at Ealing were pretty sparse and the audience wasn't getting much bigger at Harringay. On Monday 18 February, Giorgio called Stu at ICI and said, 'Tell everybody in the band that you guys are on at Station Hotel next Sunday.' We all went to Giorgio's flat, where he guaranteed us £1 each per show and suggested that we had posters made.

'I remember one night we went all over London sticking up posters with a big bucket of glue.' GIORGIO GOMELSKY

Our Tuesdays at Ealing were so badly attended that we dropped them, though Wednesdays at the Red Lion, Sutton, were going well. We talked again to Glyn Johns, who was working as an engineer at IBC studios. He encouraged us to get some songs together so he could record us.

KEN COLYER JAZZ CLUB

at Studio 51
10/11 Great Newport Street,
Leicester Square (Tube)
Open every Wednesday, Thursday,
Friday, Saturday and Sunday
All Night Sessions every Friday
Rhythm & Blues every Sunday
Afternoon with
THE ROLLING STONES
4-6.30
See Classified ads.
Pages 16-17

Ken Colyer was a trad jazz pioneer who led a number of groups and worked with Chris Barber and Lonnie Donegan.

Linda and afterwards we all went to a cafe in Soho. Pat and the baby came with us. Brian was so proud: he walked around showing everyone his son.

The next week we started what was to become our regular Sunday for several months. In the afternoon we played Studio 51, Ken Colyer's Club in Soho, and in the evening we were at the Station Hotel. Giorgio got us the Studio 51 gig – it was run by two nice women called Pat and Vi, who were always very friendly, helpful and generous to us. We drove from there

Richmond, April 1963
Giorgio Gomelsky made posters advertising the Stones at Richmond. On one of the early ones it said 'Sunday night 7.30pm – Rhythm and Bulse'.

Richmond beckons

On Sunday 24 February, we drove through snow to Richmond for our first gig at the Station Hotel. The doors opened at 7pm and we played two sets of about 45 minutes each. The first was for about 30 people at 8.15pm and then we came back on again at 9.45pm, all for £7 10s.

The following Saturday we played our last gig at Ealing. Linda Lawrence was there and Pat and the baby turned up. Brian managed to get rid of

straight over to Richmond. It was our second gig there. The audience had almost doubled from the first week.

Both Studio 51 and Richmond were great to play. Lots of Richmond fans would come over to Soho and we were beginning to earn decent money, no longer just playing for the fun of it.

Commercial Appeal

'Brian was pretty much the leader.' GLYN JOHNS

In February 1963, Glyn Johns offered to make a tape so that he could get a record company interested in us. It sounded like a good idea. Our main problem was deciding on what to record. A week or so later, after another Red Lion gig, we talked our choices over with Glyn.

WE AGREED on Monday 11 March for our first session and met Glyn at IBC Recording Studios, near BBC Broadcasting House, for a three-hour session, recording Bo Diddley's 'Road Runner' and 'Diddley Daddy', Muddy Waters' 'I Wanna Be Loved' and Jimmy Reed's 'Honey What's Wrong'. We had five minutes left, so we did a quick take on another Jimmy Reed song, 'Bright Lights, Big City'. Brian was really bowled over by these tracks. He was

more proud of them than anything else we ever recorded. Years later he would often play these songs for friends or acquaintances.

'Brian was pretty much the leader. He was certainly the spokesman for the group to me. Brian was very much concerned about the sounds that I would produce on tape. He wanted the Jimmy Reed-type sound, which was virtually unheard of in England.'
GLYN JOHNS

Glyn's boss, George Clewson, tried to interest record companies in our tape. He took it to six or seven, but everyone turned him down. The consensus was that we were not commercial enough for the pop charts. Having been so excited about the session, it was something of a letdown for all of us.

A sound man
Glyn Johns became a successful sound engineer and producer. Born in Epsom, Surrey, on 15 February, 1942, he worked with many major acts, including the Who, the Faces, Eric Clapton, Humble Pie, Joe Cocker, Led Zeppelin and the Eagles.

The IBC Session

At IBC Recording studios in Portland Place, near the BBC's Broadcasting House, the Stones recorded five songs on their two-track machine.

'Diddley Daddy'
Charlie (drums), Bill (bass), Keith (rhythm guitar), Brian (harmonica and backing vocal), Stu (piano) and Mick (vocal and backing vocal)

'Road Runner'
Charlie (drums), Bill (bass), Keith (rhythm guitar), Brian (lead guitar), Stu (piano) and Mick (double-tracked lead vocal and backing vocal)

'I Wanna Be Loved'
Charlie (drums), Bill (bass), Keith (rhythm guitar), Brian (harmonica), Stu (piano) and Mick (double-tracked lead vocal)

'Honey What's Wrong'
Charlie (drums), Bill (bass), Keith (lead guitar), Brian (rhythm guitar), Stu (piano) and Mick (double-tracked lead vocal, harmonica and maracas)

'Bright Lights, Big City'
Charlie (drums), Bill (bass), Keith (lead guitar), Brian (rhythm guitar), Stu (piano) and Mick (vocal and harmonica)

The London Club Scene

After Charlie's first gig with the other five Stones – for back then, Stu was an integral part of the band – they worked on consolidating their position around London. The number of clubs was expanding as the blues and beat bands increased. A residency became a popular way of establishing a band's reputation and developing a following.

Dates are the first time the Rolling Stones, including Bill and Charlie, played each gig.

Ealing Jazz Club, Ealing, London 12 January 1963
Flamingo Jazz Club, Soho, London 14 January
Marquee Jazz Club, Soho, London 17 January
Red Lion Pub, Sutton, Surrey 23 January
Ricky Tick Club, Star and Garter Hotel, Windsor, Berks 25 January
Harringay Jazz Club, Manor House Pub, London 7 February
Station Hotel Pub, Richmond, Surrey 24 February (from 7 April it became known as the Crawdaddy Club)
Ken Colyer Club, Studio 51, Soho, London 3 March
Wooden Bridge Hotel, Guildford, Surrey 9 March
Eel Pie Island, Twickenham, Middlesex 24 April
News of the World Charity Gala, Battersea Pleasure Gardens, London 4 May
Scene Club, Soho, London 20 June
Crawdaddy Club at Athletic Grounds, Richmond 30 June

Typical fees for a gig
Marquee Club 17 January £10
Ealing Jazz Club 19 January £3
Richmond Hotel 24 February £7.50
Crawdaddy Club 12 May £30 (guaranteed)
Crawdaddy Club 30 June £50
Twickenham Design College Dance,
Eel Pie Island 12 July £73

'In the back room there were about **500 people**, in a place designed for **100**. The music transformed them, they stood jammed together – it was like a ritual. In the half-darkness the guitars and drums started to twang and bang. Pulsating R&B. You could boil an egg in the atmosphere. Heads shake violently; feet stamp in tribal style, with hands above heads, clapping in rhythm. Like a revivalist meeting in America's Deep South. It happens nowhere else in Britain.'
PATRICK DONCASTER, *DAILY MIRROR, Sunday 9 June at the Crawdaddy Club*

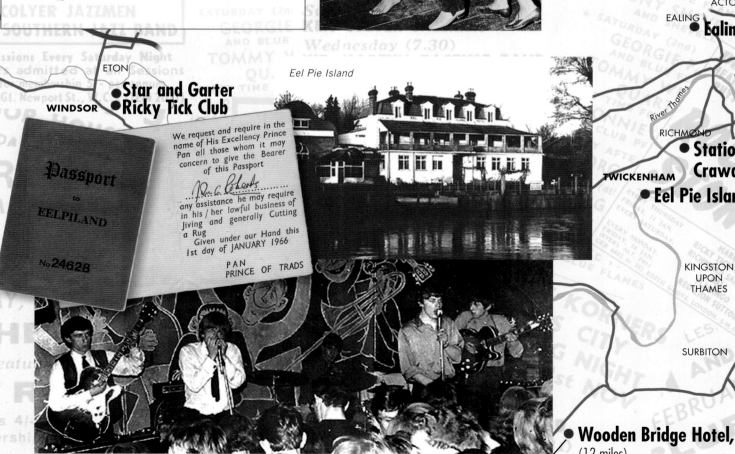

Eel Pie Island

'At our first Tuesday night residency at the Ealing Jazz Club, only six people turned up. It was so cold we played with our coats on.' MICK

The gig at the Ealing Jazz Club on 12 January, 1963, was the first time Brian, Mick, Keith, Charlie, Bill and Stu played together as the Rolling Stones.

January: 11 Gigs
Ealing Jazz Club: 12, 19, 26
Flamingo Jazz Club: 14, 21, 28
Marquee Jazz Club: 17, 24, 31
Red Lion Pub: 23
Ricky Tick Club: 25

February: 17 Gigs
Ricky Tick Club: 1, 8, 22
Ealing Jazz Club: 2, 5, 9, 12, 16, 19, 23
Red Lion Pub: 6, 20
Harringay Jazz Club: 7, 14, 21 28
Station Hotel: 24

March: 21 Gigs
Ealing Jazz Club: 2
Ken Colyer Club, Studio 51: 3, 10, 17, 24, 31
Station Hotel: 3, 10, 17, 24, 31
Red Lion Pub: 6, 20
Harringay Jazz Club: 7, 14
Ricky Tick Club: 8, 15, 22, 29
Wooden Bridge Hotel: 9, 30

April: 11 Gigs
Red Lion Pub: 3
Ken Colyer Club, Studio 51: 7, 14, 28
Crawdaddy Club, Station Hotel: 7, 14, 21, 28
Wooden Bridge Hotel: 19
Eel Pie Island: 24
Ricky Tick Club: 26

May: 18 Gigs
Eel Pie Island: 1, 8, 15, 22, 29
Ricky Tick Club: 3, 24, 31
News of the World Charity Gala, Battersea Pleasure Gardens: 4
Ken Colyer Club, Studio 51: 5, 12, 19, 26
Crawdaddy Club, Station Hotel: 5, 12, 19, 26
Wooden Bridge Hotel: 17

June: 23 Gigs
Ken Colyer Club, Studio 51: 2, 3, 9, 10, 15, 16, 23, 24
Crawdaddy Club, Station Hotel: 2, 9, 16
Crawdaddy Club, Richmond Athletic Club: 30
Eel Pie Island: 5, 12, 19, 26
Wooden Bridge Hotel: 7, 22
Ricky Tick Club: 14, 21, 28
Scene Club: 20, 27

July: 8 Gigs
Ken Colyer Club, Studio 51: 1, 8
Eel Pie Island: 3, 10, 12
Scene Club: 4, 11
Ricky Tick Club: 5

Bill and Charlie outside Studio 51

TOTTENHAM

HARRINGAY
● **Manor House Pub**
STOKE NEWINGTON

ISLINGTON

SOHO
CITY

SLOANE SQUARE
RD
CHELSEA

● **Battersea Pleasure Gardens**

LAMBETH

STREATHAM

West End venues
1 The 100 Club
2 Marquee (Oxford St)
3 Beat City
4 Roaring 20's Top Ten Club
5 Marquee (Wardour St)
6 Ronnie Scotts (briefly)
7 Jack of Clubs
8 Round House Pub
9 The Scene
10 Picadilly Jazz Club
11 Flamingo Jazz Club
12 La Discotheque
13 The Ad Lib Club
14 Notre Dame Hall
15 Studio 51, Ken Colyer Club

SOHO
OXFORD STREET
REGENT STREET
BROADWICK STREET
WARDOUR STREET
GREEK STREET
CHARING CROSS ROAD
SHAFTESBURY AVENUE
GERRARD STREET
LISLE STREET
LEICESTER SQUARE
COVENTRY ST
GLASSHOUSE ST
PICCADILLY CIRCUS
BREWER STREET

'It was wonderful to hear people playing very long versions of things like Jimmy Reed songs. They would play 10-minute versions of all sorts, "Route 66", "Pretty Thing" and "I'm A King Bee", where the solos used to get more intense and build to a climax.'
MARTIN EASTERBROOK, *fan*

'At our last gig at the Flamingo Jazz Club we stole three metal stools. We used them onstage – Brian, Mick and Keith sat on them while I sat on my "Wardrobe" bass cabinet. We would stop between songs to light up fags, drink beers and chat between ourselves. There was no stage presentation, we generally ignored the audience.' BILL

STUDIO 51
10-11 GREAT NEWPORT ST.
LEICESTER SQUARE
The Rolling Stones
EVERY MONDAY

Doin' The
CRAWDADDY

The gigs we played at Studio 51 and the Station Hotel were becoming increasingly popular. Crowds of 200 at Richmond were soon the norm. More to the point, the level of excitement we were generating was on the increase. While we played on a stage lit by just one red and one blue spotlight, the fans danced with their shirts off and climbed on the tables. It was an incredibly intense atmosphere.

'Art students from the Kingston College of Technology started coming to the Station Hotel pub. It was really a scene.' GIORGIO GOMELSKY

WE ENDED EACH SET with a Bo Diddley song, 'Pretty Thing' or 'Doin' The Crawdaddy', for 20 minutes. It became something of a ritual. It was hypnotic, some even called it tribal. The Station Hotel in Richmond was our spiritual home. The excitement in that place was electric – you could feel the energy. Our spell there, more than anywhere else, gave us the motivation to take on the world.

'A local paper asked us what we called the club. We'd never had a name. Without thinking, we said the Crawdaddy.'
GIORGIO GOMELSKY

I was still working in Streatham Hill and got flak from my boss about the length of my hair. Charlie and Stu had proper jobs and short hair, while the others had, for the time, very long hair.

Brian had more important things to worry about. Just after the IBC session, Pat Andrews went into hospital for a peritonitis operation and she returned to Cheltenham. Brian visited Linda Lawrence's family for the first time.

Linda and Brian

'Brian and I had difficulty fitting into society,' said Linda. 'He brought me to a London modelling school because he thought I would meet different kinds of people. I told him that my parents would like to meet him, and he put on a clean shirt and washed up.' Brian's domestic arrangements took another complicated turn. When Pat Andrews heard about our growing success, she decided to

Station Hotel, April 1963: Top Topham and Chris Dreja, later of the Yardbirds, were in the audience.

'The audience were barbaric. They would stand on tables and wave their arms

old son Stephen and a wife. Charlie and Stu were also used to earning money. We had to hold down jobs as well as play gigs and managed on a lot less sleep. Brian's friend Paul Jones came to Studio 51 and observed: 'You don't do many originals.' Mick replied: 'I can't write songs.' Meanwhile, life in the boys' flat continued to be unpredictable.

'Strange things happened at Edith Grove. At 2am Mick, Keith and Brian once suddenly and inexplicably hurled all their sheets and blankets out of the window into the yard and set fire to them. One night, they came home at 3am and played a pop record through one of their stage speakers at a tremendous volume.' IAN GILCHRIST, *writer who lived in the flat below in Edith Grove*

Georgio Gomelsky found us a new gig in Twickenham just down the road from Richmond. It was called Eel Pie Island and we first played there on 24 April.

'The Stones were very good in their amateur days. I was at LSE with Mick. He was attractive, even though he was ugly. That was probably his appeal. Girls usually liked his style and dress and the fact he looked interesting. He didn't go out with many girls.' CAROL HORNSEY, *fan*

return to London with the baby. She found a flat in Ladbroke Grove and began working in a chemist's shop. She stayed with Brian for a couple of days each week and he genuinely seemed to be warming towards fatherhood, buying things for both the baby and Pat. But not so much as to stop him seeing Linda. He would visit her and her family in Windsor, sometimes staying over. Linda's parents took to Brian, even lending him their car. He and Linda would go and see a local group, the Roosters, which included a young Eric Clapton and future Manfred Mann member Tom McGuinness.

'I was a real fan in 1963,' said Tom. 'I'd go and see them at the Station Hotel. I went with my girlfriend, who was at Kingston Art School

The Stones' contract with Giorgio Gomelsky to appear at the Crawdaddy.

with Eric Clapton, where we heard by word of mouth about the Stones. They drew a cross-section: mods, guys in smart Italian suits, bohemians, art students, mixed couples, everyone. The venue was a dingy, hot, sweaty function room – all tobacco-stained everywhere.'

Blues evangelists

Musically we were getting the right response. The crowds at the Station Hotel and Studio 51 were getting bigger and even more enthusiastic. Keith: 'We knew we were on the right track. We were sort of evangelists; it was pure idealistic drive that did it. We didn't give a damn about the money we needed to live on.' That might have been true for Keith, but I had the responsibility of my one-year-

A musical magnet
Barry May, writing in the *Richmond and Twickenham Times* of 13 April, 1963, said, 'A musical magnet is drawing the jazz beatniks to Richmond. The attraction is the Crawdaddy Club... Save for the swaying forms of the group on the spot-lit stage, the room is in darkness. A patch of light from the entrance doors catches the sweating dancers and those who are slumped on the floor... How sad and unfortunate that the Station Hotel is to be demolished.'
The article was all Brian had striven for. Years later, he still carried it as a good luck talisman, proof that the group he created and led were on their way to the big time at last.

about, yelling and shouting.' **HAMISH GRIMES,** *Giorgio's assistant*

THE BEATLES

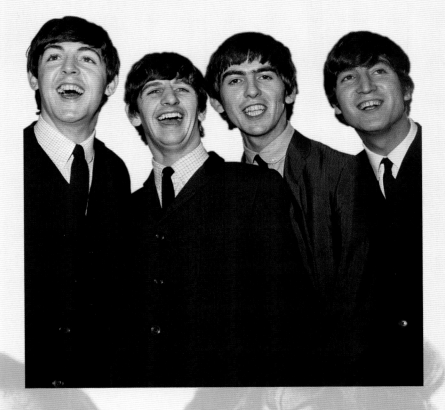

At lunchtime on Sunday 14 April, 1963, Giorgio Gomelsky went to Twickenham, where the *Thank Your Lucky Stars* TV show was recorded. With his usual opportunism he approached the Beatles, who were on the show that week, about making a film. He also suggested that they should stop in at the Station Hotel on their way back to London that night and catch the Stones' set.

This was the week the Beatles' third single was released. 'From Me To You' was the follow-up to their February chart-topper, 'Please, Please Me'. We, as usual, had played Studio 51 in the afternoon before driving down the A3 to Richmond. During our first set at the Crawdaddy I was staggered to see the four Beatles standing watching us from just six feet away. They were dressed identically, in long, black leather coats. I remember thinking, shit, that's the Beatles and I got all nervous; not like me at all.

'It was a real rave. The audience shouted and screamed and danced on tables. They were doing a dance which no one had seen up till then, but now we all know as the shake. The beat the Stones laid down was so solid; it shook off the walls and seemed to move right inside your head. A great sound.' GEORGE HARRISON

During the interval we talked with all four of them at the bar, and they ended up staying for our second set. I remember Brian asking John Lennon, 'Are you playing harmonica or a blues harp on "Love Me Do"?'

'A harmonica, y'know, with a button,' replied Lennon. Brian had been wondering how he got such a deep bottom note on 'Love Me Do' and it turned out Lennon had been much impressed with the harmonica riffing on 'Hey Baby', the 1962 smash by singer Bruce Channel. John had picked up some guidance on how to emulate the sound. John revealed to Brian that it was 'impossible to get "Hey Baby" licks from a blues harp.'

After we finished our set we packed up and Paul, John, George and Ringo all came back to Edith Grove with us. We talked for

27th May. Headline: Daily Mirror, 'BEATLE YOUR ROLLING STONE HAIR! A headmaster ruled yesterday: Beatle haircuts are IN – but Rolling Stones styles are OUT. The head, Mr. Donald Thompson has suspended eleven of his boys from Woodlands Comprehensive School, Coventry, because they wear their hair like Mick Jagger and Co. of the Rolling Stones pop group. "Long and scruffy" Mr. Thompson calls it. But yesterday he said they would return if they cut their hair neatly – like the Beatles.'

- Brian Epstein
- 'My popular music combo'
- Smart
- Clever composers
- Sitting room
- Roots in R&B
- Establishment
- Paid Hamburg dues
- Smiles
- Played the show-biz game
- Charming
- Light
- No visible cigarettes
- Your teachers bought their records
- Witty
- Strong studio sound through their mentor, George Martin
- Kept largely clear of the law
- Not really party music
- Albums subject to over-analysis

'This is what we like, being mobbed

& THE ROLLING STONES

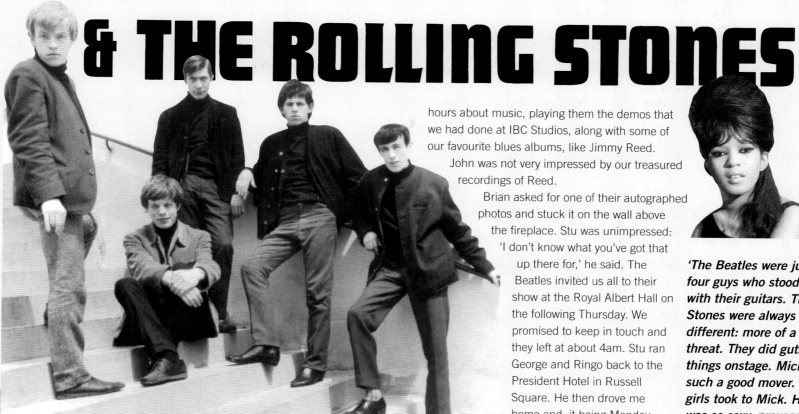

hours about music, playing them the demos that we had done at IBC Studios, along with some of our favourite blues albums, like Jimmy Reed. John was not very impressed by our treasured recordings of Reed.

Brian asked for one of their autographed photos and stuck it on the wall above the fireplace. Stu was unimpressed: 'I don't know what you've got that up there for,' he said. The Beatles invited us all to their show at the Royal Albert Hall on the following Thursday. We promised to keep in touch and they left at about 4am. Stu ran George and Ringo back to the President Hotel in Russell Square. He then drove me home and, it being Monday morning, we both had to go straight off to work.

'The Beatles were just four guys who stood there with their guitars. The Stones were always different: more of a threat. They did gutsy things onstage. Mick was such a good mover. The girls took to Mick. He was so sexy, provocative and gorgeous onstage.'
RONNIE BENNETT, of the Ronettes

- Andrew Loog Oldham
- 'Would you let you daughter sleep with a Rolling Stone?'
- Casual
- Brilliant interpreters
- Bedroom
- Roots in the blues
- Anti-establishment
- Didn't move far at first
- No smiles
- Provocative
- Attitude
- Dark
- Always visible ciggies
- They might have but wouldn't admit it
- Surly
- Lack of a real studio mentor, ALO attempting to impersonate Phil Spector
- Targeted by the law
- The ultimate party music
- Not examined in so much detail

Stones on film

After failing to secure the Beatles for a film, Giorgio decided he would shoot a 20-minute documentary of us at Richmond. He suggested we decide what to play. He also called Peter Jones at the *Record Mirror* and invited him to come and see us perform. A few days before filming, Mick, Keith and Brian went to see the Beatles at the Albert Hall. To avoid having to buy tickets, the Stones walked in the back door, carrying the Beatles' guitars; they were mobbed by girl fans.

'They invited us to one of their gigs at the Albert Hall. It was incredible for us to watch. I'd never seen hysteria on that level before. We were so turned on by those riots.'
MICK

Wasn't that the Rolling Stones you just left?" asked the taxi driver as I left a restaurant in London's Mayfair.

"Yes. What do you think of them?"

"A bunch of right 'erberts!" he replied with the cutting pertinence so typical of the London cabbie. " 'Ere, aren't they the boys they say are trying to knock the Beatles off the top?"

A popular misconception was that we were at war with the Beatles. While our busy lives prevented us from seeing much of each other, we had mutual respect and genuine admiration for the Beatles. Probably because we were so different, it made it easier for us to be friends and not feel the kind of rivalry that the newspapers had the public believe. Of course this didn't stop the press having a field day with Beatles vs Stones stories.

by people. This is what we want.' **BRIAN**

Master Manager

'I was probably 48 hours ahead of the rest of the business in getting there. That's the way God planned it.' ANDREW OLDHAM

Andrew Loog Oldham was a vital ingredient in our success. He was young enough to understand and share our outlook and he had a talent for exploiting the unexploitable. He ensured the press swallowed outrageous stories… and printed them! He set us up to be the opposite of the loveable Beatles and we became the first pop group people loved to hate.

WE WENT to the RG Jones Studios, in Morden, Surrey, on Saturday 20 April, to rehearse Bo Diddley's 'Pretty Thing' and record it for Giorgio's film. Many years later Giorgio told me we also did a Jimmy Reed song but I have no recollection of us recording it. The next day was warm and sunny and Giorgio took the opportunity to film us carrying our equipment into the Station Hotel and setting up.

We spent most of the afternoon filming. Giorgio would shout and rant, behaving just like a caricature European madcap movie director. During a break in filming, Giorgio introduced us to Peter Jones, the editor of *Record Mirror*.

'It came to lunchtime and I was first introduced to Brian and then to Mick,' recalled Jones. 'We had a couple of pints of beer. They were hungry and they didn't have any money. Brian had the group wallet and there was no money in it, but what there was, was a cutting from the local paper, a piece about the apparent success and controversy that the band were creating, and what they were about. They bemoaned to me the fact that nobody was showing any interest in them in terms of a recording contract. I said that the first thing they needed was a good manager and promised that I would see what I could do.'

Once we finished filming, it was almost time for the evening show. The crowd, as usual, were queuing to get in, well before the doors opened. Peter Jones watched the show and was immediately sold on us.

'What impressed me was Mick's animation. There was a perfect foil in the guitar playing of Keith, who didn't jump about very much, and the rather soft and nice appearance of Brian. The Stones were really very good. There was no doubting that Brian was the leader of the band. He was proud of the band. It was Brian who reigned over every single move.' PETER JONES, *Record Mirror*

The following day, Peter contacted Andrew Oldham, a young hustler who specialised in pop PR. He had worked for the Beatles for a while through Brian Epstein's organisation, North End Music Stores (NEMS). Two days after the filming, the band finally auditioned for BBC Radio's *Jazz Club*, with Carlo Little on drums and Ricky Brown on bass, as Charlie and me had to work. The following night we played our first show at Eel Pie Island.

Andrew Loog Oldham
He was the illegitimate son of Celia Oldham and Andrew Loog, a Texan of Dutch origin who served in the US Army Air Corps during the Second World War. Celia was, like Mick's mother, born in Australia and she also moved to England aged about four. She had an affair with Flight Lieutenant Loog in the spring of 1943 and he was killed in action in June 1943.

Andrew (or ALO) was born on 29 January, 1944, making him a little under a month younger than Keith. Schooled at Wellingborough Public School, Andrew grew up with his mother in north London, their life funded by Celia's lover. Andrew's career after school included a spell working for Mary Quant before he took on the world of pop.

'The combination of music and sex was something I had never encountered in any other group.' ANDREW OLDHAM

'According to Andrew, Stu just didn't look the part, and six is too many faces for the fans to remember in a photo.' KEITH

On Sunday 28 April, we played our usual double header at Studio 51 and the Crawdaddy. It was after our first set at Richmond that we were introduced to Andrew Oldham and the much older Eric Easton. 'It was the first free Turkish bath I'd ever had,' recalled Eric. 'It was absolutely jammed with people and was the most exciting atmosphere I'd ever experienced in a club. The Stones were just incredible, fantastic, fabulous. They got through to people.'

Likewise, the atmosphere struck Andrew: 'I'd never seen anything like it. You know when you're in a room with a fanatical audience. I was quite overpowered. I was mesmerised by Mick's raw sexual magnetism. I called Mick over to meet Eric. Brian came up and joined in. We simply had a chat, sizing each other up. Brian put himself forward as leader of the group and the rest seemed to accept this.'

'Andrew was dumbfounded. He looked at Mick like Sylvester looks at Tweetie Pie.'
GEORGE MELLY,
jazz musician

I think Stu summed that moment up best. 'The Stones liked Andrew. Like them, he was young, irreverent, full of enthusiasm and eager to make a fortune. He was only 19 at the time and had little experience in the high-pressure world of pop music, but that was no handicap as far as the Stones were concerned.'

The management
The next day Andrew spoke with Eric about managing them jointly. According to Andrew, 'I felt that with my knowledge of the pop world and his business experience, we could provide a good service for them.' Andrew called the Stones office – Stu's phone at ICI – and a day or so later Brian agreed to meet at Eric's office at Radnor House in

Regent Street, to discuss a management deal. Brian met Andrew and Eric several times to go over the proposed contract. Keith and Mick would wait around the corner in a Lyons Corner House; the rest of us were, of course, at work. The management contract that Brian signed helped us but did little for our association with Giorgio Gomelsky. Giorgio was, in fact, away in Switzerland attending his father's funeral. Giorgio had been good to us and while it's true there was no management deal, he deserved better.

> *'Brian and Eric liked to think they were running the whole show. My attitude was to let them get on with it, as I wanted to get on with the music-making.'*
> ANDREW OLDHAM

Brian filled us in on the contract he'd signed on our behalf. Andrew came to our gig at Eel Pie that night and we all got very excited as we talked about our future. He also dropped a bombshell, although I expect Brian knew it was coming. Andrew insisted that Stu step down from the on-stage line-up. Andrew's solution was that Stu remain for recording and be our road manager. For Brian and Mick, who were eager for success, it was a small price to pay. Stu, to his eternal credit (and very fortunately for us) agreed. He remained a Rolling Stone in our hearts and minds forever.

When we signed, only Stu and I were working. Charlie had thrown in his lot with the Stones full-time. Living at home made it easier for him to take a risk. On 2 May, Andrew told us he had booked a recording session for the following week, so we went through the limited record collection at the flat and came up with Chuck Berry's 'Come On'. Two days later, the band went to Carnaby Street, where Andrew bought us tight black jeans

Easton agent
When he and Andrew first met, Eric Easton was running a little booking agency from an office in Regent Street. He represented Julie Grant and Bert Weedon. Andrew rented some office space from Eric, who had been a performer playing the organ in the Blackpool Tower. According to Andrew, 'Eric was grey-haired, grey-suited and in his mid-thirties.' The very opposite of ALO.

and black roll-neck sweaters – our new stage gear. We did our first photo session along the Thames Embankment in Chelsea, just near the bottom of Edith Grove.

That afternoon, we performed at a *News of the World* charity gala at Battersea Pleasure Gardens. Pat and the baby were there and Brian walked around with the baby in his arms. Andrew went completely mad, telling Brian it would harm his image. Mick, Brian and Keith wore jackets over their new uniform. We wanted to retain our casual look, which didn't please Andrew either. It wasn't the last time we were at odds with him about our dress sense. It wasn't us deliberately being rebellious. We just thought that our music came first and if people liked what they heard, what we were wearing wouldn't bother them at all.

News Of the World Pop Gala

On 4 May, 1963, the Stones did their first ever photoshoot (*below*), before playing at Battersea Pleasure Gardens, by the boating pool (*right*). They faced the water, while people danced behind.

Recording Artistes?

Sunday 5 May was another pivotal moment in the band's story. We played Studio 51 and the Crawdaddy. Dick Rowe, head of A&R (Artists and Repertoire) at Decca Records, came to see us. Dick was a legend in the business, more for what he hadn't done than for what he had. He was the man who turned down the Beatles. He had no intention of letting lightning strike twice.

'George Harrison and I were judging a talent competition in Liverpool and I said, "You know, I really had my backside kicked over turning you lot down." He said, "Well, why don't you sign the Rolling Stones?" I said, "I've never heard of them. Where do they play?" "You'll find them at the Railway Hotel at Richmond." From the bright sunshine into the dark room, I couldn't see anything. I gradually began to make out what it was all about. I said to my wife, "What do they look like?" and she said, "The lead singer's very good." I was fascinated by the audience reaction and dancing.' DICK ROWE

THINGS WERE HAPPENING very fast and the rest of us were not aware of everything that was going on. The next day, Brian, Eric and Andrew signed a management contract between Impact Sound (Andrew and Eric's company) and us that was to run for three years. Brian told them about the IBC session. Andrew and Eric agreed to pay IBC £106 for the tape, which left a bitter taste with Glyn Johns. They told Glyn that Andrew planned to produce us, to which Glyn is reported to have said, 'Andrew couldn't produce juice from a bloody orange. The day you prove to me that you can produce a record, then I will come and engineer.'

Dick Rowe, Andrew and Eric met on Tuesday 7 May to talk over a deal. Later in the week, a three-year recording contract was signed by Brian on our behalf with Impact Sound. Brian saw to it that we were not always in the loop. According to Stu, 'Brian said that Mick always had a weak voice, and he had to be careful if he wanted to sing night after night. Easton said that he didn't think Mick was any good. Brian told Easton that they'd just get rid of him. I felt sure Brian

Recording 'Come On' at Olympic Studios, 10 May, 1963

would have done it. I told him not to be so bloody daft. I felt that Brian was incapable of leadership.'

On Friday 10 May, we recorded our first single. Mick said, 'I don't think "Come On" was very good; in fact, it was shit. God knows how it ever got in the charts: it was such a hype. We disliked it so much that we didn't do it on any of our gigs.'

'The Stones recorded "Come On" much too fast.' ANDREW OLDHAM

'COME ON'

Recorded
Friday 10 May, 1963
Studio
Olympic Sound Studios,
Carlton Street, London
Producer
Andrew Oldham for
Impact Sound
Engineer
Roger Savage
Release
UK Friday 7 June, 1963
Decca F 11675
Composers
a-side Berry
b-side Dixon
Highest chart position
UK No 21
Personnel
Charlie: drums
Bill: bass and
backing vocals
Keith: rhythm guitar
Brian: harmonica
and backing vocals
Mick: double-tracked
lead vocal

Chart placings
Each pop newspaper in
Britain had its own charts.
Chart placings could vary
considerably from chart
to chart and from week
to week.

For the purposes of
consistency, under
'highest chart position',
UK *Record Retailer* and
US *Billboard* charts
are used.

On 2 May 1963, Andrew Oldham booked a recording session for the following week at Olympic Sound Studios, located in Carton Street, near London's Marble Arch. The band had a problem deciding which two songs to record for their first single. They went through their combined record collections and finally came up with Chuck Berry's 'Come On'. It was taken from *Chuck Berry*, his UK album released in May 1963. For the b-side, the band decided to revisit the Muddy Waters' recording 'I Want To Be Loved', a song that they had already had a go at recording with Glyn Johns two months earlier at IBC Studios.

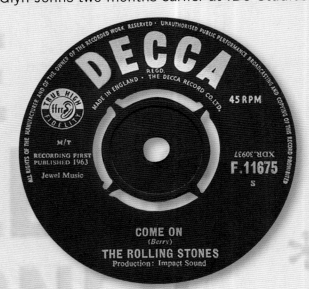

'On Tuesday 7 May, we had a rehearsal at the Wetherby Arms pub to rework "Come On" to suit our style. "Come On" ran for only one minute and 45 seconds, both sides sounded good and we were pleased with the results. At the end of the session, Roger Savage asked Andrew if he wanted to mix the tracks. Andrew didn't know what he was talking about and told him to do whatever he felt needed doing to finish off the single.' BILL

Not a come-on
Decca sent just four copies of 'Come On' to the Stones office so they had to go out and buy extra copies. Three weeks after the single had been released, the band decided they didn't like it and would no longer play it live on shows. Oldham came to watch the band at the Scene club in Soho.

'He went crazy when we didn't play "Come On" and we had a row about it. He insisted we play it at every show,' Bill recalled. The week that 'Come On' went to No 20 on the *NME* charts, each band member was paid just £25.

Olympic Studios, 10 May, 1963: 'Is that a guitar, Brian?'

'I'm the producer, and this is the first session that I've ever handled. I don't know a damned thing about recording, or music for that matter.' ANDREW

ROLLING STONES (Decca) debut with " Come On," a song and performance aimed straight at the current market for groups. Good chance of selling well. " I Want To Be Loved " is a little unusual, reasonably entertaining.

The first ever review of a Rolling Stones record was in NME.

'It's good, catchy, punchy and commercial but it's not the fanatical R&B sound that their audiences wait hours to hear.' RECORD MIRROR, *8 June, 1963*

'A bunch of bloody amateurs going to make a hit single.' MICK

We're Coming

Compared to our IBC session, 'Come On' was pure pop. In truth we would not have got a recording deal if we had carried on with the blues material. We still wanted to play the blues: they were our roots, so we played them live. After the session, Stu dropped me off at Victoria Station and I went home on the train. I had *Record Mirror* on my lap, opened at our photo. I waited to be recognised and I waited...

(Ext 28/29)

Our Ref: 01/PC/LES/MMC

13th May, 1963

Dear Mr. Jones,

THE ROLLIN' STONES

We refer to the audition of your band on Tuesday, 23rd April held by Mr. Jimmy Grant. The recording has now been played to our Production Panel with a view to general broadcasting, but we regret to inform you that the performance was not considered suitable for our purposes.

However, this is an instance when it would seem likely that it might be of help to you to know our opinions in a little more detail. I think the person who can be most helpful to you along these lines is our Music Organiser, Donald MacLean. Therefore, I suggest that you telephone his office at the above number. It will be for him to decide whether the matter is better dealt with on the telephone or, possibly, by an interview.

Yours sincerely,

(David Dore)
Assistant to Light Entertainment
Booking Manager.

David Dore of the BBC wrote to Brian to say the band had failed the Jazz Club audition.

I N MAY 1963, we played 18 gigs, not the busiest month in our short existence, but better than April. However, not all the news was good. Brian got a letter from David Dore, Assistant Light Entertainment Booking Manager of the BBC, to say that we had failed our audition.

Donald MacLean at BBC Radio told Brian that our singer sounded 'too black', but that they were interested in the group backing visiting American recording stars on radio. When Brian told us we laughed and forgot all about it.

Eric got back to Dick Rowe to tell him about the single we had cut. Andrew called Morris Clark, the publisher of 'Come On' and told him to call Dick to say that he'd heard an unbelievable version of one of his songs. On Tuesday 14 May, Eric and Andrew met with other Decca representatives and played them 'Come On'. Decca decided to rush-release the single on 7 June.

Love me two times

Brian's love life was getting ever more complicated, as he was seeing both Pat and Linda. Eventually Linda told Mick and Keith that she was thinking of leaving Brian – she had met someone she liked more. As Linda walked away, Mick ran to her and said: 'Don't go! You'll just kill him.'

'I remember Mick was always worrying about Brian's situation. He was the most sensitive towards Brian,' said Linda. The recording agreement with Impact Sound that Brian signed on our behalf was another triumph of his naivety. We got six per cent royalty from Impact, not knowing that Impact was receiving 14 per cent from Decca. Eric and Andrew were also getting 25 per cent of our 6 per cent as a management fee. Still we were not the first, nor the last, young band to fall prey to this old scam.

Two days after Brian's hero Elmore James died

Brian and Linda Lawrence

in America, Norman Jopling wrote in *Record Mirror*: 'They play and sing in a way one would expect more from a coloured US R&B team. They know their R&B inside out and have a repertoire of about 80 songs. They will, in all likelihood, be the leading R&B performers in the country.' Ironically – having just signed our deal – three record companies phoned Norman the next day, asking, 'Where can we get hold of these guys?' A typical rock'n'roll story.

June was without doubt the busiest month of our short career. We played on 20 separate days, which put Stu and I under increasing pressure at work. We also did various photo sessions and interviews for teen magazines, *Boyfriend*, *Fabulous*, *Jackie*, *Rave* and *Valentine*, along with the music press. When we arrived for one particular interview at a London hotel, everyone just stopped

talking and stared in amazement. An employee came up, asked what our business was and insisted that we leave the building. We went around the corner to an open-air cafe, where people laughed at us and nudged each other. At another interview, we were asked how we got the name. Remembering that the Beatles originally called themselves the Silver Beatles, we answered that we were originally the Silver Rolling Stones. This was one of those so-called facts that has subsequently appeared in books and articles.

Come on out

Decca released 'Come On' backed by Muddy Waters' 'I Want To Be Loved' and the *NME* said: 'Good chance of selling well.' A week later, the *Daily Mirror* said: 'After all we've heard of the Liverpool sound, here's a group from London I'm tipping for the top. Could be a capital hit.'

'Very, very ordinary. Can't hear a word they're saying and I don't know what all this is about. If there was a Liverpool accent it might get somewhere, but this is definitely no hit. I dislike it, I'm afraid!'
CRAIG DOUGLAS, *in Melody Maker*

Gotta lotta bottle
On 8 September, the Stones arrived in Birmingham to record an appearance on *Thank Your Lucky Stars*. Craig Douglas was topping the bill, and to thank him for his bad review of 'Come On', they decided a little trick was in order. He was a milkman before he made records, so the band rounded up empty milk bottles and put them outside his dressing room with a note saying 'two pints please'. Bill: 'He went mad and reported us and we were given a ticking off by the show's producers.' Ironically, his song, 'I'm So Glad I Found Her', failed to chart.

NME TOP THIRTY

On 8 June, *Disc* reported: 'The Rolling Stones are one of the new "knock-yourself-out-on-stage-and-somebody-will-sign-you-up-sometime" groups. Time will tell.' *New Musical Express* said it was 'a song and performance aimed straight at the current market for groups. Good chance of selling well. "I Want To Be Loved" is a little unusual, reasonably entertaining.'

Beat Monthly weighed in with: 'The Stones take an old Chuck Berry number and give it a group vocal for this commercially slanted disc. Harmonica is included in the backing and the whole thing moves well, but they're not able to capture all their on-stage excitement.' *Pop Weekly* said: 'Inspired by the Beatles-cum-Liverpool sound. A fast-moving, lively affair. There are so many similar sounding groups. The group has life and strength. This one only just misses.'

The night that 'Come On' was released, we played the Wooden Bridge Hotel in Guildford and on the Sunday we were back at Studio 51 and the Crawdaddy Club, so for us things didn't feel all that different. Patrick Doncaster from the *Daily Mirror* was at Richmond and his article the following week certainly helped our new release.

'I felt the Stones sufficiently dominating, interesting and important to devote my column in the Daily Mirror to them.'
PATRICK DONCASTER

'I met them at Ken Colyer's club,' said John Carter of Carter-Lewis and the Southerners. 'They were playing a lunchtime set, imagine that – the Stones playing a lunchtime gig! We had gone to the club and I really enjoyed their set. The Stones recognised us and they came over. They were asking who played 12-string guitar on "Sweet And Tender Romance". Mick

The price of vinyl
On 1 July, 1963, the price of records in the UK was increased. Singles went up to 6s 8d, EPs to 10s 9d and albums were sold at £1 12s.

reckoned it was Big Jim Sullivan, Keith thought it was Jimmy Page. Well, Mick was actually right, but funnily enough when we re-cut the song with the McKinleys we used Jimmy Page. We used to meet up with them a fair bit as we crossed over at Regent Sound. We were all starting out then.'

As the first few weeks of June slipped by, there were some really good pieces about us in the music press, including probably the first to compare us with the Beatles. Don Nicholl in *Disc* said 'The Beatles, who recommended the

	(Wednesday, July 31, 1963)	
Last This Week		
3	1	SWEETS FOR MY SWEET Searchers (Pye)
1	2	I'M CONFESSIN' Frank Ifield (Columbia)
2	3	DEVIL IN DISGUISE Elvis Presley (RCA)
5	4	TWIST AND SHOUT Brian Poole and The Tremeloes (Decca)
4	5	DA DOO RON RON Crystals (London)
8	6	TWIST AND SHOUT (EP) Beatles (Parlophone)
7	7	ATLANTIS Shadows (Columbia)
13	8	SUKIYAKI Kyu Sakamoto (HMV)
6	9	I LIKE IT Gerry and the Pacemakers (Columbia)
9	10	IT'S MY PARTY Lesley Gore (Mercury)
10	10	TAKE THESE CHAINS FROM MY HEART Ray Charles (HMV)
20	12	IN SUMMER Billy Fury (Decca)
11	13	WELCOME TO MY WORLD Jim Reeves (RCA)
12	14	DECK OF CARDS Wink Martindale (London)
15	15	YOU CAN NEVER STOP ME LOVING YOU Kenny Lynch (HMV)
16	16	THE LEGION'S LAST PATROL Ken Thorne (HMV)
19	17	I WONDER Brenda Lee (Brunswick)
22	18	WIPE OUT Surfaris (London)
—	19	BAD TO ME Billy J. Kramer (Parlophone)
28	20	I'LL NEVER GET OVER YOU Johnny Kidd (HMV)
14	20	BO DIDDLEY Buddy Holly (Coral)
17	22	SO MUCH IN LOVE Tymes (Cameo-Parkway)
28	22	BY THE WAY Big Three (Decca)
24	24	HEY MAMA Frankie Vaughan (Philips)
21	25	IF YOU GOTTA MAKE A FOOL OF SOMEBODY Freddie and the Dreamers (Columbia)
—	26	COME ON Rolling Stones (Decca)
18	27	FROM ME TO YOU Beatles (Parlophone)
—	28	THE CRUEL SEA Dakotas (Parlophone)
—	29	JUST LIKE EDDIE Heinz (Decca)
—	30	WIPE OUT Saints (Pye)

The single was released in June, but only made the UK Top 30 at the end of July.

Stones, may well live to rue the day. This group could be challenging them for top places in the immediate future.'

But success also brought its own problems. On Sunday 16 June, Giorgio told us it was to be our last show at the Crawdaddy. The brewery, prompted by the *Daily Mirror* article, was worried about the 'goings-on' at Station Hotel, as it called them, as well as the fire regulations. It insisted that the club be closed down. We were devastated. Brian immediately got in touch with Ronan O'Rahilly and arranged for us to play at his new Scene club in Soho on Thursday nights. Ronan promoted the blues in Britain managing Alexis Korner and Cyril Davies, among others. He later founded Radio Caroline, one of the original pirate radio stations.

As a result of our image, rather than our success, we were refused service in some pubs and shops. By the standards of the day our hair was very long, and

Party piece
It was around this time that Mick started going out with Chrissie Shrimpton, the younger sister of model Jean Shrimpton. 'I was introduced to Mick at a party,' she said, 'and we fell for each other immediately.'

getting longer. Added to which, Brian, Mick and Keith were not the smartest of dressers – owing to their shortage of clothes.

Scene and heard
About a week after being told that the Crawdaddy was no more, Giorgio phoned to say he'd found a new venue in Richmond. It was just up the road in the clubhouse at the athletic ground. Andrew's ability to hustle was also holding us in good stead. The coverage we got for 'Come On' was probably more than the record deserved. We convinced ourselves that 'Come On' was not very good (I think we were right, too!) and refused

'Andrew had a genius for getting things through the media… he got messages through without people knowing.' KEITH

to play it live. On June 27 Andrew came to the Scene Club and was furious with us for not playing it, he insisted we did from then on.

Peter and Gordon

'I saw the Stones at the Scene, on Paul McCartney's recommendation. Paul was jealous. He said, "The Stones really don't give a shit and don't wear suits. They don't get pushed around as much as we do." Mick talked about how they'd cut a record, he asked everyone to go and buy it and I did. Boy, did it sound terrible.' PETER ASHER, of Peter and Gordon

At the end of June, Eric phoned BBC Radio to ask if we could audition again. He also told us that he had booked us on the Everly Brothers package tour in the autumn.

'On the Everly's Tour, we'll just go wild,' said Mick. 'We're having stage gear made, but we don't know what it is yet. We've never worn a uniform in the clubs. It's going to be something really different though. Art students and college people have had these haircuts for years. They were around when the Beatles were using Brylcreem.'

The new Crawdaddy was larger than the Station Hotel, much lighter, with glass all down one side. We had to build our own stage and it also took a while to adjust to the acoustics. At our first gig about 500 people turned up, which meant we were paid better, earning £50.

Sleep deprivation

The press often remarked upon my hollow cheeks. If only they knew what my life was like. Playing four or five nights a week and then getting up at 6am for work in Streatham was taking its toll. With just three or four hours of sleep, it was no wonder I was thin. It was even worse for Stu, because he was driving us to and from home as well. He would spend the night on my couch, too tired to drive to his own home.

So far our gigs had all been around London but, in early July, we had a date booked in Kings Lynn in Norfolk. It got cancelled because we had to appear on TV's *Thank Your Lucky Stars* in Birmingham on 7 July.

THE FAN CLUB

An essential part of every beat group's activities was the fan club. The Stones' club started in Eric Easton's office, before being taken over in June 1963, by Doreen Pettifer, who ran it from her home in Surrey, under the pseudonym, 'Diane Nelson'. Terri Smith was the club's first official member. By the end of July, there were about 300 members, with more joining every day. Three months and three newsletters later, Shirley Arnold took it over as 'Annabelle Smith'. At its peak, in 1965, there were 13,000 members, about 20 per cent of whom were male.

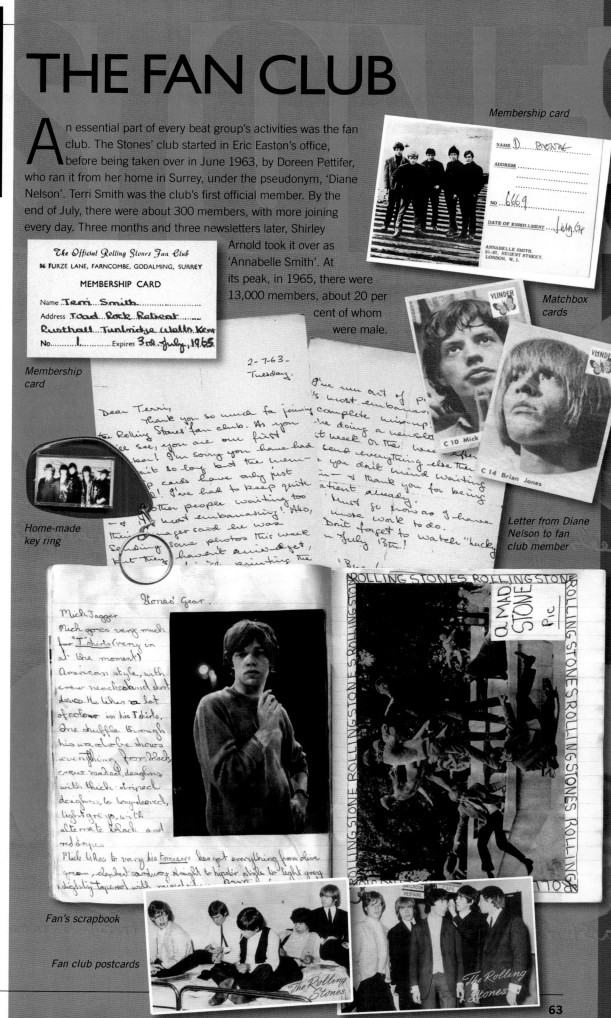

Membership card

Matchbox cards

Membership card

Home-made key ring

Letter from Diane Nelson to fan club member

Fan's scrapbook

Fan club postcards

63

Thank Your Lucky Stars

The band's first TV appearance was on *Thank Your Lucky Stars*. The show first aired in 1961 and was originally hosted by Keith Fordyce and later by Brian Matthew, Tony Hall and Pete Murray. The show's format featured bands playing their latest records in a contrived trendy set. The show also featured a weekly panel of young people who gave their views and awarded points to new records. One panelist was a girl called Janice Nicholls from the Black Country, near Birmingham. She became a regular on the show and if she liked a record she would award it top marks, announcing in her broad accent 'Oi'll give it foive!'

Janice Nicholls

Among the other guests on the Stones' first appearance were Jimmy Henney, Helen Shapiro, Mickie Most, the Cadets and Gordon Mills and the Viscounts. The set looked like the veranda of a western-style saloon. Pete Murray made some un-funny remarks about a delegation from the Hairdressers' Union wanting to see the Stones because they hadn't had a haircut since last year.

'On the afternoon of Saturday 29 June, we went with Andrew to Carnaby Street, where we were measured for black trousers and black and white dogtooth jackets with black velvet collars. We also bought blue shirts, black knit ties and blue leather waistcoats. We then went to the Annello and Davide shop and bought black Spanish boots with Cuban heels (later called Beatle boots). We wore the dogtooth jackets on Thank Your Lucky Stars *on 7 July.'* BILL

'We wanted to get on this schucky show Thank Your Lucky Stars*. If they'd dressed the way they wanted, they wouldn't have been allowed inside the TV studios. They were asked to wear uniforms of some description, so they all wore those checked jackets. But once the position had changed,* Thank Your Lucky Stars *were calling us, saying "Can we have the Stones?" and by then the Stones were going on the way they felt like appearing.'* ANDREW OLDHAM

'Though we wore this uniform, we were stunned by the hostility that our appearance provoked. One letter said: "It is disgraceful that long-haired louts such as these should be allowed to appear on TV. Their appearance was absolutely disgusting."' BILL

On 23 November, 1963, Gene Pitney appeared on the show. Mick and Keith offered him a song they had written. 'You can imagine how thrilled and suprised I was when they sang "My Only Girl [That Girl Belongs To Yesterday]" to me,' said Gene. 'I couldn't wait to cut it. I asked Andrew to arrange a recording session for me. Later, Charles Blackwell handled the session at a London recording studio, with a 30-piece orchestra, which included guitarist Vic Flick and Arthur Greenslade and we cut the song.'

The Stones on *Thank Your Lucky Stars*

7 July, 1963 Alpha Studios, Aston, Birmingham: 'Come On'
14 September Alpha Studios: 'Come On'
23 November Alpha Studios: 'I Wanna Be Your Man'
29 February, 1964 Alpha Studios: 'Not Fade Away'
30 May Alpha Studios: 'Not Fade Away', 'I Just Wanna Make Love To You'
8 August *TYLS Summer Spin* at TV Studios, Teddington: 'It's All Over Now'
5 December *Lucky Stars Special TV Show*: 'Little Red Rooster'
30 January, 1965 Teddington: 'Down Home Girl', 'Under The Boardwalk', 'Suzie Q'
27 March Alpha Studios: 'Play With Fire', 'Off The Hook', 'Everybody Needs Somebody To Love'
12 June Alpha Studios: 'I'm Alright', 'I'm Moving On', 'Route 66'
1 August Alpha Studios: '(I Can't Get No) Satisfaction'
4 September Alpha Studios: '(I Can't Get No) Satisfaction'
8 May, 1966 Alpha Studios: 'Lady Jane', 'Paint It, Black'

'The Stones sang "I Wanna Be Your Man" on television and a thousand mothers of teenage girls shuddered and turned their daughters' faces to the wall.' **LESLIE WILSON,** *journalist*

Just Another Beat Boom Band?

Despite our single only having been out a month, Andrew was already thinking of a follow-up. With a relentless schedule of gigs, our reputation and our infamy were on the increase.

ON 9 JULY, we went to Decca Studios in West Hampstead with Andrew and cut Benny Spellman's 'Fortune Teller'. But in the main it was gig after gig, usually at our regular haunts. That is, until Saturday 13 July, when Stu drove us to Middlesbrough in Yorkshire to play the Alcove Club. It was our first show outside the London area and we supported the Hollies. We were paid £55; it was a good job petrol was a lot cheaper then as it was over 500 miles from London to Middlesbrough and back! The Hollies were great and they became one of our favourite groups, working with us on many occasions. We drove back to London and, being the last one dropped off, I arrived home in the early hours very tired. It was also that week that the August edition of *Beat Monthly* came out. We featured for the first time in their popularity poll, at No 10.

One July night at the new Crawdaddy, we were playing to a crowd of around 600, when Carlo Little and Ricky Fensen (from the Cyril Davies All-Stars) turned up and sat in on a few numbers. Brian even tried to get them to join the Stones on a permanent basis, but was out-voted by the others. I was again impressed with Ricky's driving bass style and runs and I tried adding some of his ideas to my playing.

'The fans just stood there and shook all over in time to the music. It was fantastic and soon we were doing it on stage too.' MICK

We also went back to the Decca studios in West Hampstead to work with a staff producer named Michael Barclay. He was the A&R man who was responsible for launching the career of pop singer Eden Kane. Together we cut our first version of the Coasters' hit 'Poison Ivy'. We hated the result; it didn't sound like us at all. The session was not helped by the fact that we didn't get on with Michael Barclay. His approach was better suited to Eden Kane than to us. But we needed a new song for our second single, so on the evening of Stu's 25th birthday, we went to the Wetherby Arms and rehearsed. One of the songs we tried was the Shirelles' 'Putty In Your Hands'. I was also having to take time off work for things like photo sessions. We did one with Philip Gotlop at a studio in our checked jackets and another with Dezo Hoffman in leather waistcoats.

'Brian didn't have any cufflinks, so I lent him mine – they were gold, a wedding present from my wife. I never got them back. I later heard that he had given a pair of gold cufflinks to Bo Diddley.' DEZO HOFFMANN

Photographs taken by fans at Studio 51 in July 1963

'Mick, looking for all the world like a little boy lost, often wouldn't eat for days, not because he couldn't afford it, but because he just hadn't got his life organised.' **CHRISSIE SHRIMPTON**

The Beatles

Peter Jay & The Jaywalkers

The Fourmost

Manfred Mann

The Searchers

The Swinging Blue Jeans

The Dave Clark Five

The Merseybeats

Gerry & The Pacemakers

'When we started out we used to wear the same clothes on and off stage. Andrew Oldham got us to conform for a couple of TV appearances.' BILL

The Kinks

The Honeycombs

Tony Rivers & The Castaways

Sounds Incorporated

The Hollies

Brian Poole & The Tremeloes

Freddie & The Dreamers

Herman's Hermits

Paul Raven & The Twilights

The Undertakers

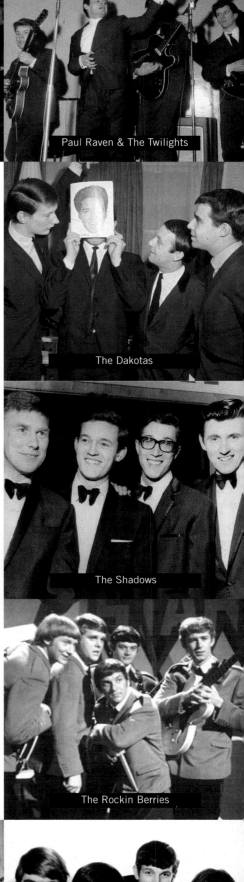

The Dakotas

Rory Storm & The Hurricanes

The Shadows

The Mojos

'In 1964 we were still wearing what we wanted, rather than "uniforms" like almost every other band. At least by then we had a few more clothes to choose from!' BILL

The Rockin Berries

Dave Dee & The Bostons

The Nashville Teens

The Tornados

Wayne Fontana & The Mindbenders

The evening of the photo session we drove to Hastings to play at a debutante's dance given by Lord and Lady Killerman. It was the coming-out of their daughter Rosanna Lampson. On the way there, Brian got really sick and was unable to play, so we cancelled our performance. He stayed in Mick's car sleeping, while we joined the party. It was the first time, but not the last, that Brian's health let us down. Long afterwards, Keith would bring up the fact that I got drunk, tried to chat up the debs and they threatened to throw me out. I was getting into the idea of there being lots of available girls!

Playing the circuit
We also played at the Corn Exchange in Wisbech, Cambridgeshire and were flattered to see our photos and posters

outside the venue. It was another first in what was fast becoming a year of them. The day following Mick's 20th birthday, we played the California Ballroom in Dunstable, Bedfordshire. It was then the realisation hit us that we could no longer play the slow Jimmy Reed numbers because the crowd just stood there in front of us and gaped. We started to concentrate our live performances on the more up-tempo songs, which seemed to work better. On Friday 2 August, 'Come On' entered the *NME* chart at No 26. Elsewhere in the paper it was reported, 'The Rolling Stones (even the name comes from a tune recorded by Negro R&B artist Muddy Waters) were formed 11 months ago to deputise for a group at London's Marquee Club. Lead singer Mick Jagger is 19, born in Dartford, Kent and is at the London School of Economics.'

OODECCA-GROUP RECORDS○●○●

THE ROLLING STONES
COME ON

F 11675

DECCA

OODECCA-GRO

'I don't have much idea about economics myself because I like money and spend it like water... mainly on clothes, Chinese food and Bo Diddley records.' MICK

It was amazing what the press printed about us; probably due as much to Andrew's efforts as to anything we might actually say to them. We were supposedly 'united in our ambitions to live on the Thames in a houseboat', while at the same time, 'Mick, Keith and Brian live in a penthouse in Chelsea. Not the scene of wild parties as you would imagine, but a place where they can all relax and work out new arrangements.'

A Whole New World

While we were becoming more professional and working harder, Brian had started to weaken under the pressure, both in his personal life and within the band. Eric took control of the group's finances away from Brian and Andrew manipulated our image in the newspapers, creating more and more hype.

BRIAN WAS SPENDING much more time with Linda. Pat Andrews was still hoping for any sort of relationship and she did everything to try and get Brian back. Eventually, though, she gave up on him and went home to Cheltenham. Brian was concerned about her capability as a mother and even asked Linda if she thought her parents might look after Julian Mark. My life also took a radical shift as I became a professional musician. I left Sparks of Streatham in August, unable any longer to hold down a job and play with the band. Everyone, friends, family said I was mad. They told me to play it safe. But I could no longer ask my workmate Jack Oliver to cover for me every time I fell asleep while at work.

'When Bill turned professional with the Stones, I didn't really mind one way or the other. He was bringing home around the same money from the group when he started as he was before. It really upset me when the boys were called "cavemen" and "dirty". You don't spend hours washing and ironing shirts, to have people turn round and call your husband dirty.' DIANE WYMAN

There was no way I could have kept working and stayed in the band. Almost every day there were things going on that I needed to be at.

The Ricky Tick moved from the old Star and Garter hotel to the Thames Hotel in Windsor on Tuesday 6 August. We were not very happy about the move. The acoustics were bad and the old place was much better – not that we would be playing places like the Ricky Tick for very much longer. On 8 August, we had woken up to the news of the Great Train Robbery, as it became known, at Cheddington in Buckinghamshire. The thieves had stolen mailbags worth around £2.6 million in the early hours of the morning. Later, while we rehearsed at the Wetherby Arms, we talked about what we would do with that kind of money. Afterwards we went to meet Andrew at Decca Studios to record tracks for our first EP. We cut Chuck Berry's 'Bye Bye Johnny', Barrett Strong's 'Money' and Arthur Alexander's 'You Better Move On'. They all sounded great and we were really pleased with them.

Richmond jazz

The next afternoon Stu drove us to Jennings Music in Dartford. Eric had done a deal with them for us to sponsor their Vox equipment and, as part of the agreement, we got a free set of gear. On 11 August, we played at the third National Jazz Festival in Richmond. We were paid £30 and were at the bottom of a bill that included Acker Bilk, Terry Lightfoot, Freddy Randall, the Cyril Davies All-Stars with Long John Baldry, and the Velvettes. We were put in as little more than a token gesture.

'Apart from the few thousand jazz fans, there were a couple of thousand Stones fans. When the gates opened, they jammed the club house to overflowing and totally nonplussed our security who didn't know what to do. It quite terrified me.' HAROLD PENDLETON, *promoter*

I saw the Stones at the Richmond Jazz Festival playing in a tent. It was rocking. I was the last one out of the tent, looking at everybody packing up the gear and I fell over a tent peg and smashed my leg. Jagger was at the front of the stage, kissing this bird [Chrissie Shrimpton].' RONNIE WOOD

We always seemed to be late leaving for gigs, which meant Stu often had to break the speed limit. The inevitable happened and a couple of days after the jazz festival, Stu had to go to court for a speeding offence. I went along with him for support, not that he really needed it. He argued his way out, saying that by just looking at the battered van anyone could see it was incapable of exceeding the speed limit. He got off with a £5 fine.

Ricky Tick and Go!

In mid-August, Eric Easton took over Brian's job of keeping the books. He paid us £18 for our previous week's work, somewhat more than Brian had been allowing us. At the same time he told us that so far 'Come On' had sold over 40,000 copies. The following day, *Melody Maker* announced 'London R&B group Rolling Stones to star in a film.' Andrew was up to his tricks, tricks that would become more and more outrageous, but effective in promoting our bad boy image. With gigs outside London, in places as far away as Northwich in Cheshire, it meant that we were getting back to Edith Grove very late. I would sometimes crash out in a chair because Stu was too tired to drive me the rest of the way home.

After a photo session on Monday 19 August, we went to Andrew and Eric's office where they played us the first pressing of the new single 'Poison Ivy' and 'Fortune Teller'. It sounded better than we remembered. We were still playing Eel Pie and the Ricky Tick in late August. We also appeared in our second TV show, ARTV's *Ready, Steady, Go!* on 23 August, performing 'Come On', which had climbed to No 20 in the *NME* chart. Also on the show were Little Peggy March, Heinz, Jet Harris, Tony Meehan and Hayley Mills. Interviewer Cathy McGowan asked: 'Brian, how do you cut your hair?'

'I cut my hair whenever necessary,' he replied, 'with a pair of scissors and two mirrors.'

Monday 26 August was due to be the release date of 'Poison Ivy'. It was decided to withdraw it as 'Come On' was still selling well and we were not really very happy with it as a follow-up. The next day we met for a rehearsal at Studio 51. When I got there I found just Andrew, Mick,

Keith, Stu and Charlie. Brian had apparently collapsed from nervous exhaustion. We decided to go clothes shopping with Andrew, before heading off to Windsor to play the Ricky Tick, without Brian – the first, but not the last time. In fact, he was still ill the next night when we played Eel Pie, so Stu sat in on piano to fill out the sound.

Scene up north

By the time we drove to Manchester, the next day, to appear on Granada's *Scene at 6.30*, Brian was much better. According to Michael Parkinson, the show's producer went into shock at seeing us. Afterwards we drove to Liverpool and went to the Cavern Club where the Big Three were recording a live E.P. August was busy, but September was even busier. We played live every day but two, and on those days we appeared on TV shows. Not that all this work seemed to be making us money. By September, we were all so broke, that Brian, who still had Eric's ear on financial matters, gave each of us £3… The joys of pop stardom!

I decided to buy a new bass guitar. I helped finance my purchase by selling my old bass cabinet and amp to Tony Chapman for £25. He

had put together a new band with Steve Carroll and some friends. They called themselves the Preachers. Brian missed a few dates in early September after he came out in blotches all over his face at an Eel Pie gig. The Paramounts supported us at one gig.

Richmond Jazz Festival, 1963: above, *Giorgio Gomelsky dancing*

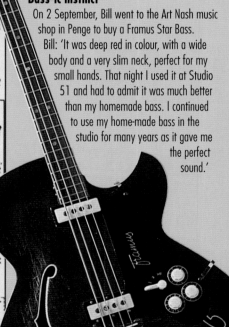

Bass-ic instinct

On 2 September, Bill went to the Art Nash music shop in Penge to buy a Framus Star Bass. Bill: 'It was deep red in colour, with a wide body and a very slim neck, perfect for my small hands. That night I used it at Studio 51 and had to admit it was much better than my homemade bass. I continued to use my home-made bass in the studio for many years as it gave me the perfect sound.'

'The Stones made us feel 10 feet tall, saying how much they liked our sound. Mick said it was crazy, us not being on record. I think our sound clicked with him because it was so blues-influenced. It was him keeping on that made us do a demo, which in turn, led to a recording contract.'
BARRY WILSON, *Paramounts drummer*

The strain of driving us around was really getting to Stu. After one gig, he took me home and Charlie ended up staying the night as well, to save Stu the extra drive to Wembley. A few days later

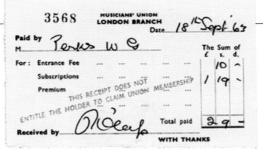

Receipt for Bill's Musicians' Union membership payment

we were booked in Aberystwyth and the second we arrived, we were pounced on by the Musicians' Union, who threatened to cancel the show if we did not become members there and then. We had a row, then reluctantly signed their forms.

From Aberystwyth we drove overnight to Birmingham, arriving at the TV Studios at 6am. The watchman wouldn't let us in, saying we were too early. Eventually he led us into a small viewing room, where we crashed out on the floor. Andrew and Brian arrived in time for rehearsals at 11am. After the show Mick and Keith went home with Andrew in his car. Stu drove Brian, Charlie and I back in the van. We were completely exhausted, having not really slept for two days.

The Stones on RSG! on 23 August, 1963, one of Bill's last live gigs playing his home-made fretless bass. Keith is playing a Harmony Meteor H70.

Ready, Steady, Go!
The Weekend Starts Here
KEITH FORDYCE
invites you to
meet a galaxy
of guest stars
INCLUDING
GERRY and the PACEMAKERS
FREDDIE and the DREAMERS
KATHY KIRBY
KENNY LYNCH
AND
THE ROLLING STONES
listen to hit discs
AND **dance**
with the teenagers in the studio
PROGRAMME EDITOR
FRANCIS HITCHING
ASSISTANTS
MICHAEL ALDRED CATHY MCGOWAN
VICKI WICKHAM
DIRECTED BY
ROLLO GAMBLE

The ITV television show that epitomised the Swinging Sixties was first broadcast at 7pm on 9 August, 1963, from TV House in London's Kingsway. Early in 1964, the show started to use Manfred Mann's '5-4-3-2-1' as the theme. Everything pointed to the fact that teenage viewers were in for something very different. Broadcasting on a Friday evening with the slogan, 'The weekend starts here', it became synonymous with the era. *RSG!* was Britain's look at the 'fab, happening' London scene; it shaped the music and fashion tastes of the nation.

On that first show were the not-quite-so-swinging Brian Poole and the Tremeloes – the band signed by Decca in preference to the Beatles. They performed their version of the Isley Brothers' 'Twist and Shout'. Also appearing in front of the 200-strong teenage crowd was Liverpudlian Billy Fury, who had first made the UK charts in 1959. On *Ready, Steady, Go!* he was promoting 'In Summer', which was to make UK No 5 the following week.

Keith Fordyce

RSG! was hosted by 35-year-old former Cambridge law student Keith Fordyce and the 19-year-old girl who became known as the queen of the mods, Cathy McGowan. Cathy became an icon of pop culture, telling viewers what was in and what was out. She also gave credence to the concept that anyone could make it, rubbing shoulders with the stars and even becoming their friend. Cathy had worked in the office of the TV company and was later quoted as saying, 'I blundered my way through each show.'

Ready, Steady, Go! *presenter Cathy McGowan (left) with singer Sylvie Vartan*

When it started, the show had two resident dancers, Theresa Confrey and Patrick Kerr, who demonstrated the latest moves, alongside the hand-picked studio audience. Scouts from the show went to clubs throughout London, like the Sabre and Crawdaddy, offering the best dancers free tickets to *Ready, Steady, Go!* The studio audience warm-up man was Paul Raven, later to find fame as Gary Glitter.

'On Sunday 18 August, we were playing to a record crowd of 800 at the Crawdaddy Club. The production team of Ready, Steady, Go! *were there looking for dancers for the show. We were introduced to them and struck up friendships. They promised to put us on the show as soon as possible.'* BILL

Above, *The Stones on* Ready, Steady, Go! *on 9 April, 1965 and,* top right, *The Beatles*

The Stones on *RSG!*

The band made 20 appearances on *Ready, Steady, Go!* Many of the songs were their hit records but they also played some less well-known material. On 1 April, 1966, *RSG!* came from La Locomotive Club, Paris, France; it featured Brian and Bill being interviewed.

23 August, 1963 'Come On'
22 November 'I Wanna Be Your Man'
27 December 'I Wanna Be Your Man'
14 February, 1964 'Not Fade Away', 'I Wanna Be Your Man', 'You Better Move On'
3 April 'Not Fade Away', 'I Just Wanna Make Love To You'
26 June 'It's All Over Now', 'Good Times, Bad Times'
7 August 'It's All Over Now'
20 November 'Little Red Rooster', 'Around And Around', 'Everybody Needs Somebody To Love' or 'Off The Hook'
31 December 'Off The Hook', 'Little Red Rooster', 'Around And Around'
15 January, 1965 'What A Shame', 'Time Is On My Side', 'Down The Road Apiece'
26 February 'The Last Time', 'Everybody Needs Somebody To Love/Pain In My Heart', 'Play With Fire', 'I'm Moving On'
9 April 'Everybody Needs Somebody To Love/Pain In My Heart', 'I'm Alright', 'The Last Time'
4 June 'Play With Fire', 'I'm Alright'
27 August 'Cry To Me', 'Mercy, Mercy', '(I Can't Get No) Satisfaction', 'Apache'
10 September 'I Got You Babe', 'Oh Baby (We Got A Good Thing Goin')', 'That's How Strong My Love Is', '(I Can't Get No) Satisfaction'
22 October 'Cry To Me', 'She Said Yeah', 'Get Off Of My Cloud'
31 December '(I Can't Get No) Satisfaction', 'Get Off Of My Cloud'
27 May, 1966 'I Am Waiting', 'Under My Thumb', 'Paint It, Black'
10 September 'Have You Seen Your Mother, Baby, Standing In The Shadow?'
7 October 'Paint It, Black', 'Lady Jane', 'Have You Seen Your Mother, Baby, Standing In The Shadow?'

'The girls were really going mad. Mick did all that jumping around that made the girls scream. We had literally thousands of letters in the office asking to see them again. The reaction to that first performance was so great that within three months, they were regulars on the show.'
CATHY McGOWAN

RSG! goes live

From April 1965, RSG! went live and was broadcast from Wembley rather than Kingsway. It meant that groups had to perform rather than mime, no problem for the Stones and many other bands, but it was clearly a challenge for some.

'The Stones turned up their amps and gave Glyn Johns a heart attack. The soundboard was almost non-existent, a mono system used the rest of the week by Muriel Young and some religious programme.' VICKI WICKHAM, *editor of RSG!*

The tapes of the shows are owned by Dave Clark of the Dave Clark Five, who acquired them in the 1980s. It's reported they have earned him a lot of money.

Ready Steady Gone!

RSG! ran until 23 December, 1966, a total of 175 episodes. By then, the premise on which the programme was built had been overtaken by a new era of beads, hair and granny glasses. The beat boom and the mod generation had finally lost ground to the Age of Aquarius and the concept album. The final show featured Mick Jagger and Chris Farlowe singing 'Out of Time' and '(I Can't Get No) Satisfaction'.

The United Kingdom,

July–September 1963

13 July Alcove Club, Middlesbrough, Yorkshire
20 July Corn Exchange, Wisbech, Cambridgeshire
27 July California Ballroom, Dunstable, Bedfordshire
2 August Wooden Bridge Hotel, Guildford, Surrey
3 August St Leonard's Hall, Horsham, Sussex
5 August Botwell House, Hayes, Middlesex
9 August California Ballroom, Dunstable, Bedfordshire
10 August Plaza Theatre, Handsworth, Birmingham, Warwickshire; Plaza Theatre, Oldhill, Birmingham, Warwickshire
11 August Richmond Jazz Festival, Surrey
12 August Cellar Club, Kingston-upon-Thames, Surrey
13 August Town Hall, High Wycombe, Buckinghamshire
15 August Dreamland Ballroom, Margate, Kent
16 August Winter Gardens, Banbury, Oxfordshire
17 August Memorial Hall, Northwich, Cheshire
19 August Atlanta Ballroom, Woking, Surrey
24 August Il Rondo Ballroom, Leicester, Leicestershire
30 August Oasis Club, Manchester, Lancashire
31 August Royal Lido Ballroom, Prestatyn, Wales
5 September Strand Palais Theatre, Walmer, Kent
6 September Grand Hotel Ballroom, Lowestoft, Suffolk
7 September King's Hall, Aberystwyth, Wales
13 September California Ballroom, Dunstable, Bedfordshire
14 September Plaza Theatre, Oldhill, Birmingham, Warwickshire; Ritz Ballroom, Kingsheath, Birmingham, Warwickshire
15 September Great Pop Prom, Royal Albert Hall, London
17 September British Legion Hall, Harrow-on-the-Hill, London
19 September St John's Hall, Watford, Hertfordshire
20 September Savoy Ballroom, Southsea, Hampshire
21 September Corn Exchange, Peterborough, Huntingdon and Peterborough
27 September Teen Beat Night 1963, Floral Hall, Morecambe, Lancashire
28 September Assembly Hall, Walthamstow, London

Until July 1963, the Stones only played in and around London at their regular club dates. When they left London to drive 260 miles to Middlesbrough, Yorkshire, it was a step into the unknown. For the next three months, the band played frequent shows throughout England and ventured into Wales, while continuing to play the London club dates, pulling in ever greater numbers of fans.

From 13 July to 28 September, the Stones played 78 shows in 76 days, earning a total of £3,592 – or £46 per show. By mid-August, Eric Easton had taken over the bookkeeping. For their first weekly wages under the new accounting scheme, each member received £18. The band also did four TV shows, two recording sessions and three photo shoots and had just three days off.

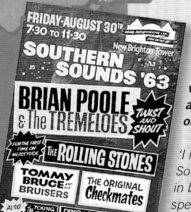

'On Friday 6 September, we played the Grand Hotel Ballroom in Lowestoft, Suffolk. Brian was sick and we played without him for a crowd of 1,200. Halfway through our show, girls started to attack us on-stage. I had half my shirt torn off, buttons ripped from my leather waistcoat and my ring pulled from my finger. The other guys suffered a similar fate. It was a great reception – the first time we were attacked on-stage.' BILL

'I must admit being a Stone and doing a day job was too much for me. Sometimes we wouldn't get home until 3 or 4am. I would have an hour or two in bed before going to work again. Bill was in the same boat. I often used to spend the night on his couch because I was just too tired to drive home.' STU

The poster for a cancelled Merseyside gig (above). The venue burned down two weeks before the Stones were due to play.

'We played the Alcove Club, Middlesbrough on 13 July, 1963. We were the support band for the Hollies, who we got on very well with. As usual we went on in our street clothes, with Brian, Keith and me sat on stools. We had a good show.' BILL

Set list

The Stones' set was changing during this period from the more bluesy oriented material they featured in the clubs, to the more upbeat R&B material that was better suited to the ballrooms.

'Shame, Shame, Shame', 'Crawdaddy', 'Tiger In Your Tank', 'Cops And Robbers', 'Jaguar And Thunderbird', 'Money', 'High-Heel Sneakers', 'I'm Moving On', 'Bye Bye Johnny', 'You Better Move On', 'Susie Q', 'Memphis Tennessee', 'Roll Over Beethoven', 'Walking The Dog', 'Poison Ivy', 'Road Runner'.

Just some of the songs played, they even did 'Come On' under duress...

76 Days Of Clubs And Ballrooms

In support...

Among the support
bands were:
The Paramounts
Russ Sainty and the Nu-Notes
The Dynatones
Peter and the Hustlers
The Barron Knights
The Cresters
The Doodle Bugs
Dave Berry and the Cruisers
The Redcaps
The Merseybeats
Lee Curtis and the All-Stars
The Hollies

'From one end of England to the other, in Stu's van, we often slept in the back of the van. Crafty Bill. For years, we believed that he couldn't travel in the back of the van because he'd be sick, so he was always allowed to sit in the passenger seat. Years later, we found out he never gets travel sick at all.' **KEITH**

'I heard the Stones at Studio 51 on Monday evenings. Boy, was it hot – unbelievably sweaty. They did tons of oldies, a lot of which I didn't know. They did "You Better Move On" extremely well. Brian used to play this big green guitar with tons of wobbly on it and Mick would do this weird hand-clapping.'
PETER ASHER

R & B
GUILDFORD
Fridays 8–11
Sessions now held at
WORPLESDON
VILLAGE HALL
August 16th
CYRIL DAVIES
HIS ALLSTARS and
LONG JOHN BALDRY
August 23rd
ROLLING
STONES

NELSONS SPORTS AND SOCIAL CLUB
presents—by Public Request

TEEN·BEAT NIGHT '63

SIX HOURS NON-STOP DANCING FEATURING
FIRST TIME IN THE NORTH-WEST—BRITAIN'S TOP RHYTHM AND BLUES GROUP

THE ROLLING STONES
Decca Recording Stars—"Come On"

THE FAMOUS LIVERPOOL SOUND—DIRECT FROM THE "CAVERN," LIVERPOOL
THE MERSEYBEATS
Fontana Recording Stars—"It's Love That Really Counts"

DECCA RECORDING STARS—"TOSSING AND TURNING," "MEMPHIS, TENNESSEE"
DAVE BERRY & the CRUISERS

TWIST AND SHOUT TO THE EXCITING RHYTHM AND BLUES SOUND OF
THE DOODLE-BUGS

FLORAL HALL BALLROOM, MORECAMBE
FRIDAY, 27TH SEPTEMBER, 1963
8 p.m. to 2 a.m.

Tickets 5/-, at the door 6/-
LATE TRANSPORT AVAILABLE

Club gigs

Studio 51, Ken Colyer Club, Soho, London 14 July, 15 July, 21 July, 22 July,
28 July, 29 July, 4 August, 11 August, 12 August, 18 August, 25 August, 26 August,
1 September, 2 September, 9 September, 16 September, 22 September, 23 September
Crawdaddy Club, Richmond, Surrey 14 July, 21 July, 28 July, 4 August,
18 August, 25 August, 1 September, 15 September, 22 September
Eel Pie Island, Twickenham, Middlesex 17 July, 24 July, 31 July, 7 August,
14 August, 21 August, 4 September, 11 September, 18 September, 25 September
Ricky Tick Club, Windsor, Berkshire 26 July, 30 July, 6 August, 20 August,
27 August, 3 September, 10 September, 24 September

STUDIO '51
10/11 GT. NEWPORT STREET
LEICESTER SQUARE (Tube)
Rhythm and Blues
Friday. 8.0
JOHN MAYALL BLUES BREAKERS
Sunday Afternoon. 4 until 6.30
THE ROLLING STONES
Monday. 8.0
Decca Recording Stars
ALEXIS KORNER
BLUES CORPORATED

CORN EXCHANGE, PETERBOROUGH
LESSEE: NORMAN G. JACOBS . PHONE 352411
Tonight [Friday]: ROLLER SKATING 6.30 to 10.30 p.m.
Friday Night is Skating Night!
Tomorrow [Saturday]: DANCING 8 to 11.45 p.m.
Norman G. Jacobs presents The South's answer to Liverpool
THE ROLLING STONES
Decca Hit Recorders of "Come On"
THE DYNATONES
ADVANCE TICKETS: 6/6. At Door 7/6. Buses at midnight for
Coates, Upwood, Yaxley, Crowland and Walton.
Coming NEXT Saturday, September 28th:
CARTER-LEWIS AND THE SOUTHERNERS
Hit Recorders of "Sweet and Tender Romance"
The Corn Exchange – Your best insurance
– against the Blues, and one of East Anglia's
Most Popular Halls. It's Part of YOUR
Fine City.

The Hollies

*Brian Poole (far left), who also missed playing
New Brighton after the venue burned down.*

'One provincial paper reported seeing on stage
"five awesome apes who perpetrated fearful
musical onslaughts".' **BILL**

With The Beatles

Mick and Keith moved into 33 Mapesbury Road, West Hampstead, London, while Brian went to stay with Linda Lawrence at her parents' house in Windsor – the end of the Edith Grove era. Chrissie Shrimpton, now 18, finished secretarial college and moved in iwith Mick and Keith. She got a job at Decca Records. Andrew was thrown out of his mother's home and joined them.

'At Mapesbury Road, we had two bedrooms between us and we shared a bathroom. All three of us were going steady.' ANDREW

As STU RECALLED, 'Keith and Mick were quite prepared to go along with anything Andrew said. They fed off each other. Edicts would be issued from the Oldham office, which were the result of the three of them.' This was the start of Brian's demise as the leader of the group. His absences didn't help his cause; neither did Mick and Keith's close friendship.

On Tuesday 10 September, Andrew arrived at our rehearsal with John Lennon and Paul McCartney. They played 'I Wanna Be Your Man'. It was to be our next single.

'We came up with "I Wanna Be Your Man" – a Bo Diddley kind of thing. I said to Mick, "Well, Ringo's got this track on our album, but it won't be a single and it might suit you guys." I knew Mick was into maracas, from when we'd seen them down at the Crawdaddy.' JOHN LENNON

Mick said, 'We didn't think that the Beatles would be prepared to give us one of their best numbers.' It probably was not their best, but cutting a Beatles song was certainly going to do us no harm.

Our live shows were more popular than ever. We broke attendance records in clubs and ballrooms and all this was without a hit record. We played the Great Pop Prom at London's Royal Albert Hall the following Sunday and our confidence was at an all-time high.

Many years later, the Beatles told us that they watched from the side of the stage and were very nervous after the reception we got. We opened the show and were followed by the Viscounts, Kenny Lynch, Susan Maughan, Shane Fenton and the Fentones, Clinton Ford, the Vernon Girls, the Lorne Gibson Trio, Arthur Greenslade and the G-Men, Helen Shapiro and Karl

Ringo, George, Paul and John in November 1963

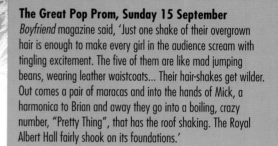

The Great Pop Prom, Sunday 15 September
Boyfriend magazine said, 'Just one shake of their overgrown hair is enough to make every girl in the audience scream with tingling excitement. The five of them are like mad jumping beans, wearing leather waistcoats... Their hair-shakes get wilder. Out comes a pair of maracas and into the hands of Mick, a harmonica to Brian and away they go into a boiling, crazy number, "Pretty Thing", that has the roof shaking. The Royal Albert Hall fairly shook on its foundations.'

Denver. To be honest, they were not the greatest competition and they received modest applause. The Beatles closed the show and need not have worried: they got an amazing reception.

Back to the clubs
That evening we were at the Crawdaddy, doing two encores; it was a world away from the Royal Albert Hall. In the following week we played Southsea, Harrow-on-the-Hill and Peterborough before we were back to our usual Sunday double-header at Studio 51 and the Crawdaddy club. Studio 51 was packed solid with 400 fans; others listened outside through the iron grilles in the pavement and danced in the street. We did several encores before leaving for the Crawdaddy. Fans had been queuing for hours as this was to be our last show there. In many ways it was a sad night, but things were moving on.

End Of An Era

We were due to start the Everly Brothers package tour. Things needed to move up a gear and so we took on John 'Spike' Palmer as an assistant to Stu, paying him £8 per week, to help spread the load.

STU COULDN'T HAVE gone on any longer without help. After one gig at the end of September, he took me home, occasionally pulling off the road and falling asleep for an hour. I would wake up, cold and miserable, wondering where we were. It was a nightmare. I woke up in Peckham and had to wake Stu to get him moving again. I then fell asleep again, only to wake up a few miles up the road to see Stu was once more sound asleep. We finally arrived at my place at 1pm, had some lunch, then crashed out in the front room for a couple of hours.

On Tuesday 24 September, we played our last residency at the Ricky Tick. Wednesday was really busy. We all went with Andrew to Decca House, then did another photo session on the Thames Embankment around Chelsea. That night we went further up the river to play our last residency at Eel Pie. The following day Brian and Linda decided to visit Brian's parents in Cheltenham.

'He thought I would please them, this quiet girl from the country,' said Linda.

That'll do nicely
On 13 September, 1963, Lloyds Bank wrote to Andrew, asking him to act as a referee for Brian, who wanted to open an account. Definitely a sign of the changing times in the band.

'Our relationship was something to be proud of. His father talked and got excited, but then his mother kept trying to cool him. They brought out pictures of Brian, and showed me his report cards. We took them to a pub. We thought that getting them out of the house would loosen them up, but they were still really tight. Brian really wanted to contact them. He would play his music for them. His mother didn't really listen, but Lewis tried to.'

Opportunity knocks
As we got closer to the tour it began to dawn on us what it was going to be like. Apart from the fact that the Everlys were huge stars, our hero Bo Diddley was also on the bill. We realised that an era was ending, and, while I could not say we were sad, there was the realisation that we were at something of a crossroads in our lives. A minor hit record, a tour and increasing numbers of fans – our world was full of opportunity. The thing was, none of us had any idea how long it would last – probably two years at the most.

63 *September*

64 *June*

Pop
Tourists

On the Thames Embankment, 25 September, 1963

The United Kingdom,
September–November 1963

The tour included two ballroom dates, 30 September and
14 October – all the Everlys dates had two shows a night.
29 September New Victoria Theatre, London
30 September Rex Ballroom, Cambridge, Cambridgeshire
1 October Odeon Theatre, Streatham, London
2 October Regal Theatre, Edmonton, London
3 October Odeon Theatre, Southend-on-Sea, Essex
4 October Odeon Theatre, Guildford, Surrey
5 October Gaumont Theatre, Watford, Hertfordshire
6 October Capitol Theatre, Cardiff, Wales
8 October Odeon Theatre, Cheltenham, Gloucestershire
9 October Gaumont Theatre, Worcester, Worcestershire
10 October Gaumont Theatre, Wolverhampton, Staffordshire
11 October Gaumont Theatre, Derby, Derbyshire
12 October Gaumont Theatre, Doncaster, Yorkshire
13 October Odeon Theatre, Liverpool, Lancashire
14 October Majestic Ballroom, Kingston upon Hull, Yorkshire
16 October Odeon Theatre, Manchester, Lancashire
17 October Odeon Theatre, Glasgow, Scotland
18 October Odeon Theatre, Newcastle upon Tyne, Northumberland
19 October Gaumont Theatre, Bradford, Yorkshire
20 October Gaumont Theatre,
Hanley, Staffordshire
22 October Gaumont Theatre,
Sheffield, Yorkshire
23 October Odeon Theatre,
Nottingham, Nottinghamshire
24 October Odeon Theatre,
Birmingham, Warwickshire
25 October Gaumont Theatre,
Taunton, Devon
26 October Gaumont Theatre,
Bournemouth, Hampshire
27 October Gaumont Theatre, Salisbury,
Wiltshire
29 October Gaumont Theatre, Southampton,
Hampshire
30 October Odeon Theatre, St Albans, Hertfordshire
31 October Odeon Theatre, Lewisham, London
1 November Odeon Theatre, Rochester, Kent
2 November Gaumont Theatre, Ipswich, Suffolk
3 November Odeon Theatre, Hammersmith, London

A 30-date tour lasting 36 days was the Stones'
introduction to that 1960s phenomenon, the
package tour. The punishing schedule would hold
the band in good stead for the future, but
it was also fun. Along with the Everlys was
Bo Diddley and after the first five dates
Little Richard was added to the bill.

*'This is a wonderful break for us and we're
looking forward to meeting the American duo.
We are coping with plenty of dates in and around
the London area. We don't hear enough about
the London scene in these days of Liverpool
domination, but we're hoping we'll
fly the flag of the capital when we
get on our tour.'* BRIAN

Don Arden, the promoter,
explained, 'The Everly Brothers
had definitely had it. I phoned
up Little Richard and said, "Richard you've
gotta help me out." He said, "Okay".
The Stones heard about the tour from Eric Easton at the
end of June, and Brian spoke for everyone.

*'They were just bringing in that not-dressing-for-the-
stage and they looked quite peculiar, but they did
a good job. They stood out. They were an easy bunch
of guys to be around but they kept to themselves as
well.'* PHIL EVERLY

*'So far, we've raved only in clubs and dance halls, but
now we're looking forward to raving on our first
theatre tour with the Everly Brothers. For us,
the big thrill is that Bo Diddley will be on the
bill. He's been one of our great influences.
It won't be a case of the pupils competing
with the master, though. We're dropping from
our act on the tour all the Bo Diddley numbers
we sing.'* BRIAN, *NME, 23 August, 1963*

Set list
The Stones' 10-minute set for
the first show:
'Poison Ivy'
'Fortune Teller'
'Come On'
'Money'

Later, 'I Wanna Be Your Man',
'Road Runner' and 'Memphis
Tennessee' were introduced.

The first show running list
The Flintstones
Compere Bob Bain
Mickie Most
The Rolling Stones
Bo Diddley
Interval
The Flintstones
Compere Bob Bain
Julie Grant
The Everly Brothers' backing
group the Nashville Three featured
Jim Gordon on drums. He later
played with Eric Clapton, most
notably on the *Layla* album.

GAUMONT THEATRE
BOURNEMOUTH
The Everly Brothers/
Bo Diddley Show
2nd Performance 8-30
SATURDAY
OCTOBER 26
STALLS
A17   15/-

The First
Package Tour

The Everly Brothers

GAUMONT - BRADFORD
Manager: D. W. J. WILLMOTT ON THE STAGE Telephone 26716
SATURDAY, 19th OCTOBER at 6.20 and 8.45

DON ARDEN ENTERPRISES LIMITED presents
RETURN VISIT OF THE SENSATIONAL

EVERLY BROS
BO DIDDLEY
With the Duchess and Jerome

ROLLING STONES
THE FLINTSTONES ★ BOB BAIN

JULIE GRANT **MICKIE MOST**

SEATS Stalls 12/6 10/6 8/6 Circle 10/6 8/6

> ### 'For us, the big thrill is that Bo Diddley will be on the bill.'
> **BRIAN**

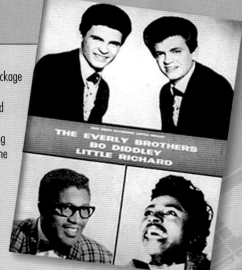

Package tours
Before stadium rock and MTV, the package tour was where teenagers saw their heroes in action. American stars found themselves at the mercy of an antiquated road system and grumbling stagehands and must have thought the UK incredibly backward. But the scenery and warm reaction from audiences was fitting compensation. Backstage was often a seething battleground, with rivalry between stars and jealousy over payment.

The visitors and their local support were allotted time according to their status and chart position. A celebrity or comedian compered, risking disheartening indifference or a barrage of abuse. Des O'Connor toured with Buddy Holly and supplied him with suitably British jokes for the audience. Bands used the house PA for amplification and borrowed equipment. However, towards the end of the 1960s, acts started to demand better sound and larger slots. With the likes of Jimi Hendrix, Pink Floyd and other groups on the scene, the days of the package tour were numbered.

'On Sunday 29 September, 1963, we rehearsed and did a soundcheck in preparation for the first night at the New Victoria theatre in London. We met everyone and we couldn't get over having the opportunity to work with such great artists. We stayed there all day, they even brought in food; we knew we were on the up. There were two shows; at 6pm and 8.30pm. The stage manager was Peter Grant, who would later manage Led Zeppelin.' BILL

'I saw them on their first tour with the Everlys and Bo Diddley and I remember being slightly disappointed when I saw them up there in suits and jackets, but that was what groups thought they had to do then.'
TOM McGUINNESS, *Manfred Mann*

'Girl after girl rushed the stage, only to be rammed back in their seats by staff.'
ROGER BENNETT, *Bristol Post, 2 October, 1964*

Accounts department
The Stones were paid £1,275 for the 30 nights (60 shows). This worked out as £42 10s for each night of the tour or £21 5s per show.

DON ARDEN ENTERPRISES LTD. present
THE FABULOUS
EVERLY BROTHERS **BO DIDDLEY**
with
'THE DUCHESS' & JEROME
THE **ROLLING STONES** **JULIE GRANT**
MICKIE MOST ☆ **THE FLINTSTONES**
Compere: **BOB BAIN**

ODEON ST. ALBANS ON THE STAGE
Manager: H. Hubball Tel. 53888.
WEDNESDAY, OCTOBER 30, at 6.45 and 9.00
Don Arden Enterprises presents
THE **EVERLY BROTHERS**
BO DIDDLEY
ROLLING STONES
JULIE GRANT
BOB BAIN THE FLINTSTONES
"Special Added Attraction" — America's Dynamic
LITTLE RICHARD
Seats: Stalls 15/- 12/6 8/6 Circle 15/- 12/6

> ## 'People said I wouldn't believe it, but nothing could have possibly prepared me for that first sight of the Stones. When I saw them, I thought they just couldn't afford to buy clothes.' **JOEY PAIGE,** *bass player with the Nashville Three, the Everlys' backing group*

Life On The Road

This tour was tremendously exciting for us, not just because it was our first, but because it included two of our heroes along with the Everly Brothers who were genuine superstars – even if they were on the wane.

THE EVERLYS HAD ALREADY chalked up four UK and US No 1s. The rest of the artists were just making up the numbers. Julie Grant had two minor hits (she was also managed by Eric Easton) and Mickie Most had staggered to UK No 45 in July 1963 with 'Mister Porter'.

Mickie would go on to find fame as a producer and record label boss. He produced the Animals (including 'House Of The Rising Sun'), Mary Hopkin, Terry Reid, Lulu, Donovan, the Yardbirds, Jeff Beck and Herman's Hermits.

On Thursday 3 October, a German group called the Rattles joined the tour and the next day Little Richard flew in to complete the line-up. That night, during the interval, we jammed backstage with Bo Diddley and the Everlys and their band. We did a lot of Elmore James songs, with Brian playing slide. You should have seen Bo's face when Brian pulled off the licks perfectly.

Little Richard closed the first half with 'Long Tall Sally', 'Rip It Up', 'Tutti Frutti' and 'Lucille'.

Bo Diddley backstage on the tour

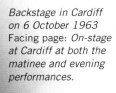

Backstage in Cardiff on 6 October 1963 Facing page: On-stage at Cardiff at both the matinee and evening performances.

'My father took me to the Gaumont Theatre, Watford. Luckily, I had tickets. I was up a drainpipe at the back, trying to get to the Stones through the gent's loo. I was dragged off and put into a Black Maria. The Stones finished playing and we must have come out during the interval. We weren't allowed back in again.' SARAH MONZANI, *Oscar-winning make-up artist and fan*

Eight days into the tour, Stu collected our new Commer van to replace the clapped-out old one, which even had windows in the back as well as seats. We played two shows in Cardiff, where Bo Diddley and Little Richard were particularly good. In fact, Richard brought the house down when he jumped off-stage, went up the centre aisle followed by members of the audience, out the front doors, then back in through a side exit and on-stage. He partly undressed and threw pieces of clothing into the crowd. He performed way past his scheduled time and his manager had to yell to him, 'Richard! Stop preaching,' to get him off.

Between houses, some local Bo Diddley fans came backstage and we chatted. One of the guys offered us some 'grass' – marijuana. We had him ejected because back then we were somewhat naive. After the show in Cardiff we drove back to London, because the following day we were going to De Lane Lea in Kingsway to cut 'I Wanna Be Your Man' and 'Stoned'.

'We all used to bowl along to the Everlys' dressing room and sort of join forces, just for kicks. Can you imagine it?' exclaimed Mick. 'That night we were singing numbers like "La Bamba" and going mad with tambourines and maracas at the same time! It really was fantastic. The Everlys really are artists. The first thing that

At Cardiff on the Everlys tour

JAMES BOND

his new
incredible
women!

his new
incredible
enemies!

his new
incredible
adventures!

BOND IS BACK!

HARRY SALTZMAN
ALBERT R. BROCCOLI
IAN FLEMING'S

FROM RUSSIA WITH LOVE

SEAN CONNERY AS JAMES BOND

DANIELA BIANCHI

RICHARD MAIBAUM — JOHANNA HARWOOD — Lionel Bart — John Barry
HARRY SALTZMAN — ALBERT R. BROCCOLI — TERENCE YOUNG
TECHNICOLOR UNITED ARTISTS

What the papers said...

'I freely admit to bewilderment at recognition of the Rolling Stones. They won great appreciation for "Poison Ivy", "Fortune Teller", their hit parade success "Come On" and "Money". But not from me.' NME, *4 October, 1963*

'The Rolling Stones followed, well applauded for "Poison Ivy" and "Come On".' MELODY MAKER, *5 October, 1963*

'We couldn't really give a verdict on the Stones, the up-and-coming young group with the caveman hairstyles, because we hardly understood a word they sang, but the teenage girls screamed and they are the ones who put such groups on the recording map.' SOUTHEND STANDARD, *10 October, 1963*

'The Stones whipped up a storm, with top rate versions of "Memphis Tennessee" and "Come On".' HERTS ADVERTISER, *1 November, 1963*

'I give the Stones about another two years.' MICK, *Ipswich Gaumont souvenir book*

strikes you about them is their professionalism.'

We had the day off on Monday 14 October, in Liverpool. In the afternoon, we all went to the cinema to see the James Bond film, *From Russia With Love*. We met Faron's Flamingos and the Mojos and later at the Cavern we met the Merseybeats. In Newcastle we went to the Club A-Go-Go. The Alan Price Combo (later the Animals) were playing – they were the hottest local group. We suggested they go to London and talk to Lionel Blake at the Scene club. We jammed with them and during the session I blew Chas Chandler's bass amp. I did say sorry to him…

We were getting a great fan reception at all of our shows, but this wasn't the case for some of the other acts; although not everyone liked us.

'The Everlys were more than brilliant. Yobbos jeered and booed but eventually even these were quietened. Their backing group were brilliant beyond words. As the show ended, they were cheered and clapped and the audience yelled for more.' DAVE BURNINGHAM, *a fan at the Bournemouth, Hampshire show*

'Having seen the Stones at the Odeon, Hammersmith, I can only say that their so-called R&B sounds as anaemic as they look and it is deplorable that they should dare to perform with artistes of the calibre of Bo Diddley and Little Richard.' J WORLEY, *non-fan, in a letter to the NME about the Hammersmith show*

After our Bournemouth gig, Stu was driving us back to London when the van went out of control on an S-bend near Salisbury. We bounced off the wall of a railway bridge, but managed to stay upright. Stu later said, 'We should have all been dead.'

One aspect of the Everlys tour that caused a number of arguments was Linda coming along to gigs with Brian. Chrissie Shrimpton was upset with Mick that he wouldn't allow her to be there.

'Chrissie would always tell me, "Oh, Linda, you can't go because we can't go." She would get real pissed off, because I would get on with Bo and the Duchess [Diddley's guitarist]. Bo was upset when we split up. Bo was so beautiful to Brian. He was getting off on teaching him things. Bo would say, "You move like this when you're on-stage." During rehearsals, he also showed Mick how to move his legs.'
LINDA LAWRENCE

Mick was also getting hassle from Kent Education Committee, who wanted to know what he was going to do about his studies. Andrew Oldham was having a difficult time too and early in the tour he went missing. He was apparently suffering from 'psycholithic' poisoning (whatever that was) and he had left for France.

My problems revolved around lack of cash; luckily Stu came to my aid and lent me £10 the night we played Guildford.

'I kind of equated Brian with Pete Best [ex-Beatle] in many ways, in that he was really the original sex symbol. Mick's looks were not in vogue at that point, but Brian was angelic.' **GRAHAM NASH,** *the Hollies and Crosby, Stills, Nash and Young*

Three days later, on 7 October, we were in the studio to cut our second single, before heading off the next morning to play Brian's home town in Cheltenham. It turned out to be a lovely place and we all teased Brian about it. He had the last laugh though, as everyone we met only wanted to talk to Brian.

The one person who didn't want to speak with him was Pat Andrews. She refused to go backstage when Stu's assistant Spike bumped into her. After the show we went to a club where Jim Gordon, the Everlys' drummer, treated us to an hour's education on how to beat the one-armed bandit machines – he had six big wins – and how to lose it all again in just 30 minutes.

Brian wrote to Eric Easton on 12 October returning some signed contracts and saying how much everyone was enjoying the tour.

Next morning Brian went to the chemist where Pat worked. He told her to contact the Stones office if there was anything she needed for the baby Mark. When she later did, he insisted that the office have nothing to do with her.

Nanker Phelge we shall be

When the Stones cut 'Stoned' – or 'Stones', according to early misprinted pressings – as the b-side to 'I Wanna Be Your Man', Brian suggested crediting it to Nanker/Phelge. The entire band would share writing royalties. Phelge came from Edith Grove flatmate Jimmy Phelge, while a Nanker was a revolting face that band members, and Brian in particular, would pull.

'I WANNA BE YOUR MAN'

After the withdrawal of 'Poison Ivy' as a follow-up to 'Come On', the band needed a new single. On Friday 10 September, they rehearsed at Studio 51 in Soho, trying to conjure up a hit record.

Mid-way through the afternoon, Andrew Oldham left Studio 51 and headed down Charing Cross Road. Opposite Leicester Square tube station he saw Paul McCartney and John Lennon getting out of a cab. The two Beatles were on their way back from a Variety Club luncheon and the 21-year-old Paul and 22-year-old John were probably a little drunk. Oldham hurried over to talk to them and soon all three were on their way back to the basement rehearsal room. Less than half-an-hour after John and Paul's arrival, the Rolling Stones had a new single.

Brian played bottleneck guitar, an entirely new sound. It was like nothing ever played before on a British record. Keith said: 'I dig that steel solo. Brian made that record with that bottleneck.' The b-side, 'Stoned', is an inversion of 'Green Onions' by Booker T and the MGs.

'John and Paul ran through "I Wanna Be Your Man" for us. Paul, being left-handed, amazed me by playing my bass backwards. Brian tried slide on it, which sounded great. It was amazing – the Beatles were No 1 in the chart with "She Loves You" and we went off that night to play the Ricky Tick Club for £67.' BILL

Facing page: *Recording 'I Wanna Be Your Man' at De Lane Lea on Monday 7 October, 1963.*

Recorded
Monday 7 October, 1963
Studio
De Lane Lea Music Recording Studios
Producer
Eric Easton
Release
UK Friday 1 November, 1963
Decca F 11764
Composers
a-side Lennon/McCartney
b-side Nanker/Phelge
Highest chart position
UK No 12
Personnel
Charlie: drums
Bill: bass
Keith: rhythm guitar
Brian: slide guitar and backing vocal
Mick: lead vocal

'It's been going down marvellously on the tour, we're just going to keep our fingers crossed.' MICK

'Not one of Lennon and McCartney's best numbers. Accent on beat, to the total exclusion of melody.' NEW MUSICAL EXPRESS

'There's a distinct rock flavour and the throaty lead voice sings well. It should do better than their last. A very probable hit, with a great guitar solo.' RECORD MIRROR

'How many more seemingly untuneful, unharmonious, badly-played cacophonies of sound are to be released? If ever a composition was murdered, unmercifully and without parallel, this is it.' ALBERT HAND, *Elvis Presley UK fan club president*

'With the record at No 21 in the NME chart, we played an afternoon show at the Co-op Ballroom in Nuneaton on Friday 15 November. It was a junior session and we had to play to a room full of 6- to 10-year-old kids having afternoon tea. They didn't appreciate R&B, so they threw cream cakes at us. It was hilarious. In the evening we played to our normal crowd.' BILL

'"Stoned", a groovy instrumental.' BEAT MONTHLY

Robbery And Hysteria

In Derby, Andrew arrived with a test pressing of 'I Wanna Be Your Man'. We loved it and so did the Americans on the tour. Knowing Andrew was coming, we all wore our uniform, the blue waistcoats and knitted ties. On tour, I often sat in the wings, watching Little Richard, Bo Diddley and the Everly Brothers. I learned something new every night. When we arrived in Liverpool, we discovered something very interesting about Brian.

'Brian said he was going to stay at a better hotel, but he never actually did. We found out that he had been drawing £5 a week extra. He had an arrangement with Easton that, as leader of the band, he was entitled to this extra payment. When we discovered this everybody freaked out, and that was the beginning of the decline of Brian.'
KEITH

ONE HAZARD OF LIFE on the road was the eagerness of fans to try and get hold of anything that belonged to us. We lost the letters off our van's number plate on a regular basis. They even broke into the dressing room when we played in Hull and stole maracas, harmonicas and tambourines. One of the support bands at this gig was Johnny Kidd and the Pirates. They stole a pair of Johnny's pirate boots; he was well pissed off – they took two right feet. This was all forgotten the next day, when we were each paid £193 4s 6d by Eric, an absolute fortune, the most any of us had ever earned in a week by a long way. The next day it was back to earth with a bump when we had a seven-hour drive in the van from Manchester to Glasgow… the joys of life on the road.

LSD not LSE

On 22 October, Mick got around to replying to Kent Education Committee. He wrote a letter explaining that he felt unable to continue his course at the London School of Economics due to the band's growing success. Mick's tutors were very good to him and told him if things didn't work out, then he could go back in a year's time.

*Playing the Sunday Star Club,
Town Hall, Crewe, on 10 November, 1963*

the fans. In Rochester, I decided to go out and try to buy some copies of the single, but I couldn't find it anywhere. The following day, I tried again. I went to Penge High Street and managed to get the last one in the shop – it was a good sign.

'The backing is wild but too prominent. The voices are lost. This may have been the intention but it was not a good one. Well, at least it's a different sound. This isn't as good as "Come On".' DJ PETE MURRAY, *Melody Maker*

The last few days of the Everlys tour went off pretty well, particularly at Hammersmith, where we had the best reception. No doubt there were lots of our fans from Richmond and around London in the crowd for that date. It was the last night of the tour and we had a party

musical *The Music Man*. No wonder we were never asked to play the Royal Command Performance.

In the Cavern

To complete the irony, we drove to a hotel in Liverpool because we were to play the Cavern Club the next night. We played a 45-minute set to a wildly enthusiastic audience. Hundreds were locked out and 25 girls fainted. I'd never seen anything like it. Three days later 'I Wanna Be Your Man' entered the *NME* singles chart at No 30.

The reaction in the clubs was getting better and better. Wherever we played people loved what we were doing and it was more fun to play the clubs and ballrooms than to play on a package tour. At Newcastle's Club A-Go-Go, one guy shouted 'Get your hair cut' and was set upon by a bunch of lads who took him outside and beat him up. Even getting in and out of clubs was becoming a headache. We had to be smuggled in and out just about everywhere we played.

In the middle of all the driving to and from shows, we went into De Lane Lea Studios in London with Eric Easton for a four-hour session (later released). We cut Barrett Strong's 'Money' and the Clovers' 'Poison Ivy' again, as well a number by Chuck Berry called 'Talkin' 'Bout You'.

'I have been offered a really excellent opportunity in the entertainment world which would not have been open to me unless I could accept at this time.' MICK, *in a letter to the Kent Education Committee*

We were beginning to get recognised in the street, which was nice, but soon began to present us with a new set of problems. After the show in Sheffield we went out on the town and found a coffee bar. We were talking to a couple of local lads when a crowd formed outside. The old guy who ran the coffee bar didn't know who we were and, not wanting trouble, threw us out. We had to make a run for it back to our hotel.

On 1 November, 'I Wanna Be Your Man' was released, which increased the level of hysteria from

backstage before driving home. The coach carrying other touring musicians, including Julie Grant and Mickie Most, was involved in a collision in Cricklewood, north London. The driver was killed and Bo Diddley's drummer – Barry Jenkins, later of the Nashville Teens – was taken to hospital. The other passengers escaped, but were shaken up.

With the tour over, it was business as usual. The next day Stu drove us the 228 miles to Preston in Lancashire. We played the Top Rank, at the same time as the Beatles were playing the Royal Command Performance in London's Prince of Wales theatre in front of the Queen Mother and Princess Margaret. While we were probably playing something like 'Roadrunner' or 'You Better Move On', the Beatles were performing ''Til There Was You' from the

De Lane Lea session
At the studios in Kingsway on 14 November, the Stones recorded three songs. For 'Money', the line-up was Charlie (drums), Keith (lead guitar and backing vocal), Brian (rhythm guitar and backing vocal), Mick (lead vocal, backing vocal and harmonica) and Bill on bass. On 'Poison Ivy', it was Charlie (drums), Keith (rhythm guitar), Brian (rhythm guitar and backing vocal), Mick (double-tracked lead vocal and a percussive instrument called the guiro) and Bill played bass and did backing vocals. Bill: 'For the life of me I can't remember what the line up was for "Talkin' 'Bout You".'

Bill: 'As usual it was our long (?) hair that drew comment.'

The United Kingdom,
November 1963–January 1964

The venues on this tour were spread far more evenly throughout England than those visited by the Stones before the Everly Brothers tour.

4 November, 1963 Top Rank Ballroom, Preston, Lancashire
5 November Cavern Club, Liverpool, Lancashire
6 November Queen's Hall, Leeds, Yorkshire
8 November Club-A-Go-Go, Newcastle upon Tyne, Northumberland
9 November Club-A-Go-Go, Whitley Bay, Northumberland
10 November Sunday Club, Town Hall, Crewe, Cheshire
11 November Pavilion Ballroom, Bath, Somerset
12 November Town Hall, High Wycombe, Buckinghamshire
13 November City Hall, Sheffield, Yorkshire
15 November Co-op Ballroom, Nuneaton, Warwickshire (matinee and evening)
16 November Matrix Ballroom, Coventry, Warwickshire
19 November State Theatre, Kilburn, London
20 November Chiswick Polytechnic, Athletic Grounds, Richmond, Surrey
21 November McIlroy's Ballroom, Swindon, Wiltshire
22 November Town Hall, Greenwich, London
23 November Leyton Baths, Leyton, London (matinee) Chez Don Club, Dalston, London (evening)
24 November Studio 51, Soho, London (matinee) Majestic Ballroom, Luton, Bedfordshire (evening)
25 November Parr Hall, Warrington, Cheshire
26 November Stamford Hall, Altrincham, Cheshire
27 November ABC Theatre, Wigan, Lancashire
28 November Memorial Hall, Northwich, Cheshire
29 November Urmston Baths, Urmston, Lancashire
30 November Kings Hall, Stoke-on-Trent, Staffordshire
1 December Oasis Club, Manchester, Lancashire
2 December Assembly Rooms, Tamworth, Staffordshire
3 December Floral Hall, Southport, Lancashire
4 December The Baths, Doncaster, Yorkshire
5 December Gaumont Theatre, Worcester, Worcestershire (two shows)
6 December Odeon Theatre, Romford, Essex (two shows)
7 December Fairfield Hall, Croydon, Surrey (two shows)
8 December Ricky Tick, Olympia Ballroom, Reading, Berkshire (matinee) Gaumont Theatre, Watford, Hertfordshire (evening – two shows)
11 December King and Queen Hall, Bradford, Yorkshire
12 December Locarno Ballroom, Liverpool, Lancashire
13 December Hillside Ballroom, Hereford, Herefordshire
14 December Epsom Baths, Epsom, Surrey
15 December Civil Hall, Guildford, Surrey
17 December Town Hall, High Wycombe, Buckinghamshire
18 December Corn Exchange, Bristol, Gloucestershire
20 December Lido Ballroom, Winchester, Hampshire
21 December Kayser Bondor Ballroom, Baldock, Hertfordshire
22 December St Mary's Hall, Putney, London
24 December Town Hall, Leek, Staffordshire

26 December Selby's Restaurant, Hanover Street, Mayfair, London
27 December Town Hall, Reading, Berkshire
28 December Club Noreik, Tottenham, London
30 December Studio 51, Soho, London
31 December Drill Hall, Lincoln, Lincolnshire
3 January, 1964 Glenlyn Ballroom, Forest Hill, London
4 January Town Hall, Oxford, Oxfordshire
5 January Ricky Tick, Olympia Ballroom, Reading, Berkshire

Five thousand, three hundred and fifty-four miles – that's how far the Stones went in the van driven by Stu in the two months between finishing the Everly Brothers package tour and starting a UK tour with the Ronettes in early January 1964. They played 58 shows in 62 days, managed five recording sessions, appeared on five TV shows, did a pilot for another TV show that never aired and had seven days off. One of which was Christmas Day, 1963.

'While the noise they make is tremendous, the appearance is stupefying. Onstage they wear high-heel boots, tight pants, black leather waistcoats and even ties, except for Mick, who wears his shirt with collar detached. Off-stage, they wear a jumbled assortment of jeans, silk cardigans, camel jackets or sloppy sweaters. None of the slick suits sported by Billy J or Gerry of the Pacemakers.' CYNTHIA BATEMAN, *Preston newspaper, November, 1963*

'The Stones were late, arriving in an old van and a shooting-brake-type vehicle. One of the group wiped condensation off the window of the shooting brake and peered out. He looked like a frog. Jagger's neck was filthy. I asked the group to sign their autographs upon the back of the Beatles' Please Please Me *album, to which Brian replied "We are trying to outdo these". The attendance on the night was between 700 and 800. The Stones were reluctant to leave the stage at the end of the night, preferring to "jam".'* DAVE EDGLEY, *club co-organiser*

5,354 Miles

Money – that's what they want

With a single under their belts and another climbing the charts, the Stones were able to command more money. During November they earned an average of £117 per gig, which rose to £154 in December and January. The Stones' first £200 gig was at the Lido Ballroom in Winchester on December 20.

And in support...
The Rattles
Frankenstein and the Monsters
The Crestas
The Escorts
Mike Sagar and the Tornados
The Valiants
The Liverbirds
Wayne Fontana and the Mindbenders
The Ricky Allen Trio
The Exchequers
Gerry and the Pacemakers
The Detours
The Original Checkmates
The Overlanders
Pete McClaine and the Clan
The Art Tilburn All-Stars
Group One
Glyn Johns and the Presidents
The Graham Bond Quintet
Georgie Fame and the Blue Flames
The Yardbirds
The Strangers
The Big Three
The Sheffields
Vance Arnold and the Avengers
Karen Young
The Vantennas
Johnny Tempest and the Cadillacs
The 4 Plus 1
The Downliners Sect
Jimmy Powell and the Five Dimensions

'The Assembly Rooms erupted to a crescendo of female screams. Five lads with a pulsating beat streaming from their amps. Lads with more hair hanging over their ears and around their shoulders than the Beatles ever had, produced the biggest audience appeal that there has ever been here. When you consider the talent that has stepped onto this stage, the Beatles, the Big Three, the Bachelors, Screaming Lord Sutch, the Bruisers, you have an idea of the impact made by the Stones'.
TAMWORTH HERALD,
6 December, 1963

RICKY TICK CLUB
OLYMPIA BALLROOM, READING
Sunday, January 5th, 3-530
ROLLING STONES

'In Sheffield, we again wore casual clothes and played to 3,000 fans. It was a wild crowd and we had a really great show.' BILL

Gerry and the Pacemakers

'For us, Monday 18 November was a day off, so I went shopping in Penge and bought three new albums: Bo Diddley Rides Again, More Chuck Berry and Chet Atkins' Workshop. On the way home, it started to pour with rain. I began decorating the sitting room and I got an early night for a change.' BILL

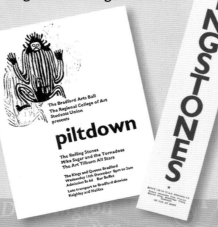

STUDIO '51
10/11 GT. NEWPORT ST.
LEICESTER SQUARE
RHYTHM & BLUES every
Friday, 8 till Midnight
THE DOWNLINERS SECT
Sunday Afternoon, 4 until 6.30
THE ROLLING STONES

TOP of the POPS
HILLSIDE BALLROOM
ROSS ROAD, HEREFORD
FRI. 13TH DEC.
9 p.m. to 12.30 a.m.
COME ON! to our
XMAS PARTY with the
ROLLING STONES
PLUS
THE VALIANTS
ADM. 7/6   REFRESHMENTS
LICENSED BAR (app. for)

'The Stones drew an even bigger crowd than the Beatles here. Is this an omen that they are to be soon crushed by the Stones?' **KILBURN TIMES**, *25 November, 1963*

We Like It

As my first year as a Rolling Stone drew to a close, we began to see the results of months of hard work touring, recording and appearing on television. And all of this was done without us writing any of our own material. Ironically, one of Mick and Keith's first compositions was not released by the Stones, but was recorded by American star Gene Pitney.

O N 17 NOVEMBER, we mimed to 'I Wanna Be Your Man' on *Thank Your Lucky Stars*. Gene Pitney was also on the show and we met him in the dressing rooms. Mick and Keith played him a song they had written called 'My Only Girl'.

Andrew had been encouraging them to write their own songs for some time, although the story that he locked them in the flat until they wrote some material is just another Rolling Stones myth.

promoter Robert Stigwood and was to kick off in February 1964 for a month, immediately after we finished the Group Scene Tour 1964 with the Ronettes. A few days after Eric's announcement, 'I Wanna Be Your Man' dropped two places on the *NME* chart to No 23 and a week later it vanished from the chart completely.

For the rest of November and most of December, we interspersed gigs with appearances on *Ready Steady Go!* and *Thank Your Lucky Stars*,

Walk Alone', had all reached UK No 1. Naturally, he insisted on closing the show, while we ended the first half. By the time we played at the Fairfield Hall in Croydon, fans were leaving during the interval, which meant Gerry suffered the indignity of playing to a half-empty house. After the show we all went back to my parents' place in Blenheim Road for a bit of a party.

'A deafening reception greeted the Stones, who jerked about the stage looking, with their eccentric hairstyles, like tufted moorhens. They somehow managed to make themselves heard above the frenzied screaming of the packed house. Hysterical girls howled successfully for an encore.'
LOVATT LINDSEY, *The Croydon Advertiser*

Filming a BBC pilot programme at St Michael's Hall, Lower Sydenham on 19 December, 1963

'I changed the whole thing. That song wasn't right for the market. I put it into the ballad-type thing that I was doing.' GENE PITNEY, *on 'That Girl Belongs To Yesterday'*

Three days later, we went into Regent Sound Studios in Denmark Street, London with engineer Bill Farley, Andrew Oldham and Gene Pitney to cut a demo version of the song he would later release as 'That Girl Belongs To Yesterday'. Gene, Mick and Keith eventually rewrote the chorus.

The fall and rise
Eric told us we were booked on a tour with John Leyton, whose hits included 'Johnny Remember Me'. It was co-promoted with manager/producer/

Promotion for the Croydon gig

FAIRFIELD HALLS in the **FAIRFIELD HALL** CROYDON
Saturday, 7th December
6.15 & 8.45
John Smith presents
THE **ROLLING STONES** **GERRY AND THE PACEMAKERS**
THE **ORIGINAL CHECKMATES**
plus FULL SUPPORTING COMPANY
PRICES 10/6 8/6 6/6 5/-
watch for further announcements

helping our single back into the *NME* chart. It rose steadily – thank goodness. Our improving pay meant that we were also staying in better hotels. At the beginning of December, we played shows within driving distance of Manchester and we liked staying in the Grand Hotel, although I am not sure what they thought of us. Increasingly, we were getting mobbed at the venues, fans tearing at our clothes and hair. I regularly lost the buttons off my jackets.

Closure
In early December, we did a short run of gigs with Gerry and the Pacemakers, playing Worcester, Romford, Croydon and Watford. Gerry's first three singles, 'How Do You Do It', 'I Like It' and 'You'll Never

The freedom to choose

Abortion in Britain was outlawed in the 19th century, when many women died as a result of botched attempts. Despite medical advances, it remained illegal until the 1960s. After a fierce debate on the morality of abortion, the Abortion Act became law in much of the UK on 27 October, 1967, by which time the risk of unwanted pregnancy had significantly diminished. The contraceptive pill was introduced in the UK in 1961 and was associated with the Swinging Sixties and greater sexual freedom. It's now used by around 100 million women worldwide.

Two days after we played Croydon, Linda found out that she was pregnant with Brian's baby. By all accounts, Linda's parents took the news well and urged Linda and Brian to go to Cheltenham to tell his parents about their expected grandchild, which they did the following Sunday. Well, not quite, according to Linda: 'We went through the whole visit and never told them. Finally, when Brian wrote and told them about it, they denied it and cut me right off. They thought I was terrible because I was pregnant, but they'd accepted me before. I had slept in their house. It wasn't the way they expected it. I felt very bad, and Brian freaked out.' Later in the month, Brian and Linda considered an abortion. Charlie's girlfriend, Shirley, took the couple to see a doctor, who asked if they were in love. They said they were and he advised,

'Go home then, we're not going to do it.'

The period leading to Christmas gave us a little bit of time off and we played gigs that allowed us to stay at home most nights. We also filmed the pilot for a BBC TV show at St Michael's Hall, Lower Sydenham, a place the Cliftons had played regularly. Other artists on the show included Rolf Harris and Dusty Springfield. It never aired and is just another lost BBC tape, but we did get paid £52 10s. The penultimate gig before Christmas was at St Mary's Hall in Putney and our support band were the Detours, who later became the Who. Just before we took to the stage, Pete Townshend saw Keith swing his arm in a wide arcing motion, a gesture that inspired Townshend's famous windmill strum. It was just over 12 months since my first gig as a Rolling Stone. We had played 268 gigs since Charlie joined the band: not a bad year's work.

Pete Townshend's trademark 'windmill'

Meaty Christmas

Christmas was nearly a disaster after Brian and I both got food poisoning. We had a gig on Christmas Eve in Leek, Staffordshire and, as there was nothing to eat, Stu bought some meat pies, which tasted okay at the time. On the way home, however, Stu had to keep stopping on the motorway so that Brian and I could be sick. We finally arrived back home at 7am on the morning of 25 December… Happy Christmas. The festive issue of *Record Mirror* ran a Stones advert which offered a 'Happy Christmas to the starving hairdressers and their families.'

'I Wanna Be Your Man' was at UK No 15 in the *NME* chart at Christmas and went up the following

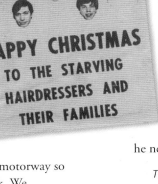

HAPPY CHRISTMAS TO THE STARVING HAIRDRESSERS AND THEIR FAMILIES

week to No 12. Our hard work promoting it was paying off. We recorded a *Ready Steady Go!* on the afternoon of 27 December. The show featured a 13-year-old boy from America: Little Stevie Wonder. Many years later we would tour America with Stevie. Andrew had a spot as the guest DJ – he was such a brilliant self-publicist! We were always on the lookout for new stage material and learned 'I Can Tell' and Chuck Berry's 'Carol' at Studio 51 on 30 December. For New Year's Eve we were in Lincoln and stayed at the White Hart Hotel. After the gig and a drink, I went to bed. Mick, Keith and Brian had other ideas. They dressed Brian in a sheet to make him look like a ghost, turned out the lights in the hallway and came knocking on my door. I opened it, took one look at this ghostly apparition and said, 'Go to bed, Brian, and stop messing about.'

'You bastard!' Brian said, 'It's taken us an hour to get this together.' After lunch at the hotel the next day, we drove to Manchester to appear on the first ever *Top of the Pops*. Before we started the tour with the Ronettes we played a few gigs around the south and backed Cleo Sylvester on the old Teddy Bears' song, 'To Know Him Is To Love Him', at Regent Sound. The b-side was an instrumental featuring us and Mike Leander on piano, entitled 'There Are But Five Rolling Stones' and credited to the Andrew Oldham Orchestra. It was good to know how he saw us. Oh yeah, and he never paid us.

Thirteen-year-old Little Stevie Wonder

Ready, Steady, Go!
The Weekend Starts Here
KEITH FORDYCE invites you to meet a galaxy of guest stars
America's boy phenomenon
LITTLE STEVIE WONDER
AND
THE ROLLING STONES
Listen to hit discs dance with the teenagers in the

It's No 1... It's TOP OF THE POPS

If you are British and under 55, then it is guaranteed you will have watched *Top Of The Pops*. It is an institution, the longest-running music show on British television. The very first programme aired on Wednesday 1 January, 1964 and the Stones were on it.

T he *Radio Times* announced: 'The performers whose songs are popular in the charts will mime to their discs, a departure from standard BBC policy. The idea is to replicate the sound of the popular track. No two performances are the same, but this performance is the one that made it a hit.' The Stones appeared on *Top Of The Pops* on numerous occasions ever since. The dates below mark the first performance of each new release during the 60s.

Debut *TOTP* appearances for new releases

1 January, 1964 'I Wanna Be Your Man'
27 February 'Not Fade Away'
1 July 'It's All Over Now'
11 March, 1965 'The Last Time'
10 June 'I'm Alright'
2 September '(I Can't Get No) Satisfaction'
14 October 'Get Off Of My Cloud' from *Charlie Is My Darling*
19 October 'Get Off Of My Cloud'
20 January, 1966 '19th Nervous Breakdown'

3 February '19th Nervous Breakdown'
14 April 'Paint It, Black'
22 September 'Have You Seen Your Mother, Baby, Standing In The Shadow?'
26 January, 1967 'Let's Spend The Night Together'
21 December 'She's A Rainbow' and '2000 Light Years From Home'
23 May, 1968 'Jumpin' Jack Flash'
10 July, 1969 'Honky Tonk Women'

After 'I Wanna Be Your Man', the only 1960s single not featured on *Top Of The Pops* was 'Little Red Rooster'. The band's management was then in dispute with the BBC. Eric and Andrew fell out over some BBC bookings that Eric had made, which Andrew refused to honour. This ended in a legal wrangle with the BBC, but by the time 'The Last Time' was released, things had been resolved.

On 6 July, 1967, the show featured Mick, Keith and Brian in the Beatles' film for 'All You Need Is Love'.

Three weeks later, on 30 July, Peter Whitehead filmed a promo for 'We Love You' with Mick, Keith and Marianne Faithfull in a church hall in Essex. Coming in a period when the Stones were targeted by the authorities for drug busts, it was a timely adaptation of the 1960 movie *The Trials Of Oscar Wilde*. Andrew offered it to *Top Of The Pops* but was turned down.

Jimmy Saville was the show's first DJ.

Mick signs autographs outside the BBC studio.

'After filming the first edition of Top Of The Pops, we headed to the outskirts of Manchester to drive home to London. We stopped at a small Chinese restaurant, the only place open late at night. After 40 minutes, the food hadn't arrived. We were all impatient, put £10 on the table, shouted a few curses and left. Suddenly the chef burst out of the kitchen brandishing a meat cleaver and screamed at us, "Come black, you flucking blastards". We bolted for the door, jumped in the van and raced up the road. We could hardly stop laughing, that is until we realised how hungry we were.' BILL

Hairy Pudding Basins

'They may be the shape of things to come. Who would have thought that half of Britain's teenagers would end the year with heads like hairy pudding basins?' wrote Ian Marlowe in the *Daily Sketch*. 'Their success seems to lie in their offhandedness. "We just please ourselves," they say. But remember, millions of teenagers in 1964 may end up looking like them.'

WE WERE USED to being written about in the music press, but now we were featured in the national papers. Mr Marlowe's views were typical of the reaction we were causing by early 1964. Not that it bothered us: we loved the publicity. It sold records and filled our live shows with screaming girls and wannabe boys. We all laughed at the *Daily Sketch* before we drove to Oxford with Andrew.

We took two chauffeur-driven cars, as the van had broken down. On the way we stopped at a service station for some food. Almost immediately we got sarcastic comments about our hair and dress. There were about 40 people there, so we ordered a fried egg to be served to everyone in the place and each person was told that it was from us. Everyone became very British, nodding at us and smiling, saying, 'Oh – thanks very much.'

Two nights later we met the Ronettes on the first night of our short tour together. The Ronettes, who were lovely, had recently got to UK No 4 with 'Be My Baby'. A few days after the tour started they entered the chart with another Phil Spector production, 'Baby I Love You' (Ronnie Bennett later married Phil).

'They didn't warm up to us, we couldn't get these guys to talk to us. I asked Andrew Oldham why the boys were ignoring us. "Darling, we'd all love to talk to you, but we got a telegram that forbids us to talk to you." "Who from?" I asked. "From Phil, darling," he replied. "He said there would be dire consequences if we did." "That may be the way Phil feels, but Phil's not here. You tell the Rolling Stones that if they don't start talking to us there'll be dire consequences from us."' RONNIE SPECTOR, *in her autobiography, Be My Baby*

According to Keith, things began to look up later in the tour: 'There was no direct competition within the band for pulling chicks. The only time I remember Mick and I in any slight competition was with the Ronettes, when Mick wanted to pull Ronnie, and ended up with her sister Estelle.'

We enjoyed touring with the Ronettes and the exposure did us no harm, although there was a less positive side. 'We're not always happy about playing theatres,' admitted Mick. 'Sometimes the lights are so strong that we cannot see the audience and that bothers us. Sometimes I wish we could return to the clubs where we started out, just to play there again for old times' sake. We had some really raving sessions in those days.'

Five dates into the tour we were back in the studio cutting 'Not Fade Away'. It was the same day as our first EP was released (that's an extended play, 45 revolutions per minute, vinyl record to anyone under 35).

The United Kingdom, *January 1964*

Italics indicate non-tour gigs.

6 January Granada Theatre, Harrow on the Hill, London
7 January Adelphi Theatre, Slough, Buckinghamshire
8 January Granada Theatre, Maidstone, Kent
9 January Granada Theatre, Kettering, Northamptonshire
10 January Granada Theatre, Walthamstow, London
11 January *Baths Hall, Epsom, Surrey*
12 January Granada Theatre, Tooting, London
13 January *Barrowlands Ballroom, Glasgow, Scotland*
14 January Granada Theatre, Mansfield, Nottinghamshire
15 January Granada Theatre, Bedford, Bedfordshire
16 January *McIlroy Ballroom, Swindon, Wiltshire*
17 January *City Hall, Salisbury, Wiltshire*
18 January *Pier Ballroom, Hastings, Sussex*
19 January Coventry Theatre, Coventry, Warwickshire
20 January Granada Theatre, Woolwich, London
21 January Granada Theatre, Aylesbury, Buckinghamshire
22 January Granada Theatre, Shrewsbury, Shropshire
23 January *Pavilion, Lowestoft, Suffolk*
24 January *Wimbledon Palais, Wimbledon, London*
25 January *California Ballroom, Dunstable, Bedfordshire*
26 January De Montfort Hall, Leicester, Leicestershire
27 January Colston Hall, Bristol, Gloucestershire

The Group Scene '64 tour opened at the Harrow-on-the-Hill Granada on Monday 6 January. The package tour visited 14 places in 22 days, playing two shows a night, not that the band had any spare time. On days off, the Stones played other gigs, including a second visit to Glasgow, only this time the band flew; a sign of changing times.

The set at Salisbury differed from the version they used on the tour. It was closer to their roots. They played 'Come On', 'I Wanna Be Your Man', 'Talkin' 'Bout You', 'Poison Ivy', 'Fortune Teller', 'Pretty Thing', 'Love Potion No 9', 'Route 66', 'Roll Over Beethoven', 'Road Runner' and 'Memphis Tennessee'.

The Stones got £125 for each night on the tour. They were commanding more at some of the one-off shows. At the Barrowlands gig the band got £270 and at Wimbledon Palais they earned £273. An old friend of the Stones, UK R&B pioneer Cyril Davies, died of leukaemia the day of the Slough show, 7 January, 1964.

'On Wednesday 15 January, Stu, Spike, Brian and I drove by van to Bedford, while the others went by car. On the way a stone shattered our windscreen, making the rest of the journey very cold and uncomfortable. We drove back to London after the gig, still minus a windscreen, in a snowstorm, in zero visibility; it was one of the worst drives we ever had.' BILL

A few days after the Stones played Aylesbury, two 14-year-old girl fans wrote to the manager, asking if they could see the band's dressing room. They visited it a few weeks later and touched and kissed the door handle.

'They look like refugees from a barber's shop and dress like gentlemen of the open road.'
NORTHAMPTONSHIRE EVENING TELEGRAPH

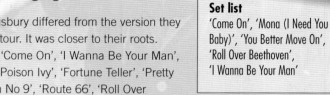

Set list
'Come On', 'Mona (I Need You Baby)', 'You Better Move On', 'Roll Over Beethoven', 'I Wanna Be Your Man'

Running order
The Cheynes
Compere Al Paige
Dave Berry and the Cruisers
   (replaced by Lee Curtis
   All-Stars at some gigs)
Johnny Kidd and the Pirates
   (added to some gigs)
The Ronettes
Interval
The Swinging Blue Jeans
Marty Wilde and the Wildcats
Bern Elliott and the Fenmen
   (added to some gigs)
The Rolling Stones

In Coventry, Patrick Dane and the Quiet Five, the Barron Knights and Freddie and the Dreamers played with the Ronettes and the Stones. Patrick Dane and the Quiet Five played at Epsom, Johnny Carr and the Cadillacs at Salisbury and the Four Aces (not the American group) were also in support.

The Group Scene '64 Tour

'THE ROLLING STONES' EP

Recorded
'Bye Bye Johnny' (Berry)
8 August, 1963
'Money' (Gordy jr/Bradford)
14 November
'You Better Move On'
(Alexander) 8 August
'Poison Ivy' (Lieber/Stoller)
14 November
Location
Decca Studios, West
Hampstead 8 August
De Lane Lea Studios,
Kingsway 14 November
Producer
Andrew Oldham 8 August
Eric Easton 14 November
Engineer
Unknown
Release
UK Friday 10 January 1964
Decca DFE 8560
Highest chart position
Record Retailer EP
chart No 1

A few days into the tour with the Ronettes, the Rolling Stones released their first EP. It entered the *NME* singles chart on 18 January, mid-way through the tour. It was in the singles chart for 11 weeks and spent a full year in the EP chart, topping the chart for 14 weeks. Having failed to be released as the second single, 'Poison Ivy' was re-recorded for the EP in November.

The liner notes of the EP were an insight into how Decca viewed their young protégés. 'Whichever way the present musical trends develop, the Stones are likely to stay in there, swinging at the top with their uniquely refreshing contribution to popular music…' Well, they got that bit right!

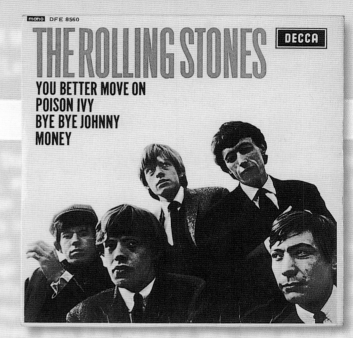

'We've been using "You Better Move On" in our act for ages and it has always gone down well. That's why we decided to record it.' MICK

'Without doubt it was "You Better Move On" alone that was responsible for catapulting this EP into the best-selling singles chart. Had it been released as a single, it may have well reached the very top. It could have been their first UK No 1.' ROY CARR

'Brian and I sang backing vocals to Mick's double-tracked lead vocals on "You Better Move On".' BILL

'Mick and Charlie were in the usual padded cells. Brian, Keith and Bill were huddled round a central mic, with their amps buried under a pile of soundboards. Four titles were put on the master tape and the one I really dug the most was "You Better Move On", a beautiful slow belter.' ANDREW OLDHAM

'Ten days after we released the EP, my old mates the Paramounts released a version of "Poison Ivy", which hung around the lower reaches of the chart for seven weeks, getting to UK No 35. "Money" had got as high as UK No 14 for Bern Elliott and the Fenmen in December 1963, which is why they were added to the John Leyton tour.' BILL

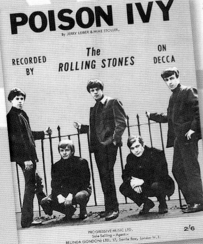

Shake, Rattle And Rolling Stones

On Friday 24 January, 1964, Decca issued George Bean's 'Will You Be My Lover Tonight' with 'It Should Be You' on the b-side. Both were Jagger/Richards compositions, released before Gene Pitney's 'That Girl Belongs To Yesterday'. It has the distinction of being the first UK single to feature songs written by Mick and Keith. The producer was Andrew.

'George Bean was a hardcore Stones fan and former drinking partner of mine from the early days at Ealing Blues Club.'
JAMES PHELGE

THE RECORD WAS ONE of Andrew's many early attempts to become a pop producer, spurred on no doubt by his hero worship of Phil Spector. What is interesting about Mr Bean's record is the fact that both sides are very slushy, romantic beat ballads, an early feature of Mick and Keith's compositions.

On the day of the record's release, we went to Regent Sound to cut demos of more of Mick and Keith's songs. We did 'I'd Much Rather Be With The Boys', 'Each And Every Day Of The Year' and 'Sleepy City', all for a measly £2 or £3 each from Andrew.

'It was Andrew who really forced Mick and I to sit down and get through that initial period where you write absolute rubbish,' said Keith. 'You rewrite things you've heard and other people's songs, until you start coming up with songs of your own. Andrew made us persevere.'

'Andrew's pushing Mick and Keith to write songs was what really caused Brian to be left behind.' GLYN JOHNS

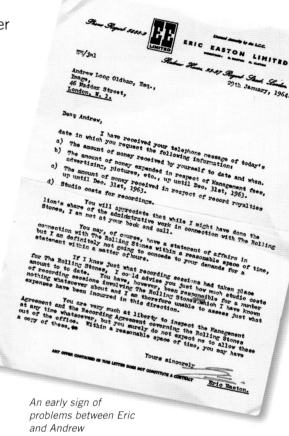

An early sign of problems between Eric and Andrew

'I think everyone got turned onto the idea of writing songs by the Beatles. It was like, if the Beatles can write, we can write.' MICK

On the same day, Eric told us he had been approached with a movie idea. We met with a man from Border Films, one Michael Winner. I cannot remember what the film was about, but I know it was nothing like *Death Wish*.

Just before we started the John Leyton tour, there were the first signs of a rift between Andrew and Eric. Andrew called Eric several times demanding details of money matters, to which Eric replied in writing. I suppose at the time we were uncertain as to the ins and outs of such things, but it wouldn't be long before we began to find things out the hard way.

Back at the Hall

Three days before the tour began, we headlined at the Royal Albert Hall – less than five months since we had been an opening act. Our success was even surprising us. Also on the bill were Jet Harris, the Swinging Blue Jeans, Brian Poole and the Tremeloes and Dusty Springfield. It was a charity pop show run by *Valentine* magazine and the audience went wild.

'The Stones are real ravers,' gushed *Valentine*,

'and were a huge success at the great pop prom.' Another review said, 'Mick launched into his now-famous dance routine as the group began to play. He kicked his legs back and forth, arched his neck and waved his arms. Keith clutched his instrument like a pike, and charged across the stage. Brian and Charlie both shook their heads and their hair cascaded wildly. Charlie thumped his drums with great gusto and bounced up and down on his stool. Brian attacked his guitar with renewed vigour. Bill just stood there and grinned.'

'They wail, they thump, they look like scarecrows.'

REVEILLE *magazine,*
2 February, 1964

The run-up to the John Leyton tour was very busy. On Monday 3 February, we made our band debut on BBC Radio's *Saturday Club*, although Charlie, Brian and I had backed Bo Diddley on the show the previous September. The engineers at the Playhouse Theatre in Charing Cross were old BBC types, and the mics were even older. Andrew wanted us to reproduce our sound, but had a lot of difficulties dealing with the old hands. We eventually recorded 'Come On', 'Roll Over Beethoven', 'Memphis Tennessee', 'I Wanna Be Your Man' and 'You Better Move On' for the show that went out on the following Saturday morning. Presenter Brian Matthew admitted: 'I think perhaps a little bit mistakenly I found their attitude in the studio, as apart from their music, extremely truculent.'

Witness protection

The next day we were back at Regent Sound Studios with Bill Farley and Andrew to cut some tracks. Pretty soon Phil Spector arrived, followed by two of the Hollies, Graham Nash and Allan Clarke. A little later Gene Pitney came direct from Heathrow Airport with duty-free brandy. Everyone got involved in playing something. Pitney played piano, while Spector and the Hollies banged coins on empty bottles and played tambourines and maracas. We cut 'Can I Get A Witness' with Stu on piano and then Gene played on 'Little by Little'.

'I took a fifth of Cognac over to the studio, and told the Stones that it was my birthday, and that the custom in my family was that when anybody had a birthday, everybody had to drink a whole glass until the bottle was empty. We ended up with a hell of a session. I played piano and Phil Spector played empty Cognac bottle, and we played on the b-side, which was "Little By Little".' GENE PITNEY

Inspirational bottle
Recording at Regent Sound on 4 February. *Top:* Phil Spector and the Stones with Gene Pitney seated. *Above:* Andrew stands far left and Gene Pitney far right.

We then worked up a song called 'Now I've Got A Witness', before the whole session degenerated into silliness. No doubt Gene's drinks helped us to cut 'Andrew's Blues' (sometimes called 'Song For Andrew' and far too dirty to be released), and then 'And Mr Spector and Mr Pitney Came Too', but we all had a great time. It's often said that we recorded 'Not Fade Away' at this session, with Phil Spector playing maracas, but Andrew used this as publicity, although he was more impressed than the media were.

Two days later, we were at Pye Studios near Marble Arch to record a TV commercial for Kellogg's Rice Krispies. We invented a short Jimmy Reed-style track. We had a good laugh doing it and they paid us £400 too.

The night before the tour began, we taped ATV's *The Arthur Haynes Show*, at Elstree Studios, playing 'I Wanna Be Your Man' and 'You Better Move On'. It really was all go.

The John Leyton Tour,
January–March 1964

Gigs in italics were not a part of the package tour

31 January, *Public Hall, Preston, Lancashire*
1 February *Valentine Charity Pop Show, Royal Albert Hall, London*
2 February *Country Club, Hampstead, London*
5 February *Locarno Ballroom, Willenhall, Staffordshire*
8 February Granada Theatre, Edmonton, London
Club Noreik, Tottenham, London (all night)
9 February De Montfort Hall, Leicester, Leicestershire
10 February Odeon Theatre, Cheltenham, Gloucestershire
11 February Granada Theatre, Rugby, Warwickshire
12 February Odeon Theatre, Guildford, Surrey
13 February Granada Theatre, Kingston-upon-Thames, Surrey
14 February Gaumont Theatre, Watford, Hertfordshire
15 February Odeon theatre, Rochester, Kent
16 February Guildhall, Portsmouth, Hampshire
17 February Granada Theatre, Greenford, Middlesex
18 February Rank Theatre, Colchester, Essex
19 February Rank Theatre, Stockton-On-Tees, Durham
20 February Rank Theatre, Sunderland, Durham
21 February Gaumont Theatre, Hanley, Staffordshire
22 February Winter Gardens, Bournemouth, Hampshire
23 February Hippodrome Theatre, Birmingham, Staffordshire
24 February Odeon Theatre, Southend-on-Sea, Essex
25 February Odeon Theatre, Romford, Essex
26 February Rialto Theatre, York, Yorkshire
27 February City Hall, Sheffield, Yorkshire
28 February Sophia Gardens, Cardiff, Wales
29 February Hippodrome Theatre Brighton, Sussex
1 March Empire Theatre, Liverpool, Lancashire
2 March Albert Hall Theatre, Nottingham, Nottinghamshire
3 March Opera House, Blackpool, Lancashire
4 March Gaumont Theatre, Bradford, Yorkshire
5 March Odeon Theatre, Blackburn, Lancashire
6 March Gaumont Theatre, Wolverhampton, Staffordshire
7 March Winter Gardens, Morecambe, Lancashire

John Leyton

A week after finishing the Group Scene '64 tour, the Stones joined another package. Between the two tours, the band played four gigs, recorded three TV shows and had three recording sessions. The tour played 29 venues in 29 days, performing twice-nightly.

The Stones' first EP was at No 19 in the *NME* singles chart and rose to No 15 during the tour. John Leyton's first record, the Joe Meek-produced 'Johnny Remember Me', topped the charts two years earlier. He was then a fading recording star. 'Make Love To Me' entered the chart for just one week, Leyton's last hit single. The Stones were paid £4,142 17 shillings for the 29 dates – just £142 per show... Ah, but think of the exposure, boys!

'The first night of the tour coincided with the Beatles arriving in New York for their first tour. After we finished in Edmonton we drove the few miles to the Club Noreik in Tottenham where we played an all-nighter. We had a marvellous reception and we always loved playing there, as it was more like one of the old club gigs.' BILL

'Mike Berry's band the Innocents were a four-man group that included Colin Giffin (guitar), and Dave Brown (bass), who later formed the End. Later still they became Tucky Buzzard. I produced both bands from the mid-1960s to the early 1970s.' BILL

ALL NITE RAVE
MIDNIGHT to 6 a.m.
CLUB NOREIK
HIGH ROAD, TOTTENHAM, N.15
PRESENTING
SAT., FEBRUARY 8th
THE ROLLING STONES
SAT., FEBRUARY 15th
THE HOLLIES
PLUS!
Two Supporting Guest Combos
EVERY WEDNESDAY
Non-stop Dancing
from 7.30—11 p.m.
Apply Club Noreik for Membership
Coach parties welcomed

Touring with John Leyton

'In York I noticed that Jet Harris has a whole crate of light ale in his dressing room. I was told he had one each night, and drank the lot all by himself! I was also amazed when I found out that he didn't play his bass on stage, but that he mimed to it, while Billy Kuy of the Innocents played Jet's parts, hidden behind the curtains'. BILL

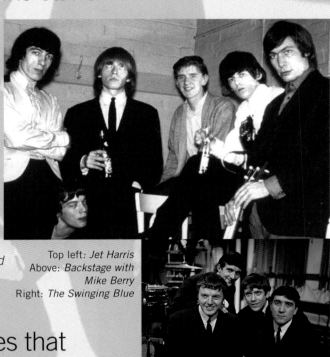

'On the last night, Jet Harris got drunk and throughout his set told dirty jokes to a stunned audience. As if responding to Jet's performance, Billie Davis' poodle walked onstage, peed on Jet's spot-lit vocal mike stand while he was singing and walked off.' BILL

'We all got on well with Coca-Cola and fags but no drugs in those days. We would be pretty well trapped wherever we went, so we just played silly buggers. The girls mostly screamed at Brian, as he was the smart mod. Their rhythm sound was what sounded the best – I didn't rate Jagger as a singer at all. I couldn't really see the appeal!' MIKE BERRY

'At Romford, Mick was in the middle of a number when a hysterical teenager rushed towards him from the wings, sobbing, with her arms outstretched. Mick ducked quickly, caught her in a fireman's lift and carried her back to the wings, where she was taken away by an attendant. Mick carried on with the song as though nothing had happened.' STU

Top left: *Jet Harris*
Above: *Backstage with Mike Berry*
Right: *The Swinging Blue*

'Five young men with hairstyles that make the Beatles appear bald.'
THE LEICESTER MERCURY

'At one time, I was going to insist that the Stones wore decent suits on stage but, when I started talking about it, they gave the impression of having suddenly gone stone-deaf, so I gave up.' THEATRE MANAGER, *the Gaumont theatre, Watford*

Sneers And Smears

press by and large supported us: 'On-stage, the Stones have changed. Their dress is somewhat modified, and the last time I saw them, on a TV show, they were actually quite smart,' reported *Pop Weekly* in February. 'Whatever people say about them, the fact remains that they've filled ballrooms and dance halls with crowds greater than those at some of the Beatles shows.' We were forever being tackled about our looks and clothing; Brian's comments at the time were typical of our response to the constant criticism: 'We know about the sneers and the smears. It seems that people who've never met us, or even heard us play, take a great delight in taking the mickey. Our view is simple. We wear our hair long because we like it that way. We wear clothes that appeal to us because we simply won't get involved in the midnight-blue mohair uniforms worn by so many others.'

'We aim to please the fans and it seems that we are succeeding.' BRIAN

Fifty-eight shows in 29 days, all without a night off, would have been hard enough but, on top of that, we travelled to and from just about all of them in the van – we didn't even know what a limo was back then. When not performing, we were in and out of TV and recording studios.

ON THURSDAY 13 FEBRUARY, Andrew had us back at Regent Sound Studios to cut two more of Mick and Keith's songs. We did 'Try A Little Harder' and 'Some Things Just Stick In Your Mind' and again Andrew paid us a fee of just £3 each.

The following day, we did publicity photos in London on the Thames Embankment and on a boat. These were extensively used over the next year, throughout the world. Later in the day Decca, very generously, gave each band member a solitary copy of the new single, 'Not Fade Away', which was due out the week after.

We appeared on BBC Radio's *Pop Inn*, at the Paris Studios in Regent Street, on Tuesday 18 February. We chatted and played 'Not Fade Away'. When we finished we had to fight our way out of the studios. The fee was 10 guineas.

Our ever-increasing popularity made us a target for some sections of the media. We were also less than loved by most parents and members of the Establishment. Promoters were not that enthusiastic about us, although they liked the money we made them.

'Promoters who had seen pictures of us used to get the dead needle for no reason at all. It was assumed that we weren't capable of putting on a show, because we didn't press our pants or comb our hair. Quite unfairly, we were described as unreliable.' KEITH

It was the national press who were the most conservative in their outlook. The music

Record Mirror, 18 January, 1964, enthuses about the new sounds.

'NOT FADE AWAY'

Not Fade Away
The Rolling Stones
Little By Little (UK)

The one minute and 42 seconds of 'Not Fade Away' is classic pop-rock. A homage to Buddy Holly by way of Bo Diddley, it is the first record where Mick really sounds like Mick.

The single entered the *NME* chart at No 10 a week after its release, giving an indication of the popularity of the Stones. The band appeared on *Top of the Pops* on 27 February, which helped boost its chart placing the next week.

The inspired US pairing of 'Not Fade Away' with 'I Wanna Be Your Man' prompted one critic to write: 'They [America] never knew what hit them!' The single entered the US Hot 100 on 2 May, 1964, eventually making it into the lower reaches of the Top 50.

'On Saturday 22 February, we shot a Top Of The Pops film on a rocky beach at Weymouth in Dorset. We mimed to "Not Fade Away" in hats, coats and scarves, as it was freezing cold. They rolled stones down the cliffs – pop video 1964-style.' BILL

'The Stones were not very punctual. They'd arrive very late. Then they'd spend half an hour lazing about, having an official tea break. The actual recording was usually done very quickly. They were a funny-looking bunch, but you could hardly find a more professional lot. Their arrangements were worked out in advance and they knew exactly what sort of sound they wanted to get.' BILL FARLEY, *engineer*

DECCA
MADE IN ENGLAND
Southern Music Ltd.
XDR 32719
F 11845
℗ 1964
NOT FADE AWAY
(Petty, Hardin)
THE ROLLING STONES
Production: Impact Sound

'The rhythm thing was based around the Buddy Holly song. We brought the rhythm up and emphasised it. Holly used that Bo Diddley beat on his version, but because he was only using bass, drums and guitar, the rhythm is sort of throwaway. Buddy played it very lightly. We got into it and put the Diddley beat up-front.' BILL

LONDON
Distributed By London Records, Inc.
Nor Va Jak Music, Inc.
BMI
Time: 1:50
DR 32719
Made in U.S.A.
45-LON 9657
Production:
Andrew Loog Oldham
NOT FADE AWAY
(Petty; Hardin)
THE ROLLING STONES

'The first takes were too fast. It's a common error among performing groups not familiar with recording in the studio. I insisted on them slowing it down. This time it worked.' ANDREW OLDHAM

A little pastiche
'Little By Little' is a pastiche of Jimmy Reed's 'Shame, Shame, Shame', injected with the feel of the Stones R&B live shows at the time. '"Little By Little" sounds just like the Louisiana blues I've been hearing since I was a little kid,' said Jerry Lee Lewis in March 1964. 'They sure do it real well.'

US b-side
'I Wanna Be Your Man'
Recorded
Friday 10 January, 1964
Studio
Regent Sound Studios
Producer
Andrew Oldham for Impact Sound
Engineer
Bill Farley
Release
UK Friday 21 February, 1964
Decca F 11845
US Friday 6 March, 1964
London 45-LON 9657
Composers
a-side Petty/Hardin
UK b-side Phelge/Spector
US b-side Lennon/McCartney
Highest chart position
UK No 3
US No 48
Personnel
Charlie: drums
Bill: bass
Keith: lead guitar
Brian: harmonica
Mick: double-tracked lead vocal, claps, tambourine and maracas

NOT FADE AWAY
Recorded on DECCA F11845 by
THE ROLLING STONES

What the papers said...
'The effect I get is of a group which hasn't the talent to sing in harmony so they do it in unison,' reported *Melody Maker*. 'Their saving grace is that they sing in English rather than American.'
'The Stones are on the beat with "Not Fade Away", which is in the modern idiom,' said the *Daily Mirror*.

THE ROLLING STONES—NOT FADE AWAY (Nor Va Jak, BMI) (1:50)—Another hot GB group that proves how deep the r.&b. roots have gone over there. Flip: "I Wanna Be Your Man" (Gil, BMI) (1:44).
London 9657

Latest hit!
The Rolling Stones
NOT FADE AWAY
#9657
LONDON
RECORDS

103

Media Hype

WOULD YOU
GO WITH A

Constant touring, coupled with the media attention, was beginning to do the trick. We were the bad boys of pop, an image carefully crafted by Andrew. People may not have liked us, but they couldn't fail to notice us.

AFTER PLAYING BOURNEMOUTH, we drove to Birmingham next morning to record *Thank Your Lucky Stars*. We broke down at Amesbury in Wiltshire – incessant touring was taking its toll on the van too. We had a temporary repair in a garage, but it wouldn't go into reverse gear, so we all had to push it out of the garage. Charlie, in his usual laconic manner, muttered: 'It's just as well we don't have to drive to Birmingham backwards.' After the TV programme and a show at the Hippodrome in Birmingham, we headed for London, making one of our frequent stops at the Blue Boar service station on the M1 motorway, a touring band's home away from home.

Shows around London, on the Monday and Tuesday, gave us the chance to record tracks for our first album at Regent Sound Studios. A wonderful article at the end of February by Judith Simons in the *Daily Express* was a pretty accurate representation of how the dailies saw us.

'They look like boys whom any self-respecting mum would lock in the bathroom. But the Stones, five tough, young, London-based music-makers with doorstep mouths, pallid cheeks and unkempt hair, are not worried what mums think. They have taken over as the voice of the teens.

'Watching them as they perform onstage, with the glazed expression of sleepwalkers, no adult would credit that they come from good homes. They now knock up £1,500 a week between them. The time will come when they will want to capture the ear and the lolly of older age groups and unless

they change their present image, this will be impossible.' Judith, you hadn't counted on our audience growing old with us!

The response from the audiences got even wilder as the tour went on. It was not unusual for girls to make a run for the stage and try and get to one of us. The success

> 'Even my own mother thought I was ridiculous, but what can she say now, with all this money rolling in?' **BRIAN**

of 'Not Fade Away' coupled with the negative reaction of the national newspapers seemed, if anything, to make the fans love us even more.

Brian, when not on the road, lived with the pregnant Linda and her parents in

Windsor. Often Brian could not contain his jealousy of Linda's male friends. On one occasion she went to a party and got Brian so enraged that he gave her a black eye; they told her parents she had walked into a door. Brian had no cause to be this way with Linda. Shortly after this occurred, another girl who Brian was seeing found out she too was pregnant by him. Her name was Dawn Malloy: 'I was Brian's girlfriend for about three months,' she said. 'I used to go on tour with the group and stay at the hotels with Brian.'

Dad's wheels

Getting to and from gigs was a little easier as Mick was driving his dad's Ford Consul. Some of us would go with him, while the rest went in the van. Often we ended up at a party somewhere. Years

Down the M1 apiece
'The Blue Boar – the place where you can meet the stars for the price of a cup of tea,' reported *Fabulous* in April 1964. 'You'll find it at Long Buckley, on the Birmingham end of the M1. The all-night cafe that the stars head for after one-nighters in the Midlands. Sunday is star-spotting day. You'll find most of the next Saturday's *Thank Your Lucky Stars* guests relaxing there after recording the show in Birmingham. The Stones are on the road most of the time, but they belt back to London at every opportunity, so the Blue Boar is a natural stopping-off point for them.' The picture is from 23 February, 1964.

LET YOUR SISTER ROLLING STONE ?

● BILL WYMAN

● BRIAN JONES

● KEITH RICHARD

● CHARLIE WATTS

later, I received a letter from Joan Scott-Allen: 'We met at my home in Beeston, Nottingham, some three decades ago. It was a one-night stand of artists who appeared at the Albert Hall, Nottingham. Mike Berry's mum and I are good mates. When she left the UK for the States she asked me to keep an eye on her two boys who were in showbusiness, hence why I was asked to open my home that night. I'll never forget you and Charlie Watts sitting in my kitchen drinking out of jam jars because we'd run out of glasses!'

When the John Leyton tour ended, Charlie and Shirley went to Gibraltar. Diane, Stephen and I went to stay at the Brown Derby Hotel near Lyndhurst in the New Forest, Mick and Chrissie went to Paris, Brian toured Scotland and Keith

stayed in Mapesbury Road. We had a whole week off, which was wonderful. It was the first seven days I'd had to myself since I joined the Stones.

Coleman's balls
It was during this week that Andrew claimed to have given Ray Coleman the famous line, 'Would you let your daughter go with a Rolling Stone?' Ray changed 'daughter' to 'sister' when the headline appeared in the *Melody Maker* of 14 March. Whether or not he said this to Roy is beside the point. There is no doubting Andrew's skill at promoting our bad boy image. Instead of hustling for a few column inches, he was now a conductor, skillfully orchestrating the media to play up whichever aspect of our image he chose.

'I don't particularly care either way whether parents hate us or not. They might grow to like us one day. We don't set out to try to be grizzly. I can tell you this much – my parents like me.' MICK

'If parents begin to like the Stones, the teenagers who made that group will begin to feel they're losing them to older people, and discard the group. I've made sure the Stones will not be liked too much.'
ANDREW OLDHAM, *March 1964*

The day after the *Melody Maker* article appeared we were due to play the Invicta Ballroom in Kent, only there was a problem. Charlie was still in Gibraltar. Despite all our efforts, no one could contact him; we were resigned to finding a substitute drummer. Someone suggested Micky Waller, who had played with Cyril Davies and Marty Wilde, and he agreed to play for £16. It was the only time, thank goodness, I ever played a Stones gig without Charlie. Jimmy Page, later of Led Zeppelin, came backstage after the show for a chat. We had just heard from ALO and Eric that we were to tour America in June and that was all we could talk about. The big league was beckoning and the only thing standing in our way was 58 gigs in the next two-and-a-half months.

United Kingdom, *March-May 1964*

15 March Invicta Ballroom, Chatham, Kent
17 March Assembly Hall, Royal Tunbridge Wells, Kent
18 March City Hall, Salisbury, Wiltshire
21 March Whitehall, East Grinstead, Sussex
22 March Pavilion, Ryde, Isle of Wight, Hampshire
23 March Guildhall, Southampton, Hampshire (two shows)
25 March Town Hall, Birmingham, Staffordshire (two shows)
26 March Town Hall , Kidderminster, Worcestershire (two shows)
27 March Ex-Serviceman's ClubWindsor, Berkshire
28 March Wilton Hall, Bletchley, Buckinghamshire
Club Noreik, Tottenham, London (all night)
30 March Ricky Tick Club, Plaza Ballroom, Guildford, Surrey (matinee)
Olympia Ballroom, Reading, Berkshire (evening)
31 March West Cliff Hall, Ramsgate, Kent
1 April Locarno Ballroom, Stevenage, Hertfordshire
3 April Wimbledon Palais, Wimbledon, London
4 April Leas Cliff Hall, Folkestone, Kent
5 April Gaumont Theatre, Ipswich, Suffolk
(two shows, Stars Of 1964 tour)
6 April Royal Hotel Ballroom, Lowestoft, Suffolk
8 April Empire Pool, Wembley, Middlesex,
(Ready, Steady Go! Mod Ball)
9 April McIlroy's Ballroom, Swindon, Wiltshire
10 April Leyton Baths, Leyton, London
11 April Pier Ballroom,Hastings, Sussex
12 April Fairfield Halls, Croydon, Surrey (two shows)
16 April Cubi-Club, Rochdale, Lancashire
17 April Locarno Ballroom, Coventry, Warwickshire
18 April Royalty Theatre, Chester, Cheshire
22 April Carlton Ballroom, Slough, Berkshire
24 April Gaumont Theatre, Norwich, Norfolk
(two shows, All-Stars 1964 tour)
25 April Odeon Theatre, Luton, Bedfordshire
(two Shows, All-Stars 1964 tour)

26 April Empire Pool, Wembley,
London (matinee and evening,
NME Poll Winners' Concert)
27 April Royal Albert Hall , London (two shows,
Top Beat Pop Prom)
28 April Publica Hall, Wallington, Surrey
30 April Majestic Ballroom, Birkenhead, Cheshire

1 May Imperial Ballroom, Nelson, Lancashire
2 May Spa Royal Hall, Bridlington, Yorkshire (two shows)
3 May Palace Theatre, Manchester, Lancashire (two shows)
7 May Savoy Ballroom, Southsea, Hampshire
8 May Town Hall, Hove, Sussex
9 May Savoy Ballroom, Catford, London
10 May Colston Hall, Bristol, Gloucestershire (two shows, Brian
played only second)
11 May Winter Gardens, Bournemouth, Hampshire (two shows)
13 May City Hall, Newcastle upon Tyne, Northumberland (two shows)
14 May St George's Hall, Bradford, Yorkshire (two shows)
15 May Trentham Gardens, Stoke-on-Trent, Staffordshire (two shows)
16 May Regal Theatre, Edmonton, London (two shows, All-Stars
1964 tour)
17 May Odeon Theatre, Folkestone, Kent (two shows, All-Stars
1964 tour)
18 May Chantinghall Hotel, Hamilton, Scotland
19 May Capitol Theatre, Aberdeen, Scotland (two shows)
20 May Caird Hall, Dundee, Scotland (two shows)
21 May Regal Theatre, Edinburgh, Scotland (two shows)
23 May Leicester University, Leicester, Leicestershire
24 May Coventry Theatre, Coventry, Warwickshire (two shows)
25 May Granada Theatre, East Ham, London, (two shows)
26 May Town Hall, Birmingham, Staffordshire (two shows)
27 May Danilo Theatre, Cannock, Staffordshire (two shows)
28 May Essoldo Theatre, Stockport, Cheshire (two shows)
29 May City Hall, Sheffield, Yorkshire (two shows)
30 May Adelphi Theatre, Slough,
Buckinghamshire (two shows)
31 May Empire Pool, Wembley, London
(matinee and evening, *Pop
Hit Parade)*

After finishing the John Leyton tour the band had a week off. The day after Ray Coleman's famous article appeared in the Melody Maker, the Stones began a hectic series of dates that took them the length and breadth of Britain.

During these two-and-A-half months the band earned an average of £324 per night, more than double the amount from similar gigs at the end of 1963. It was also more than twice what each member earned nightly on the John Leyton tour. During this ten-week period, the band was grossing around £2,000 per week from gigs as well as TV and radio appearances. The five band members and Stu were being paid a total of around £800 per week. Each musician earned an average of £154 each week, while Stu picked up £25 - the average weekly wage in Britain was a little over £16. At the end of May, Andrew Oldham, with his usual exaggeration said, 'The Stones earn £3,000 per week if they're fully booked, and that doesn't include record royalties. This is only the beginning.'

'One of the most bizarre shows we ever did was at the Royalty theatre in Chester. It was more like Music Hall than rock'n'roll. To open the show, a Miss Olivia Dunn played songs at a piano on the dancefloor in front of the stage. She was followed by a group of sailors who announce every song with a supposedly funny comment. Things like: "And now! The fish-fryer's delight! 'Mashed Potatoes'" (a song that was popular in America at the time). While all this was going on – we were in fits of laughter, watching from the side of the stage – Olivia remained seated at her piano. In the interval before we went on, she played again. The crowd went crazy when we started our first song. They all rushed to the front, trampling Miss Dunn and her piano; she disappeared under a mass of bodies, never to be seen again! BILL

☆ March dates
★ April dates
☆ May dates

North, South, East And West

COLSTON HALL, BRISTOL
SUNDAY, MAY 10th, at 5.30 and 7.45 p.m.
...ern Scene presents by arrangements with Malcolm A. Rose

The Rolling Stones
★ JOHNNY CARR AND THE CADILLACS ★
★ MIKE TOBIN AND TH...
MILLIE and the NO...
★ THE AVON CITIES ★
★ Christine Marlowe ★
GENE VINCENT and T...
TICKETS: 12/6, 10/6, 7/6, 5/- from C...
and Western Scene Offic...

ALL NITE RAVE
MIDNIGHT to 6 a.m.
CLUB NOREIK
HIGH ROAD, TOTTENHAM, N.15
Telephone: 2...
PRESENTING
SATURDAY, MARCH 14th
THE ANIMALS
SATURDAY, MARCH 21st
FREDDIE & THE DREAMERS
SATURDAY, MARCH 28th
THE ROLLING STON...
PLUS !
Supportin...

RICKY TICK R & B CLUB
PLAZA BALLROOM GUILDFORD
EASTER MONDAY AFTERNOON, 3-5.30
Rolling Stones
EVERY TUESDAY 7.30-10.30
Rhythm & Blues
FRIDAY ...8-11
... d
...e
...11 p.m.
...ship

PALACE THEATRE - MANCHESTER
SUNDAY, 3rd MAY, 1964
TWO CONCERTS
JOHN SMITH presents The Fabulous ALL STAR SHOW
THE ROLLING STONES
—NOT FADE AWAY—
PETE McCLAIN · THE FOUR JUST MEN · **SUNLINERS**
THE SWINGING HI-FOUR
THE OVERLANDERS · **McKINLEYS**
JULIE GRANT
Compere: DAVID HAMILTON

CITY HALL,
Northumberland Road, Newcastle upon Tyne, 1.
WEDNESDAY, 13th MAY, 1964
at 8.45 p.m.
AUSTIN NEWMAN presents
THE ROLLING STONES SHOW
AREA 5/-   SEAT   LL
Booking Agents: A. E. Cook, Limited, 5-6 Saville ...
Newcastle upon Tyne (Tel. 2-2901).
This Portion to be retained.

WINTER GARDENS BOURNEMOUTH
THE ROLLING STONES and Co.
at 8.40 p.m.
STALLS 12/6   STALLS 12/6   MON. 11th MAY, 1964
A 38   A 38

The Rolling Stones Show
SOUVENIR PROGRAMME
Austin Newman presents

The Rolling Stones

ALBERT A. BONICI and ANDY LOTHIAN, JNR. present
Star Parade
MARK PETERS AND THE SILHOUETTES · PETER AND GORDON · THE ROLLING STONES · FREDDIE AND THE DREAMERS · DAVE BERRY AND THE CRUISERS · MILLIE AND THE...

John Smith presents
The Rolling Stones
The Rattles
Fairfield Hall, Croydon

Set list
Songs included:
'Talkin' 'Bout You' (often the opener)
'Poison Ivy'
'Walkin' The Dog'
'High Heel Sneakers'
'You Can Make It If You Really Try'
'I'm A Kingbee'
'Pretty Thing'
'Cops And Robbers'
'Jaguar And The Thunderbird'
'Don't Lie To Me'
'Roll Over Beethoven'
'You Better Move On'
'Road Runner'
'Route 66'
'I Just Want To Make Love To You'
'I'm All Right'
'Beautiful Delilah'

At the start of this period the band often finished their set with 'Bye Bye Johnny'. Later on 'Not Fade Away' and then 'I Wanna Be Your Man' would close the set.

And In Support...
The Marauders
Denny Laine and the Diplomats
Group Z
Barron Knights
Wayne Fontana and the Mindbenders
Mike Sarne
Alex Harvey Band
Chris Farlowe and the Thunderbirds
Jet Harris
Big Dee Irwin
Terry Judge and the Barristers
Mike Berry
The Falcons
The League of Gentlemen
Billie Davis
The Rattles
Mickey Finn and the Bluemen
The Innocents
Miss Olivia Dunn
Dene Hunter and the Sunliners
The Le Roys
The Lou Prager Orchestra
Heinz and the Saints
Pete McClaine
The Mandrakes
Mark Anthony and the Avengers
Four Just Men
The Swinging Hi-Four

Millie Small and the No Names
Julie Grant
Overlanders
Gene Vincent and the Shouts
Avon Cities
Christine Marlowe
Mike Tobin and the Magnettes
Gamblers
Ray Bush Rhythm and Blues Band
Johnny Carr and the Cadlilacs
The Echoes
Keith Powell and the Valets
Peter Jay and the Jaywalkers
Chris Carlsen
David John and the Mood
Cliff Bennett and the Rebel Rousers
Applejacks
Dave Berry and the Cruisers
Mark Peters and the Silhouettes
Caravelles
The Monarchs
Freddie and the Dreamers
Simon Scott
Peter and Gordon
Pat Wayne and the Beachcombers
The Outlaws
Dave Dee and the Bostons
The Johnny Quantrose Five
The Barracudas
The Bachelors

'The Odeon Theatre, Rochester, has gone the way of so many cinemas, and is now a branch of Boots the Chemist. The stage, on which you performed, would have straddled an area that now extends from the 'After Shave' display, to the 'Johnny' counter. What can this mean? We should be told.' Jeremy Miles, *News Editor of South Kent Newspapers in a letter to Bill in 1983*

'We'd rather starve than have our nuts shaved'
BRIAN, *in the Daily Mail 6th March, 1963...*

'I'm sure Brian was talking about our heads!'
BILL, *2002*

Stereo Stones

Three days after we played Chatham, in Kent, we were in a London studio, recording a series of four programmes for Radio Luxembourg to be aired in April. In all, we cut 14 tracks, which were a good cross-section of our live material at the time.

The Radio Luxembourg songs
'Bye Bye Johnny', 'I Wanna Be Your Man', 'Diddley Daddy', 'Little By Little', 'Look What You Done', 'Mona (I Need You Baby)', 'Not Fade Away', 'Now I've Got A Witness', 'Pretty Thing', 'Walking The Dog', 'You Better Move On', 'Reelin' and Rockin'', 'Roll Over Beethoven' and 'Route 66'.

THE DAY AFTER THE Luxembourg show, we taped an experimental stereo radio show for the BBC at the Camden Theatre in London, which aired on 9 May, 1964. The audience had been recruited from the Flamingo Jazz Club. Georgie Fame and the Blue Flames played first and after a quick soundcheck, we played 'Route 66', 'Cops and Robbers', 'You Better Move On' and 'Mona'.

'Charlie Watts crept up on the stage behind the Blue Flames' drummer and stood entranced, hypnotised by every drum beat,' reported *Top Boys* magazine in March 1964. 'Keith and Bill sat chatting in the front row of the stalls and showed one another their new LP buys like a couple of excited kids. Then Brian Jones arrived and chatted

to Adrienne Posta, whose new single is written by Mick and Keith, and who follows the boys around at every opportunity. Mick sat in the back row of the empty theatre, fidgeting with impatience.'

On Good Friday, March 27, after playing in Windsor, we went to Adrienne Posta's 16th birthday party. Peter (Asher) and Gordon (Waller), Millie Small (famous for 'My Boy Lollipop') and singer Jimmy Justice were there, while Paul McCartney brought along his friend John Dunbar and girlfriend Marianne Faithfull. This was the first time Mick met Marianne.

'Rumour has it that Mick spilt champagne over Marianne's dress to get her attention, but she was in love with John Dunbar and ignored him. I didn't see it happen and Mick definitely can't remember!' BILL

Radio waves
On the day after Adrienne's party, Radio Caroline began broadcasting from a ship 'somewhere in the North Sea'. On the same day we played the Wilton Hall, Bletchley, and then drove back to north London to play Club Noriek , where we went on stage at 3am. On Easter Sunday, Brian sat in with the Yardbirds at the

Posta pin-up
Adrienne Posta's Decca single, 'Shang-A-Doo-Lang', was written by Jagger and Richards, and produced by Andrew Oldham. Adrienne later appeared in *Up The Junction* and *Here We Go Round The Mulberry Bush*.

When pirates ruled the air waves
From early 1964, outfits like Radio London, Radio 390, Radio King and Radio Caroline, started by Ronan O'Rahilly, filled the gap left by the lack of decent music programmes on the BBC and the patchy service from Radio Luxembourg. Transmitting from off-shore, the pirates weren't answerable to UK authorities and couldn't be shut down. Radio Caroline broadcast from the *Mi Amigo* ship, pictured top right, with DJs *(right)* including Dave Lee Travis (wearing policeman's hat) and Tony Blackburn *(second from right)*. Screaming Lord Sutch's Radio Sutch broadcast from an old sea fort *(near right)*. Their decline began in 1967, when the government passed a new law making real outlaws of the pirates. The BBC also introduced music station Radio 1, recruiting DJs from many of the pirate stations.

365 Rolling Stones

On Friday 10 April, the Andrew Oldham Orchestra single '365 Rolling Stones (One For Every Day Of The Year)' with 'Oh, I Do Like To See Me On The B-Side' was released. Charlie and Bill played on both sides of this single. Unfortunately, Andrew failed to realise that this was a leap year — there were 366 days in 1964! The b-side is a rare writing credit indeed. It is Oldham/ Watts/Wyman.

Bill: 'I don't think it has made either Charlie or me a lot of money.'

> '*Dear Sir, I am not a square, but when I saw the Rolling Stones on television the other night, I was shocked and disgusted. I used to like them but now their act of being different has gone too far. With their hair, they look like something from a horror film. If television gave X-certificates, then this would surely qualify.*'
> ANN COOPER, *letter to Beat Monthly magazine, April 1964*

We're in the money

Early in the month Brian left Linda's parents and moved to a flat at 13 Chester Street, Belgravia, London. Money was less of a problem than it had been a few months earlier, although our weekly wage fluctuated quite dramatically. In April we were paid £201, £184, £121 and £77. Not that we were complaining – to earn nearly £600 in a month was amazing back in 1964.

'More than 40 girls and two boys fainted during a performance by the Stones. Some were treated for cuts from bottles. The hall resembled a battlefield.' A RAMSATE PAPER

Crawdaddy, as their singer Keith Relf was ill. On the Tuesday after the Easter weekend we played Ramsgate in Kent. Local newspapers described what was becoming the norm at our gigs.

Margate's *Thanet Times* reported: 'The effect they had on the young audience was astounding. At one point during the evening, first aid personnel were kept busy dealing with relays of young girls overcome with emotion. A separate room was set aside and they were laid in rows on the floor until they had recovered from their hysteria.'

Andrew continued to feed the press such outrageous stories that it beggars belief they took it all so seriously. London's *Evening Standard* reported Andrew saying, 'They don't wash too much and they aren't all that keen on clothes. They don't play a nice-mannered music, but raw and masculine. People keep asking me if they're morons.' Some fans even began responding to his taunts.

Stone not alone

On 11 April, it finally came out that Bill was married. *The Evening Standard* broke the story. 'This is the married Rolling Stone. He is Bill Wyman, 21 years old... The one who resembles Charles I,' wrote Maureen Cleave. 'The secret has been miraculously kept since the Stones, who have very long, floppy hair and dress eccentrically to the point of messiness, became well-known.' *The Sunday Mirror* also ran the story and, as usual, they managed to get many of the facts wrong — nothing new there, then. 'Pop stars hiding their wives for fear of fans' jealousy are slowly realising that marriage won't necessarily muck up their careers,' said Jack Bentley. 'The latest pseudo-bachelor to stop telling his wife to pretend they're just good friends is Bill of the Stones. He has been married to Ann [Diane], from Penge in Kent [London], for 18 months [four-and-a-half years], and they have an eight-month-old son [two years and two months].

Marriage revelations by members of other groups have not harmed their popularity. Bill's confession shouldn't make the slightest difference to sales of his group's new LP.'

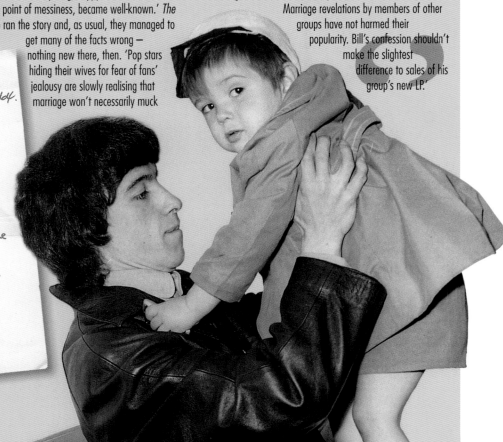

A La Mod

As well as playing ballrooms, theatres and clubs – gigs which increasingly got out of hand – we performed at the *Ready Steady Go!* Mod Ball at the Empire Pool, Wembley. We were to stand on a huge revolving rostrum and mime to our first song. We ran to the stage through a security corridor, which promptly collapsed.

THE MOD BOOK OF THE STONES BOYFRIEND EXTRA!

WE FOUGHT OUR WAY towards the stage, listening to 'Walking The Dog' play while 8,000 fans stared at the empty stage. We finally made it onto the rostrum just as the song was ending.

Charlie had to use the same drums as the Dakotas and the Fourmost because of limited changeover time between acts. We were pulled into the crowd throughout the set and, when we finished, we were unable to leave the moving stage for 30 minutes. We fought our way backstage with the help of security men. None of the other acts had a reaction like this. It was a glimpse of the way things were going to be for a very long time.

We played Rochdale on 16 April and the gig was abandoned before we even got on stage, as the club owners and police feared for the safety of audience and band.

'A 13-year-old girl fainted and couldn't be revived and was taken to Rochdale Infirmary for treatment. Outside, over 1,000 youngsters were clamouring to get inside, but generally, the 50 police and two dogs kept them under control.'
ROCHDALE PAPER

The next day our first long-playing record was due to be released and hysteria levels were set to get even higher.

When the Stones finally made the stage at the Mod Ball on 8 April, they mimed their whole set.

Ready, Steady, Go! Mod Ball

This is the night of the year when 8,000 mods (note for squares: mods are the smartest fashion-conscious teenagers) congregate in aid of children's charity in the **Empire Pool, Wembley**, to dance to the top pop names. It's a live show in every sense of the word. Stand by for excitement!
INTRODUCED BY
KEITH FORDYCE
WITH
Cathy McGowan
AND
Michael Aldred
CILLA BLACK
The **FOURMOST**
FREDDIE and the **DREAMERS**
KATHY KIRBY
BILLY J. KRAMER
and the **DAKOTAS**
KENNY LYNCH
MANFRED MANN
The **MERSEYBEATS**
The **ROLLING STONES**
The **SEARCHERS**
SOUNDS INCORPORATED
PROGRAMME EDITOR FRANCIS HITCHING
EXECUTIVE PRODUCER
ELKAN ALLAN

Mod generation
Mod was not just a fashion, it was a lifestyle. Short for 'modernists', it was a term used to describe kids into jazz, R&B, Vespa motor-scooters, smart shirts and sharp suits. Hair was short on boys and girls wore a bob to match their miniskirt. Its peak was in the mid-1960s.

1964. Wednesday:-
Went up to Wembley Empire pool for the Mod Ball on T.V. Went over marvellously & we were mobbed on the live show & in the T.V. spot – & none of the other groups were touched

Andrew Loog Oldham's creativity reached new heights with the band's first album, heights he was never to scale again. His belief in himself and the band prompted the bold stroke of creating a cover with no name, just a photograph. It was unheard of. He would have probably removed the Decca logo if they had let him get away with it.

Nine cover versions, one original by Mick and Keith and two group compositions (one with a little help from Phil Spector) make up the Stones' debut album in the UK. It was all cut at Regent Sound, one of the least sophisticated (but cheapest) studios in London. There were few overdubs and the album comes as close as you can get to the live sound of the band at that time; all the songs were honed to perfection during a year of non-stop touring.

'It was really just the show we did on-stage, recorded in one take – as it should be!' **BILL**

Stu played piano on 'Tell Me' and 'Can I Get A Witness', and organ on 'Now I've Got A Witness' and 'You Can Make It If You Try'. Gene Pitney played piano on 'Little By Little', while Phil Spector played maracas.

On Tuesday 24 March, journalist Penny Valentine met with Andrew, Charlie, Mick and Keith in Andrew's office, where they listened to the first test pressings of the album. 'It is easily the most knockout thing the boys have ever done. This is probably the first time that something of the excitement that the Stones generate on stage has been captured on disc,' wrote Penny. Charlie was obviously excited too: 'This is the first time we've heard it. Can you wonder we're so thrilled?'

'I do like the abum really. I think it's good. It's something that we've always wanted to do, to record these numbers and I hope that we'll be proved right.'
KEITH

'I like the way it sounds. I don't think my contribution is all that fantastic, but the LP has got our sound.'
CHARLIE

'It's very good, because it reflects the Stones, which is what we intended to do.'
BRIAN

Top ten LPs

1	(—)	**THE ROLLING STONES** The Rolling Stones, Decca	
2	(1)	**WITH THE BEATLES** Beatles, Parlophone	
3	(3)	**WEST SIDE STORY** Soundtrack, CBS	
4	(2)	**PLEASE PLEASE ME** Beatles, Parlophone	
5	(—)	**SESSION WITH THE DAVE CLARK FIVE** Dave Clark Five, Columbia	
6	(8)	**BLUE GENE** Gene Pitney, United Artists	
7	(4)	**STAY WITH THE HOLLIES** Hollies, Parlophone	
8	(5)	**MEET THE SEARCHERS** Searchers, Pye	
9	(—)	**A GIRL CALLED DUSTY** Dusty Springfield, Philips	
10	(7)	**IN DREAMS** .... Roy Orbison, London	

'It's the kind of stuff we like playing. The real R&B fans will know what we're doing on it, and even others should. We've tried to get the kind of sound we like, and I think we've done that.' **MICK**

Recorded
3 January; 4, 24, 25 February, 1964

Studio
Regent Sound Studios, London

Producer
Andrew Oldham/Eric Easton for Impact Sound

Engineer
Bill Farley

Cover design and photography
Nicholas Wright

Release
UK Friday 17 April, 1964
Decca LK 4605

Highest chart position (time on chart)
UK No 1 (51 weeks)

Stones through the window
The album's release prompted Decca to create a window display, the band's first, featuring the album and EP at Alex Strickland's Soho Record Centre on the corner of London's Dean Street and Old Compton Street.

'We cut everything in mono. It came out in the UK as a mono album, but was released as "reprocessed stereo" in the US.' BILL

'It is the classic album of white rock, because, like Presley's Sun sessions, it was the first of its kind and it has the startled, breathless intensity of doing it for the first time. It pointed pop music in a new direction.' DAVID DALTON, *US-based rock journalist*

'Their singles have a strange appeal but their LP is a stinker. The result is shaky, the essential blues links are missing, their approach is ham-handed rather than uninhibited and the voices and rhythm seem strained and unsure, never relaxed and confident. At times they sound as jerky as a shunting goods train. It's a flop.' MIKE NEVARD, *Daily Herald, April 1964*

'A final word of praise to Andrew Loog Oldham, who recorded the sessions – he's living up to his boast that he'd be the top independent recording manager in Britain by November this year!' NME, *April 1964*

'Another highlight album and a cast-iron cert for hitsville.' BEAT MONTHLY MAGAZINE, *May 1964*

Jimmy Reed

Rufus Thomas

Slim Harpo

Under the influence

'I Just Wanna Make Love To You' Written by Willie Dixon and recorded by Muddy Waters in April 1954.

'Route 66' Originally a US R&B chart hit for the King Cole Trio in June 1946. The Stones' version took its inspiration from Chuck Berry's 1962 version.

'Honest I Do' US R&B Top 5 hit for Jimmy Reed in October 1957 and his biggest hit, at US Hot 100 No 32.

'I Need You Baby (Mona)' A Bo Diddley original from 1957.

'I'm A King Bee' A Slim Harpo original from 1957.

'Carol' A US R&B hit for Chuck Berry in September 1958, it also made US No 19 in the Hot 100.

'Can I Get A Witness' Marvin Gaye had a US R&B and Hot 100 hit in November 1963 backed by the Supremes.

'You Can Make It If You Try' A US R&B Top 5 hit for Gene Allison in January 1958, also hitting US No 36 in the Hot 100.

'Walking The Dog' A US R&B Top 5 and US Hot 100 Top 10 hit from October 1963 for Rufus Thomas.

First LP **THE** **Terrific LP** **ROLLING** **DECCA LP** **STONES** DECCA

ENGLAND'S NEWEST HIT MAKERS
THE ROLLING STONES

FREE full color photo of THE ROLLING STONES inside

To herald the group's arrival in the USA, the album's title was amended and, more significantly, the band name was on the cover. The US album debut was released on London Records in May and was essentially the UK album with 'Not Fade Away' substituted for Bo Diddley's 'I Need You Baby'. Initial pressings were shipped from the UK as promotional copies ahead of the American release.

'Because their primary interest at that time was blues, most of the tunes on that album are familiar. Still, a certain aura of excitement is present on these cuts that make them seem distinctly the Stones, even today. From the point of view of original material the first album offered no great promise.'
JOHN LANDAU, *Crawdaddy magazine*

'This is the hardest rhythm and blues the Stones (or anyone) ever recorded. Besides "Not Fade Away", it has another Berry marvel, "Carol", another strong original, "Tell Me", and some first-rate Chicago blues.' **ROLLING STONE MAGAZINE RECORD GUIDE**

POP SPOTLIGHT
THE ROLLING STONES
London LL 3375 (M); PS 375 (S)
This, the latest of the British invaders, is the toughest sounding. (That's been the pattern so far, each group with a harder approach than the almost gentle Beatles.) The Stones have more country in their instrumentation, more rock in the beat and a decidedly Negro orientation in the sound and mood of their singing. Their single has shown no spectacular movement on the chart, but heavy TV and promotion should do much.

The ROLLING STONES are more than just a group – they are a way of life. A way of life that has captured the imagination of England's teenagers, and made them one of the most sought after groups in Beatdom. For the Stones have their fingers on the pulse of the basic premise of "pop" music success – that its public buys sound, and the sound is what they give you with this their first album; a raw, exciting basic approach to Rhythm and Blues which, blended with their five own explosive characters, has given them three smash hits and an E.P. that stayed in the single charts for fifteen weeks. In the eight months since the Stones embarked on their pop career, they have not only chalked up major chart successes, but smashed attendance records on tours the length and breadth of the country. They have emerged as five well rounded intelligent talents, who will journey successfully far beyond the realms of pop music. And in this album there are twelve good reasons why.
Andrew Loog Oldham.

The album liner notes were the same in the US and Britain, an evocative echo from the beat boom era and an indication of the unique style of Andrew Oldham.

The Stones launched their American debut with a New York press conference.

America's first impression of the Stones

US release
May
London P5375 and LL3375
Chart entry
26 July, 1964
Highest chart position
US No 11
Weeks on chart
US 12 weeks

Dear Diary...

Thursday: –
Left at lunchtime for Rochdale. Brian & I got
in O.K. but then couldn't get out. 2000 inside the club
& 5000 outside & police everywhere. Couldn't play
or we would have got killed. Went back to Manchester
& went to Mr Smiths & saw the Dallas boys.

'Their private thoughts are noted by Bill Wyman, who keeps a daily diary.' RAVE MAGAZINE, *April 1964*

April 1964, the first the world knew of my diary. What a good job I decided to keep one. Mick, Keith and Charlie are forever telling people to check things with me, as I'm the only one who really remembers what happened.

THE DAY OUR FIRST album was released was the day after the fiasco of the cancelled gig in Rochdale and the papers were full of the story.

We played the Locarno Ballroom in Coventry in the evening and the organisation was about as efficient as it had been in Rochdale. We were greeted by 1,800 screaming fans, everyone was

pushing and a riot erupted. The whole audience went mad, girls were climbing onto the revolving stage and within minutes we were taken off. The staff used a fire extinguisher to quieten the crowd so we could do two half-hour sets.

The Locarno's manager Brian Thompson said: 'One girl fainted and fell to the floor and I was worried about her safety. It was then that I used the extinguisher to help clear a space and get her out. It had the desired effect.'

'I feel that the management could have used less stringent methods in quietening the crowd. I was sprayed with a fire extinguisher and kicked and kneed in the stomach by the bouncers.'
MISS CT FALLON, *fan*

On 18 April, we played in Chester. Keith and Charlie drove home in the car with Mick, who was reported to the police by an indignant motorist for driving dangerously at 12.30am in Wolverhampton. Police later dismissed the allegation, but Mick was charged for driving the car without insurance, licence or name and

Ready Steady Go! up for an international award: the band in Geneva on 19 April with Kenny Lynch and Cathy McGowan

address in the registration book. He was the first to follow in Stu's footsteps – but not the last.

Ready, steady for awards

Next morning the five of us, together with Andrew, Eric and Stu, met at London Airport. We were joined by Kenny Lynch, Cathy McGowan and Michael Aldred along with 40 *Ready, Steady, Go!* dancers for a trip to Montreux, Switzerland. *RSG!* was the British entry for the International Golden Rose TV Awards. Hundreds waved goodbye from the airport roof as we took a charter flight to Geneva. We boarded a large steamer for a five-hour trip down the lake to Montreux. Andrew had a portable record player which he played very loudly all the way.

The next afternoon we rehearsed at the casino for an evening gig in front of about a thousand Swiss teenagers who seemed to be in shock: they had no idea how to react to us. Back at the hotel bar, we celebrated with Kenny Lynch playing piano, Brian on guitar and me on double bass. Eric Easton joined in on piano as we played old standards.

Bill sent home a postcard of the steamer on Lake Geneva

'Here in cuckoo-clock-land, the mountains are still echoing to the sound and impact of the British teenager. The climax of ITV's pop invasion were the Stones. The show was a roaring success, but the sight of Beatle haircuts and hipster jeans on the staid streets has caused the Swiss to stop and stare in amazement. When the judges announced their awards, there was no mention of British beat shows.'
DAILY MIRROR, *April 1964*

It was our first overseas trip as a band and great fun – although I wasn't sure I liked it when a taxi driver said 'Non, mademoiselle', when I tried to get into his over-crowded cab. We arrived home on 20 April, the day BBC 2, the third TV channel in Britain, went on the air. Our album was selling better than we hoped. Judith Simons wrote in the *Daily Express* of 22 April, 'The Rolling Stones have knocked the Beatles from the UK No 1 LP spot. Their new LP, released six days ago, is No 1,

the position held by the Beatles since 10 May last year. The Beatles' two LPs have sold 1.45 million in 11 months. The Stones' LP has sold 110,000 since last Friday.' Mind you, not everyone seemed happy at our success.

'A free haircut awaits the next artist or group to be top of the pops. The Stones are the worst. One of them looks as if he's got a feather duster on his head.' WALLACE SNOWCROFT, *president of the National Federation of Hairdressers*

In the *Daily Herald* on 25 April, Mike Nervard got personal. 'The missing links. Their album is a hit, but not with me. They look like a cross between Neanderthal Man and 18th-century cut-throats. Their stage manner is almost ape-like, and their music primitive.' I think he went a bit far. I wonder if anyone would get away with writing like this today? Mick was forthright.

'We are completely unmoved by criticism,' he said. 'We are not worried about obvious sensationalism on the way we look and dress. I never did like wearing a suit, but maybe I will when I'm about 25. We have our hair trimmed about once every three months.'

Our old supporter, Patrick Doncaster at the *Daily Mirror*, jumped to our defence – at least, I think he did.

'Everything seems to be against them on the surface. They're called the ugliest group in Britain. They're not looked on very kindly by most parents or adults in general, but an awful lot of people love those five talented, shaggy-as-Shetland-ponies lads.'

'We like the Rolling Stones records, but think that they are really going bald and have to wear their hair like that so it doesn't show.' PAT AND LINDA, *fans, in a letter to NME, 24 April, 1964*

We played the *NME* poll winners' concert at the Empire Pool, Wembley on the following

Rehearsing in Montreux, 20 April

Saturday. We chatted with the Beatles when we were all backstage; John Lennon was very complimentary about our album.

Also on the bill were the Swinging Blue Jeans, the Dave Clark Five, Cliff Richard, Manfred Mann and the Searchers. We performed 'I Just Want to Make Love To You', 'Not Fade Away' and 'I'm All Right'.

A year ago to the day we had been playing to an audience of just a few hundred people at the Ricky Tick in Windsor; now we had a wonderful reception from over 10,000 fans. Even the Beatles later admitted that the scale of the response to our performance had freaked them out. An American DJ called Murray The K taped the concert for his WINS New York radio show, which helped to introduce us to a wider audience in the USA.

'Nobody could hear a note of music. Even my eldest son couldn't say what they were playing but said it didn't matter as they were *"just fab anyway!" Of course, it was fascinating seeing screamers close to, with their hands over their ears or clawing at their open mouths, tears in their eyes and, now and then, making hasty emergency exits!'* JACINTH WHITTAKER, *reporter, April 1964*

We were playing in Birkenhead when we found out two fans with tickets for the show had been badly injured in a car accident. We went to the hospital to try and cheer them up. Mick was caught speeding on the way and then realised that only his father was insured to drive the car.

Back at the Majestic Ballroom, as the opening chords of 'Not Fade Away' sounded, the crowd went crazy, stampeding towards the stage. We dropped everything, vaulted Charlie's drums and ran for dear life. Fortunately, the police herded us into one of their vehicles and got us away safely, leaving poor old Stu to retrieve our gear.

May was even busier: we played 26 different venues during the month. It also seemed impossible, but the fans' reaction was getting even more intense. They went to extraordinary lengths to get tickets. Forgeries were turning up at some venues, while some fans wrote begging letters with the most amazing threats. The *Yorkshire Post* reported: 'More than a hundred letters were delivered yesterday, most of them pointing out that death is imminent for the writers unless tickets are available. Yesterday's black market price was £2 2s for a 6/- ticket.'

None of us knew how long all the hysteria would last: 'I reckon that if it all ended tomorrow,'

'I beg and implore you to let me have tickets for the greatest, most fabulous and one and only Stones, or I shall die.' A FAN LETTER, *in the Yorkshire Post*

Fans at Bridlington, 2 May, 1964

said Brian, 'we will have enough put by to let us live in luxury for four years or so.'

Early in May, he and Linda visited his parents, but didn't tell them that Linda was seven months into pregnancy. Around the same time, Keith met a model named Linda Keith and they began a relationship that lasted for nearly two years. Andrew Oldham also had sex on his mind, but his thoughts were geared towards marketing us in America. 'Pop music is sex and you have to hit them in the face with it,' he told *Vogue* in May.

There was also a non-stop round of interviews in both the music and national press. If you delve back through these stories,

'Pop music is sex and you have to hit them in the face with it.' ANDREW OLDHAM, *Vogue, May 1964*

there are many inconsistencies. We quite often made things up; it helped to relieve the monotony.

Charlie was probably the most consistent in what he said, although he and his mother disagreed over his shirts: he said he had 200, she reckoned 50 – which is still an awful lot of shirts. They weren't the only things he liked:

'If I was a millionaire, I'd buy vintage cars just to look at them because they're beautiful,' he said in May. He's never learnt to drive, but he did buy a very expensive 1930s-era Lagonda in 1983.

Not Berry nice

On 9 May, we had a gig at the Savoy Ballroom in Catford, a local one for me. At almost the same time, Chuck Berry and Carl Perkins were playing at the Finsbury Park Astoria in North London – we wanted to be there. We got backstage (having hit records opened doors) and tried to meet Chuck. We sent him a message, but he refused to come out; we were told he had a girl in his room.

Carl Perkins, backed by the Nashville Teens, impressed us with his show. We went backstage again and this time got into Chuck's dressing room only to find he hadn't had a girl in there at all. He'd been in there cooking his dinner on a small portable stove.

We were now very late for our Catford gig, so Stu drove across London as fast as possible. When we arrived it was mayhem and impossible for us to get in the regular way. The promoters led us through a private house, next to the ballroom, through the garden, over the fence, and in a back way. Backstage looked like a casualty department – girls were everywhere, sprawled out on the stairs, in the corridors and inside the rooms.

A few weeks later, Mick and Charlie were in a hotel elevator. It stopped, the door opened and there stood Chuck Berry. He stepped in, saw Mick and Charlie, turned his back and when the doors opened, he walked out without speaking. Funny man, Chuck.

No ties

Our appearance was beginning to get us into all sorts of scrapes. With hindsight, I am sure that the media stirred people up, causing them to take offence before we'd even done anything. In Bristol we went for lunch in the Grand Hotel's restaurant. Keith was wearing a sweater,

'Too-scruffy' Stones are refused lunch

by ROGER BENNETT

Pop idols The Rolling Stones were refused lunch in the restaurant of Bristol's Grand Hotel this afternoon because they looked too scruffy.

Singer Mick Jagger wandered into the restaurant wearing a grey striped sweatshirt and jeans at 1.20 p.m. to be met by the tail-coated head waiter Mr. Dick Court.

"Excuse me, sir, but we cannot serve you unless you wear a tie and jacket. We can arrange to lend you suitable clothes if you wish to eat here," Mr. Court told him.

Jagger retired to the cocktail bar. "I'm not going to dress up in their clothes," he said. "We dress like this, and that's that."

Mr. Court said: "I realise the gentleman is something of a celebrity among the young people, but that does not change the position. I would feel compelled to refuse service to anyone—even a king—if he did not dress correctly. It is a strict rule of the hotel."

Stones road manager Ian Stewart was annoyed at the ban. "We are guests here, and we have paid well for accommodation. Why should they refuse us food?"

Drummer Charlie Watts, wearing a tie and brown jacket, said: "I suppose they'd serve me, but I'm not going in there alone."

And the Stones trooped off in search of steaks at a nearby restaurant.

Mr. M. E. T. McFedyen, hotel manager, said: "We insist on this rule—otherwise guests in the restaurant could be embarrassed. We accept the modern vogue in dress—button-up shirts and so on—but not jeans and T-shirts."

The Rolling Stones eventually lunched—off curried prawns—at the Bali restaurant in Park Street, Bristol.

Promoter Terry Olphin, who took them there, said: "We created quite a sensation when we arrived. There were girls hanging out of the windows all up the street."

Mick looks wistfully into the restaurant inside the Grand Hotel.

Mick a striped sweatshirt and corduroy trousers, Stu a blue pullover, while Charlie and I wore coloured sweaters. We were refused permission to eat by the head waiter, Dick Court. His reason? We had no ties and Mick didn't have a jacket. They offered us lightweight fawn jackets and maroon ties.

Mick was outraged, telling the *Mail*, 'I had no intention of wearing borrowed clothes to eat in my hotel.' The report stirred up correspondence in the paper. 'Congratulations to the head waiter,' wrote one Judith Scholes to the letters page. 'I am not a square, and love the Beatles, but the Stones must learn to conform.' Sorry if you are still waiting, Judith.

She wasn't alone. For example, take what Maureen Cleave had to say in the *Sheffield Telegraph*. It's laughable now, but by the standards of those times, we were that outrageous. Teenagers could get themselves in a row just for mentioning our name at home: 'Parents do not like the Rolling Stones. They do not want their sons to grow up like them; they do not want their daughters to marry them. Never have the middle class virtues of neatness, obedience and

'ROLLING STONES' POP GROUP REFUSED LUNCH. YOU MUST WEAR COLLAR AND TIE, SAY HOTEL MANAGEMENT

FRED'S CAFE

MENU
CHEESE ROLLS £2-10-0 EACH
TEA 15/- A CUP
FRUIT CAKE QUID A SLICE

"Crikey, your prices are up a bit since celebrities started dining 'ere, aren't they, Fred...?"

punctuality been so conspicuously lacking as they are in the Rolling Stones.'

Amid all the mayhem of constant touring, we were getting excited about our upcoming first trip to America. Two weeks before we set off, we made another trip to Scotland.

'Police are taking special precautions in preparation for tonight's invasion of the Chantinghall Hotel in Hamilton by more than 2,000 teenagers.' SCOTTISH DAILY MAIL, *18 May, 1964*

The Hamilton gig was more memorable than most, even by our standards. We arrived to find a riot in full swing, mostly caused by hundreds of fans with forged tickets. Said promoter Ronnie Kirkwood: 'This is frightening. I expected about 2,000 people, and instead, we have about 4,000 fans trying to get in to see the show.'

Once inside the venue, we found the stage was surrounded by a 10-foot-high wire fence, added to which the temperature inside was unbearable. Ambulance men treated more than 300 fans. We went onstage at 11.15pm and ended up playing stripped to the waist, drenched with sweat

(no wonder so many fainted). Fans tried to climb the wire and we were prevented from playing after just 15 minutes.

'It was the worst night in all my 18 years,' said one fan identified as Miss B. 'When the Rolling Stones came onstage, everybody charged and a number of us girls were trampled underfoot. The next thing I remember was being hauled over a barrier, which ripped my new skirt to pieces. When I came around in the car park, my leg was cut from top to bottom and also I had a badly sprained ankle. In that condition, after fainting twice because of the heat... I had to queue for over two hours to get my coat. Never again.'

'In 30 years as an ambulance man, I have never experienced anything like this. The scenes were incredible.' GAVIN LANG, *Commandant of the Ambulances*

While we were in Scotland, one of the most ridiculous stories of our entire career – and we've had far more than our fair share – began doing the rounds. 'Rumours have spread like wildfire, throughout the north, that Mick is soon to have a sex-change operation in Sweden,'

'They're my boys. I like their version of "I Just Want to Make Love To You". They fade it out just like we did. One more trip and they'll have it. Believe me, I'll come back one more time and then I won't need to come back no more.' MUDDY WATERS, *Melody Maker, 23 May, 1964*

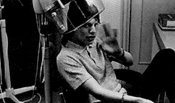

reported *Combo* magazine in May. 'Phone calls... and letters have poured into our offices, asking for a denial or confirmation of this rumour.'

University challenge
On Saturday 23 May, we played Leicester University. It was a great show for us and the audience loved it too. It was more like a club gig than the bigger shows we were used to. We played for a long time, doing old material and blues songs. Charlie almost had a fight with the promoter, who tried to pull the power on us and stop the show.

On 31 May, we played the Pop Hit Parade at the Empire Pool, Wembley along with Adam Faith, Wayne Fontana and the Mindbenders, Julie Grant, the Hollies, the Merseybeats, the McKinleys and the Undertakers. We rehearsed in the afternoon and got a chance to read the Sunday papers. They were full of the usual ridiculous stories; one in the *Sunday Citizen* grabbed our attention. They quoted a headmaster, Mr EW Minter of Chippenham Secondary Modern: 'When most of the boys started sporting Stones hair-dos, I sent them straight home. I announced that unduly long hair was untidy and likely to be unhygienic. I asked those concerned to get their hair cut. Most did, but there were six or seven I thought necessary to send home, with a request that their parents get it cut. No parent has protested.'

Long hair horror
'I thought for a moment he was a girl. I think hair that long on a boy is disgusting,' a Cliff Richard fan told the *Daily Mirror*, 14 May, 1963.

After the Wembley show, it was off home to finish packing for our trip to America the next day. Maybe they would treat us differently, although if we could have read one Toronto paper we would have been put right.

'Those who think the Beatles caused an uproar when they arrived in New York had better take to the bomb shelters when the Stones arrive. They are hard to describe. They don't believe in bathing (it's bad for your health), they wear dirty old clothes, their hair is twice as long as the Beatles' and they never comb it. London Records invested $85,000 in the quintet.' THE TELEGRAM, *Toronto, Canada, May 1964*

And so it was on 1 June, 1964, the day before Charlie's 23rd birthday, that Diane, Stephen and I went to London Airport. There were screaming fans charging all over the place. The police did their best to protect us as girls swarmed around.

Come home soon
'Americans – brace yourselves,' the *Chicago Sunday Times* had reported on 1 January, 1964. 'In the tracks of the Beatles, a second wave of sheepdog-looking, guitar-playing Britons is on the way.'

Invasion of the British
The British took over the American music scene in 1964. The US charts were dominated by the sound of Britain's beat groups and in particular the Beatles. Today, everyone assumes the Stones were in the vanguard of the British invasion. In fact, they were one of the less successful British bands in America in 1964. The Beatles had five US No 1 songs, along with five US Top 10 and four US Top 20 hits that year. Manfred Mann topped the chart with 'Do Wah Diddy Diddy' and the Zombies made US No 2 with 'She's Not There'. The Dave Clark Five (four US Top 10 singles), Gerry and the Pacemakers (two US Top 10 entries) and even Billy J Kramer (two US Top 10 songs) did better. Bands such as the Searchers, the Kinks and the Animals, who topped the American charts with 'The House Of The Rising Sun' in late summer, did at least as well.

Their idea of driving us around the back was scuppered when we arrived separately and the fans spotted all of us, except Brian. Screaming girls surrounded Mick; girls pulled Keith away from his police guard. He had to stand for a few moments, hugging and kissing fans, before he escaped. Airport staff finally got us into a private lounge. Mick and I sat on the floor playing with Stephen and his toy cars. We eventually said our goodbyes and flew to New York on BOAC flight 505.

June **64**

Rolling
Stones

ONLY APPEARANCE IN TH...

One Nigh...

SAT., JUNE...

Omaha

America
Calling

Outside the Hotel Astor, New York City, 2 June, 1964

WELCOME TO AMERICA

'They're so… so… far out!' GIRL FAN, *Kennedy Airport*

As our descent began, Brian was asked what he thought of his first glimpse of New York. 'It looks like a bigger version of Balham [a London suburb].' We landed at 3.30pm and were genuinely shocked to find about 500 screaming fans waiting for us. Fifty policemen tried to hold them back, but some broke through and two fans gave us carnations from their garden.

One of us said, 'The natives appear to be friendly. We don't need the beads and trinkets after all,' but I can't remember who it was. In the airport, workers and passengers couldn't believe their eyes. There were cries of 'Get your hair cut!', 'Where are the razors?' and 'Are you the Beatles?' We were taken to a large lounge for our first American press conference. Inside were 87 press people presided over by Murray The K. Our American PR man had the bright idea of bringing along two English sheepdogs. Inevitably one reporter asked us if we washed. Brian as quick as a flash raised his arms like the Statue of Liberty and asked: 'Wanna smell?' At the press conference Charlie admitted that he was 23 the next day, not 22 as the official biographies had it.

Bob Bonis, our tour manager, said: 'The Stones arrived and the reception was unbelievable. Everyone said, "what a great staged reception", but it wasn't staged. We were hoping to get them in quietly.'

'The flowers' scent brought relief to many press corps who feared that the Rolling Stones arrival from customs might precede a wind change.' DOUG McCLELLAND, *Record World*

These are the good guys
Bill: 'We were introduced to a dull bunch of DJs called the WMCA Good Guys, who looked like six cropped-haired, overgrown college kids. They presented us with gigantic T-shirts, tailor-made for Orson Welles.'

We were to be put into five separate limousines to be interviewed by reporters en route to the hotel. There were hundreds of fans behind wooden barriers, all screaming and waving signs. Several girls broke through the cordon as the cars slowly moved off. The police fought to hold the fans back and one girl was almost struck by the leading car. Our convoy with its police escorts raced out of the airport followed by dozens of cars and cabs. Some drove alongside, bombarding us with roses, love notes and stuffed animals.

'I was to share the car with Mick and a huge sheepdog. The fans became hysterical, suddenly; they broke through and came screaming towards the cars. They yelled for the cars to start moving and we jumped into the slowly-moving vehicles. Mick, the sheepdog and six other reporters jumped into the car we were in. I sat on Mick's lap and the dog sat on mine.' HILDA SKARFE, *Song Hits magazine*

At the Hotel Astor near Times Square, there were only four policemen guarding the entrance and they couldn't control the crowd that swarmed over the cars. The police were pulling us out, saying: 'Run, it's every man for himself.' Mick and I dashed into the lobby along with the sheepdog and Hilda Skarfe, followed by about 70 screaming girls, with the police not far behind. Within seconds it was bedlam: bellboys dropped cases and guests ran for cover. We ran into a laundry closet by mistake, becoming trapped; we started to suffocate. Some photographers and police tried to keep the door open for air. Finally officers dragged us to a heavily-guarded elevator; Mick turned to Hilda and said: 'By the way, I don't think we've been formally introduced.'

Hotel America

We had been given double rooms on the third floor. Each room had twin beds and we shared: Brian and I; Mick and Keith; Stu and Eric; and Charlie and Andrew. Every time we looked out of our windows there would be screams from the 200-odd fans below.

We did another press conference at the hotel and had to answer more silly questions, before fighting our

Rolling Stones Dig Charles

NEW YORK — There's a touch of nobility among the Rolling Stones, the English group currently the latest musical imports touring the U. S.

Upon arrival last week at Kennedy International Airport, newsmen asked them what prompted them to sport such unusually long and distinct hair. "Why this is a style set by Charles the First," was the reply.

Asked what American artists have influenced their moving musical style, the answer was "Bo Diddley and Chuck Berry."

Billboard features Bill and the boys

The Stones were finally talked into having photos taken with one of the old English sheepdogs, which they all thought was pretty corny.

way through fans to be driven to radio station WINS for an interview with Murray The K on his *Swinging Soirée*. We were live on air for three hours, talking, joking and reading commercials. What really freaked everyone out was when we asked each other for fags. After drinks at the Peppermint Lounge (where Joey Dee and the Starlighters made their name with the US No 1 single 'Peppermint Twist'), we finally got to bed at 1.30am.

We were woken at 8am and had our first American breakfast, which included English muffins (we'd never seen a muffin in England like it). At 10am we went to WMCA for another radio interview. Mo Shulman from London Records and Bob Bonis, our US tour manager, who we took to immediately, accompanied us.

Mr Wyman is unwell

After we did another press conference I was feeling out-of-sorts, having practically lost my voice. The doctor diagnosed laryngitis and gave me a painful penicillin injection and a throat spray and charged me $25 (that was a first, paying for a doctor). I stayed in the hotel on his advice, while the rest of the boys went out sightseeing. At 11.30pm, we were driven to *The Les Crane TV*

Stones at large
In NYC the Stones were able to explore the area around the hotel without *too* much trouble, save for shocked looks and occasional cat-calls from passers-by.

Show, our first in America. We were on live for an hour with people phoning in with questions. Though it was hardly a good time for our fans – it all got a bit bitchy after a while, with Les Crane trying to take the mickey out of us; we rose above it and were back at the hotel by 3am.

We were up early again and checked out of the hotel, only to find that Keith had lost his passport. We fought our way through fans and were driven in limos to Kennedy Airport. We took a six-hour flight on a Boeing 707 to Los Angeles. On arrival, we once again found fans waiting, who gave us a great welcome.

'The radio station announced the Stones were coming. We had to go to Wallach's Music City to find their album to see who they were. Mick and Keith came off the plane first. [My friend] Candy and her blonde girlfriend ran over. Then Bill came off and grabbed my hand and we went running off down the hallway. That's when he introduced himself to me. We went downstairs where limousines were waiting. Candy and the girl she was with got in the limousine. Bill let go of my hand, got in the car and drove away. I didn't see Bill until his next visit.' KATHY (WEST) TOWNSEND, *16-year-old fan, 1964*

Hollywood Squares

Limos took us to the Beverley Hilton, where we checked into our four double rooms. The cost of a room back then at the Beverley Hilton was just $27 a day. In the afternoon we went to the ABC Studios to film a TV show. Dean Martin's kids asked for our autographs.

THERE WAS A STRANGE atmosphere on set; we were treated more like a comedy act than a band. Joey Paige, whom we'd met on the Everly Brothers tour, stayed to see the show and he was a welcome friendly face. We then broke and all went to eat at a local restaurant before returning to record our performance for ABC TV's *Hollywood Palace Show*, compered by Dean Martin.

We recorded 'Not Fade Away', 'I Just Want To Make Love To You', and 'Tell Me', playing all three live. Keith broke one of his guitar strings during 'Not Fade Away', although in the end all they broadcast on the show was 45 seconds of 'I Just Want To Make Love To You'. Dean Martin, who appeared to be drunk throughout the show, persistently tried to get cheap laughs at our expense. 'Their hair isn't long, it's just smaller foreheads and higher eyebrows.'

> ③ ⑥ ⑦ **HOLLYWOOD PAL-ACE—Variety**
> The host is Dean Martin, who introduces the singing King Sisters and their daughters; the Rolling Stones, English rock 'n' roll group; comedian Joey Forman; Bertha the Elephant and her daughter Tina; the singing girls from SHARE, a Hollywood charity group made up of celebrity wives; and comic acrobat Larry Griswold. Les Brown conducts. (60 min.)

Dean Martin's show was old-fashioned variety, even including animal acts

'Dean Martin was a little out of it and made an awful lot of fun of the band. The producer gave them money to go out and buy themselves uniforms. We said, "They don't wear uniforms." Dean Martin and I got into an argument, and Keith was about to pop him one with his guitar.' BOB BONIS, US tour manager

Dejected, we returned to the hotel with Joey Paige, who took us to some local clubs on Sunset Strip, which helped get us out of our mood. The next morning we went shopping with Andrew, who took us to Beau Gentry on North Vine Street in Hollywood, where we bought clothes.

Joey Paige had a friend named Marshall Leib who sang with Phil Spector on the Teddybears' 'To Know Him Is To Love Him'. The two of them took us to Malibu Beach. The weather was sunny and very warm and we spent the afternoon having fun.

We went to the RCA Recording Studios, and met Jack Nitzsche, Phil Spector's arranger. Backing singers Jackie De Shannon and Darlene Love were doing vocals on a new record.

The following day, we found fans waiting for us at the elevators and in the lobby. We were surprised, as non-guests were not allowed to wander around English hotels. We took a bus the 62 miles to the Swing Auditorium out in San Bernardino, California, for our first ever US gig. We

The band go shopping in Beau Gentry, Hollywood, where Bill spent $90 on 4 June.

got a really good reception. Keith explained: 'It was a gas. They knew the words and were really bopping, especially when we did "Route 66".'

Limos took us back to the airport at 7am. Being used to touring in Britain, it was a shock to realise that distances in America were so vast. We flew to San Antonio to play the State Fair. On the bill was George Jones (the great country singer), as well as Bobby Vee. His saxophonist was Bobby Keys, who went on to play regularly with us over the next three decades. It turned out he was born on exactly the same day as Keith. Which, as you will see, accounted for a lot...

The concert was in the open air, on a makeshift stage. Everyone got a poor reception from a crowd of cowboys and kids. We went on after some performing monkeys. People didn't know whether to take us seriously or not.

'Bobby Vee's band were dressed in mohair suits, high-roll collar shirts, silk ties and hand-made shoes. At this point, everybody dressed alike and we did these little steps. What was the deal with these English bad boys? They came on-stage and they weren't dressed alike. That impressed me more than anything, apart from the fact that they were singing one of Buddy Holly's songs "Not Fade Away". I was born in Lubbock – Buddy's hometown.' BOBBY KEYS

The evening show was no better than the matinee, but we gave Bobby Keys a laugh. Brian said: 'All American groups change their clothes before going on-stage.' Bobby told him that was just the way they did it. Bobby remembered Brian saying 'Well, we can do that.' Then we all switched clothes with each other and went on-stage and played.

A bunch of girls
The next day we were to play the State Fair again, so we had the morning off and spent it around the pool. Hotel residents stared, hardly able to believe their eyes. A resident complained that girls were at the pool swimming and sunbathing topless. Some time later, six very friendly local girls joined us. One got very excited and tried to pull Brian's hair off, saying that she thought it was a wig. Back at

the venue Bobby Vee had decided to take a leaf out of our book, sort of: 'Breaking with tradition, Bobby Vee went onstage wearing Bermuda shorts,' said Bobby Keys. 'He could – he was the lead vocalist. So I said, "OK, man, if they can do it, shit! So can I." I damn near got fired over that.'

We had most of the next day off and spent it shopping and bar-hopping. I was amazed in one: the jukebox was full of Jimmy Reed records. Charlie and Stu went out with some local guys in a jeep. 'We drove along a dried-up river bed, looking for rattlesnakes,' said Stu. 'Fortunately, we never found any. Charlie has a big thing about guns and we later found him wandering around in a dazed fashion amid a huge armoury in a local gunsmith. He was deeply moved.'

Radio blues
We flew from San Antonio to Chicago and appeared on WMAQ's *Jack Eigen Show*. He asked us lots of stupid questions – a typical experience on that first tour. Afterwards, we listened to him on the car radio making fun of us. A woman caller accused us of being dirty and of not combing our hair. Eigen replied, 'They may have more in their group than they think,' implying we had fleas.

'He had this negro on,' Mick told the *Chicago Daily News*, 'and he kept saying how much he liked the negroes, the phoney bum.'

Anyway, what did we really care? We were going to Mecca that night.

'It was a lot better than Clacton, but I still kept my clothes on.' **BILL**, *on Malibu*

North America, *June 1964*

5 June Swing Auditorium, San Bernardino, California
6 June State Fair, San Antonio, Texas (matinees and evenings)
7 June State Fair, San Antonio, Texas (matinees and evenings)
12 June Excelsior Fair, Minneapolis, Minnesota
13 June Omaha Auditorium, Omaha, Nebraska
14 June Olympia Stadium, Detroit, Michigan
17 June Westview Park, Pittsburgh, Pennsylvania
19 June State Farm Arena, Harrisburg, West Virginia
20 June Carnegie Hall, New York (matinee and evening)

If anyone has told you they saw the Stones on their first US tour be sceptical… Be very sceptical. Apart from Carnegie Hall, where the band sold out, other crowds were mostly small. San Antonio had reasonable numbers, mostly because Bobby Vee was on the bill and it was the State Fair. In Minneapolis, there were about 400 people and Omaha just 650; Detroit and Harrisburg had audiences of less than a thousand each – in stadiums with a capacity 10 times that size.

Eric Easton had gone to New York to organise the tour in mid-May with the General Artist Corporation. He signed an agreement between the Stones and a firm called the Souvenir Publishing and Distributing Company for both the US and Canada, which ran for two years. He also arranged for Bob Bonis to be the tour manager.

When the tour was first announced in the US, the opening date was scheduled to be Portland, Oregon. Other cities that narrowly missed out on a visit from the Stoneboys, as they were often referred to in the North American press, were Chicago, Indianapolis, Louisville, Charleston, Washington DC, Philadelphia and Providence, and Vancouver in Canada.

Set list
The repertoire included:
'Route 66' (usually the opener)
'Not Fade Away'
'I Wanna Be Your Man'
'High Heel Sneakers'
'I'm All Right'
'I Just Want To Make Love To You'

And in support…
San Bernardino
The Cascades
San Antonio
Bobby Vee and George Jones
Carnegie Hall
The Counts, Kathy Carr
Jay and the Americans

A plaque presented to the Stones in America

'A friend of mine, Norman Weiss, asked me as a special favour, to take care of these wise guys who had horrible reputations and were coming in from England. I wasn't interested in going on the road any more, so he showed me this article headed "Would You Let Your Sister Go With A Rolling Stone?" I said, "That's a great sales pitch" and agreed.'
BOB BONIS

'We realised we were well on the way when we were offered an American tour. It seemed that at last we were going to play for the people who really knew our kind of music.' BILL

Coast To Coast –
The First US Tour

'I have never heard screaming like it. Girls got up on their seats, and bedlam broke out' STU, on the Carnegie Hall gig

'There were less than a thousand in Detroit, which was understandable, as the show had only been promoted for three days. However, they were very enthusiastic and jumped about all over the place. There were quite a few black kids here, which was very encouraging.' BILL

'The Stones are different in every respect from their predecessors. They are wilder, shaggier in appearance, more casual in dress. A rebellion against society, authority, convention and parenthood. They have overwhelmed the American teenagers with their image, catching newspapers and magazines with empty biographical files. They turned Carnegie Hall into a teenville heaven.' JACKIE KALLEN, *Teenville magazine*

The last word to Bill:
'From the start we always had very good morale, but it did almost collapse during the first American tour, which was a disaster. When we arrived, we didn't have a hit record or anything going for us. All the other English groups that had ever been there had at least one or two big hits to their credit. We had nothing except that we were English.'

Watch out USA...here they come!
THE ROLLING STONES
They're great! They're outrageous! They're rebels! They sell!
THEY'RE ENGLAND'S HOTTEST!...BUT HOTTEST GROUP!

THE BEST SELLERS

HOT SINGLE!
NOT FADE AWAY

Over 170,000 LP's sold in England!

LONDON

Trouble at Carnegie Hall
'Bill was a little dissatisfied with the way the American tour had gone. But he said that the Stones had enjoyed this concert, which was a bit more like England. However, he said that the Stones had intended to do at least three more songs, but they'd been stopped by the officials, who told them that if they did anything more, they would not be allowed to go on with the evening performance. As we wished Bill luck and got up to go, a policeman yelled out that "If anyone in the ******* room shook the ******* Venetian blind or raised it to look at the ******* crowd outside, the ******* evening show would be cancelled". So far as we know, nobody shook the blind.' *Meet The Rolling Stones* magazine

BIG ENTERTAINMENT SCOOP!
The Rolling Stones
IN PERSON! ONLY APPEARANCE IN THIS AREA!
One Night Only!
SAT., JUNE 13, 7:30 P.M.
Omaha Auditorium
ADMISSION:
Advance, $2.00 — At Door, $2.50

BIGGER Than The BEATLES
Presented by Rowan & Isaacson

Oh my God
Omaha was not ready for the Stones — just 650 people turned up at a gig that could accommodate 15,000 and the press was scathing.

'They clumped with stony-eyed nonchalance down the ramp of the plane that had carried them from Minneapolis,' wrote Robert McMorris in the *Omaha World Herald* on 14 June. 'Then, the scraggly-haired performers, surrounded by a cordon of Omaha police, waded stoically through squeals of welcome emanating from 200 youthful greeters. Fans stormed the police barricade to rub a hand in unkempt hair or to touch a cheek. A girl cried, "I touched him, I touched him". Her companion, eyes bright, said, "They're wonderful". Said one girl, "They're so ugly, they're cute".'

In the same edition, Denman Kountze wrote: 'The Stones seem to be nothing more or less than typical red-blooded English boys. These characters wear their hair long and uncombed, their clothes are dirty and they appear to be strangers to a bathtub. You see them roaming around in packs. It's hard to tell the girls from the boys because they dress the same way. Our teenagers look like angels compared to them.'

Bill recalled: 'We were always amazed that people hated us. They never realised that while they were afraid of us, we were just as afraid of them.'

San Antonio State Fair, 6 June

'To get the Stones rolling is simply a matter of bullying, threatening, pleading and bribing. Then getting down on your knees and praying that they'll turn up in time.'
STU, *1964*

2120 SOUTH MICHIGAN AVENUE

After the disappointment of the Jack Eigen radio interview, the band went to 2120 South Michigan Avenue, Chicago, the home of Chess Records. The Rolling Stones' recording sessions at Chess were more akin to visits to a shrine. Mick and Keith were still 20 years old, Brian was 22, Charlie a year older and Bill was 27.

In the early 1940s, two Polish-born brothers, Leonard and Philip Chess (originally Czyz) owned a number of Chicago nightclubs. They bought into the established Aristocrat record label in 1947 and had their first major success with Muddy Waters' 'I Can't Be Satisfied'.

Chess And Checker R&B US No 1s

Chess 1458	Jackie Brenston 'Rocket '88'	1951
Checker 758	Little Walter 'Juke'	1952
Chess 1531	Willie Mabon 'I Don't Know'	1952
Chess 1538	Willie Mabon 'I'm Mad'	1953
Checker 811	Little Walter 'My Babe'	1955
Checker 814	Bo Diddley 'Bo Diddley'	1955
Chess 1604	Chuck Berry 'Maybelline'	1955
Chess 1653	Chuck Berry 'School Day'	1957
Chess 1683	Chuck Berry 'Sweet Little Sixteen'	1958
Checker 1105	Little Milton 'We're Gonna Make It'	1965

Ironically, the label's two biggest blues stars, Howlin' Wolf and Muddy Waters, never did manage to top the US R&B chart. The Wolf's biggest hit was 'How Many More Years', which made US No 4 in early 1952; the best for Muddy was a US No 3 in 1954, with 'I'm Your Hoochie Coochie Man'.

Nearly two years later, Leonard and Phil bought out their original partner and renamed their label Chess. With the new name came a rash of new signings, including Jimmy Rogers, Eddie Boyd, Willie Mabon, Memphis Slim and Howlin' Wolf. In 1952, a subsidiary called Checker was formed, home to Elmore James, Little Walter, Memphis Minnie and Sonny Boy Williamson. By 1955, Chess had crossed over into the white rock'n'roll market through Chuck Berry and Bo Diddley. On the back of the label's success, a new breed of blues men came along, led by Otis Rush and Buddy Guy.

Much of the label's success can be attributed to the excellent work of A&R man, composer, performer and general Mr Fix-it, Willie Dixon. His bass playing, coupled with Fred Below's peerless drumming, were pivotal to the Chess sound. They were brilliant in creating that tight-yet-loose trademark that epitomises Chess records throughout the 1950s and early 1960s. The key to the label's early success was their ability to pick up records that were originally recorded by other studios, including Sam Phillips' Memphis-based Sun Records. Jackie Brenston's 'Rocket 88' was leased from Sun by Chess in early summer 1951. It is often cited as the first rock'n'roll record.

Leonard Chess

Phil Chess

'They wanted to work in Chess Studios in Chicago with Ron Malo. It was done very much against Andrew's wishes.' STU

'Andrew didn't know anything about blues. The cat who really got it together was Ron Malo, the engineer for Chess. He had been on all the original sessions.' MICK, *1968*

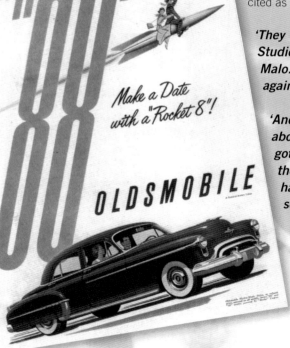

The Oldsmobile Rocket 88 inspired Jackie Brenston's 1951 song.

'We went to Chess for the first time on Wednesday 10 June. We set up our equipment; my bass guitar lead was plugged into a wall socket, of all things. Ron Malo got a good sound almost immediately and we worked for four hours, cutting four tracks. We knew pretty well which numbers we wanted to get in the can and the atmosphere was so marvellous that we got through them in double-quick time. We were thrilled to be visited by guitarist Buddy Guy and songwriter Willie Dixon, who tried to sell us some of his songs.' BILL

'The blues is at the heart of popular music and Chess Records are at the heart of the blues.' BUDDY GUY

'The next day we helped Stu unload the equipment from the van, when who should appear beside us but the great Muddy Waters himself. We were staggered, lost for words. What shook us even more was when he helped us carry our things into the studio. Muddy very definitely was not up a ladder painting the studio, he was a major star at this time and had been for years. We recorded all afternoon and evening, finishing around midnight. During "Down The Road Apiece", Chuck Berry walked in and stayed a long while chatting to us. He was the nicest I can remember him ever being, but don't forget, we were recording his songs!' BILL

The recordings
10 June, 1964
'It's All Over Now' The Valentinos
'I Can't Be Satisfied' Muddy Waters
'Stewed And Keefed' Nanker Phelge
'Time Is On My Side' Irma Thomas
11 June, 1964
'If You Need Me' Solomon Burke (written and also recorded by Wilson Pickett)
'High Heel Sneakers' Tommy Tucker
'Look What You've Done' Muddy Waters
'Down In The Bottom' Muddy Waters (written by Willie Dixon)
'Confessin' The Blues' Chuck Berry
'Down The Road Apiece' Chuck Berry
'Around And Around' Chuck Berry
'Empty Heart' Nanker Phelge
'Tell Me Baby' Big Bill Broonzy
'2120 South Michigan Avenue' Nanker/Phelge
Stu played organ on three tracks and piano on another five, including the great boogie piano on 'Down The Road Apiece'.

'That guitar player ain't bad.'

MUDDY WATERS, *on Brian*

'The biggest advantage of recording strong rhythm and blues in Chicago was that the engineers were a lot more used to that sort of music. I don't think anyone anywhere could record this type of music as effectively as they did in Chicago. We almost got the sound captured on "Memphis" on one number.' CHARLIE, *Mersey Beat, July 1964*

'I played the bass riff for "2120 South Michigan Avenue" and then everyone picked up on it. It was credited to Nanker/Phelge.' BILL

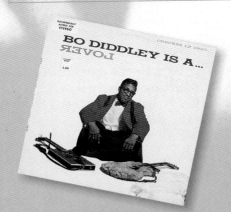

'I was talking to Bo Diddley on the telephone at the recording studio and we joked a bit about America, and then he got very serious and sad about how hard it is for the Negro to make it here in the States, unless he's in jazz.' BRIAN, *Chicago Daily News, 20 June, 1964*

'Swing on, gentlemen, you are sounding most well, if I may say so.' CHUCK BERRY

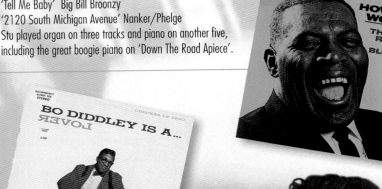

'TELL ME (YOU'RE COMING BACK)'

Recorded
24 or 25 February, 1964
Studio
Regent Sound Studios
Producer
Andrew Oldham
Engineer
Bill Farley
Release
US Saturday 13 June, 1964
London 45-LON 9682
Composers
a-side Jagger/Richard
b-side Dixon
Highest chart position
US No 24
Personnel
Charlie: drums
Bill: bass, backing vocals
Keith and Brian: guitars, backing vocals
Mick: lead vocals
Stu: piano
Brian: tambourine

Richard vs Richards
Keith's name was shortened to Richard in the early days of the band by Andrew, who thought it sounded better. Keith reverted to Richards in the late 1970s.

The Stones' second US single was released mid-way through the first US tour, on 13 June. Both sides were taken from the debut album and 'Tell Me' has the distinction of being the first Jagger/Richard composition to appear as a Stones single release. The record spent 10 weeks in the US charts and was the highest placed of the first three US 45s.

Mick and Keith were definitely influenced by the Beatles and British beat boom bands. The single was a long way from the band's blues roots; its affinity with other British invasion material secured its US release as the follow-up to 'Not Fade Away' and contributed to the song's US chart success. American audiences were more used to the sound of Mersey Beat, the Dave Clark Five and the Searchers.

'Tell Me' was also the second Stones single to be released in Holland. It made it to No 11 in the Dutch singles chart in November.

In glorious colour
Bill: 'A colour sleeve was unheard of in England at the time. They were only found on EPs. The sleeve shows the mis-spelling of "want to" on the b-side. Strangely, it was correctly spelt on the record itself.'

'There are very few cover versions of the song. One, by the Termites, was released in February 1965 (when it sank without trace), and the other by Cleveland punk band the Dead Boys featured on their 1978 album We Have Come For Your Children.*'* BILL

What the papers said...
On 27 June, *Record World* reported, 'This looks like the big one this week. It starts with a slow beat that builds, shifts and then builds again. The singing and off-beat instrumentation will captivate teen listeners.' Another paper said, '"Tell Me" is a much-requested track from their sizzling LP and it's a haunting rock-a-cha-cha that picks up steam each time around.'

Pop Weekly was also tracking the single's performance: '"Tell Me" sold 130,000 and moved into the Top 100 fast and then slowed down.'

ROLLING STONES—TELL ME (Southern, ASCAP) (2:35) — I JUST WANT TO MAKE LOVE TO YOU (Arc, BMI) (2:15)—Neanderthal music at its best. The British group offers a crude chant and the rockiest sound around. Flip features lead in r&b groove. Sustained guitars beat with hand-clappin' makes it r&b with British accent.
London 9682

'In June 1964, Bob Neuwirth, Dylan and I were in a hotel, trading songs. I don't recall who started singing "Tell Me", but we sang it together.'
TONY GLOVER, *Koerner, Ray and Glover*

'"Tell Me" featured on the soundtrack of Martin Scorsese's Mean Streets *in 1973.'* BILL

A Great New Sound!
THE TERMITES
sing **TELL ME**
(Written by MICK JAGGER and KEITH RICHARD)
on ORIOLE CB 1989

Will America Love Us?

After the euphoria of the first gig in San Bernardino, things quietened down as we travelled across the States. We needed Andrew's creative promotional abilities to make America love us... by getting the press to hate us!

BEFORE OUR SECOND DAY of recording at Chess, Andrew arranged a press conference, not at a regular venue, but on a traffic island in the centre of Michigan Avenue. This was one of Andrew's most inspired stunts and it worked like a dream. There were shrieking girl fans and many onlookers who caused a traffic jam. We were moved on by the police, but we achieved exactly what we wanted – masses of media coverage.

'The Rolling Stones, a form of British blight related to the Beatles, tried to hold a news conference in the middle of Michigan Avenue, and ran into a square cop. "Get out of here or I'll arrest the bunch of you," thundered the cop. A squadron of their squealing teenage girl fans and onlookers stared as if they were at Lincoln Park Zoo.'
CHICAGO DAILY NEWS

'Americans think we're freaks, but time will change that.' Andrew's comment was something that we all agreed with. That evening we had dinner with Richard Christiansen from the *Chicago Daily News*: 'When the Stones came down from their hotel rooms to dinner, they were in an expansive mood. They read the newspaper stories about them and Mick had just said that their trip was turning into a ball, when a fat man wandered into the dining room, took one look at them and shouted, "Hey, how about those guys? Is there a

'There's nothing we parents can do about this craze. Ministers and psychiatrists say it's healthy.'
JL KOPENGA, *mother of the Stones US fan club president, 14-year-old Judy*

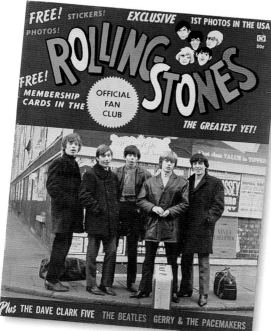

barber in the house? Ha, ha."

'It was not funny to the Stones: "What's the matter, stupid? Can't you do any better than that? Our taxi driver already gave us that one! Beat it, baldy. Jealous? Get out, you slob. You're nothing." They hooted and hissed... The fat man fled.'

It wasn't an untypical situation for us, only this time a reporter was around to capture it for posterity. As Mick remarked, 'They think they're the first to say it. The other one they like to ask is if we're gathering any moss. Big joke. If you scream back at them, they stagger back to the bar. Simple idiots.'

Later, Brian stuck two fingers in his nostrils, pushed down his nose and pulled a Nanker, 'I use Whiter Than White face cream, but I'm still black.'

This got Keith going.

'Negroes are the only ones here who haven't made fun of us,' he said. 'They accept you as individuals. All the others point at us because we have long hair and they ask stupid questions.'

Fair play
After two wonderful days at Chess, we flew to Minneapolis to play the Excelsior Fair. The show had been booked late, which partially accounted for the small crowd. The reception was similar to our first English ballroom dates – one of curiosity and disbelief.

The day our second US single came out, we flew to Omaha, Nebraska, arriving at Eppley Airfield at 2.30pm, to be greeted by about 200 fans. At the Music Hall, we had a little run-in with the law. In Omaha, alcoholic beverages were prohibited by law and a cop looked in our dressing room and saw a whisky bottle. He made us pour the bottle and the rest of our drinks down a sink.

'I was only drinking Coca-Cola. I refused to pour mine away, thinking why the fuck was an American cop telling me to pour the national drink down the bog? The cop pulled a gun on me. A very strange scene to me, a cop ordering me at gunpoint to pour a coke down the john.' KEITH

The show was as badly attended as the night before – Mr McMorris of the *Omaha World Herald* was not particularly impressed: 'To us older folk, the first Stone who poked his shaggy head through the curtain was a sight that belonged to a science-fiction movie. The guitar player came out in a kind of crouch. He maintained this stance throughout the concert. He stared at the crowd with furtive, almost hostile eyes. Was this the creature from the black lagoon? He was followed on-stage by four other seedy, unlikely-looking heroes.' Later that night the *Hollywood Palace Show* we had recorded with Dean Martin was on TV and we were furious at the way they had portrayed us. Mick immediately got on the phone to London, and screamed at Eric for booking our appearance.

Dean Martin

'It was a good job the sheriff's office riot squad were there.'
SAN BERNARDINO SUN TELEGRAPH,
7 June, 1964

'They could appear on the Hollywood Palace Show *on condition that they could not perform on another TV show for 21 days before or after their appearance. Consequently, their appearance, headed by an alcoholic, was anything but helpful for their popular image.'* JACKIE KALLEN, *Teenbeat magazine*

As we became popular in America, they re-ran the complete spot many times, substituting comperes who said more favourable things about us. In truth, we had the last laugh. On a later US tour, Brian had an affair with one of Dean Martin's daughters.

Motor city

On the day that Nelson Mandela was sentenced to life imprisonment in South Africa, we played the 13,000 seat Olympia Stadium in Detroit. There were less than 1,000 people when we went onstage at 6pm, but at least they were enthusiastic. The *Detroit Free Press* reported: 'Their records aren't selling well, and DJs only play them occasionally. Back they may come, with more promotion, but wait and see what the reaction is.' As I commented at the time, 'We'll be back this autumn and sell out. Only the past few generations had short hair. Wars did it. The army.'

Mick, Brian, Keith and Andrew went off to a do: 'The party was a lively one and the four foreigners fitted in perfectly,' wrote Jackie Kallen in *Teenbeat* magazine. 'The only difference was the length of their hair and their noticeably British accents. Before the evening was over, Mick and Brian explained that they were staying over an extra day in Detroit, and were interested in seeing the sights and doing some shopping. My friend and I offered to be their guides.' Later, I ended up at the hotel with Jackie, her girlfriend Pat Powell and a local DJ, Terry Knight (who went on to manage Grand Funk Railroad) doing interviews.

With no show the next day we planned to go to Canada. At least, we would have, if Keith had found his passport; the officials refused him entry without it. Mick and Keith went out with Jackie and her friend instead.

'We set out the next morning in my '64 Mustang, and headed straight for Belle Isle, where they took turns trying to drive on the other side of the road. Next we stopped at Hudsons downtown to shop and then back to my house for a home-cooked meal. Everything American was new and fascinating to them.'** JACKIE KALLEN

Mo Schulman, from London Records, took Stu, Charlie and I to a local record store. They allowed us to help ourselves to records and I got eight albums. In the evening, Mo, Bob Bonis and I went to the Playboy Club for drinks, and then on to another club called the Brass Rail – I was getting into this American touring!

After the show, we drove to Cleveland, where unfortunately nobody had thought to make a hotel reservation. Finally at 5am, we found somewhere to stay. Up at 9.30am, we appeared on *The Mike Douglas Show* and then spent the day driving to Hershey, arriving at midnight.

'There we get a special plane, and fly 15 miles to Harrisburg, because we're supposed to arrive by air,' remembered Brian. Total insanity! They even had a small banquet in the terminal in our honour. Harrisburg was a disappointment with only 1,300 – albeit enthusiastic fans – in a 17,000 seater arena. We drove to New York, finally arriving at the Park Sheraton Hotel at 2.30am.

We were up early for *The Clay Cole Show*, which also featured Neil Sedaka, Leslie Miller and Bobby Fontaine and the Eggheads. We then went straight to Carnegie Hall for a matinee. Dozens of fans attacked us and we only managed to get in with the help of the police. For our first ever New York show, Murray The K introduced us individually. The audience went crazy, and rushed forwards; many got on-stage before being caught.

As Rita Paulk of *Fabulous* magazine reported, 'Suddenly the curtain went up and the Rolling Stones strolled on stage, paused a second, then swung into "Route 66". There was a quiet pause, then the audience went wild. I kept getting the peculiar feeling that they had just walked into my living room and started playing for me alone. "I Just Want To Make Love To You" stopped the show.'

'Brian Jones stepped up to the microphone, harmonica in hands. He might have blown air into it, but what came out was raw soul! The air around was electric with pulsating blues. I have never seen performers anywhere who could touch them.' The scenes were more frenetic than on most US dates.

'Jelly beans, flowers, toilet paper and messages flew through the air and were strewn on the stage. Banners and flags were waving. Girls were swinging their arms, shrieking, standing on their chairs and gyrating.' MEET THE ROLLING STONES MAGAZINE, 1964

Brian said what we were all feeling. 'I've never seen anything quite like this. It's marvellous, but it scares me a bit at the same time.' After the show, police found fans hiding in phone booths, closets, hallways and rest rooms. Prisoners in our dressing room, the management and police tried to persuade us to cancel the evening show, but we refused. As a compromise we agreed to go on before Jay and the Americans. The management warned that if anybody moved towards the stage, left their seat, or stood on a chair, the performance would be stopped immediately.

We'd barely finished when we were herded off stage as Murray The K announced Jay and the Americans. Unfortunately, many fans ran out of the hall and across the street to our hotel. By the time we got back, there was a shrieking mob in the lobby. The police managed to push us into the elevator while keeping the fans out. Perhaps America was going to love us after all.

Right: In Rolling Stones Monthly, every last detail concerning the Stones was lapped up by eager fans. The first issue was published on 10 June, 1964; it was produced until November 1966.

Back Home

Ready to return to London after the great gig at Carnegie Hall, we spent our last day in America besieged in our hotel. Our overnight BOAC flight to London left JFK at 8pm. We were looking forward to getting home.

'America was strange. I enjoyed the trip, but I couldn't live there. Their outlook was outdated. The funny thing was, the kids had never heard of Muddy Waters. They've got the greatest blues singer living among them and they don't even know.' MICK, *Heathrow press conference*

WE LANDED IN London at 7.30am. Eager to get off, we were told to leave the plane last because of hundreds of waiting fans. Keith and I had both bought guns in Texas and I had concealed mine in my underpants. I think Keith did the same. We successfully negotiated customs and gave a well-attended press conference.

Charlie commented: 'We were exhausted for most of the US tour, because of the tremendous amount of travelling. We appealed more to the coloured audiences than to other teenagers, because we wanted to play their type of music, a sound we have always admired. The white

teenagers go more for beat and ballads than they do for R&B.'

Reg King, Andrew's driver, arrived in Andrew's new Chevrolet with Chrissie Shrimpton, who was there to meet Mick. They all left along with Keith and reporter Chris Hutchins. Keith showed Chris his gun and talked about our future.

I went straight home and tried to relax because that evening we were going to Oxford University. We had a gig! By 9.30pm there were a hundred fans outside Magdalen College, chanting 'We want the Stones.' The police moved in and the fans started chanting, 'We love you policemen!'

We played two sets, supported by the Falling Leaves, Sadler, Arnold and Gould, Freddie and the Dreamers, John Lee Hooker and the Tubby Hayes Band. We were shattered. I didn't get home until 10am and I fell straight into bed. I really needed sleep.

Ch… ch… changes

The next day Diane told me about a modern two-bedroom flat, 9 Kenilworth Court, over a garage opposite Beckenham Grammar School in Penge. At £7 a week, it was very expensive for the area, but we looked at it and decided to take it.

The following day I went to the Waldorf Hotel for lunch with Eric, Andrew and the rest of the boys. We met with a solicitor to talk over making the Stones a limited company. I also discussed changing my name officially from Perks to Wyman by deed poll. A few days later, Mick and Keith left the flat in Mapesbury Road, which had been burgled while we were away, and moved to 10a Holly Hill in Hampstead. Andrew also moved – to Ivor Court, Gloucester Place – setting up home and office there. Chrissie Shrimpton started working for him as a secretary.

That Thursday we recorded for *RSG!*, playing 'It's all Over Now'. The programme aired the day after, coinciding with the single's release.

'On our present strength, I think the Stones can count on lasting at least two more years. If there's nothing new on the way, then we can literally go on indefinitely.' KEITH

Bill adopted his stage name permanently when he made the offical change from Perks to Wyman.

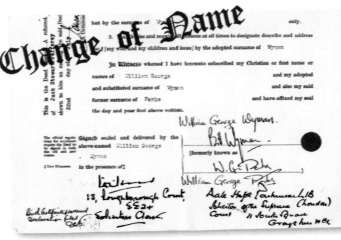

'IT'S ALL OVER NOW'

The day the Stones arrived in America, they did two major press conferences and then went to radio station WINS to appear on Murray The K's *Swinging Soiree* show. After the programme had gone off air, Murray played them a single by the Valentinos, Bobby Womack's group. He suggested the band cover 'It's All Over Now' as their next single and they all agreed it was a good idea. Mid-way through the tour, the Stones recorded the track at Chess studios in a two-day session.

The Valentinos' version came out in early 1964 and was a very different-sounding record. The Stones came at the song from a perspective that worked perfectly when coupled with Ron Malo's brilliant engineering. 'It's All Over Now' is all about the sound of the record. The intro makes it the perfect radio track, grabbing your attention and never letting go.

The single went straight into the *NME* chart at No 7 the week after its release. In America it ran into censorship problems over the words 'half-assed games' and many DJs cut that part out.

The Stones with Murray The K

'*The Stones have gone all country and western. "It's All Over Now" (echoes of Roy Orbison) is a happy canter in the country style, which is going to cause some soul-searching among the fans.*'
ROBERT BICKFORD, *Daily Mail*, 26 June, 1964

'*An irreverent person has hinted that this sounds fractionally like the Beverly Hillbillies. This person has a point. It's less exciting than a lot of the stuff they sing. There is some good guitar but it lacks drive. The pace is that of a jogtrot through a country lane.*'
MAUREEN CLEAVE, *Evening Standard*, 27 June, 1964

'*We like the sound of it. We didn't think it sounded country and western until we read it. It's the 12-string guitar and harmonising that do it. We don't want to do the same old thing every time, or people would get fed up with it.*' BILL

Fry's Shooting Star award

'On Tuesday 7 July, we won a UK silver disc for "It's All Over Now". There was only one copy: Brian got it.' **BILL**

Recorded
a-side 10 June, 1964
b-side 25 February, 1964
Studios
a-side Chess Studios
b-side Regent Sound Studios
Producer
Andrew Loog Oldham for Impact Sound
Engineers
a-side Ron Malo
b-side Bill Farley
Release
UK Friday 26 June, 1964
Decca F 11934
US Saturday 25 July, 1964
London 45 LON 9687
Composers
a-side B and S Womack
b-side Jagger/Richard
Highest chart position
UK No 1
US No 26
Personnel
Charlie: drums
Bill: bass
Keith: lead guitar
Brian: guitar
Mick: lead vocals, tambourine

this week's record
No. 208
top ten

1	IT'S ALL OVER NOW	THE ROLLING STONES	F 11934
2	HOLD ME	P.J. PROBY	F 11904
3	IT'S OVER	ROY ORBISON	HLU 9882
4	SOMEONE	BRIAN POOLE & THE TREMELOES	F 11893
5	I WON'T FORGET YOU	JIM REEVES	RCA 1400
6	HELLO DOLLY	LOUIS ARMSTRONG	HLR 9878
7	RAMONA	THE BACHELORS	F 11910
8	IT HURTS ME / KISSIN' COUSINS	ELVIS PRESLEY	RCA 1404
9	SHOUT	LULU AND THE LUVERS	F 11884
10	BAMA LAMA BAMA LOO	LITTLE RICHARD	HL 9896
SPOT OF THE WEEK	TOBACCO ROAD	THE NASHVILLE TEENS	F 11930
	ALONE WITH YOU	BRENDA LEE	05911
	LONELY HEART	CARL PERKINS	05909

'I'm not too keen on the record. It's all right, but I just don't know. There's just something.' **BRIAN**

June **64**

March **65**

Going Global

'Brian, I love you!'

Jury Service

Back from America our lives continued at the same hectic pace. We had some time off planned, but before that we were booked to appear on a TV show that was compulsive viewing for much of the nation.

ON 26 JUNE, 'It's all Over Now' came out and we played an all-nighter at Alexandra Palace. Backstage at the show, Brian told Mike Ledgerwood from *Disc*, 'If I can get everything arranged in time I'd like to return to New York and Los Angeles where I have friends in the music publishing business. There were some new arrangements they have that I'd like to have a go at. I might even do some demo discs if I get the chance.' Brian always had more plans than he ever realised; it was the tragedy of his life.

The next day we were all shattered, but still had to go to the BBC studios in Shepherds Bush to record. *Juke Box Jury* attracted an audience of around 12 million every week. We were expected to push that up to 20 million. On arrival we discovered fans had been queuing all day to get a seat in the theatre.

David Jacobs, the compere, came to our dressing room and acted in a very off-hand manner. As usual, our reputation preceded us. On the show we were played eight songs, among them was the Searchers' 'Someday We're Gonna Love Again', the Everly Brothers' 'The Ferris Wheel', Freddie & the Dreamers' 'Just For You' and Elvis's 'There's Gold In The Mountain'. The tracks weren't that good and we voted most songs as 'misses'; one of us, I forget who, described Elvis's song as 'dated'.

'I disagree that the Stones on *Juke Box Jury* were a disgrace. They spoke their minds. When the Beatles appeared, they voted everything a 'hit' so as not to spoil their public image. Well done, Stones.' **DAVID BALDWIN,** *in a letter to the NME*

We thought the show went off pretty well, although it was hard to find five different things to say about each record. After we'd finished, there was just an hour before we went to another studio to film *Top Of The Pops*. The following week, *Juke Box Jury* aired and it was clear we had been optimistic, as our appearance on the show caused the usual amount of controversy.

'Never in the course of human history has so much drivel been spouted by so few in front of so many.' RUSSELL FORGHAM, *in a letter to the NME*

In the *Daily Sketch* (19 August, 1964), Robert Ottaway wrote, 'When the Stones slumped into their chairs as panellists on *Juke Box Jury*, many tut-tutting elders took it as a declaration of war. When the Stones

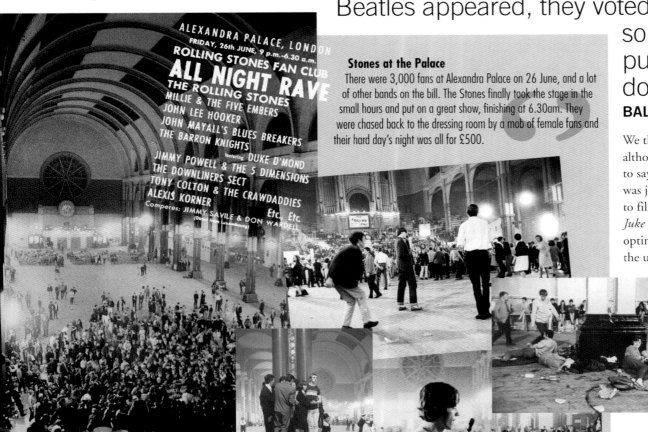

Stones at the Palace
There were 3,000 fans at Alexandra Palace on 26 June, and a lot of other bands on the bill. The Stones finally took the stage in the small hours and put on a great show, finishing at 6.30am. They were chased back to the dressing room by a mob of female fans and their hard day's night was all for £500.

ALEXANDRA PALACE, LONDON
FRIDAY, 26th JUNE, 9 p.m.-6.30 a.m.
ROLLING STONES FAN CLUB
ALL NIGHT RAVE
THE ROLLING STONES
MILLIE & THE FIVE EMBERS
JOHN LEE HOOKER
JOHN MAYALL'S BLUES BREAKERS
THE BARRON KNIGHTS
featuring DUKE D'MOND
JIMMY POWELL & THE 5 DIMENSIONS
THE DOWNLINERS SECT
TONY COLTON & THE CRAWDADDIES
ALEXIS KORNER
Etc, Etc.
Comperes: JIMMY SAVILE & DON WARDELL
(Direct from Luxembourg)

Left: *Mick and Chrissie leaving for Ibiza*; Right: *Charlie settles into his flat in Ivor Court.*

opened their mouths, their strangulated vowels couldn't have been identified in the *Oxford English Dictionary*. Many thought they needed an interpreter. Some called for the resignation of the Minister of Education. The fury was all on the adult side.'

At the time I said: 'Some people take these programmes too seriously. Producer Barry Langford was happy and said it was marvellous. The audience was okay too. People knew what to expect when they invited us to be on the show. They didn't want a sophisticated panel and they didn't get one. If some of the viewers didn't like it,

they should have switched off. I don't care what they thought.' I think I'll stick with that. Brian said he thought our appearance harmed us, but I don't see how it could have done.

Summer holidays

Our holiday started on Monday 28 June and we certainly needed it. Mick and Chrissie, Charlie and Shirley, and Keith and Linda planned to go to Ibiza, but Linda had a car accident and ended up in hospital. Keith decided to stay with her. When the others got to the airport, Charlie realised he had forgotten his passport. He and Mick joined the girls later.

I stayed at home and spent time with Stephen and Diane; Keith came and stayed on Sunday 5 July. I recorded him on my tape recorder playing some nice country blues songs on my 12-string guitar. He did four tracks including 'Brown Girl', on which he sang. When we got up next morning, we found that 'It's All Over Now' was No 1. Brian had learned to like it too. 'I'm not jumping about like an idiot, but I'm very pleased,' he said. 'I feel like I do after I've had a good meal – satisfied. I didn't like the number when I heard it on a radio, but I like it now.'

Keith and I walked to Beckenham and back that day and were bothered by lots of fans; now even the most ordinary journey was becoming a problem for us. In the late afternoon, Keith met with Brian in London. They gatecrashed the Beatles' party at the Dorchester hotel, for the premiere of *Hard Day's Night* and were welcomed with champagne.

Andrew Oldham and Eric Easton were kept busy on business matters, including

Saville or servile – after being interviewed by Penny Valentine, the Stones did a photo session with DJ Jimmy and his Rolls Royce on 16 July.

the incorporation of Rolling Stones Limited on 1 July, 1964.

Back to work

We played on Saturday 11 Jul, at Spa Royal Hall, Bridlington. We were a bit stiff after our lay off, but soon got back into it. This was the gig at which Brian used his Vox Teardrop guitar for the first time. There was some fighting in the crowd, and many girls fainted – things were back to normal on stage. July was otherwise anything but a typical month: we only played nine gigs – the quietest month since we'd started playing together.

With time off, Charlie moved from his parents' house in Kingsbury to Ivor Court in Gloucester Place, becoming Andrew's neighbour. His rent was £54 3s 4d per month. Stu also bought a Jaguar, the first of us to have a new car.

A fun article appeared in *Disc*, where Penny Valentine wrote, 'Bill was in a very good mood because he had that morning succeeded in the new Stones game.'

The rules were simple, as I told her: 'We sit in these very plush hotels and see how long we can stay there before someone asks us to leave. I sat in the Hilton waiting for Charlie for 10 minutes and nobody said a word.'

TOP RANK
MAJESTIC BALLROOM
FINSBURY PARK, N.4
(Opp. Finsbury Park Station)   STA 2676
WEDNESDAY, JULY 15th
Open 7.30 p.m.   Admission 4/-
THE GROUP THAT UNGASSED
'THE STONES'
THE PRETTY THINGS
WEDNESDAY, JULY 22nd
ALEXIS KORNER'S
BLUES INC., BAND

After the rigours of US touring, on top of a hectic UK schedule, the Stones had a relatively easy period on their return. It was well deserved. They had played 120 gigs since January, as well as doing numerous TV appearances, radio shows and recording sessions. During the summer there were two mini-tours and a trip to Holland for the band's first proper European gig.

Set list
Drawn from the following.

'Walking The Dog'
'Route 66'
'High-Heel Sneakers'
'Around And Around'
'If You Need Me'
'You Can Make It If You Try'

'Not Fade Away'
'Can I Get A Witness'
'It's Alright'
'I'm A Kingbee'
'I Just Wanna Make Love To You'
'It's All Over Now'

And in support...
John Lee Hooker
John Mayall's Bluesbreakers
Kenny Lynch
The Downliners Sect
Jimmy Powell and the Five Dimensions
The Echoes
Simon Scott
The LeRoys
The Executives
Mandrakes
Tony Colton and the Crawdaddies
The Mysteries
Lulu and the Luvvers
Ray Kennon and the Guvnors
The Sabres
Tom Jones and his Band
Patrick Dane and the Quiet Five

Prince and the Paupers
Danny Clarke and the Jaguars
The Falcons
The Worryin' Kind
Ray Anton and the Peppermint Men
Westcoasters
Ryles Brothers with Dallas
Gene Vincent and the Shouts
The Avengers
Marty Wilde and the Wildcats
Tony Rivers and the Castaways
Kremlins
The Ken Turner Orchestra.
The Barron Knights
The Redcaps

The Falcons featured 17-year-old Roy Wood, later of the Move, on guitar.
The Executives starred Tony Ashton, later of Family and other bands.

The United Kingdom/Europe, *June–August 1964*

Italics indicate two performances.

22 June Magdalen College, Oxford University, Oxfordshire, Commemoration Ball
26 June Alexandra Palace, London, Fan Club All Night Rave
11 July *Spa Royal Hall, Bridlington, Yorkshire*
12 July *Queens Hall, Leeds, Yorkshire*
18 July Beat City Club, Oxford Street, London
19 July *Hippodrome Theatre, Brighton, Sussex*
24 July Empress Ballroom, Blackpool, Lancashire
25 July Imperial Ballroom, Nelson, Lancashire
26 July *De Montfort Hall, Leicester, Leicestershire*
31 July Ulster Hall, Belfast, Northern Ireland
Flamingo Ballroom, Ballymena, Northern Ireland
1 August Pier Ballroom, Hastings, Sussex
2 August Longleat House, Warminster, Wiltshire
7 August Athletic Ground, Richmond, Surrey *(4th National Jazz and Blues Festival)*
8 August Kurhaus, Scheveningen, The Hague, Holland
9 August New Elizabethan Ballroom, Belle Vue, Manchester, Lancashire

10 August Tower Ballroom, New Brighton, Cheshire
13 August Palace Ballroom, Douglas, Isle of Man
14 August Wimbledon Palais, London
18 August *St George's Hall, New Theatre Ballroom, Guernsey, Channel Isles*
19 August *St George's Hall, New Theatre Ballroom, Guernsey, Channel Isles*
20 August *St George's Hall, New Theatre Ballroom, Guernsey, Channel Isles*
21 August *Springfield Hall, St Helier, Jersey, Channel Isles*
22 August *Springfield Hall, St Helier, Jersey, Channel Isles*
23 August *Gaumont Theatre, Bournemouth, Hampshire*
24 August *Gaumont Theatre, Weymouth, Dorset*
25 August *Odeon Theatre, Weston-super-Mare, Somerset*
26 August *Odeon Theatre, Exeter, Devonshire*
27 August *ABC Theatre, Plymouth, Devonshire*
28 August *Gaumont Theatre, Taunton, Somerset*
29 August *Town Hall, Torquay, Devonshire*
30 August *Gaumont Theatre, Bournemouth, Hampshire*

Back On The Road Again

The Stones at the Richmond Jazz Festival, 7 August

Mini-tour
On this tour at the end of August the running order of the shows was: Worryin' Kind, Overlanders, Barron Knights, *Interval*, Five Embers, Millie Small and the Stones. Julie Grant substituted for Millie Small and the Five Embers and on the first show the Paramounts appeared. For the last show Long John Baldry and the Hoochie Coochie Men were added. In the band was a young Rod Stewart.

WALKING THE DOG
Recorded at Haven of THE ROLLING STONES

4th National JAZZ FESTIVAL
7th, 8th & 9th AUGUST, 1964

Live at the Wimbledon Palais, 14 August

RHYTHM & BLUES JAZZ and GOSPEL..
4th National JAZZ & BLUES FESTIVAL
* * *
8·9·AUGUST
ATHLETIC ASSOCIATION GROUNDS......
RICHMOND
AFTERNOONS 5s.
EVENINGS 10s.
ALL DAY 12s.6d.
EVENING NEWS & STAR

'Some groups give performances, but we have a rave. A mad, swaying, deafening, sweating half-hour of tension or excitement, which gives us just as big a kick as the kids.' **BRIAN**

new flat with two policemen to make a statement. While they were questioning me, one of them noticed the gun I had got in America. They asked if I had a gun licence and wanted to know how I got it into the country. I told them I had packed it in my suitcase. They said it was a prison offence to have a gun without a licence, but if I let them hand it in at the police station, nothing more would be said. I didn't need to think about it – I gave them the weapon, the end of my gun-toting days.

Another little Jones

On 23 July, 1964, Linda gave birth to Brian's fourth illegitimate child. Bizarrely, they gave him the same name as Pat Andrews' child, Julian Mark.

'There was a time when they were gonna get married. They actually told people,' said Shirley Arnold, our fan club president in the UK. 'Maybe Brian did want to get married and settle down, but he never quite made it. I was going to be chief bridesmaid. Linda and I went out one afternoon and she was looking at wedding dresses. Then they just split up. She decided to stay at home with her mum and they left each other again.'

The day after the birth, we played the Empress Ballroom, in Blackpool, Lancashire. A great gig, or so we thought – we were being paid £750, our best-ever fee, for two 25-minute sets. There were over 7,000 people packed into the ballroom and our first set went off fine. During the second, a gang of drunken Scots, mostly Glaswegians, started fighting their way to the front, where they started spitting at us. Keith warned them more than once to stop, they ignored him and he kicked one of them in the head.

There's A Riot Goin' On

One of the more terrifying moments playing live with the Stones was when a gig got totally out of control in Blackpool. There'd been no indication that it was going to be different to any other show.

A FEW DAYS BEFORE THE Blackpool gig, *Today* magazine ran an article that revealed what our parents thought about us now we were becoming successful. They were asked if playing with the Stones had changed us in any way.

'Brian has always been a little unconventional. What infuriates me, however, is the implication that the boys don't wash, that they're scruffy and dirty. As a matter of fact, Brian is a bit of a pest when he comes back home because he's always washing his hair. I think Brian still believes I disapprove of the Rolling Stones. But he's got a good brain – better than my own – and I wish that it was being put to better use. He uses his intelligence now, of course, but his brain is quite definitely under-worked.' LEWIS JONES, *Brian's father*

'And there's the business about the name. Our name is Perks, but Bill changed his to Wyman because I suppose he thought it sounded better for the business. It would have been nice if he'd kept his real name, though.' WILLIAM PERKS, *Bill's Dad*

The next week was almost too eventful for my liking and not just with Stones activity. We had a few gigs, did some recording and I had time to go to the Framus factory with Stu to get a new bass.

Having just moved flat, I had to clear up our old place and, while I was doing it, I managed to set fire to the chimney. The fire brigade put it out and I then had to go back to the

'Trouble erupted the moment the Stones slouched on stage. Suprisingly, the group seemed quite oblivious to the frequent outbursts of senseless violence that their mere presence seemed to ignite.' ROY CARR, *writer and member of the support band the Executives*

The papers were full of the riot.

'I certainly didn't hit anybody. I simply made an aggressive movement with my guitar.'

KEITH, *Daily Express, 1964*

'It was very nearly the date on my gravestone,' remembered Stu. 'Keith still thought he was God and that he could kick one of these guys and get away with it. The rest of the band already turned, realising they had to get off stage. I just pushed Keith and said, "For fuck's sake get out of here while you're still alive." We could hear cymbals going through the air, thumps as all the amps got smashed up and then there was the most glorious crash of all time – there'd been a grand piano on the stage. The cops sent for reinforcements. About 50 of them went in with truncheons. Charlie wasn't using his drums. He'd borrowed a kit from this guy, who was sitting there crying over his lovely Ludwig.' Stu arrived at the band's hotel later

that evening to return our kit, or rather the fragments that remained. 'This is your amp… and here's your guitar… as he gave us bits of wood and stuff.'

Mick said: 'We were scared stiff. Nothing like this has ever happened before. You cannot expect people to put up with having their property smashed up like that.' Brian couldn't understand it. 'Everyone seems to think that we are always out to be antagonistic and to put their backs up. It just isn't true! All we want is for people to accept us and our music. Not to look on us as freaks.'

With typical understatement, Charlie commented: 'All we want is to get on with our music.' In truth, back then I thought it was the most terrifying night of my life and probably the rest of the band would have agreed. Keith denied hitting anyone, but that certainly was not true. Little were we to know what we would face before the decade was out – not that at that point it ever crossed our minds that we would still be playing in five years. I would be almost 33 by then; no one had a career as a rock star at that age.

The following day we played Preston and it was a more normal crowd, a good gig in which the fans went home happy. The next stop after that was Leicester, where Mick celebrated his 21st birthday. It was business as usual here too, so was our visit to Northern Ireland soon afterwards.

Press darlings

Looking back, it is amazing that the press took all the bullshit stories that Andrew fed them. The naivety is difficult to appreciate. It really was a very different world. For us, life was the road, giving the press endless opportunity to write trivia. They had an insatiatable appetite for minutiae; obviously we sold papers and magazines. August began with a case in point – one of Andrew's most ridiculous publicity scams to date.

'Many secret Rolling Stones recordings have been insured under a £10,000 policy taken out by their manager Andrew Oldham. They are covered against loss, theft and accident. The tapes are kept in a locked cupboard in Oldham's office-cum-bedroom. They include the Stones' next LP, which will be issued at the end of the year. Also covered in the policy are master recordings of all songs which they have released so far, plus several more tapes they don't want issued yet and 18 Mick Jagger/Keith Richard compositions.'
MIKE GRANT,
Rave magazine

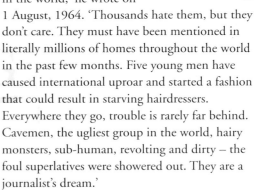

The late Ray Coleman, who helped me with my book *Stone Alone*, summed it up brilliantly in *Melody Maker*: 'They have become the most talked-about, turbulent group in the world,' he wrote on 1 August, 1964. 'Thousands hate them, but they don't care. They must have been mentioned in literally millions of homes throughout the world in the past few months. Five young men have caused international uproar and started a fashion that could result in starving hairdressers. Everywhere they go, trouble is rarely far behind. Cavemen, the ugliest group in the world, hairy monsters, sub-human, revolting and dirty – the foul superlatives were showered out. They are a journalist's dream.'

Eric Easton was booking our shows well in advance which meant we were getting less than our level of success deserved by the time we played. But Eric liked to keep us working: the more we worked, the more he and Andrew earned. Back then it really paid being a manager – but we had more fun.

Nice place, your lordship

Our first gig in August, at Hastings pier, earned us £300, less than half what we made at the

Blackpool riot. And less than a third of what we would earn the next day – but, then again, we were playing for the nobility. The venue was Longleat House, the Marquis of Bath's residence. We lined up with Tony Rivers and the Castaways, and Danny Clarke and the Jaguars. It was estimated that there were between 16,000 and 25,000 people at the gig and somewhere between £2,000 and £3,125 in gate receipts (and he charged 2/6 for parking a car). Lord Bath paid us £1,000.

A police chief complained about the gig in the *Daily Mirror*: 'I feel it's a bad state of affairs. We could easily have had some dead on our hands.' Lord Bath responded in the same newspaper: 'I don't see what the police are bellyaching about. I thought the show went off in an orderly way.'

Besides gigs we also taped 'Carol', 'Tell Me' and 'It's All Over Now' for a US show, *The Red Skelton Hour*. This aired on 22 September, helping promote our second US tour which was to begin in late October. A few days later we taped the first anniversary show of *Ready Steady Go!*

On Saturday 8 August, we played a beautiful venue in Holland called the Kurhaus. It was an opera house in The Hague and it turned into a disaster. As soon as the curtains opened the crowd went berserk. 100 police were moved in position to protect us and it ended with chandeliers being broken and tapestries torn from walls. After two numbers the leads were pulled from our mics and we

ended up as spectators to a riot. Stu was right in the firing line and got hit by a bottle.

'The police formed a chain like fire-fighters and when a teenager came forward, he was passed along, thumped and thrown out of the door and down some steps, where there were more waiting to help him on his way. I have never seen policemen so vicious as they were that night in Holland.' STU

Back home, our gigs were a cross between a war zone and a hospital waiting room. Boys would fight and girls would faint. Whatever happened it got us into more trouble with the media. It even reached the point in the Isle of Man where they had a police dog on stage to guard us: 'Rex certainly helped as a deterrent,' a police superintendent said. 'He stuck at his post for 20 minutes, then he started to fidget and he was taken away. We decided that the beat music and the screaming was getting him excited.'

The Stones are a menace

On 14 August, the *Five By Five* EP was released and an interesting piece appeared in *Record Mirror*

Longleat House

the following day. It was an early sign that Andrew was thinking of moving in another direction. Then again, he maybe had an inkling that we were too, and he would become obsolete.

'The Stones are now their own publicists. They've got past the stage of needing any pushing. There's no challenge in it for me. I've sold my publicity business, which was too much of a strain. I no longer care about clothes. I've made a lot of money and spent most of it. What I want to do is produce records and be an artiste myself.' ANDREW OLDHAM, *Record Mirror, 15 August, 1964*

Three days later, in the *Daily Sketch*, Andrew was back on form. He neatly summed up the reason for our popularity:

'The boys love them because they don't care a brass monkey for authority. The girls go for them because they're sexy. They change their girlfriends with dizzy inconstancy. Going steady is strictly for the clerks. Their language is spiced with swearwords. They drink, and don't take much water with it.

'Life is lived for the moment and is lived to the hilt, in a basic and somewhat selfish concentration on

At the Kurhaus gig riot in Holland, Stu was hit on the head by a bottle.

'These performers are a menace to law and order, and a result of their formula of vocal laryngitis, cranial fur and sex is the police are diverted from bank robberies, murders and other forms of mayhem, to quell the mob violence that they generate.' **DAILY MIRROR,** *August 1964*

their immediate appetites. The older generation cannot live as they do. They have commitments, mortgages, insurance, dangling pensions and that, I believe, is why there is this unreasoning hatred of the Stones. The Stones have a sense of menace in their behaviour.'

Channel-hopping

Our Channel Islands tour was fairly uneventful by our standards, other than a guy pelting us with eggs and tomatoes. However, we did have a little trouble on the plane home. We were climbing up the steps of our plane when the air hostess said in a stage whisper, 'Well, boys, have you washed today?' She then added, 'When did you last have a haircut?' From then on we let her have it, continually asking her for things, making her run up and down the aisle. Eventually she started crying and the airline later told us that they would never have us flying with them again. Brian said afterwards that we should have bought the airline to teach them a lesson. I think he may have overestimated the size of our accounts just a little. My bank balance stood at £28 8s 5d.

We had a new member of staff, Mike Dorsey, who had been employed by Eric to drive us and take care of various duties. He met us at the airport, and his first remark became his trademark, 'Hello, chaps.' All of us liked him from the start. He drove us to Dorchester where we checked into the King's Arms Hotel. That evening we were to play Bournemouth for the first night of our mini-tour of the southwest. It was the familiar round of running, hiding, playing, screaming, travelling and sleeping. While we were playing away, Mick and Keith were once again burgled.

We were off for the first few days of September before starting our next UK package tour. We put in a couple of days in the studio and recorded 'Off The Hook', among other songs.

As tears go by

A song written by Mick, Keith and Andrew, the first with Mick and Keith's name on, charted to make the UK Top 10. Marianne Faithfull's 'As Tears Go By', with its haunting arrangement by Mike Leander, had been released two months earlier, on 19 June. 'Miss Lonely Sobs Into The Pops,' said the *Daily Mail*.

'I played guitar on Marianne's version and Mick's original demo of "As Tears Go By",' said session guitarist Big Jim Sullivan. 'Mick wasn't at Marianne's session, it was just Andrew. Back then, I was a bigger star than the Stones!'

FIVE BY FIVE EP

Recorded
11 June, 1964
Studio
Chess Studios, Chicago
Producer
Andrew Oldham
for Impact Sound
Arranger
The Rolling Stones
Engineer
Ron Malo
Release
UK Friday 14 August,
1964
Decca DFE 8590
Composers
'If You Need Me'
Pickett/Bateman/Sanders
'Empty Heart'
Nanker/Phelge
'2120 South Michigan
Avenue' Nanker/Phelge
'Confessin' The Blues'
Brown/McShann
'Around and Around'
Berry
Highest chart position
UK No 1
Record Retailer EP chart
Personnel
Stu: organ on 'If You Need
Me' and '2120 South
Michigan Avenue'

While the Stones were shifting further away from their roots, this EP, recorded at Chess, is a eulogy to their own blues beginnings. They were clearly inspired by recording at Chess. The sound that was created by engineer Ron Malo was perfect when added to the young-guns-on-hallowed-ground approach of the Stones.

Whatever the sleeve says, it was the Stones and Ron Malo who produced this brilliant record. Andrew was not on that particular wavelength. Stu played organ on 'If You Need Me' and '2120 South Michigan Avenue'.

On 7 August, the *NME* announced that sales of 'It's All Over Now' had reached the half-million mark, and the advance orders for *Five By Five* were 180,000. The EP reached No 7 on the *NME* singles chart and failed by just three places to emulate the Beatles' *Twist And Shout* EP, which made UK No 4 in August 1963. The Beatles and the Stones were the only two bands in the sixties to achieve such strong sales with their EPs.

'This new EP was recorded in Chicago during their recent American tour and is yet another showcase for their exciting vocalising and unique instrumental sound. And by way of saying "thank you" to you, their friends and fans, we have included an extra track on this, their latest disc outing.' ANDREW OLDHAM, *from liner notes on Five By Five*

'We were awarded our third silver disc for the EP on Wednesday 30 September. As was usual back then there was only one copy. It was my turn to get an award, as we took it in turns.' BILL

'This EP is full of vitality, appeal and authority'
NEW MUSICAL EXPRESS, *July 1964*

'Over the years, rumours have been spread that Muddy Waters played on a longer version of "2120 Michigan Avenue". It has been said that he played guitar towards the end of the track. Not true. He did not play with us in the Chess studios – not that we would have minded.' BILL

this is the rolling stones on route to america where they cut their new E.P. released this week on decca DFE 8590

FIVE BY FIVE
THE ROLLING STONES

BRITAIN'S TOP EPs

1 FIVE BY FIVE
(1) The Rolling Stones (Decca)

2 LONG, TALL SALLY
(2) The Beatles (Parlophone)

3 WONDERFUL LIFE
(3) Cliff Richard (Columbia)

4 THE ROLLING STONES
(5) The Rolling Stones (Decca)

11 ALL MY LOVING
(8) The Beatles (Parlophone)

12 LOVE IN LAS VEGAS
(9) Elvis Presley (RCA Victor)

13 BEATLES HITS
(-) Beatles (Parlophone)

14 SONG OF THE HEART—Volume Two
(-) Jim Reeves (RCA Victor)

The band's fourth major UK package tour featured brother and sister soul duo Inez and Charlie Foxx as the principal support band. The couple came from Greensboro, North Carolina, and had a US Top 10 hit in the summer of 1963 with 'Mockingbird'.

Set list

Chosen from:
'Not Fade Away'
'Everybody Needs Somebody To Love'
'I Just Want To Make Love To You'
'Pain In My Heart'
'Walkin' The Dog'
'Down The Road Apiece'
'If You Need Me'
'Time Is On My Side'
'Around and Around'
'I'm All Right'
'I'm A Kingbee'
'Route 66'
'Little Red Rooster'
'Off The Hook'
'Around And Around'
'The Last Time'
'It's All Over Now'
'Carol'

Running order

Innocents
Don Spencer (Compere)
Mike Berry and the Innocents
The Mojos
Interval
The LeRoys
Simon Scott and the LeRoys
Inez and Charlie Foxx
The Rolling Stones

For the last show, Marty Wilde and the Wildcats replaced Mike Berry, the Echoes replaced the Mojos and Kenny Lynch was added.

The Foxxes were playing the UK, where the track wouldn't be a hit until 1969. As usual, the tour took in two shows a night and the plan was to split the tour profits three ways, so that promoter Robert Stigwood received 40 per cent, the Rolling Stones 40 per cent and Eric Easton got 20 per cent. As a result, the Stones took just £50 per week and the following year ended up in the High Court suing for what they thought was their share, about £12,000, a fortune back in 1964.

'A few days after the tour ended we went to Eric's office for a meeting. Robert Stigwood arrived and presented us with an end-of-tour gift, one small portable black-and-white TV set. Mick and Keith took immediate possession of it... it was never seen again.' BILL

'This tour is the biggest thing the Stones have done yet. Our repertoire for the tour consists of about 20 numbers, from which we choose eight every night.'
MICK, *MELODY MAKER*, 12 September, 1964

Charlie Watts backstage with Charlie Foxx

5 September Astoria, Finsbury Park, London
6 September Odeon, Leicester, Leicestershire
8 September Odeon, Colchester, Essex
9 September Odeon, Luton, Bedfordshire
10 September Odeon, Cheltenham, Gloucestershire
11 September Capitol, Cardiff, Wales
13 September Empire, Liverpool, Lancashire
14 September ABC, Chester, Cheshire
15 September Odeon, Manchester, Lancashire
16 September ABC, Wigan, Lancashire
17 September ABC, Carlisle, Cumbria
18 September Odeon, Newcastle upon Tyne
19 September Usher Hall, Edinburgh, Scotland
20 September ABC, Stockton-on-Tees, Durham
21 September ABC, Kingston upon Hull, Yorkshire
22 September ABC, Lincoln, Lincolnshire
24 September Gaumont, Doncaster, Yorkshire
25 September Gaumont, Hanley, Staffordshire
26 September Gaumont, Bradford, Yorkshire
27 September Hippodrome, Birmingham, Staffordshire
28 September Odeon, Romford, Essex
29 September Odeon, Guildford, Surrey
1 October Colston Hall, Bristol, Gloucestershire
2 October Odeon, Exeter, Devonshire
3 October Regal, Edmonton, London
4 October Gaumont, Southampton, Hampshire
5 October Gaumont, Wolverhampton, Staffordshire
6 October Gaumont, Watford, Hertfordshire
8 October Odeon, Lewisham, London
9 October Gaumont, Ipswich, Suffolk
10 October Odeon, Southend-on-Sea, Essex
11 October Hippodrome, Brighton, Sussex

The Fourth With The Foxxes

For Ten Pins

The package tour was a sell-out and chaos surrounded our every move. Mike Dorsey made life easier by driving us to gigs, rather than us having to use the van, or Mick having to drive. Things were getting slightly better organised and our presence in a town was no longer a surprise to police and promoters.

A NEW-FOUND pleasure on this tour was ten-pin bowling. Quite often, we arranged for the alley to be opened especially for us after a gig. Over the course of the tour we got pretty good at it. The authorities were also getting good, or better, at preparing for our arrival:

'Edinburgh police have drawn up plans to cope with crowds expected when the Stones come to town. Organisers are recruiting 20 extra men to augment the Usher Hall's 45 stewards.' SCOTTISH DAILY MAIL, *12 September, 1964*

'The Stones escaped by climbing over a 10-foot high wall. They scaled a ladder and dropped into the empty backyard of the Swan Hotel, where a police van spirited them away.' NORTHERN DAILY MAIL, *15 September, 1964*

'A 60-strong riot squad held back the fans who tried to mount the stage. Several girls fainted.' SHEFFIELD PAPER, *25 September, 1964*

'TIME IS ON MY SIDE'

Recorded
a-side 10 June, 1964
b-side 12 May, 1964
Studios
a-side Chess Studios, Chicago
b-side Regent Sound Studios
Producer
Andrew Oldham
Engineers
Ron Malo and Bill Farley
Release
US Saturday 26 September, 1964
London 45-LON 9708
Composers
a-side Meade
b-side Jagger/Richard
Highest chart position
US No 6

The fourth American single was not released in Britain in the same format. Someone got confused in crediting it to Meade and Norman: the writer was in fact Norman Meade (aka Jerry Ragovoy). Recorded as a b-side by Irma Thomas in early 1964, it was to be the Stones' highest-placed US release until the eighth single.

'It begins with Stu playing organ as though he were in church, then what seems to be a whole chorus crashes in. The song is taken at a very slow pace, but is to me one of the best things the Stones have ever done. Keith takes a great solo. Mick said this is the big moody one, after all the excitement, and the kids go mad.' NME, *November 1964*

Amid all the excitement in Scotland, Andrew got married: 'Student Sheila sent her father, psychoanalyst Dr Sidney Klein, a telegram from Glasgow to tell him she'd married 20-year-old Andrew,' said the *Daily Express*. 'He thought she was abroad. They had been spending two weeks in Scotland, qualifying for a marriage licence.' Andrew said: 'We had to do it this way. Her parents don't like me.'

In Hull ABC, Pathé filmed us miming to 'Around and Around'. It's a good indication of what we and our audience were like live at that time. Imaginatively entitled *Rolling Stones Gather Moss*, it was shown as a six-minute short at cinemas. All in all,

On 16 September, Andrew Oldham married Sheila Klein at a Glasgow registry office.

Out and about in Paris on 20 July

the tour was far less arduous than the last – we only did 32 venues in 37 days this time.

The tour was coming to a conclusion, early in October, when Dawn Malloy, Brian's ex-girlfriend, gave birth to his fifth illegitimate child. Brian would do nothing to help Dawn or their son, so the office had her sign a letter.

'I have received a cheque for £700 from Andrew Loog Oldham Ltd, paid to me by the said company on behalf of Brian Jones, in full settlement of any claims arising, damages and inconveniences caused by me by the birth of my son, and I understand completely that the matter is now closed and that I will make no statement about Brian Jones or the child to any member of the press or public.'

The £700 was deducted from Brian's earnings.

'I had our baby adopted. I've realised that the love which Brian claimed to have for me didn't exist. I'm not really sure if mine did either. It was all a foolish mistake.' DAWN MALLOY, *the Sunday People, July 1969*

With the tour over, Charlie secretly married Shirley Shepherd at Bradford Register Office on 14 October, witnessed by friends Andy and Jeanette Hoogenboom. They celebrated with a champagne lunch at a country inn near Ripon and returned to London by train. He didn't even tell us about it for a few weeks.

Parisian Stones
A few days later we did a TV show in Belgium and then flew to Paris for our first French press conference and another TV show. We had to borrow equipment, as Stu and Spike, who were driving from Brussels, got delayed. Fortunately, we only mimed, as there was no bass I could borrow. We did 'Carol', then our most popular song in France.

We went to a café for a drink. Some young French

Shirley and Charlie married on 14 October.

guys made fun of us; one asked, 'Are you the Supremes?' That was enough for Keith. Before the guy had stopped smiling, Keith was across the table and punched him in the face – fortunately they upped and left.

We rehearsed the following afternoon for our gig at Olympia. Our support act was Vince Taylor, who had decamped from Middlesex to France, where he was treated as a rock messiah. His band included Prince Stanislas Klossowski de Rola, better known as Stash. He was later to be a friend of the band – of Keith and Brian in particular. It was also while we were in Paris that we met Robert Fraser, an art dealer, another who later played a part in our story.

Ready for the States
Back in London, we had a couple of days to get ourselves together for our second US tour. Mick had to shop as the airline had lost luggage containing his favourite clothes on the way home from France. Would the US be better this time?

The Stones found they were more popular in the 'with it' areas of New York and California. The Midwest was a very different place in the 1960s, far less sophisticated and not as aware of fashion and trends.

'Charlie insisted on taking his own drum kit and Brian took his Teardrop Vox guitar. We hired Fender Amps so that we could get closer to our sound. Touring then was a whole lot more do-it-yourself than it is today.' **BILL**

I would have been 14 years old at the time (making me 52 now!). I heard about the concert on KRLA, Dave Hull, the Hullabalooer, I listened constantly hoping to win various contests to meet various British groups. As the Stones came out, everyone stood up on the folding chairs and screamed for the entire concert. It was nearly impossible to hear them (in grown-up hindsight, I know that the sound system was probably inadequate for that type of venue as compared to today), but who cared! Just the chance to catch a glimpse of them up close was why we were there. My parents had come to accept that I was "British invasion crazy" and willingly took us to the concert. However, I did have to pay for the $5 myself from my baby-sitting money.' MARY SNYDER, *fan, 2002*

'Rolling Stones Out Tweedle Beatles.'
LOUISVILLE COURIER JOURNAL,
15th November, 1964

Set list
Songs taken from:
'Tell Me'
'Around and Around'
'Off The Hook'
'Time Is On My Side'
'It's All Over Now'
'I'm All Right'
'Not Fade Away'
'If You Need Me'
'Carol'
'I'm A Kingbee'

And in support
Sacramento
The Righteous Brothers
Keith Allison and the Goodnighters
Jody Miller
Tony Bigg
Long Beach
Dick and Dee Dee
Jimmy Clanton
The Spats
The Vibrants
The Soul Brothers
San Diego
The Misfits
Joel Scott Hill
Invader
Milwaukee
Alan Black
Fort Wayne
Shangri-Las
Dayton
Ivan and the Sabers

North America,
October–November 1964

24 October Academy of Music, New York (matinee and evening)
26 October Memorial Auditorium, Sacramento, California
31 October Swing Auditorium, San Bernardino, California
1 November Civic Auditorium, Long Beach, California (matinee)
   Balboa Park Bowl, San Diego, California (evening)
3 November Public Hall, Cleveland, Ohio
4 November Loews Theatre, Providence, Rhode Island
11 November Milwaukee Auditorium, Milwaukee, Wisconsin
12 November Coliseum, Fort Wayne, Indiana
13 November Wampler's Hara Arena, Dayton, Ohio
14 November Memorial Auditorium, Louisville, Kentucky (two shows)
15 November Arie Crown Theatre, Chicago, Illinois

'My friends and myself dressed up like English schoolgirls and faked the British accent, which my photos depict. We were sooo excited that we forgot our fake British accents within a few minutes! The screaming was strictly "American teenage" dialect.' Mary Snyder, fan

'The old Long Beach Auditorium is no longer there was just exactly that, a wooden-floored large auditorium that had no balconies, just folding chairs on the floor, almost like a local gymnasium. Today there is a large convention center, Seaport Village and the Queen Mary in that very location.' – Mary Snyder

A Q 46
LONG BEACH AUD.
ORCHESTRA $5.00
November 1

NOW... NO. 1 IN ENGLAND
WHY HAVE THOUSANDS OF EUROPEAN TEENAGERS RIOTED?
BECAUSE OF
THE ROLLING STONES
LEAVING ENGLAND TO APPEAR ON THE ED SULLIVAN SHOW IN NEW YORK, OCTOBER 25. DIRECT TO SACRAMENTO FROM ED SULLIVAN SHOW FOR THEIR FIRST WEST COAST APPEARANCE THIS TOUR...TO BE IN A SHOW AT...
The Memorial Auditorium
Sacramento, California, U.S.A.
MONDAY, OCTOBER 26, 1964 – 8 P.M.
Tickets available at Tower Record North and on Broadway College 46 Shop, Southgate

KRLA tell Mi pull out SHIRT

Good Around The Outside

ACADEMY OF MUSIC
126 EAST 14th ST. N.Y.C.
Saturday Matinee
SID BERNSTEIN Presents
"THE ROLLING STONES"
IN CONCERT
ORCHESTRA
OCT. 24
2:00 P.M.
1964
EST. PRICE $6.61
FED. TAX .56
CITY TAX .33
TOTAL $7.50

New York – So Good We Went There Twice

We arrived at JFK at 1.50pm on 23 October and were greeted by 500 fans yelling 'We want the Stones'. DJ Ed Rudy tried to do a live commentary on our return to the States, but was almost drowned out by the screaming of our admirers.

'Believe it or not, that is the sound of an invasion. The most controversial of invading British balladeers is a quintet called the Rolling Stones. And while they may not gather any moss, they certainly are raking in a lot of good, green American money, gathering hundreds of thousands of teenage fans in the process. The Stones are different, not only from the American groups, but even very different from their own countrymen. They are not really very neat in appearance, and one of them has been known to appear on-stage in grease-stained slacks and another customarily sings in a sweatshirt.' ED RUDY

AFTER BEING INTERVIEWED and appearing on Ed Rudy's radio show, we were put in Cadillacs to go to the Hotel Astor. As usual, the lobby was a sea of fans. The police and security guards eventually got us in. This time we had the entire seventh floor to ourselves, while Andrew and Sheila stayed at an apartment belonging to Bob Crewe, the producer of the Four Seasons, who were huge in the 1960s.

Having settled in, we did more press conferences and met English DJ Scott Ross, who worked at WBIC Radio, New York. He became a firm friend of the band. We rehearsed for *The Ed Sullivan Show*. Getting into the studio was a

headache; we all felt quite at home.

Birthday Bill
The next day was my 28th birthday (officially my 23rd) and we spent the morning rehearsing. We were guests on Murray The K's radio programme and taped six songs for *Clay Cole's TV Show*. That just left one further show at the Academy of Music on Broadway, to which another performance was added due to incredible demand.

'It was a totally wild concert,' said Allen Jones in the book *Blinds and Shutters*. 'People were throwing all these objects onto the stage and then the management came on and said, "Hold everything, stop. That's it. Any more jelly beans and we stop the show." Then they wheeled on these huge arc lights, turned them on the audience and left them switched on for the rest of the concert.'

We spent 25 October in rehearsal, yet again, and played 'Around And Around' on the Sullivan programme, returning after 20 minutes to perform our new US single, 'Time Is On My Side'.

'Ed told us that it was the wildest, most enthusiastic audience he'd seen any artiste get in the history of his show,' Mick said. 'We got a message from him a few days later, saying, "Received hundreds of letters from parents complaining about you, but thousands from teenagers saying how much they enjoyed your performance."'

The Stones on The Ed Sullivan Show

In the *Toronto Globe and Mail* that December, Dennis Braithwaite told a different story: 'Ed Sullivan wrote to say that he agreed with my description of the Stones as a grubby lot, and to pledge, "So help me, the untidy Stones will never again darken our portals."'

Released on Bill's 28th birthday and timed to coincide with the band's second US tour, *12 x 5* was only released in America, an expanded rendering of the UK-only EP, *5 x 5*. Two of the tracks, including a new Mick and Keith song, 'Grown Up Wrong', were recorded less than a month earlier. Without doubt, the standout tracks are those recorded in Chicago.

'This is the new Rolling Stones album, and it's the best they've ever done (except for the one they're about to make).'
ANDREW OLDHAM, *in 12 x 5 sleeve notes*

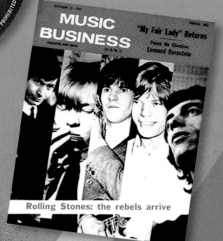

Rolling Stones: the rebels arrive

'Unlike many of the original material-based groups, the Stones developed slowly as songwriters. This album, which was pretty much a comedown from the first, presented some particularly bad material, amid fine original and traditional blues.'
JOHN LANDAU, *Crawdaddy magazine, May 1967*

Around in Germany

A few weeks later, the Stones' first album came out in West Germany. Entitled *Around And Around*, it contained seven of the tracks on *12 x 5*, plus singles and EP tracks. On side one were the songs 'Around And Around', 'Good Times, Bad Times', 'It's All Over Now', 'Empty Heart', 'Confessin' The Blues' and 'Not Fade Away'. On the other side German fans could hear 'Bye, Bye Johnny', 'You Better Move On', 'I Wanna Be Your Man', '2120 South Michigan Avenue', 'If You Need Me' and 'Poison Ivy'.

Side one
1. 'Around and Around'
   Berry
2. 'Confessin' The Blues'
   McShann/Brown
3. 'Empty Heart'
   Nanker/Phelge
4. 'Time Is On My Side'
   Meade
5. 'Good Times Bad Times'
   Jagger/Richards
6. 'It's All Over Now'
   B and S Womack

Side two
1. '2120 South Michigan Avenue' Nanker/Phelge
2. 'Under The Boardwalk'
   Resnick/Young
3. 'Congratulations'
   Jagger/Richards
4. 'Grown Up Wrong'
   Jagger/Richards
5. 'If You Need Me'
   Pickett/Bateman/
   Sanders
6. 'Susie Q' Broadwater/
   Lewis/Hawkins

Recorded
Side 1: 1, 2, 3
(11 June, 1964), 4 (10 June, 1964), 5 (25 February, 1964), 6 (10 June, 1964) Side 2: 1 (11 June, 1964), 2 (2 September, 1964), 3 (12 May, 1964), 4 (28–29 September, 1964), 5 (11 June, 1964), 6 (28–29 September, 1964)

Studios
Side 1: 1, 2, 3, 4, 6 (Chess Studios, Chicago), 5 (Regent Sound Studios, London) Side 2: 2, 3, 4, 6 (Regent Sound), 1, 5 (Chess Studios)

Producer
Andrew Loog Oldham for Impact Sound

Engineers
Bill Farley at Regent Sound
Ron Malo at Chess Studios

Cover photography
David Bailey

US release
Saturday 24 October, 1964
London LL 3402

Highest chart position (time on chart)
Billboard US No 3
(20 weeks)

Do Your Thing

From New York we flew cross-country to Sacramento, California, for our second gig. We liked playing California: the audiences there loved us.

THE SECOND GIG of the tour was in Sacramento on 26 October. This was another good show from our point of view, with 4,500 of our most enthusiastic fans. At one point the promoter threatened to stop the performance. From Sacramento we flew to LA where we had an evening off. Mick and Keith went to see Etta James, while I went out with Joey Paige and Marshall Leib. The next day we were off to Santa Monica to appear in a film. When we got to the Civic Auditorium, we saw Jack Nitzsche conducting the band that was backing all the other acts. It was a great

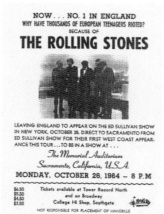

NOW... NO. 1 IN ENGLAND
WHY HAVE THOUSANDS OF EUROPEAN TEENAGERS RIOTED?
BECAUSE OF

THE ROLLING STONES

LEAVING ENGLAND TO APPEAR ON THE ED SULLIVAN SHOW IN NEW YORK, OCTOBER 25. DIRECT TO SACRAMENTO FROM ED SULLIVAN SHOW FOR THEIR FIRST WEST COAST APPEARANCE THIS TOUR... TO BE IN A SHOW AT...

The Memorial Auditorium
Sacramento, California, U.S.A.
MONDAY, OCTOBER 26, 1964 – 8 P.M

$6.50
$5.50   Tickets available at Tower Record North
$4.50   and on Broadway
$3.50   College Hi Shop, Southgate

NOT RESPONSIBLE FOR PLACEMENT OF HANDBILLS

'I'm gonna make the Rolling Stones wish they'd never come to America.'
JAMES BROWN

group that included Leon Russell (piano), Sonny Bono (percussion), Nino Tempo (sax) and Glen Campbell (guitar). We sat around watching the other acts perform, but only Diana Ross and the Supremes came over and introduced themselves.

Later in the afternoon, we heard that James Brown wanted to close the show, but the powers that be insisted we do the honours. James Brown

'People love you because of what you do on stage, so just go out there and do it and forget about James Brown. Go do your thing – that's what I do.' MARVIN GAYE

vowed that he was going to 'make the Rolling Stones wish they'd never come to America.' The next day we were back at the venue watching all the other acts perform. We sat backstage and witnessed an incredible set from James Brown and his Famous Flames, during which all the acts were going crazy, as were the audience out front. It made us very nervous, knowing that we had to follow him. We went to the dressing room to get ready, where Chuck Berry and Marvin Gaye reassured and encouraged us.

Get on up

We got a fantastic reception from the 5,000 fans as we walked on the stage, just us with our two guitars, bass and drums. We played 'Around and Around', 'Off The Hook', 'Time Is On My Side', 'It's All Over Now' and

Teens international
The Stones played TAMI (Teen Age Music International), a show compered by surfers, Jan and Dean, held on 28 October.

'I'm All Right'. The crowd loved it and then we, along with all the other performers, did a version of 'I'm All Right'/'Get Together' with Jack Nitzsche's band. As we walked off the stage, James Brown walked up to us and shook our hands, saying how he loved our performance. From then on we became good friends and often met up on tour.

'They're tough, kinda uncompromising, no pandering to an audience. They just get on with the job. The Stones are rough, musically, sort of musical gangsters and that's a compliment.' DENNIS WILSON, the Beach Boys, January 1965

'Unless someone teaches guitar chords to chimpanzees, the visual ultimate has been reached in the Stones.' MICHAEL DREW, *Milwaukee Journal*

On Saturday 30 October, we went shopping again at Beau Gentry, on Hollywood's North Vine Street, where I bought a jacket. Later that day, we went to a party at Phil Everly's house. By this time, the Stones' American Fan Club had a membership of 80,000, even though we hadn't had a major hit there. We also had our own fan club in California, where we were undoubtedly more popular than anywhere else. Our shows at San Bernardino, and at Long Beach and San Diego (on the same day) were great.

Recording the LA way

The following day, we were back in Los Angeles to record at RCA studios in Hollywood, a very different experience from working at Chess.

'The atmosphere and studio, plus the fact that we knew we had good material, made the session a good one,' said Keith on 14 November. 'We didn't think it would work out at first, as the studio is so gigantic we were terrified to use it. Then Andrew hit on the idea of putting us in one corner, shutting off the main lights and just using a spotlight, to make it more cosy. The control room was also in darkness. A bit mad, but it did the trick.' We worked with Dave Hassinger as engineer and Jack Nitzsche played keyboards on some tracks.

On 3 November we flew to Cleveland, where the mayor said that our performance was immoral and no teenagers should see us. It was a poorly-attended gig, in part because of the mayor's comments, but also because of the presidential election – Lyndon B Johnson was re-elected that night. We played Providence, Rhode Island, the

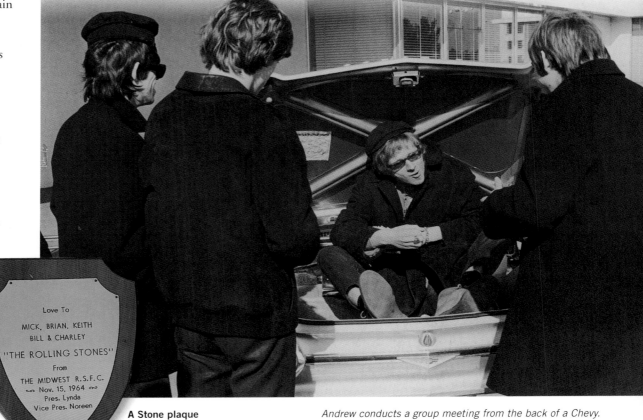

Andrew conducts a group meeting from the back of a Chevy.

A Stone plaque
The *Milwaukee Journal* thought the Stones were chimps, but the band's American fan club loved them – even if they spelt Charlie's name wrong.

Love To
MICK, BRIAN, KEITH
BILL & CHARLEY
"THE ROLLING STONES"
From
THE MIDWEST R.S.F.C.
Nov. 15, 1964
Pres. Lynda
Vice Pres. Noreen

Andrew Oldham: 'The time they use aftershave is the time they'll slip.' November, 1964

night after, before a few days off in New York. Shortly afterwards we flew to Chicago to record at Chess again with Ron Malo.

On 10 November, the day before we were to play in Milwaukee, Brian phoned Mike Dorsey at 7am to say he was feeling ill. Mike called the house doctor who insisted Brian went to Chicago's Pasavant Hospital; he had a high temperature, bronchitis and was suffering from extreme exhaustion – the first one of us to really show the strain. Brian's constitution was undoubtedly the weakest.

Later that day I bumped into Les Paul, the brilliant guitarist whose record I had bought 11 years earlier to play on my first record player. I spent hours talking with him. We played Milwaukee without Brian and it was a fairly small crowd. The Mid-West had really not cottoned onto us as yet.

For the next three gigs, we were without Brian. The audiences were wild and I'm sure some of them didn't notice Brian was not there

as Keith worked extra hard to make up for his absence. By the time we played Chicago on 15 November, our last night of the tour, Brian was back and feeling much better. The following day, he, Mick and Charlie flew home while Keith and I stayed on in New York for an extra two days. We flew home with Andrew and a puppy that a fan had given Keith.

The smart band
Musician and producer Jack Nitzsche: 'They were the first rock'n'roll band I met that were intelligent. They could all talk, which was the most impressive thing about them. There was no guidance at all on those records and very little need for it. This

was the first time a band got together and just played. They changed my whole idea of recording. Nobody had the big ego thing about keeping a song a certain way. That changed me. That was the first really free feeling I had in the studio.'

'LITTLE RED ROOSTER'

Recorded
2 September, 1964
Studio
Regent Sound Studios
Producer
Andrew Oldham
Engineer
Bill Farley
Release
UK Friday 13 November, 1964
Decca F 12014
Composers
a-side Dixon
b-side Nanker/Phelge
Highest chart position
UK No 1
Personnel
Charlie: drums
Bill: bass
Keith: guitar
Brian: slide guitar and harmonica
Mick: lead vocals

Howlin' Wolf

The fifth UK single became the Stones' second British chart topper, despite the fact it was a blues song and released on Friday 13 November. It's a classic written by Willie Dixon and first recorded by Stones influence Howlin' Wolf for the Chess label in 1961. The Wolf's recording features the brilliant Hubert Sumlin playing the classic slide guitar riff. For the Stones, Brian plays excellent slide. Play both versions back to back – they're a mirror. The Wolf howls while Mick purrs... it's what the blues are about: S E X.

London Records passed on releasing 'Rooster' in America, which displeased the band. With its blatant sexual undertones, London probably felt there was every chance that American radio would have banned it.

'People say "Little Red Rooster" is too slow. I don't see why we should have to conform to any pattern. We thought just for a change, we'd do a nice, straight blues on a single. What's wrong with that? It's suitable for dancing. It just depends who you're dancing with. Charlie's drumming makes it good for dancing.'
MICK, *Melody Maker, 28 November*

'There is one outstanding crackeroo, the much-hailed and long-awaited "Little Red Rooster". This is the best all-round single to come from the Stones.'
POP WEEKLY MAGAZINE, *14 November, 1964*

Dave Thompson was at the session on 2 September. Known by the band as 'Scottish Dave', he had met them when they toured in Scotland. He moved to London and ended up living in Brian's flat.

'I did some lyrics for "Off The Hook", like, "Phone disconnected 'cause she couldn't pay the bill," and Bill said, "Why not make it unpaid bill?"'
DAVE THOMPSON

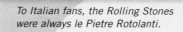

THE ROLLING STONES

F 12014

little red rooster

off the hook

LE PIETRE ROTOLANTI

DECCA

To Italian fans, the Rolling Stones were always le Pietre Rotolanti.

Due to an argument with the BBC about performances booked by Eric that Andrew did not want to honour, the Stones did not appear on *Top Of The Pops* when the record was at UK No 1. 'The Stones' "Little Red Rooster" was UK No 1 in *Record Mirror*,' reported the paper on 12 December, 1964. 'The record was not played, nor did the Stones appear. Readers hit out with, "I think this is a direct snub to the Stones and their fans." Another said: "Fans want an explanation, an apology and rolling BBC-type heads. Fast!"'

'When people get to this stage in a career, they can record the national anthem and still reach the Top 10.' COMBO, *November 1964*

'If it wasn't the Stones, I wouldn't give it much hope, because it's not all that commercial.' NEW MUSICAL EXPRESS, *13 November, 1964*

Recording Little Red Rooster

Time Out

When I got back from the States I discovered it was my turn to have been burgled. My mum and dad told me about it on the phone, but there is still nothing to prepare you for the actual mess. Diane and Stephen were away in South Africa visiting her relatives and it took me all day to clean up.

Centrepiece from Rolling Stones Monthly *magazine, December 1964*

AFTER I PICKED THEM up from the airport early on the Friday morning, I returned to London for our *Ready Steady Go!* appearance.

Shortly after we finished the show, Keith collapsed. He quickly recovered but told us that he hadn't really slept for five nights – the beginning of a habit. We then had to drive out to Wembley to play the Glad Rag Ball along with the Animals, Long John Baldry and Humphrey Lyttelton. It was here that Charlie's wedding came to light. A reporter from the *Daily Express* asked Charlie if he and Shirley were married. 'I emphatically deny I am married,' replied Charlie. 'It would do a great deal of harm to my career, if the story got around.'

But the truth came out and Shirley admitted: 'We have wanted to marry for about a year, and just didn't dare. The months went on and we decided we could not live separately any longer. I'm terribly happy being Charlie's wife. It's just wonderful. I really don't know what it's like being married to a Stone yet. We have only spent five days together in all and then we couldn't be seen out together. My parents like him an awful lot. I intend to finish my college course and, in about 18 months time, I may teach. It's all a bit up in the air at the moment.' Charlie said he hadn't dare tell us as he thought we'd be angry.

Time off

We didn't play any gigs for the rest of November. We

| Heart Of Stone |
| The Rolling Stones |
| What A Shame |

'HEART OF STONE'

The Stones' fifth US single was also their first issued on either side of the Atlantic with original numbers by Mick and Keith on both sides.

'We wrote several originals, including a thing called "What A Shame". It wasn't quite the same atmosphere [at Chess] this time, because it was a Sunday, and nobody was about. Sunday in Chicago is like Sunday in Scotland – dead.'
MICK, *MELODY MAKER, 28 November, 1964*

Recorded
a-side 2 November, 1964
b-side 8 November, 1964
Studios
a-side RCA Studios
b-side Chess Studios
Producer
Andrew Oldham
Engineers
a-side Dave Hassinger at RCA
b-side Ron Malo at Chess
Release
US Saturday 19 December, 1964
London 45-LON 9725
Composers
Jagger/Richard
Highest chart position
US No 19
Personnel
Stu: piano on a-side

HEART OF STONE
(Richard; Jagger)
THE ROLLING STONES

Mick Jagger had Dutch fans for tea.

He and Linda were having real problems and Brian was also taking all sorts of amphetamines, drinking more and had taken up smoking marijuana. Brian's illness in America was the result of his lack of self-control coupled with his less-than-strong constitution.

'He kept trying to talk me out of all the things he was doing that he thought were bad. But he thought they were good for him. He needed them just to cope.' LINDA LAWRENCE

The situation was serious enough for Brian to have to issue a denial that he was quitting the band: 'I'm not on my last legs through ill-health and I'm not leaving the Stones,' he commented in *Disc* on 12 December. 'I felt ill during our American tour, and I wasn't enjoying very good health when we arrived back in Britain. That's why I had to take things easy for a while.'

The couple's relationship couldn't withstand Brian's excesses but the break up was still a tragedy for Brian. People have said that Linda was the love of Brian's life and I think it was true. She constantly gave to Brian and never asked for anything in return. I think Brian knew that he was hurting Linda and I think he knew that he couldn't control himself. He was wild, he wanted more and he knew that if

Santa calling at hospital

Mr. Jim Green, licensee of the Railway Tavern, Lower Sydenham, his wife May and a group of customers are playing Father Christmas to patients in the Children's Hospital, Sydenham, on Sunday.

They will take along parcels of sweets for the children as well as several large toys for the hospital's permanent toy chest.

The sweets and toys were bought with money from a pile of pennies at the Railway Tavern which customers built up for eight months. The pile was knocked down by Bill Wyman, one of the Rolling Stones. It contained more than £38.

A competition to guess how much was in the pile and a competition for a pound note signed by Mr. Wyman brought the total to £54 10s.

Charity night at the pub
Bill visited a Sydenham pub on December 15 to help out a charity appeal for a local hospital. He met some of his older admirers and donated a signed pound note.

he took Linda along with him, he would ultimately harm both of them.

A year to remember
We had played 206 gigs in 1964, often performing twice nightly. We were on TV, radio and often in the studio. We went to America twice, performed in Europe for the first time, had four US singles, two UK No 1s, a UK No 1 album and one that hit US No 11. I expect at this point all five of us were in the same boat financially. Ironically, only Stu and Andrew Oldham owned a car. Inevitably, we all wondered if it could get any better?

did a few TV and radio shows and it made a nice change to get some time to do our own thing. Brian spent about a week in bed, with very bad sinus problems. I managed to work in the studio with my old mates, the Herd, and met with the Cheynes (whose drummer was Mick Fleetwood), with a view to recording. One night I got a call from the Herd to say they were playing at Wallington Public Hall and Jimmy Reed was supporting them. I went over and watched Jimmy. He was brilliant, sat on a chair playing his guitar and singing all those great songs.

December was the quietest month since we had formed. In fact, our only live gig was at the

billmickkeithbriancharlie
GREETINGS
billmickkeithbriancharlie

Fairfield Halls in Croydon on 4 December, a great one for me as it was so close to home. We did do some TV, including the New Year's Eve *Ready Steady Go!* special and a pre-recording for the US TV Show *Shindig* at Shepperton studios. We played 'Heart Of Stone', 'Suzie Q' and 'Little Red Rooster'; the show aired in January and March 1965.

She's gone
Mick and Brian did go to Paris for a few days, but the rest of December was a difficult one for Brian.

'I'm a pretty sensitive sort of person. I always have been. When the Stones are knocked, I feel it personally.'

BRIAN

All aboard
The Stones took the train to their Irish gigs, *clockwise from left*, Mick, Brian and Charlie.

New Year, New Places

THE TOPS WITH YOU

I started 1965 by letting one of our fans see some of the stuff I had collected since we started. I began in order to show my son Stephen that his dad had been in a band. I thought that we would have a couple of years, maybe four at a pinch. Well, we'd had two so far and I had already collected a lot.

O N NEW YEAR'S DAY, an American fan, staying in London, called me at home, and I invited her and her friend around to spend the afternoon with Stephen, Diane and I. Amy Goodman came just a few days before we were due to start an Irish tour: 'He showed us boxes he had kept filled with scrapbooks and clippings,' she said.

The three-date tour began on 5 January in Belfast. We took the train to play Dublin the next day and Cork the following night. Our support acts were the Banshees, the Checkmates, and Twinkle and the Gonks. A young Bob Geldof came to see us in Dublin: 'My sister brought me with her mate, Michelle,' he recalled. 'There was a sort of foyer that the Stones came through and there were kids waiting. I was quite young, but I remember one girl just went ape-shit – really freaked me because I hadn't seen it before. They came in really fast and Brian put his arm around her and said "Come on." Later, the Stones signed a couple of autographs and my sister got hers signed, which we still have. We sneaked in and watched the soundcheck.'

On the drive to Cork, we stopped at a small army surplus shop in a village. Mick, Keith, Charlie and Andrew went inside to look around. The proprietor refused to serve them, and talked about 'having not forgotten Oliver Cromwell'.

'Mick was balancing on the footlights and Andrew said, "Get on with it." Mick or Keith turned round and said "Fuck off". This was exactly what we expected the Stones to be like. Then we got thrown out.' **BOB GELDOF**

They exchanged insults, and walked out, but Andrew peed against the shop front. The owner burst from the shop, and chased them to the cars; he jumped onto the bonnet of the car I was in and

Dear Eric,

We left Los Angeles at 8.0.p.m. on Tuesday, January 19. It is now 6 a.m. on Thursday, January 21. You are currently enjoying Wednesday, January 20, your time now being 10.0 p.m.

It has, as I understand it, always been our policy to work together in a spirit of harmony and understanding—so, together in a spirit of harmony and understanding—so, WHERE IS OUR WEDNESDAY? Your yesterday is our yesterday but, while you sit back in your far-off country and are contented to enjoy your today (Wednesday, January 20), we sit here and ponder our strange transit from Tuesday to Thursday.

I trust you will rectify this matter as early as possible and won't steal another day from us.

Sincerely,
BRIAN.

Brian's puzzle

Brian decided to write to Eric Easton when the Stones rolled over the date line. It was a brilliant letter that showed Brian's wit and intelligence at its sharpest. When the band flew from LA to Australia, they 'lost' a day. Brian didn't mention they'd get the day 'back' when they crossed the line the other way.

started to kick the windscreen wipers off. We left hurriedly but in hysterics.

A day away

Back from Ireland, we played the Commodore Theatre, Hammersmith, on Sunday 10 January. Rolling Stones Ltd promoted these shows.

We appeared with the Quiet Five, Julie Grant, Zoot Money's Big Roll Band, Tony Jackson (ex- Searchers) and the Vibrations, the Original Checkmates and Marianne Faithfull.
Two days after

our second album came out, we left Heathrow to fly to Los Angeles on the first stage of our journey down under. We were going to tour Australia and New Zealand.

Before heading to Australia we had fixed another recording session at RCA in Hollywood with Dave Hassinger: 'We did two Mick and Keith compositions, "The Last Time" and "A Mess Of Fire" (renamed "Play With Fire") and three old blues numbers,' said Andrew at the end of January, 'but I had to go back to Hollywood to do some more work on the tapes before deciding which one to use as the next a-side.'

Dionne Warwick

'The Stones will make a one-week tour of New Zealand in February. Their hair is much longer and twice as shaggy as the Beatles,' the New Zealand *Herald* reported. 'They will be accompanied by American singer Roy Orbison and Dionne Warwick, a Negress.' Bill: 'A "Negress". It is amazing to think just how very different attitudes were, 40 years ago. In the end, however, Dionne didn't come on the tour.'

'I was relieved that my seat in the balcony was close enough to one of the house PA speakers to be able to hear the Stones above the screaming girls.' STEPHEN CARTER, *fan*

That Tuesday, 19 January, we flew to Hawaii and then on to Fiji before landing in Sydney, 18 hours later. It was Thursday in Australia! During the course of the flight we crossed the International Date Line. It gave us all a laugh trying to work out how we 'lost' a day.

'After weeks of breathless anticipation, I have just returned from witnessing yet another historical event in the cultural development of this nation. At 8.27am the Stones raced down the gangway of their aircraft, onto Australian soil. They neither paused nor waved to 2,500 squealing fans. Long, thin legs pumping like pistons, they dashed to the customs shed. A few fans caught a glimpse. The great majority saw nothing. It was over in seconds. One big policeman reflected, "You know, 10 or 15 years ago we'd have lumbered those blokes on a vagrancy charge for impersonating females."' AUSTRALIAN TV TIMES MAGAZINE, *27 January, 1965*

"FOR ROLLING STONES THEY'VE GATHERED AN AWFUL LOT OF MOSS!!"

Good to know that Australia was just like everywhere else. Andrew saw it slightly differently, but then he always did: 'The boys and I were moved as we stood on the steps of the airliner,' he told the *NME* on 29 January, 'which had brought us to this distant land, receiving a tremendous welcome from those warm-hearted and wonderful colonials.'

After a press conference with the usual questions, ('Is it true you don't wash?') we went to the Chevron Hilton hotel in Kings Cross. They had booked us a whole floor. The following day we spent relaxing before our first show that evening at the Manufacturers' Auditorium of the Agricultural Hall.

The Rolling Stones take their first look at Sydney.

Stu played piano on 'Everybody Needs Somebody To Love', 'Down The Road Apiece' and 'What A Shame', and organ on 'Time Is On My Side'. Jack Nitzsche played piano on 'Down Home Girl' and a toy electric piano ('Nitzsche-phone') on 'Pain in My Heart'.

'It's a very fine LP, with the Stones well into their rootsy, true R&B style, with no concessions made to commercialism or the hit parade. There's a fantastic atmosphere to most tracks and this helps the group to sound more live than on any previous record.'
MERSEY BEAT, *16 January, 1965*

The Stones were unusual for a British band in the 1960s in that they recorded much of their material in America. On the second British album, seven of the 12 tracks were recorded in America. It gave the material a different sound.

The band said...

'"You Can't Catch Me" is my favourite. It has a fantastic heavy beat which builds up like a locomotive coming up behind you.' KEITH

'"I Can't Be Satisfied" is my favourite track. I played bottle-neck guitar on it and it has one of the best guitar solos I've ever managed.' BRIAN

'I play six-string bass on "Down Home Girl" and "Pain in My Heart". It gives a fantastic treble effect.' BILL

The Stones loved American music – not that they were unusual in that – but they turned a passion for blues and R&B to their advantage in a way that almost no other British band had done. The sound they got at Chess and RCA set them apart from the rest and it gave them a cachet, especially among more discerning English fans. This was happening at a time when trends in record buying were subtly changing. It was the dawning of the 'Rock Era'.

The Stones in the studio recording their second album.

'I put Mick there deliberately. I didn't want the others to think he was getting special treatment because he was a friend of mine.'
DAVID BAILEY, *sleeve photographer*

Under the influence

'Everybody Needs Somebody To Love'
A Solomon Burke original that made No 58 in the US R&B chart in August 1964.

'Down Home Girl'
A 1964 single by little-known New Orleans recording artist Alvin Robinson.

'You Can't Catch Me'
Chuck Berry's song that Bill saw in the film *Rock Rock Rock* in 1957.

'Time Is On My Side'
The b-side of Irma Thomas' summer 1964 US No 52 hit, 'Anyone Who Knows What Love Is'.

'Down The Road Apiece'
From Chuck Berry's version of this 1940 Western swing classic by way of 1947 and Amos Milburn.

'Under The Boardwalk'
The Drifters made US No 4 and UK No 45 in the summer of 1964 with this classic.

'I Can't Be Satisfied'
A Muddy Waters track from 1948.

'Pain In My Heart'
Otis Redding's third (minor) US hit recorded in 1963 and written by Naomi Neville (a *nom de plume* of Allen Toussaint).

'Susie Q'
Dale Hawkins from Louisiana had a hit with this in 1957 for the Checker label.

Solomon Burke

Irma Thomas

Dale Hawkins

Word art or what?

'Mr Oldham should remember he is recording the Stones, and not his ego,' R Kearsley of Leeds wrote to *Melody Maker* on 6 February. When you read Oldham's sleeve notes you certainly realise that he was on another planet:

'A day in May at Richmond came to the treen, two showbiz genties with ideas plenty for the Stones, Easton and Oldham named they were,' he wrote in the Rolling Stones No 2 sleeve notes. *'The rest is not history so I'll tell you 'bout it. Records followed, so did fame, Beatles wrote a song for them that got to No 10. Tours of the country and fame at large the Stones were here, and we'll be back with you when break commercial is over. (This is the Stones' new disc within. Cast deep in your pockets for loot to buy this disc of groovies and fancy words. If you don't have bread, see that blind man, knock him on the head, steal his wallet and lo and behold you have the loot, if you put in the boot, good, another one sold!) Back to the show, all was on the go, fame was having its toll of sweat and grime of a million dimes, ah! What a lovely war, man, Easton called a meet one day; Stones arrived. "Columbus went to America, so shall we!", so we went, naturally.'*

Fans were quick to respond to Andrew's hype, 'I'm delighted with the record, but amazed at the drivel Andrew Oldham has written on the back,' wrote Broderick Beauchamp to *Record Mirror* on 30 January, 1965. 'All I can say is that people have been locked up for less than this.'

In another letter, this time to *Melody Maker*, R Kearsley of Leeds wrote: 'How far will Andrew Oldham's obsession with Phil Spector take him? The Stones' new LP seems to be a testing ground to discover how many weird sounds he can produce on each track.'

Brian with the Drifters

Yes, a great LP, and well worth delving into your savings—or utilising that Christmas record token.

Side one
1. 'Everybody Needs Somebody To Love'
   Russell/Burke/Wexler
2. 'Down Home Girl'
   Leiber/Butler
3. 'You Can't Catch Me' Berry
4. 'Time Is On My Side' Meade
5. 'What A Shame'
   Jagger/Richards
6. 'Grown Up Wrong'
   Jagger/Richards

Side two
1. 'Down The Road Apiece'
   Raye
2. 'Under The Boardwalk'
   Resnick/Young
3. 'I Can't Be Satisfied'
   Morganfield
4. 'Pain in My Heart' (Neville)
5. 'Off The Hook'
   Jagger/Richards
6. 'Susie Q'
   Broadwater/Lewis/Hawkins

Recorded
Side 1: 1,2 (2 Nov, 1964), 3 (28–29 Sept, 1964), 4,5 (8 Nov, 1964), 6 (28–29 Sept, 1964)
Side 2: 1 (11 Jun, 1964), 2 (2 Sept, 1964), 3 (10 Jun, 1964), 4 (2 Nov, 1964), 5 (2 Sept, 1964), 6 (28–29 Sept, 1964)

Studios
Side 1: 1,2 (RCA, Hollywood), 4,5 (Chess Studios, Chicago), 3,6 (Regent Sound, London)
Side 2: 1,3 (Chess), 2,5,6 (Regent Sound), 4 (RCA)

Producers
Andrew Loog Oldham for Impact Sound

Engineer
Bill Farley (Regent Sound Studios), Ron Malo (Chess Studios), Dave Hassinger (RCA)

Cover photography
David Bailey

Release
UK Friday 15 Jan, 1965
Decca LK 4661

Highest chart position (time on chart)
UK No 1 (37 weeks)

'We're very good friends of the Stones. We like their work and spend a lot of time with them when they're in town. The album's great, but I don't like five-minute numbers.' **JOHN LENNON**

Over 34 shows, the Stones played to around 100,000 people which did wonderful things for their popularity in Australasia and did record sales a lot of good too. Like everywhere else, a generation were waking up to a new era of music, one in which the kids had a lot more sway.

The Pacific, *January–February 1965*
Two shows per venue, except Auckland there were three.

22 January Manufacturers' Auditorium, Agricultural Hall, Sydney Showground, Sydney
23 January Manufacturers' Auditorium, Agricultural Hall, Sydney Showground, Sydney
25 January City Hall, Brisbane
26 January City Hall, Brisbane
27 January Manufacturers' Auditorium, Agricultural Hall, Sydney Showground, Sydney
28 January Palais Theatre, St Kilda, Melbourne
29 January Palais Theatre, St Kilda, Melbourne
30 January Palais Theatre, St Kilda, Melbourne
1 February Theatre Royal, Christchurch (NZ)
2 February Civic Theatre, Invercargill (NZ)
3 February Town Hall, Dunedin (NZ)
6 February Town Hall, Auckland (NZ)
8 February Town Hall, Wellington
10 February Palais Theatre, St Kilda, Melbourne
12 February Centennial Hall, Adelaide
13 February Capital Theatre, Perth

'By the time we toured Australia we had already released nine singles, which certainly helped with our initial popularity.' BILL

'I received a letter from my sister [Eva Jagger] saying, "I solemnly advise you to take earplugs, because after the last concert I saw, my doctor had to treat me for perforated eardrums".' MRS R SCUTTS, *Mick's aunt, 22 January, 1965*

'At Inverell, my home town, grown-ups reckon Mick has the face of a Barwon River cod and a mouth like a barbed-wire gate. They say the Stones are unwashed and horrible. Well, they might be untidy, but there's nothing wrong with that. The kids at school would throw me in the creek if they knew I'd met the Stones. It's the most wonderful night of my life.' PATRICIA LESLEY, *Sydney fan*

HARRY M. MILLER
presents

BIG BEAT '65
★ THE ROLLING STONES   ★ ROY ORBISON
★ THE NEWBEATS
★ RAY COLUMBUS AND THE INVADERS

NEW ZEALAND TOUR - 1965

'Screaming, hysterical girls were trampled underfoot when 3,000 fans of the Stones went berserk today, when the beat group arrived by air at Sydney.' SYDNEY EVENING NEWS, *21 January, 1965*

'Some of them have the appearance of pantomime dames who left the theatre hurriedly without removing their wigs. Others have the delicate, sensitive look of young schoolboys, the morning after a hectic party.' AUSTRALIAN TV TIMES, *on the Stones, 27 January, 1965*

Set list
'Not Fade Away'
'Walking The Dog'
'Under The Boardwalk'
'Little Red Rooster'
   (introduced by Charlie)
'Around and Around'
'Heart Of Stone'
'It's All Right'
'Time Is On My Side'
'It's All Over Now'

Running Order...
Chris Hall and the Torquays
(Sydney only)
Compere Don Linden
The Newbeats
Ray Columbus and the Invaders
Roy Orbison
The Stones
The Flies played in Melbourne
and the Clefs played Adelaide.

In A Land Down Under

'They're Shockers. Ugly looks, ugly speech, ugly manners.'
SYDNEY MORNING HERALD

'They seem as intelligent as any group of youths their age.' BRISBANE PAPER, *25 January, 1965*

'The nine-day tour of New Zealand proved to be much quieter than their rave reception in Australia. Reason may well be that the Conservative government-controlled radio stations feature few pop programmes. Consequently, the Stones sound hasn't saturated New Zealand airwaves as it has in other countries.' JUDY WADE, *NME, 19 February*

'Six bodyguards flanked the Stones, and at the end whisked off their charges while the sound system blared "God Save The Queen". A thin blue line of police repelled boarders from the ground floor.' AUCKLAND HERALD, *8 February, 1965*

'Invercargill is the end of the earth. There are 28 rooms in this hotel, and only two baths between everybody. The last meal you can get is supper, and that finishes at 7pm.' MICK, *NME, 5 February, 1965*

Below left: *Roy Orbison, just before the second show in Sydney*

PAN PACIFIC PROMOTIONS
HARRY M. MILLER *proudly presents*
THE 'BIG BEAT' SHOW OF '65

'The hotel people couldn't understand it when I asked for an electric fire in my bedroom, because it was 90 degrees outside. I have got very thin blood.' KEITH, *NME, 29 January*

'I signed the Stones for A$12,500 a week, for which they had to give up to 13 performances a week, and paid for the accommodation and economy airfares for five Stones and three managers. Over a three-week tour of Australia and New Zealand it added up to an outlay of almost A$100,000, but we grossed about A$250,000 at the box office. Perhaps I was a little mean when I refused to allow them to bring their own amplifiers as excess baggage.' HARRY M MILLER, *promoter*

'Australia is a gas. We didn't think it would be anything like this. We're doing marvellously out here. This is more like a holiday with work, rather than a tour with a few days off.' BRIAN, *Melody Maker, 25 January, 1965*

Laundry Service

Brian was right when he said our tour Down-Under was a gas; it was more like a holiday than working. We were used to a routine of shows night after night when we toured in the UK. Even our American tours were harder than it was in Australia and New Zealand. We played 16 nights in 26 days... and it was summer! Having just left a cold English winter behind made it all seem even better. I took many hours of footage on my new movie camera.

ON THE DAY OF OUR first Sydney show, Brian, Keith and Andrew went boating in Sydney Harbour and got involved with some local lads who tried to capsize their boat.

'The boys shouted, "Go home Stones" and "Look at the white suntans",' reported the *Northern Daily Mail* on January 23. 'The Stones called back, "Come over here and say that", so the boys rowed towards them. As the boats drew close together, both groups started splashing each other with oars. One of the boys dived into the water, grabbed the Stones' boat and started rocking it, trying to turn it over. Brian jumped in to try and do the same to the boy's boat. Within seconds, the other two boys were in the water, rocking the Stones' boat. During a scuffle Brian was pushed under the water, but managed to duck two of his attackers.

'Andrew then told the schoolboys to move off and they swam back to their boat and rowed off. He said later, "The attack was quite unprovoked. We didn't want to fight, but we were forced into it. Luckily, neither Brian nor Keith were hurt." One of the schoolboys, Simon Pockley, commented, "They asked for it. Anyway you couldn't call us Stones fans."'

Exploring Australia

Our reception at the Agricultural Hall at Sydney Showground was great, and pretty much set the tone for all our Australian gigs. The press, as usual, was intent on making us out to be the bad guys. When we got to Brisbane, we stayed at Lennon's

Brian, Andrew and Keith got into a fight with local lads.

Hotel and found that Manfred Mann, the Kinks and the Honeycombs were also staying there, as they were on a rival promoter's tour. Brisbane was great, helped by the fact that a local DJ Bill Gates befriended us. He took us to his house and we sat round his pool. The next day he took the rest of the boys, Andrew and Mike Dorsey for a picnic on the Brisbane River. Keith paddled a surfboard, Charlie just laid around in the sun and the others went water-skiing. I got a girl reporter to drive me up into the hills and then went to a place called Mount Tambourine in Toowoomba; that night we were all a little sunburnt when we played Brisbane's City Hall.

Paul Jones from Manfred Mann and I went with two girls for a drive in the morning. The others went to Surfers' Paradise, but I was still happier away from the water and spent the day sightseeing. On their trip back there was an accident; Andrew braked and Keith hit his head on the windscreen – he was lucky not to have been really hurt.

We returned to Sydney for more shows, playing the Agricultural Hall again on 27 January. We were all anxious to get back to the hotel – Brisbane had taken it out of us – but promoter Harry Miller had organised a party at his home. Mick and Brian had already gone to bed and the rest of us were having a drink at the hotel when a frantic Harry called just before midnight and summoned us.

The Stones top the Australian charts.

None of us wanted to go and Mick was furious. We arrived to find that much of Sydney's polite society were there. Brian made a big effort to be nice, especially to the girls, and the rest of us tried hard to be pleasant, all except Mick, who got a bottle of champagne and sat on the floor in the corner. After a while, we tried to cheer him up, but he would have none of it, telling us to 'fuck off'. Unfortunately he said it a little loudly, at the same time as there was a lull in the conversation.

Everything went even quieter and then people started to make their excuses and leave. We had done little to further Harry's position among Sydney's elite. At least it meant we got to bed early.

Please, Mr Porter

In Melbourne for three days, Brian and I shared a suite and a lounge with a bedroom each. It was in Australia that we started to refer to the girls we picked up on tour as 'laundry'. We had a lot of fun at the John Batman Motor Inn, getting 'laundry' sent up by the porters. We would see girls from our window waiting outside the hotel, ring down to the porter and tell him which ones we wanted.

While we were in Melbourne, Andrew celebrated his 21st birthday. Looking back it's difficult to believe that he was so young when all this was going on, younger even than most of the band. There is little doubt that his age worked to our advantage. He knew the market, he understood what they wanted and was able to mould us into an effective reflection of teenage taste. Two days after Andrew's birthday, we flew to Christchurch where we were to begin the New Zealand leg of our tour.

It proved to be the total opposite of Australia. Not that they didn't appreciate us, but more that everything in New Zealand seemed to be shut – at least it was when we wanted anything. Not only that, but we were booked into the United Service Hotel in Cathedral Square, supposedly the best in town. It was a dump, so lacking in amenities that we had to wash out our own socks and shirts. We complained later that there were too few bathrooms – not that they would have had time to do anything about it. We moved on two days later to Invercargill. It was even more shut. All the other

Flights were a great time to relax and contemplate away from the mayhem of the tour.

'A thousand youngsters waited two hours in the rain at the airport to welcome the Stones in from Australia.' **NEW ZEALAND DAILY EXPRESS,** *1 February, 1965*

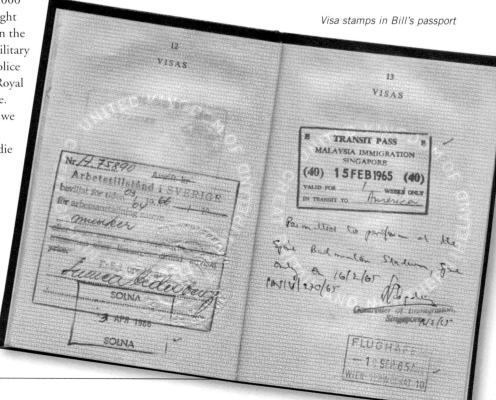

Above: *A plaque presented by the fans in Victoria*
Left: *Bill and Stu sightsee in Rotorua, New Zealand on 7 February.*

cities we went to in New Zealand proved to be similar. Only Auckland had any real nightlife; elsewhere we went to bed early most nights. To cap it all, I got a bad eye infection.

We returned to Australia and did another night of shows in Melbourne, before moving on to Adelaide and Perth in the west of the country.

East meets West?

We left Western Australia and flew to Singapore for our first-ever gigs in the Far East. After Australia, Singapore seemed so exotic. We were welcomed by a large crowd of European, Chinese and Malayan fans in incredibly hot weather. As we walked down the steps of the plane, we were instantly drenched in sweat from the humidity. It was like walking fully-clothed into a shower.

We were driven to the Singapura Hotel and settled in. I took a shower, changed into fresh clothes, walked out onto the balcony and was immediately just as sticky and sweaty as before.

We had lunch at Government House with Deputy High Commissioner Philip Moore and his family. In the beautiful grounds, we had a wonderful meal with dozens of dishes that we thought were very exotic.

'The atmosphere was fantastic. Straight out of Somerset Maugham.' MICK, *Beat Instrumental magazine, April 1965*

'Mick has forgotten to mention the best part of that lunch. There we were, all dressed up to the nines, drinking cocktails and saying the right things for once, when Mick drops a clanger by swearing in the middle of talking to the High Commissioner.' KEITH, *Beat Instrumental Magazine, April 1965*

Getting the opportunity to visit Singapore was fantastic and going to Government House a real bonus. It made us all realise that we were moving up into a different league.

In the evening we did two shows at the Badminton Stadium, watched by 10,000 fans at each. Tight security came in the shape of the Military Police, Navy Police and Women's Royal Air Force Police. After the show we were invited to promoter Freddie Yu's apartment for drinks.

Included with the drinks were about a dozen attractive 'ladies of the night', provided especially for our benefit. There was no doubt about it – life in the East had its attractions.

Hong Kong blues

The next day we flew to Hong Kong for a four-hour layover, just time for a great Chinese lunch and some shopping. Most of us bought Pentax cameras which cost us a fortune in customs duty when we got back to the UK. We returned to the airport and flew to Japan and held a press conference at Tokyo airport. There was a large welcoming committee as well as lots of fans everywhere. Charlie spent most of the time worrying if he would meet up with Shirley who had flown from London to Los Angeles, our destination after Toyko. Mick and Keith were going back into the studio to work on 'The Last Time', while the rest of us did our own thing.

'When we touched down, she was not at the barrier, so he phoned the hotel. She was not there either. That was it. He stormed through the customs barrier without even waiting to be cleared, grabbed a record company executive by the scruff of his jacket and whisked him over to the nearest taxi. "Where's Shirl?" he panted. "We've booked her into another hotel," said the executive. Charlie rushed him into the taxi and off they sped.' STU

Visa stamps in Bill's passport

'The crowd at the airport was one of the biggest ever to have welcomed any entertainers to Singapore.' STRAITS TIMES,

17 February, 1965

STEREO ELECTRONICALLY RE-PROCESSED PS 420 LONDON

THE ROLLING STONES, NOW!

Under the influence

All the covers, except 'Oh Baby (We Got A Good Thing Goin')', had already been released by the band. 'Oh Baby' was written by Barbara Lynn Ozen and released on the Jamie label, simply as Barbara Lynn. It peaked at US No 69 on the Hot 100 in the summer of 1964.

The sleeve notes on *The Rolling Stones, Now!* were the same as *Rolling Stones No 2* in the UK. They contained the immortal Oldham words, 'Cast deep in your pockets for loot to buy this disc of groovies and fancy words. If you don't have bread, see that blind man, knock him on the head, steal his wallet and lo and behold you have the loot.' A few days after the band returned home from Australia, the newspapers cottoned on to Andrew's advice.

"The stuff about the blind man has nothing to do with us. We didn't write it. The first we knew about it was when we saw it on the record sleeve.' MICK

'Protest Over "Rob Blind" Advice On Rolling Stones Disc.' DAILY EXPRESS

'You can see a lot of sicker things on TV. I'm sorry if the blind people are upset, but it's not as if it is the only sick joke in the world.' KEITH

As the Australian tour finished, the third American album was released. It featured seven tracks from the band's second UK album, the other five were a mix that included 'Little Red Rooster', not released as a single in the USA.

The version of 'Everybody Needs Somebody To Love' that appears on the album is in fact a studio run-through that was used by mistake. It is somewhat faster than the other version and has some harmony vocals. Lulu and the Luvvers released a version of 'Surprise Surprise' in April 1965 that failed to chart.

'Another winning package from the hot British group, as they offer a programme of blues, barrelhouse, boogie and country-oriented material.' BILLBOARD magazine, 13 February, 1965

POP SPOTLIGHT

THE ROLLING STONES, NOW!
London LL 3420 (M); PS 420 (S)
Another winning package from the hot British group as they offer a program of blues, barrel house, boogie and country-oriented material. They perform the material with authority and feeling as witnessed in "Down the Road Apiece," "You Can't Catch Me" and the Bo Diddley Sound in "Mona." "Oh, Baby" sounds like a hot single. Their hit single "Heart of Stone" is included.

'Stones "Rob A Blind Man" Cover Starts Row' DAILY SKETCH

'I am told that this inscription was intended to be humorous, but I am afraid this jargon does not make sense to me.' SIR EDWARD LEWIS, *Chairman of Decca records*

'Keith's performance is enough to make him the best recorded hard rock lead outside of Berry himself.' JOHN LANDAU, *Crawdaddy magazine, 1967*

LONDON STEREOPHONIC
PS 420
Side 1
THE ROLLING STONES NOW

1. EVERYBODY NEEDS SOMEBODY TO LOVE (Russell, Burke, Wexler)
2. DOWN HOME GIRL (Leiber, Butler)
3. YOU CAN'T CATCH ME (Berry)
4. HEART OF STONE (Jagger, Richards)
5. WHAT A SHAME (Jagger, Richards)
6. MONA (I NEED YOU BABY) (McDaniels)

THE ROLLING STONES
Produced by Andrew Loog Oldham for Impact Sound
(ZAL 6691)
Made In U.S.A.

Side one
1. 'Everybody Needs Somebody to Love' Russell/Burke/Wexler
2. 'Down Home Girl' Leiber/Butler
3. 'You Can't Catch Me' Berry
4. 'Heart of Stone' Jagger/Richards
5. 'What A Shame' Jagger/Richards
6. 'Mona (I Need You Baby)' McDaniel

Side two
1. 'Down The Road Apiece' Raye
2. 'Off The Hook' Jagger/Richards
3. 'Pain in My Heart' Neville
4. 'Oh Baby (We Got A Good Thing Goin')' Ozen
5. 'Little Red Rooster' Dixon
6. 'Surprise, Surprise' Jagger/Richards

Recorded
Side 1: 1, 2, 4 (2 November, 1964), 3 (29 September, 1964), 5 (8 November, 1964), 6 (3 January, 1964)
Side 2: 1 (11 June, 1964), 2, 5 (2 September, 1964), 3, 4 (2 November, 1964), 6 (29 September, 1964)

Studios
Side 1: 1, 2, 4 (RCA, Hollywood), 3, 6 (Regent Sound, London), 5 (Chess Studios, Chicago)
Side 2: 1 (Chess), 2, 5, 6 (Regent Sound), 3, 4 (RCA)

Producer
Andrew Loog Oldham for Impact Sound

Engineers
Bill Farley at Regent
Ron Malo at Chess
Dave Hassinger at RCA

Cover photography
David Bailey

Release
US Saturday 13 February, 1965
London PS.420 stereo/LL 3420 mono

Highest chart position (time on chart)
US No 5 (29 weeks)

Cathy McGowan subjects Mick to interrogation.

'Super Answer, Mick!'

We arrived in Los Angeles early in the morning of 18 February. Charlie and Shirley left almost immediately to fly to Miami to stay with friends. Brian and I left soon after to return to London. Mick, Keith and Andrew went to RCA studios to redo the vocals on 'The Last Time', which we had decided to release as our next single. Mick flew home the following day.

'Hollywood is quite a pleasant town, very picturesque. But it houses a terrible lot of phonies. Even the waitresses want to become film stars. If you mix with the right people, however, you'll have a great time. I like the new single a lot. It's far more commercial than "Little Red Rooster". We're all satisfied with it.' MICK, *NME, 26 February, 1965*

THE EVENING THAT MICK got home, he went to the Ad Lib Club and met up with the Beatles. Keith and Andrew were flying from New York to Paris for a couple of days. After having all week to recover, we had a date to appear on *Ready Steady Go!* on Friday 26 February, the day the new single was released. We had rehearsals from 11am onwards and then taped the show that went out that evening. We mimed to 'Play With Fire' and Cathy McGowan interviewed Mick. She kicked off by asking him, 'How did you enjoy the tour?'

'Very much, actually.'

'You know when you're going to come on, we get hundreds of letters from girls, asking me if I'd give them to you, and the kind of things they want to know is, how many times *do* you wash your hair?'

'About twice a week.'

'And who cuts it for you?'

'Usually Keith, but sometimes other people.'

'And who cuts Keith's?'

'Keith cuts his with a mirror.'

'And mums write in to me and say, how many times do they take a bath?'

'If it's a hot country, every day.'

'That's a super answer, Mick! Do you think if you got married, it would affect you as a person, and your popularity?'

'It might do. I only fancy unmarried people, so why should anyone fancy a married me?'

'That's quite true! Anyway, let's hear the a-side of the new record.'

We then mimed to 'The Last Time'. Keith Fordyce said, 'Let's round off with a great number from the Stones, called "Everybody Needs Somebody To Love"'. We played it live, during which Mick got pulled over by fans; we continued as the show faded out.

Just writing about Mick's interview brings back memories of how good a show *Ready Steady Go!* was and what a bad interviewer Cathy was. She always put forward the sort of questions that the audience wanted to ask. Cathy was a fan herself and her technique was totally based on that simple idea.

With 'The Last Time' in the shops, we were busy with promotional duties, wherever we could get a plug. We did the Eamonn Andrews TV show, Radio's *Top Gear* with Brian Matthew and *Pop Inn,* and, the following Thursday, *Top of The Pops.*

MICK JAGGER LIPS Order now !

Be in with the in-crowd, order now, new self adhesive, easy stick-on Mick Jagger lips, fab gear, Showbiz, yeh, yeh, rave of the week. Medium, large, small available.

Full details from your local lip dealer!

P.S.—Group singers! These lips help you get that true R. & B. feel.

No self-respecting Stones fan would be without a pair of their own Jagger lips.

'THE LAST TIME'

The sixth UK single was the third UK No 1 in a row and the first Mick and Keith UK a-side. It was the band's sixth US single, released there two weeks after it came out in the UK.

But, strictly speaking, it wasn't written by Mick and Keith. They based it on a 1955 record on the Vee Jay label by the Staple Singers called 'This May Be The Last Time'. On the Staples Singers' recording, it is listed as traditional, arranged Staples.

'Play With Fire' features only Mick, Keith, Phil Spector (acoustic guitar) and Jack Nitzsche (guitar and harpsichord). Everyone was so tired at the session and a number of different versions were recorded. Chrissie Shrimpton probably delivered the wrong master tape to Decca for them to release.

In 1968, *Rolling Stone* asked Mick about 'Play With Fire': 'There are lines about getting your kicks in Knightsbridge and Stepney, and a rich girl whose father's away, and there is a suggestion that the guy in the song is having an affair not only with the daughter, but with the mother?'

'Ah, the imagination of teenagers!' replied Mick. 'Well, one always wants to have an affair with one's mother. I mean, it's a turn on.'

Recorded
18 January, 1965
(a-side vocals re-recorded 18 February)
Studio
RCA Hollywood
Producer
Andrew Loog Oldham for Impact Sound
Engineer
Dave Hassinger
Release
UK Friday 26 February, 1965
Decca F 12104
US Saturday 13 March, 1965
London 45 9741
Composers
a-side Jagger/Richard
b-side Nanker/Phelge
Highest chart position
UK No 1, for three weeks
US No 9

'"Play With Fire" remains as an extremely underrated and atmospheric social cameo of life on the King's Road in the mid-1960s.'
ROY CARR, *Rolling Stone magazine, October 1968*

'The big difference is that our version was faster and Mick sang it as a love song, whereas Pop Staples was singing to God. I have no idea where Keith or Mick heard the song; it's not the sort of thing that got played on the radio. I think they may have bought a Staples Singers' album on one of our many record-buying trips while touring in America.' BILL

'This must give the Stones a bumper hit. It's a good Stones track, beefy, beaty and instant foot-tapping material. You can remember the tune after one spin.'
RECORD MIRROR, *26 February, 1965*

'A tremendously gutsy sound with a storming, thumping beat. The strident, vibrant rhythm envelops Mick's forceful vocal, while the melody is repetitive to the point of hypnosis... In complete contrast, Mick sings the wistful lyric of "Play With Fire" with an insidious and compelling backing.'
DEREK JOHNSON, *NME, 26 February, 1965*

'We wrote "The Last Time" when we had a few weeks off. Mick and I played around with it for days because we weren't happy with the first title we thought up, which was "The Last Time".'
KEITH, *Beat Instrumental, April, 1965*

According to the Italian sheet music, it could be 'The First Time', not the last.

65
March
December

Travellin'
Band

The Stones arrive at JFK on 27 October, 1965,
to begin their fourth US tour.

The United Kingdom, *March 1965*

Glyn Johns, using a mobile recording unit hired by Andrew Oldham, recorded the first three dates.

5 March Regal Theatre, Edmonton, London
6 March Empire Theatre, Liverpool, Lancashire
7 March Palace Theatre, Manchester, Lancashire
8 March Futurist Theatre, Scarborough, Yorkshire
9 March Odeon Theatre, Sunderland, County Durham
10 March ABC Theatre, Huddersfield, Yorkshire
11 March City Hall, Sheffield, Yorkshire
12 March Trocadero Theatre, Leicester, Leicestershire
13 March Granada Theatre, Rugby, Northamptonshire
14 March Odeon Theatre, Rochester, Kent
15 March Odeon Theatre, Guildford, Surrey
16 March Granada Theatre, Greenford, Middlesex
17 March Odeon Theatre, Southend-on-Sea, Essex
18 March ABC Theatre, Romford, Essex

The fifth UK package tour was an intense two-week, two-shows-a-night affair. It featured some of the usual package suspects along with American all-girl group, Goldie and the Gingerbreads, and Manchester's finest, the Hollies.

'In Edmonton, Charlie was brought to the mic by Mick to introduce "Little Red Rooster". His opening words were lost in the screams of the crowd. Later, in the dressing room, we asked him what he had said: "I thought about it for a long time and then I eventually decided to say 'Hello Edmonton'. I shall obviously have to rehearse something more punchy".' BILL

'At Edmonton, the Hammond organ of the Gingerbreads broke down and I helped out, playing bass guitar in the wings of the stage so the audience didn't see me.' BILL

Set list
Songs taken from:
'Everybody Needs Somebody To Love'
'Pain In My Heart'
'Down The Road Apiece'
'Time Is On My Side'
'I'm Alright'
'Little Red Rooster'
'Route 66'
'The Last Time'
'I'm Moving On'

Running order
Compere: Johnny Ball

The Konrads
Dave Berry and the Cruisers
The Hollies
Interval
The Original Checkmates
Goldie and the Gingerbreads
The Rolling Stones

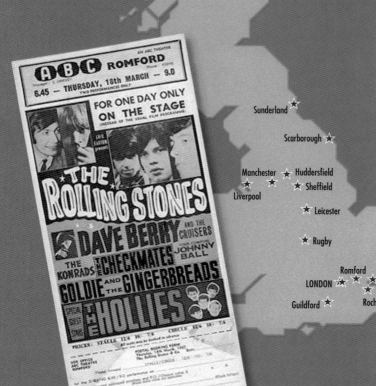

'This tour is pretty mad and it's doing ridiculous business. Fans have got a new thing going – the suicide wish. Girls have started jumping out of the balconies now.' **KEITH,** *Melody Maker, 13 March, 1965*

'The show was a tremendous success. After the show, the Stones left as "God Save The Queen" was played.' CHARLES FIELD, *general manager, Rugby Granada, 13 March, 1965*

'Modern youth, the Stones and such, are something one has to live with and understand.' DR RAMSEY, *Archbishop of Canterbury, 12 March, 1965*

Hollie-Days
1965

Take three girls

Three Manchester girls, Pam Johnson (14), Pam McClore (15), and Kathy Healey (17), stayed outside the band's hotel all night before the Palace Theatre gig, and the day and night after too. They then hitched 125 miles in trucks to Scarborough on 8 March, eating just a bar of chocolate between them. They were at the band's hotel in Scotch Corner the following day.

Bill: 'We found the three girls asleep in a telephone box outside the hotel. Mick, Brian and I spent 30 minutes on the hotel steps, lecturing them and trying to persuade them to return home. We sent them off with money for a meal and promised that if they returned home, we would arrange a meeting later with all of us. They were still there later that night after we did the show, tired and frozen. We gave them another telling off and arranged some accommodation for them. Mick found a phone number and called Pam Johnson's mother, to say the girls were alright. On 10 March, we sent them by train to Huddersfield to be met by their parents.'

'This is taking fan fever a bit too far. Their parents must be worried silly, but what can we do?' BRIAN, *Daily Express*, 10 March, 1965

The Hollies

By the time this tour started, the Hollies had already scored with seven UK hit singles, five of them making the Top 10. Three months after the tour, 'I'm Alive' became the first of their two UK No 1 singles.

'There was an incredible difference between the depth of emotion expressed for the Stones and for us,' said member Graham Nash. 'We could certainly drive them crazy but then it reached a brand new level when the Stones came on – it was somehow deeper and darker than Beatlemania.'

'In Scarborough, we chatted to the Hollies, who were dissatisfied with their business arrangements. We suggested that they try to control their publishing and do a better deal. Graham Nash and I talked about this in Los Angeles at a party on 16 October, 1989. He said they had taken our advice and never looked back.' BILL

'I am a housewife aged 40 and I thoroughly enjoy the music of the Stones, but I simply cannot stand their appearance. It is slovenly and unkempt, and their hair is positively unnatural. As they have a considerable influence on the youth of today, I think they should be made to have their hair cut and smarten themselves up.' MRS J STREET, *letter to NME* 12 March, 1965

'Long hair on young men looks effeminate and there is seldom any attempt to keep it clean. Therefore, it's unsanitary. Extra long hair on boys is unnatural. If they want to make charlies of themselves on TV or stage, they're entitled to do so, but they must respect their obligation to society. I think that male entertainers on stage should have the courtesy to wear a suit.' DEREK JOHNSON, *NME*, 12 March, 1965

Goldie and the Gingerbreads

The Gingerbreads were an all-girl band from New York led by Goldie Zelkowitz. They had their one and only hit in the UK in the spring of 1965. Alan Price of the Animals produced 'Can't You Hear My Heart Beat', by John Carter and Ken Lewis of the Ivy League. It made UK No 25. Goldie went solo early in 1966 and by 1969 was fronting the rock band Ten Wheel Drive under the name Genya Raven.

The Hollies

Dave Berry

Goldie and the Gingerbreads

'Not only did I survive machine gun and bomb attacks on the cinema during the war, but I also managed to come through the live Stones concert here unscathed.' ALF SHARP, *projectionist, ABC Theatre, Romford, 18 March, 1965*

Grand Hotels

Hotels proved to be a bit of a problem throughout our tour with the Hollies. We were often unwelcome guests.

NEW MUSICAL EXPRESS

NME TOP THIRTY

FIRST-EVER CHART IN BRITAIN
—AND STILL THE **FIRST** TODAY!

(Wednesday, March 10, 1965)

Last	This			Highest Position	Weeks in Chart
Week					
8	1	THE LAST TIME	Rolling Stones (Decca)	2-	1
1	2	IT'S NOT UNUSUAL	Tom Jones (Decca)	5-	1
2	3	I'LL NEVER FIND ANOTHER YOU	Seekers (Columbia)	8-	1
3	4	SILHOUETTES	Herman's Hermits (Columbia)	4-	3
5	5	I'LL STOP AT NOTHING	Sandie Shaw (Pye)	4-	5
4	6	GAME OF LOVE	Wayne Fontana and the Mindbenders (Fontana)	6-	3
9	7	COME AND STAY WITH ME	Marianne Faithfull (Decca)	4-	7
8	8	DON'T LET ME BE MISUNDERSTOOD	Animals (Columbia)	6-	4
7	9	I MUST BE SEEING THINGS	Gene Pitney (Stateside)	5-	7
24	10	GOODBYE MY LOVE	Searchers (Pye)	2-10	
11	11	YES I WILL	Hollies (Parlophone)	7-11	
10	12	FUNNY HOW LOVE CAN	Ivy League (Piccadilly)		6

The Stones played Huddersfield as 'The Last Time' went to No 1

TWO DAYS INTO THE TOUR, the Grand Hotel in Manchester refused to accommodate us: they wouldn't even even give a reason. We stayed at the Midland instead, which was fine until the day we were due to leave.

Mick went down to the grill room for lunch, but was refused because of his lack of jacket and tie. Any annoyance was quickly forgotten when we heard that 'The Last Time' had gone to UK No 1.

Princess when I had an urgent need to use a toilet. The chauffeur stopped at the Francis Service Station in Romford Road in Stratford, East London and I went to ask if I could use their lavatory.

The attendant said, 'There isn't a toilet.' I replied, 'This is a big garage, and there's service bays and showrooms, so there must be one.'

'Get off my forecourt!' CHARLES KEELEY

The day after we sorted out the three runaway girls, we had a problem at the Scotch Corner Hotel, and it was of our own making. After we checked out of our individual rooms we kept one so we had somewhere to pass the afternoon. We were bored and ordered afternoon tea; pretty soon it got silly. We started writing things on the walls, throwing cakes and treading biscuits into the carpet. We made a real mess and were eventually thrown out. I have to say it was stupid, but I swear it was the only time we ever trashed a hotel room. There were other bands who made us look almost saintly on that score. On 11 March, the *Daily*

He said, 'There isn't a toilet, so get off my forecourt.' I was bursting to go, but returned to the car and told the others what had happened. Mick took my hand and said, 'Come on Bill, we'll find you a toilet.' Then Mick, Joey Paige (who was in London promoting the single that I wrote for him), Brian and myself went back and again asked to use the toilet. The attendant freaked out and started screaming at us, 'Get off my forecourt! Get off my forecourt!' Brian started dancing around, pulling a Nanker face, singing, 'Get off my foreskin!' We were told to leave,

'Get off my foreskin!' BRIAN

Mirror reported: 'The Stones were banned from the Scotch Corner Hotel. The bill was £56 and they added five guineas for damages.'

To pee or not to pee
Just over a week after we played the last night of the tour, an incident occurred that has become part of Stones folklore – and it was all my fault. We were driving back to London in an Austin

so walked across the forecourt into the adjoining side road, went about 10 yards and peed against the wall.

On our way back across 'his' forecourt we yelled a few insults, then got into the car and continued on our way home... and thought no more about it. Later, we heard that a customer, Eric Lavender, and the petrol station attendant, Charles Keeley, had reported us to the police.

The next day I went to see a Harley Street specialist about my eyes. They had continued to give me problems since New Zealand and were the reason that I was wearing dark glasses at night. A few days later, we recorded *Thank Your Lucky Stars* in Birmingham. Once again, my bladder nearly got me into trouble. On the outskirts of town I needed to go to the toilet, much to the boys' amusement. We stopped in a deserted area and I peed up against a fence. Halfway through, a policeman shone his torch on me and enquired as to what I was up to. He warned me not to do it again, and let me go – after I finished peeing.

A few days later, Keith, who was still living at Holly Hill in Hampstead, was charged with three driving offences at Bow Street Magistrate Court. Mike Dorsey acted as a witness. It was written up in the *Daily Express* on 25 March: 'Keith pleaded guilty to three motoring summonses, failing to produce his driving licence and insurance at a police station and driving without L-plates. When the L-plates were stolen from his car, he did not realise it. Mike Dorsey said that items disappeared from their van and cars with monotonous regularity. Peter Sheridan said there had been a burglary at Keith's flat last year. His licence and

Fans who had waited outside the Stones' hotel were unlucky— their idols were taken in through the garage.

Above and left: *The Stones in Scandinavia*

insurance certificate were stolen. Later a suitcase containing some of his clothes was found.'

On the same day as the report appeared, we flew from London to Copenhagen, Denmark for our first European tour. On arrival at Kastrup Airport, we had a great reception from about 2,000 fans and hundreds of photographers.

'Hundreds of young people stood screaming at the airport… it was on a par with visits of heads of state. Fans Lis Petersen and Tove Andersen got permission to walk all the way up to the plane, and presented the Stones with a bouquet of roses each. The Stones had to fight their way through the masses to get to the waiting cars.' EKSTRABLADET, *Denmark, 26 March, 1965*

We were driven to the Royal Hotel, where we checked into the 19th floor, reserved solely for us. The view from the windows was wonderful. In the evening Charlie and I went to the Tivoli Gardens and saw a very good concert by the Oscar Peterson Trio, Erroll Garner and Ella Fitzgerald. We went backstage afterwards and met Erroll Garner.

War and peace
President Lyndon B Johnson sent the first 3,500 US Marines into South Vietnam at the end of March 1965. Their role was to be 'purely defensive' but, by the time the conflict ended, there would be 45,000 Americans dead. The Vietnam War was to play a significant part in the history of rock music. Protest songs and the whole hippy scene were closely allied to the anti-war movement in America.

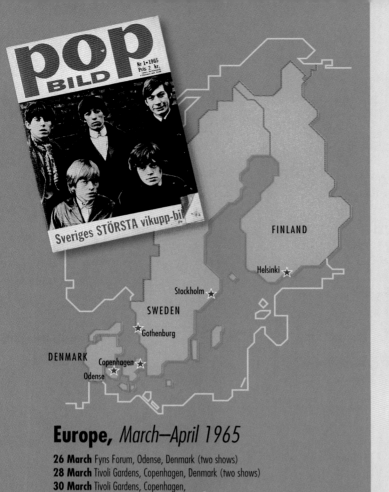

Sveriges STÖRSTA vikupp-bil

FINLAND

Helsinki ★

Stockholm ★

SWEDEN

Gothenburg ★

DENMARK

Copenhagen ★

Odense ★

Europe, *March–April 1965*

26 March Fyns Forum, Odense, Denmark (two shows)
28 March Tivoli Gardens, Copenhagen, Denmark (two shows)
30 March Tivoli Gardens, Copenhagen, Denmark (two shows)
31 March Masshallen, Gothenburg, Sweden (two shows)
1 April Kungliga Tennishallen, Stockholm, Sweden (two shows)
2 April Kungliga Tennishallen, Stockholm, Sweden

The Stones' very first European tour was a short but enjoyable trip to Scandinavia. It also passed off relatively calmly and without major incident, except for Mick and Bill being electrocuted at the first gig!

'We flew to Odense and we were driven to the venue for rehearsals and a soundcheck in the afternoon. During the rehearsals, both Mick and I received very bad electric shocks. I tried my bass and amplifier out while Mick was testing the microphones. There was no earth on the amplifier and suddenly Mick and I became the earth. I got an electric shock and fainted. I was out for a few minutes. When I regained consciousness, I was wet all over with perspiration. Horrible.' BILL

'I touched two microphones simultaneously and couldn't let go of them. I was knocked back, I can tell you. I felt like I had just been in a fight. Bill was knocked unconscious by the shock but, like us, carried on afterwards.' MICK, *Disc, 3 April, 1965*

'Several weeks ago, when it was published that the Stones should stay at the Park Avenue in Gothenburg, the hotel management got an unusual request. A businessman wanted to buy the sheets that the Stones would be sleeping on. Why? He is thinking of cutting them up into pieces and selling them to fans.' AFTONBLADET, *29 March, 1965*

'I am very glad to be here in Copenhagen. We live in one of the best hotels I have ever been in. We have a 16-room suite.' KEITH, *NME, 2 April, 1965*

'We went to a Servicemen's Club and got smashed out of our heads. Next morning we woke up to find a great drunken picture in all the papers. But it's a great place.' BRIAN, *NME, 2 April, 1965*

'Charlie said nothing.' NME, *2 April, 1965*

Set list
'Everybody Needs Somebody To Love'
'Pain In My Heart'
'Tell Me'
'Around And Around'
'Time Is On My Side'
'I Just Want To Make Love To You'
'It's All Over Now'
'Little Red Rooster'
'Route 66'
'The Last Time'

'Everything's swinging up here and as this call is not reverse-charged, can you tell me who is No 1 this week? We are? That's half-a-crown I've lost!' **MICK**, *NME, 2 April, 1965*

Scandinavian Shocker

Stu poses proudly with the graffiti-covered van.

was 'The *NME* Poll Winners' Concert' in front of a capacity audience of 10,000.

Other acts included the Moody Blues, Georgie Fame, the Seekers, Donovan, Them, the Animals, and the Beatles. We closed the first half and the Beatles closed the show. We played 'Everybody Needs Somebody To Love/Pain In My Heart', 'Around and Around' and 'The Last Time.'

And the family came too

After three days off, we went to Paris. I took Diane and Stephen with me for their first taste of being away with the band. We played Musicorama at the Olympia theatre as part of a bill that included Les Jets, Vince Taylor and Evy and Rocky Roberts. Our set was made up of the usual material, but we included 'Carol', which was very popular in France.

We did two more nights at the Olympia, playing 'Doin' The Crawdaddy', which had hardly been aired since our early club gigs. It went over very well. We were paid a lot of money for these three shows, FF 27,252 ($5,000), and were given eight first-class return air fares.

'Four days in Paris with the Stones seems like a couple of years.' NICOLE PORTIER, *Disc, 24 April, 1965*

Only 72 hours later, we were off to another French-speaking area, Montreal in Canada. We were to begin our third North American tour.

Winning Streak

Before we went to Scandinavia there was press speculation, probably fuelled by Eric and Andrew, that CBS were interested in signing us. Our recording contract with Impact and Decca was due to expire in May. Eric and Andrew wanted a better deal, not just for us but for themselves.

'Decca have outbid America's CBS for the millionaire Stones. Decca confirmed that terms have been agreed.' EVENING NEWS, *30 March, 1965*

NME Poll Winners

'Unconventional, controversial, call them what you will,' said *NME*, 'but there can be no denying that the Stones' popularity has progressed in leaps and bounds since they appeared in a guest capacity in last year's *NME* concert. Today, breathing down the necks of the Beatles for recognition as the most dynamic act in the music business, the Stones return — and as poll winners in their own right.'

MAURICE KINN
presents the
new
MUSICAL EXPRESS
1964-65 ANNUAL
POLL-WINNERS ALL-STAR CONCERT
SUNDAY, APRIL 11th, 1965
EMPIRE POOL, WEMBLEY
OFFICIAL PROGRAMME PRICE **1/6**
20 Pages

THE MILLIONAIRE STONES? My personal bank account was only showing a credit of £91 2s 4d.

While Andrew was being Mr Businessman attempting to get us an improved recording contract, Mick and Keith were hanging out with John Lennon.

'Neil Aspinall and I went to Mick and Keith's house,' Lennon told the *NME* in April, 'and played records all night. We must have outstayed our welcome, because when the time came to go home, our hosts had gone to bed.'

Early in April, we did our first photo shoot with Gered Mankowitz; we would often use Gered over the next couple of years. On 11 April, we played our first UK show in three weeks at the Empire Pool, Wembley. It

Bill, Diane and Stephen in Paris

North America, *April–May 1965*

23 April Maurice Richard Arena, Montréal, Canada
24 April YMCA Auditorium, Ottawa, Canada
25 April Maple Leaf Gardens, Toronto, Canada
26 April Treasure Island Gardens, London, Ontario, Canada
29 April Palace Theater, Albany, New York (two shows)
30 April Memorial Auditorium, Worcester, Massachusetts
1 May Academy of Music, New York (matinee)
   Convention Hall, Philadelphia, Pennsylvania (evening)
4 May Georgia Southern College Auditorium, Statesboro, Georgia
6 May Jack Russell Stadium, Clearwater, Florida
7 May Legion Field Stadium, Birmingham, Alabama
8 May Coliseum, Jacksonville, Florida
9 May Arie Crown Theater, Chicago, Illinois
14 May New Civic Auditorium, San Francisco, California
15 May Swing Auditorium, San Bernardino, California
16 May Civic Auditorium, Long Beach, California
17 May Convention Hall, San Diego, California
21 May Civic Auditorium, San Jose, California
22 May Radcliffe Stadium, Fresno, California (matinee)
   Municipal Auditorium, Sacramento, California (evening)
29 May Academy of Music, New York (two evening shows)

The third North American tour was then the Stones' most prolonged spell away from home. They were beset by hassles with hotels, trouble with fans, an unsympathetic press, worries back home and arguments among themselves; the first signs of a serious divide in the band. Brian began to feel like he was on the outside. Oh yes, and in Long Beach, the Stones were very nearly killed.

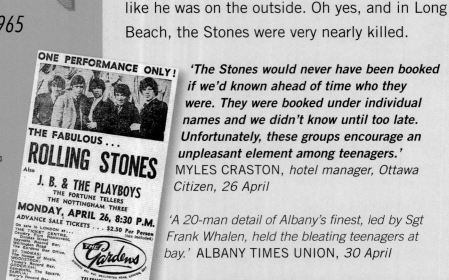

'The Stones would never have been booked if we'd known ahead of time who they were. They were booked under individual names and we didn't know until too late. Unfortunately, these groups encourage an unpleasant element among teenagers.' MYLES CRASTON, *hotel manager, Ottawa Citizen, 26 April*

'A 20-man detail of Albany's finest, led by Sgt Frank Whalen, held the bleating teenagers at bay.' ALBANY TIMES UNION, *30 April*

'A DJ from WLCY and police chief Willis Booth warned the large, restless crowd that unless order was maintained, the Stones portion of the programme would be cancelled. The announcement brought jeers and an increase in the bombardment.' CLEARWATER SUN, *7 May*

'It was a return engagement for the Sheriff's Office riot squad. Many of the deputies wore ear plugs.' RON PLOTKIN, *San Bernardino Sun, 16 May*

'Adults who saw it shuddered in apprehension. Some grown-ups called it "frightening".'
WILF BELL, *Ottawa Citizen, 26 April*

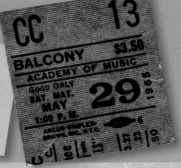

Support bands
Opening acts included:
Toronto
David Clayton Thomas and the Shays
London
The Runarounds, the Nottingham Three, the Fortune Tellers, JB and the Playboys
New York
The Knickerbockers, the Sundowners
Philadelphia
Herman's Hermits, Little Anthony and the Imperials, Bobby Vee, Freddy Cannon, Bobby Freeman, Reparata and the Delrons, Brenda Holloway, the Hondells, the Ikettes, the Detergents, Billy Stewart
Statesboro
The Roemans
Clearwater
The Intruders, Pam Hall and the Catalinas, the Canadian Legends
Birmingham
Sonny James, Marty Robbins, the Beach Boys, the Righteous Brothers, Cannibal and the Headhunters, the Premiers, Skeeter Davis, Del Reeves, Archie Campbell
Jacksonville
The Righteous Brothers, the Newbeats
San Bernardino
The Buschmen, the Driftwoods, the Torquays, the Byrds
Long Beach
Don and the Deacons, the Vibrants, the Dartells, the Byrds, Paul Revere and the Raiders
Fresno
The Ladybirds, the Cindermen, the Road Runners, the Byrds

Trouble
Tour
1965

Set list
Songs chosen from:
'I'm Alright'
'The Last Time'
'I Wanna Be Your Man'
'Not Fade Away'
'Time Is On My Side'
'Little Red Rooster'
'Off The Hook'
'Everybody Needs
  Somebody To Love'
'Around And Around'

London lights out

The Stones went on stage in London at 8.30pm and played to about 3,000 fans. Many had driven up from Detroit and gave the band a great reception. Things were going fine until the police cut off the power mid-way through the set. 'The police just created an antagonistic atmosphere,' Bill told the *London Free Press* on 27 April. 'The kids were just enjoying themselves. The police acted in a typical small-town way. They just panicked.'

Mick said: 'Our instruments wouldn't work, and the place was dark. There was a riot, but it wasn't our fault. We're always the ones to get the blame.'

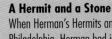

'Mick walked on first, waved and began to adjust the mic. He wore a white shirt, rust-coloured suede jacket and really stylish, modish pants. He wore flat brown shoes and was fantastic-looking. The other four came on from both sides. Brian wore a white shirt under a red top and white slacks. Looking at his boots, I'd never noticed before how small his feet are. Keith wore a regular suit, white shirt and boots. Charlie had on a suit with a blue shirt. Bill wore black slacks and a leather jacket. They fired away with "Everybody Needs Somebody To Love", followed by "Around And Around". My favourite spot, after they went into "Off The Hook" was when Mick did his famous dance.' MARTHA AARONS, *fan, Long Beach, 16 May*

'Our police were harassed and vilified in a way that was most uncomplimentary and I would not subject them to this again and I will not approve another show of this type.' POLICE CHIEF WILLIS BOOTH, *Clearwater, 7 May*

'In Long Beach, we nearly lost our lives.' STU

'We were directed to an exit, but it was too narrow for the limo. We made for another one: too narrow again and 6,000 kids tore down on us. I thought we'd be crushed. Dozens of teenagers were on the car's roof and bonnet, with more trying to pile on. The car was surrounded and bodies were jammed against the sides and windows. Girls looked terrified and fought for breath. We lay on the floor and pushed on the roof with our feet with all our strength to keep it from caving in. The police started swinging their long batons, hitting at everything, as they tried to restore order. There were several casualties. One girl lost fingers on one hand and another had her foot crushed. It was horrible.' BILL, *on leaving the Civic Auditorium, Long Beach, in NME, 21 May*

Below left to right: *the Stones, the Byrds and Herman's Hermits*

A Hermit and a Stone

When Herman's Hermits and the Stones played in Philadelphia, Herman had just gone to US No 1 with the appalling 'Mrs Brown You've Got A Lovely Daughter'. Herman probably thought that he should top the bill.

'They were better than I've ever seen them before, and I like them, but they don't seem to like me,' complained Herman (Peter Noone) in *Melody Maker* on 15 May. 'They never came over to me to say hello, except Mick. You'd think that when you're 3,500 miles away, and on the same show, they might at least say hello. But they're still fabulous.'

Watery hermits

'I wish people would stop asking us what we think of them,' said Mick of the Hermits. 'We don't think of them at all. We think their music is wet and watery and not significant.'

'They were on stage a mere 25 minutes, during which time they mixed obscene gestures with inaudible singing.' MORRIS DUFF, *Toronto Star, 26 April, 1965*

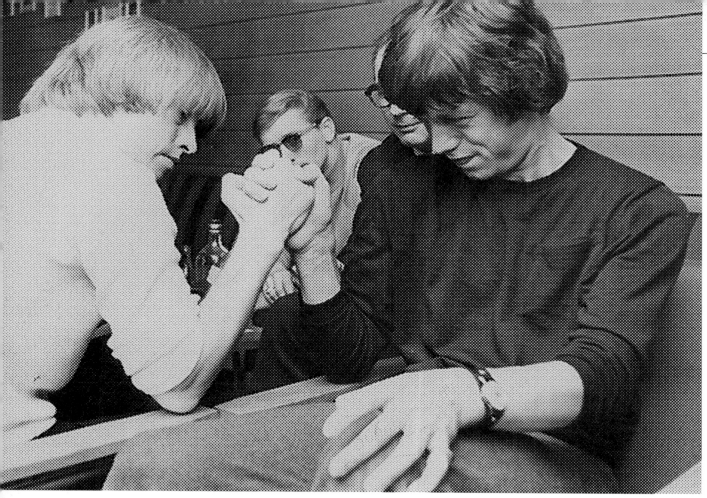

The day after the Sullivan show aired, we rehearsed for *The Clay Cole Show* and went to a London Records party. We drove through Central Park followed by a convertible with five guys in it. They called us faggots and when we got to the club Brian yelled, 'Let's get the colonists.' Mick, Keith and Brian jumped into the convertible and started beating them up. Charlie, Scott Ross and I went into the club while they fought outside. When we left, there was more trouble.

'There were all these fans outside the club. Keith just got the hump at something and he just booted one of them in the mouth.' FRANCESCA OVERMAN, *New York, friend of the band*

We played Statesboro next, once home to Blind Willie McTell, the great blues singer, and then headed south to Florida for a gig in Clearwater. There were two more shows down South, after which we were due to fly back North to play Chicago and record at Chess.

LBJ GBH
While we were staying in the Gulf Motel in Clearwater, Brian had a girl spend the night with him. Next morning, she arrived at

Bad Trip

Apart from our unpopularity with hotel managers, our visit to Canada went off reasonably well. But Brian was starting to get upset, with Keith and Mick in particular. For a little while, he had begun to sense that he was losing his grip on what he still felt in his heart was his band.

WHILE WE WERE IN CANADA, Brian called Scott Ross, our DJ friend in New York. 'He said he was not going to go to the recording session in Chicago. He wanted to come directly to New York,' said Scott. 'I tried to talk him out of it, or at least have him realise that it was a pretty big decision and it had implications if he didn't show up, but he didn't care.

'He just said he couldn't do it, he wasn't in the frame of mind to do it. He was angry, despondent, all sorts of things. He came to New York and stayed with me for about three days. He talked about it a lot. He felt like he was being cut out.' Brian didn't miss the sessions, but this turned into a bad trip for Brian in more ways than one.

Party Crewe
We relaxed in New York, going to a party in an apartment owned by producer Bob Crewe. We met George Shearing, the blind, English-born jazz pianist, and he was charming. The next day we recorded *The Ed Sullivan Show*, miming to 'Little Red Rooster', 'The Last Time', 'Everybody Needs Somebody To Love' and some of '2120 South Michigan Avenue' on the play-out.

'The Stones are the soul of British beat music. I was driving along in my car. I have a TV installed and suddenly on the screen came the Stones singing my song, "Everybody Needs Somebody To Love". What a knockout!' SOLOMON BURKE, *Beat Instrumental magazine, August 1965*

'Mick Jagger cannot sing – even Ringo can sing better than him.' DEVOTED RINGO FAN, *Pop Shop, 24 April, 1965*

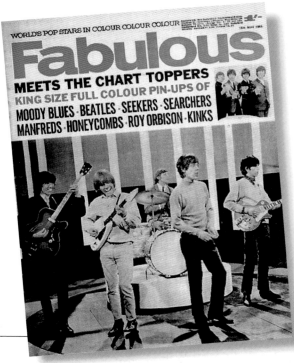

the pool where we were all sunbathing. She was bruised and told us that Brian had beaten her up.

Mike Dorsey, our road manager, promptly disappeared into the motel to have a word with him. Blows were exchanged and Brian ended up with a couple of cracked ribs – much to everyone's satisfaction. I covered up for Brian, telling the press he had been practising karate around the pool when he had an accident.

High-flying daddy

One day I called home and Diane told me that she and Stephen had gone shopping in Penge. A neighbour asked Stephen, 'Where's your daddy, Stephen?' 'Oh! My daddy lives in an aeroplane.'

We flew to Chicago on the morning the English Sunday papers were full of unwelcome news about Charlie. He was to be taken to court by a 19-year-old named Christine White, the daughter of a London taxi driver, who alleged Charlie had fathered her child. It was a total scam and the case was dropped a couple of months later.

After our Chess session in Chicago, we were happy to fly to Los Angeles. Californian fans always gave us a great welcome and we enjoyed hanging out in LA. For once the weather was cold, but we didn't really care as we spent the next two days recording at RCA.

'We did the Temptations' "My Girl". I don't mind admitting that it took me a while to twig exactly what I was supposed to do. The notes and musical content were straightforward enough, but it was just the timing which had me foxed for a while. It seemed as if I was playing at the wrong speed and on the wrong beat. As it happened, I was doing the right thing all along, but I had to wait until the playback to hear how well it was fitting in.' BILL, *Beat Instrumental magazine, August 1965*

All the Californian gigs were great, despite our near-death experience at Long Beach. Our main support band was the Byrds. As our Californian shows began, their cover of Bob Dylan's 'Mr Tambourine Man' entered the US Hot 100 and a month later, it was No 1. 'The Byrds are quite nice fellows – very English types, really. Long hair and all that,' said Mick. We also did a TV show, *Hollywood A-Go-Go,* with Chuck Berry.

It was after our Long Beach gig that Brian took what was probably his first LSD trip. He and I went to a club on Sunset Boulevard and as we got out of the car Brian said the whole ground was covered with snakes. He jumped along the pavement, trying to avoid them. Later, when we got back to New York for the last gig of the tour, Brian and Scott Ross tripped together a couple of times.

Bob Bonis remembered one of the other little incidents that amused us in America: 'I was getting Keith out of his room and he hid two girls on the balcony. I was always security conscious and I locked the balcony door. We went off to play the date, about 100 miles up the coast. When we got back there were freezing girls still on the balcony. Keith figured they'd get out, but they were five floors up.'

As our California gigs were coming to an end, we recorded a slot for the *Shindig* TV programme. Sonny and Cher, Jackie De Shannon, Bobby Sherman and, at our insistence, Howlin' Wolf were also there. Today it is difficult to comprehend the enormity of seeing a black performer on what was very much a white TV show. The producer of *Shindig* was expatriate Englishman Jack Good, who produced UK TV shows and wrote for *Disc*. He would constantly refer to Wolf, in his very proper accent, as 'Mr Howling'. Wolf played 'How Many More Years', a

The Stones sit at the feet of the Wolf.

performance which must have been a revelation to many watching the show. While we were rehearsing, revered 1930s blues singer Son House and his manager came by the studio.

'Brian Jones was watching me and then came up and tapped me and said, "Excuse me, who is the old man that Wolf thinks is so special? Wolf is in awe of him." And so I said, "That's Son House". And he turned to me and said, "Ah, the one that taught Robert Johnson".' DICK WATERMAN, *manager of Son House*

Dick also recalled how we were draped all over a Rolls Royce as we sang 'Satisfaction'.

There were five days before we had to go to New York. Brian and I stayed in LA, where he spent most of his time in the clubs. Stu went to Yosemite National Park, Death Valley and Las Vegas, Charlie went cross-country to Gettysburg in order to look at some Civil War sites and Mick and Keith went off to the Arizona desert.

We did three shows at the Academy of Music in New York and then we went on to a party at the Ondine club. Afterwards, Brian, Charlie and I went back to the City Squire hotel, while Mick and Keith went on to a friend's place.

The jangly guitars and soaring harmonies of the Byrds created the perfect West Coast sound.

'We were 30 minutes late getting to San Diego, so the Byrds stayed on to keep the audience entertained. By the time we got there, they had run out of their own numbers and were playing ours. What a gas.' MICK

'(I CAN'T GET NO) SATISFACTION'

(I Can't Get No) Satisfaction
The Rolling Stones
The Spider And The Fly (UK)

The seventh single in both the UK and the US, this was the first to top the charts on both sides of the Atlantic. It is without doubt the most famous intro in rock music – the perfect rock riff of the 1960s?

'We wrote it in Tampa, Florida, by a swimming pool. It was Keith's initial idea.' MICK, *Rolling Stone magazine, October 1968*

'"Satisfaction" was actually written in Clearwater, Florida. Keith woke up in the middle of the night with the riff in his head and put it down on tape. In the morning, Mick said the words were, "I can't get no satisfaction."' BILL

On Monday 10 May, they went to Chess Studios at 1pm and worked until 10pm. 'Satisfaction' was among the tracks cut.

'I didn't think much of "Satisfaction" when we first recorded it. We had a harmonica on then and it was considered to be a good b-side or maybe an LP track.' KEITH, *NME, 3 September, 1965*

'I heard a demo of the original track before the fuzz tone was put on and it was Brian on harmonica. I made a bet with Mick, Keith and Brian that it was going to be the biggest record the Stones had ever had, even before the fuzz tone was put on.' SCOTT ROSS, *DJ and friend of the band*

Two days later, the band went to RCA Studio in Hollywood with Dave Hassinger and reworked 'Satisfaction'.

'Charlie put down a different tempo, and with the addition of a fuzzbox on my guitar, which takes off all the treble, we achieved a very interesting sound.' KEITH, *NME, 3 September, 1965*

'After we listened to the master, we discussed whether or not it should be the next single. Andrew and Dave Hassinger were very positive about it, so we put it to the vote. Andrew, Dave, Stu, Brian, Charlie and I voted yes, while Mick and Keith voted no. It became the next single by the majority vote.' BILL

'"The Under-Assistant West Coast Promotion Man" was a good-natured jibe at George Sherlock, the London Records promo man who accompanied us on our first American tour. The track is based on Buster Brown's 1960 hit "Fannie Mae", which also inspired the Beach Boys' "Help me Rhonda".' BILL

TRITONS

Delle rubriche radiofoniche "ALTO GRADIMENTO.. "SUPERSONIC.. grande successo dei (disco Fonit-Cetra International) con

(I can't get no) SATISFACTION

Testo originale e Musica di M. JAGGER - K. RICHARD

Edizioni Musicali MARIO AROMANDO s.r.l. - Milano

US b-side
'The Under-Assistant West Coast Promotion Man'
Recorded
a-side 12 May, 1965
US b-side 10 May, 1965
Studios
a-side and UK b-side RCA Hollywood
US b-side Chess Studios, Chicago
Producer
Andrew Loog Oldham for Impact Sound
Engineers
Dave Hassinger at RCA
Ron Malo at Chess
Release
US Saturday 6 June, 1965
London 45 9766
UK Friday 20 August, 1965
Decca F 12220
Composers
a-side Jagger/Richard
b-sides Nanker/Phelge
Highest chart position
US No 1, for four weeks
UK No 1, for two weeks

faces of today : sounds of tomorrow
spots, not gauze, and peepers of truth
an audience in a sea of fear
for big daddy doesn't relate any more
this does : so float into tomorrow

Out Now!

(I can't get no)
SATISFACTION
b/w The spider and the fly

THE ROLLING STONES

F 12220

produced by andrew loog oldham

DECCA

Decca House   The Decca Record Company Limited
Albert Embankment · London SE1

ROLLING STONES—(I CAN'T GET NO) SATIS- FACTION (Immediate, BMI)**—THE UNDER AS- SISTANT WEST COAST PROMOTION MAN** (Immediate, BMI)—Hard-driving blues dance beat backs up a strong vocal performance. Hot follow-up to "The Last Time." Flip is a clever music business lyric and idea. Well done and funny. Watch lyric at ending.   **London 9766**

'Satisfaction...' was nominated the greatest pop single of the last 25 years in *Rolling Stone*, 1988.

'At this time, everybody was smoking dope. Mick and Keith went into some room at the apartment and they were smoking in there. We didn't have anything outside, so I started kicking on the door. Mick opened it and said, "What do you want?" I said, "What have you got in there? Can we have some?" and he said, "Oh, we can't do that." I said, "Oh! You're a big star now," and I started pushing on the door. We were yelling at each other and I grabbed him and pushed him up against the wall.'
SCOTT ROSS, *New York DJ*

Home again

Back from tour, Diane and I went house-hunting and decided to buy the Oaks, at Keston Park Estate, near Biggin Hill in Kent. While our domesticity was fairly ordinary, Brian was meanwhile facing a legal onslaught by two ex-girlfriends. Eric Easton had received a letter from Brian and Brian (Solicitors).

Left, *Pat Andrews and Julian,* and right, *Linda Lawrence and Julian*

'We have been instructed on behalf of Miss Lawrence as respects Affiliation Proceedings against Mr Lewis Brian Jones, a member of the Rolling Stones group. Our client alleges that he is the father of the child born to her on 23 July, 1964. We have now made an application to the Law Society for a Legal Aid Certificate to enable our client to institute proceedings before the Local Magistrate's Court for maintenance payments…

'Our client instructs us that she would be prepared to accept a lump sum in full and final settlement of your Client's liability in this matter. Naturally, we would not want Mr Jones to agree to this before consulting his Solicitor.'

On 3 June, Pat Andrews began proceedings against Brian.

On the move

Keith and Mick had moved out of their flat in Hampstead and had been staying at the Hilton Hotel since getting back from America. Keith decided to go to Brian's for a few days and Mick went to stay with photographer David Bailey. He met Jacqueline Bissett, who was posing for Bailey.

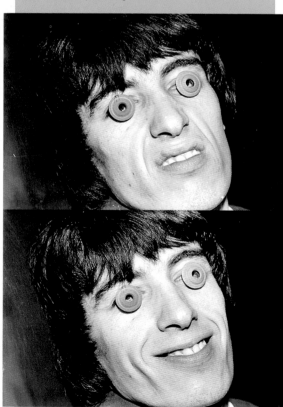

'David told me to come back in six months, when I'd done something with myself. I was big, fat and lumpy in all the wrong places and that might have been that, had not Mick walked in. "Put her on your back and let's try it again," the photographer suggested to the pop idol. The resulting picture was seen by millions and Aberdeen-born Jacqueline Bissett was launched.'
JACQUELINE BISSETT, *Evening News, February 1970*

A week or so later, Mick moved into a new flat at 13a Bryanston Mews East in London W1. Keith moved to 5 Ambassador House, Carlton Hill, a North London tower block.

'Just because Keith and I aren't sharing this flat, everyone thinks we've had a bust-up,' Mick told the *NME* on 24 July, 1965. 'There's absolutely no truth in that. It's simply because we couldn't find a flat suitable for the both of us. I'd like to get out in about three months and find something permanent.

While Andrew Oldham gave free copy to the Music Echo, *the Stones were going upwardly mobile in* Fabulous.

'I'd like two bedrooms, a large double one and a smaller one, a very large living/dining room, a kitchen and a bathroom. You know the type of place I mean, old-fashioned furniture, fur rugs and big thick curtains, and a woman who can cook for me. That's a necessity.

'I'm a bit hopeless when it comes to the old bacon and eggs. I definitely won't be throwing parties. I don't mind going to other people's, but I'd rather do without the mess. Of course, I'll have the rest of the Stones round, and my other friends will be very welcome.'

GOT LIVE IF YOU WANT IT EP

The first track is 'We Want The Stones', consisting entirely of the audience chanting the title, for which the Stones claimed publishing royalties by listing it as a separate number (perhaps the most audacious piece of publishing ever). 'I'm Moving On' was a cover of a 1950 US Country Chart No 1 by Canadian artist Hank Snow.

'The EP captures on wax the unadulterated in person excitement of a Stones stage show. Side one opens with the audience insistently chanting, then the Stones give us a snatch of the already-familiar "Everybody Needs Somebody to Love". The first of the record's four main titles is "Pain In My Heart", a pounding big-sounding blues ballad. This is followed by an insidious, throbbing R&B treatment of "Route 66". Clashing cymbals, shrilling harmonica and whining guitar feature behind Mick's lead vocal on "I'm Moving On", which opens side two. Last track is the number which inspired the whole thing, "I'm Alright", a fast group vocal offering, with a guitar ringing out the instrumental melody line true as a bell. This is the Stones as they sound on stage, and very good it is too.' UK PRESS OFFICER, *Decca Records*

'The balance is far from perfect. If you're looking for seething tension, an electrifying atmosphere and spine-tingling excitement, you'll find them all on this disc.' NME, *28 May, 1965*

'The whole record raves from start to finish. Much of the recording quality is lost, but the atmosphere makes up for everything.' BEAT INSTRUMENTAL, *June 1965*

'As a Stones fan, I am very disappointed with their latest EP. The songs themselves are very good, what I can hear of them, but on side two, the Stones are almost impossible to hear because of the screaming. Please Stones, don't go live again.' JENNIFER MATTHEWS, *fan*

'Just listening makes you feel as though you're actually in a club with the Stones, dancing, listening and sweating.' **RECORD MIRROR,** *5 June, 1965*

The third Stones EP title is based on 'I've Got Love If You Want It', recorded in 1957 on Excello Records by Slim Harpo, one of the Stones' favourite blues men. Live recording techniques in 1965 were primitive. The warts-and-all sound of the Stones playing live is fascinating as a historical document, but not too much else.

'We all knew that the sound that we were getting live and in the studio was not what we were getting on record – the difference was light years apart.' **KEITH**

Side 1
1. 'We Want The Stones'
   Nanker/Phelge
2. 'Everybody Needs Somebody to Love'
   Russell/Burke/Wexler
3. 'Pain In My Heart'
   Redding/Walden
4. 'Route 66' Troup

Side 2
1. 'I'm Moving On' Snow
2. 'I'm Alright'
   Nanker/Phelge

Recorded
5 March, 1965, Regal Theatre, Edmonton, London; 6 March, Empire Theatre, Liverpool and 7 March, 1965 Palace Theatre, Manchester

Producer
Andrew Loog Oldham for Impact Sound

Engineer
Glyn Johns

Release
UK Friday 11 June, 1965
Decca DFE 8620

Highest chart position
Record Retailer EP No 1

Getting live makes the front page.

The United Kingdom/Europe
June 1965

15 June Odeon Theatre, Glasgow
16 June Usher Hall, Edinburgh
17 June Capitol Theatre, Aberdeen
18 June Caird Hall, Dundee
24 June Messehallen, Oslo, Norway
25 June Yyteri Beach, Pori, Finland
26 June KB Hallen, Copenhagen, Denmark
(two shows)
29 June Baltiska Hallen, Malmo, Sweden
(two shows)

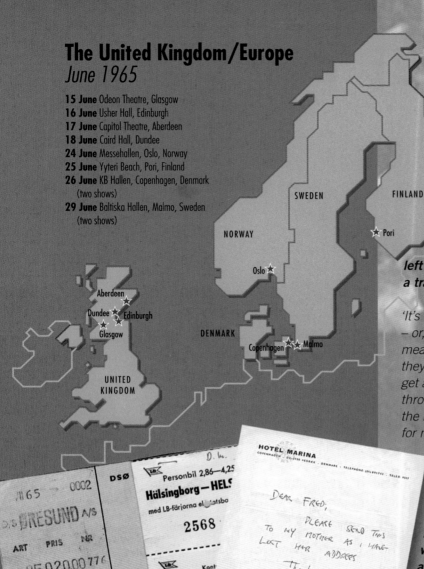

The band played two four-date mini-tours in the second half of June. The first was to Scotland, accompanied by the Hollies, which gave the Stones the chance to relax at the world-famous Gleneagles Hotel. Their return visit to three Scandinavian countries and a first show in Norway did a great deal to enhance the Stones' already considerable reputation in Europe.

'The four concerts in Scotland by the Stones left behind more than 120 wrecked theatre seats and a trail of debris and disorder.' NME, *9 July, 1965*

'It's true we did get a lot of bad publicity in Scotland – or, at any rate, the fans did. They don't mean to break the seats. In many cases, they stand on them to see better. Sure you get a couple of fellows who come along to throw tomatoes, but nobody turns up with the idea of wrecking the joint. It's difficult for me to judge. I've never been in the middle of a Stones audience, have I?' MICK, *NME, 9 July, 1965*

'We're really sorry that we're late and that you had to wait so long for us. But now we're here and I believe the concert will be a smasher. I'm happy to see you all.' MICK, *Turku Airport, Finland*

'In Finland, we played one open-air concert to 15,000 people. It was only dark between about 12.30am and 2am. The concert was held on a beach and the nearest road was several miles away. We had to get to the beach by driving over the sand dunes in a jeep. What a ride. All the people who came slept on the beach in tents. What a scene!' MICK, *Disc, 10 July, 1965*

Top, *Bill on stage on 25 June and*, above, *Oslo Airport, 23 June*

Support bands in 1965
Glasgow
The Hollies, the Original Checkmates, the Cannon Brothers
Aberdeen
Doris Troy, the Drumbeats (local band)
Dundee
The Hollies, Doris Troy, Mike and the Shades, the West Five, the Modells

The Tartan To The Midnight Sun

Money Matters

Our four nights in Scotland caused the usual organised chaos, but the second trip to Scandinavia was less eventful in the way of riots and mania, although Keith had language problems. The business side of the Stones was beginning to take an ominous turn with the growing involvement of Allen Klein.

AFTER OUR FIRST SHOW in Glasgow we were driven to Gleneagles Hotel in Perthshire. It was an old-style establishment, with a famous golf course, well away from screaming fans. It was safer for us to be there and we had a chance to unwind over the four nights we spent at the hotel. We even managed a few rounds of golf before a photoshoot.

We began our Scandinavian tour in Norway and then played in Finland. One night we went out to eat; Keith ordered soup, but it didn't arrive with the food. He got angry and asked for it again, pointing at the menu. The waiter arrived with a meal on a plate. Keith went ballistic, flinging the plate full of food onto the dance floor and storming out. We realised that he hadn't been ordering soup at all;

he'd asked for 'supper'. Soup wasn't on the menu.

While Charlie and I came home after the end of our Scandinavian dates, Mick, Keith and Brian stayed on. I went with the family to Lymington for a break. On our return, the rest of the Stones agreed to loan me £6,000 so that I could buy the house in Keston.

Business was also very much on Andrew and Eric's minds. They had met with their respective lawyers to discuss how they would work with us in the future. A couple of days later, Andrew flew to the US. 'Satisfaction' was at US No 1. After a night in New York, he flew to Miami to attend the Columbia Records convention. Here Andrew met Allen Klein for the first time, and Klein's lawyer, Marty Machat. Klein was a New York music industry accountant who obviously impressed Andrew with his approach to business. Shortly after, Andrew wrote to Klein:

'You are hereby authorised to negotiate on my behalf as the producer of the Rolling Stones and the co-manager of said group for a new phonographic recording agreement. I will inform the other manager, Eric Easton, and the artists who comprise the Rolling Stones that you have been exclusively retained by me for such purposes. Inquiries from record companies will be directed to you and all negotiations and submissions of negotiations will be submitted to me and my solicitor in England, David Jacobs. For your services, we agree to pay you 20 per cent of the gross compensation paid pursuant to the agreement we enter into, that is either guaranteed, paid or earned under the agreements you negotiate. It is understood that your appointment hereunder is exclusive and can be revoked by you or myself by giving each other prior written notice of no less than 90 days.'

(I can't get no) SATISFACTION
THE ROLLING STONES

LONDON RECORDS · Produced by Andrew Loog Oldham for Impact Sound

Court in the act

On Thursday 22 July I went to East Ham Magistrates Court, London and appeared in No 1 court. It was my first experience of being prosecuted. Mick and Brian were in the dock with me, while Charlie and Keith sat at the back of the court in a show of solidarity. As a result of the toilet incident at the garage, all three of us were summoned to appear for using insulting behaviour. I was further summoned for using obscene language. We all pleaded not guilty.

'At about 11.30pm on 18 March, 1965, a Daimler car stopped in the road outside the Francis Service Station, Romford Road, Forest Gate, West Ham, London. Wyman used disgusting language in asking the garage attendant if he could use the toilet.' PROSECUTING COUNSEL KENNETH RICHARDSON

'When the car pulled up outside, Wyman, wearing dark glasses, got out and approached the staff kiosk. Then this shaggy-haired monster looked into the kiosk.' CHARLES KEELEY

'There were cries from the public gallery, when Keeley referred to Wyman as a "shaggy-haired monster".' DAILY SKETCH

'The behaviour of the young man annoyed me. He enquired where the toilets were, using obscene language.' CHARLES KEELEY

'After being told the public lavatory was being reconditioned, the attendant was going to direct Wyman to the staff toilet, when he saw eight or nine youths and girls getting out of the car.' PROSECUTING COUNSEL KENNETH RICHARDSON

'We didn't have time to go to the dressing room after the show, because as soon as the curtain fell, we had to leave the stage and rush to the car to avoid fans.' BILL

'We were laughing a lot because Mr Keeley's behaviour was so comical. We are rather more mature than that. None of us urinated.' BRIAN

'I think we were top of the hit parade at the time and we were discussing our forthcoming American tour. We had every reason to be happy. I've never been in a bad enough mood to want to hit anyone. We have played in many places from Texas and Miami, to Helsinki and this is the first time we have been in any trouble with the police.' MICK

'This is a trivial case and you are making a mountain out of a mole-hill.' DEFENDING COUNSEL DALE PARKINSON

We were all found guilty of using insulting behaviour in which a breach of the peace might have occurred. We were fined £5 each, and ordered to pay 15 guineas costs. We all gave notice to appeal. I was found not guilty of using obscene language.

BOW STREET MAGISTRATES COURT

'I kept out of trouble. I was asleep in the back seat of the car, man.' CHARLIE

Andrew and Brian at Decca House on 29 July, when the band went to sign a new recording contract.

Andrew wrote again to Klein the next day, appointing him 'business manager and advisor for myself and all artists I represent in the phonograph record industry.' The letter went on: 'In the event of such [contract] termination, you will continue to receive your 20 per cent of all sums either guaranteed or received or earned based on agreements or negotiations entered into prior to the termination of this agreement. This agreement is limited to the United States and Canada and you are not to participate in any record earnings outside the United States and Canada.'

We knew absolutely nothing about these arrangements. Life was just rolling along for us. Like me, Charlie was getting himself on the property ladder, oblivious to the fact that the rest of our lives would be affected by what Andrew and Allen Klein were arranging behind our backs. I am sure that Mick and Keith didn't

really know the full extent of things at this point in the proceedings. Our minds were focused on our music and, to be honest, on simply having a good time. Charlie put down a 10 per cent deposit (£885) on a 16th-century property that had once belonged to the Archbishop of Canterbury. The Old Brewery House in Lewes, Sussex, was to be his and Shirley's first proper home together.

'We can't understand why he prefers an old place like this to something modern.'
CHARLES WATTS SNR

On Monday 26 July, 1965, Mick's 22nd birthday, we all went to a meeting at Andrew's office in Ivor Court, London. From there we went to the Hilton hotel to meet Allen Klein for the first time. Klein held court in his suite, offering us his and Andrew's vision for the future of the band. While I was as interested as anybody in improving our financial position, I suggested that we should have our own lawyer look over all the documents before we signed anything.

A little while after this meeting, I discovered that Andrew had already signed Letters of Agreement that Klein had prepared for him. We were committed without ever having a chance to discuss it or verify anything that was agreed. Events unfolded over the next few days that

ought to have made us all think more closely about our financial futures.

Fractions

The next day we had another meeting with Andrew, Allen Klein and an accountant. We found out that Impact Sound (Andrew and Eric) had been receiving a 14 per cent royalty from Decca on our records, and only paying us six per cent to share between us. Of this, Andrew and Eric were taking a 25 per cent management fee (leaving us with four-and-a-half per cent against their nine-and-a-half per cent). We were told that this would be changed on the new contract. Andrew had never mentioned any of this to us before, and it had been going on since May 1963. Perversely, it was this type of thing that made the others believe that Klein was righting the wrongs… But, oh, how wrong we would be.

We went to Decca House with Klein's lawyer, and had a meeting with executives. Klein told us all not to say anything,

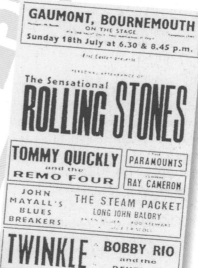

UK mini-tour

Among the support acts was Steam Packet, a group that included Long John Baldry, Brian Auger, Rod Stewart and Julie Driscoll. At the London Palladium gig, I used my new Vox Teardrop 'Wyman Bass' for the first time. It was built with small frets and fingerboard to make playing easier with my small hands.

16 July, 1965 Odeon Theatre, Exeter, Devon (two shows)
17 July Guildhall, Portsmouth, Hampshire (two shows)
18 July Gaumont Theatre, Bournemouth, Hampshire (two shows)
25 July ABC Theatre, Great Yarmouth, Norfolk (two shows)
26 July ABC Theatre, Leicester, Leicestershire
1 August Palladium, London (two shows)

'Don't be so fucking mercenary! We got to trust someone.' KEITH, *overriding*

Bill's misgivings about Klein

'I didn't feel comfortable with Klein, a feeling that never changed.' BILL

Rolling Stones Ltd accounts

The band's first set of accounts from Rolling Stones Ltd made interesting reading. From performances (shows, TV, radio and merchandising) they earned £82,605 15s 7d gross. From all their activities they made a profit of £9,922. Mick received royalties of £342 16s 9d from PRS (the Performing Rights Society), for BBC radio, BBC TV and ITV. Interestingly, he received three-twelfths of all Jagger/Richards songs and from Nanker/Phelge songs, a tenth of 'Empty Heart', two-fifteenths of 'It's Alright', one twelfth of 'Little By Little', the same from 'Now I've Got A Witness', four-twelfths of 'Play With Fire' and a twelfth of 'Stoned'. He also got six-twelfths of '2120 South Michigan Avenue', which was an instrumental. An artist royalty statement prepared much later from London Records for Nanker Phelge Music Ltd showed a profit of $65,317.93 (1 March–30 June, 1965). This worked out as $13,063.58 each. This was not paid to the Stones for some time.

suggesting our being there was a show of strength. After the meeting, Brian said to me that he too felt uneasy about Klein.

Not that we didn't need improvement in our financial affairs. My bank account was in the red that morning and I suspect that others weren't a lot better off. For all the talk of our millionaire life styles, we were often short of cash.

On Thursday 29 July, 1965, we went to Decca with Andrew and Allen in order to sign a new recording contract in Decca's boardroom. We met Decca chairman Sir Edward Lewis and various other top executives. We were each presented with a cheque for £2,500, which was our first year's guarantee on the deal. We were guaranteed a further 10 annual payments of $7,000 from Decca

Records (UK) from 30 July, 1965, to 1 July, 1974. The following day we had a number of letters of 'agreement' sent to us by Andrew, which in fact were written by Allen Klein, that effectively locked us into arrangements that we did not fully comprehend. Not one of us had them checked independently by our own lawyers.

My fears about Allen Klein proved to be well-founded.

Fanzine fun

The Stones fan club produced a newspaper. In the first edition, Bill contributed descriptions of the band for the front page, a chance for him to become the 'youngest member' of the Stones. Elsewhere in the magazine, there was a feature on the Stones' homes and news of 'Satisfaction' hitting US No 1.

Stone Age

VOLUME 1 No. 1   Free to all Members

Brian Jones

Owner of CHELTENHAM GIRLS' SCHOOL. One of the best dressed stars on the scene today. Affectionately known to his confederates (see Charlie Watts) as "Haystack Head".

Keith Richard

Young, virile Keith voted NO. 9 most handsome star of 1965 by Esther Chamberlain. Interests are tracing various cases and trunks containing clothes, left all over the London area.

Charlie Watts

Oldest member of group. Great interest in horses (see facial structure at close range). Appearance generally "scruffy". NOT on list of most handsome stars of 1965.

Mick Jagger

Referred to as "THE GOVERNOR" by his backing group (who are thinking of replacing him with Ray Columbus). Seasoned taxidermist, whose hobbies include palmistry and dental nursing.

Bill Wyman

Youngest member of the group. Pipped JAMES BROWN as "Hardest working man in Show Business 1965". Commonly referred to as "MAN MOUNTAIN WYMAN". Interests — Laundry and Prize Fighting.

out of
our heads
THE ROLLING
STONES*

MONO LL 3429   LONDON

'Isn't it something the way the Stones are practically taking over where the Beatles left off? I used to think the Stones were the world's worst, but after hearing their latest album, I take it all back.' DICK SUMMER, *DJ, Teen Screen magazine, September 1965*

The day after the band received their advance cheques from Decca, the fourth US album was issued. It was the first to be dominated by band originals, although only three were written by Mick and Keith. In choosing the five cover versions, they picked out the very best R&B singers to cover in a further move away from the blues.

'This album saw Jagger and Richard begin to flex their writing muscles which, up until then, had been mainly of the 96-pound weakling variety. There was nothing weak – or even very imitative – about "Satisfaction" and "The Last Time".' RALPH THOMAS, *Toronto Daily Star, July 1967*

'"That's How Strong My Love Is" is Jagger's best pure soul vocal.'
DAVE MARSH AND JOHN SWENSON,
Rolling Stone Record Guide

PICK HITS

OUT OF OUR HEADS
THE ROLLING STONES—London LL 3429.
A hit single makes a hit album—if the artists are the Rolling Stones. Actually, the big one ("Satisfaction") doesn't come until side two, but before it are such rousers as "Mercy Mercy" (not Mersey, Mersey), "Good Times" and "I'm All Right." The group may soon have the No. 1 single and LP. Out of sight!

Under the influence

'Mercy, Mercy' Don Covay's version reached US No 35 in late 1964.
'Hitch Hike' Marvin Gaye's second US Hot 100 entry in January 1963 eventually got to US No 30 and US R&B No 12.
'That's How Strong My Love Is' Recorded by Otis Redding, the song entered the US Hot 100 in January 1965 as the b-side of 'Mr Pitiful' and climbed to No 74.
'Good Times' Sam Cooke's recording made US No 11 in the summer of 1964.
'Cry To Me' The oldest of the covers on the album made US No 44 in early 1962 and R&B US No 5 for Solomon Burke.

Marvin Gaye, whose 'Hitch Hike' the Stones covered

COVER STORY

A PANTHER PIXTAR ON
BRIAN JONES
of The Rolling Stones

Edited by
DAVID ROGERS

1/6

HIT PARADE
THE ROLLING STONES
2/-

romeo
for young romance
FOUR BIG ROLLING STONES PAGES
KATHY CRAWFORD
TONIGHT

POP WEEKLY
Nº 45
1/-

Fabulous
MEETS THE UNDER 21'S
11 KING SIZE FULL COLOUR PIN-UPS
ESCORTS CHICK. G. MIKE SMITH B.J.K. ETC

POP WEEKLY
Nº 46
1/-

LIFE WITH THE **Rolling Stones**
WHY PARENTS HATE US
WHY WE HATE UNIFORMS

rave
THE FRANK LOOK AT TODAY'S POP WORLD · DECEMBER

OUR OWN STORY
BY THE
ROLLING STONES
As We Told It To Pete Goodman

ALONE WITH THE STONES 24 PRIVATE HOURS!!!
TEEN
fax
and PIX
DEVILS or DARLINGS? HAVE THEY GONE TOO FAR?
Mick "Lips" Jagger
WE HATE THOSE NASTY LIES!
SECRET PIX 200 VERY INTIMATE!?!
PLUS
BILL
KEITH'S
CHARLIE'S
MICK
BRIAN

ROLLING STONES
FREE! PHOTOS!
STICKERS!
EXCLUSIVE 1ST PHOTOS IN THE USA
FREE! MEMBERSHIP CARDS IN THE OFFICIAL FAN CLUB
THE GREATEST YET!
Plus THE DAVE CLARK FIVE · THE BEATLES · GERRY & THE PACEMAKERS

rave
JANUARY 2s 6d
HAPPY NEW YEAR FOR A HAPPY NEW YOU!
INSIDE 100 PIN-UP PEOPLE!
WHO WILL WIN YOUR HEART IN 1965?

Fabulous
A SWINGING STAR MOBILE
FREE INSIDE
FAB GETS MOBILISED
TWINKLE WRITES JUST FOR YOU

BRAVO
Sie kommen!
BRAVO-Tournee mit den Rolling Stones

LLOYD THAXTON'S
TiGER beat
COLLEEN CORBY
THE P.J. PROBY UNTOLD SHOCKER!
America's Answer to THE BYRDS
DAVID McCALLUM
WHO'S THE BOSS?
HERMAN

RINGO STARR AND BRIAN BENNETT TALK DRUMS
BEAT INSTRUMENTAL MONTHLY
NOVEMBER 1964 No. 19
TOO MANY KNOBS SAY MANNS
ARE MANAGERS REALLY NECESSARY?
STONES' Playing Secrets
WELSH BEAT

POP WEEKLY
1/-

POP
NUMBER SEVEN Week Ending October 9th
RUDOLF RASMUSSEN SPORT

DISC weekly
PROBY writes to the QUEEN
BEATLES X-RAYED!
STONES FILM! Shooting next year
DUSTY WITH THE HEAT ON!

muziek express

Fabulous
YOUR TOP TWENTY
PLUS KING SIZE COLOUR PIN-UPS OF WALKERS · GEORGE · PAUL · MICK · DAVID McCALLUM · DAVE DAVIES · GENE PITNEY · PART TWO DOUBLE PAGE PIN-UP OF PAUL RYAN · ALSO FABULOUS FREE COMPETITION INSIDE

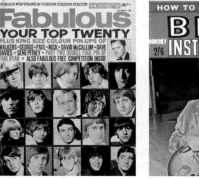

HOW TO SELL YOUR SONG
BEAT INSTRUMENTAL MONTHLY
APR 1966 No. 36
2/6

LLOYD THAXTON'S
TiGER beat!
THE STONES ARE YOU FOR OR AGAINST?
HERMAN'S MOVIE LIFE STORY
HOW TO MEET THE BEATLES THIS SUMMER!
ENGLAND'S GREAT

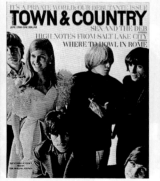

TOWN & COUNTRY
SEX AND THE DUB
HIGH NOTES FROM SALT LAKE CITY
WHERE TO HOWL IN ROME

George Hamilton – ein Filmstar zieht in's Weiße Haus
ok
Bond verliert den letzten Kampf

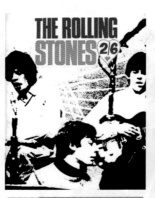

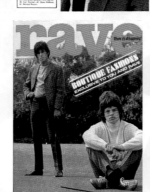

197

We Must Have Been Out Of Our Heads

On the day *Out Of Our Heads* was released, I got my house loan from the Bradford and Bingley Building Society, borrowing a further £6,000 at seven per cent over 20 years. Two days later, we had the Annual General Meeting (AGM) of Rolling Stones Ltd, and there were more letters and articles of agreement between ourselves, Allen Klein's company (ABKCO), Andrew, Decca, London Records and Nanker Phelge Music.

THE DAY AFTER THE MEETING, we started a three-week holiday and Andrew Oldham was quoted in the *Daily Express* on our new business arrangements:

'Under the terms of a deal concluded by our American business manager, Mr Allen Klein, the Stones are guaranteed three million dollars over the next five years.'

Meanwhile Mick and Chrissie went on holiday to Morocco. Somewhat surprisingly, given the pending court case, Brian and Linda Lawrence went with them. They all stayed at the Hotel Minzah in Tangier.

From left, *Donald Cammell, Robert Fraser, Deborah Dixon, Linda Lawrence, Brian and Ali, who was employed by Fraser.*

saying, 'Brian and Linda went to Tangier together for a holiday. The decision was made very suddenly.' According to Linda, the press speculation soured the holiday.

Moroccan-roll
London art gallery owner Robert Fraser, model Deborah Dixon and her artist and director boyfriend Donald Cammell were also staying at the hotel. They later acted coldly towards Linda

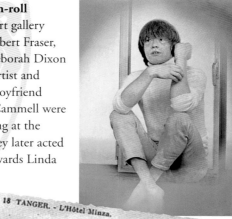

18 TANGER. - L'Hôtel Minza.

'Brian thought Morocco was amazing. The whole way of life seemed to attract him. Morocco was a place where he could forget all that had happened back in England.' LINDA LAWRENCE

Keith and his Linda went on holiday to the south of France, while Diane, Stephen and I went to stay with my brother John, who was in the air force in Germany.

The press found out about Brian's trip and, as usual with a Stones story, had a field day. They quoted Linda's mother

Frampton comes alive
Peter Frampton was born at Stone Park Nursing Home, Beckenham, Kent on 22 April, 1950. In his early years, he lived in Penge. Peter went to Bromley Grammar School and in his second year, aged 12, he joined a local group called the Truebeats. He went on to play with the Preachers and the Herd and became a superstar in the 1970s. He teamed up with Bill again in the 1990s to play with the Rhythm Kings.

(4) 'It is impossible to do Isle of Man on 8 [September]. We need record. Must record between 5 and 10 [September], Cancel date.'

Eric replied to the burst of demands:

'I cannot understand how the cables were supposed to have been sent by Mick since I have spoken to him on the telephone this morning at his flat in London. He has just returned from Tangiers and was surprised to hear that cables had been sent to me bearing his name. He has no idea of what is going on in New York. Neither have I, for that matter.'

Eric wrote at length explaining various aspects of the business arrangements. Whatever the truth of who decided to send what and who knew about it

Studios, with Glyn Johns. Playing guitar was Peter Frampton, a young neighbourhood friend of mine. The next day I was back at IBC working with a band called the End, cutting 'I Can't Get Any Joy' and 'Hey Little Girl'.

Soon after, we met with Klein and Andrew in London. We were there to discuss Eric, whose arrival heralded a full-scale row. Klein accused him of cheating us and told him he was no longer handling our bookings, which in future would be done by Tito Burns.

'We decided on an American as our new business manager because when you are handling world-wide transactions, America is the only place to work from and it's very useful to have a man on the spot,' Keith told the *NME* on 3 September. In *Disc* magazine he added, 'Eric Easton was just too tired. We couldn't get anything done. He's not all

'The group scene will disappear in six months, with the exception of the Beatles, the Stones and the Animals.' ALLEN KLEIN, *NME, 27 August, 1965*

and Brian after reading press reports.

Brian freaked out and became paranoid as he worried about never getting away from the press. He came back on his own and Linda returned with the others. Robert gave her a huge lump of hash to carry home – she had no idea what it was and blithely walked through customs.

Eric continued to deal with General Artist Corporation (GAC) about our tour and we appeared on *Shindig* to perform 'Down The Road Apiece', taped back in May. On 13 August, Eric wrote to Andrew at Klein's New York office. The letter was in response to the following four cables that he had received from Mick, Keith and Andrew:

(1) 'In order to secure the written consent of the Stones required for contracts on the proposed English tour please forward forthwith all contracts and pertinent details to Allen Klein. The Stones will not be the promoters.'

(2) 'In order to secure the written consent of the Stones required for contracts on the proposed German tour, please forward forthwith all contracts and pertinent details to Allen Klein.'

(3) 'We direct that you desist from holding our money at GAC [General Artist Corporation]. It is our money isn't it?'

in advance, it was the beginning of Eric's end.

Next day, Keith and his girlfriend Linda returned home from France. He and Mick met up at Heathrow and flew to New York to join Andrew. The rest of us were blissfully unaware of these behind-the-scenes manoeuvrings that were to have such far-reaching consequences. The three of them went to see the Beatles at Shea Stadium and attended the after-show party. They also met with lawyers from London Records and Decca Records, along with Klein's lawyer, Marty Machat.

On Friday 20 August, 'Satisfaction' came out in England, which precipitated a round of TV appearances to promote the single, which had already topped the US charts. Two days later we played a gig in Scarborough, along with Lulu and the Luvvers. We were paid £950, three times what we earned a year earlier.

I continued working on my own projects. I cut 'Tomorrow' with Bobbie Miller at IBC

that young and after the strain of our last two US tours, he couldn't make the third one due to illness. It's been a very happy relationship. Klein is young and knows what's happening. We'll keep in touch by phone.' Mick added that 'it had been more or less decided for several months'.

In true music business style, the bullshit machine had also kicked into overdrive on another front: we were *definitely* going to be film stars!

'The Stones have signed an agreement for their record company Decca to finance five films to be made over the next three years. The minimum budget is £1,700,000.'
EVENING NEWS, *27 August, 1965*

McCartney and Lennon at Shea Stadium, New York: Keith, Andrew and Mick watched the show.

IMMEDIATE RECORDS

A NEW RECORD COMPANY OF TOMORROW TODAY

As Allen Klein appeared on the scene, Andrew was making plans to further his own ambitions. In the week that he wrote endless letters about various aspects of the Stones' business arrangements, he formed Immediate Records with Tony Calder, whose background was, like Andrew's, in PR. Although Immediate sometimes lacked decent recorded material it was never short of a good promotional punchline.

'Whatever people thought about Andrew, he had enormous flair and was very much the man on the ball at the time.' KEITH ALTHAM, *NME journalist and press agent*

Tony Calder, Andrew Oldham and Mickie Most

O n 20 August, the day of the label's first release, there was a launch party attended by Mick, Eric Clapton, Mike Clark (drummer with the Byrds) and Nico, who would later sing with the Velvet Underground. The label's first single, 'Hang On Sloopy' by the McCoys, reached UK No 5.

The McCoys first appeared on American Bert Burns' Bang label and Andrew, shrewd as ever, leased the rights for $2,000. Andrew naturally made a great deal about his association with the Stones and, in particular, Mick and Keith, but it wasn't until Immediate's 18th release in October 1965 that the two

of them were involved with the label. They wrote 'Wastin' Time', the b-side for comedian Jimmy Tarbuck's first release; it is without doubt as bad a record as the label ever put out, a complete dud.

Mick also produced 'Though It Hurts Me Badly', the b-side of PP Arnold's '(If You Think You're) Groovy'. Andrew and Mick co-produced the b-side of Nicky Scott's debut single.

'Andrew thought anything was possible if you put enough echo on it.' KEITH

Glyn Johns also had a single released on the label, 'Mary Jane', written by Jerry Lordan and produced by former Shadows drummer Tony Meehan. It failed to chart. Jimmy Page, later of Led Zeppelin, was a significant member of the Immediate family. He produced, played on and arranged many of the singles. Among his production credits was September 1967's 'I'm Your Witchdoctor' by John Mayall's Bluesbreakers with Eric Clapton.

The label folded in February 1970 with Amen Corner's 'Get Back' the last of their 84 singles to be released in October 1969. Immediate had 24 UK Top 50 hits, of which nine went UK Top 10. 'Out of Time' by Chris Farlowe and '(If Paradise is) Half As Nice' by Amen Corner went to UK No 1.

Session man Jimmy Page

Happy to be a part of the industry of human happiness
Mick and Keith wrote tracks in bold

10/65	IM018	'Someday'/**'Wastin' Time'**	Jimmy Tarbuck	(producer ALO)
1/66	IM023	**'Think'**/'Don't Just Look At Me'	Chris Farlowe	(producer ALO/Mick/Keith) No 37
2/66	IM025	**'So Much In Love'**/'Our Soul Brother'	Charles Dickens	(producer ALO)
5/66	IM033	**'Sittin' On The Fence'**/'Baby I Want You'	Twice As Much	(producer ALO) No 25
6/66	IM035	**'Out Of Time'**/'Baby Make It Soon'	Chris Farlowe	(producer Mick) No 1
10/66	IM038	**'Ride On Baby'**/'Headlines'	Chris Farlowe	(producer Mick) No 31
1/67	IM045	**'Back Street Girl'**/'Chain Reaction'	Nicky Scott	(producer ALO/Mick)
5/67	IM049	**'Yesterday's Papers'**/'Life Is But Nothing'	Chris Farlowe	(producer Mick)
7/68	IM071	**'Paint It, Black'**/'I Just Need Your Loving'	Chris Farlowe	(producer Mick)
7/68	IM078	**'Out Of Time'**/**'Ride On Baby'**	Chris Farlowe	(producer Mick)

Knackered!

September began with us recording a *Ready Steady Go!* Rolling Stones special. Mickie Most performed 'Johnny B Goode' and Chris Farlowe sang 'In The Midnight Hour'. After a performance by Goldie and the Gingerbreads, I introduced the Preachers (with Peter Frampton), who sang 'Hole In My Soul', followed by Manfred Mann.

'On the TV monitor was Andrew, clad in bobcat waistcoat, miming to Cher's voice and benevolently patting Mick on the head. Mick mimed a reply via Sonny's line. The Sonny and Cher send-up was just one of the hysterical highlights in the Stones take-over of RSG!' KEITH ALTHAM, *NME, 10 September, 1965*

On board the train to Ireland

THE DAY AFTER RECORDING we were off to Ireland where we were to be filmed by director Peter Whitehead for a documentary about the band called *Charlie is My Darling*.

'What I liked most about that film was the fact that when the Stones were talking they were really quite inarticulate,' Whitehead told *Films and Filming* magazine in February 1974. 'There was a kind of groping. There was an extraordinary inability to describe what they were doing. In fact, Brian Jones was the only one who was really articulate.'

On the night of our arrival, we played two shows in Dublin's Adelphi theatre. It was the first time that we had performed 'Satisfaction' live on stage. The *Daily Mirror* reported the expected chaos: 'As the Stones finished "Satisfaction", fierce fighting broke out between fans and theatre attendants, stopping the show. Bill was knocked to the floor, an arm badly sprained, as screaming girls and boys stormed the stage.

'Mick was lifted off his feet and pushed through a door at the side of the stage. His jacket was torn to shreds. Andrew Oldham cracked his head as he fought to clear the teenagers off the stage. Keith, Charlie and Brian ran out of the stage door into a waiting car.

'A minute later, Mick and Bill joined them, chased by screaming girls. As the car pulled away, some teenagers who had tried to get into the Stones dressing room were still fighting backstage.'

'This was one of the most frightening scenes that I have seen at a beat show. All the boys are rather shaken up, particularly Bill. His arm is quite badly strained. The drum kit was smashed to pieces.' ANDREW OLDHAM, *Daily Mirror, 4 September, 1965*

Stones for sale
At Sotheby's rock'n'roll and film memorabilia auction on 21 August, 1980, a double-sided 12-inch Emidisc acetate went on sale. It featured the Stones' recording of 'I'm Free' on one side and the Everly Brothers' version of 'Let It Be Me' on the other.

'There was this incredible transformation from dressing room to stage. Suddenly they were there and bang.' PETER WHITEHEAD, *Films And Filming magazine, February 1974*

The next day we played the ABC Theatre in Belfast and from there we travelled direct to Heathrow, transferring onto a flight to Los Angeles. Later that same evening, we went to RCA Studios in Hollywood to record with our favourite engineer, Dave Hassinger. We worked all night with Jack Nitzsche and cut 'Get Off Of My Cloud' and three other tracks. Brian and I later went out to the clubs with Kathy Townsend, who was my girlfriend in Los Angeles.

'We went to the Trip Club,' she remembered. 'All the important people on the club scene were coming over and getting to know you.'

Back in the studio

The following evening we returned to RCA. We cut 'I'm Free', 'Lookin' Tired' and two other tracks with Jack. During the session I had to have a doctor come in, as I was feeling ill from exhaustion. I think I was burning the candle at both ends – actually, I know I was.

We flew back to the UK overnight and arrived home on the morning of Wednesday 7 September. We freshened up and then returned to Heathrow to catch a flight to the Isle of Man to play the Palace Ballroom. Mick and Keith had insisted that Eric cancel this gig, but we were contractually obliged to play it. We were knackered. When we flew back from Douglas the following day, we found Klein had deposited $47,326.85 into each of our personal accounts at the Chemical Bank, New York. This sounds like a lot of money, but we had sold a phenomenal amount of records worldwide by this point. On a

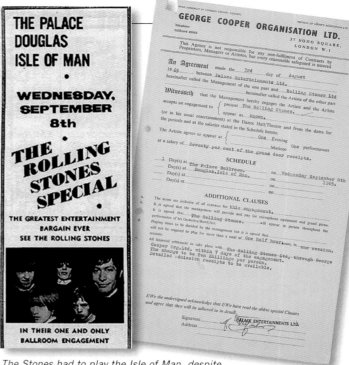

The Stones had to play the Isle of Man, despite their protests – the organisers had a contract to prove it.

Germany calling

Germany's introduction to the Stones was a riotous five-city affair with a sixth night tacked on in Vienna, Austria. Five thousand screaming fans greeted the Stones as they flew into Düsseldorf... and many water cannons greeted the fans.

11 September, 1965 Münsterland Halle, Münster, West Germany (two shows)
12 September Gruga-Halle, Essen, West Germany (two shows)
13 September Ernst Merck Halle, Hamburg, West Germany (two shows)
14 September Circus Krone-Bau, Munich, West Germany (two shows)
15 September Waldbuhne Halle, West Berlin, West Germany
17 September Wiener Stadthalle, Vienna, Austria

Support bands The Rackets, Didi and the ABC Boys, Team Beats, the Rivets

Programme for the tour

'In West Berlin,' remembered Bill, 'our dressing rooms were in the old military bunkers and backstage there were police with dogs everywhere. The crowd was estimated at between 21,000 and 23,000.' On 17 September, the *Daily Telegraph* reported, 'Damage to the open-air theatre, which looked like a battlefield, was estimated at £27,000.'

When the band got to Vienna, they played to 12,500 fans, 'but not before the police received a phone call that a bomb would explode before we appeared on stage,' said Bill. 'Some fans were arrested, and about 800 police stopped what might have been a riot.'

'I have seen nothing like this since the old days of a Nazi or Communist rally.' ESSEN POLICEMAN, *Daily Mail*, 13 September, 1965

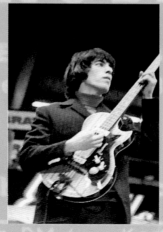

Food served to the band backstage.

Anita Pallenberg

personal level, it was a good day for Brian, as Linda Lawrence withdrew the summons she had issued against him. She and Brian broke up not long afterwards.

Brian was soon involved with another girl. In the interval between shows in Munich, Brian met Anita Pallenberg. The daughter of Lutheran parents, Anita was brought up in Rome, Italy. She was expelled from boarding school, studied graphic design in Germany and then became a photographer's assistant in New York, before taking up modelling. She was to be a major force in Brian's life.

The band flew home from Vienna on Saturday 18 September, too late to catch a session we had recorded for BBC radio's *Saturday Club*. Besides 'Satisfaction', we'd played Buster Brown's 'Fannie Mae' – that was the one which inspired 'The Under Assistant West Coast Promotion Man'.

The original… Not the best?

We also came home to a rather strange story about the Stone Brothers from the West Country. They claimed they owned the name the Rolling Stones, having registered it under the Companies Act in November 1957.

'We are the original Rolling Stones. We live in Bristol and do a cabaret turn at dances. We now bill ourselves as the Stone Brothers – the Rolling Stones, but we still want to establish our right to the name of the Rolling Stones.' BRIAN STONE, DAILY MAIL, *24 September, 1965*

Nothing ever came of their claim. I'm sure no one would have been confused by the two sets of Stones. At the end of the week, on the day we started a UK package tour, Mike Dorsey left us. He was replaced by Tom Keylock, whose first job was to drive us to the Astoria gig in Finsbury Park. That same day, our third UK album was released. Called *Out of Our Heads*, it differed quite considerably from the US version which had come out six weeks earlier.

out of our heads

Out Of Our Heads was the first Stones album to be issued in the UK in stereo. The UK version dropped six of the US tracks and introduced six different titles, three of which were Mick and Keith compositions.

Before the album was finished, test pressings of each track were made to ensure they were the correct masters.

Under the influence

Of the three different cover versions on the UK release, 'Oh Baby' had appeared on *The Rolling Stones Now!* in the USA. The others were 'She Said Yeah', originally recorded by Larry Williams in 1959, whose 'Short Fat Fannie' was a US R&B No 1 in 1957, and 'Talkin' 'Bout You', a Chuck Berry a-side in 1961.

Side one
1. 'She Said Yeah' Christy/Jackson
2. 'Mercy Mercy' Covay/Miller
3. 'Hitch Hike' Gaye/Stevenson/Paul
4. 'That's How Strong My Love Is' Jamison
5. 'Good Times' Cooke
6. 'Gotta Get Away' Jagger/Richard

Side two
7. 'Talkin' 'Bout You' Berry
8. 'Cry To Me' Russell
9. 'Oh Baby' Ozen
10. 'Heart of Stone' Jagger/Richard
11 'The Under Assistant West Coast Promotion Man' Nanker/Phelge
12. 'I'm Free' Jagger/Richard

Recorded
Side 1: 1, 6 (September 5 or 6, 1965), 2, 4 (10 May, 1965), 3 (2 November, 1964), 5 (13 May, 1965)
Side 2: 1 (5 or 6 September, 1965), 2 (13 May, 1965), 3, 4 (2 November, 1964), 5 (10 May, 1965), 6 (6 September, 1965)

Studios
Side 1: 1, 3, 5, 6 (RCA, Hollywood), 2, 4 (Chess Studios, Chicago)
Side 2: 1, 2, 3, 4, 6 (RCA), 5 (Chess)

Producer
Andrew Loog Oldham

Engineers
Dave Hassinger at RCA
Ron Malo at Chess

Cover photography
David Bailey

Release
UK Friday 24 September, 1965
Decca SKL 4733

Highest chart position (time on chart)
UK No 2, 2 October, 1965 (UK 24 weeks)

The United Kingdom,
September–October 1965

24 September Astoria Theatre, Finsbury Park, London
25 September Gaumont Theatre, Southampton, Hampshire
26 September Colston Hall, Bristol, Gloucestershire
27 September Odeon Theatre, Cheltenham, Gloucestershire
28 September Capitol Theatre, Cardiff, Wales
29 September Granada Theatre, Shrewsbury, Shropshire
30 September Gaumont Theatre, Hanley, Staffordshire
1 October ABC Theatre, Chester, Cheshire
2 October ABC Theatre, Wigan, Lancashire
3 October Odeon Theatre, Manchester, Lancashire
4 October Gaumont Theatre, Bradford, Yorkshire
5 October ABC Theatre, Carlisle, Cumberland
6 October Odeon Theatre, Glasgow, Scotland
7 October City Hall, Newcastle upon Tyne, Northumberland
8 October ABC Theatre, Stockton-on-Tees, Durham
9 October Odeon Theatre, Leeds, Yorkshire
10 October Empire Theatre, Liverpool, Lancashire
11 October Gaumont Theatre, Sheffield, Yorkshire
12 October Gaumont Theatre, Doncaster, Yorkshire
13 October De Montfort Hall, Leicester, Leicestershire
14 October Odeon Theatre, Birmingham, Staffordshire
15 October Regal Theatre, Cambridge, Cambridgeshire
16 October ABC Theatre, Northampton, Northamptonshire
17 October Granada Theatre, Tooting, London

On some dates, the Moody Blues were added to the line-up.

Twenty-four dates in 24 days and two shows every night... it was just like the old days.

'Things on this tour were much better organised, although we were still getting plenty of screaming girls and over-zealous fans. One thing that made it easier for us was the fact that we stayed in hotels well away from where we were actually performing. After we played in Carlisle we stayed in Kelso, two hours drive to the north. After our show the following night in Glasgow we went to a hotel in Peebles, which was an hour south, but on the way to our next night's gig in Newcastle.' BILL

Among the support bands on the tour were the End, who were working with Bill. He produced their first single, 'I Can't Get Any Joy', which came out on Philips the same day as 'Get Off Of My Cloud' was released in the UK. The End failed to chart. The main support act were the Spencer Davis Group, who had scored with three minor hit singles. Three weeks after the tour ended they released a cover of 'Keep on Running' by Jamaican singer Jackie Edwards and topped the UK singles chart. The track featured 17-year-old Stevie Winwood playing organ.

The Spencer Davis Group

Set list
'She Said Yeah'
'Mercy Mercy'
'Cry To Me'
'The Last Time'
'That's How Strong My Love Is'
'I'm Moving On'
'Talkin' 'Bout You'
'Oh Baby'
'Satisfaction'

Just Like The Old Days

'GET OFF OF MY CLOUD'

The eighth single on both sides of the Atlantic came out earlier in the US, where 'Satisfaction' had already begun to slip down the chart. 'Get Off Of My Cloud' became the second Stones single to top the charts on both sides of the Atlantic and their fifth UK chart-topper in a row. This was a feat only previously achieved in Britain by Elvis and the Beatles.

Keith has said it was kind of rushed, in the desperate drive to have a follow-up that maintained their chart momentum. But it is easy to see why it was so popular and not just because the Stones themselves were on the crest of a wave. Mick's lyrics and Keith's melody make it a great pop record.

Dave Hassinger became a recording engineer in 1959, at a time when rock'n'roll was all very tame. He worked with such artists as Bobby Rydell, Brenda Lee and Bobby Darin, ensuring that he recorded the singers louder than the orchestras backing them. He went on to work with Sam Cooke and the Johnny Mann Singers.

'A mutual friend, Jack Nitzsche, recommended me to them. After the first session they told everyone that I was great and made a big deal of coming out to Hollywood specially to record with me.'
DAVE HASSINGER

On the US b-side, 'I'm Free', tambourine was played by Mississippi-born James Alexander, a session musician who also worked with Sam Cooke, the Bar-Kays and Isaac Hayes. Mick and Keith share the vocals on UK b-side 'The Singer Not The Song.'

There have been around 30 covers of the a-side including versions by the Flying Pickets (1982) and Crap Bloke (1998). Sheryl Crow included it in her live set in the 1990s.

Stones' 'Cloud' Shines in Poll

LONDON — The Rolling Stones' "Get Off My Cloud" won top place by a six-nation voting panel in the European Pop Jury program, part of the European Broadcasting Union's "Radio in Europe" week. The Stones' disk was one of the U. K. record entries.

Sweden, Norway, Finland, Belgium, Switzerland and Britain took part, each entering a record from its own country and one foreign. Runner-ups were "Yesterday" by the Beatles, entered by Finland, and "Eve of Destruction" by Barry McGuire, entered by Switzerland.

A total of 1,200 voters took part, 200 at each country's station studio. The program was heard simultaneously in all six countries.

The Stones were a Europe-wide hit with the single.

US b-side
'I'm Free'
Recorded
a-side 5 September, 1965
UK b-side 5 or 6 September, 1965
US b-side 6 September, 1965
Studio
RCA Hollywood
Producer
Andrew Loog Oldham for Impact Sound
Engineer
Dave Hassinger
Release
US 25 September, 1965
London 45 9792
UK 22 October, 1965
Decca F 12263
Composers
All songs by Jagger/Richard
Highest chart position
US No 1, for two weeks
UK No 1, for three weeks

STONES SCORE A DOUBLE TOP IN THE CHARTS

THE Rolling Stones jumped to the top of the hit parade yesterday — on both sides of the Atlantic.

In Britain, the pop group's disc "Get Off Of My Cloud" toppled Ken Dodd's "Tears" which had been top for six weeks.

And in America the record took over from Beatle Paul McCartney's "Yesterday."

Pop Thirty—see Page 26

The single made a splash in the papers

NME TOP THIRTY

FIRST-EVER CHART IN BRITAIN
—AND STILL THE **FIRST** TODAY !
(Wednesday, November 10, 1965)

Last Week	This Week			Highest Position	Weeks in chart
1	1	GET OFF OF MY CLOUD	Rolling Stones (Decca)	3-	1
2	2	YESTERDAY MAN	Chris Andrews (Decca)	6-	2
16	3	MY GENERATION			
15	4	1-2-3	Len		
7	5	IT'S MY LIFE			
4	6	HERE IT COMES AGAIN			
11	7	THE CARNIVAL IS OVER			

The new single went down well with reviewers.

ROLLING STONES — GET OFF OF MY CLOUD (Gideon, BMI)—Another wild, far out beat number which will have no trouble topping their "Satisfaction" smash. Rocks all the way with exciting vocal work. Flip: "I'm Free" (Gideon, BMI).
London 9792

Civilisation's End

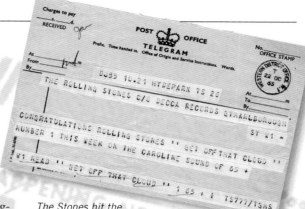

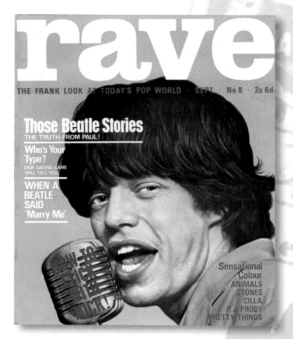

Mid-way through our tour with Spencer Davis, an interesting article came out in *Rave* magazine. It gave a rare and candid insight into how Brian saw things at this point in his life. Brian's views on marriage were, for the time, particularly revolutionary.

'The most important thing in my world is my work. Of course, I like a good time, but these days I get very conscious of doing nothing. I have a different attitude to people now, too. I've found out that if you adopt a friendly attitude to anybody, they can become a friend. This is because I've learnt to respect people even though I may not really like them. I'm quite shy about girls although that may surprise you. I always have been frightened of getting too involved. It's the thought of marriage that I hate. I think in these modern days, it would be a good idea to have one-year marriage contracts that you could renew only if you wanted to. Everything for me is so temporary that I can't think ahead for more than a year.'
BRIAN, *Rave Magazine*, October 1965

BRIAN ALSO TALKED about opening a boutique and becoming a film producer. Looking back, it's possible to see the signs that Brian knew he was being sidelined. Perhaps he had an inkling that his long-term future was not with the Stones. According to another music paper, Mick also needed to consider his options.

'How good a singer is Mick? He has serious shortcomings. He relies far too much on gestures, some of which border on the vulgar. The time may yet come when Mick will have to have a private talk with himself, and decide whether his future lies with the Stones or whether he will one day have to make it on his own.'
POP WEEKLY, *2 October, 1965*

This was no new story, but one that kept reappearing. The pop media found it difficult to think of different things to write about us and relied on recycling old stories. Having said that, Mick did a pretty good job of feeding the press.

'The more records we sell, the more money there is for me and I like money. The novelty of the group routine has worn off. I like the idea of being someone.' MICK, *Record Mirror, 14 October, 1965*

Mick and Keith also had fairly direct views on marriage, as they told the *News Of The World* on 31 October. 'Boys don't think of marriage until it's forced on them.' said Keith.

Mick quipped: 'Marriage isn't on my mind. It's simple to keep single if you're as infantile as I am.'

With the tour over, all of us were preoccupied with our own lives. Brian bought a Rolls Royce (registration DD666) and Charlie and Shirley

moved into the Old Brewery, Lewes.

The following week, I celebrated my 29th birthday and did a photo session for Vox endorsing the new 'Wyman Bass' which I'd recently started playing. Two days later we were off again to America to begin our fourth US tour.

Sign of the Times

We arrived in New York about four hours late. There were still hundreds of fans waiting at the airport to meet us. We got into downtown New York to see a 100-foot tall, illuminated billboard in Times Square, advertising our new US album *December's Children*.

We held a press conference the following day, fielding the usual dumb questions from reporters with preconceived notions. Bob Dylan dropped by – he and Brian hung out a lot while we were in the New York area. Brian was jamming in his room some weeks later, with Dylan, Robbie Robertson and Bobby Neuwirth, when the power failed. They switched to playing acoustic guitars by candlelight, the great lost jam, as it has since been called. The

Brian and Bob Dylan

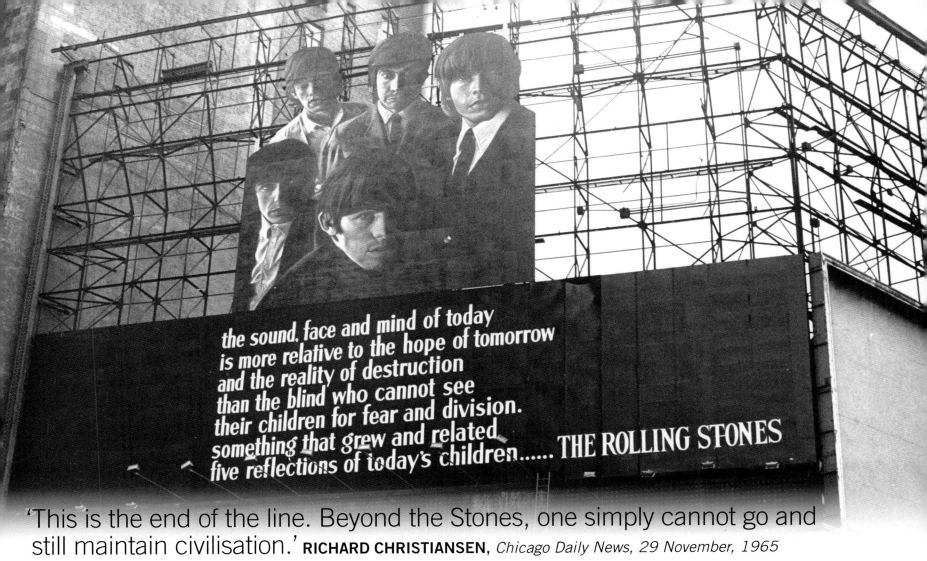

the sound, face and mind of today is more relative to the hope of tomorrow and the reality of destruction than the blind who cannot see their children for fear and division. something that grew and related five reflections of today's children...... THE ROLLING STONES

'This is the end of the line. Beyond the Stones, one simply cannot go and still maintain civilisation.' **RICHARD CHRISTIANSEN,** *Chicago Daily News, 29 November, 1965*

Mick and Keith song-writing in their hotel, New York City, 1965

New York power failure lasted 12 hours and was the biggest in American history. It also blacked out parts of nine states.

We flew by charter plane to Montreal in Canada for our first gig of the tour. Keith had lost his passport in New York and we had to smuggle him through Canadian Immigration by crowding the area and continually moving around. The officials could not count how many were actually in our party.

'The first time I ever saw the Stones perform was at the Forum in Montreal in October 1965. It was only afterwards, when I happened to walk past the bus terminal that I glimpsed what had really just happened. There in the station were hundreds of youths, all speaking French, waiting to complete their pilgrimage by plunging back into the cold of northern Quebec. I had never seen so much long hair in one place in my life.' ROBERT CHRISTGAU, *in The Rolling Stone Illustrated History of Rock'n'Roll, 1980*

Keith with typical frankness told *KRLA Beat* magazine, 'I will never move to the States because I couldn't stand hamburgers every day.' The writer Tom Wolfe said, 'The Beatles want to hold your hand, but the Stones want to burn your town.'

'There is something elegantly sinister about the Stones. They sit before you like five unfolding switchblades, their faces set in rehearsed snarls, their hair studiously unkempt and matted and the way they walk and the way they talk and the songs they sing, all become part of some long, mean reach for the jugular.' PETE HAMILL, *New York Post*

Live at the Academy, NYC, 6 November

Brian gets into mischief in the back of a bus.

The Stones' fourth US tour was by far the biggest of their career up to that point. They played 37 venues in 38 days. There were concerts in 20 different states, along with appearances in Washington, DC, and Canada. The band played matinees and evening shows on six different days and had only seven days off in almost eight weeks away from home.

North America, *October–December 1965*

29 October Forum, Montréal, Quebec, Canada
30 October Barton Hall, Cornell University, Ithaca, New York (matinee)
    War Memorial Hall, Syracuse, New York (evening)
31 October Maple Leaf Gardens, Toronto, Canada
1 November War Memorial Auditorium, Rochester, New York
3 November Auditorium, Providence, Rhode Island
4 November Loews State Theater, Newhaven, Connecticut (two shows)
5 November Boston Gardens, Boston, Massachusetts
6 November Academy of Music, New York (matinee)
    Convention Hall, Philadelphia, Pennsylvania (evening)
7 November Mosque Theater, Newark, New Jersey (two shows)
10 November Reynolds Coliseum, Raleigh, North Carolina
12 November Memorial Auditorium, Greensboro, North Carolina
13 November Coliseum, Washington, DC (matinee)
    Civic Center, Baltimore, Maryland (evening)
14 November Civic Coliseum Auditorium, Knoxville, Tennessee (matinee)
15 November Coliseum, Charlotte, North Carolina
16 November Municipal Auditorium, Nashville, Tennessee
17 November Mid-South Coliseum, Memphis, Tennessee
20 November State Fair Youth Center, Shreveport, Louisiana
21 November Will Rogers Stadium, Fort Worth, Texas (matinee)
    Memorial Auditorium, Dallas, Texas (evening)
23 November Assembly Center, Tulsa, Oklahoma
24 November Civic Arena, Pittsburgh, Pennsylvania
25 November Milwaukee Auditorium, Milwaukee, Wisconsin
26 November Cobo Hall, Detroit, Michigan
27 November Hara Arena, Dayton, Ohio (matinee)
    The Gardens, Cincinnati, Ohio (evening)
28 November Aire Crown Theater, McCormick Place,
    Chicago, Illinois (two shows)
29 November Coliseum, Denver, Colorado
30 November Veterans' Memorial Coliseum, Phoenix, Arizona
1 December Agrodome, Vancouver, British Columbia, Canada
2 December Coliseum, Seattle, Washington
3 December Memorial Auditorium, Sacramento, California
4 December Civic Auditorium, San Jose, California (two shows)
5 December Convention Hall, San Diego, California (matinee)
    Sports Arena, Los Angeles, California, (evening)

F an mania hit hard on this tour. There were several abandoned concerts and the police had their work cut out trying to control what were the largest audiences the Stones had so far played to in America. They performed to over 250,000 people on a tour that put them into a different league in America.

'On the tour we grossed around $500,000, and earned $50,418.62 each. We didn't see the money at the time, which was a pity, as when I got home at the end it I had £170 in my current account.' BILL

'When the Stones came on stage the excitement level was very high. Usually within the space of two songs, the first aid places backstage would be full of fainting and hysterical teenagers. Whatever magic was there was in the band's performance. The police presence was enormous, but very unprofessional. At the slightest disturbance the show was stopped, the house lights would go up and the local sheriff would be on stage. To this day I can't hear those songs without feeling the bass line running up my leg. Bill told me that the reason he played the bass with the neck straight up was so that he could shade his eyes from the spotlights and be able to see the girls in the front row. You could see him pulling the girls while he was still on stage.' GERED MANKOWITZ, *photographer*

'It was a great concert, but the thing that marred it was a group of big tough policemen, who threw a girl bodily out of a door just for taking a picture.' GWYNNE BUTTLE, *fan, Detroit, 26 November*

And in support...
At most gigs the support bands were the Rocking Ramrods, Patti LaBelle and the Blue Belles and the Vibrations. The Embers played some shows.

Set list
'Get Off Of My Cloud'
'Everybody Needs Somebody
 To Love'
'Play With Fire'
'Mercy Mercy'
'Around And Around'
'The Last Time'
'That's How Strong My Love Is'
'Satisfaction'

Twenty-State Rock

Catching some sun in San Diego

'The Texas State Security Guard called and said, "How do we protect your guys?" We said, "Put up a moat," and so they did. It was 15-feet wide, filled with water, with a stage-length barricade, and nobody could swim the moat. It was like a gigantic swimming pool in front of the stage.'
BOB BONIS, *tour manager*

'My friends, Ron Martin, Brian Lee and I lived in a little town called Leaksville 30 miles north of Greensboro. Since only one of us had turned 16, he drove to the Memorial Auditorium. We arrived and saw the marquee: "Tonight! The Rolling Stones!" Our tickets had cost the staggering sum of five dollars. We were dressed like three 1950s nerds, we all had crewcuts (two of us were on the high school football team) and I had on my new, three-piece herring-bone suit. Most of the audience looked the same – nicely dressed. The five English gentlemen were dressed like I wanted to dress; I was immediately struck by how thin they were. I saw Brian Jones and decided he was pretty cool and would be a positive image for me in my own rock band. The band cranked up with a number before Mick said anything to the audience. At that point in the Stones' career Mick seemed organically connected to the band. There was no wild screaming and yelling. The polite audience, dressed like they were at a garden party, clapped warmly after each song. A special treat of t he evening was the band performing their recent hit "Satisfaction." We were waiting to see how Keith did the opening intro. We were really surprised that he was actually playing the riff on a guitar since some of our friends had speculated that it was a saxophone. I followed their career throughout the 1970s and 1980s, but that 1965 concert was how I always remember the Rolling Stones.' JOHN MARSHALL CARTER, *fan*

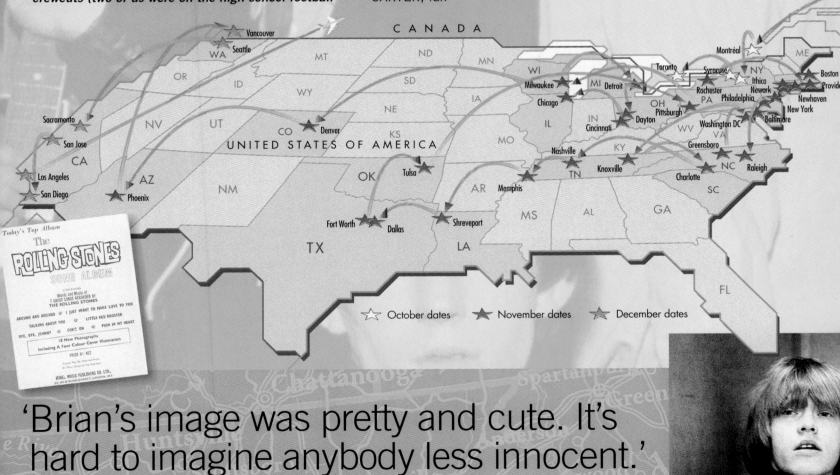

'Brian's image was pretty and cute. It's hard to imagine anybody less innocent.'
GERED MANKOWITZ, *photographer*

Side 1
1. 'She Said Yeah' Christy/Jackson
2. 'Talkin' 'Bout You' Berry
3. 'You Better Move On' Alexander
4. 'Look What You've Done' Morganfield
5. 'The Singer Not The Song' Jagger/Richard
6. 'Route 66' (live) Troup

Side 2
1. 'Get Off Of My Cloud' Jagger/Richard
2. 'I'm Free' Jagger/Richard
3. 'As Tears Go By' Jagger/Richard/Oldham
4. 'Gotta Get Away' Jagger/Richard
5. 'Blue Turns to Grey' Jagger/Richard
6. 'I'm Moving On' (live) Snow

Recording
Side 1: 1, 2, 5 (5–6 September, 1965), 3 (8 August, 1963), 4 (11 June, 1964), 6 (5–7 March, 1965) Side 2: 1 (5 September, 1965), 2 (6 September, 1965), 3 (26 October, 1965), 4, 5 (5–6 September, 1965), 6 (5–7 March, 1965)

Locations
Side 1: 1, 2, 5 (RCA, Hollywood), 3 (Decca Studios, London), 4 (Chess Studios, Chicago), 6 (recorded live in London, Liverpool or Manchester) Side 2: 1, 2, 4, 5 (RCA), 3 (IBC studios, London), 6 (recorded live in London, Liverpool or Manchester)

Producer
Andrew Loog Oldham

Engineers
Ron Malo at Chess
Dave Hassinger at RCA
Glyn Johns at IBC and at live shows

Cover photography
Gered Mankowitz

Release
US Saturday 4 December, 1965 London LL 3451

Highest chart position (time on charts)
US No 4 (22 weeks)

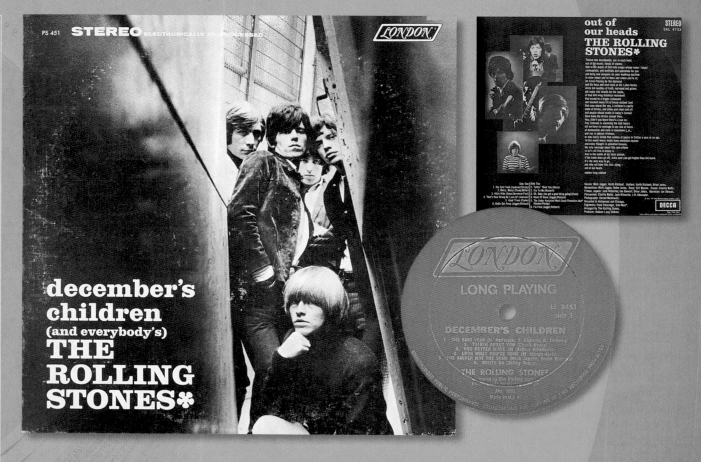

'December's Children isn't an album, it's just a collection of songs.' MICK JAGGER, 1968

This strange mixture of an album was the band's fifth in the US. It was recorded at various locations between August 1963 and October 1965. Its 'hip' title was coined by Andrew Oldham and was probably only relevant in that it was released in December.

'Blue Turns to Grey' had been written by Mick and Keith late in 1964. It was first recorded by Dick and Dee Dee as the b-side to an Andrew Oldham-produced single on Warner Brothers that December. In February of 1965, the Mighty Avengers, again produced by Oldham, cut it as the a-side of their Decca single.

The arrangement on this version was by John Paul Jones. In March 1966, Cliff Richard also cut a version at Abbey Road with the Shadows and reached UK No 15.

No one can remember if Keith was in the studio the day before the Stones left for their fourth American tour. In all probability it was just Mick working with Mike Leander. Mike did the arrangement for a string quartet, which worked brilliantly on the Stones version.

'"As Tears Go By" hit UK No 9 for Marianne Faithfull in late summer 1964. When Mick decided to cut it, he did so at IBC Studios with Andy producing and Stones' old friend Glyn Johns as engineer.' BILL

POP SPOTLIGHT

DECEMBER'S CHILDREN
(And Everybodys)
Rolling Stones. London LL 3451 (M); PS 451 (S)

With "Get Off of My Cloud" featured, the unique group has another top-of-the-chart entry. Along with the hit, the pop blues-rock material is tops as witnessed by "Blues Turn to Gray" and "She Said Yeah." A beautiful ballad featuring a solo by Mike, backed by full rich strings, has the potential of the Beatles' "Yesterday."

Under the influence
Only one song on this album was a cover that had not appeared on any other Stones release – Muddy Waters' 'Look What You've Done'.

Call Me Indestructible

The American tour confirmed our increasing popularity. We were also causing outrage in the press much as we had done in Britain. We finished the trip in fine style, although at one point we almost had to find a new guitarist.

DURING OUR STAY AT THE City Squire Hotel, over-enthusiastic fans did around $50,000 worth of damage.

Brian phoned Anita Pallenberg early in the tour and asked her to join him. She arrived in Miami on 19 November and stayed for a week. Shortly after Anita went home, an article appeared in *Newsweek* magazine:

'The Stones talk mean. With their jack-knife profiles, junior Rasputin coiffures, and cockney calls for "girlie action", they have been cast as the bad boys of popland. What people see is five hipless moppets dressed like carnival coxcombs. You could be kind and call it music.' I think we said something like 'bollocks' when someone showed it to us. But not everyone thought that we were an awful bunch. When we got to Denver in Colorado, we found that the Governor, John A Love, had officially declared that date Rolling Stones Day throughout the state.

While we were in America, I asked Allen Klein about my Chemical Bank account and he gave me a cheque book. Brian and I went shopping and used some cheques to buy things. However, when Klein learnt of our expedition, he went beserk. He shouted, 'You mustn't write cheques against the accounts.' I never really worked out why.

Back to the USA

Anita, who had flown back to England, probably to do a job, hardly had time to unpack before she headed back to LA with Chrissie. Mick and Brian chartered a plane so they could fly from Seattle to LA to meet them. We had our usual enthusiastic fans in California, of which 4,500 nearly witnessed a tragedy when we played the Memorial Auditorium, in Sacramento. Towards the end of the show, Keith touched the microphone stand with his guitar. There was a blinding blue flash and he ended up flat on his back, out cold. The promoters closed the curtains as police and medical attendants swarmed all over the stage. Keith came round within a few minutes and seemed none the worse for wear. All his guitar strings were severed and the ends were curled up, melted like fuse wire. Keith was taken to hospital, where doctors claimed that it was the thick rubber soles of his Hush Puppy shoes that had saved his life. Mr Indestructible had survived an early scare.

'The British quintet knows what it is doing every minute. But so does Father Time. One fine day, they'll all be sitting around their solar-heated pad, telling their grandchildren about those "It's what's happening, baby," days.' STEVE VIVONA, *San Diego Evening Tribune, 6 December, 1965*

'AS TEARS GO BY'

As Tears Go By
The Rolling Stones
Gotta Get Away

On Saturday 18 December, 1965, Keith's 22nd birthday, the ninth Stones US single came out. A total departure from the band's usual records, it's probably only Mick who appears on the a-side.

'We didn't think of doing it, because the Rolling Stones were a butch blues group. But Marianne Faithfull's version was already a big, proven hit song... It was one of the first things I ever wrote.' MICK

'Among the 60 or so covers of "As Tears Go By" are versions by PP Arnold in 1968, Joe Pass in 1972 and Twice As Much, who did it in 1966.' BILL

We were planning our next release when the disc jockeys of the nation decided for us

Over 500,000 sold in seven days

Released as a single by public demand

AS TEARS GO BY
45-9808
THE ROLLING STONES

from their hit album december's children (and everybody's)

LONDON®

ROLLING STONES—AS TEARS GO BY (Essex, BMI)—Mick Jagger goes it solo, a la Paul McCartney, on the beautiful folk-flavored ballad associated with Marianne Faithfull. Baroque, semi-classical smash hit! Flip: "Gotta Get Away" (Golden; BMI). **London 9808**

Recorded
a-side 26 October, 1965
b-side 5 or 6 September, 1965
Studios
a-side IBC Studios London
b-side RCA Hollywood
Producer
Andrew Loog Oldham
Engineers
Glyn Johns at IBC
Dave Hassinger at RCA
Release
US 18 December, 1965
London 45 9808
Composers
a-side Jagger/Richard/Oldham
b-side Jagger/Richard
Highest chart position
US No 6, 25 December, 1965

On Sunday 5 December, an audience of 3,700 queued for five hours to see the afternoon show in San Diego. Nikki Smith, president of the local Stones fan club, came backstage and presented us with home-sewn shirts that were far too big.

In the evening, we flew by charter plane to Los Angeles for a show at the Sports Arena, our last of the tour. We earned a massive $30,000, then our biggest-ever pay day, when we played to 15,000 fans. Days later, American TV man Dick Clark was quoted as saying, 'The Stones are slipping.'

The day before the last gig, our new album came out, appropriately entitled *December's Children (And Everybody's)*. Once the tour was over,

there were some more recording sessions lined up. But we got the chance to take a break and unwind. Keith used the time to get into the saddle in the American hills.

Head for the hills

Gered Mankowitz, Allen Klein's nephew, Ronnie Schneider (who worked in Klein's office) and Keith flew to Phoenix and went on an overnight horse-ride into the McDowell Mountain. Maybe Keith was living out his childhood Roy Rogers-inspired fantasies.

'We got kitted out in cowboy gear and were armed to the teeth with side guns and Winchester rifles. A guide took us to a place on the Apache reservation called Green River. We stayed overnight, cooking steaks and baking potatoes on an open fire.'

GERED MANKOWITZ

Keith going way out west

Keith had to get back to Los Angeles all too soon as we were needed for a photo shoot. According to Gered, it was about time they headed back. 'Apart from looking like the James gang, we stank to high heaven, having been in the saddle for 48 hours and nowhere near a bath.'

We did a shoot with Guy Webster in Hollywood, which included some pictures that were used on the *Big Hits* album. The next day we were back in RCA's Hollywood studio for another three days with Dave Hassinger.

'We recorded 10 numbers, all written by Mick and Keith,' said Charlie that Christmas. 'I think that musically they are the best thing that we've ever done.'

Stu was kept very busy throughout the sessions, as he always was. He not only played, but was also nipping out for food and drink and laying on a constant stream of instruments. He got me a six-string bass that I played on one number, as well as a sitar for Brian.

'Gibson let us have quite a few Fuzz Tones,' said Stu. 'We only used fuzz on a couple of tracks, but Keith gets carried away and tramples them underfoot when he's raving about on stage. We've gone through quite a few like that.'

The tracks we laid down at RCA included '19th Nervous

'Our previous sessions have always been rush jobs. This time we were able to relax a little, take our time.' **KEITH,** *Beat Instrumental, February 1966*

Breakdown', 'Goin' Home', 'Sittin' On The Fence', 'Ride On Baby' and 'Take It Or Leave It'.

'Keith and Mick acted as musical directors until the others got the gist of the numbers and then it was a free-for-all with everyone chipping in with their own particular ideas. Charlie Watts was in great form and played the bongos and conga drums like a native. He also tried his hand (and arm) on a set of gigantic timpani which an orchestra had left behind. Brian, Stu and American session player Jack Nitzsche took it in turns to play the harpsichord, piano or organ. Brian told me that there is a keyboard instrument on every track recorded. He and Stu handled the groovy numbers while Jack Nitzsche played on the slower tracks.'
KEVIN SWIFT, *Beat Instrumental, February 1966*

Lakeside Stones posing for Guy Webster: photos from the shoot were used on the Big Hits *compilation.*

As soon as we had finished, Brian and Anita flew to the Virgin Islands for a five-day holiday, before going on to New York to meet up with Bob Dylan. Charlie and I flew overnight to London. When we got back, customs gave Charlie a good grilling and ended up charging him £60 duty.

Linda Keith flew to Los Angeles to join Keith, while Mick and Chrissie Shrimpton went on holiday to Jamaica. They arrived home in time for Christmas and for Mick to have his first taste of hassle from customs officers… Soon it would be a familiar fact of life for all of us.

'Customs men kept them more than an hour. They slit open wrapped Christmas presents.' EVENING STANDARD, *24 December, 1965*

Brian and Anita returned to England on 27 December – four days before we were back to work taping the *Ready Steady Go!* New Year's Eve special.

1966
And All
That

At the Century Plaza Hotel in LA, Brian had been
shopping during a visit in July 1967

A Happy New Year?

January 1966 was something of a relief as we had some time to ourselves. It was a chance to get things organised in our personal lives. I pursued interests outside of the band and my major domestic priority was the move to our new house in Keston. Diane and I shopped for new furniture, carpets and other things that we had not previously been able to afford. We also got a nanny for Stephen.

AROUND THE SAME TIME, Keith had carpets fitted in his flat. Brian and Scottish Dave, who was staying with him, were living a slightly more Bohemian lifestyle.

'Brian's flat was like Aladdin's cave. Records, bottles, souvenirs, books and even a huge amplifier were liberally scattered about the room. There seemed to be a struggle going on inside him. Something that wanted to break out in a creative form.' RECORD MIRROR, *12 February, 1966*

'I've been here a year and spent a total of about three months in the place. I'm moving soon. I want to get a big flat in London, then a large house with a minstrel gallery. I'm going to build a Go-Kart track in the grounds. I'd like to put down all this rubbish that has been started about Anita and me. I'm getting rid of my Rolls Royce soon. I'll probably get one Mini for Anita and one for me.' BRIAN, *Record Mirror, 12 February, 1966*

'I'm not personally insecure, just unsure. I would like to write, but I lack confidence.'

BRIAN, *Record Mirror, 12 February, 1966*

Brian and Anita

On 3 February, 1966, the band aired '19th Nervous Breakdown' on the BBC's Top Of The Pops.

Could You Walk On The Waters? Decca hastily denied that this was going to happen, telling *NME* on 14 January, 'We would not issue it with that title at any price.'

In mid-January, a summons was issued to Brian as a result of Pat Andrews, who was now 21, seeking maintenance for Brian's son. Brian was told to pay £2 10s per week, along with some £78 costs.

'The Bench finds it deplorable that the four-year-old boy should not have been recognised and helped by his father up till the present date,' said magistrate Sir John Cameron. 'I find it impossible to understand his attitude. If we could make a larger order, we would do so.'

While Brian continued to be a rebel without a cause, in the words of his friend Dick Hattrell, he had a great deal of self-knowledge, as an illuminating interview with *Record Mirror* revealed:

'I'm so contradictory. I have this need for expression, but I'm not certain what it is I want to do. I need encouragement. If someone told me I could write and egged me on, I suppose I could do it. It's like jumping in at the deep end and not knowing which way you are coming up.

'I enjoy being with the Stones. It gives me satisfaction. I take music seriously and it allows me to express myself. I made a mess of my life earlier. I chucked away a career at university because I didn't like the school rules. The uniform bit wasn't me. My life has been all escapism.'

With no live gigs in our schedule, we had more time to socialise. I often went to the Scotch of St James club, as did Brian and Mick. We met with old friends Glyn Johns, Otis Redding, Keith Moon and John Entwistle of the Who and Patti Labelle and the Bluebells, who were over here on tour. Another hangout was the Cromwellian club, where I saw Lee Dorsey perform.

One night we went to a party at Mick's flat. John Lennon, George and Ringo were there. It was a chance to catch up, as we hadn't seen each other in months. On other evenings, if you were in the Kings Road, you were likely to have seen Mick and Chrissie having dinner at Casserole, one of their favourite haunts.

Groundhog day

My projects outside of the Stones included producing Bobbie Miller, the End and John Lee's Groundhogs. This was blues guitarist Tony McPhee's band, the name a combination of John Lee Hooker and McPhee's favourite Hooker track. Glyn Johns and I produced the Groundhogs' 'I'll

Never Fall In Love Again', which came out a couple of weeks later on the Planet label. At a Bobbie Miller session at IBC Studios, we cut a track called 'Stu-Ball' with me on bass, Tony Meehan (ex-Shadows) on drums, Keith playing guitar and Stu on piano. This was the b-side of Bobbie's Decca single, 'Everywhere I Go', released in March. It wasn't a hit, which is why it's now worth £75. If you find one at a car-boot sale let me know. I haven't got a copy.

Andrew's audacity

With Allen Klein in the equation, our relationship with Andrew had altered, but this didn't stop his audacity when it came to promoting us. He told the *New Musical Express* that the title for our new album was going to be

'This rebel thing has gone now. Life is a paradox for me.' BRIAN,
Record Mirror, 12 February, 1966

Darling Charlie
Mick, Keith and Bill went to Andrew's office to watch a preview of *Charlie Is My Darling*. It included some brief live performance

footage ('The Last Time' and 'It's Alright') and showed the band jamming backstage on 'Maybe It's Because I'm A Londoner.' Bill:
'We seemed to spend most of our time getting in and out of limos. The soundtrack included "Get Off Of My Cloud", "Heart Of Stone", "Satisfaction" and "Goin' Home".'
'This is a revealing glimpse into life on the road,' wrote Chris Welch in *Melody Maker* on 22 January. 'Filmed by Peter Whitehead in Ireland, there are riot scenes, hilarious fan comments and not always flattering interviews with the Stones. Charlie leaves a trail of incomplete sentences behind a cigarette smokescreen and Brian, talking about a film he hopes to make, is suddenly left speechless when a voice asks if he knows the meaning of 'surrealism'. Some of the best moments include a drinking scene with Mick and Andrew, Mick doing an accurate send-up of Elvis Presley and a nasal interpretation of George Harrison's guitar playing.'

'19TH NERVOUS BREAKDOWN'

US b-side
'Sad Day'

Recorded
a-side 8 December, 1965
UK b-side 26 October, 1965
US b-side 9 December, 1965

Studios
a-side and US b-side
RCA Hollywood
UK b-side IBC Studios, London

Producer
Andrew Loog Oldham

Engineers
Glyn Johns at IBC
Dave Hassinger at RCA

Release
UK Friday 4 February, 1966
Decca F 12331
US Saturday 12 February, 1966
London 45 LON 9823

Composers
a-side Jagger/Richard
UK b-side Jagger/Richard/Oldham
US b-side Jagger/Richard

Highest chart position
UK No 2
US No 2

Marking a change to the pattern of Stones releases, '19th Nervous Breakdown' was first issued in the UK. It was the ninth British single and the tenth in America. It was also indicative of a new trend in pop singles, running for four rather than the usual three minutes. Lacking the immediacy of the musical hooks of 'Satisfaction' or 'Get Off Of My Cloud', it faltered at UK and US No 2. The single did hit No 1 on the *NME* chart, where it stayed for three weeks.

Nancy Sinatra's 'These Boots Are Made For Walking' took the No 1 slot on the *Record Retailer* chart. Nancy later made amends by recording 'As Tears Go By' as a track for her *Boots* album. The US b-side, 'Sad Day', written while the band was on tour, has Jack Nitzsche on piano and Brian on organ.

'If it was possible for a disc to climb higher than No 1, here's one that would. This is by far and away their best-ever release. Watch it top the charts, not only in Britain, but also all over the world. There's a Chuck Berry-style guitar intro, setting the up-tempo pace for the whole side. The Stones provide some interesting sounds here with zoom bass and fuzzbox guitar. The lyrics by Mick and Keith stand in a class of their own, and are typical of their unique, humorous songwriting style.' DECCA PRESS RELEASE, *28 January, 1966*

'If someone told me they were going to write a song called "19th Nervous Breakdown", I would say they must be out of their minds, but here it comes. It's a rollicking piece. Some of the words get lost in the exuberance, but it's a big hit.' DAILY MIRROR, *3 February, 1966*

'I'm pleased to say that when it comes to the Stones' records, it's getting increasingly hard to find new words of praise to lavish on them. Technically, especially when straining to hear Mick's voice surface from the backing, it's not the best.' DISC, *5 February, 1966*

'At the time Glyn Johns did a remix of the song which brought Mick's vocal out more, but Andrew rejected it.' BILL

'I didn't like this when I first heard it. I was surprised they came out with such a weak record. But the Stones have reached the snowballing stage, when they can have a hit with pretty well any release.' ERIC BURDON, the Animals, *19 February, 1966*

ROLLING STONES — 19TH NERVOUS BREAKDOWN (Gideon, BMI)—With "As Tears Go By" falling off the chart, the hot group offers this raucous rocker that will fast replace it. Flip: "Sad Day" (Gideon, BMI). **London 9823**

'"19th Nervous Breakdown" is a putdown of the kind of thoroughly spoiled, neurotic debutante who infests the periphery of rock's café society, looking for expensive cheap thrills and a bit of rough.' **ROY CARR,** *music journalist, 1976*

Tattoo Phew!

Cars were very much on our minds early in 1966. Keith bought a brand-new, dark blue Bentley S3 Continental Saloon (registration JLP 400D), while I bought a Morris Minor 1000 Traveller (MYR 242D). Both of us had been taking driving lessons. I had been a driver since my Air Force days, but I needed a civilian licence.

KEITH TOOK HIS TEST on 8 February and failed, which meant his chauffeur was still in a job.

By early February I had moved to my Keston house. It was such a change from Penge – I could see people riding horses and there were foxes in the garden. It seemed a lifetime away from where I had grown up. We had a house-warming party and invited the rest of the band and their girlfriends. Keith was away in Paris, but Andrew Oldham, all of Spencer Davis' group and singers Paul and Barry Ryan were among those who came.

Stones in colour

On 11 February, we left Heathrow at noon and flew direct to New York. We stopped off to promote our new single on Ed Sullivan's show, before travelling on to Australia for our second tour. Mick and Chrissie flew together, while Shirley Shepherd came with us. The show went well and was the first colour broadcast on American TV. We played 'Satisfaction' as well as '19th Nervous Breakdown'. Mick and Keith returned to the stage to perform 'As Tears Go By'.

Saucy devil

After New York we flew to Los Angeles and on to Sydney via Honolulu and Fiji. Once again we crossed the dateline and lost another day. Australia proved to be very welcoming, especially the girls.

In Adelaide an amazing thing happened to us – and it wasn't on stage. We were all around the hotel's small and deserted swimming pool when two slightly plain-looking girls joined us. We chatted and one of them told us that she had a tattoo. As we couldn't see it, we asked her where it was. In an instant, she took off her bikini bottom and showed the tattoo to us. It was all around her lower regions and from a distance it looked like a flower patterned bikini bottom. Looking closer, we were amazed to see a little red devil sitting on her pubic mound. This kept us amused for weeks whenever it came up in conversation – and it often did! Mick, who would regularly call the music press to tell them

Soaking up the Australian sun on 28 February, 1966

of our exploits down under, left our encounter with the young lady out of his reports.

'In just one day, we're all getting sun burned, except Bill. Biggest news of the week is that Brian used the word "Christ" on a radio show the other day. The press here really got at us for that. They don't like us very much. We got stoned a couple of times and went to a party given by some DJ the other day. It was a gas. We have to stay on-stage each performance, until the police come to help us get away.' MICK, *Disc, 26 February, 1966*

Thomas organ
On 5 February, Charlie Cobbett from Jennings of Dartford delivered a Thomas organ to Bill. It was advance payment for his endorsement of the new 'Vox Wyman' bass.

The Stones arrived in Sydney on 16 February to begin their second tour of Australia and New Zealand. They were back after taking the longest break in performing since their formation. The band's popularity was assured, as Decca had already released 13 singles, six EPs and four LPs in Australia – the Stones were indeed big Down Under.

The Pacific,
February–March 1966

18 February Commemorative Auditorium, Sydney (two shows)
19 February Commemorative Auditorium, Sydney (two shows)
21 February City Hall, Brisbane (two shows)
22 February Centennial Hall, Adelaide
23 February Palais Theatre, St Kilda, Melbourne (two shows)
24 February Palais Theatre, St Kilda, Melbourne (two shows)
25 February Palais Theatre, St Kilda, Melbourne (two shows)
26 February Palais Theatre, St Kilda, Melbourne (two shows)
28 February Town Hall, Wellington (NZ)
1 March Civic Theatre, Auckland (NZ)
2 March Capitol Theatre, Perth

O n the first tour, promoter Harry M Miller had been less than generous with the band's baggage allowance. This time the Stones really made up for it. They arrived with 72 pieces of luggage and 110 pieces of equipment. Supporting the Stones throughout the short tour were the Searchers.

'On Sunday 20 February, we were staggered to find out that the Searchers all went to church.' BILL

'We traversed Australia with the Rolling Stones, a combination as weird as teaming up Vlad the Impaler with Mother Theresa.' FRANK ALLEN, *the Searchers*

'On 17 February, we recorded Channel 9's Bandstand Special in Sydney, which aired three days later. We mimed to "I'm Moving On", "Get Off Of My Cloud", "Play With Fire", "19th Nervous Breakdown" and "Satisfaction". Then Mick and Keith did "As Tears Go By".' BILL

'When the Beatles were here seats were damaged. This was worse than the Beatles – several seats were pierced by stiletto heels.' WELLINGTON DOMINION DOORMAN

'On this tour we grossed $59,136; [UK agent] Tito Burns received $5,913; Klein and Andrew each received $5,321. The Stones each earned $7,063 after expenses – but we didn't receive it at this time.' BILL

Set list
'The Last Time'
'Mercy Mercy'
'She Said Yeah'
'Play With Fire'
'Not Fade Away'
'The Spider And The Fly'
'That's How Strong My Love Is'
'Get Off Of My Cloud'
'19th Nervous Breakdown'
'Satisfaction'

Local support bands
Max Merritt and the Meteors
Tony Barber
Marty Rhone
The Four Fours

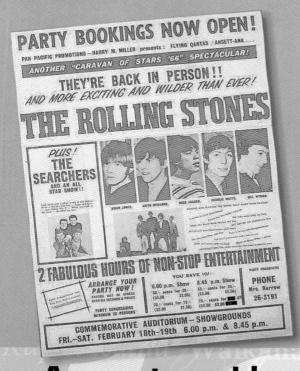

Australia And New Zealand

Good Blokes!

While we were away in Australia an article appeared in *Disc* in which we gave our opinions on each other. Looking back on it and knowing all the incredible things that were to happen over the next few years, it's a fascinating picture.

CHARLIE ON BRIAN 'My first impression of him was just of a very good guitar player. He's basically a very quiet bloke. He likes being left alone – not on his own though. He's really a very soft person. People don't know him. I know him really only as someone I play with. He can be very funny – when he feels like it. He's one of these people who, if he's feeling a bit ill or tired, likes to be left alone. He's fairly quick-tempered but he gets over it. Like all of us, he's a bit moody. I think he's generous to people he wants to be generous to.'

MICK ON KEITH 'Very untidy and very forgetful – that's Keith. I still don't know what he's thinking at any time and he really is one of my closest friends. From time to time, we've had little arguments. As I said, he's forgetful and he doesn't remember to bear a grudge. He can stay awake much longer than me. He's very good about the group. Very optimistic. People find it difficult to know Keith. Sometimes he's shy and other times he can't be bothered to take an interest in people.'

ME ON MICK 'He was very friendly when I first met the group, a lot quieter and less confident. Now he's more difficult to get on with. He's always been very close to the rest of the group and at no time have we been scared that he was going to quit and turn solo. He gets depressed sometimes and we have to bear with it. He's a bit careful with money – not extravagant like Keith. I also think Mick's a romantic – very much so. When the group eventually breaks up I think he'll do something completely different.

KEITH ON CHARLIE 'Charlie ain't awkward. He hasn't changed much since I met him first except that he's a lot happier since he got married. Charlie's a very deep thinker. It's hard to tell if he's listening to a conversation or thinking about something else. When you think he hasn't heard a thing you've been talking about, he'll start discussing the subject a couple of hours later. But he's not that deep that we don't know him – although he still surprises us. When I first met him he was playing with Alexis Korner. We asked him over to join us when we were earning £2 a night each. I'm glad he came – he's a good bloke.'

BRIAN ON ME 'I'm very fond of Bill. In fact I often feel very paternal towards him. He gets drunk more easily than the rest of us. He's more difficult to understand because he's married and until recently lived a very reserved home life. I'm considered the mad raver of the group and he's the opposite. He's older than the rest of us and more stable. Rather matter-of-fact. He picks things up more easily than the rest of us. We take the mickey out of Bill a lot but he takes it well. He's pretty well-organised. Bill is very concerned with money and he's very precise with things.'

KEITH ALTHAM COMMENTED in the *NME* mid-way through February, 'It is virtually impossible to write an article on the Stones without Andrew getting in on the act, as the Stones have practically become a projection of his own ego.'

In fact, Andrew was becoming a little removed from our activities. Immediate Records was taking up more and more of his time. By they end of February, they had issued 29 singles, of which ALO himself had produced 11.

We recorded for three days at RCA with Dave Hassinger, cutting more than 20 tracks. Among them were 'High And Dry', 'It's Not Easy', 'Lady Jane', 'Long Long While', 'Out Of Time', 'Paint It, Black', 'Under My Thumb' and 'If You Let Me'. Jack Nitzsche was there and played on many of the songs. Brian was at his creative peak with the band around this time. While the songs were all written by Mick and Keith, it was Brian's musical abilities that made those recordings sound so much better than they might otherwise have done.

Left, *Mick and Keith at RCA studios and,* below, *Keith, Bill and Andrew*

From LA To West Wittering

When the tour finished, I went with Brian and Bob Bonis to LA, while the others stopped over in Fiji for a holiday with Shirley. Brian and I amused ourselves with a string of girls who hung around our hotel. When Andrew and Tito Burns flew in from London the fun and games stopped. The rest of the band arrived in California. It was time for work.

Soon after arriving home from LA, I had a call from Allen Klein to discuss my US dollar account at New York's Chemical Bank. He suggested that I drew a $40,000 cheque and deposited it with my local Barclays Bank in Penge to 'see what would happen'. I didn't realise that he was using me as a guinea pig for the rest of the boys. I was eager to get my hands on the money so I went along with it. Barclays in Penge submitted an application to

'Brian's contribution can be heard on every track of those recordings at RCA. What that guy didn't play, he went out and learned. You can hear his colour all over songs like "Lady Jane" or "Paint It, Black". In some instances it was more than a decorative effect. Sometimes Brian pulled the whole record together.'
ANDREW OLDHAM

the Bank of England for permission to regard these funds as available for investment. I called Klein in New York to discuss the transfer. He told me that he was dealing with it. (Even this 45-minute call cost me £44 – a small fortune at the time.)

On 30 March, Barclays wrote:

As you are aware, we have endeavoured to obtain a preferential rate for the conversion of your dollar cheque which we sent for collection. The Bank of England can find no record of the authority for opening USA accounts or for the sale of Nanker Phelge Ltd and advise us that they require the authority number for the opening of the account and for the sale of Nanker Phelge Ltd.

'We regret troubling you in this matter, but this request has come from the Bank of England. You told us that the Bank of England authority was obtained, so presumably the authority number is known.

The truth of the matter is that Klein was making it up as he went along, including the sale of Nanker Phelge for some obscure legal reason. During April he transferred money to the others in different ways, while mine was still tied up by the Bank of England.

Brian had stayed on in New York with Andrew for a few days and when he did finally get home to his flat he had misplaced his keys. He let himself in by putting his fist through the window. A few hours later *NME* journalist Keith Altham turned up to interview him.

'I found the front room had been officially declared a disaster area. Spencer Davis was seated beneath a standard lamp, wearing Brian's newly-acquired rose-tinted spectacles, Stevie Winwood was in a green stetson, Spencer's road manager Dave was there and Tom Keylock was drinking bitter from a pudding bowl. Brian produced a wooden zither-like instrument, which proved to be a dulcimer you'll be hearing more of, as Brian revealed it had been included on several tracks recorded in Los Angeles. Brian phoned Dial-A-Meal and ordered lunches from a nearby mobile restaurant. He produced a monstrous great red sitar from the corner of the room, stood it on end, and started tuning it.' KEITH ALTHAM, *NME, 25 March, 1966*

Keith had not been back from America for long before he finalised the purchase of his own house.

Classical wannabe

On Friday 11 March, 1966, a curious album came out on Immediate. Called *Today's Pop Symphony* it was credited to the Aranbee Pop Symphony Orchestra – the name a pun on R&B – which, it was claimed, was directed and arranged by Keith. Among the tracks were 'Play With Fire', 'Mother's Little Helper', 'Take It Or Leave It', and 'Sittin' On A Fence'.

'It's just something I've always wanted to do,' Keith told the *NME* on 11 March, 1966.

'He's trying to prove he's a musician and not just a rock'n'roll guitarist,' Mick commented in the same edition of the music newspaper.

There is no doubt that Keith had very little to do with this project. It was another of Andrew's attempts to put him and Mick in the limelight. At the time, Keith was probably the least visible member of the group. At least one paper, *Record Mirror*, was taken in by the stunt.

'Anyone who thinks that Keith's talents are limited will be forced to think again when they hear any tracks from this,' it marvelled on 12 February, 1966. 'He takes 10 quality pop songs and under his direction they perform them in near-classical style.'

'I have not slept for 50 hours. Do you think that you could come around tomorrow afternoon?' BRIAN, *to a writer for Rolling Stone Monthly, April 1966*

Stamps issued by the Stones fan club

The Stones in pieces

In March, a merchandise company reported its sale of 1,449 boxes, each containing a dozen Stones jigsaw puzzles, between June and November. Our five per cent royalty amounted to £43 12s 5d.

Before we left to tour Australia, Keith had gone to view a house called Redlands, which was in West Wittering, Sussex.

He bought it for £17,750 and still owns the house to this day. Keith stays there whenever he is over in the UK. Redlands went on to become one of the most famous – or perhaps infamous – homes in rock'n'roll history. The estate agent's brochure paints a very different picture of the house:

Redlands occupies a particularly pleasant and secluded situation on the edge of the village of West Wittering, about six miles south of Chichester. A charming period residence, it is reputed to be some 600–800 years old and at one time was believed to have been owned by the Bishop of Chichester. A house is alleged to have been erected on the site in AD 100 and reference to the property was made in the Domesday Book. A Saxon moat completely encircles the house. The house is scheduled as a building of special architectural and historical interest.

On 26 March, we flew to Amsterdam in Holland to begin our European tour. Arriving at midday, we were driven to the Hotel Naaden, where we checked in and relaxed.

Boys And Their Toys

Brian was a Roller Stone – and the others also bought flash motors. Some ended up in accidents, but that the band could purchase them was a sign of their success.

All of the members of the band were given a Ferrari at the end of a tour.

Brian's Rolls-Royce

Mick bought his Aston Martin DB6 in April 1966. It came complete with a record player installed.

Keith and his Bentley, bought in 1966 at the same time as Bill bought his Morris Traveller.

A few months after buying the Morris, Bill purchased his MGB sports car.

Bill had, below left, a Mercedes, below right, a Citroën Maserati and, right, a Morris Traveller.

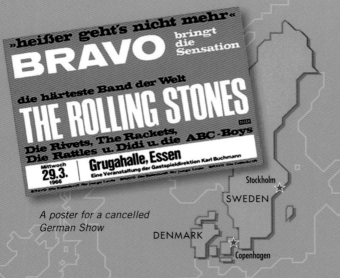

A poster for a cancelled German Show

By today's standards the spring 1966 European tour was short and sweet – if you ignore the odd riot, fist fight and Mick's trip to hospital.

At seven different venues in five countries, audiences averaged between 1,500 and 2,500. The Stones played to around 22,000 fans in total, a fraction of the number that would watch them at a single show, as the band graduated to stadiums in the 1970s.

MAANDBLAD muziek expres PRESENTEERT
ROLLING STONES
SLECHTS één OPTREDEN IN NEDERLAND:
Zaterdag 26 maart 8 uur in de
BRABANTHAL - DEN BOSCH
BEAT-BLITZEND VOORPROGRAMMA
BINTANGS • BUMBLE BEES • OUTSIDERS
FERRARIS • PETER AND THE BLIZZARDS
Aankondigingen: JAN VAN VEEN (Veronica)
ENTREEPRIJS: ƒ 10.—

Europe, *March–April 1966*

26 March Braband Hall, The Hague, Holland
27 March Palais des Sports, Brussels, Belgium
29 March Olympia Theatre, Paris, France (two shows)
30 March Salle Vallier, Marseille, France (two shows)
31 March Palais d'Hivers, Lyon, France (two shows)
3 April Kungliga Tennishallen, Stockholm, Sweden (two shows)
5 April KB Hallen, Copenhagen, Denmark (two shows)

Fighting fans

The tour was marked by violence. In Brussels, the police had difficulty controlling 2,000 teenagers.

In Marseille, during the second show, in front of 1,200 screaming fans, someone threw a piece of wood, from a chairback, which hit Mick over the right eye while he was singing 'Satisfaction'. The cut was serious and Mick had to go to hospital. It was just as bad in Lyon.

The Stones were banned from three auditoriums in Copenhagen, following the riots that had marred their last visit to Denmark.

'Last June the Beatles were in this concert hall and there was no police force at all,' wrote Maurice Curt in *Le Progress* of April 1966. 'Does this mean that the Stones are considered to be outlaws or dangerous leftists?'

Mick – hit in Marseille

Accounts department

This tour grossed $59,910 before expenses. Tito Burns received $5,991; Allen Klein and Andrew Oldham each received $5,391; the band earned $6,216 after expenses (not paid at the time).

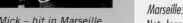

Hallo, Bonjour, Hej and Goddag

'We were all totally captivated by Brigitte, especially Brian. We chatted for a while and she told us how much she'd enjoyed the show.'

BILL, *on Ms Bardot*

Brian holding the band's Bravo award and Keith clutching his passport.

Bardot starring in Two Weeks In September

Bardot stuns the Stones

After the Paris shows the band returned to the hotel. There they learnt Brigitte Bardot and some friends were popping by to see them. They all waited with some excitement for her arrival. When she walked into the suite, accompanied by six young men, she totally dominated the gathering. Bill: 'Once she left we all talked about how amazing she looked. She asked us to appear in the film *Two Weeks In September*. We turned her down because we were supposed to be doing our own film… which never appened.'

'Good concert. All the kids leaping about and screaming, with the police giving them plenty of truncheon.' **KEITH,** *NME, 1 April, 1966*

April In Paris

As we started our European tour, one of the Rolling Stones Ltd's accounts was showing a debit of £3,746, with £5,461 owed in various outstanding bills. Another showed a credit of £105 0s 3d. While we were obviously earning a lot more, the financial state of the Rolling Stones business was probably far less rosy than people imagined. I don't want to sound like I'm complaining. I just say all this with hindsight and a sense of history.

THIS WAS A TIME when bands gave little thought to 'the business'. Most groups were in their early twenties and were into having a good time – and so was I.

One aspect of touring that continued to improve was the accommodation. In Paris, for instance, we stayed at the Georges V. Waiting for Brian at the hotel when we checked in was Anita. After settling in we decided to go shopping and I almost got myself killed. I was hassled by some fans and went to rejoin the rest of the boys, who were waiting in our cars on the other side of the road. Being English and used to driving on the left, I looked the wrong way and thinking the road was clear, I ran across. Halfway over there was a screech of brakes, and there was a car inches away from me.

Instinctively, as the bumper touched my legs, I put one hand on the bonnet and vaulted to safety over the front of the car. It wasn't until later, when I talked to the others, I realised how lucky I'd been.

'Our cars threaded their way through the group of photographers and autograph hunters. As we accelerated off, one persistent youth attached himself to the tail fin of the car.' KEITH ALTHAM, *NME, 1 April, 1966*

Hair was even an issue in France

Brian and I got ourselves into trouble with Andrew when we were interviewed on Ready, Steady, Go! *live from Paris.*

'Accelerate now. I want to see him bounce.' BRIAN

'We stopped at the traffic light and the youth jumped off, pursued by Mike Gruber, the American road manager. As the traffic moved off again, Mike returned to the car and the youth resumed his position. In this manner, we travelled through Paris, followed by an auxiliary motorcade of fans and photographers in cars and taxis.' KEITH ALTHAM, *NME 1 April, 1966*

After the Lyon gig, everyone except Brian and I flew home. We went back to Paris for some fun. Anita was still there and we had a good few days seeing the sights and the clubs. I got a call from journalist Keith Altham, who was still in Paris, to tell me that *Ready Steady Go!* was being filmed at La Locomotive club in Paris, featuring the Who and the Yardbirds. The show's producer invited us to appear on the show, which we did. The fact that we

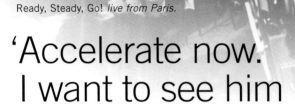

went on totally pissed Andrew off. He was so annoyed he even wrote to the two of us.

'Although I am quite sure your motives were innocent, I would be grateful if in future you could refrain from appearing on TV shows such as Ready Steady Go! *without consulting me. As it happens, I was put in an embarrassing position as I had spent the last month trying to get you to do a show from Paris. I had explained that this was impossible because you would either be on holiday or travelling. The real reason was I did not want you to do RSG! as I have been negotiating with Rediffusion for us to do our own special. To have you turn up on their TV show rather made a mockery of my plans. You are supposed to be the number two group in the world and I do not want you just dropping in on TV shows. If you feel that your personal points of view are not put across properly to the public, I would be quite happy to arrange for you to be interviewed.'*

Back in London, Mick and Jack Nitzsche dropped into a recording session of the Troggs. Their appearance in the studio was later mentioned in the *Troggs Tapes*, widely bootlegged and the very stuff of rock legend. In a drunken Troggs session, throughout which tapes were left running, the Troggs can be heard taking swearing to new heights – or depths, depending on your point of view – as they attempt to get some music down on tape. The session that was recorded on the tapes was the inspiration for some of what appeared in the classic rock 'n' roll spoof film *Spinal Tap*.

DAY... and NIGHT

The Stones shopped and partied around Swinging London in the hippest and happeningest places, as the austere 1950s were swept away by a colourful cavalcade of bright young people.

Centre of the teenage shopper's universe was Carnaby Street, where dedicated followers of 'groovy' fashion swung by His Clothes and John Stephen. On the Kings Road there was the Chelsea Antique Market, Countdown, Guy and Granny Takes A Trip. Chelsea Cobbler was on Fulham Road, Anello and Davide on Oxford Street, Lord John on Great Marlborough Street and Quorum was to be found on Radnor Walk.

We're night clubbin'

The club scene boomed in the 1960s. The music business had its own club in the Speakeasy. The Stones liked the Bag O'Nails in Kingly Street, Soho, and Duke Street's Scotch of St James. Other major clubs were Blaise's in Queensgate, the Cromwellian on Cromwell Road, Dollys on Jermyn Street, In Place on Allsop Place, the Pickwick Club on Great Newport Street, Elbow Room on Carlisle Street and Tiles of Dean Street.

Side one
1. '(I Can't Get No) Satisfaction' Jagger/Richard
2. 'The Last Time' Jagger/Richard
3. 'As Tears Go By' Jagger/Richard/Oldham
4. 'Time Is On My Side' Ragovoy
5. 'It's All Over Now' B and S Womack
6. 'Tell Me' Jagger/Richard

Side two
1. '19th Nervous Breakdown' Jagger/Richard
2. 'Heart Of Stone' Jagger/Richard
3. 'Get Off Of My Cloud' Jagger/Richard
4. 'Not Fade Away' Petty/Hardin
5. 'Good Times Bad Times' Jagger/Richard
6. 'Play With Fire' Nanker/Phelge

Producer
Andrew Loog Oldham

Engineers
Ron Malo at Chess Studios, Chicago
Dave Hassinger at RCA, Hollywood
Bill Farley at Regent Sound, London

Cover photography
Guy Webster
Gered Mankowitz

Cover design
Andrew Loog Oldham

Release
US Saturday 2 April, 1966
London NPS 1

Highest chart position (time on chart)
US No 3 (35 weeks)

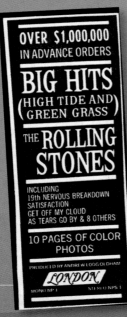

The band's sixth US album came out four months after *December's Children* and, not surprisingly, contained no new material. It was especially well-packaged for the time, in full colour with 10 pages of photos on the inside. Much was made in the trade press that the album's packaging was created by Andrew Loog Oldham… But then, Andrew never missed a trick.

Oldham's original title for the album was *Can You Walk On The Water?* Though Decca firmly squashed this particular idea, Andrew managed to get a good few column inches of promotional copy.

'Both brutal and beautiful, this is one of the finest rock'n'roll collections ever assembled.' **DAVE MARSH AND JOHN SWENSON**, *Rolling Stone Record Guide*

The album carried a suggested list price of $4.79 for mono and $5.79 for stereo – was stereo really that much more expensive?

'Farewell to the first golden era.' LILLIAN ROXON, *Rock Encyclopaedia*

BIG HITS (HIGH TIDE AND GREEN GRASS)
THE ROLLING STONES—London NP 1.
Label has a beautiful package replete with many full color photos of the teen idols. The bands are the biggest hits the fellows made and that means "Satisfaction," "Time is On My Side," "Get Off My Cloud," etc.

Big British hits
The UK version of the album came out on Friday 4 November, 1966, and was the band's fifth British LP. The running order reflected its later release and the different hits that the band had enjoyed at home. It also had 14 tracks.

US version

Side one
1. 'Have You Seen Your Mother, Baby…'
2. 'Paint It, Black'
3. 'It's All Over Now'
4. 'The Last Time'
5. 'Heart Of Stone'
6. 'Not Fade Away'
7. 'Come On'

Side two
1. '(I Can't Get No) Satisfaction'
2. 'Get Off Of My Cloud'
3. 'As Tears Go By'
4. '19th Nervous Breakdown'
5. 'Lady Jane'
6. 'Time Is On My Side'
7. 'Little Red Rooster'

Highest chart position (chart entry)
UK No 4 (12 November)

Time on chart
UK 43 weeks

Easter Holidays

1966 NME CONCERT
MIGHTIEST EVER !

THOUSANDS upon thousands of fans converging on the massive Wembley Empire Pool for the biggest pop show in the world on Sunday . . . the staggering, the breathtaking NME Poll-winners Concert with its dazzling host of stars—Beatles, Stones, Walkers, Who, Dusty, Dave Dee, Roy Orbison, Cliff, Shads . . . and many others !

After our few days in Paris, we met up in Sweden to finish off the European tour, then we travelled home for Easter and some more time off. I went to Pye Studios, near Marble Arch, on the following Tuesday to produce a single for Moon's Train. On almost any evening you would find one or several of us at the Scotch of St James club. We were still having problems with money, both personally and as Rolling Stones Ltd. Our account now showed a debit of £2,827 and outstanding bills of £11,495. Klein needed to resolve these issues, so we could concentrate on music.

The NME poll winners' concert at Wembley on May 1, 1966

O N THURSDAY 14 APRIL, we did *Top Of The Pops*, where we performed 'Mother's Little Helper', a track from *Aftermath*, which was coming out the next day.

On the same day, the Searchers released 'Take It Or Leave It', a Mick and Keith composition which also came from *Aftermath*. It struggled to UK No 31. Bands like the Searchers were beginning to slip out of fashion.

On Saturday 6 April, Keith officially took possession of Redlands, having had around £16,000 transferred by Klein from his Chemical Bank account (my money was still tied up by the Bank of England). I went with my parents to look at a house in Beckenham. They

Tara Browne

liked it and I offered £7,750 for it. This was the first home they ever owned.

Away to Norway

I went with Diane and Stephen for a short holiday to Scandinavia. While I was away, Mick and Chrissie and Brian and Anita flew to Dublin for their friend Tara Browne's 21st birthday party, held at his mother's home. I used to hang out with Tara at the clubs in London along with Keith Moon; we had some really fun times together. When Mick got home from Ireland, he bought a navy blue Aston Martin DB6 with the registration TKK 4D. It came with dark, push-button windows and a record player. All of us took a very welcome opportunity to spend time at home for the rest of April. Keith even bought himself a puppy.

NME winners

Sunday 1 May marked our first gig in about four weeks. We played the *NME* Poll Winners' concert at Wembley. Others on the bill included the Beatles, the Spencer Davis Group, Dave Dee, Dozy Beaky Mick and Titch, Cliff Richard and the Shadows, the Walker Brothers, the Who, the Yardbirds and Crispian St Peters. We played 'The Last Time', 'Play With Fire' and 'Satisfaction' to an amazing response.

'The Beatles and Stones refused to face the cameras. They said that the sound system was not good enough. ABC TV paid £8,000 to film the concert. The Beatles and Stones will be missing,' DAILY MIRROR, *on the poll winners' concert, 2 May, 1966*

The following day Brian received a phone call from Anita, who was in London to do some photographic modelling. They met up and just a few days later she moved in with Brian.

Movie moves

In the UK 'Paint It, Black' was the first single from our new album, *Aftermath*. To promote it we went to Birmingham to record *Thank Your Lucky Stars*. We closed the programme by miming to our new single. Compering the show was Jim Dale and appearing with us were Tom Jones, the Morgan-James Duo, Deano, the Londonaires, the Koobas, Ronnie Carroll, Lorne Leslie, and the Kentuckians.

The next day, Andrew did an interview with the *NME* and told them that *Back, Behind and In Front* was no longer to be made into a Stones film.

A new way

Aftermath, which came out on 15 April, 1966, was a subtle move in a different direction for the Stones – one that was embraced by other groups as well. The Beatles' *Rubber Soul* had signalled something of a change for them and *Revolver* was to come out three months later. In America, the Beach Boys' seminal *Pet Sounds* was already finished and would be released four weeks after the Stones' album.

Side one
1. 'Mother's Little Helper'
2. 'Stupid Girl'
3. 'Lady Jane'
4. 'Under My Thumb'
5. 'Doncha Bother Me'
6. 'Goin' Home'

Side two
1. 'Flight 505'
2. 'High and Dry'
3. 'Out Of Time'
4. 'It's Not Easy'
5. 'I Am Waiting'
6. 'Take It Or Leave It'
7. 'Think'
8. 'What To Do'

Recorded
All tracks recorded at
RCA Studio, Hollywood
Side 1: 2, 3, 4 (6–9 March,
1966), 1, 5, 6 (8–10
December 1965)
Side 2: 1, 2, 3, 4, 5, 8
(6–9 March 1966), 6, 7
(8–10 December 1965)

Composers
All tracks Jagger/Richard

Producer
Andrew Loog Oldham

Engineer
Dave Hassinger

Cover photography
Guy Webster
Jerrold Schatzberg

Cover design
Sandy Beach
(aka Andrew Oldham)

Release
UK Friday 15 April 1966
Decca KL 4786

**Highest chart position
(time on chart)**
UK No 1 (28 weeks)
US No 2 (26 weeks)

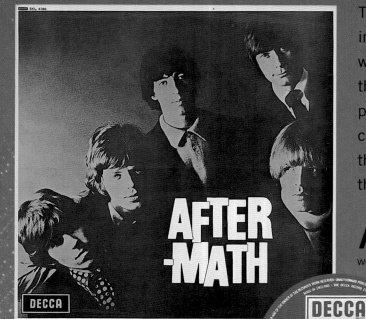

The band's fourth UK album was a milestone in that Mick and Keith wrote every track. It was also the culmination of the adrenalin rush that had been their first three years as a professional band. It showed the band's chauvinism in its full flowering, an attitude that was to carry them through the rest of their careers.

A*ftermath* replaced the soundtrack of *The Sound of Music* at the top of the UK album charts. After the Stones' eight-week run at the top *The Sound Of Music* went back to UK No 1. This was not surprising – Julie Andrews' hit spent a total of 70 weeks at the top.

'The album was to have been the soundtrack for the never-filmed feature Back, Behind And In Front. *Nicholas Ray, director of* Rebel Without A Cause, *was to direct it, but the deal fell through when Mick met him and didn't like him.'* BILL

'It's been great working with the Stones, who, contrary to the countless jibes of mediocre comedians all over the world, are real professionals and a gas to work with.' DAVE HASSINGER, *album liner notes*

'Mick and Keith write about things that are happening. Everyday things. Their songs reflect the world about them. I think it's better than anything they've done before.' ANDREW OLDHAM, *in Disc, 16 April, 1966*

The alternate US sleeve design was by Steve Inglis.

American Aftermath

Aftermath came out in the US on Saturday 2 July, 1966. It was the Stones' seventh US album and had the catalogue number London PS 476.

Side one
1. 'Paint It, Black'
2. 'Stupid Girl'
3. 'Lady Jane'
4. 'Under My Thumb'
5. 'Doncha' Bother Me'
6. 'Think'

Side two
1. 'Flight 505'
2. 'High and Dry'
3. 'It's Not Easy'
4. 'I Am Waiting'
5. 'Goin' Home'

'This album does the best job yet of alienating the over-twenties. The reason – they attempt to sing.' BRYAN GRAY, *Desert News, 19 August, 1966*

'Goin' Home' was written in the States. Charlie played brushes on a bass drum, Mick was on harmonica and Stu provided piano. At 11 minutes and 35 seconds, it was the longest rock song on an album at that time.

'I don't like the album cover Andrew did.' BRIAN, *Melody Maker, 23 April, 1966*

DECCA

'Instead they have bought the rights to a British novel, *Only Lovers Left Alive*, by David Wallis and filming may begin as soon as August. The Stones will be playing leading character roles and not portrayed as a group.'

'The Stones will be paid nearly £300,000 for eight weeks work. Filming starts in August. Decca are financing the film, based on a book by Dave Wallis called Only Lovers Left Alive. *In the novel, the grown-ups commit suicide and teenagers turn Britain into a fascist jungle.'* ALAN GORDON, *Daily Mirror, 11 May, 1966*

Mick, Keith and Brian did an interview with the *Record Mirror*, which showed early signs of Keith's new, more confident, persona.

'I suppose you can say we're rich. We've reached the stage where we can go out and buy anything we want. We don't have to worry about money anymore.' KEITH, in *Record Mirror, 8 May, 1966*

Keith, Allen Klein and Mick

Mick was elected to be an honorary president of the Trans A Society of St Andrews University, a post that had been held by distinguished politicians in the past.

On a slightly more mundane level, Mick bought Keith a large Atco motor lawn mower from Selfridges and had it delivered by train to Redlands.

Home and away
During the second half of May, Diane and I went to Majorca for a short

'I've worked out that I'd be 50 in 1984. I'd be dead! Horrible isn't it. Halfway to a hundred. Ugh! I can see myself coming onstage in my black, windowed, invalid carriage with a stick. Then I turn round, wiggle my bottom at the audience and say something like "Now here's an old song you might remember called 'Satisfaction'".'
MICK, *Disc, 21 May 1966*

holiday, while Brian made a couple of trips to stay with friends in Marbella. The rest of the band were occupied with socialising, along with the usual round of music paper interviews. At one of these Mick speculated on the horror of being 50 in 1984, which most of us would have agreed with or, at least, almost agreed with. On the other hand, the prediction that he would still be performing 'Satisfaction' was absolutely right.

Home from Spain, I found that my mineral-blue MGB sports car (KLH 604D) had been delivered. Things were looking up. I had finally

Mick was invited to be a president of the Trans A Society at St Andrews University – he was in very distinguished company.

Aftermath, the essential fashion accessory

| Paint It, Black |
| The Rolling Stones |
| Long Long While |

'PAINT IT, BLACK'

US b-side
'Stupid Girl'
Recorded
6–9 March, 1966
Studio
RCA Hollywood
Producer
Andrew Loog Oldham
Engineer
Dave Hassinger
Release
US Saturday 7 May, 1966
London 45 LON 901
UK Friday 13 May, 1966
Decca F 12395
Composers
Jagger/Richard
Highest chart position
US No 1, for two weeks
UK No 1, for one week

The US single sleeve

'Don't ask me what the comma in the title is for – that's Decca's.' KEITH

The 10th UK and the 11th US single editions came out a week apart and topped the charts on both sides of the Atlantic. 'Paint It, Black' is a great track, combining the simplicity of a great pop hook with a driving rock sound. It marked the end of the Stones' first phase as a pop band and, at the same time, was a call to arms for every other group that aspired to making it as a rock outfit. UK success was assured with advance orders of 200,000 in the week before the single came out.

The single featured Brian on sitar and acoustic guitar, Keith playing electric guitar, Charlie on drums, Mick on vocals and Bill on bass and organ pedals.

'While we were in the studio I started messing about on the Hammond doing a piss-take of Eric Easton, who had once played professionally. Charlie immediately took up the rhythm and Brian played the melody line on sitar. I played normal bass on the record and on listening back to it, I suggested Hammond organ pedals. I lay on the floor under the organ and played a second bass riff on the pedals with my fists, at double-time. Funnily enough it was never credited as a Nanker Phelge composition – I can't think why.' BILL

What the papers said...

'A glorious Indian raga-rock riot that will send the Stones back to UK No 1 and probably give pop the biggest punch up the Punjab since Peter Sellers met Sophia Loren.' MELODY MAKER, 14 May, 1966

'Opens quietly, then suddenly erupts into a thumping, crashing beat that almost makes the disc vibrate off the turntable. Highlight of the routine is the use of the sitar and Mick and Keith have written the number with a strong Eastern slant.' NME, 13 May, 1966

'Long Long While' is a great soul ballad, typical of Otis Redding or Solomon Burke. In the UK, Frank Sinatra's 'Strangers in the Night' knocked the Stones from the top spot, the second single from a Sinatra to stand in their way. In the US, 'Paperback Writer', by the Beatles, took over at the top.

'On "Paint It, Black", I used a flattened third in fret position. The sound you get from a sitar is a basic blues pattern, which results in the flattening of the third and seventh as a result of the super-imposition of primitive Eastern pentatonic [five note] scales on the well-known Western diatonic.' BRIAN, in Beat Instrumental magazine, June 1966

Dylan in Manchester

A much-bootlegged recording of Dylan was made on his 1966 tour when he played Manchester. It was officially released in the late 1990s. When Dylan went electric in the second half of the show, the die-hard folk fans could be heard to boo and jeer. Towards the end, an audience member cried, 'Judas!' Shocked but defiant, Dylan responded, 'I don't believe you. You're a liar.' He ordered his band, 'Play fucking loud!' They ripped into a thunderous 'Like A Rolling Stone'.

resolved my problems with the Bank of England over the transfer from the Chemical Bank. I did have one momentary worry when a girl I had spent time with in Denmark contacted the Stones' office to say that she had given birth to my child. On hearing when the child was born, I pointed out that her arithmetic was two months out. I never heard another word from her.

Soon after 'Paint It, Black' came out, the press was again comparing us with the Beatles. This time we were accused of copying their use of the sitar. Brian was typically forthright in our defence.

'What utter rubbish. You might as well say that we copy all the other groups by playing guitar. Also, everyone asks if it's going to be the new trend. Well, personally, I wouldn't like it to be. You don't have to get that weird Indian sound from a sitar. Take "Norwegian Wood". Atmospherically, it's my favourite track by the Beatles. George made simple use of the sitar and it was very effective.'
BRIAN, *in Beat Instrumental magazine, June 1966*

Like A Rolling Stone

At the end of May, Diane and I went to the Royal Albert Hall and met up with the others and their girlfriends to see Bob Dylan in concert. He did the first half of the show on his own, playing an

Yellow Submarine

On Wednesday 1 June, Brian helped out at the recording of the 'Yellow Submarine' single. He clinked glasses. Marianne Faithfull was there too. They both sang along with the Beatles on the backing vocals.

acoustic guitar. After the interval Dylan returned, and was supported by a full group (the members of which would soon be calling themselves the Band) to play an all-electric set. This didn't go down well with some of his folk fans, but we really enjoyed it.

We spent June getting on with ordinary life. I managed to develop some of my photographs in Stu's darkroom. Keith was often seen around town and frequently ate at La Terrazza restaurant, sometimes with Mick. We had to take our passports to the office for our American visas, which at this time was a pretty straightforward process for us. One day Mick collapsed from overwork, although none of us could figure out why, as we weren't working. A week later, he moved from Bryanston Mews East to 52 Harley House, W1.

Brian spent much of his time shopping. Encouraged by Anita, he was beginning to experiment with his dress. He always was more fashion-conscious than the rest of us. In the evening, he could often be found eating at Alvaro's Restaurant in Chelsea. Charlie and Shirley, meanwhile, relaxed at their home in Sussex.

On June 23, we flew from Heathrow to New York to start our fifth American tour.

The items on Keith's restaurant bill from La Terrazza included pot and dancing girls.

'Stone Brian and Beatle George Harrison both turned up wearing gay striped jackets, at different times – fortunately for the airport. The Stones, who were off to America for a month, were seen off by hundreds of screaming fans. Trend-setter Brian's blazer was lemon and blue with pink stripes.'
DAILY MIRROR, *24 June, 1966*

There were over six months and three US Top 10 singles between the Stones' fourth and fifth North American tours. They visited 20 states, Washington, DC and Canada. On this tour they played in Virginia, Missouri, Oregon, Utah and Hawaii for the first time. The band played fewer shows than previously, but grossed more, earning around $750,000 overall from this trip.

North America, June–July 1966

24 June Manning Bowl, Lynn, Massachusetts
25 June Cleveland Arena, Cleveland, Ohio (matinee)
  Civic Arena, Pittsburgh, Pennsylvania (evening)
26 June Coliseum Washington, DC (matinee)
  Civic Center, Baltimore, Maryland (evening)
27 June Dillon Stadium, Hartford, Connecticut
28 June Memorial Auditorium, Buffalo, New York
29 June Maple Leaf Gardens, Toronto, Canada
30 June Forum, Montréal, Quebec, Canada
1 July Marine Ballroom, Steel Pier, Atlantic City, New Jersey
2 July Forest Hills Tennis Stadium, Queens, New York
3 July Convention Hall, Asbury Park, New Jersey
4 July Under The Dome Theater, Virginia Beach, Virginia
6 July War Memorial Hall, Syracuse, New York
8 July Cobo Hall, Detroit, Michigan
9 July State Fairgrounds Coliseum, Indianapolis, Indiana
10 July Arie Crown Theater, McCormick Place, Chicago, Illinois
11 July Sam Houston Coliseum, Houston, Texas
12 July Kiel Convention Hall, St Louis, Missouri
14 July Winnipeg Stadium, Winnipeg, Canada
15 July Civic Auditorium, Omaha, Nebraska
19 July PNE Forum, Vancouver, Canada
20 July Center Coliseum, Seattle, Washington
21 July Memorial Coliseum, Portland, Oregon
22 July Memorial Auditorium, Sacramento, California (two shows)
23 July Davis County Lagoon, Salt Lake City, Utah (matinee)
  Local venue, Phoenix, Arizona (evening)
24 July Civic Auditorium, Bakersfield, California (two shows)
25 July Hollywood Bowl, Los Angeles, California
26 July Cow Palace, San Francisco, California
28 July Honolulu International Centre, Honolulu, Hawaii

Tickets sold for between $2.50 and $5 at most venues, with only New York reaching prices of around $10 for the most expensive seats. As a result, the Forest Hills gig in New York was around three-quarters full. The only really disappointing date was St Louis where just 4,500 of the 10,500 seats were sold; it was the first time the band had played the city.

'This was the most prolonged demand of physical endurance I have ever seen police confronted with during my 33 years of service. Sixty police officers were hampered by the Stones themselves, who made offensive remarks and rude gestures at them. Proportionately, the trouble was a lot worse than the Beatles' show three years ago. As soon as the rock'n'roll hits its tempo, the fans are gone. The bumps and grinds are really what you would expect an adult to be watching in a burlesque show. It is not only vulgar, it is disgusting. It's a tribal dance. Its purpose is to get the youngsters sexually excited. The Stones would not be welcome in the city in the future.' CITY POLICE INSPECTOR FC ERRINGTON, *Vancouver Sun, 20 July, 1966*

'Mick sang passionately and danced with gyrations that would do credit to a stripper.' CHICAGO DAILY NEWS, *11 July, 1966*

Set list
The song pool on this tour was:
'19th Nervous Breakdown'
'Not Fade Away'
'The Last Time'
'Get Off Of My Cloud'
'Paint It, Black'
'Stupid Girl'
'Lady Jane'
'That's How Strong My Love Is'
'The Spider And The Fly'
'Time Is On My Side'
'Satisfaction' (This was the regular closer)

Support bands in 1966
In general, the other acts were the McCoys (their 'Hang On Sloopy' was a UK hit on Immediate), the Standells ('Dirty Water' was Stones-like) and the Tradewinds ('New York's A Lonely Town'). Others who made occasional appearances included the Ugly Ducklings, the Rogues, the Syndicate of Sound and the Ronettes.

Satisfaction Guaranteed

'Stones' Roll 'N' Rock, Almost Try 'Knuckle' Sock

Portland, Ore. (UPI)—The mop-topped British rock 'n' roll quintet, the Rolling Stones, rolled into town Thursday night, threatened a television cameraman with a "knuckle sandwich" and appeared later before some 10,000 hysterical teen-agers.

They shouted and stomped their way through a list of current rock 'n' roll hits, including one which has been banned at several radio stations, "Satisfaction."

Mick Jagger, 22, leader of the Stones, did calisthenics, turned his microphone upside-down and led his fans in a chorus of squeals.

One young girl was carried out of the Portland Coliseum by a policeman after trying to charge the stage as Jagger sang "Not getting any satisfaction or girlie action" from the hit.

K-poi presents...
The INCREDIBLE
ROLLING STONES
(ONE SHOW ONLY)
THURS. NITE -- JULY 28th
INTERNATIONAL
CENTER ARENA
Tickets $6.50, 5.50, 4.50, 3.50, 2.50
BOX OFFICE OPENS TODAY

KOL Radio 1300 Presents
The **Rolling Stones**
plus
"DIRTY WATER"—THE STANDELLS
"HANG-ON-SLOOPY"—THE McCOYS
"Little Girl"—The Syndicate of Sound
WED., JULY 20-8 pm
SEATTLE CENTER COLISEUM
Prices 5.00—4.00—3.00—2.00
TICKETS ON SALE TUESDAY!
SHERMAN-CLAY TICKET OFFICE
1424-4th AVE, SEATTLE
And Suburban Agencies

HUBBUB PRODUCTIONS PRESENTS
ONLY NEW ENGLAND CONCERT
FIRST U.S. APPEARANCE 1966
THE
ROLLING STONES
FRI., JUNE 24
8.30 P.M.
MANNING BOWL
LYNN, MASS.
TICKETS $5.00 - $4.00 - $3.00

Direction George A. Hamid
AMERICA'S GREATEST AMUSEMENT BARGAIN
STEEL PIER
ATLANTIC CITY, N.J. — SHOWPLACE OF THE NATION
Now Open for the Season
DIONNE WARWICK
DANCING
Frankie Lester directing
BILLY MAY BAND
ALL FOR ONE LOW ADMISSION
COMING—1 DAY ONLY
July 1—First Eastern Appearance
THE
ROLLING STONES

CONVENTION HALL
BOARDWALK
ASBURY PARK, NEW JERSEY
9:45 P.M.
SUNDAY EVE. JULY 3
1966
$5.00
THE ROLLING STONES

'Whether or not you dig the Stones' sounds in the world of modern music, they're what's happening, baby.'
OREGON JOURNAL, *22 July, 1966*

'The young nubiles surged forward, arms undulating like tentacles of sea anemones writhing in warm fluid. Mick is a phenomenon of utter sexuality, beyond simple distinctions of maleness or femaleness.' TORONTO DAILY STAR, *30 June, 1966*

'I didn't particularly like the Stones and went out of curiosity. I've never screamed so much in my life and I've never had so much fun.' **LIZ VARGO,** *fan at Asbury Park, 3 July, 1966*

Dirty But Cool

When we arrived in New York we went to New York's West 79th Street Marina for a press conference on board a 110-foot yacht, the *SS Sea Panther,* hired by Allen Klein. One of the photographers there was Linda Eastman (who went on to marry Paul McCartney). She wrote an article in an American magazine about her night out with Mick.

THERE WERE THE USUAL round of dumb questions to which we responded with our usual mixture of coolness and humour and – if all else failed – by telling the truth. A reporter from the *New York Post* asked Keith, 'Have you gotten tired of girls, with the masses of birds that throw themselves at you?'

'Why should I?' said a surprised Keith. 'I'm only 22.' After sailing around for a while, we returned to the hotel to freshen up. I got a phone call from musician John Hammond, who was at a studio recording. He asked me if I'd like to play bass on some tracks. Brian came along as well. I played alongside guitarist Robbie Robertson (of the Band). We cut three tracks, including 'I Can Tell' and 'I Wish You Would', later released on John Hammond's 1967 album *I Can Tell*.

Bob Dylan joined us at the studio and later invited everyone back to his apartment for drinks. We walked to his flat, stopping off at a couple of delis and other small shops on the way. To my amazement, as one of our party was being served, the others – including Dylan himself – shoplifted items. When we arrived at the flat, there was

All aboard the Sea Panther *with*, inset below, *Mick with Linda Eastman*

Another gig –
another riot

Top of all the pops
The Stones' 'Satisfaction' was one of the most programmed songs of the year on US radio and television. As something of a contrast, the other big one in the same period was 'Ballad Of The Green Beret', a patriotic song by Staff Sergeant Barry Sadler.

already a bunch of people there, drinking and smoking pot.

In the morning I phoned Klein and told him about the Hammond session. He was angry with me for doing it, telling me that there would be tax implications. He agreed that John could give me a credit on the album, but insisted I should not get a session fee – sometimes it seemed like he didn't want things to work for us.

Chaos and consent
Later in the same day, we played our first show to 15,000 in Lynn, a Boston suburb. The show degenerated into a riot when some of the fans

the time to take a bow – and taken to a car for a quick getaway, often straight to the airport. The security at times felt claustrophobic. Our lives revolved around the gig, limos and hotel rooms. Sometimes we would sneak away, like Charlie and Keith did in New York. They went to Greenwich Village and got in a hell of a lot of trouble with Mike Cornwell and Mike Gruber, our tour managers.

'I'm old enough to do as I please!' KEITH

'The Stones are good but grubby, they're dirty but cool, they're tough. Tough, for the benefit of old fogies over 20, is good.' A GIRL FAN, *on the Hartford show, 27 June, 1966*

tried to storm the stage; the police ended up using tear gas – welcome back to America. From Boston we took a chartered plane to Cleveland. This was a pattern that continued throughout the tour. There was very little time off for us as we spent our time criss-crossing America. Whichever venue we went to play, the routine was the same. As soon as we finished, we were bundled off the stage – with barely

Going up in the world
The magazine for which Linda Eastman was photographing the Stones ran an article on New York debutantes. One of them, Alexandra E Chalice met the Stones and this piece of high-society gossip was the basis for the magazine's lead story.

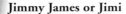

The only trouble with Keith's angry statement was that we couldn't do what we wanted – not when we had so many fans wanting to get us whenever we went out.

Our Forest Hills show in New York was to be one of the most important gigs on the whole tour, but only about 9,500 seats were sold in the 14,000 capacity stadium. We flew to and from the venue by helicopter – it was a great ride to downtown New York. It may have looked like Balham from the Boeing 707 we had taken to the US on our first tour, but the city looked much more exotic from a thousand feet.

Jimmy James or Jimi
After we got back from the gig, we went to a club to see a guitarist who called himself Jimmy James. John

Hammond told me he was amazing and he was absolutely right – it was Jimi Hendrix. was in fact Keith's girlfriend, Linda, who told Chas Chandler of the Animals to check him out. It was as a result of this that Chas took Jimi to England.

While we were in New York, Brian and I saw quite a bit of our friend Scott Ross. One night we went over to his place where a party was in full swing. Scott was out of it on LSD and Brian ended up staying all night, while I went back to the hotel. The following morning Brian, Scott and two of the Ronettes drove to Jones Beach.

'On the way there, we jumped into the back of a parked milk truck and stole milk. Then we went to a bakery store and stole some doughnuts. We ate them with milk on the beach, fell asleep and got terribly sunburnt – even the Ronettes, and they are black.' SCOTT ROSS, *DJ and friend*

It was later that day that Brian got into trouble over an incident with the American flag. At the War Memorial Hall in Syracuse New York, we were making our way back under the stage after performing when Brian noticed a dirty and tatty

That'll do nicely
At the end of June 1966, Barclays Bank introduced Barclaycard, the first British credit card. It was a landmark in finance. Credit had existed in the US for decades and the UK version was based on Bank Americard, since renamed Visa.

'MOTHER'S LITTLE HELPER'

The Stones' 12th US single came out the day the band played Forest Hills.

'**M**other's Little Helper' is Mick and Keith's ode to tranquillisers and was partially written during the band's fourth US tour. Brian plays electric dulcimer on 'Lady Jane', which was covered in the summer of 1966 by David Garrick, Tony Merrick, the Zombies, and Trini Lopez.

Recorded
a-side 8–10 December, 1965
b-side 6–9 March, 1966
Studio
RCA Hollywood
Producer
Andrew Loog Oldham
Engineer
Dave Hassinger
Release
US Saturday 2 July, 1966
London 45 LON 902
Composers
Jagger/Richard
Highest chart position
US No 8

old American flag lying over a boiler pipe. He took it, saying that he wanted it as a souvenir. Almost immediately the police, who were escorting us, set upon us. We were pushed around and bundled into an office, where the police snatched the flag from Brian and started giving us a hard time. They were yelling at us, accusing us of insulting the American flag and threatening to throw us all in jail. We finally calmed them down and they let us go. The incident was later grossly exaggerated in many of the newspapers.

Back in the lone star state

We returned to Texas for the first time since June 1964. At Houston's Coliseum, we played to around 6,500 screaming fans. In mid-tour we had a few days off, so we headed for Los Angeles, our favourite American city. We stayed at the Century Plaza Hotel and during our time there we went shopping and visited the clubs, particularly the Whisky A Go-Go on Sunset Boulevard. At this time, we long-hairs were still very much a novelty and the whole band, Brian most of all, found it annoying when people stared.

Our first gig after our short rest was in Vancouver and we were 90 minutes late starting, as our plane broke down in Portland. This put the crowd in a difficult mood, one the police couldn't control. Police inspector FC Errington was very unhappy about our visit, as the *Vancouver Sun* reported on 20 July:

'Sixty police officers were hampered by the Stones themselves, who made offensive remarks and rude gestures at the police. Proportionally, the trouble was a lot worse than the Beatles three years ago.'

After two good shows in Sacramento on 22 July, we flew to Salt Lake City, Utah. We were playing poker in the back of the plane. Mick, Brian and Keith were sitting on one side of the aisle, Charlie, myself and two others were on the other side. All of a sudden, there was a loud crack from the window next to Brian. All three of them

screamed and charged up the aisle to the front of the plane. The rest of us were in hysterics, watching them panic. When they were assured that everything was secure, they returned to their seats. But we all suffered pains in our ears, as there had been a sudden decompression. The pains only went away when the plane descended to a height of about 8,000 feet. It was the first air scare for all of us: it wouldn't be the last.

Hollywood nights

One of the highlights of this tour was our sell-out gig at the famous Hollywood Bowl. A total of 17,500 fans were there. Afterwards, Sunset Strip was filled with many hundreds of kids, all high on our gig – and a whole lot more besides, I expect.

We trekked up the coast for our second show in San Francisco, our first in the city since May 1965.

We played at the Cow Palace, so named because it was a livestock exhibition hall and it certainly smelt like it. This was our penultimate show of the tour; our last was in Hawaii.

We played the last night in Honolulu and took some days out for a brief holiday before heading back to Los Angeles. Chrissie and Shirley – who had flown out to join us in Hawaii – stayed on in Los Angeles. Diane also flew out to LA for a holiday in a rented house in the hills.

Charlie and Shirley take time out in Hawaii on 30 July, 1966.

Drag Queens To Witches

Diane and I returned home on 22 August, via New York. Waiting for me was another new car, a Mercedes 250 S Saloon (KYM 585D) with black windows. Domesticity was on Mick's mind as well. He applied to Fortnum and Mason for credit, after stopping his account with Selfridges due to their poor service.

A REVEALING ARTICLE WAS featured in *Rave* magazine. In the piece about the band that month, writer Dawn James noted that she made a perfectly innocent request of our office and it was the response which was telling.

'Brian seems to have disappeared from the public eye. He doesn't feature very much in the Stones' present image. Once, the rather weird, long-haired, almost mythical Brian, was the most talked-of and popular Stone. We asked the Stones' office for an interview with him.' DAWN JAMES

Andrew replied to her enquiry, 'No, you cannot see him, or phone him and he cannot give you any quotes'.

Brian really was not popular with Andrew. He hadn't been since the start. Andrew's relationship with Mick and Keith, 'the unholy trinity' as Stu always called it, pushed Brian closer to the edge of the group. Charlie and I had never been the centre of attention, which was more understandable – which rhythm section ever is? Brian's paranoia fuelled the situation and his drug-taking, on the increase at this time, did nothing to alleviate his problems. When his relationship with Anita was

TAMI or not TAMI
On 7 August, 1966, the film of the TAMI (Teen Age Music International) show was released in the UK under the name *Gather No Moss*. It featured four songs performed by the Stones.

'In a more gracious age, Anita would have been called a witch.' CHRISTOPHER GIBBS

added to this mix, you had a cocktail for which there was no cure. While Brian's difficulties were nothing new, his work on *Aftermath* had been recognised by everybody and certainly gave him encouragement in the short term. Towards the end of August, he and Anita, along with their friend Christopher Gibbs, went to Morocco on holiday. It's easy with hindsight to say that this period was a watershed for Brian but the writing was on the wall. While Brian was in Morocco he supposedly fell in the bathroom and broke his wrist. According to Christopher, Brian and Anita fought the whole time they were away.

On his return from Morocco, Brian visited Dr Martin Hynes at Harley Street, and then went to see Mr Phillip Lebon, a specialist, about his broken wrist. He was also unhappy with Anita and, sometime in the month, had a short affair with Marianne Faithfull. Mick did too. It was the beginning of his relationship with her.

How to act
Another aspect of our career was taking precedence over our music. In preparation for the filming of *Only Lovers Left Alive,* we were being coached in acting by a Miss Mary Phillips. It would be fascinating to know what she really thought of us, but she was far too polite to tell. Keith was busy furnishing Redlands and had lots of things made, including two lioness skin

Keith backstage at the Cow Palace, San Francisco on July 26

rugs and one wildebeest skin mat. He bought a rabbit-skin rug and a grey wolf-skin rug – it was all very tasteful.

On Thursday 8 September, I spent the day at Keston; Charlie was in Lewes and Mick went to the Mill House in Sonning, near Reading, with a view to buying it.

Together with Andrew and Sheila Oldham, Keith and Stu, Mick flew to Los Angeles. They worked with Dave Hassinger at RCA to finish our new single, 'Have You Seen Your Mother, Baby, Standing In The Shadow?'.

The following day the rest of us flew to New York and the others flew

in from LA. We were due to record an appearance on *The Ed Sullivan Show*, but first we had to do the cover shoot for 'Have You Seen Your Mother'.

What a drag

We dressed in women's clothing in a studio and photographer Jerry Schatzberg took us to a side street off 3rd Avenue and shot the famous photographs that promoted the single. At the same time we recorded a short film clip. We were nicknamed Sarah (Mick), Molly (Keith), Flossie (Brian), Millicent (Charlie) and Penelope (me).

Our new PR

Leslie Perrin was born in Manchester in 1920 and after service in the RAF during the Second World War, he worked in a silk-screen printing company. He became a freelance journalist and was one of the founder team members of the *New Musical Express*.
In March 1950, he began working as a publicist for bandleader Johnny Dankworth. His clients included Nat King Cole, Frank Sinatra and Cliff Richard and the Shadows.

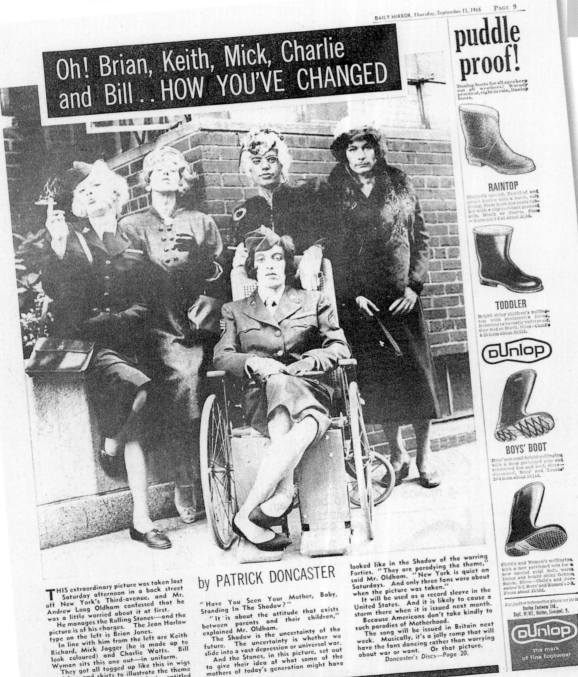

That evening I was taken to Andy Warhol's studio with a girlfriend. It was crowded with people and the whole place was filled with silver balloons. Brian and I flew back home together on the Sunday. He and Anita were moving into a new flat at 1 Courtfield Road in London.

There was a slight but significant shift in our relationship with Andrew – indicating a change in our situation. We no longer needed the type of PR that he was so good at. We had gone from needing a striker to a goalkeeper. We employed Leslie Perrin, a PR man who could defend our position, rather than promote it.

The first three weeks of September were free. I did some work in the studio with Moon's Train and the End, but mostly I relaxed – apart from the day I almost poked my eye out with a screwdriver while working in the garden. I still bear the scar. Keith continued to frequent Alvaro's Restaurant, mostly with Linda Keith and friends. Sometimes Brian and Anita joined him.

I often spent evenings at Scotch of St James or Tiles club. By Thursday 22 September, it was back to work. We were rehearsing for our upcoming UK tour and we needed to. We hadn't played live for almost two months.

Girls together outrageously

The Mirror ran a story about the cross-dressing antics of the band in the States. Even slipping into a skirt was national news if it was a Rolling Stone who was doing it.

'HAVE YOU SEEN YOUR MOTHER, BABY, STANDING IN THE SHADOW?'

'We tried trombones, saxes and every permutation of brass, before the trumpets. Everything else dragged.'
KEITH, *in NME, 23 September, 1966*

Written by Mick and Keith on their last US tour, the Stones' 11th UK and 13th US single was released in both territories at the same time. With its clear Phil Spector overtones, it was expected to be another No 1 – all the UK music press said so! Unfortunately, nobody expected Jim Reeves' 'Distant Drums' to be such powerful competition. The Stones floundered at UK No 5.

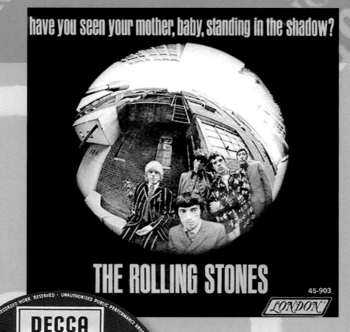

The song's US TV debut was on Ed Sullivan's show on Sunday 11 September, 1966. Besides 'Have You Seen Your Mother', the band also played 'Lady Jane' and 'Paint It, Black'. Mick sang live to backing tracks, as Brian couldn't play guitar because of his hand injury.

The single fared even worse in America. The Stones were moving away from the format of US Top 40 radio and it was airplay that drove chart positions.

'Keith always felt that the incorrectly mixed version was released as the single. The rhythm section is buried in the mix and it failed to create as much excitement as we all felt it should have done. Although we took longer to record and mix this single than any of our previous releases, Keith always felt it needed more – this was the beginning of the future!' BILL

Recorded
a-side 3–11 August, 31 August and 8 September, 1966
b-side 3–11 August, 1966
Studios
RCA Hollywood 3–11 August and 8 September, 1966; IBC Studios London 31 August, 1966
Producer
Andrew Loog Oldham
Engineers
David Hassinger at RCA
Glyn Johns at IBC
Release
UK Friday 23 September, 1966
Decca F 12497
US Saturday 24 September, 1966
London 903
Composers
Jagger/Richard
Highest chart position
UK No 5
US No 9
Additional personnel
Jack Nitzsche: piano

What the papers said...

'Another fantastic disc from the Stones, with such a complexity of startling sounds that it'll leave you breathless.' NME, *23 September, 1966*

'I don't know what this is all about, but it doesn't really matter, since it's one of the most exciting records the Stones have made. The most certain UK No 1 they've ever had.' DISC, *24 September, 1966*

'The new single is a knockout and should be nestling in the UK No 1 spot in double-quick time. It's only justice that sound engineer Dave Hassinger should get a credit.' RECORD MIRROR, *24 September, 1966*

A review of the US edition of the single

THE ROLLING STONES—HAVE YOU SEEN YOUR MOTHER, BABY, STANDING IN THE SHADOW? (Prod. by Andrew Oldham) (Writers: Jagger-Richard) (Gideon, BMI)—Invigorating rhythm rocker from the group will skyrocket to the top of the charts in short order. Has all the ingredients necessary to follow their string of past hits. Flip: "Who's Driving My Plane" (Gideon, BMI). **London 903**

The United Kingdom,
September–October 1966

Two shows everywhere (except the Royal Albert Hall).

23 September Royal Albert Hall, London
24 September Odeon Theatre, Leeds, Yorkshire
25 September Empire Theatre, Liverpool, Lancashire
28 September Apollo Theatre, Manchester, Lancashire
29 September ABC Theatre, Stockton-on-Tees, Durham
30 September Odeon Theatre, Glasgow, Scotland
1 October City Hall, Newcastle upon Tyne, Northumberland
2 October Gaumont Theatre, Ipswich, Suffolk
6 October Odeon Theatre, Birmingham, Staffordshire
7 October Colston Hall, Bristol, Gloucestershire
8 October Capitol Theatre, Cardiff, Wales
9 October Gaumont Theatre, Southampton, Hampshire

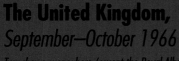

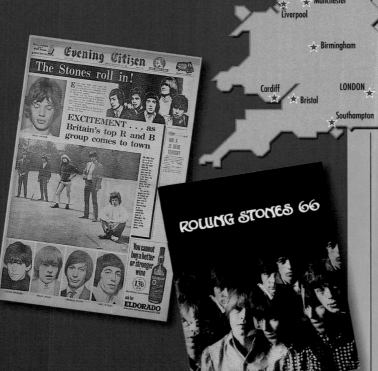

Evening Citizen
The Stones roll in!

EXCITEMENT . . . as Britain's top R and B group comes to town

You cannot buy a better or stronger wine 13/6 ask for ELDORADO

ROLLING STONES 66

Excluding the *NME* poll winners' show in May, these were the Stones' first live UK dates in almost a year. It was a 12-date, big-city tour with Ike and Tina Turner as the principal supporting act.

'We haven't toured here for a year. We are seeing everything with a new light and doing much more. All of a sudden, I am very interested in everything again. Touring all the time around one country or another abroad, you get blasé about the kids. Consequently, you often give an indifferent performance. Now I'm finding myself determined to do my best. We thought the fans would have grown up and away from us in a year, but there are some out there that are so young. Do you know there are girls of nine and 10 in the front rows?' MICK, *Disc*, 1 October, 1966

Bird(s) for the Yardbirds' roadie

'The Yardbirds' road manager tried to get into the theatre after the show to collect their gear. The police nabbed him and said he'd be nicked if he went in. We all leapt out of the coach and said he was with the show. No joy. He spent the night in jail.' PETER JAY, *Record Mirror*, 8 October

'Linda and Celia hitched to eight places on the tour: Albert Hall, Leeds, Newcastle, Ipswich, Birmingham, Bristol, Cardiff and Southampton. I had no one to go with and I couldn't really afford to go anyway. Lin was very lucky as they got backstage. While they were hitching round the country, I just sat at home moping because they were seeing the boys. I cried nearly every night. I wanted to see Brian so much and I couldn't, but they could. It really was upsetting. Anyway, while they were hitching, the Yardbirds' road manager stopped and gave them a lift for the last 20 or so miles to Southampton.' A FAN'S DIARY

Set list from...
'Paint It, Black'
'Under My Thumb'
'Get Off Of My Cloud'
'Lady Jane'
'Not Fade Away'
'The Last Time'
'Have You Seen Your Mother, Baby?'
'Satisfaction'
'19th Nervous Breakdown'
'Mother's Little Helper'
'Stupid Girl'
'Flight 505'
'Out Of Time'
'It's Not Easy'
'I'm Alright'
'Time Is On My Side'

And in support...
Peter Jay and the New Jaywalkers
Ike and Tina Turner (featuring the Kings of Rhythm Band, the Ikettes, Jimmy Thomas and Bobby John)
Interval
The Yardbirds (featuring Jeff Beck and Jimmy Page)
The Rolling Stones (Compere Long John Baldry)

Touring With The Turners

'Girls rushing onstage stopped the show twice. Officials pleaded in vain with hundreds of fans to go back to their seats. Fifty girls fainted in the pandemonium.'
DAILY SKETCH, *24 September, 1966*

What the papers said...

'A total of 6,500 people watched. Each seat was filled and scores stood in the gods. Fifty girls fainted and were treated by the St John's Ambulance Brigade. Charlie has grown a moustache, Bill had his hair cut and Brian's locks are beginning to curl. Only the Stones could have followed Ike and Tina Turner.'
DISC, *1 October, 1966*

'The sight of a 14-year-old schoolgirl with her mini-skirt hitched up over her thighs, being flung, legs kicking, through swing doors, like a gangster in a B-picture brawl, no longer makes me feel sick. Girls crying as bitterly as if they'd just seen their parents killed in a road accident, when all they wanted was just to touch one of the Stones, no longer brings a lump to my throat. I saw mass hysteria at close hand. It was not a pleasant sight. Hardly a word of the Stones' lyrics was heard above the shrill screams. The violent volume from the amplifiers blasted each tune into inaudible anonymity.' PEOPLE, *9 October, 1966*

Accounts department

Gross Receipts		£27,586.3.7d
Less	Long John Baldry	£270
	Peter Jay and the Jaywalkers	£720
	The Yardbirds	£2,300
	Ike and Tina Turner	£6,183.3.1

(including Air Fares £3,589.11.0d and excess baggage charges of £439.12.1d)
After commissions and the band's tour costs, Rolling Stones Promotions Ltd made a Net profit of £615.17.7d.

Ticket prices at the Royal Albert Hall were 17/6d, 15/-, 10/6d, 7/6d, and 3/6d.

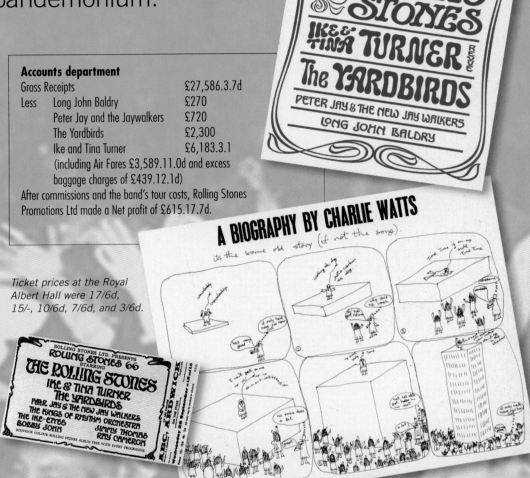

'The tour has been an enormous success because it's brought the young people back again. It was getting all draggy and quiet. We were in danger of becoming respectable. Now the new wave has arrived, rushing the stage just like old times.' **KEITH,** *NME, 14 October, 1966*

Taxing Times

The opening night of our UK tour was at the Royal Albert Hall in London. The show almost got halted because fans stormed the stage – it was good to be back. Afterwards, we returned to the Kensington Palace Hotel for a press reception. We were each presented with four gold discs for sales in America.

At the Kensington Palace Hotel the band received gold discs.

THERE WAS A PARTY attended by John Maus and Gary Leeds from the Walker Brothers, Keith Moon and John Entwistle from the Who, Chris Curtis of the Searchers, Vicki Wickham and Cathy McGowan from *Ready Steady Go!*, Peter Asher of Peter and Gordon and Paul Samwell-Smith, ex-Yardbirds.

As the tour continued around the UK, Glyn Johns recorded some of the dates with a view to releasing a live album. The Ike and Tina Turner Revue was brilliant – especially the Ikettes. Lead singer with Peter Jay and the New Jaywalkers was 18-year-old Terry Reid, who later found success in America; he had a wonderfully soulful voice. The Yardbirds, featuring Jeff Beck and Jimmy Page, were nearing the end of their time together. A few days after finishing their dates with us, they flew to America for a four-week tour. Jeff managed to play two gigs before he pulled out, feigning illness, and he was then sacked. Jimmy always claimed it was the worst tour he had ever done.

I drove myself to some of the gigs in my new Mercedes and was almost killed on the road between Glasgow and Newcastle. Mike Gruber and Ikettes Rose and Pat were in the car when we suddenly came upon the scene of a terrible accident, with jack-knifed trucks and trailers strewn across the oily tarmac. There were bodies covered in sheets on the grass. The driver in front of me stopped his car to see what had happened, I slammed on my brakes, hit the oil and ran into the back of him. My radiator was smashed and I lost all the water. It was impossible to drive it further , so we pushed it up onto the verge. A few minutes later the boys came by in their car and we squeezed in with them. We treated it as a huge joke.

Stony broke

The public would never have believed that our company was short of money. Rolling Stones Promotions had an income tax assessment of £4,200, which was due on 8 September. Three weeks later it was still unpaid and the Inland Revenue was getting nasty. All the while that we were in the red at the bank, the press carried stories of our fabulous wealth.

'Backstage, the Stones heard that in New York, their American business manager Allen Klein had announced his fantastic estimate for their overseas earnings of $20 million in the next 12 months. This is made up of earnings from discs, personal appearances and two films.' DAILY MIRROR, *29 September, 1966*

Klein, it was reported, had cabled us to say that next year we would all be millionaires. I, for one, don't recall seeing the cable.

On the day we played Bristol, a legal case against Beat Publications, the publishers of *Rolling Stone Monthly,* was concluded. They had published some material without permission from us. The terms of the settlement included an undertaking not to publish the magazine after the November issue. There was also an undertaking to pay us royalties.

Mick's mind was very definitely not on business affairs. Marianne Faithfull, who had been seeing Mick for about a month, came to Bristol. She had split up with her husband, John Dunbar, who was looking after her

one-year-old son. According to Gered Mankowitz, 'I saw Marianne and Mick outside, holding hands and walking by the river in the dawn. As far as I know, that was the first night they'd spent together.' I am pretty sure that it's not true but it made for a good story.

There was continuing press speculation about our prospective film, fuelled no doubt by Klein talking of our anticipated earnings. We were in the dark, as was everyone else at the time. We wanted to do something new and it seemed to all of us to be a logical direction for the band – well, with the probable exception of Charlie.

Left, *Charlie and moustache and,* below, *Keith and Bill*

'I entice the audience. I do it in every way I can think of. I hate the people who just sit there and don't scream. Since the screaming started, a lot of people have talked about it, but none of them has really gone into it. What I'm doing is a sexual thing. I dance and all dancing is a replacement for sex. My dancing is pretty basic sexuality. What really upsets people is that I'm a man and not a woman – I take my jacket off and sometimes I loosen my shirt – what I do is very much the same as a girl striptease dancer.'
MICK, *Sunday People, 9 October, 1966*

Live on Top Of The Pops *in October 1966*

'We seem to have been talking about making a film for years. Among ourselves it has been a topic of much discussion for a long time. Of course, we have known that negotiations have been in an advanced stage. But now it's been finalised, we are more excited than ever. It is a big step forward in the group's career, perhaps the biggest yet. Now we have to prove ourselves and this is the challenge. We have every confidence in our ability. We are really looking forward to it. I have even started running films at home. In my new flat I have a huge studio, and I'm making a point of seeing several films each week when possible.' BRIAN, *Melody Maker, 8 October, 1966*

Brian hired *Goldwhiskers, Springtime For Samantha* and *Polygamous Polonius.*

Fan reaction was wild throughout the tour. The press had an insatiable appetite for stories about our audience and us.

'There's so many of them, there can't be anything wrong with what they do. If there is, then the whole country must be in a bad way. We belong to a generation that's separate from any other. We believe in what we're doing. We're happy to have the kids screaming for us. It gets me down to think that a lot of them will one day disappear into the drab nest. I hope all of them won't. If only the whole world could stay young.' KEITH, *Sunday People, 9 October, 1966*

When the tour finished, everyone thought it had been a great success. We were still at the point in our careers where we were not sure how the future would work out. We had been going for a little under four years and I think all of us, in the backs of our minds, wondered how much longer it would last. The tour certainly confirmed that the British public still loved us, even if 'Have You Seen Your Mother' was not turning out to be such a strong single. Andrew also had doubts and fears about the future. There was just a hint of relief in Andrew's comment to a London paper.

'The Stones are not slipping. Not after this tour, as every police force in the country will tell you.' ANDREW OLDHAM, *Evening Standard, 10 October, 1966*

'I know a few groovy middle-aged people, but not many.' KEITH, *Sunday People, 9 October, 1966*

When the tour finished, Brian and Anita went to Paris and I went shopping in Penge. I needed some new clothes and went to Watts the Tailor. Mick and Keith spent time in the studio with Glyn Johns, running through the tapes to see what we could use for a live album.

I flew to Madrid with Glyn to discuss a deal for the End with a Spanish record company. Two plain-clothes policemen, who must have thought we looked a little weird in our Edwardian-style clothes, followed us around Madrid. We didn't know that Michael Aldred, one of the *Ready Steady Go!* presenters, had been arrested just a week before for his outlandish dress.

For the rest of the month, I did some more recordings with Moon's Train and the others worked on mixing the live songs. I had some more acting lessons, while Mick, who wanted to broaden his musicial talents, took piano lessons. Marianne often stayed with Mick at Harley House. One day Ian McLagan of the Small Faces dropped round.

"Ronnie [Wood], Steve [Marriott] and I went to Mick Jagger's flat on the Marylebone Road one evening,' wrote Ian in his book *All The Rage*. 'Mick led us into the bedroom, where Marianne Faithfull was quietly reading a book of poetry in bed and he and Ronnie left the room to get some drinks.

'Steve and I sat on the bed passing a joint and listening while she read us a poem from the book. It was a beautiful moment and she read well, but what made it more memorable for us was her tits unintentionally popped out of her nightdress a couple of times as she read. It didn't seem to bother her in the slightest and we were delighted. She remembers that evening differently these days and even recalls us setting up our musical equipment and performing. The truth is there was only one performance and the equipment was all hers.'

On top of all this excitement, I was 30 on 24 October… and still going strong.

A change is gonna come

On 4 November, *Big Hits (High Tide And Green Grass)* came out in the UK with a slightly different track listing from the American release. It certainly marked the closing of a chapter in our career; from then on things were going to be different. In the press there was much talk about our failure to make UK No 1, including some comment from other pop stars.

'I just didn't think this was good enough. It wasn't as well-constructed or as commercial as other records they've made, but I really can't see this affecting them in any way at all. The Stones are big enough to cope.' ERIC CLAPTON, *Disc, 5 November, 1966*

'The record basically went over the top of their fans' heads. It was too hippy and those photos showing the Rolling Stones in drag put the youngsters off a bit.' BOBBY ELLIOTT, *of the Hollies, Disc, 5 November, 1966*

On 8 November, we started recording at Olympic Studios in Barnes and worked for the rest of the month. Among the tracks we cut were 'Miss Amanda Jones', 'All Sold Out', 'Ruby Tuesday', 'Yesterday's Papers', 'She Smiled Sweetly' and 'Trouble In Mind'. The latter was really us just messing about on an old blues song. Brian, who loved these old numbers, was in control of the track.

Anita arrives from Munich on 2 December, 1966.

While we were recording, people would drop by the studio, more often than not friends of Mick, Keith and Brian. They included Marianne, Anita, Prince Stash, a friend of Keith's who was called 'Spanish' Tony Sanchez, photographer Michael Cooper, Robert Fraser and the comedians Peter Cook and Dudley Moore.

Button-hole camera

On Monday 14 November, after an all-night session, we drove to Primrose Hill, in north London, so Gered Mankowitz could take shots for the cover of our upcoming album, *Between The Buttons*.

Playing with fire

Anita filmed *A Degree Of Murder* in Munich and early in November, Brian joined her. Their photo sessions caused trouble, which he made worse: 'These are going to be realistic pictures. The meaning is there is no sense in it.'

Bill: 'Sometimes he did the most stupid things, that he instinctively knew would land him in trouble with the press, with us, his family and just about everyone else. It was attention seeking in part. His dissatisfaction with his role and position in the group spurred him on to more and more destructive behaviour.'

SHE has the heart of a Stone . . . Rolling Stone guitarist Brian Jones. He is clad as one with a heart of stone, in a Nazi SS uniform. A doll lies fallen at their feet, near an ornament showing another swastika.

These are the clothes Jones and his girl friend, German actress Anita Pallenberg, both born in the war year of 1942, chose to wear for a publicity photographer in Munich.

"These are going to be realistic pictures," said Jones. "The meaning of it all is there is no sense in it."

Modern art pioneer
Robert Fraser (pictured in his gallery with Peter Blake pictures) brought modern art to London. He provided space for many artists new to the UK, including Andy Warhol, Roy Lichtenstein and Richard Hamilton. Nude drawings by Jim Dine shocked non-Swinging London and Fraser was prosecuted and fined. The pop elite loved this champion of Pop Art, who counted the Stones, the Beatles and Dennis Hopper among his friend. In the 1970s, drugs took over his life and he declined. He died of AIDS in the 1980s.

'We piled them into Andrew's Rolls and headed for Primrose Hill in North London. When we reached the top of the hill, there was this well-known London character called Maxie – a sort of prototype hippy – just standing on his own playing the flute. Mick walked up to him and offered him a joint and his only response was "Ah – breakfast!"'
GERED MANKOWITZ, *on Between The Buttons cover photo shoot*

Mick's love and sex life was becoming increasingly complicated. He booked a holiday for late December in Jamaica with Chrissie but was secretly seeing a lot of Marianne. We all waited for the problems to begin. Mick saw Marianne a lot more in December, which resulted in him cancelling the holiday with Chrissie.

On Tuesday 6 December, Keith and Brian flew to Los Angeles for a 10-day holiday, staying at Jack Nitzsche's house in Hollywood. Two days later I went to the Scotch of St James club and met a pretty young Swedish girl named Astrid Lundstrom. I then went on to the Bag O' Nails Club, not thinking too much more about her. Charlie and Shirley's Christmas break was spent in America. The couple travelled there on board the *Queen Elizabeth II* from Southampton. On arrival in New York, they took the train to Florida; Charlie has always enjoyed taking the train.

Overs

The inevitable happened between Mick and Chrissie. They broke up after a row on 18 December. She attempted suicide and was admitted to the Greenway Nursing Home in Hampstead. By coincidence, the date of their split was also Keith's birthday, not that it played any part in their break-up.

That same evening, I went to the Scotch of St James once more and then off to to the Bag O'Nails, where I met Astrid again. It was the birthday of the Animals' Chas Chandler and we spent some time there with him and his girlfriend. A group of his friends went back to Chas' flat in Kensington. Everybody was smoking joints, as did Astrid and I. As we talked, we both got very stoned. I was also pretty drunk. When Astrid wanted to leave, I offered to drive her to Onslow Square, where she was staying with friends. I have no clear recollection of the drive.

The following day, another bizarre rumour started circulating. In the US, it was reported that Mick had died. Our new PR man, Les Perrin, phoned the *Melody Maker* and offered them a statement.

One of Gered's outtakes from the photo session for Between The Buttons

On 15 December, 1966, the UK fan club sent out 7,200 Christmas cards.

'Mr Jagger wishes to deny that he is dead and says that the rumours have been grossly exaggerated. It all apparently started when a Los Angeles radio station announced that Mick had died in London.' LES PERRIN, *in Melody Maker, 24 December, 1966*

With Christmas approaching, Astrid went home to Sweden and I must admit I thought of her a lot over the holiday period, which was unusual. Most of the time, the girls I met had just drifted in and out of my life until that point. My homelife with Diane was going even further downhill and our relationship was all but over.

Christmas break time

On Christmas Eve, Brian and Anita flew from London to Paris where they joined Keith and Linda for the Christmas holiday. It was almost the end of 1966, a year in which we had six million-sellers – '19th Nervous Breakdown', 'Paint It, Black', 'Have You Seen Your Mother…' and 'Mother's Little Helper'. There were also the albums, *Aftermath* and *Big Hits*. What was to happen next? It was anyone's guess – but I guarantee no-one would have guessed correctly.

I heard the news today
On the evening of 18 December, Tara Browne, Mick and Brian's friend, died in a car crash in London. His accidental death was immortalised in The Beatles' song 'A Day In The Life'.

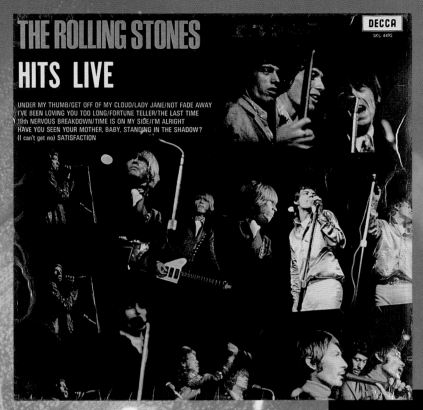

THE ROLLING STONES
HITS LIVE

UNDER MY THUMB/GET OFF OF MY CLOUD/LADY JANE/NOT FADE AWAY
I'VE BEEN LOVING YOU TOO LONG/FORTUNE TELLER/THE LAST TIME
19th NERVOUS BREAKDOWN/TIME IS ON MY SIDE/I'M ALRIGHT
HAVE YOU SEEN YOUR MOTHER, BABY, STANDING IN THE SHADOW?
(I can't get no) SATISFACTION

DECCA
SKL 4495

This is a rare export-only version of the album with a slightly different cover from the US release.

A s an album it is a filler, perhaps it was even viewed as a chance to cash in before the ride came to an end. The LP features an introduction by the live show's compere, Long John Baldry. Glyn Johns was assisted by three technicians in its recording.

'A blockbuster album that can't miss. The first live recording by the Stones is sure to be much in demand. Indeed in the concert are their smash hits "19th Nervous Breakdown", "Have You Seen Your Mother" and "Satisfaction". Their "Under My Thumb" is really a powerhouse.' BILLBOARD MAGAZINE, *17 December, 1966*

The band's eighth US album came out just in time for the Christmas market and was duly rewarded when it entered the charts on New Year's Eve, 1966. It was supposedly recorded at the Royal Albert Hall during the Stones' autumn tour of England. However, much of the album was not recorded live at all. Some tracks featured overdubs from Mick, Keith and Stu; others were studio recordings with added crowd noise.

Got some live bits!
Some of the tracks were rather less than live. It appears that 'I've Been Loving You Too Long' was recorded between 11 and 12 May, 1965, at RCA Hollywood with Dave Hassinger. 'Fortune Teller' was laid down on 9 July, 1963, at Decca Studios in West Hampstead. Both these songs had crowd atmosphere added. 'Lady Jane', 'I'm Alright', 'Have You Seen Your Mother' and 'Satisfaction' all benefited from various amounts of overdubs at Olympic Studios in mid-October.

Side one
1. 'Under My Thumb'
   Jagger/Richard
2. 'Get Off Of My Cloud'
   Jagger/Richard
3. 'Lady Jane'
   Jagger/Richard
4. 'Not Fade Away'
   Petty/Hardin
5. 'I've Been Loving You Too
   Long' Redding/Butler
6. 'Fortune Teller' Toussaint

Side two
1. 'The Last Time'
   Jagger/Richard
2. '19th Nervous
   Breakdown'
   Jagger/Richard
3. 'Time Is On My Side'
   Ragavoy
4. 'I'm Alright' McDaniel
5. 'Have You Seen Your
   Mother, Baby'
   Jagger/Richard
6. '(I Can't Get No)
   Satisfaction'
   Jagger/Richard

Recorded
Live in London (23 September, 1966), Newcastle (1 October, 1966) and Bristol (7 October, 1966) with overdubs at IBC Studios and tracks not performed on tour

Producer
Andrew Loog Oldham

Engineer
Glyn Johns

Technicians
Mr Lyon-Shaw, Mr Stoat and Mr Smith

Cover photography
Gered Mankowitz

Cover design
Stephen Inglis

US release
Saturday 10 December, 1966 London PS 493 and LL 3493

Highest chart position (time on chart)
US No 6 (11 weeks)

January **67** July

Dusted
And
Busted

Backstage at the London Palladium, 23 January, 1967

Self Assessment

A wedding and a parting started 1967 and, as the year unfolded, there would be a bust, a flop, a trial, a refusal, African travels, an appeal, a tour, a single and an album – and all before the end of June.

INTERVIEWED IN THE first week of 1967, Mick took stock and talked of where we might be going. Instinctively, we all felt that this would be a year of change, and as everyone knows, change is difficult to handle. It's something we all deal with in different ways and the Stones were no exception.

'It's true we didn't sell so many discs in England during 1966 as in the previous year, but neither did the other groups. As far as abroad goes, America is okay and we broke the Italian and German markets in 1966. We haven't quietened down. It's madder now than ever before. We couldn't possibly go on doing ballrooms and cinema appearances all the time. All the groups seem to be cooling off in this respect.'
MICK, *Disc, 7 January, 1967*

Mick also confirmed that he and Chrissie had parted. Stu, on the other hand, was getting hitched. He married Cynthia Gaisford, Andrew Oldham's secretary, on the Monday after New Year's Day. All of us went to a party at Stu's house.

A wedding can bring matters to a head in other relationships and Stu's certainly did with Diane and me. The next day we had a major row, which ended with us deciding that we should part. Our relationship had been going wrong for a while and and – I make no excuses – success had changed me.

Diane wanted to go and live with her relatives in South Africa. She decided to leave Stephen with me.

On 9 January, I drove the two of them to London Airport, from where she flew to Durban. I then drove Stephen and myself home. It was a difficult journey.

A different kind of change was occupying Mick's mind at that time: 'What does worry me is that there's nobody coming up to match the sort of popularity that the Stones and the Beatles have had in the past,' he told *Melody Maker* in January 1967.

On the day 'Hey Joe', Jimi Hendrix's first single, entered the UK charts, I went to see him

'If anyone is going to match our success and that of the Beatles, I know and you know that it'll be someone completely new that we've never heard about.'

MICK, *Melody Maker, 7 January, 1967*

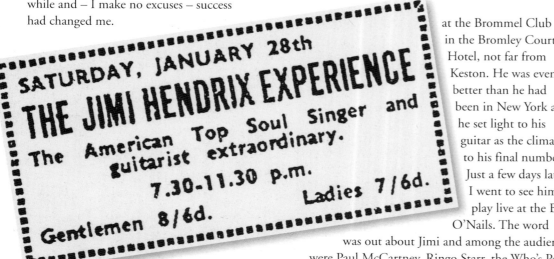

SATURDAY, JANUARY 28th
THE JIMI HENDRIX EXPERIENCE
The American Top Soul Singer and guitarist extraordinary.
7.30-11.30 p.m.
Ladies 7/6d.
Gentlemen 8/6d.

at the Brommel Club in the Bromley Court Hotel, not far from Keston. He was even better than he had been in New York and he set light to his guitar as the climax to his final number. Just a few days later I went to see him play live at the Bag O'Nails. The word was out about Jimi and among the audience were Paul McCartney, Ringo Starr, the Who's Pete

Townshend and John Entwistle, Eric Clapton, Lulu, the Small Faces, Donovan, the Animals and Georgie Fame.

Charlie ponders

Just before our new single hit the shops, Mick and Charlie did some interviews. Charlie set the scene for what was to come in 1967. To be honest, he was almost certainly thinking that the next few months would be a little less traumatic than they turned out to be. 'Our scene really is the recording scene,' said Charlie in an interview with *Record Mirror* that month. 'Producing and writing and playing – trying to keep ahead of the rest. This is much more exciting than the show-business aspect.'

'LET'S SPEND THE NIGHT TOGETHER'

The 12th single release in the UK and the 14th in the US, it was banned by many radio stations (some bleeped out 'night') and Ed Sullivan forced the band to change 'the night' to 'some time'. It simply asserted what most pop singles had been suggesting for years, without really saying so.

Keith played bass on the a-side. On the b-side, Brian played piano and recorder and Bill played bowed double bass.

'I like the other side, "Ruby Tuesday", better. The a-side is a dancy, strong beat and this is very melodic and sounds a bit like Chopin in parts.' MICK, *Disc, 7 January, 1967*

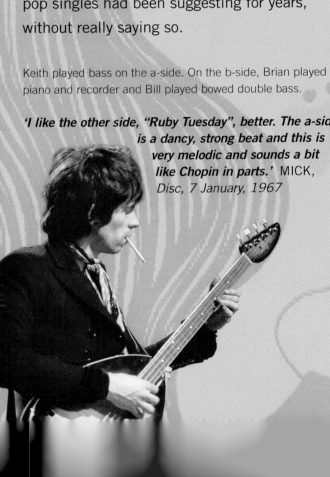

'I don't disapprove at all. You can't hear many of the words. I don't think it's corrupting – it might be a very innocent night.' STANLEY DORFMAN, *Top Of The Pops producer, Daily Mail, 10 January, 1967*

> THE ROLLING STONES—LET'S SPEND THE NIGHT TOGETHER (Prod. by Andrew Loog Oldham) (Writers: Jagger-Richards) (Gideon, BMI) —RUBY TUESDAY (Prod. by Andrew Loog Oldham) (Writers: Jagger-Richards) (Gideon, BMI)— Two blockbuster sides with equal top of the chart potential. First is a raucous dance number that builds to a wild frenzy. If exposed, this should prove the major side. Flip is an interesting Jagger-Richards composition combining the baroque sound with a groovy dance beat. **London 904**

'I always say "Let's Spend The Night Together" to any young lady I'm taking out. What it means is: shall we spend the evening together? If people have warped, twisted, dirty minds, I suppose it could have sexual overtones. The song isn't really very rude. When you hear it, you'll realise this. The rest of the words aren't rude. There are a few slightly rude bits, but I've covered them up.' MICK, *Melody Maker, 7 January, 1967*

'"Ruby Tuesday" is a wonderful song. It's just a nice melody, really. And a lovely lyric. Neither of which I wrote, but I always enjoy singing it.' MICK, *1995*

Hot new releases from Decca
On 6 January, Decca issued a press release: '"Ruby Tuesday" is a sad and ironic song of lost love ideally interpreted by Mick's impassioned vocal and a delicate backing. It's full of depth and maturity that reflects the talent of the Mick/Keith combination. On "Let's Spend The Night Together" all the Stones trademarks are in evidence — wild Mick vocal, great percussion from Charlie and some superb instrumental and vocal support from Brian, Keith and Bill. An irresistible beat, catchy chorus and some great lyrics are going to mark this side for plenty of attention! Certainly they've again come up with the kind of magic that's bound to make these two of the biggest hits of this new year. Both sides will be promoted on TV shows both sides of the Atlantic.'

Recorded
a-side November 1966
b-side 16 November, 1966
Location
Olympic Studios, London
Producer
Andrew Loog Oldham
Engineer
Glyn Johns
Release
UK Friday 13 January, 1967 Decca F 12546
US Saturday 14 January, 1967 London 45 904
Composers
Jagger/Richard
Highest chart position
UK No 3
US No 1, for one week. 'Ruby Tuesday' officially made the top. 'Let's Spend The Night Together' was US No 55

13 FRIDAY Spending Some Time Away

To avoid travelling on Friday 13 January, we all flew TWA to New York a day early, except Mick. He ignored the superstition and, while nothing happened on the flight, we were out of luck with Ed Sullivan, who took offence to the lyrics of 'Let's Spend The Night Together'.

AFTER ARGUING THE TOSS, Andrew and Allen Klein eventually agreed that Mick would sing, 'Let's spend some *time* together'. We appeared live on Sunday and did 'Ruby Tuesday' first and then the offending number, suitably cleaned-up.

Having shot the show, we returned to London and I went to the Bag O'Nails, where I bumped into Astrid again. She didn't seem that keen to talk. Stephen had started at his new school and I was trying to find out what Diane's intentions were. On Friday 20 January, *Between The Buttons* came out in the UK.

I took Peter Frampton to the Scotch of St James, where we met Astrid and her girlfriend Kerstin. Peter and I took the girls back to their flat, where each couple disappeared into separate rooms. We gave Peter a lift to Victoria station to catch the last train home (he was only 16!). I suppose I can take the blame for introducing Peter to the wonderful world of rock'n'roll. The following day we had to be in London for an early afternoon rehearsal for *Sunday Night At The London Palladium*. We had succumbed and were going to appear on that bastion of British light entertainment. To this day, I'm not sure why

we agreed to do it.

Mick sang and the rest of us mimed. We were paid £1,500 to perform 'Ruby Tuesday', 'Let's Spend The Night Together', and 'Connection' to 9.25 million people. It was a big audience for the time.

'They arrived with all their music on a tape. Their manager sat alongside me checking the sound level. I was so disappointed in my dealings with them. Not only were they late for rehearsal but I was confronted with ill-mannered, studied rudeness.' ALBERT LOCKE, *Palladium producer, Evening News, 25 January, 1967*

Glyn Johns, Mick and Andrew Oldham discuss the merits of doing the Palladium roundabout.

'The show's so bad we couldn't rely on them to get the sound we wanted.' KEITH, *on recording Sunday Night At The London Palladium*

We refused to go onto the roundabout at the end of the show. All the performers and the show's host, Dave Allen, were supposed to grin inanely and wave as the stage revolved slowly. Andrew Oldham wanted us to do it but we refused and he and Mick had a furious row. Our appearance on the programme generated a torrent of letters to the press; the ones to the *Daily Mirror* were fairly typical.

'It is too late to prevent this record ['Let's Spend The Night Together'] *going on the market but, for goodness' sake, let us ban any sequels before the entire business has a harmful effect on our nation as a whole.'* JANET DE CRANER, *of Polegate, Sussex, in a letter to the Daily Mirror, 25 January, 1967*

'The way they were dressed, they looked as if they came out of a circus.' F FITCH, *in a letter to the Daily Mirror, 25 January, 1967*

'They should take a lesson from the real stars like Gracie Fields, Margot Fonteyn and Frankie Vaughan, none of whom would dream of being so rude to either their fellow artists or the public.' MISS JOAN H GADD, *of Sandford-on-Thames, Oxford, in a letter to the Daily Mirror, 25 January, 1967*

Perhaps the times weren't a-changin' after all. 'Personally, I didn't want to do it,' reasoned Charlie in *Melody Maker*, 'and I'm not sure why we did. I suppose it was a challenge. It's always done more harm than good to anybody I've ever seen on it.'

'I've hundreds of thousands of kids watching my show. I won't stand for anything like that with a double meaning. Either the song goes, or the Stones go.' ED SULLIVAN

'The only reason we did the show was because it was a good national plug. Anyone who thought we were changing our image to suit a family audience was mistaken.'
MICK, *NME, 28 January, 1967*

The row rumbled on for weeks. You would have thought we had committed a major crime. The older half of the nation felt insulted, while the younger half couldn't care less. Paul McCartney videotaped the show and Mick and Keith watched it at Peter Asher's place. They all had a good laugh.

Let's mime together
We did the usual round of promotional work, miming to 'Let's Spend The Night Together' on *Top Of The Pops*. I went on to the Bag O' Nails and met up with Astrid. Paul McCartney, his uncle and Beatles' staffer Neil Aspinall, joined us at our table. When I drove her home, Astrid told me Paul had been playing footsie with her. We sat in the car near her flat and talked. Paul arrived, saw us and drove around for some time before giving up and driving away.

On Sunday 29 January, Glyn Johns, Astrid and I flew to Madrid to meet with Sonoplay Records about our recordings with the End and other projects. Mick flew to Italy, joining Marianne at the San Remo Music Festival. They took a few days holiday in the south of France before returning to London. In San Remo, Mick and

Marianne were photographed together, making their romance public.

Brian did an interview with Keith Altham for the *NME* which showed how his philosophies were shaping up at the time. 'Why should we have to compromise with our image? You don't simply give up all you have ever believed in because you've reached a certain age. Our generation is growing up with us and they believe in the same things we do. I hope they won't require a show like the *Palladium*. Some of those we like most are the hippies in New York, but nearly all of them think like us and are questioning some of the basic immoralities in present-day society – the war in Vietnam, persecution of homosexuals, illegality of abortion and drug-taking.

'The photographs taken of my flat in a terrible mess recently was another misrepresentation. A company was filming in the room and we pushed everything into one corner to make room for the crew. We were not aware that the photographs being taken were for publication in a paper. You've seen my flat. I don't live in that kind of mess normally. I've complained to the Press Council about the whole episode.'

Sings and roundabouts
While Mick was in France and I was in Madrid, Charlie was at home in Lewes with Shirley. Brian and Keith were doing the clubs and found time to take guitar tuition. A frustrated Andrew got our

Stones at the London Palladium, 23 January

Mick and Marianne in San Remo

accountant Stan Blackbourn to telex Ronnie Schneider in Klein's office to ask for funds. In all, they needed $100,000 to cover recording.

Andrew needs to know if the $20,000 has been cabled? He also requires $80,000 to clear recording session fees, otherwise there will be a breach of contract. They have refused credit. Andrew said the money would come from publishing. Please cable same today. This telex is on Andrew's instructions.

Recorded
3–11 August, 1966 at RCA,
Hollywood and November,
1966 at Olympic, London

Composers
All songs Jagger/Richard

Producer
Andrew Loog Oldham

Engineers
Dave Hassinger at RCA
Glyn Johns at Olympic

Cover photography
Gered Mankowitz
(front photograph)

Cover design
Charlie Watts
(rear illustrations)

Release
UK Friday 20 January,
1967 Decca SKL 4852.
US Saturday 11 February,
1967 London LL 3499
mono and PS 499 stereo

Highest chart position
(time on chart)
UK No 3 (22 weeks)
US No 2 (9 weeks)

Personnel
Mick Jagger: guitar,
harmonica, keyboards
and vocals
Brian Jones: guitar,
keyboards, sax and vocals
Keith Richard: guitar,
keyboards and vocals
Charlie Watts: drums
Bill Wyman: synthesizer,
bass, keyboards and vocals
Ian Stewart: piano
and organ
Nicky Hopkins: piano
Jack Nitzsche: piano and
harpsichord

'Andrew told me to do the drawings for the LP and said the title would be between the buttons. I thought he meant the title was *Between The Buttons*, so it stayed.'
CHARLIE, *Melody Maker, 4 February, 1967*

The 6th British and 9th US album came out three weeks earlier in the UK. It was unique among British albums in that it contained no hit singles. In the US, 'Let's Spend The Night Together' and 'Ruby Tuesday' replaced two tracks on the British release, making it a stronger album. It is one of the lesser-known LPs, which is a pity as it contains some strong songs. It divided opinion among critics then and it still does now.

'Andrew's influence was on the wane and this was his production swan song with us. He still had dreams of being an English Phil Spector, if only by cranking up the reverb to 11. Production subtlety was not Andrew's bag.' BILL

Many tracks began at RCA and were overdubbed and mixed in London. It took longer – technology allowed experimentation and flexibility, something the Stones embraced. 'Yesterday's Papers' is the first song written by Mick on his own for a Stones album. On 'Something Happened To Me Yesterday', Brian played sax. It was a take-off of the UK TV personality Dixon of Dock Green.

'I don't like Between The Buttons *very much. It just isn't any good. "Back Street Girl" is about the only one I like.'* MICK, *Rolling Stone magazine, October 1968*

'*Between the Buttons*'!
(To understand this little rhyme you first must tap your foot in time. then the buttons come much nearer and the Stones you see more clearer.)

The sleeve – for and against

'The Stones' sleeves never seem to look very much different, but this one is more clever and more subtle than the rest. The back of the sleeve is far more unpretentious than is the current group trend.' RECORD MIRROR, *28 January, 1967*

'The new LP is their greatest yet and the sleeve photography is fantastic. But must we have Charlie's scribblings on the back? I even prefer Andrew's dreaded poems or, better still, an informative sleeve note.' AJ GRIFFEN, *in a letter to Disc, 4 February, 1967*

What the papers said...

'Every LP by the Stones has been a hot chart item and this latest collection will be no exception. Their hard-driving beat is evident throughout and their hits add immediate sales appeal. "Miss Amanda Jones" and "Cool, Calm And Collected" are outstanding in this winning package.' BILLBOARD MAGAZINE, *11 February, 1967*

'It is an eccentric album to say the least, with self-conscious undercurrents of sex, drugs, alcohol and excessive English whimsy. Except for the Valse Musette "Back Street Girl" and the jerky "Connection", this album sounds more like a bunch of vaudevillian Kinks out-takes than a bona fide Stones collection.' ROY CARR, *music journalist, 1976*

'Not every group that has a hit record is worth listening to and a lot of groups that don't, are. Five years from now, what will remain? What will we still be able to listen to? I think we'll always be able to listen to the Stones and, most especially, Between The Buttons.' JON LANDAU, *Crawdaddy magazine, May 1967*

'They have that one quality which sets the Stones in a category all their own: a strong personal contact with the listener. Unlike the Beatles, who touch mainly the mind, the Stones touch the emotions and the gut.' TORONTO DAILY STAR, *July 1967*

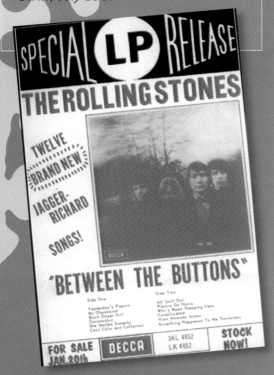

Home from France, Mick was annoyed by an article in the *News Of The World* on Sunday 5 February. It published a five-part exposé about drugs and pop stars. The paper referred to Mick having taken LSD at the Roehampton home of one of the Moody Blues – in fact, the journalist had confused Brian with Mick in May 1966 and made other mistakes. The paper reported 'Mick' (actually Brian) saying, 'I don't go much on LSD [he'd said marijuana] now the cats [these were fans] have taken it up. It'll just get a dirty name. I remember the first time I took it. It was on our tour with Bo Diddley and Little Richard [wrong again] … Later at Blaises [a club], Jagger showed a friend and two girls a small piece of hash. He invited them to his flat for "a smoke".'

Mick made a statement. 'I am shocked that a responsible newspaper like the *News Of The World* can publish such a defamatory article about me. I want to make it quite clear that this picture of me is misleading and untrue and the only way to prevent this libel being repeated is for my lawyer to take immediate legal action in the High Court.'

A day in the life
On Friday 10 February, the Beatles were at Abbey Road along with a 40-piece orchestra to record the 24 bar gap in 'A Day In The Life' on *Sgt Pepper*. Mick and Marianne, Keith, Mike Nesmith (the Monkees) and Donovan joined them. The whole thing was filmed but was not shown by the BBC as it thought the song was drugs related.

roundabout incident. They went on it with five life-size dummies of us created by Gerald Scarfe. So it's untrue to say we never appeared on the bloody roundabout.

Something for the weekend
I saw a lot of Astrid, mostly at the Bag O'Nails, although our relationship seemed to be going nowhere. She joined the band at Olympic Studios on Saturday 11 February, where we had started working on new tracks. We cut a couple of versions of a track with the working title 'Blues 1'. She and I went back to the Mayfair Hotel for the night.

'Everyone is fallible, but the teenager of 16 to 18 knows their own mind. I don't have any real moral responsibility to them. They'll work out their own moral values for themselves.' MICK, *to Eamonn Andrews*

That same day we were to appear on the Eamonn Andrews show. The Musicians Union insisted we play 'Let's Spend The Night Together' live rather than mime to it. We all felt they were trying to make an example of us. It was an accepted procedure to mime on this type of show; they just seemed to want to wrap us up in red tape. There was not enough time to rehearse the new number, so we did 'She Smiled Sweetly' from *Between The Buttons*. Eamonn asked Mick if he felt any responsibility for his fans. The question was typical of the position we were in. It wasn't our music that mattered; it was our values and lifestyles. Mick was made a spokesman for a generation at just 23.

Later that evening, on *Sunday Night At The London Palladium*, Peter Cook and Dudley Moore appeared. They had become our good friends and decided to have a bit of a laugh over the

Meanwhile, a bunch of people drove down to Redlands for the weekend, arriving around 11pm. In the party were Mick, Marianne, Keith, art dealer Robert Fraser, Fraser's Moroccan servant Ali, photographer Michael Cooper, antique dealer Christopher Gibbs, David Schneiderman (a Canadian also known as Acid King David) and Nicky Cramer, a hippy from Chelsea. George Harrison and Patti Boyd joined them there.

'Everyone was hungry, so we cooked eggs and bacon. I was really tired. I sat in an armchair, reading a book. After midnight, people were chatting, listening to records and reading books.' KEITH

A very ordinary beginning to an extraordinary weekend.

Dud and Pete with dummies

Redlands on Sea

In a career filled with controversy, the Redlands drug bust is a grade A scandal. It is the very stuff of which rock mythology is made. The legend could only have been bettered if George Harrison had also been caught! The chain of events started about an hour before Keith and the rest of the party got to Redlands. Bill was not there, nor were Charlie or Brian. Perhaps the best way to tell the tale is through the words of those who were.

The story broke in the *News Of The World* on 19 February, a week after the incident. The newspaper failed to name names, merely saying: 'Several stars, at least three of them nationally known names, were present at the party.' They later revealed details when the case came to court.

'At 10pm, a reader telephoned our offices. He told our reporter, "I've got some information about a party some of the Stones are holding in West Sussex." At 3am, the caller arrived at our offices and repeated his information in fuller detail. He rejected our suggestion that he should go to the police, saying, "I want to remain anonymous. But I think the police should know." A senior executive of this newspaper contacted Scotland Yard and was advised that the proper course was to give the information to drug squad officers connected with West Sussex. Police were informed.' NEWS OF THE WORLD, *2 July, 1967*

Patti Boyd

'The party broke up around 5am and the married couple left. I slept in an armchair downstairs.' KEITH

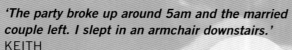

'It was the first time that we'd been to the house at West Wittering and I can't remember why we were invited. It didn't seem to be a special party; it just seemed to be friends of Keith.' **PATTI BOYD**, *then wife of George Harrison*

'At 11am, detailed information was given to Detective Sergeant Stanley Cudmore and he and his colleagues obtained from the local magistrates the warrants necessary to carry out the raid.' NEWS OF THE WORLD, *2 July, 1967*

The front page of the News Of The World, *2 July, 1967*

'I woke up around 11am. Schneiderman was up and dressed when I awoke. Mohammed was in the kitchen. I went into the garden for an hour or so. I had no idea what the rest of the guests were doing indoors, but went back in because I heard there was talk of a beach party. Except for two, all the guests went in Schneiderman's Minivan. Later on during the afternoon, everybody went on a minibus mystery tour around West Sussex.' KEITH

'We had a quasi-cultural expedition to the house of Edward James, the father of English surrealist art, at West Dean on the Downs. In the evening we went back to the house and sat around talking, playing records and watching TV. Everything was perfectly respectable.' CHRISTOPHER GIBBS

Ali cooked a meal, and at about 7.30pm, everyone ate and watched *Pete Kelly's Blues* on TV. At 7.55pm, Chief Inspector Gordon Dineley, with 18 other

Keith with David Schneiderman, on the beach at West Wittering

> ### 'A lot of cars drove up the lane to Redlands. I heard the police had been. A lot of people were staying there, but there was no noise.'
> **JUDITH KING,** *Redlands neighbour*

officers, drove up the narrow lane leading to Redlands. They knocked on the door and waited. A woman police officer looked through a drawing-room window after several minutes. As the police were about to make their own entry, Keith opened the front door. After they explained their purpose, the officers were received civilly.

A warrant to search

Everyone was in the drawing room, where Keith was shown the warrant, issued under the Dangerous Drugs Act of 1965. All the guests were searched and the police later said that they noticed a very strong, sweet, unusual smell. Detective Constable John Challen went to a bedroom where he found a green jacket on the back of a chair. They looked in the pockets and found four tablets inside a plastic phial with a label written in Italian. Mick admitted that the coat and tablets were his.

'Yes, my doctor prescribed them.' Asked who the doctor was he said, 'I think it is Dr Dixon Firth but I can't remember.' Mick said he was not sure where the doctor lived but thought it might be Knightsbridge. Mick told the police he used the tablets 'to stay awake and work'.

A police officer found a dark-coloured jacket behind the drawing room door. Eight green capsules were found in the right-hand jacket pocket and Robert Fraser said, 'I have trouble with my stomach. I got them on prescription from a doctor in London.' When he was asked which doctor, he replied it was one of three doctors but he did not know the address of their surgery. He was searched and a small box containing 24 white tablets was found in his trouser pocket. Robert said, 'I am a diabetic. These are prescribed by my doctor.' He said he thought his diabetic card might be upstairs, but a search failed to find it. He was told by a senior police officer that the tablets looked like heroin and replied, 'Definitely not.'

On Schneiderman, the police found a tin containing pieces of a brown substance, a decorated wooden pipe with cannabis resin, an envelope of small particles of a brown substance and a ball of similar material. They found a pudding basin beside a bedside table containing ash. They took away 29 items, including cigarettes, four candlesticks, soap and the suspicious cigarette butts.

They found sticks of incense and a tin containing what appeared to be more of the substance. They opened airline mustard sample packs and miniature bars of soap from hotels. If dangerous drugs were found to have been used and they couldn't be traced to anyone, they said,

Keith would be held responsible. 'I see, they pin it all on me,' replied Keith.

Just after 8pm, Keith phoned solicitor Timothy Hardacre in London and informed him that a police search was in progress at Redlands.

'Police officers entered premises in the Chichester area under the authority of a warrant issued under the Dangerous Drugs Act. Several persons were interviewed and certain articles brought away from the house.' WEST SUSSEX POLICE STATEMENT

'We were supposed to go to Redlands on the day of the bust, but they called and said, "Don't bother to come – we've just been busted." Brian and I stayed in London to do music for **A Degree Of Murder.'** ANITA PALLENBERG

Timothy Hardacre and publicist Les Perrin got to Redlands as quickly as they could. Robert Fraser, his servant Ali and David Schneidermann returned to London. Fraser advised Schneidermann to get out of the country as quickly as he could and he did so later that night.

There has been speculation ever since about Schneiderman's role. Some suggested he tipped off the newspaper. No-one has ever been able to establish the truth or otherwise of these rumours.

'It was just an ordinary weekend by the sea.' CHRISTOPHER GIBBS

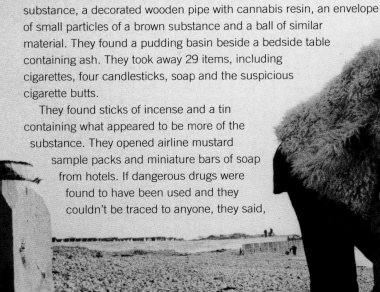

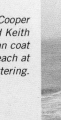

Michael Cooper photographed Keith in his Afghan coat on the beach at West Wittering.

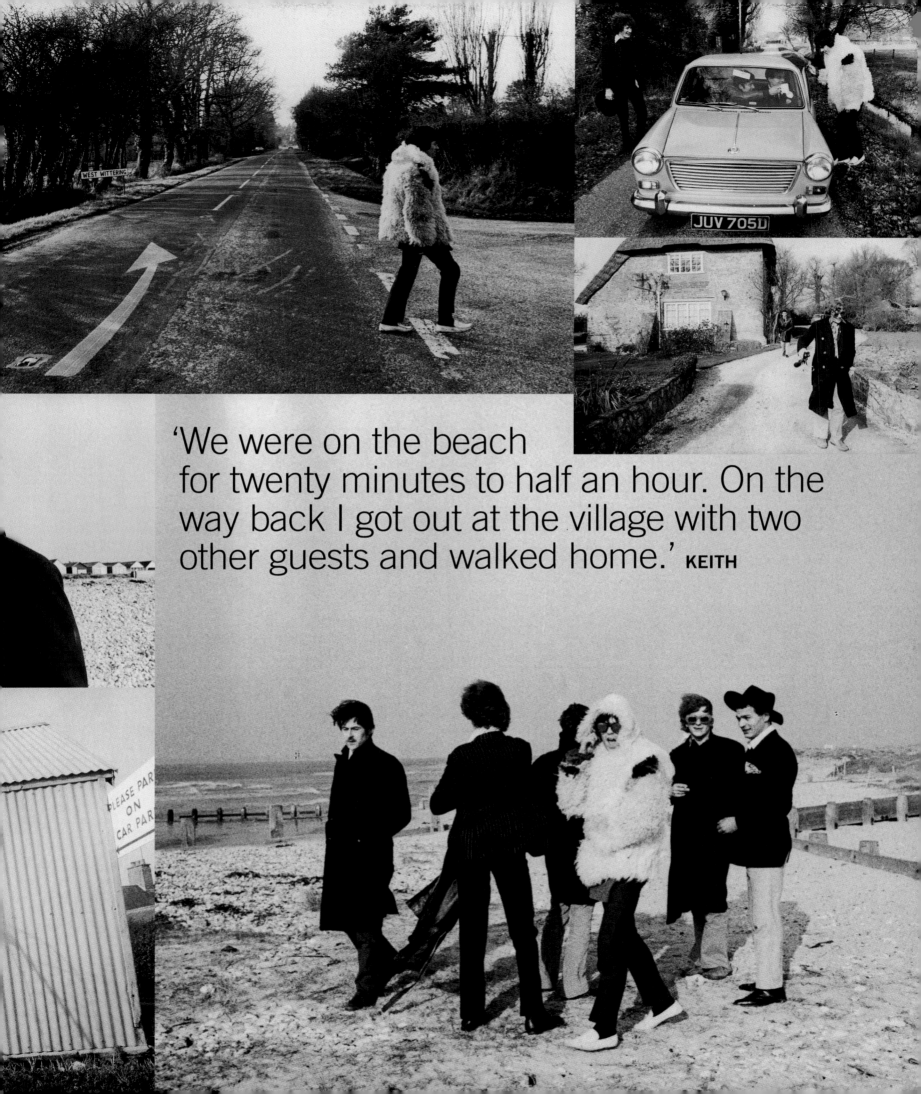

'We were on the beach for twenty minutes to half an hour. On the way back I got out at the village with two other guests and walked home.' **KEITH**

Life Goes On

Brian, Charlie and I heard about Mick and Keith's weekend when we got to Olympic on Monday. We were continuing to record, trying to get enough material for a new album. Mick and Keith tried to make light of it, but it was obvious that they were worried, although I'm not sure that they could have imagined the full extent of what was to happen.

ON TUESDAY, MICK, KEITH and Timothy Hardacre met with leading counsel Victor Durand, QC, to talk about the situation following the bust. He stressed the magnitude of their problem, which must have worried them greatly.

We continued recording at Olympic throughout the following week and often during these sessions John Dunbar (Marianne's ex) and a Greek friend of his called Alexis Mardas came to the studio. They convinced Mick and Keith that they could do amazing visual effects using coloured lights and magnetic fields that we could use on our forthcoming tour. They managed to get various sums of money for these projects, but there always seemed to be a problem when we asked to see examples of their work. Mardas was known as Magic Alex; as far as I could see the only magic he that performed was making our money disappear. Maybe John Dunbar was getting his own back.

Cross-border talks

Eleven days after the bust, Tom Keylock flew from Lydd Airport near Folkestone in Kent to Le Touquet with Keith's Bentley and then drove to Paris. Mick and Marianne went to the ballet for the world premiere of Roland Petit's *Paradise Lost*, starring Rudolph Nureyev and Margot Fonteyn. Three days later Keith flew to Paris and was joined there by Brian and Anita.

They stayed at the Georges V, where they were joined by Deborah Dixon, the American girlfriend of film director Donald Cammell. On Monday 27, Keith, Brian, Anita, Deborah and Tom Keylock left Paris in Keith's Bentley and began their long drive south to North Africa. Their plan was to meet up with Mick, Marianne, Michael Cooper, Robert Fraser and Christopher Gibbs at the El Minzah Hotel in Tangier. Everyone thought it would be better if Mick, Keith and Brian were out of the country. With the

press interested in their every move, it kept prying eyes at a safe distance.

Before they reached the Spanish border, Brian was taken ill (no one is quite sure whether it was his asthma or pneumonia) and was admitted into the Centre Hospitalier d'Albi in Tarn, near Toulouse. Having been told that he'd have to stay there for a number of days, he insisted that the rest of the party, who had checked into a local hotel for the night, should continue their journey without him.

Brian celebrated his 25th birthday alone in hospital. Keylock drove Keith, Anita and Deborah across the border into Spain, travelling down the east coast, stopping off at Barcelona. Here things got a little out of hand when Keith's Diners Club card was refused. The waiter insisted on seeing his passport, so Tom Keylock went to get it. While he was gone Keith, Anita and Deborah were taken to police headquarters and interrogated. They were released at 6am and got to their hotel where there was a message waiting for them from Brian asking Anita to return to Toulouse. She ignored the request.

Beaton man

My problems were of an altogether more mundane nature. I had telexed Klein asking him where the money was that he had promised me – I was down to just £26 9s 10d in my current account. Astrid was still playing hard to get, but I was getting closer.

On 1 March, Deborah Dixon decided to return to Paris, leaving Keylock to drive Keith and Anita from Barcelona to Marbella. It was to be a fateful stay in the south of Spain. This is where their affair well and truly began. Ironically, at this time, Brian and Keith were really getting along well, Keith would usually stay at Brian's place when he was in London. The three of them had a lot of fun together, fuelled by their collective intake of drugs. Brian, no stranger to paranoia, stuck in the French

Mick and Marianne at the ballet on 23 February, 1967

hospital, was getting worried about Anita. He sent a telegram to the Stones office on 2 March:

Feeling almost fully recovered. Must leave here as soon as possible for Tangier assuming no complications. Very unlikely. Please book flights 1st class from Toulouse via Paris to Tangier early next week and mail tickets immediately. Also notify others of arrival and ask them to wait for me. Will recuperate fully in sun. Love Brian.

Three days later and Keith and Anita were still in Marbella, having a good time while Brian stayed in hospital. Anita decided to fly back to Toulouse to see him, while Keith and Keylock took the ferry to North Africa and continued to Tangier. Checking in to the El Minzah hotel they met up with Christopher Gibbs, Robert Fraser, Michael Cooper, Paul and Talitha Getty. On Tuesday 7 March, Brian checked out and flew with Anita to London. Brian checked in to the West London Hospital for further tests. The next day news of his solo work appeared.

A still and poster for A Degree Of Murder

'Brian has added a new dimension to his career by writing and producing the soundtrack of Germany's entry in the Cannes Film Festival. It's titled Mord Und Totschlag, **screened in English as** A Degree Of Murder. **The production was made by Hower Films of Munich and produced-directed-written by German ace Walter Schlondorff, who won the Critics' Award at Cannes and the Golden Gate Award in San Francisco,'** LES PERRIN, *press release,10 March, 1967*

'In writing and producing the track, I used a series of different groups, from one musician to 10. I ran the gamut of line-ups from the usual brass line-up to using violin and banjo. Mostly they were session men, but some of the group helped out. I myself played sitar, organ, dulcimer, harmonica and harp.' BRIAN, *10 March, 1967*

On Saturday 11 March Brian was discharged from hospital. Brian, Anita and Mick flew to Tangier and joined the rest of the party at the El Minzah. The whole party drove down to Marrakesh to continue their holiday at the Hotel Es Saadi. Here by all accounts the drug of choice was LSD, with everyone tripping together. Brian was getting increasingly suspicious about Anita and Keith. Attempts by Brian to keep Anita took a bizarre twist when he brought some local whores back to the hotel, where he wanted Anita to join them in bed. Though she was pretty wild, this was too much, even for Anita. It made her easy prey. On cue, it was Keith to the rescue.

Keith shot by Cecil Beaton on 15 March, 1967

While they were in Marrakesh they met the legendary British photographer, Sir Cecil Beaton. He was quite taken by Mick and found the whole gang of them absorbing, if only for an evening. The next morning Cecil photographed Mick and Keith in the hotel grounds.

The relationship triangle was coming to a head at the hotel. Anita was openly flaunting her affections and Brian was getting very upset. Even Mick, who normally liked to avoid confrontation, couldn't drag himself away. Keith and Tom Keylock (who was still Brian's chauffeur), cooked up a scheme to get Brian out of the way. Marrakesh scene veteran Brion Gysin was duped into taking Brian out into the Djemaa el Fna, the big central square, to record Moroccan music, drink mint tea and buy souvenirs. With Brian out of the way, Keith and Anita split. Premeditated – or spur of the moment as Keith

'I took Mick through the trees to photograph him in the midday sun... He is sexy, yet completely sexless. He could nearly be a eunuch. As a model he is a natural.' SIR CECIL BEATON

Marrakesh excess

'We met Ahmed on our first trip to Marrakesh. He used to export these very fancy Moroccan leather shoes, which had very thick leather soles and looked like clogs. It was just a cover for bringing in hashish. Brian showed me this one time – he peeled off this thin little piece of leather and it was just solid green. The whole of the sole of the shoe was made of hashish.'
DONALD CAMMELL

claims? Who knows? As in any break-up the truth gets massaged to suit the on-going lives of those involved.

Keylock drove Keith and Anita to Tangier. They boarded a ferry for Malaga where Spanish customs gave them all a good going-over. On finding them gone, Brian immediately flew to Paris to seek consolation. He stayed with Donald Cammell. Mick flew home from Casablanca on Thursday 16 and was met at the airport by Marianne. After Brian left Marrakesh, Keith and Anita returned to continue their holiday, flying back separately to London on March 22; Brian met Anita at the airport. From there they went home together to what must have been an awkward time.

Hearts and money

The band would never be the same again. It was one thing Brian taking an extra £5 a week when we were starting out. This was a betrayal on a totally different scale. While Brian was always slightly detached from the very earliest times, he had, if anything, become closer to the heart of the Stones through his friendship with Keith, but now that was all over.

I was busy sorting out the terms of my divorce from Diane. She had decided to move to South Africa and I agreed to pay her £50 per week for 10 years, with a three-year advance payment as a lump sum (£7,300), leaving seven years of monthly payments. Astrid and I had become much closer; she seemed to like me after all. We were holidaying in Cornwall while Brian, Anita and Keith were fighting it out in Morocco.

On Saturday 18 March, the press was full of stories about Mick and Keith being among four people to be summoned by the police following the raid on Redlands. Police disclosed no details of the summonses and refused to reveal the names of the other two people involved. The court hearing had been fixed for 10 May in Chichester. The story rumbled on for a number of days.

'Mick is accused of unlawfully possessing amphetamine tablets. Keith is accused of allowing premises to be used for smoking Indian hemp.' DAILY MIRROR, *21 March, 1967*

Between the emotional and the legal was the financial – we were still having trouble getting money from Klein. Throughout their stay in Morocco, the others had been badgering Klein for money. On 22 March, accountant Laurence Myers telexed Ronnie Schneider:

Have still not received the $10,000 re: Stones that you promised to send last week. Kindly look into this urgently.

On the day Keith returned to London, we rehearsed at Sound Techniques in preparation for our European tour. We had not played live for nearly six months and so apart from the need to add some new material, we also needed to be sure we were tight. The next afternoon we flew to Copenhagen, Denmark, arriving at 6pm local time. We then flew on to Malmö in Sweden, where we were met with a very heavy drugs check at customs. Swedish customs officers searched the Stones and 16 pieces of luggage. The customs officers belonged to a mobile unit known in Sweden as the Black Gang because of their reputation for finding smuggled goods, particularly narcotics. The *Evening News* of 25 March reported, 'They ordered Mick to unscrew the back of a heavy chest, the key of which had been lost. Mick and Bill were taken into separate rooms for a search. The Stones were delayed nearly an hour.'

'They were looking for pot and they went through every bit of clothing we had. Even our underclothes. I shouted I wanted a witness in there with me, so they didn't bother.'

MICK, *Evening News, 25 March,* **1967**

A good going-over from Swedish customs on 24 March, 1967

This tour included the Stones' first shows in Italy, Greece, and Poland (then behind the Iron Curtain); these were the band's first proper gigs in nearly six months. There were riots everywhere, with the notable exception of Germany.

'It was our idea to go to Poland – I wanted the kids there to have the chance to listen to us. I don't see why half of Europe should be left out. It really won't be worth our while money-wise, but it's a start. I think our records will be on sale there in a few years. The kids get the records from western European countries and they hear us on the radio. I'd love to go to Leningrad' MICK, *Melody Maker, 22 April, 1967*

'When we checked out of our hotel in Warsaw we found that our hotel bill came to exactly the same amount as our proceeds from the concerts the night before.' BILL

Set list from:
'Let's Spend The Night Together', 'The Last Time', 'Paint It Black', '19th Nervous Breakdown', 'Lady Jane', 'Get Off Of My Cloud', 'Yesterday's Papers', 'She Smiled Sweetly', 'Under My Thumb', 'Connection', 'Ruby Tuesday', 'It's All Over Now', 'Goin' Home', 'Satisfaction'

And in support...
Acts included: the Easy Beats, the Creation, the Batman (Didi & the ABC Boys), & Achim Reichel (Ex-Rattles) the Move, and Red & Black (Warsaw)

Europe, *March–April 1967*

25 March Idrottens Hus, Helsingborg, Sweden (two shows)
27 March Vinterstadion, Orebro, Sweden (two shows)
29 March Stadthalle, Bremen, West Germany (two shows)
30 March Sporthalle, Cologne, West Germany (two shows)
31 March Westfallenhalle, Dortmund, West Germany
1 April Ernst Merke Halle, Hamburg, West Germany (two shows)
2 April Stadthalle, Vienna, Austria (two shows)
5 April Palazzo Della Sport, Bologna, Italy (two shows)
6 April Palazzo Dello Sport, Rome, Italy (two shows)
8 April Palazzo Dello Sport, Milan, Italy (two shows)
9 April Palazzo Dello Sport, Genoa, Italy (two shows)
11 April Olympia Theatre, Paris, France (two shows)
13 April Congress Hall, Palace Of Culture, Warsaw, Poland (two shows)
14 April Hallenstadion, Zurich, Switzerland
15 April Hautreust Hall, The Hague, Holland
17 April Panathanaikos Football Stadium, Athens, Greece

Peace, man
Helsingborg: 'Mick nearly got beaten up, but stepped out of the way as the police charged the stage.' *Disc*
Orebro: 'Two thousand fans threw bottles, stones, chairs and fireworks at the stage. Five teenage girls and a policeman were injured in the tumult.' *Reuters*
Vienna: 'Police detained 154 Austrian beat fans after a riot. Smoke bombs were thrown in the 14,000 capacity Stadthalle.' *Daily Mirror*
Rome: 'Police foiled an attempt by 200 fans to storm the Stones' dressing room after the show. One youngster was injured.' *Reuters*
Paris: 'Riot police dispersed a 2,000 strong crowd of mini-skirted and leather-jacketed fans chanting the names of the Stones.' *Evening News*
Warsaw: 'The Stones triggered something that western politics could never incite – riots! Outside the Palace Of Culture in Warsaw, I witnessed 10,000 crazy Polish teenage fans locked out.' *NME*
Zurich: 'Screaming teenamges ripped up chairs and iron railings, which they hurled at the baton-waving police. Dogs and firehoses were brought in to keep the rioting fans at bay.' *Daily Mirror*
In contrast to the trouble on the Stones tour, 200,000 Americans gathered on 15 April to protest against violence, and the Vietnam War, in New York and San Francisco.

Below, *Riots in Zurich*

Riot Time

Local Customs

The problem with customs in Sweden was just the beginning. Our troubles continued throughout our European tour. Not that it wasn't expected, given the publicity surrounding the Redlands bust. In Paris things got very difficult and not just with over-zealous customs officials.

'I don't know what they thought we might be smuggling. Once they searched me right down to my underwear. I don't think we are doing anything wrong. I wouldn't kill anyone. That would be wrong. I wouldn't steal from anyone. That would be wrong. You see, we're not criminals. We're believers. I believe – that's all.' BRIAN, *in the New York Times 14 April, 1967*

Trouble abroad

A master of soundbites before they were invented, Winston Churchill declared of Europe 1946, 'An iron curtain has descended across the continent.' The Allies of the Second World War fell out, America and Britain aligning themselves against the USSR. The Stones in Warsaw were in the middle of the Cold War, between austere East and decadent West. And America supported the overthrow of the leftist Greek government in 1967, the coup in which Bill found himself embroiled when he visited Athens with his son Stephen.

WE WERE IN THE vanguard of changing times. Our attitude angered many who saw us as a threat to society. First it had been our hair and then our clothes. By early 1967 it was just us.

We were in Paris to play at the Olympia theatre. Mick wore a floor-length satin gown that zipped up the front. We went back to our hotel where we found that money, clothes, cameras and radios had been taken. Chief suspects were two over-friendly waiters, but the hotel would hear none of it, refusing any responsibility. We went to the airport in the morning.

'One official was throwing his weight about. Trouble started when the Stones handed their passports to a representative to save time. The official started shouting and Mick asked him to calm down. The official went berserk. A traveller explained everyone had to carry his own passport.' LES PERRIN, *in the Daily Express, 13 April, 1967*

a punch up at the airport

From TONY CONYERS, Paris, Wednesday

THE Rolling Stones were involved in a punch-up at Le Bourget airport today when they clashed with a French immigration officer at the passport control.

The official suddenly started talking rapidly to the group in French. None of the Stones could understand a word.

Leaving from Warsaw airport

'If they had an official who spoke English at the barrier this would never have happened,' Mick told the *Daily Mirror* on 13 April.

'There was no record of any incident,' commented an official from French Immigration. 'Had there been any serious dispute it would certainly have been in our records.'

One noticeable change to touring was the fact that more people came with us. Besides Stu, we had Tom Keylock and Jo Bergman on the tour – Jo worked in our office in London. There were four other crew members, along with Charlie Cobbett who worked for Vox and whose role was to look after our amplifiers.

Curtain call

From Paris we went to Warsaw to play two shows. Nothing could have prepared us for what it was like behind the Iron Curtain. On arrival, there

'A punch caught Keith. The official aimed one at Mick.' **LES PERRIN,** *on French airport staff, Daily Express, 13 April, 1967*

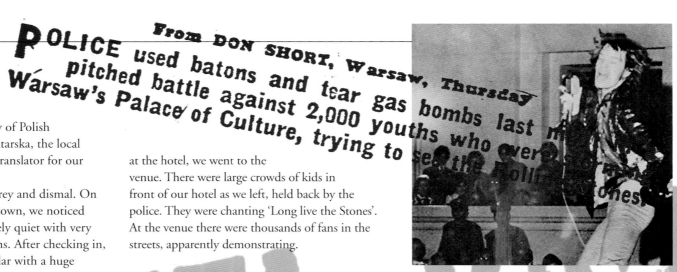

POLICE used batons and tear gas bombs last night in a pitched battle against 2,000 youths who overran Warsaw's Palace of Culture, trying to see the Rolling Stones. *From DON SHORT, Warsaw, Thursday*

were 100 fans waiting to greet us at the airport, where the buildings looked like army Nissan huts. A party of Polish security men and Madame Katarska, the local promoter and our guide and translator for our stay, met us in a tin hut.

Warsaw was depressingly grey and dismal. On our drive to the best hotel in town, we noticed that the streets seemed strangely quiet with very little traffic and few pedestrians. After checking in, I found my room was triangular with a huge circular concrete pillar in the centre of the room, which I had to negotiate whenever I wanted to go to the bathroom. Everybody was in and out of each other's rooms to see who had the best one – none of them were any good. There was no TV,

at the hotel, we went to the venue. There were large crowds of kids in front of our hotel as we left, held back by the police. They were chanting 'Long live the Stones'. At the venue there were thousands of fans in the streets, apparently demonstrating.

Come all ye faithful

Once inside, we found that the tickets for our shows had not been put on sale. They were given to loyal party members. This meant all the real fans were outside, unable to get tickets. but the

Mick in Sala Kongresowej (Congress Hall), Warsaw

away, backed by armoured cars with machine-guns. It was worse than it had been during the UK riot in Blackpool when those Glaswegians had gone nuts.

'ICANTGETNO, ICANTGETNO.'

POLISH FANS, *calling for 'Satisfaction'*

just a radio, which we couldn't hear anything on – the stations appeared to be jammed.

Dinner was fairly basic and cost a fortune. We wanted to go for a walk, but weren't allowed out by the secret police. Behind every pillar was a plain clothes agent. After completing a press conference

audience seemed to get into it as we went along. Towards the end of our set they began chanting, 'Icantgetno, Icantgetno,' it took a while for us to realise that they wanted 'Satisfaction'!

After we came off stage, we heard that the fans outside had been rioting. There were scores of police and military. The police were on horses and chased the fans

'One of the famous modern music groups, the Stones, gave two concerts in Warsaw. The young English artists performed their best songs and the audience, consisting of mainly young people, received the performance with enthusiasm, which was too noisy. Some of the fans outside tried to mislead officers to get in. More than 200 tickets were confiscated. The resourceful forgers had forged them, selling the tickets for an enormous profit.' THE OFFICIAL POLISH NEWS AGENCY

Back in the hotel, we decided to get our own back on the authorities as best we could. We arranged for a van with windows to be sent for us and got in with boxes of our singles and EPs. We drove around the city. Whenever we saw groups of kids in the streets, we would slow down and throw records out to them. Once all the records were gone we returned to the hotel, feeling very much happier.

Coup de Greece

We finished off our tour in Athens, Greece, at the Panathinaikos Football Stadium. Things were about to change, according to our leader.

'We've virtually given up one-night stands,' Mick told the *Melody Maker* in April. 'The one-night scene is just dead terrible – there's just not enough entertainment value in tour shows now. The people need something more interesting. I have got some ideas on how to change things – to do something different, but I don't want to say what they are. It would be very expensive and it's so difficult to tell whether it would be a success. We shall never tour America again. It is very hard work and one bring-down after another. You have no idea of how terrible it is unless you've been through it.'

After playing Athens, the rest of the band went home. Astrid and Stephen had come with me and the plan was to stay on for a holiday. We moved from our hotel in the centre of Athens to the suburbs, staying in a beach house.

We had been spending the day relaxing when we heard gunfire coming from Athens, across the bay. I called the Greek promoter's office to ask what was happening. I was told that troops commanded by Colonel Georges Papadopoulos had occupied government buildings in Athens and successfully overthrown King Constantine. He also told us that a 6pm curfew had been imposed and under no circumstances were we to leave our place after that time. All communication with the outside world had been cut off – we couldn't even contact the Stones office by phone, telegram or letter. There was nothing to do but wait. On Sunday 23 April, we managed to get a flight back to London.

At the Greek airport I was approached by several British newsreel crews who begged me to take film to London. I'm glad I turned them down, as we were thoroughly searched before boarding. There could have been another Stone in court.

MICK JAGGER

on the end of an era

Bill and Stephen at Athens airport

The following day, Brian flew out to Cannes for the launch. Brian checked into the Martinez Hotel and went to see Anita in a final attempt at reconciliation. Keith stayed in his room, deciding to let them fight it out. A good tactic, as Brian failed to get her to change her mind.

Brian returned home after the premiere, leaving Keith and Anita on the Riviera. Keylock was there, having driven Keith's Bentley to Nice. Keith flew back from Nice on 9 May to make his court appearance.

Anita and Brian in Cannes

Linda Brian?

Brian, in a bizarre twist, started seeing Keith's ex, Linda Keith. They spent time together in the Cotswolds. A few days later, Anita went to Cannes for the launch of *A Degree Of Murder*. Tom Keylock drove Keith's Bentley over. Astrid and I went to the Bag O'Nails, where we met up with Brian. Meanwhile, Elvis and Priscilla got married in Las Vegas: the everyday lives of rock stars.

Three days in May

On Tuesday 9 May, Keith met Mick at Simpsons restaurant in the Strand for lunch. They were there to discuss arrangements for their court appearance the following day. After lunch they drove to Redlands, the scene of the crime, and spent the night there.

The hearing was to take place in Chichester. Extra police had been drafted in to cope with two coach-loads of fans that were expected. Using walkie-talkies, the police guarded all the entrances. They closed the first floor public gallery half-an-hour before the case began.

Mick and Keith travelled from Redlands to the court in a chauffeur-driven car. There was only a small waiting crowd, a few carrying cards saying 'Legalise marijuana'. Les Perrin and Robert Fraser were already there.

Mick was in a green jacket, white shirt and dark grey floral tie, Keith wore a navy blue jacket and pink tie and Robert Fraser was in a light grey suit. Chairman of the hearing was Basil Shippam, prosecuting counsel was Anthony McCowan and defending counsels were Michael Havers, QC and Geoffrey Leach.

Keith was accused of permitting his home to be used for the purpose of smoking cannabis resin. Mick was summoned for being in unauthorised possession of four tablets of amphetamine sulphate and methyl amphetamine hydrochloride. Robert Fraser was accused of being in unauthorised possession of heroin, contrary to the Dangerous Drugs Act 1965 and faced a second summons for having in his possession eight capsules of methyl-amphetamine hydrochloride [stimulants].

When the Court adjourned for lunch, Mick and Keith came out to screams, cheers and even boos from a crowd of about 600, mostly kids and housewives. Mini-skirted girls grabbed at Mick's hair and coat and six policemen helped them to reach their car. They all went to a local hotel for lunch, before Mick and Keith returned to Redlands to change.

Mick came back wearing a charcoal grey jacket, while Keith changed into a green one. After lunch, the court heard various statements from both the prosecution and the defence, as the question of who had tipped off the police was raised.

On the court steps in Chichester

Mick and Keith leaving court

All three elected to go for trial by jury, the date was set at 27 June and the venue was to be West Sussex Quarter Sessions. They were released on £100 bail.

Mick and Keith dodged a hundred waiting fans by being smuggled out of the back door of the court, They were driven to Redlands, after which Keith went to Heathrow to fly to Paris and Mick went back up to London.

Brian busted

While all of this this was taking place, I was at home in Keston with Astrid and Brian was himself being busted at his flat in Courtfield Road, South Kensington. At 4pm, drug squad detectives led by Detective Inspector Benny Lynch arrived with a search warrant. Brian was there with his Swiss friend Prince Stash.

Two detectives walked up a small flight of stairs into the house, while 10 others positioned themselves on nearby street corners and across the road. After Brian opened the door, all 12 detectives went into the flat and spent the next 40 minutes searching the place thoroughly. One of the police officers that

'I suffer from asthma. The only drugs I have are for that.' BRIAN

made the search described the room where the drugs were found as 'rather like a dance hall for holding parties in'. Brian was asked if he had any drugs, on prescription or otherwise and he told the police about his asthma.

The police found 11 suspicious objects, including two metal canisters, two pipes, two cigarette ends and a chair castor used as an ashtray. In total, just over 50 grams of a suspicious substance were found, making up to 10 cigarettes. Brian was shown one of the items by detectives and a phial bearing traces of cocaine. He admitted to using dope, but not to taking the hard drug.

He left the house wearing a dark-coloured three-quarter length coat with a silk scarf knotted round his neck. Detectives walked either side of him, and the rest of the squad followed. Brian and Stash sat in the back of a police car with a detective on either side. They were driven to Kensington Police Station, where

they were charged under the Dangerous Drugs Act with unlawful possession of approximately 50 grams of cannabis resin. Solicitors Joynson-Hicks represented Brian and both he and Stash were released on bail. The two were ordered to appear at West London Magistrates' Court the following morning at 10.30am. Brian left for the Odeon Cinema, Marble Arch, with four friends.

Jones in court

Brian and Stash were driven to the court in Brian's silver-grey Rolls Royce. Outside the courtroom a crowd of about a hundred, including shop girls and girls in school blazers, were waiting. The two were smuggled into court through a back way an hour before the hearing. Brian wore a navy blue mod suit with bell-bottom trousers and flared jacket, white shirt, a white spotted tie, and Cuban-heeled boots. Extra police were on duty. Two teenage girls were among 13 people in the public gallery.

Brian outside West London Magistrates Court

Magistrate ER Guest heard from defending counsel James Kingham that he would be quite happy for a three-week remand.

Brian and Stash were remanded on £250 bail each, charged with unlawful possession of 50 grams of Indian hemp and the case was adjourned until 2 June. By the time they left the court a crowd of 150 had gathered outside. The police had to force a way clear for them to get to the car.

Brian went with friends to the Speakeasy and then on to the Bag O'Nails. I was in RG Jones studio with the End. Mick was at Olympic studios where the Beatles were recording 'Baby You're A Rich Man'. He sang backing vocals at the closing of the song.

'Yes, it is hash. We do smoke. But not the cocaine, man. That is not my scene. I am not a junkie.' BRIAN

Country Life

After the hearings it was back to work again, not that I think any of us were that enthusiastic. Mick and Andrew were at Olympic on 16 May and the rest of us were there from the following day. We were working on ideas for a new album and spent the next five days laying down tracks.

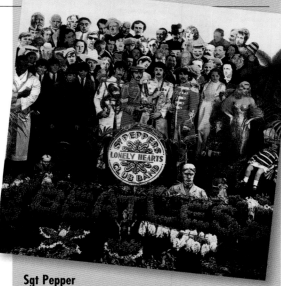

Sgt Pepper
On June 1, the Beatles released *Sgt Pepper's Lonely Hearts Club Band*. 'The "Welcome The Rolling Stones" was something Michael Cooper and Peter Blake put in,' said Paul McCartney. 'They sort of asked us if we minded and we said, "No, no, not at all."'

AMONG THE THINGS we layed down were two intriguingly-titled pieces: 'Telstar II' and 'Manhole Cover'. We also did 'She's A Rainbow' with Nicky Hopkins on piano. John Paul Jones, later the bass player with Led Zeppelin, arranged the strings.

We recorded mostly in the evenings and through the night. This allowed Mick to hire a chauffeur car one day to take Marianne and Christopher Gibbs and view a house called Stargroves near Newbury in Berkshire. He fancied the idea of living in the country.

'We were shown round the house by this incredibly stuffy old baronet, who thought we were the most loose and disreputable bunch of people he'd ever come across, especially when Mick stole some 19th-century photograph of the house and stuffed it in his pocket.' CHRISTOPHER GIBBS

Mick had Stargroves valued. The property comprised a mansion, two cottages and 40 acres of land and was valued at £28,000. Charlie was on the move too. He had decided to buy Peckhams, in Halland, near Lewes, for £25,000. Not to be outdone, Brian began looking at houses in the country. Tom Keylock drove him to Beulah, in South Wales and then on to Nansladron Farm in St Austell, Cornwall. He also had a valuation and survey done on Aston Somerville Hall, near Broadway in Worcester, not far north of his home town of Cheltenham. All this required money, as Charlie was forced to remind Allen Klein by telex in June:

What has happened to the money for my house?

On Friday 2 June, 1967, Charlie's 26th birthday, Brian and Stash were back in court. The authorities were told that detectives searching Brian's flat had found marijuana, methedrine and cocaine.

Brian and Stash followed Mick and Keith in electing for a jury trial. Six days later, Brian was in the studio, not with the Rolling Stones, but with John, Paul, George and Ringo.

'I liked Brian. We asked him to one of our sessions and to our surprise he brought along a sax. He turned up in this big Afghan coat at Abbey Road. We said, "We've got a little track here" and he played sax. It was a crazy record, "You Know My Name, Look Up The Number". It's a funny sax solo – exactly what we wanted, a ropey sax, kind of shaky. Brian was very good like that.' PAUL McCARTNEY, in Blinds And Shutters, a book of Michael Cooper photographs, 1989

We were all back at Olympic the next night and on 12–13 June. Recording was put on hold as Mick, Marianne, baby Nicholas and his nanny went on holiday to Tangier, staying at the El Minzah Hotel. Mick checked in as P Gunning.

The Monterey Festival took place in California between 16–18 June and Brian decided to go. The day after it finished, I joined the Royal Horticultural Society – no, I was not trying to learn how to grow marijuana at home.

Mick got back from Tangier on 25 June. He and Marianne, and Keith and Brian joined the Beatles at Abbey Road for the filming of their contribution to the *Our World* TV programme linking five continents live by satellite. The Beatles performed 'All You Need is Love'.

The next day Keith shopped for clothes at Chelsea's Granny Takes A Trip. Tom Keylock drove Mick, Keith and Robert Fraser to Redlands. Leslie Perrin and three solicitors checked into a Chichester hotel. They were due in court the next morning.

Mick and Marianne holiday in Tangiers

HIPPY MEETS HOLLYWOOD

On 15 June, Brian decided pretty much on the spur of the moment to fly to California to attend the Monterey International Pop Festival.

This was a three-day affair that took place at the Monterey County Fairgrounds, a hundred miles south of San Francisco. The men behind it were producer and record label boss Lou Adler and John Phillips of Californian band the Mamas and the Papas. Their 'Monday, Monday' had topped the American charts a year earlier.

Today we look back at the festival as the embodiment of the hippy ideal, but many of the San Francisco bands then at the forefront of the West Coast sound saw it as an attempt by Southern California – and the Hollywood set in

'Brian, in a mind-shattering gold lamé coat festooned with beads, crystal swastika and lace, was the unofficial king of the festival.' **NME,** *24 June, 1967*

particular – to muscle in on their scene. Not that it stopped them playing the festival. Lou Adler called them the Ungrateful Dead.

'Those 400 miles [between LA and San Francisco] marked the difference between a neon wasteland and the most important underground in the nation.'
VILLAGE VOICE

This was Otis Redding's first major appearance before a predominately white crowd. He was apprehensive, but the audience loved him. On Sunday, Brian introduced Jimi Hendrix on stage. The night before, Brian had dropped acid in a tepee with Dennis Hopper – 18 months before the actor made *Easy Rider* with Peter Fonda.

Michelle Phillips and, behind, *Cass Elliot: the Mamas*

'This is a great scene. The people are so polite and talk to me and say they like the way I'm dressed.' **BRIAN,** *in NME, 24 June, 1967*

Festival line-up

Day one: 16 June, 1967
The Association, the Paupers, Lou Rawls, Beverly, Johnny Rivers, Eric Burdon and the Animals, Simon and Garfunkel

Day two: 17 June
Canned Heat, Big Brother and the Holding Company, Country Joe and the Fish, Al Kooper, the Butterfield Blues Band, Quicksilver Messenger Service, the Steve Miller Band, the Electric Flag, Moby Grape, Hugh Masekela, the Byrds, the Butterfield Blues Band, Laura Nyro, Jefferson Airplane, Booker T and the MGs (with the Mar-Keys), Otis Redding

Day three: 18 June
Ravi Shankar, the Blues Project, Big Brother and the Holding Company, the Group With No Name, Buffalo Springfield, the Who, the Grateful Dead, the Jimi Hendrix Experience, Scott McKenzie, the Mamas and the Papas

Above right: *Brian with Nico*

Right: *the Grateful Dead*

Below: *Buffalo Springfield with David Crosby*

Summer of love

For many, Monterey marked the start of the Summer of Love. Brian was there with Nico, the German singer who was signed to Immediate and had worked with the Velvet Underground. Rock history has cast Monterey in the shadow of its successor, the 1969 Woodstock festival, but some think it was a truer embodiment of flower power. Elsewhere, it wasn't all peace and harmony. On 17 June, China detonated its first H-Bomb.

MONTEREY INTERNATIONAL POP FESTIVAL
JUNE 16·17·18
MONTEREY COUNTY FAIRGROUNDS, MONTEREY, CALIF.

In the Court of Judge Block

In front of a full public gallery, Mick and Keith gave the impression they were unconcerned as they and Robert Fraser sat in the dock.

The charges were read out as they sat before 61-year-old Judge Leslie Block and the all-male jury. Fraser was the first to stand trial. He pleaded guilty

The case attracted more mature crowds less given to screaming than regular Stones fans.

to possessing 24 heroin tablets and not guilty to having eight capsules of methyl-amphetamine hydrochloride [stimulants]. Prosecuting QC Morris did not want to deal with the possession of the capsules. For the defence, Mr Denny said that Fraser had been working hard and been given heroin tablets about 12 months previously. He thought he could control his use of heroin but he found he became hooked.

'At no time did he supply or sell or give any other person any quantity of heroin whatever.' MR DENNY, *defence*

Mick and Keith leave Redlands for court.

On Tuesday 27 June, Astrid and I decided to spend the day at home in Keston. Brian, Charlie and I had talked to Mick and Keith and we decided it would serve no purpose for the band to be at court. If anything, our presence would be more a hindrance than a help.

Robert Fraser at an earlier court appearance in November 1966, fined for exhibiting 'indecent' paintings

While Charlie and I had both smoked marijuana, drugs as such were not our scene. If either of us had been caught with dope, we would have been in deep water too. Back then, marijuana was like Communism, an evil threat to civilised Western society.

What I have written here about Mick and Keith's day in court has been researched from literally hundreds of contemporary reports and conversations among ourselves. I want once and for all to tell the whole, unembellished story.

The morning of the hearing, Tom Keylock drove Mick, Keith and Robert Fraser in the Bentley to a secret rendezvous with the police. They were taken to the courthouse in Chichester, some 45 minutes before their hearing. There was no screaming welcome from 50 or so people gathered near the back entrance.

For the prosecution, Detective Sergeant Stanley Cudmore said that in November 1966, Fraser had been fined £20 and ordered to pay £50 costs, for 'exposing to public view an indecent exhibition of paintings' by American Pop artist Jim Dine (though why they had to bring the earlier offence up wasn't clear). Dr John Craigmore, witness for the defence, told the court, 'At the moment he is cured of his addiction and there is no reason why he should go back.'

Despite further defence, Fraser was found guilty and remanded in custody, to be sentenced after cases were heard against Mick and Keith.

Mick was first up after lunch. His defence was 44-year-old future UK Attorney General, Michael Havers. For the prosecution, Malcolm Morris, QC said, 'In a case of this sort, it is right that I should say that you will decide this case entirely upon the evidence which you hear in this court.'

Michael Ansell, a scientific officer at the Metropolitan Police laboratory, said that the four tablets contained substances known during the war as Benzedrine. They were prescribed for slimming. Mr Havers called up Louis Priest, a specialist on poison and drugs. Priest, who was an administrative

'It may be that some of you have heard something about Mr Jagger, because he is somebody who may well be known to some of you.'
MALCOLM MORRIS, QC, *addressing the jury*

assistant at the Pharmaceutical Society of Great Britain, told the court that the drug could be used for tiredness, convalescence, travel sickness and fear of heights. The dosage was one to four tablets a day.

Dr Raymond Dixon Firth, Mick's doctor since July 1965, had told him that they were alright to take in an emergency, but were not to be used regularly.

Dr Firth was asked, 'From your point of view was he properly in possession of them?' He replied, 'Certainly.'

Mr Havers submitted that Firth's verbal agreement amounted to issuing a prescription. Mick's case hinged upon this argument. But Judge Block ruled, 'The evidence given by Dr Firth does not in law amount to the issue of a prescription by a qualified practitioner.'

After an adjournment, during which Mr Havers decided not to address the jury, the judge began his summing up.

Marianne, accompanied by Tom Keylock, arrives to see Mick in jail.

'I have to direct you to say there is no defence to the charge and ask you to retire and consider your verdict.' JUDGE BLOCK

The jury took just six minutes to elect a foreman and return their verdict. They found Mick guilty. The defence asked for a certificate to appeal on a point of law. 'Yes, Mr Havers, and may I wish you luck' replied the judge.

'Blest be the man who spares these stones.'
WILLIAM SHAKESPEARE, *from his tombstone inscription*

Just before the court adjourned, Keith (now more soberly dressed in a pale pink T-shirt and jeans) returned in his Bentley from Redlands. He had a suitcase containing a change of clothes for Mick, who travelled to Lewes with Robert Fraser and four other men in a prison van. It swung through the gates of the jail at 7pm. Mick was taken to the remand wing and allowed to see his solicitors. They took him a book on Tibet and two on modern art.

Mick asked for 40 Benson and Hedges cigarettes and was offered an evening meal before lights went out at 10pm. A jigsaw puzzle was sent in to him. He was allowed to keep his own clothes while he was in jail.

The papers made the most of Mick's wait to hear his sentence.

'It's cold in here.'
MICK

Mick and Robert Fraser were woken up at 7am and ate breakfast alone in their cells. When they arrived at court, they were handcuffed. They waited in a cell beneath the courtroom during Keith's trial. Marianne, who had just finished a run at the Royal Court Theatre in

Chekhov's *Three Sisters*, arrived in Chichester early in the morning. She entered the courthouse by a rear entrance and was told that she could see Mick after the sentencing.

Keith arrived at court in his Bentley, fully aware that the outcome was not looking promising for him. Malcolm Morris once again faced Michael Havers across the court. A new jury of 11 men and one woman was then sworn in.

The prosecution case was straightforward. In Keith's home, traces of cannabis resin had been found in some ash on a table, in pipes, in a pudding basin in one bedroom and in substances found on one of the guests who had since left the country. He said that incense was being burned to mask the smell, that the woman guest was under the influence of marijuana and that Keith could not have failed to notice her behaviour. Evidence about the 'mystery girl' (in fact Marianne) was allowed by Judge Block after the defence objected that she would be tried in her absence.

Keith and his solicitor take the Bentley from Redlands to the court.

'I have never known anything of this sort happen before. This is almost Star Chamber.' MICHAEL HAVERS, *on Marianne's involvement in the case*

Morris went on to talk about how this young woman was naked except for a fur-skin rug, sitting between two men on a sofa. A briar pipe bowl in the room was found to contain traces of cannabis resin. There were cigarette ends and ash, containing Indian hemp and cannabis. He told the court about David Schneiderman, who was searched and had cannabis resin on him. A warrant for his arrest had been issued by 14 February but, the court heard, he had already left the country.

Police witnesses were then called.

'The woman was in a merry mood and one of vague unconcern.' DETECTIVE CONSTABLE EVELYN FULLER, *on Marianne*

'When she got to the bedroom door, she allowed the rug to fall to the ground. She had nothing on. I heard a laugh from a man in the bedroom, who was using the phone. I saw her naked back.' SERGEANT JOHN CHALLON

Keith had lunch at a local hotel, while Mick and Robert Fraser ate in their cells. Mick had prawn cocktail, roast lamb, strawberries and cream sent in from a local hotel. He and Robert shared a bottle of Beaujolais.

Robert Fraser and Mick

After lunch Havers told the court, 'A well-known national newspaper gave information which led to the raid at Redlands. Who tipped off the paper? When you hear which paper it is suggested it is [*News Of The World*], you may find difficulty in accepting them as well-known guardians of the public morals. The week before the raid, it published an article. The consequences were a writ for libel served upon the *News Of The World*.'

The lawyer went on, 'In the remaining five days, Mr Jagger was followed wherever he went or whatever he did. Can you think of any better way to kill off the ensuing libel action? Schneiderman was at the party loaded to the gunwales with cannabis resin, the only man at the party found to have

cannabis on him, but by the time the charges were made, he had gone. Was the girl high on cannabis? I wonder if the jury has stopped to consider that the story of the girl's movements was given so that they could draw the inference she was smoking cannabis. She is not on trial. She is a girl who remains technically anonymous and I hope she will remain anonymous. She is described as a drug-taking nymphomaniac, with no chance of saying anything in her defence. Do you expect me to force that girl to go into the witness box with no chance to refute the allegations?'

'If I can't call the girl,' concluded Havers, 'and Mr Richards is in agreement with this, I will not call anyone else.'

At the end of the second day, Marianne briefly saw Mick in the cells. She gave him newspapers, magazines, fresh fruit, a game of draughts, 60 cigarettes and a science-fiction book. After slipping away, she was driven to Redlands. Michael Cooper smuggled in a miniature camera to photograph Mick, possibly for the Stones' next album cover. The police confiscated his film after he snapped Mick through the cell door. Keith spent a few minutes with Mick and Robert Fraser and returned to Lewes prison.

The press loved it… It was a headline writer's dream.

The following day, Keith wore a black four-button Regency-style mod suit trimmed with black braid. A few moments before the hearing was due to begin, Mick and Robert Fraser arrived at the court. They were again handcuffed to one another.

'When a number of prisoners who represent a security risk are being moved together it is desirable for them to be handcuffed.' THE HOME OFFICE

Taking the witness stand, Keith gave details of the events leading up to and including the bust. For the prosecution, Morris said that Havers 'spoke about various things and, in the course of that opening speech, made it quite clear that your defence was that Schneiderman had been planted in your weekend party as part of a wicked conspiracy by the *News Of The World*? Is that any part of your defence or not?'

Keith said, 'Yes it is, sir.' Mr Morris finished the prosecution with further questions along the same lines and some enquiries about the unnamed girl in the rug.

Keith Richards

'Remember that you are not trying the News Of The World, as you are not trying the young lady in the rug. You are trying Keith Richard.' MR MORRIS

In his summing-up, Judge Block told the jury to put out of their minds any prejudice about Keith's views on petty morals and said they should not be prejudiced by allegations about the lady who was in some condition of undress. The issue facing them was comparatively simple.

'You have to be satisfied cannabis resin was being smoked in the house when the police went there and you have to be satisfied Richard knew it. You are trying a man who is well known in the entertainment world and inevitably in circumstances like these there has been an enormous amount of publicity.' JUDGE BLOCK

The jury retired at 2.25pm, returning 55 minutes later to find Keith guilty of knowingly allowing cannabis resin to be smoked at his house.

Michael Havers gave pleas in mitigation for Mick and Keith. After a 10-minute retirement, Judge Block returned to pass sentence. Mick and Robert Fraser were led into court to join their friend. Keith was jailed for 12 months and ordered to pay £500 towards costs. He raised his eyes to the ceiling, then stood down from the dock, pale and silent. He was led to the cells with the sound of 'oohs' and 'aahs' from the public gallery.

Fraser was sent to prison for six months and ordered to pay £200 costs and then it was Mick's turn. He had gripped the dock rail tensely as the two jail sentences were passed on his friends. Now, left alone in the dock, he looked around the court nervously.

Mick was jailed for three months and ordered to pay £100. He went pale at the sentence, swayed and almost collapsed. Mopping his brow, he put his fist to his forehead and

started to cry. He walked at a snail's pace, shaking his head in dismay and whistling softly, towards the cells. As details of the sentences spread to the 600 waiting outside there were yells of, 'Let them go', 'Shame' and 'Unfair'.

Mick and Keith were granted certificates to appeal against their convictions. Twenty minutes after they had been sentenced, Marianne arrived at the court in Keith's Bentley. She wore dark glasses and a black trouser suit. Pale and crying, she pushed her way to the double gates guarded by police. She spent 15 minutes with Mick in his cell.

A police Land Rover emerged from the double gates as a decoy to fool press and public. Mick and Keith used the front entrance, surrounded by about 10 police officers. A handful of fans watched them trudge dejectedly across the pavement to a police vehicle. Mick held back tears, while Keith stared stonily ahead, biting his lower lip. A policeman was handcuffed to Mick and Keith and Robert were handcuffed together.

We were all phoned at home by the office to be told of the sentences. Allen Klein was also called. Our office sent a telegram to Rome to inform Anita of Keith's sentence. I told the newspapers, 'Unless our record company puts out an old record, we have nothing new in the bag.' It was hard to take in. Brian flew to Rome to see Anita and win her back.

Just before 8pm, a grey and blue prison minibus, escorted by a black Maria, drove up to Brixton prison. Inside were the three new prisoners. Mick was to be left at Brixton. A few minutes later, the minibus departed for Wormwood Scrubs, where the other two were to be incarcerated. Mick and Keith's solicitors worked until after midnight on their appeal forms.

The Establishment had won, they had got their own back on us. We had in their eyes got above ourselves and we needed bringing down.

Clockwise from left: Mick in Melody Maker, *on his way to Brixton prison and Marianne outside the court.*

Melody Maker

July 8, 1967 9d weekly

JONES PLUS BASIE?

TOM JONES will be seen again on this week's Top Of The Pops, Their excerpt from the Dot World TV programme will be shown on the programme (Thursday).

BEATLES 'WORLD' TV REPEAT

THE BEATLES will be seen again on this week's Top Of The Pops, Their excerpt from the Dot World TV programme will be shown on the programme...

MICK JAGGER

has been sentenced to imprisonment for three months. He was charged with being in possession of four benzedrine-type tablets, acquired in Italy and recommended by the Italian manufacturers as a remedy for travel sickness. Mick Jagger has appealed against the conviction and sentence and has been granted bail until the hearing of the appeal. Because the case has aroused public interest to such a large degree, many national newspapers have passed comment. The Melody Maker has read them all and we find ourselves, a little surprisingly, handing not one flower, but a large bouquet to The Times. For last Saturday, The Times ran a leader on the Jagger case. It was objective, informed, and fair. Thankfully, it lacked hysteria. One of the most telling passages ran... "If, after his visit to the Pope, the Archbishop of Canterbury had bought proprietary airsickness pills on Rome airport, and imported the unused tablets into Britain on his return, he would have risked committing precisely the same offence." The Melody Maker, unasked by the Rolling Stones, thanks The Times. The Melody Maker bows to The Times. The Melody Maker has a message for The Times: KEEP SWINGING!

OPERATION MONKEE

turn to centre pages

Free Stones

As Mick and Keith were languishing in jail, our friends the Who had an emergency meeting, as a result of which they decided to record two Keith and Mick songs the following day to draw attention to the jailed Stones. More than 200 chanting teenagers protested outside newspaper offices in Fleet Street. Chanting 'Free the Stones' and 'We want love', they were eventually dispersed by police with dogs. Meanwhile, at a dancehall in Bognor Regis, the DJ turned off the lights, played 'The Last Time' and urged the crowd to think about Mick and Keith.

The poster adorned thousands of bedrooms.

'Be cool for a moment and be serious. Cast your thoughts to a courtroom where three young men were deprived of their freedom. Let's have three minutes silence for some of the country's finest talent.' DJ, Bognor Regis

'The court that convicted Jagger and Richard set out merely to make an example of them. This is unjust.' JOHN WOLFE, *the Who's road manager, in Evening Standard, 30 June, 1967*

'Teenagers wept, I read, when Jagger and Richard were sentenced. I decline to imitate them. I prefer to applaud.' CHARLES CURRAN, *Evening News, 30 June, 1967*

THE FOLLOWING DAY, there were urgent moves to get the appeal documents completed for submission to the Court of Criminal Appeal, in the hope that the plea for bail could be made before a judge.

Protests continued in Fleet Street, with the *News Of The World*'s offices being the focus of most of the attention. Spontaneous demonstrations broke out all over London. The Who's drummer Keith Moon, his girlfriend Kim and the band's road manager John Wolfe drove in Keith's Bentley to the West End and joined the protesters. Their comments reflected how most young people of the generation felt at news of the sentences.

The Who support their friends.

It took just 24 hours for the Who to record, press and deliver 'The Last Time' and 'Under My Thumb' into the shops.

At the High Court, Lord Justice Diplock, Justice Braben and Justice Waller took 25 minutes to hear an appeal from Michael Havers, QC and Geoffery Leach. They granted Mick and Keith bail in their own recognisance of £5,000 each, plus two sureties each of £1,000, supplied by Leslie Perrin and book keeper Stan Blackbourn. Their appeals could not be heard until the autumn, which meant they had to stay in England while they were on bail, surrendering their passports. Robert Fraser remained in jail.

Les and Stan left the High Court to finalise the release of Mick and Keith from prison. Mick left Brixton at 4.25pm. He waved and smiled to a group of photographers and a handful of young girls, before being whisked away in Keith's Bentley, driven by Tom Keylock.

At 5.08pm, they arrived at Wormwood Scrubs to collect Keith, reappearing at 5.15pm. From prison they went to meet their legal team in King's Bench Walk. They went for a quiet drink in the nearby Feathers Pub in Fleet Street. Mick had on his trouser belt a

button badge reading 'Mick Is Sex', which was probably the last thing on his mind. He had really had a scare. He sipped a vodka and lime, while Keith drank a whisky and coke from a half-pint glass.

The Daily Record *of 30 June, 1967, was just as interested in the girl in a rug as in the Stones.*

Special Announcement

The WHO consider Mick Jagger & Keith Richard have been treated as scapegoats for the drug problem and as a protest against the savage sentences imposed on them at Chichester yesterday. The WHO are issuing today the first of a series of Jagger/Richard songs to keep their work before the public until they are again free to record themselves.

"THE LAST TIME" and "UNDER MY THUMB"

written by Mick Jagger & Keith Richard

TRACK 604006

'I just went dead when I was sentenced. I could think of nothing.' MICK, *Daily Mail, 1 July, 1967*

'I was so stunned at the sentence that I went limp. I thought of nothing. Later, I wept. You don't know the feeling.' KEITH, *Daily Mail, 1 July, 1967*

In keeping with the spirit of the time, someone had the idea of doing a concert and using the proceeds to buy flowers for the judge.

'With an audience of 100,000 we might charge everybody to raise £25,000, We could send a lot of flowers to Judge Block, some to all the hospitals in the country and the rest of the proceeds we could give to good causes. We want to show our forgiveness with love and charity.' IC ROSS, *in the Times, 1 July, 1967*

Not everyone felt the same, Charles Curran, in the *Evening News* of 30 June, decided that Mick and Keith were not worthy of anyone's pity: 'Teenagers wept, I read, when Jagger and Richard were sentenced. Well, I decline to imitate them. I prefer to applaud. I hold that people who break the law

ought to be punished. The law that Jagger and Richard broke is not a trifle, either. Look at Jagger and Richard. Each of them is a millionaire at 23. They have so much money that, by comparison with them, the Count of Monte Cristo looks like a pauper.

'Neither, in my opinion, has any talent. Because they are untalented, they arouse the enthusiasm – and collect the money – of youngsters like themselves. When a celebrity goes off the rails, the public takes a lot of notice.

'Jagger and Richard must accept that there is no help for that. It is an occupational hazard – like housemaid's knee.'

William Rees-Mogg

Editor of the *Times* William Rees-Mogg wrote an eloquent piece under the headline 'Who Breaks A Butterfly On A Wheel'. This was written entirely in defence of Mick: Keith was not even mentioned.

'The Rolling Stones are one of Britain's major cultural assets, who should be honoured by the kingdom instead of jailed.' ALLEN GINSBERG, *poet, in a letter to the Times of 12 July, 1967*

Flaming June, as it's sometimes called, came to an end. There was no question that this was going to put a strain on the band. Personal relations between Keith and Brian could not have been worse. There was the uncertainty of the appeal and Mick and Keith seemed strangely short of new material. Allied to which our relationship with Andrew was at an all-time low, not to mention Mr Klein's total control on all aspects of the finances… The situation was not good.

Roll on the summer of love.

Mick and Keith released on bail and, right, Keith Moon and girlfriend Kim Kerrigan join the demonstrators

August **67**

68 December

Oh, What A Circus

An outtake from the Beggars Banquet shoot. It took place at Sarum Chase, 23 West Heath Road, Hampstead, London, on 7 June, 1968.

Idol Young

We were the talk of the nation and few of our fans probably gave much thought to what we felt as individuals. Jail was a real fear for Brian, Mick and Keith. The future for Charlie and I was in jeopardy and there was nothing that we could do about it.

FOLLOWING WILLIAM REES-MOGG'S piece in the *Times*, there was a groundswell of public opinion that went along with the notion that if Mick and Keith were jailed they would be seen as martyrs to a cause, which would do little or nothing for the anti-drug movement. The press was divided. The popular press viewed the whole thing as a scandal, a full-blown, drug-taking orgy. The more serious press followed the lead set by the *Times*, debating the issue sensibly.

A Mr Green of Somerset wrote to the *Times* quoting the Shropshire poet AE Housman:

'Oh who is that young sinner with the handcuffs on his wrists?
And what has he been after that they groan and shake their fists?
And wherefore is he wearing such a conscious-stricken air?
Oh, they're taking him to prison for the colour of his hair.' AE HOUSMAN, *Collected Poems, 1939*

On 3 July, Brian checked into a Hampshire health clinic called Forest Mere Hydro. He badly needed help; the drugs and his own demons were taking their toll. Forest Mere said it could do nothing for him and he left for the Priory Nursing Home in Richmond two days later.

'Brian has been admitted into a London nursing home suffering from severe strain.' EVENING NEWS, *6 July, 1967*

Mick and Keith returned to Redlands to work on songs and learned their appeal would be brought forward to 31 July. Brian's court appearance would follow

Mick arrives at court for his appeal hearing as fans wait to hear the verdict on 31 July.

in October.

My own life was taken up with preoccupations about my son, Stephen. Diane heard that Astrid was living with us at Keston and returned from South Africa to take him back. I met Diane at her father's flat and for Stephen's sake I agreed to her demands. The two of them flew to South Africa a fortnight later.

Things quietened down on the drug trial front, but not before the BBC intimated they were to cut Mick and Keith out of the Beatles' film of *All You Need Is Love* on *Top Of The Pops*. Their manager, Brian Epstein, was incensed and threatened to withdraw it.

'I would object most strongly if cuts were made from the film. The Beatles want Mick and Keith in.' BRIAN EPSTEIN, *Beatles manager*

Astrid and I visited Brian at the nursing home and then went on to Olympic studios. We were there most evenings and late into the night during the middle two weeks of July. Sometimes Mick and Keith were

Popular opinion was behind the Stones.

there, other times not. It was all fairly loose. For the first time, our discipline in the studio had gone – it wasn't a surprise, given all that was happening.

Three days after checking out of the Priory on 24 July, Brian flew to Málaga to stay at a friend's villa with new girlfriend Suki Potier and Nicky, Tara Browne's widow. Just two days later, Robert Fraser's conviction was upheld by the court. It was hardly a good omen for Mick and Keith.

At 10am on July 31, Lord Chief Justice Lord Parker, Lord Justice Winn and Mr Justice Cusack entered the court. Keith had chicken pox and was forced to stay in a separate room, so only Mick stood in the dock. Michael Havers was again representing them. His defence of Keith prompted Lord Parker to say, 'It would be unsafe to allow the conviction to stand. Judge Block erred in not warning the jury there was no proper evidence other than purely tenuous evidence that the girl clad only in a rug had smoked cannabis and that Richards must have known about it.' Keith was free.

Mick, head bowed, face reddened, heard his conviction upheld but his sentence was quashed.

'If you keep out of trouble for the next 12 months, what has happened will not go on your record as a conviction. Whether you like it or not, you are an idol of a large number of the young in this country. You have grave responsibilities.' LORD PARKER

Outside the court, in the Strand, a crowd of about 300 received the news quietly, while Mick and Keith left the building by a small door leading into the judge's quadrangle and drove away. Keith flew to Rome to join Anita, where she was starring alongside Jane Fonda in *Barbarella*, directed by Roger Vadim. Mick picked up Marianne and flew from Battersea heliport to Spain's Hall near Ongar, in Essex, to record ITV's *World In Action* show. Also on the show were William Rees-Mogg, Father Thomas Corbishley, Baron Stow Hill (former Home Secretary, Sir Frank Soskice) and Dr Robinson (Bishop of Woolwich). Mick was seated outside on a garden seat and defended himself very well.

'In the public sector, to do with my work, I have responsibilities. But my personal habits are of no consequence to anyone else. Until recently, attempted suicide was a crime. Anyone who takes a drug, a very bad drug such as heroin, commits a crime against himself. I cannot see how it is a crime against society.' MICK, *World In Action*

The papers were full of their own, subjective, opinions on the judgement. The *Daily Sketch* typified one point of view: 'Mick had his three month prison sentence reduced to a conditional discharge not because the appeal judges took a tolerant line on cannabis smoking, but because he had four pep pills on him with medical approval. The *Sketch* shouldn't have to spell this out. Lord

Mick and Marianne with Desmond Guinness in Ireland

The tenth US album, entitled *Flowers*, was a hotchpotch of previously issued tracks plus three previously unreleased songs. The latter included a cover of Smokey Robinson's 'My Girl', which the Temptations had taken to the top of the US charts in January 1965.

'Mick and Keith's idea of a joke was that Brian's flower should have no leaves on the stem. Truth is, I never got it.' **BILL**

Side one
1. 'Ruby Tuesday'
2. 'Have You Seen Your Mother, Baby'
3. 'Let's Spend The Night Together'
4. 'Lady Jane'
5. 'Out Of Time'
6. 'My Girl' (Robinson/White)

Side two
1. 'Backstreet Girl'
2. 'Please Go Home'
3. 'Mother's Little Helper'
4. 'Take It Or Leave It'
5. 'Ride On Baby'
6. 'Sitting On A Fence'

Recorded
Side 1: 6 (31 Aug–2 Sept, '66)
Side 2: 5, 6 (8–10 Dec, '65)

Composers
All tracks Jagger/Richard, except where indicated

Studio
Side 1: 6 (IBC, London)
Side 2: 5,6 (RCA Studios, Hollywood)

Producer
Andrew Loog Oldham

Engineers
Dave Hassinger at RCA
Glyn Johns at IBC Studios

Title concept
Lou Adler

Photography
Guy Webster

Graphics
Tom Wilkes
The Corporate Head

Released
Saturday 15 Jul, '67
London PS 509

Highest chart position
US No 3

Parker should have done it. But he didn't.'

An article in the *Daily Telegraph* was more worrying for us: 'Findings in the High Court on Jagger will confront the American authorities with a dilemma if he seeks a visa to visit the USA in the next 12 months.' It was not something any of us had really focused on. We were more concerned with whether Mick and Keith would get sent to prison. A US immigration ban would be a disaster – it could all be over.

In August, we behaved like normal people and took holidays. Brian went to Marbella, Mick and Marianne to stay with Desmond Guinness in Ireland, while Astrid and I visited Charlie and Shirley in Lewes. Keith was in Rome with Anita. Brian had trouble paying his hotel bill at the Marbella Club; he couldn't get the $300 cabled from Klein's office. He ended up borrowing money from a Major Dawson. Even more worrying was the fact that rumours began circulating that Brian was leaving the band. Word had got out that his involvement in recording was only minimal.

'WE LOVE YOU'

Recorded
a-side 13, 21 June, 2 and
19 July, 1967
b-side 12, 13 June and
2 July, 1967
Studio
Olympic Studios, London
Producer
Andrew Loog Oldham
Recording personnel
Glyn Johns: engineer
Eddie Kramer:
second engineer
Andy Johns: tape operator
Release
UK Friday 18 August, 1967
Decca F 12654
US Saturday 2 September,
1967
London 45 905
Composers
Jagger/Richard
Highest chart position
UK No 8
US No 14 'Dandelion'
US No 50 'We Love You'
Additional personnel
Nicky Hopkins: piano

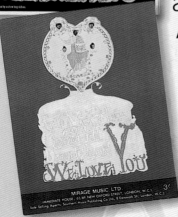

It was the unlucky 13th UK single as this double a-side only managed to make No 8. It was the band's worst showing since 'I Wanna Be Your Man' in November 1963. In America, it was their 15th single and 'Dandelion' was promoted as the lead side, but here too it was singularly unsuccessful. It was conceived of as a thank-you to fans loyal to Mick, Keith and Brian during their court appearances.

'The tape played backwards at the end of "We Love You" is the last few bars of "Dandelion" and we took the warder's footsteps from an actual prison sound effects tape.' MICK, *NME, 12 August, 1967*

'"We Love You" – well, it's funny. It's last month's message for this month! I had a piece off one of the Goons' LPs I wanted them to use for the sound of the prison gates. We seldom turn up together at the studio. "We Love You" was a case of creating the music in the studio, although Mick and Keith had had the basic idea for some time.' BILL, *NME, 12 August, 1967*

In shops next week?

THE SOUND of a prison warder's footsteps echoing down a long corridor and firmly shutting a cell door introduces "We Love You" —one side of the new Rolling Stones' single expected to be in the shops by August 18.

SESSIONS

Written by Mick Jagger and Keith Richard "We Love You" and "Dandelion" were completed by the Stones "and friends" at extra recording sessions in July inbetween Mick and Keith's court appearances. "We Love You" features all four Stones with a little help from their friends who sound at times like the Beatles.

'On 19 July, Keith arrived at London Airport from Paris at 4.30pm and was driven to Redlands and on to Olympic. We all met at the studio early in the evening. John Lennon and Paul McCartney did backing vocals on "We Love You".' **BILL**

What the papers said...

'"We Love You" is as simple as "All You Need Is Love", but the musical holocaust surrounding it is so cleverly produced, you will be able to listen to it again and find new ideas. It will need a family favourites fiasco like Humperdinck's "Release Me" to stop this making No 1.' NME, *12 August, 1967*

'When are the Stones not the Stones, children? When they are the Beatles, of course.' DISC, *19 August, 1967*

'Production-wise, "We Love You" is very complex. I wouldn't say it was Beatles-influenced at all.' JIMI HENDRIX, *DISC, 9 September, 1967*

'The Stones show signs of running out of gas. "Dandelion" and "We Love You" are excruciatingly bad. They seem to have decided to ape the Beatles, but they've run amok and found nothing.' TORONTO DAILY STAR, *9 September, 1967*

'The word "love", as we use it, means an all-embracing emotion for the rest of humanity. It should be possible to found a society on the principle of helping others. People pay you back by helping you. I would like to see more freedom. There are too many restrictions upon personal liberty.' MICK, *NME, 12 August, 1967*

Rolling Wilde
On Sunday 30 July, Peter Whitehead filmed Mick, Keith and Marianne at a church hall in Essex for a promo based on the trials of Oscar Wilde. Mick (in make up, *above*) played Oscar, Marianne wore a wig to play Wilde's friend Bosie and Keith was the Marquis of Queensberry. *Top Of The Pops* banned the film, which was shown in the US and Germany.

Trials And Tribulations

Rock journalist Keith Altham interviewed me for the *NME* in August 1967. 'Mick now feels that he is old enough to get into something new. I know that Charlie couldn't care less but, if Mick and Keith suddenly decided on something different, I suppose we would do it. Our fans have got married and turned into a record-buying public rather than one which goes to stage shows.' I certainly got that part wrong.

UNDERCURRENTS OF INTRIGUE within the band, as well as with Andrew, made it difficult to work or be creative in the studio. It was the worst possible environment to record an album. On one occasion, photographer Gered Mankowitz found the atmosphere at Olympic so tense, he couldn't get any decent pictures and just upped and left.

On 25 August, Mick and Marianne boarded the Maharishi's special train at Paddington along with the Beatles, Patti Boyd and Jane Asher. Seen off by a whole mass of press, they were going to Bangor in North Wales to attend the Maharishi's conference at a teacher training college. The rest of us were back at Olympic that evening trying to carry on, continuing the pattern in which nearly every night somebody was missing. Brian often just didn't show up for a few days. As it turned out, Mick was soon back from finding inner enlightenment: the trip to Wales had been cut short after Brian Epstein was found dead in his flat from an overdose of sleeping pills. Mick returned to discover his flat had been burgled.

Right, *Mick and Peter Asher on their way to enlightenment.*

Paul McCartney, below, chats with Mick at Euston Station prior to the departure for Bangor.

Inner light
Maharishi Mahesh Yogi impressed the Beatles and the trendy set of the mid-1960s. The fabulous foursome followed him to India and transcendental meditation caught on as a great way to relieve stress.

'It's all right leaping about the stage when you're 20 but when you get to 25 or 26 it gets a bit embarrassing.' **BILL**, *in NME, August 1967*

Checking Charlie's aftershave?

The Loog goodbye

We lost our manager too, although less dramatically. We split with Andrew, who had pretty much given up on us and, in the press, he was very positive about the break-up. We all felt that our relationship had run its course.

The band needed sound financial management (not control like Klein wielded over us), but not Andrew's creative skills. Nor did we require his limited production abilities. We had long ago learned what he knew about production and were all far more confident in the studio. It was a sign of the times that we 'artists' sought to control our own

On one of Keith's trips to Europe to see Anita, Redlands was burgled. Keith was so angry that he phoned Klein and insisted that a high wall be built around his home. It cost around £20,000 but Keith felt better as it discouraged thieves, fans and police alike from breaking in.

Despite the apparent generosity of Klein towards Keith, our company finances were dire. With monotonous regularity telexes were being sent to Ronnie Schneider in Klein's office about our lack of cash. On 7 September, one was sent by our accountant Laurence Myers.

With hindsight, there's no doubt that we should have paid more attention to our financial affairs. Charlie and Shirley finally moved to Peckhams in Halland, not far from their previous home. A few days later all of us, except Mick, met up with photographer Michael Cooper at London Airport on Wednesday 13 September. We were off to shoot the cover of our new album at Pictorial Productions in Mount Vernon, New York.

Immigration at Kennedy Airport initially refused Keith entry to America before allowing him a deferred entry. He underwent further examination at the immigration offices on Broadway the next morning. Mick, who had been in Paris with Marianne, flew in on a later flight to meet the same fate as Keith. The drug trial was the problem. They were given permission to stay until 17 September, but were told that US Immigration would study reports of their cases before deciding whether or not to allow them in again. Our worst fears were becoming a reality.

'We can all stay. The chap who gave us the visas even asked for an autograph.' MICK, *Daily Mirror, 15 September, 1967*

During our stay we met with Klein and talked about the situation with Andrew. Klein assured us that everything was going to be okay and that his control of our business affairs was well in hand. It was agreed that if we needed smaller, everyday kind of items to have the bills sent to

Photographer Michael Cooper (far right) and Brian attended one of the Maharishi's lectures.

'We split because we got to a stage of mutual boredom.' ANDREW OLDHAM

(production) destiny. Andrew said, 'They were not puppets, they were people. Whatever else is said about them, they were as close to professionalism as any five artists can get. We split because we had no need of each other anymore. As people we went in different directions. It came at a time when everybody was working out their lives.' But our next album proved we desperately needed a guiding hand.

September was just as disorganised. Going into the studio was just like going to the office, only there was no one to tell us off if we showed up late or didn't show up at all. During all the madness, I was also producing the End.

Lack of money on Rolling Stones likely to result in writs being issued against them at any moment. You have had details of monies required for weeks. Also you have had and agreed a monthly budget. These repeated delays in transferring funds result in a great deal of time wasting by Stan and myself. Also unnecessary extra costs to say nothing of bad feeling on the part of the creditors. Rolling Stones revised 1966 accounts sent to Allen Klein some weeks ago. These must be approved and submitted to the revenue in near future.

the London office. We returned home to the normal pattern of intermittent recording and doing our own thing.

Mid-way through October, the papers reported a merger between the Stones and the Beatles. It was one of the more ridiculous ideas to come out of a ridiculous period, sparked off by a casual conversation between Mick and Paul McCartney. 'At the moment we are just exchanging views to see whether we can work something out between us,' said Paul of his talks with Mick.

'A multi-million pound business merger between the Beatles and the Rolling Stones is being planned. As part of the prospective deal, both groups would be their own bosses, become joint owners of recording studios and act as a powerhouse for new talent.' NEWS OF THE WORLD, *15 October, 1967*

The day after this story broke, Andrew and Eric Easton were in the High Court. Eric was suing Andrew and seeking the appointment of a temporary receiver to look after financial aspects of their former partnership. He also sued Decca Records and Nanker Phelge Music. Andrew, the Stones and Decca Records opposed the claim.

I sentence you...
Brian's day in court was 30 October. Prince Stanislaus Klossowski de Rola (Stash) was there on a separate charge. He was quickly discharged, as the prosecution offered no evidence. Brian pleaded guilty to possessing a quantity of cannabis without authority and permitting his premises to be used for the smoking of cannabis. His denial of two charges of unlawfully possessing Methedrine and cocaine was accepted by the prosecution.

James Comyn, defending Brian, pleaded with the court not to send him to jail. He said that Brian had taken cannabis but had nothing to do with hard drugs. Walter Neustatter, a court-appointed psychiatrist, said that time spent in jail

'I hope that this will be an example to young people who attempt to try drugs.' BRIAN

'There are no plans to replace him in the Stones, if he has to serve his sentence.' *DISC, on Brian, 4 November, 1967*

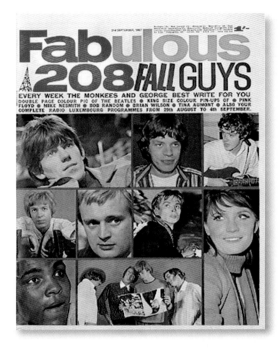

would destroy Brian. Harley Street specialist Dr Flood told the court that Brian was under his care at a nursing home for nearly three weeks in July. He told the court that Brian's attitude was that of a potential suicide. Brian was remorseful in court.

The judge jailed Brian for nine months for permitting his flat to be used for smoking cannabis. He was further sentenced to three months for possession of cannabis and and ordered to pay £265 10s costs. Brian showed no sign of emotion as he was led away from the dock and James Comyn gave notice of appeal. The chairman of the magistrates rejected his appeal for bail.

Tom Keylock went directly from the court to pick up Mick and Keith and take them to London Airport, where they met up with Glyn Johns and Ronnie Schneider. They were off to New York to mix and master our new album. While they were *en route*, about 40 people staged a protest march

All the news that fits
Rolling Stone was first published on 9 November, 1967. Bill: 'The San Francisco-based newspaper — or is it a magazine? — has devoted tens of thousands of words to covering us. In the first issue, founder Jann Wenner wrote, "We have begun a new publication reflecting what we see are the changes in rock'n'roll..." There have certainly been a few.'

against Brian's jail sentence. They walked from World's End, in the Kings Road, to Sloane Square, politely marshalled by six policemen. Scuffles broke out at Sloane Square, where two girls and six men (including Mick's brother, Chris) were arrested for abusive and insulting behaviour, obstruction and damage to a police van.

The papers were quick to nail their colours to their own mastheads. The *Daily Sketch* was fairly typical of the anti-drugs-but-too-harsh-a-sentence camp. 'The sentence on Brian is too severe. It's a few months too many. Don't get the *Sketch* wrong. We are not joining the legalise-cannabis brigade. Far from it. We do not consider smoking cannabis to be as harmless a pastime as drinking a pint of beer.'

At the High Court later that morning, Brian's QC asked judge Mr Justice Donaldson to grant bail, pending an appeal against Brian's sentence. The two psychiatrists repeated their trial evidence. Having spent the previous 24 hours in jail, Brian was freed on bail from Wormwood Scrubs at 7pm. The whole question of Brian's drug case was another spanner in our works. America could be out of bounds to Brian even if he was not jailed. He had pleaded guilty and this was probably enough for US Immigration to deny him a visa.

'Mick and Keith are having talks with Allen Klein in New York. News of Brian's case was phoned to them.' DISC, *4 November, 1967*

Court out
The court case with Eric Easton reached temporary resolution in early November when Mr Justice Buckley ordered a freeze on our American earnings until a partnership agreement has been decided between Andrew and Eric. He banned Andrew from making any attempt to get hold of American earnings. He also accepted undertakings from Decca to freeze earnings in Britain by suspending payments of

Chris Jagger

royalties. The judge said that Andrew could have behaved with a great deal more frankness, and refused him any costs. It had the hallmarks of something that would run and run.

Astrid and I flew to New York for a break on 13 November and then on to Bermuda to stay with my brother Paul, who had moved there. While in Manhattan we shopped and had a meal at Allen Klein's New Jersey home. Dinner was a struggle and the only thing of real interest to come out of it was I learned that my song, 'In Another Land', was to be released as a single. 'It's the only love song on *Satanic Majesties*,' said Klein.

The story of our joining forces with the Beatles rumbled on into late November when *Fabulous* magazine ran a story about a recording studio that we were to jointly own and manage. 'Mick Jagger's brother Chris, 19, has been given the plum job of running the super-studio. If the project materialises, the studio is expected to be the world's No 1 showpiece for recording techniques and the development of new talent.' It went on to say that Paul McCartney had approved plans to buy the old Majestic Theatre in Clapham Common, South London because it was within easy reach of Surrey, where George Harrison, Ringo Starr and John Lennon lived. It was so typical of the period — a pipe dream — which is easy to say with the benefit of hindsight, but I did think it at the time. I had just turned 31 and felt much older than Brian, Mick and Keith.

While we were in Bermuda, 'In Another Land' became our 16th American single. A week later our new album came out in Britain and America.

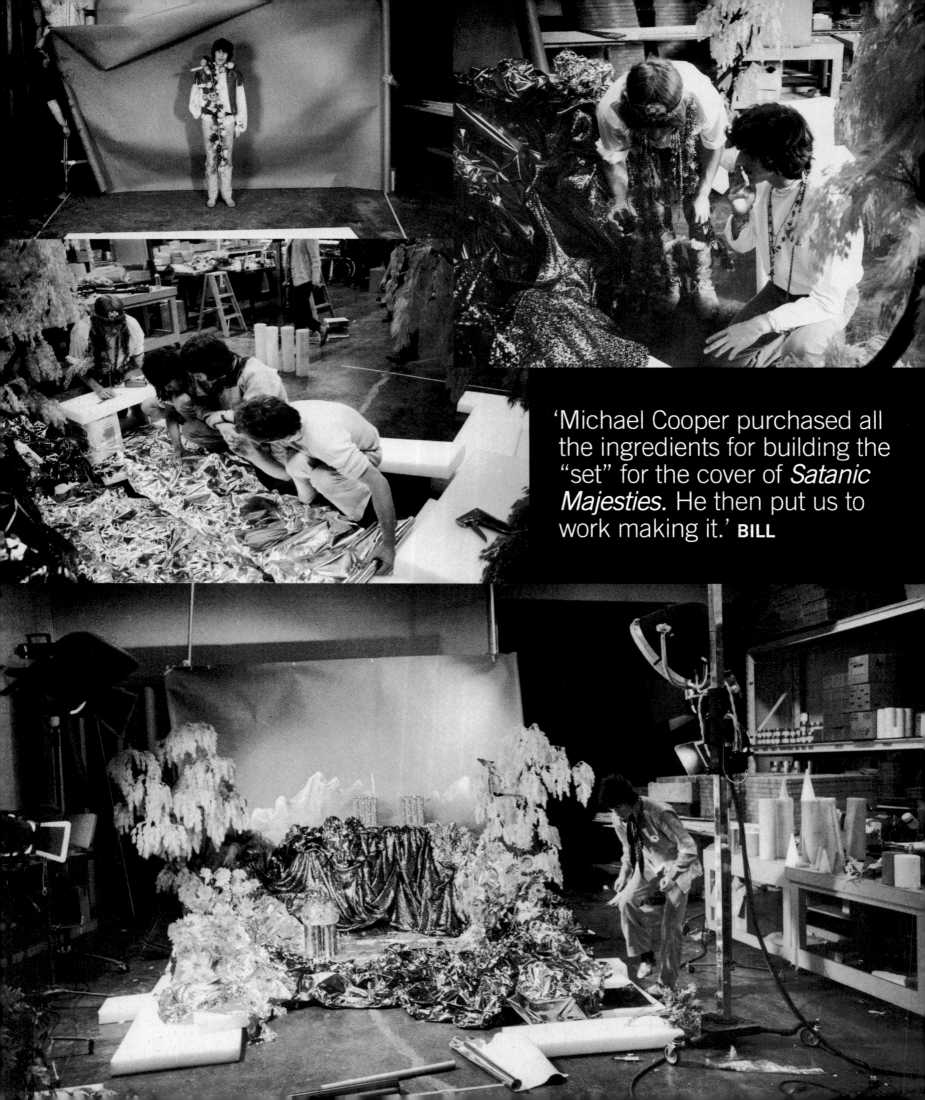

'Michael Cooper purchased all the ingredients for building the "set" for the cover of *Satanic Majesties*. He then put us to work making it.' **BILL**

Side one
1. 'Sing This All Together'
2. 'Citadel'
3. 'In Another Land' (Wyman)
4. '2000 Man'
5. 'Sing This All Together (See What Happens)'

Side two
1. 'She's A Rainbow'
2. 'The Lantern'
3. 'Gomper'
4. '2000 Light Years From' 'Home'
5. 'On With The Show'

Recorded
February, May–October, 1967

Composers
All songs Jagger/Richard, except where indicated

Studio
Olympic Studios, London

Producer
The Rolling Stones

Recording personnel
Glyn Johns: engineer
Eddie Kramer: second engineer

Design
Michael Cooper

Artwork
Michael Cooper (front photograph)
Tony Meeviwiffen (back illustration)

Release
UK Friday 8 December, 1967 Decca TXS 103
US Saturday 9 December, 1967 London NPS 2

Highest chart position (time on chart)
UK No 3 (13 weeks)
US No 2 (13 weeks)

Additional personnel
Steve Marriott: vocals 'In Another Land'
John Paul Jones: string arrangements 'She's A Rainbow'
Nicky Hopkins: piano '2000 Light Years From Home'

Her Britannic Majesty's Secretary of State Requests and requires . . .

The words on the inside of a British passport, if not the sentiment, were the inspiration for the title of the band's seventh UK and 11th US album. It was also the first album to receive simultaneous release on both sides of the Atlantic.

'It's just another album. It's different from the others we've done and it's different from the next we will do. But it's still just an album. The work on this album is not a landmark or a milestone or anything pretentious like that. All we have tried to do is make an album we like, with some sounds that haven't been done before.' MICK, *Melody Maker,* 9 December, 1967

Their Santa-nic majesties
The album was originally to be called *Cosmic Christmas*. The Stones even cut a track called 'We Wish You A Cosmic Joke'.

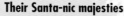

'It might best be described as a kind of show, a voyage into the beyond, an abstract musical experience to capture the new dimension in music the Stones and Decca Records have come up with. Featuring one of the most inventive album covers ever produced, this is the first time 3D photo prints have been used in which the figures move. Artist-photographer Michael Cooper designed the Beatles' Sgt Pepper sleeve. He and the Stones staged the cover photograph. The 3D and cover art cost ran in excess of $25,000.' LESLIE PERRIN, *Decca press release, December 1967*

'Mick Jagger arrived at the studios when they were working on Their Satanic Majesties *and said he wanted a load of unusual sounds that had never been done before. I had a nosh and finally thought of something using echo. I plugged it all in and finally got it to work. I got Mick to listen and he said, "Great, half-a-dozen more like that and we're okay."'* GLYN JOHNS, *Melody Maker, 29 June, 1968*

'Doubtless there is some innocent explanation for Mick saying, "Where's that joint?" at the beginning of "Sing This Song All Together".' RECORD MIRROR, *December 1967*

'There was absolutely no idea behind Satanic Majesties. *No, it's wrong to say there is or was no idea at all, there was, but it was all completely external. It was done over such a long period of time that eventually it just evolved. It took almost a whole year to make, not because it's so fantastically complex that we needed a whole year, but because we were so strung out. Plus, we didn't know if we had a producer or not. Sometimes Andrew would turn up, sometimes he wouldn't. We never knew if we would be in jail or not. Keith and I never sat down and played the songs to each other. We just made that album for what it is. I was happy when it was finished. I breathed a sigh of relief because we finally completed it.'* MICK, *Rolling Stone magazine, October 1968*

'Sometimes I think it was a miracle we produced anything under the pressures and emotional upheavals within the group. We had to find a switch of direction. The era which bred the Liverpool boom in pop music was over. More than ever before it meant you must stand or fall by your product.' CHARLIE, *Rave magazine, February 1969*

'Their Satanic Majesties Request could and should do for the Stones what *Sgt Pepper* did for the Beatles.' **RECORD MIRROR,** *December 1967*

'The only time Brian looked like coming into his own, was when they did that awful Satanic Majesties, where he got the chance to dabble with the mellotron. It was a terrible shame. He'd do anything. He would turn up at the studio with saxophones and he even played harp on a number. There was one in the back of the studio for an orchestral session. He sat down and fiddled with it, and got something out of it fairly easily. The talent and ability were there, but he just screwed himself up.' STU

'Satanic Majesties *is a bad idea gone wrong. The idea of making a truly druggy answer to the cherubic joyousness of the Beatles'* Sgt Pepper *was silly enough. Doing so by fuzzing up some pretty good songs with tape loops and early synthesizer experiments is thoroughly unforgivable. Only "2000 Man", "In Another Land" and "She's A Rainbow" redeem this one.'* THE ROLLING STONE RECORD GUIDE

'What is so obviously and desperately needed to turn the whole thing into good Stones is the instrumental and vocal style that has made the Stones so potent in the past.' JON LANDAU, *music writer, February 1968*

'The making of this album was THE rock'n'roll circus, well before we had the idea of a real one. Every day at the studio it was a lottery as to who would turn up and what – if any – positive contribution they would make when they did. Keith would arrive with anything up to 10 people, Brian with another half-a-dozen and it was the same for Mick. They were assorted girlfriends and friends. I hated it! Then again, so did Andrew and he just gave up on it. There were times when I wish I could have done, too.' BILL

The naming of songs

On Friday 15 September, acetates of possible masters were cut for each of the band. The tracks were (with final titles in brackets): 'Aftermath' ('2000 Light Years From Home'), 'God Bless You' ('Sing This All Together'), 'After Five' ('Citadel'), 'Pieces', 'Flowers' ('She's A Rainbow'), 'Flowers In Your Hair' ('Gomper'), 'No Title', 'Dream Pipe', 'Flying High' ('The Lantern'), 'Bill's Tune' ('In Another Land') and 'Surprise Me'.

'On 13 and 14 September we went to a studio at Pictorial Productions, Mount Vernon, New York, with Michael Cooper, where he explained his ideas for a 3D photo. We helped to prepare the studio set until late, then returned to the hotel.' BILL

'IN ANOTHER LAND'

In Another Land
Bill Wyman
The Lantern (The Rolling Stones)

Recorded
a-side 13 July, 1967
b-side February, May–
October 1967
Studio
Olympic Studios, London
Producer
a-side Bill Wyman
b-side The Rolling Stones
Engineer
Glyn Johns
Release
US Saturday 2 December,
1967
London 45 907
Composer
a-side Bill Wyman
b-side Jagger/Richard
Highest chart position
US No 87

In the same week as the album was released, *In Another Land* came out. The logic behind releasing this as a Bill Wyman solo single has never been fully understood. Allen Klein's assertion that it was 'a love song' probably says more about his musical insight than anything else.

'In early July, I sat at home playing the Thomas organ and wrote "In Another Land", which was a bit spacey, but interesting. I made a demo on my home tape recorder. On 13 July, nobody but Charlie, Nicky Hopkins and I turned up at the studio. We were thinking of leaving when Glyn said, "Do you have a song we can do?" I sat at the piano and played "In Another Land" and they all liked it. We put a basic track together and got a good master on tape. I was worried when it came to adding vocals. In the end, I suggested tremolo on my voice. The Small Faces were recording next door and Glyn asked Steve Marriott to come in and help. We sang it together and it turned out good. The track was given the working title "Acid In The Grass".' BILL

'Wyman goes solo in this off-beat piece of rock ballad material that should prove a monster. It's a weirdy that can't miss.' BILLBOARD, *2 December, 1967*

'SHE'S A RAINBOW'

She's A Rainbow
The Rolling Stones
2000 Light Years From Home

Recorded
February, May–
October 1967
Studio
Olympic Studios, London
Producer
The Rolling Stones
Engineer
Glyn Johns
Release
US Saturday 23 December,
1967
London 45.906
Composers
Jagger/Richard
Highest chart position
US No 25

No UK singles were released from *Satanic Majesties*, but 'She's A Rainbow' became the 17th US single of the Stones' career.

On Tuesday 19 December, Stu collected Keith's Mellotron from the band's warehouse and took it to the BBC Television Centre for the Stones to use for their appearance on *Top Of The Pops* the next day. The show aired on 21 December and featured both 'She's A Rainbow' and '2000 Light Years From Home' as promotion for the album.

'In February we cut "Loose Woman", which was an early version of "2000 Light Years From Home".' BILL

Set of lead figures from Bill's collection

A Miller's Tale

WORLD VOCAL GROUP

1 BEATLES	8234
2 Beach Boys	5648
3 Monkees	4297
4 Rolling Stones	1626
5 Bee Gees	1508
6 Jordanaires	1367
7 Four Tops	1100
8 Diana Ross/Supremes	965
9 Shadows	

On the weekend that Satanic Majesties came out, the NME poll had us at number four on the World's Best Group list. It was a sign of the times, a sign that times were anything but good for us. The album did make US No 2, but this had more to do with the fact that it hit the Christmas market than anything else. We knew in our hearts that we had failed to deliver and we would need to do a lot better next time. At least there was Christmas to look forward to – Astrid and I had decided to go to Sweden.

The boys send a heartfelt thanks to their fans.

BEFORE WE COULD ALL relax, there was the small matter of Brian's appeal. He drove around Cornwall and Devon, staying in Penzance and Dartmouth, in the run-up to his appearance. Friends had dinner with him at the Tandoori restaurant in Chelsea the night before the hearing. It must have been a difficult evening, as Brian was scared stiff of going to prison. He knew it was a likely outcome with bad implications for him and the band.

On Tuesday 12 December, Brian sat before Lord Chief Justice Parker and two other Law Lords. According to medical testimony, the prison sentence had affected him so deeply that he was potentially suicidal. Brian was given three years probation, with the condition that he should receive treatment. He was also ordered to pay the maximum fine of £1,000.

'We are all pleased he is free. All we want to do now is put it behind us and get down to some hard work.' ROLLING STONES SPOKESMAN, *NME, 16 December, 1967*

'I will not treat him as a celebrity. To me, Brian is the same as any other offender who has been placed on probation.' WILLIAM HORNUNG, *probation officer*

Having won his appeal the question remained, would US Immigration allow Brian into America? More immediately, by way of celebration, Brian had dark windows and an eight-track stereo tape recorder fitted into his Rolls Royce. Any celebrations were short-lived: the next day, Brian's new chauffeur, John Coray, found him collapsed at his rented flat in Chesham Street, Chelsea. John rushed him to St George's Hospital, where he spent about an hour in the casualty department. He refused to stay longer, despite the doctor's protestations that he should spend the night under observation.

'I was feeling terribly exhausted and fainted. I'm much better now and that is why I didn't stay in hospital.' BRIAN, *Daily Mirror, 15 December, 1967*

Brian went to the Priory for a check up and was advised to go on holiday. After we made an appearance on *Top Of The Pops*, Brian and Linda and Keith flew to Colombo, Ceylon (now Sri Lanka) to stay with Stash. Astrid and I flew to Sweden. Keith, who had just celebrated his 24th birthday, went to Tangier and then Marrakesh with Anita. Charlie and Shirley were at their new home in Sussex. Mick and Marianne flew to the Bahamas. We were all away over the festive season, with our thoughts that New Year's Eve very much on the previous year. While everyone else seemed to be in a state of permanent euphoria, we were in a constant state of flux. We all thought 1968 would be better... but would it?

'Five boys who have made personal fortunes, who have tasted adulation and fame. The changes are there for their friends to see. But whatever they do, or are, millions will regard them as being musical outsiders, unable to join the Beatles on that very special plane of mass acceptance.' BEAT INSTRUMENTAL MAGAZINE, *January 1968*

Beat Instrumental's take on our musical acceptability was not far out, as *Satanic Majesties* made us keenly aware. We needed someone to

Mr Jimmy

Jimmy Miller was born in New York in 1942. His father, Bill Miller, was a theatrical impresario who wanted Jimmy to become a lawyer. The lure of music was too strong and Jimmy sang and recorded as a member of the Anglos, who recorded 'Incense' in 1965. Chris Blackwell of Island Records invited Jimmy to produce the Spencer Davis Group in England. Jimmy went on to work with Traffic and Spooky Tooth. He co-wrote 'I'm A Man' with Stevie Winwood, which the Spencer Davis Group took into the Top 10 in the UK and US. Jimmy died aged 52 in October 1994.

produce and guide us and Jimmy Miller was being talked about as the man for the job.

'We chose Jimmy because, unlike so many other record producers, he does not have an ego problem. He will do what we want and not just what he wants.' MICK, *Rave magazine, February 1969*

Debt relief

Amid our musical uncertainties, Brian was more concerned about how he was going to pay his solicitor's bill of £8,667 (about eight times the average annual income in 1968). Mick was busy house-hunting. He visited Stargroves twice in January and also joined the Country Gentleman's Association, probably in anticipation of the move to a rural location. He also took possession of a flat in London's Chester Square. A few weeks later our office, run by Jo Bergman, moved to Maddox Street, W1.

In early February, a story appeared in the *Toronto Telegram* headed 'It's High Time The Stones Acknowledged This Debt', under which

'All Along The Watchtower'

On Sunday 21 January, 1968, Brian was at Olympic Studios where Jimi Hendrix was recording Bob Dylan's 'All Along The Watchtower'. Dave Mason, who was having a sabbatical from Traffic, and Jimi played acoustic guitars, while Brian (who played piano on an early take) switched to percussion. Bassist Noel Redding left the session and Jimi played a small Framus bass that Bill had given to assistant engineer Andy Johns.

'The story that Otis originally wrote "Satisfaction" is completely false. We took the Rolling Stones record and then cut our version of what we thought we heard.'
STEVE CROPPER, *guitarist, Booker T and the MGs, Rolling Stone magazine*

was written, 'It is now almost two months since Otis Redding was killed in that tragic plane crash. They've had plenty of time and many opportunities to make a confession but they've remained stubbornly and disgustingly silent… They did *not* write "Satisfaction", nor did they even record it first. "Satisfaction" was written by Otis Redding who sold it to Mick for a measly $10,000. The Stones were visiting Memphis and heard Otis cutting the song. They begged him to sell it to them.' This story was total crap. The first time we visited Memphis was on 17 November, 1965, six months after we recorded 'Satisfaction'.

This was one of the more bizarre stories about us. I'm not saying we didn't encourage them and sometimes we made things up at interviews, but the 'Satisfaction' story went a bit far. A few weeks after this story ran, *NME*'s Keith Altham came to a rehearsal at RG Jones in Morden. Mick duped Altham, telling him I was in hospital with a broken knee and we would begin a world tour as soon as I recovered. I had felt unwell early in February, when I had an anxiety attack and my local doctor came to the house to examine me. The sleeping pill he gave me freaked me out and I paced the floor until it wore off. Drugs of almost any sort have never really been my scene. During that rehearsal, I was feeling unwell again and went to see a specialist. It turned out that my problems lay in my anxiety about Stephen. I was missing him very badly.

We rehearsed and recorded with Jimmy Miller off and on for much of early March, Brian only showing up some of the time. On Tuesday 12 March, I was messing around on the electronic keyboard playing a great riff I'd found. As Charlie,

Session pianist Nicky Hopkins

Brian and I were jamming, Mick and Keith walked in and said, 'Keep playing that, it sounds great, and don't forget it.' And we didn't forget. It was to become our next single – 'Jumpin' Jack Flash'.

'The idea was exactly the same as I had for Traffic when they hid themselves away from the world for three months in the country cottage before they emerged as a group. I wanted to be in sympathy with what the group were doing. Most of all I wanted the Stones to be themselves, not my idea of what they should be. It also had the very practical reason that you waste less time when you get in the recording studio.'
JIMMY MILLER, *Rave magazine, February 1969*

Keith recorded some song ideas onto his new Philips cassette recorder in the middle of March and played us one of the demos in the studio. We

'Keep playing that, it sounds great – don't forget it.' **MICK,** *to Bill, on 'Jumpin' Jack Flash'*

ON SALE FROM
8th MARCH 1968

All records on this folder will be
played on RADIO LUXEMBOURG
from TUES. MARCH 5th — for full
details see RELEASE SHEETS.

Introducing...

THE END

produced by
Bill Wyman

MALCOLM ROBERTS
—
THE ROYAL GUARDS MEN

Bill's outside interest – the End

couldn't get the same feeling that Keith had on his demo. Charlie had an antique box (made for a street vendor) that contained a tiny snare and small cymbal. He sat on the floor playing his miniature kit while Keith played acoustic guitar, which sounded great. Keith's cassette recorder, with its small microphone, was used to record their playing. We were all knocked out by the crude homemade sound, so it was transferred direct onto the four-track to add overdubs. Known then as 'Primo Grande', the song became 'Street Fighting Man'.

Charlie's girl

The following night, as we continued working on the song, Shirley Watts went into labour at a nursing home in Hove. She gave birth to her and Charlie's only child, Seraphina, on 18 March. Mick finally purchased Stargroves and immediately embarked upon extensive and costly renovations, as the whole place was in very bad shape. Maggie Phillips, who worked in our office, found a London residence for him – 48 Cheyne Walk in Chelsea – which Mick bought for £50,000. Still feeling unwell, I went for further check-ups with the doctor, who confirmed that there was nothing physically wrong with me. When I wasn't working on a Stones session in late March and April, I was often at Decca's West Hampstead studio cutting more songs with the End, along with engineer Gus Dudgeon. A single I co-wrote for them came out on Decca in early March. 'Shades Of Orange' had very favourable reviews but sank without trace. I was disappointed, as I felt it was a good song and the band had done a great job with it.

Business affairs were very much on all of our minds, things remained unclear. At the beginning of April, solicitor Michael Oliver wrote to Klein to seek clarification on a number of issues. Much of the letter concerned our earnings from tours, recording and publishing and how it had been paid to us. Mick was also trying to get us a little more organised. He asked Jo Bergman to write to us all and outline the plans for the rest of the year. There was more recording pencilled in and also talk of a US tour in the last quarter of the year. The only problem with that, as far as I could see, was a potential US Immigration ban.

On Saturday 20 April, Michael Lindsay-Hogg (former director of *Ready Steady Go!*) and four camera crews were at Olympic Studios to film us. We had our faces painted and mimed to 'Jumpin' Jack Flash'. The following weekend we went into the countryside for more filming, including us miming to 'Child Of The Moon'. Later we drove back to Olympic Studios for drinks, where we were again filmed playing 'Jumpin' Jack Flash'.

In early May, we had some time off to do our own things. Brian put in a bid to buy Nansladron Farm in Cornwall, complete with its livestock. By 9 May, we were back in Olympic working on more tracks for the new album. We played the *NME* Poll Winners' concert on 12 May, 1968, our first gig in what seemed like forever.

HAIR

Long, straight, curly, fuzzy, snaggy, shaggy, ratty, matty...

The stage musical *Hair* became a huge hit with its pounding soundtrack, rebellious lyrics and good-looking cast – *Hair* had everything. Except a plot. Its Broadway run began on 29 April, 1968 and the bold sexuality – upfront and, briefly, full-frontal – predictably outraged the Establishment. It's a tame night out by modern standards, though 'Age Of Aquarius' is an enduringly popular evocation of hippy idealism, albeit a sanitised version to satisfy theatre-goers.

'JUMPIN' JACK FLASH'

Jumpin' Jack Flash
The Rolling Stones
Child of The Moon

The second in the 'remarkable riff' series of singles that has become the Stones' trademark over the years was originally conceived by Bill sitting at a keyboard in R. G. Jones' studio on 12 March, 1968. It was honed to perfection over several sessions in March and early April at Olympic Studios. The band's 14th UK and 18th US single was made under the guidance of new producer Jimmy Miller.

I t was one of the most important records of their career, possibly the most important. Had they not come up with the goods at this moment, the drift downwards might well have continued. Keith's guitar was tuned to an open E, lending a fantastic ringing quality to his playing. It really cuts through on the radio. It was also a "single only" release and didn't feature on a regular Stones album.

'Being a drummer, I was very rhythm-minded.'
JIMMY MILLER, *producer, 1979*

Recorded
12 and 29 March,
11 and 20 April, 1968
Studio
Olympic Studios, London
Producer
Jimmy Miller
Engineer
Eddie Kramer
Mixing
George Chkiantz
Glyn Johns
Release
UK Friday 24 May, 1968
Decca F 12782
US Saturday 1 June, 1968
London 45 908
Composers
Jagger/Richard
Highest chart position
UK No 1, for two weeks
US No 3

'After waiting two weeks to see the Stones at UK No 1 on Top Of The Pops, what do we get but the Go Jos [dance troupe] prancing about and the Stones' faces superimposed on them a few times. On phoning the BBC to ask why they were not on, I was told they were only there to play the records and they didn't know what I was complaining about because they showed their faces.' LINDA PHILLIPS, *in a letter to Record Mirror, 6 July, 1968*

Ironically, given Bill's involvement in the song's creation, it was Keith who played the bass. Bill played organ, Brian guitar and Jimmy Miller sang backing vocals with Mick and Keith.

'You shouldn't worry, it's doing fine. I hear it about once an hour [in LA] on both KRLA and KHJ. The Stones' magic is still tangible, but an appearance here wouldn't hurt. Any chance of that, or has Brian's bust postponed that indefinitely?' JUDY SIMS, *Teenset magazine, 3 June, 1968, in a letter to the Stones London office*

What the papers said
On 21 May, 1968, the *Daily Sketch* said, 'The Stones have taken a step back. Their new single takes them back to the era of "Satisfaction" nearly three years ago. Welcome back.'

Melody Maker concurred: 'An important release for the Stones which will prove one way or the other whether they are still a major chart force. My guess is they've got a No 1 with the most commercial Stones single in a long, long time.'

The *NME* said: 'It's vintage Stones. The Stones have a unique flair for taking a basically simple formula and turning it into a miniature epic.' The *Daily Express* on 11 May was even more direct: 'The Stones are back at work.'

'This raucous single with its driving rhythm in strong support should fast top the sales of "She's A Rainbow",' said *Billboard* on 1 June, 'and put them right back at the top of the Hot 100.'

Déjà Vu

We badly needed a hit record. It had been nearly 18 months since we had a US or UK Top 3 single. Our reputation was now based on anything but the music. It was not to be a smooth ride. Trouble was looming once again and it had Brian firmly in its sights.

W**E ALL MET AT MICK'S** flat before being driven to Wembley for our surprise appearance at the *NME* Poll Winners' concert on 12 May. The bill included Status Quo, Don Partridge, Love Affair, the Association, Lulu, the Shadows, Cliff Richard, Amen Corner, the Herd, the Move, Dusty Springfield and Scott Walker. Compere Jimmy Saville kept hinting at a big surprise and when he announced us, the crowd went crazy; we played 'Jumpin' Jack Flash' followed by 'Satisfaction'.

'The Stones came rolling back into the limelight and thousands of teenage fans screamed a welcome. For a moment the 10,000 fans were silent in amazement. Then they went wild as the group started to play. Some leapt on their seats, screaming. Others showered the group with tulips. At one point, Mick threw his shoes into the audience during a frantic dance.' DAILY MIRROR, *13 May, 1968*

Wembley, 12 May, 1968

'Mick is probably the greatest performer to have emerged from the pop world. Erotic, mercurial, destructive, narcissistic, violent – as he rubbed his naked stomach during last Sunday's concert at the Empire Pool, Wembley, any doubts about his pre-eminence were swept away in an orgasm of shouts and cries.' TONY PALMER, *Observer, 19 May, 1968*

It certainly felt like we were back.

Ten days before 'Jumpin' Jack Flash' hit the shops, Leslie Perrin made an announcement: 'The Rolling Stones invite you to meet them at 46a Maddox St, London W1, on 15 May at 3.30pm. We have arranged this magazine and periodical conference to afford you the opportunity of interviewing them.' It made us seem like celebrities and our confidence started to return.

A Byrd in the car

Some days later, Mick hired a limousine to take the Byrds, who were playing UK concerts, to see Stonehenge. The following day, we had a board meeting at which Michael Oliver was appointed to be our new solicitor. We all went for lunch together, something we hadn't done in a long while. We then met up with girlfriends and wives to see *2001 – A Space Odyssey* and were totally knocked out by the film.

We spent the next few days at Olympic. The new album was beginning to take shape and it sounded great. But, as is so often in life, just when you think it's safe to get back in the water, the sharks appear. Not surprisingly, it was Brian they were after.

On the night of 20 May, Brian took a sleeping pill. At 7.30am the next morning, four officers from Chelsea police station arrived at his flat. A constable knocked on the door and rang the bell, while shouting through the letterbox. As Brian didn't answer, a policeman climbed into the flat

through a refuse hatch and let the other three in. They found Brian sitting on the floor, dialling a number on his bedroom telephone. Told they had a search warrant, Brian replied, 'I was first going to telephone for my solicitor.'

'I've been knocking on the door for about 10 minutes. Why didn't you open the door?' asked the constable.

'You know the scene, man. Why do I always get bugged?' was all that Brian could reply.

They searched the bedroom, the smaller bedroom and the kitchen, but found nothing. In a bureau in the lounge, they discovered a ball of blue wool in a drawer. The policeman pulled the wool apart to reveal a piece of brown substance inside. 'Oh, no,' said Brian, 'This can't happen again, just when we're getting on our feet.' When asked if the wool was his, he replied, 'It could be.' The police then cautioned Brian.

'Why do you always have to pick on me?' BRIAN

lounge. Brian explained, 'The phial was prescribed to me some time ago and the jar was left by someone after a party the other night.'

Brian dressed and was taken to to the station where he was formally charged. Shortly before 10am, Brian, pale and unshaven, arrived at Marlborough Street Magistrates Court wearing a dark grey, striped jacket over an open-necked psychedelic shirt, red trousers, and fawn boots. He was charged with possessing a quantity of cannabis under the Dangerous Drugs Act. Mr Nicholls, defending, said, 'Jones has a complete answer to this, which will be disclosed in due course.' Brian was remanded on £1,000 bail and on a surety of a similar amount given by Fred Trowbridge, our book-keeper, until 11 June.

The fact that the police had secured a warrant with no evidence showed the arrest was part of a carefully orchestrated plan. Brian and the Stones were being targeted in an effort to deter the public from taking drugs. We knew this was going on and it did little for our morale, even for Charlie and me who were clean.

Brian took his instruments and clothes from the flat to Redlands in a chauffeur-driven car to stay with Keith. Mick joined them later. The two really did sympathise with Brian's plight and were all too aware that they could be next.

Constable: 'Well, this officer, as you have seen, has found it in this drawer with this piece of brown substance inside. Does it belong to you?'

Brian shrugged his shoulders and made no reply.

Constable: 'When Prentice [another police officer] showed me the wool, you seemed to immediately recognise it.'

Brian: 'Why do you always have to pick on me? I've been working all day and night promoting our new record and now this has to happen.'

Constable: 'Is this your flat?'

Brian: 'No. I've just been staying here for about two weeks, while the place I have bought is being decorated.'

Constable: 'I am arresting you and you will be taken to Chelsea police station where you will be charged with possessing cannabis.'

Brian: 'I never take the stuff. It makes me so paranoid.'

The police also found a used phial in a toilet bag and a jar filled with coloured material in the

You need hands...
It's somewhat spooky, or perhaps trippy, to discover there are 11 hands in this publicity photograph, *below*, shot by Michael Cooper. Who supplied the extra, manicured hand — was it he, or was it she? Nobody knows...

Shoot The Beggars

We were being filmed in the studio while recording our latest album. When we finished we took some time off, a welcome break from everything.

AROUND OF INTERVIEWS coincided with the release of our new single. Mick did the majority. He told *Melody Maker* that he hoped the, as yet unnamed, album would be out on 26 July, his birthday. He later told *Disc* that we would like to play live again but we wouldn't be going back to the old routine of travelling around the country doing shows night after night.

We also did interview tapes for 35 US radio stations, knowing that we needed to pull out the promotional stops. With the bust hanging over Brian there was obviously a question mark hanging over our immigration status. We recorded off and on through the end of May, with Brian commuting from Redlands. In nearby West Wittering, Brian frequented the New Roman Way Club. He was trying hard to stay off drugs, but his intake of booze was increasing dramatically. One night at the club, he bought a

bottle of brandy, three bottles of Liebfraumilch, three bottles of Beaujolais and 100 Benson and Hedges cigarettes (not that he consumed them all). He was also drinking vodka and whisky in large quantities.

Christopher Gibbs, who was decorating Mick's new Chelsea home that May, suggested we name our upcoming album *Beggars Banquet*. This inspired an idea for a cover shot, which was arranged for early June. Even by our standards, it was over-the-top stuff. We rented Sarum Chase, a house at 23 West Heath Road, Hampstead. The

room was decorated in medieval style, complete with a huge banquet table. For good measure, a suckling pig was placed on the table. The photograph was used on the inner sleeve of *Beggars Banquet*.

On 5 June, French director Jean-

The new wave director
One of the most famous names in French cinema, Jean-Luc Godard, was born in 1930. He revolutionised film-making as a leading figure in the French new wave. His seminal work was *A Bout de Souffle* (*Breathless*), released in 1960. It was a loose, fragmented approach to storytelling which shook the Establishment.

'I do not see the difference between documentary and fantasy.' JEAN-LUC GODARD

Country house retreat
The Stones drove up the M1 to a place called Swarkestone, near Derby, on 8 June. Keith and Tom Keylock were travelling in the Bentley at speeds of 90-120mph, trying to lose Astrid and me in the Mercedes (not that they managed it). At Balcony Field, there was a 17th-century ruin where we posed in a variety of clothes. After we finished the band drove back to London for a recording session at Olympic.

Luc Godard began filming us in the studio for his film *One Plus One*. We were working on 'The Devil Is My Name' (later 'Sympathy For The Devil'). We signed a contract which said that the film would go ahead even if Brian was imprisoned following his trial. We needed to be pragmatic about our future.

We recorded over a few nights. On 10 June, around 4.15am, the heat of the film crew's arc lamps set fire to the studio ceiling. Everyone was rushing around trying to put it out, while Jimmy Miller and I ran to save master tapes and put them in his car. Fortunately, the fire brigade soon had the situation under control and the sessions did not become the great lost Stones album.

Brian was back to court in the morning, with our talisman, Michael Havers, QC, as defending counsel. Brian made an eight-minute appearance and elected to go for a jury trial at the court of Inner London Sessions. He had no travel restrictions and flew with Suki Potier to Málaga in Spain. The trial was put off until 26 September, allowing Brian more time to worry and to take stock

of what this all meant for his future, both with the band and as an individual.

On 22 June, I was at Olympic working on some mixing with the End when Jimmy Page came into the studio. He played me three or four tracks he'd done with the Yardbirds. They sounded so powerful – a completely new style for them. He revealed the Yardbirds were going to split up and he was going to form a new group and use those tracks. Led Zeppelin was the band, to be managed by Peter Grant, the stage manager on the Everly Brothers package tour.

Stephen returns

We finished the month pretty much as we began, in the studio working on the new album. Stephen flew from Durban for a holiday with Astrid and me. He was very thin and looked unwell. He told me he'd had really bad toothache for some time, but that his mother had said he would have to wait until he came to England for treatment. The dentist took out four teeth and filled several others. Over the course of the month that Stephen was with us, I resolved to keep him in England and fight Diane for his custody.

Brian and Suki Potier went to Tangier and stayed at the El Minzah Hotel on 4 July. Two days later, Mick, Marianne and Jimmy Miller flew to Los Angeles to join Glyn Johns, who was mixing *Beggars Banquet*. Charlie and Shirley joined them three days later. On 20 July, Keith, Anita, Michael Cooper and Gram Parsons joined the party. Parsons had got to know Keith in London while being a member of the Byrds. He had, in fact, defected from the Byrds while in London as he did not want to tour South Africa with the band, some say at the urging of Mick and Keith. He was to become a satellite of the Rolling Stones, and Keith in particular, over the next few years.

Gram, Mick, Keith, Anita and Michael Cooper went to Joshua Tree National Park in the California Desert where, according to Marianne, they all took mescaline. It was a few days after this that photographer Barry Feinstein was asked by Mick and Keith to photograph a lavatory wall they had found in Los Angeles for the cover of *Beggars Banquet*. The idea was controversial and totally freaked out our record company.

Above, *the Joshua Tree National Park, where Keith, above right and right, and Gram Parsons were said to have taken mescaline together.*

Taste And Wealth

While everyone was away, I was busy house-hunting. I decided Keston was not for me and I looked at a number of properties, including one in Suffolk. We were also having ongoing problems with Klein over money.

THINGS WERE STAGGERING FROM bad to worse on the financial front. The telexes flying across the Atlantic to Klein's office were getting ever more desperate. In one, accountant Fred Trowbridge informed Ronnie Schneider that our travel agent was threatening court action unless £1,406 was paid.

In another, of 19 July, Fred outlined the problems in simple language:

'We have made numerous attempts to contact you on the telephone. We are making a further attempt between 10.15am and 11am (your time). The position has now reached crisis point. I need money now. As follows: Overdraft (now): £3,180 17s 9d. Creditors: £7,284 8s 0d. Less paid £277. Total: £7,007 8s 10d. Plus new Les Perrin's bill, £157 10s 0d. Total £7,164 18s 10d. Plus monthly quota £2,610. Total: £12,955 16s 7d. Yes, Allen, I need £12,955 16s 7d, now. Please await.'

to America? 'Yeah, well, we can and we do want to. I think we should do something more. We're working on a new kind of show.' When asked whether we would be back to tour in California, Mick was pretty forthright: 'California is like an amateur night burlesque show.' But it was nothing compared to his views on the other side of the States. 'I hate New York. It's artificial, an out-of-date farce. One of the most horrible, one of the most totally awful communities I've ever been in my life. Apart from Warsaw. But you can't really count Warsaw 'cause it's just poverty-stricken and New York isn't. I hate it.'

At the beginning of August, Brian and Suki Potier stayed at the Es Saadi Hotel in Marrakesh. Brian decided he wanted to make a recording of Moroccan musicians and arranged for recording engineer George Chkiantz to fly out to join him. On the balcony of their Marrakesh hotel in front

The artwork for Brian's Jajouka album

The master musicians

Stones' friend Brion Gysin was the one who guided Brian Jones and George Chkiantz to where they could record a local musician named G'Naoua in Marrakesh, Morocco, and also the Maalimin Musicians. The three of them captured the Master Musicians of Jajouka in the Atlas Mountains. Klein kept these tapes for some time, but seemed totally disinterested in the project and never got a deal together for Brian. Finally, he shipped the tapes back to the Stones office in June 1969.

> ## 'I don't want to come back and do any more of the rock'n'roll spectacle kind of thing.' MICK, *on US tours*

A week later we had a reminder letter from the collector of taxes for £13,639. It also threatened legal action. At the end of July, one of Fred's telexes really summed up the absurdity of it all:

'When Stu bought the organ and asked Ronnie [Schneider, Klein's nephew] for the cash, Ronnie told him to pay it out of the money already sent to him and he would reimburse for same. Stu is still waiting. He needs the £2,000 as he is flat broke. This is urgent.'

So while our solicitors were on the case, our road manager and pianist was actually funding the Rolling Stones.

Mick was asked by *Eye* magazine in Los Angeles about our tour plans. Were we able to come back

of Suki Potier and George Chkiantz, Brian suddenly keeled over. He had blacked out – George was shocked, but Suki assured him that it was quite a common occurrence. She told him Brian would be back to normal if he slept for a while. They put Brian on the bed and when he awoke he remembered nothing of what had happened.

On their return, Brian and Suki visited Cotchford Farm, in Hartfield, Sussex (40 miles southeast of London), the former home of *Winnie The Pooh*

World musician
The album finally came out three years after Brian made the recordings, on 8 October, 1971, as a kind of Rolling Stones tribute to the guitarist. Al Vanderburg designed the cover.

author AA Milne. Brian put in a bid of £28,750 (the asking price was £31,500). The old farmhouse had two reception rooms, a breakfast room, six bedrooms, a garage block and staff flat, ornamental gardens, a paddock, a pool and 11 acres of woodland. William the Conqueror reportedly once lived in Cotchford and it was thought that parts of the house dated back to the 13th century.

Unfit for children

Being summer-time, the silly season for the press was in full swing. A rumour started that I was leaving the Stones to be replaced by Eric Clapton, who was to quit Cream later in the year. Apart from the obvious fact that Eric doesn't play bass. It's possible that the press picked up on gossip about Brian, and Eric could have been linked with us in that way.

The debate about the *Beggars Banquet* album sleeve raged on, filling many column inches of the music press. Mick even told the *NME* that we had suggested putting the album in a brown paper bag marked 'Unfit For Children'. He also said we hoped to play live again soon, something I very much wanted to do – I really missed it.

'We've got this album with 10 groovy numbers, all of which we're dying to play live. All we want is for someone to give us the opportunity to play somewhere. It could all work out very groovy.' MICK, *Disc,* 14 September, 1968

The other big story was that Mick's first full-length film would feature Anita Pallenberg as his leading lady. 'Lucky old Anita,' quipped Mick. 'She's okay. We're all one big family.' The *NME* also described her as the former girlfriend of Brian and Keith. Wrong – she was still very much Keith's girl.

'Keith was trying to sabotage my movie because he was jealous of Mick with Anita,' said Donald Cammell, director of *Performance*. 'Anita was having the time of her life. She'd go home to Keith, who'd be terribly jealous when he heard she'd been in bed with Mick.' Although of course this was for a scene in the movie.

Girl On A Motorcycle, in which Marianne appeared nude, premiered in London. It starred Alain Delon and has been described as 'Wonderful, unmitigated trash'. Maybe a little harsh but it was very much a film of its time.

Amid the madness of court cases and financial chaos, Charlie lived quietly in his new home in

'STREET FIGHTING MAN'

| Street Fighting Man |
| The Rolling Stones |
| No Expectations |

The 19th US single was taken from *Beggars Banquet* and issued over three months before the album. Its comparative lack of success was partly due to many radio stations banning it.

Studio
Olympic Studios, London
Producer
Jimmy Miller
Engineer
Glyn Johns
Release
US Saturday 31 August, 1968 London 45 909
Composers
Jagger/Richard
Highest chart position
US No 48

The original colour sleeve with a picture of a street demonstration was withdrawn after a few days. Now it is the most sought-after original packaging of all the Stones' releases. It is worth up to $9,000, but beware – forgeries abound.

'I'm rather pleased to hear they have banned "Street Fighting Man", as long as it's available in the shops. The last time they banned one of our records in America it sold a million.' MICK, *London Evening Standard, 4 September, 1968*

'Street Fighting Man'—violence fear

NEW YORK, Monday
THE new American single by the Rolling Stones, "Street Fighting Man," a track from their new album, has been banned by many radio stations.

The single is running into a lot of problems over radio plays. Many stations have refused to play it and the Chicago stations banned it altogether last week because they feared it could incite even more violence in the city, where the Democratic Convention was held amid scenes of extreme police brutality.

The record is a strong, hard 12 bar bluesy 'number, reminiscent of early Stones' recordings featuring heavy guitar chording.

Chicago riots
The release coincided with massive demonstrations in Chicago, where the police had to use tear gas to break up anti-war demonstrations. The mayor of Chicago, Richard Daley, was accused of adopting 'Gestapo tactics' on the streets of the city.

THE ROLLING STONES
STREET FIGHTING MAN

'Subversive? Of course we're subversive.' KEITH, *Rave magazine*

STONES' HOMES

I first tried to buy a house in Petersfield, Sussex, with no success. While I was viewing a property near Margaretting in Essex, on 15 July, the estate agent told me about Gedding Hall.

Mick's country home was Stargroves.

The Hall, near Bury St Edmunds in Suffolk, was due to go on the market the next morning. It took Astrid and me an hour to drive there and our first thought was that we were at the wrong place. The Hall looked so beautiful and expensive.

We plucked up courage, reaching the Hall through the long drive in the grounds. The main building was surrounded by a beautiful moat with ducks on it. The owner was away and a gardener showed us around the outside. I agreed we would try to buy it. The only thing that would stop us was if it were falling down inside.

On Sunday 21 July – when Mick and Keith were in the US – Astrid and I went back to visit Gedding Hall. We met owner Geoff Allen, who showed us around the lovely house. I was shocked to see a signed photo of the Kray brothers (Ronnie, Reggie and Charlie) on top of the TV in the lounge. Geoff said they were great friends of his and often visited.

Charlie, left, *in Lewes and*, above, *Peckhams.*

We offered £41,000, although a member of the Queen's household was also interested and had offered more. Geoff was a self-made man and said that he preferred to sell it to someone similar. As we were leaving, he told us we could visit Gedding as often as we wished. We returned home, elated. All I had to do was raise the money. I did it by taking out three separate loans.

All of us were lucky enough to buy some wonderful homes over the years – far too many to show all of them here.

Cotchford Farm, Brian's home, above and right

Keith lived in Redlands, above, and in Cheyne Walk, right.

Gedding Hall was Bill's home.

Halland. His lifestyle, much like mine, was a million miles from how people thought the average pop star spent their time. With his guns, Civil War uniforms and some bullets that were supposed to have been shot at the Battle of Little Big Horn, Charlie, like me, indulged in collecting. One of his other passions was Georgian silver. 'I've got some nice silver,' he said, 'but I've never paid £200 for a bit. I like to find bargains in junk shops, and I don't just buy stuff because it's supposed to be good – but because it *is* good.'

I was having trouble with Diane, who had flown back to the UK to contest custody of Stephen. It's a situation that no parent relishes and I am sure Diane had Stephen's best interests at heart. It was just

that the two of us saw those interests differently.

On the day that Che Guevara died in Bolivia, we were all rehearsing at the warehouse studio we bought in Bermondsey, southeast London. It never ceased to amaze me that we might not see each other for weeks, or play together for months, but we would get straight back in the groove as soon as we met up again. It was a real mix of spontaneity and familiarity, our unique aspect. The sum of the parts was always our strength. We were

CAMPAIGN BOOK

picking up on what Mick had said about getting back on the road and we were in the frame of mind to become the Rolling Stones again, rather than just Mick, Keith, Brian, Charlie and Bill.

Cordial invitations

Mick and Marianne hit the headlines again when it was announced that Marianne was expecting a baby. There was endless debate about the fact that they weren't married. We were characterised as ruining the nation's morals. My worries were all

Back in court

Thursday 26 September and Brian was back in court with Michael Havers. He looked drained, the strain was almost intolerable and his late-night drinking sessions didn't help much. There was a jury of 10 men and two women and the chairman of the court was one Reginald E Seaton. Brian, charged with possessing 144 grains of cannabis, gave his address as Redlands, West Wittering, Sussex, and pleaded not guilty.

The crux of Brian's defence was that the cannabis had been found in a flat in which items had been left behind by previous owners.

Brian told the court, 'The first thing I heard in the morning was a loud knocking. I tiptoed to the front door and looked through the spy hole. I remember seeing three men of the type I do not usually see. I panicked. I tiptoed back to the bedroom and was deciding whether or not to call my solicitor.'

touched the stuff since the year before.

He had lunch with Suki Potier and Tom Keylock before the court reconvened. Brian was cross-examined about the effects of cannabis on his personality and it was explained that he had been having treatment. The chairman said, 'If you think

'I don't knit. I don't darn socks and I don't have a girlfriend who darns socks.' BRIAN

The prosecution alleged that the drug was found in a ball of wool, to which Brian replied, 'I would easily have had time to dispose of anything I should not have had. When the ball of wool was shown to me, I was absolutely shattered. I felt everything swimming. I did not have the slightest knowledge that the ball of wool was in the flat. It was such an important time in the group's life. We had not had a record out in a long time and we were just promoting one. We had the feeling that this new record was going to lead us on the road back to success.' Brian went on to explain that cannabis made him feel very paranoid and that he had not

the prosecution has proved without a doubt that the defendant, Brian Jones, knew the cannabis was in his flat, you must find him guilty. Otherwise, he is innocent.' The jury retired to consider its verdict, returning 45 minutes later.

'Guilty,' said the foreman. Brian staggered back, muttering, he was near to collapse. Young girls in the public gallery gasped and sobbed. One began to cry. Brian just said, 'No, no, no. It can't be true.'

Amazingly, Reginald Seaton said, 'I think this was a lapse and I don't want to interfere with the probation order which already applies to this man. I am going to fine you according to your means. You must keep clear of this stuff. You really must watch your step. You will be fined £50 with £105 costs. For goodness sake, don't get into trouble again or it really *will* be serious.' Seaton clearly did not agree with the jury's verdict and acted sensibly to deal with it. Brian left the court hand-in-hand with Suki and danced a jig with her. Mick and Keith, who were also there, drove away in the Bentley. Our show was still on the road.

'I will state till my death that I did not commit this offence,' said Brian.

Keith, Suki, Brian and Mick outside court

wrapped up with the purchase of Gedding Hall. House-buying is never easy and I was stretching myself to the absolute limit to get the home of my dreams. We finally moved in on 30 October, spending much of the night in darkness, as all the light fittings had been removed. I needed money for my house purchase and getting it from Klein was like drawing teeth. Brian needed money too, to pay his court costs. Fred Trowbridge telexed Ken Salinsky (Klein), on 25 October:

Berger Oliver are screaming for the balance of Bill's money. What is happening to those cheques? What about Brian's £6,000? Has Mick's film contract been sorted out yet?

As we continued to rehearse in November, the idea of the *Rock'n'Roll Circus* TV show began to take shape. We met director Michael Lindsay-Hogg to discuss it further. At this stage, it was just the germ of an idea. By 16 November, we were

'Jimmy Miller sat down at the drums and remained there playing on the take. Charlie was not happy but was graceful about it. Mick and Keith played acoustic guitars, I played piano, Bill was on bass and Brian lay on his stomach in the corner reading an article on botany throughout the proceedings. I then overdubbed the organ.' AL KOOPER, *from Back Stage Passes And Backstabbing Bastards*

We finally settled on an acceptable cover for *Beggars Banquet* and everything was focused on its release. Like 'Jumpin' Jack Flash', it needed to do well. Our office made enquiries with the Tower of

cinematic mish-mash.' Our TV appearance generated controversy, but at least people were talking about us *and* our music: 'Angry viewers swamped London Weekend TV switchboards after the Stones sang "Sympathy For The Devil",' reported the *Sunday Express*.

The press reception for the album launch was on 5 December. Our real beggars' banquet, for 70 guests from the media, was a candle-lit affair in a room that looked the part. Serving wenches were there to wait at our tables. After we finished eating, Mick stood up and said, 'Well, I hope you've all had enough to eat and drink. And I hope you've all enjoyed yourselves. But we didn't invite you here just to eat

'You are cordially invited to a Beggars' Banquet … It should be a very good scene.' ROLLING STONES OFFICE MEMO,

on the Beggars Banquet launch party

back at Olympic with Jimmy Miller. One outcome of our rehearsals was a new song, 'You Can't Always Get What You Want', with Al Kooper on organ and piano. Al had been with the Blues Project and Blood, Sweat and Tears (a band Mick really liked).

David Frost, Mick and Mary Whitehouse

London about holding our album launch party at the historic castle, but they turned us down and we settled on an appropriately-named hotel room. Our office sent us a memo about it:

You are cordially invited to a Beggars' Banquet next Thursday, 12.30pm, at the Elizabethan Rooms, Gore Hotel, 190 Queensgate. This is the press party which Decca are paying for, but which we are organising. It will be for lunch and Mick suggests that everyone wear appropriate costumes, as we will be doing photographs after lunch and possibly TV.'

In the third week of November, Brian completed the purchase of Cotchford Farm. Marianne, seven months pregnant, with complications, went into a nursing home. A few days later she miscarried a baby girl.

As Mick and Marianne dealt with the sadness of losing the baby, we took a break from rehearsing but, unfortunately, not for long. David Frost booked us for his *Frost On Saturday* show. We performed 'Sympathy for the Devil', with Brian playing organ, tying-in with the premiere of Jean-Luc Godard's *One Plus One*. I go along with *British Weekly*'s verdict: 'A semi-incoherent

and drink and enjoy yourselves, did we?' Mick calmly picked up a meringue pie and slapped it in Brian's face, who was sitting beside him. All the guests hurled pies at us, principal guest Lord Harlech (chairman of the British Film Board) and each other. Keith didn't arrive until the end.

'Thanks again for the banquet. As usual the newspaper accounts were almost totally inaccurate.' LORD HARLECH, *from a letter to the Stones, 17 December, 1968*

Rolling Stones
Beggars Banquet

R.S.V.P.

The eighth UK and 12th US album came out a year after *Satanic Majesties* and that's where the similarity ends. Where the former was indulgent, lacking in clarity and far away from Stones' roots, *Beggars Banquet* was a focused, blues-based tour de force. The Stones were back on track. Ironically its chart performance was somewhat worse than *Satanic Majesties*. History has served *Beggars Banquet* far better. It's been called the greatest rock'n'roll album of the 1960s. Start debating…

The album's gestation was at RG Jones studios in south London, where the Stones began rehearsing with Jimmy Miller on Wednesday 21 February, 1968. It was finalised in Los Angeles during three weeks in July, when Jimmy and Glyn Johns, watched over by Mick, completed the mix at Sunset Sound studios. It was right around the corner from the giant RCA studios on Sunset Boulevard.

It came out almost head-to-head with the Beatles' *White Album*, which was released on 22 November. That undoubtedly harmed its chances of topping the chart and it had a fight on its hands in the traditional UK Christmas sales stampede. It was kept from No 2 by *The Best of The Seekers* and the Beatles took the No 1 spot.

'The Stones have unleashed their rawest, ludest, most arrogant, most savage record yet. And it's beautiful.'
CARL G. BERNSTEIN, *Chicago Sun Times, 26 January, 1969*

Additional personnel
A gospel choir from Watts was added to 'Salt Of The Earth' in Los Angeles during mixing.
Nicky Hopkins: piano
Dave Mason: guitar and mandolin
Rocky Dijon: congas
Anita and Marianne: backing vocals, 'Sympathy for the Devil'
On 'No Expectations', Brian played bottleneck. It was his last significant contribution to a Stones song.

The devil is one of my names
With the album taking six months from rehearsals to final mix, it was inevitable that the band did many versions of the songs. The Stones also recorded a number of songs during the sessions that never made the final cut. In March they worked on 'Street Fighting Man' (then 'Primo Grande') and in April 'Stray Cat Blues'. In May they did 'No Expectations', 'Dear Doctor', 'Parachute Woman', 'Factory Girl' and 'Salt of The Earth' (originally 'Silver Blanket') and in June, 'Sympathy For The Devil' (then 'The Devil Is My Name'), 'Jig Saw Puzzle' and 'Prodigal Son'.

'They are very demanding. They will keep working at a thing until it's right. But I don't mind that. I think it's the right way.' NICKY HOPKINS, *22 March, 1969*

'We were cutting "Sympathy For The Devil" the night before Robert Kennedy was shot [5 June] and we had to change some of the lyrics because of it.' JIMMY MILLER, *14 December, 1968*

What the papers said…

'The Stones have returned and they are bringing back rock'n'roll with them.' JANN WENNER, *Rolling Stone magazine, 10 August, 1968*

'The album bristles with the brand of hard, raunchy rock that has helped to establish the Stones as England's most subversive roisterers since Fagin's gang in Oliver Twist. *In keeping with a widespread mood in the pop world,* Beggars Banquet *turns back to the raw vitality of Negro R&B and the authentic simplicity of country music.'* TIME MAGAZINE, *11 October, 1968*

'This album is to Beatles as Courbet to Manet, Michelangelo to Tintoretto, Realism to Expressionism.' INTERNATIONAL TIMES, *15 November, 1968*

'…the mixed bag of topics put to music include the Bible, Satan, street riots and, of course, sex. I find it the best Stones disc to date.' SUNDAY MIRROR, *1 December, 1968*

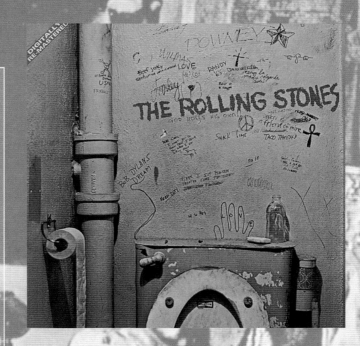

Under the influence
Mikhail Bulgakov's novel *The Master and Margarita* inspired 'Sympathy For The Devil'. The feel of 'Stray Cat Blues' came from the Velvet Underground's 'Heroin'. Of 'Salt Of The Earth', a Stones press release said, 'It's the Stones' hymn of praise to the two billion ordinary hardworking people who keep the world alive and well and living in space.'

The original Rolling Stone?
The press pack said, '"Prodigal Son" is a traditional blues first recorded in 1927 by Rev John Wilkinson.' The truth is that the song was first recorded in September 1929 as 'That's No Way To Get Along' by Robert Wilkins, *left*, an

idiosyncratic writer/performer from Memphis who cut the first known song entitled 'Rolling Stone' on 7 September, 1928. He recorded until 1935 and turned to God in the late 1930s. He became a minister for the Church of God in Christ in 1950. In 1964, he was rediscovered during the folk-blues revival and died in 1987.

Cover story

One of the most interesting aspects of the album was its on/off release date, coupled with the row that developed over the cover. On 9 April, Jo Bergman wrote to the Stones: 'Dear Lads, From the nerve centre of this vast, sprawling mini-Empire. 1: Recording until middle of May to complete work on the album. 2: Tentative release date, 31 May for the album release.'

On 1 June, Mick told *Melody Maker*, 'I hope the new album will be released on my birthday, 26 July.' On 6 July, *Rolling Stone* reported, '*Beggars Banquet* will be the title of the next Stones album, Mick announced in London.'

Barry Feinstein shot the infamous photo of a graffiti-covered lavatory wall in Los Angeles on 26 July. In early August, the news came through to the Stones office that both Decca Records and London Records refused to release the album with the graffiti and the toilet.

By 10 August, *NME* was predicting, 'The Stones new album *Beggars Banquet* is now completely finished and is scheduled for release by Decca in mid-September.'

But by 7 September, 'There is still no release date for *Beggars Banquet*. It could be a Christmas release,' said a band spokesman in *Melody Maker*.

Time (11 October) said, 'The Stones hint that the cover of their next album may make the bathroom wall of *Beggars Banquet* look cute by comparison. It's subject: the Pope.'

'The Stones lost their fight to keep a photograph of a lavatory wall on their new LP,' reported the *Daily Mail* on 30 October. 'Now a new sleeve, in the form of an invitation card, has been designed.'

Other artwork concepts for the Beggars Banquet cover

Side one
1. 'Sympathy For The Devil'
2. 'No Expectations'
3. 'Dear Doctor'
4. 'Parachute Woman'
5. 'Jig Saw Puzzle'
Side two
1. 'Street Fighting Man'
2. 'Prodigal Son'
3. 'Stray Cat Blues'
4. 'Factory Girl'
5. 'Salt Of The Earth'
Recorded
February–July, 1968
Composers
All tracks Jagger/Richard
Studio
Olympic Studios, London
Producer
Jimmy Miller
Engineers
Glyn Johns and Eddie Kramer, with Alan 'Irish' O'Duffy on some sessions
Design
Tom Wilkes
Photography
Michael Joseph
Release
UK Friday 6 December 1968 Decca SKL 4955
US Saturday 7 December, 1968 London PS 539
Highest chart position (time on chart)
UK No 3 (12 weeks)
US No 5 (13 weeks)

THE ROCK'N'ROLL CIRCUS

The first the world knew of Mick's idea to make *The Rock'n'Roll Circus* was in mid-November when the *Daily Mirror* carried a piece about the proposed TV programme.

'The Stones are to produce their own TV spectacular for sale all over the world. They will star in an hour-long show, which will cost £20,000 to make. Worldwide sales are likely to earn them about £250,000.' DAILY MIRROR, *13 November, 1968*

Ten days later the *NME* said: 'It was revealed this week that three TV companies are already negotiating for the British screening rights. However, it will not now be ready for Christmas transmission. The Stones plan to show it to prospective buyers on 1 January, 1969. The Stones themselves are financing the project, which stems from an idea of Mick's.'

Unfortunately, costs soon started to get out of hand and the budget for the TV show was estimated at £31,686 by production company Colourtel. But with the proposed sales that were talked about, it looked like a good deal.

Astrid and I were staying at the Londonderry House Hotel, where the rehearsals were to take place. Jimmy Miller and Glyn Johns were busy mixing the backing tracks that we were to use at Olympic. Tony Visconti (who later produced David Bowie and T Rex) conducted a small orchestra in the recording of 'Circus March (Entry Of The Gladiators)', 'Trapeze Music', 'In And Out Of Commercials', 'Wild Tuba', 'Clown Effects', 'Drum Rolls' and 'Fanfare'.

Rock'n'roll invite
The tickets were distributed by the Rolling Stones fan club and by the *NME*. They were printed on gold metallic cards that featured a wood-cut of a galloping elephant in green.

You are invited to the Rolling Stones' Rock and Roll Circus on Wednesday, 11th December, 1968 at the studios of Intertel Television, Wycombe Road, Wembley, Middlesex. Nearest tube: Stonebridge Park (Bakerloo line) 12.30 – 15.30 Costumes Provided

'There's not much to say about **The Rock'n'Roll Circus** *debacle except that it was terrifying. Mick and Charlie never said hello to me. I conducted the little circus band and they played tambourines behind them. From time to time they whispered to each other while looking at me, so I assumed they were saying what a dick I was. Well, that's what it seemed like to a 24-year-old kid from Brooklyn.'* TONY VISCONTI, *2002*

Some of our favourite acts were asked to appear – the Who, Taj Mahal, Jethro Tull, Eric Clapton and Marianne Faithfull among them. Johnny Cash was invited but declined. The Isley Brothers and Traffic couldn't make it. Mick also asked John Lennon to come along. On the first day of rehearsals Mick, dressed in a black bearskin coat, was asked by the *Evening News* what it was all about. 'We decided to put up the money for the spectacular ourselves so that we had complete control of the production. We have never tried producing a show before. If we aren't pleased with the result we will scrap it.'

Rehearsals began on 10 December, 1968. Yoko Ono (as a witch) came with John and his son Julian. At Intertel Studio A that day were the Who, Jethro Tull, clowns, a tiger in a cage, model Donyala Luna (who was filmed with the tiger), a cowboy, Mick (dressed as a ringmaster), Brian, Keith, Charlie and I. We dressed as circus characters, with me as a clown.

Other guests were classical pianist Julius Katchen (who had been engaged to play Brahms) and French violinist Ivry Gitlis (who performed Paganini's 'First Violin Concerto' and later played country fiddle while Yoko Ono wailed). Marianne, along with members of Robert Fosset's Circus, including a fire-eater (Danny Kamara), was also there.

There were two midgets, Norman McGlenn and Willie Shearer. Anita Pallenberg was to appear as a bearded lady, but it didn't happen. Taj Mahal, who had flown in from America to play, failed to secure work permits so they only rehearsed with us. Lennon, Eric Clapton, Mitch Mitchell and Keith played John's 'Yer Blues'. For some reason, Keith ended up as the bass player in this supergroup, christened the Dirty Mac (Lennon's play on Fleetwood Mac). The director was Michael Lindsay-Hogg,

the man who had worked with us on our promo films; he also directed the Beatles' promotional film for 'Hey Jude'.

'If anyone had told me we would have been doing this kind of thing six years ago I would have said they were mad. But here we all are, thoroughly enjoying ourselves with clowns, midgets, acrobats and classical musicians. Yesterday Lennon and Clapton were jamming all the old rock'n'roll numbers, with Mick singing the vocals to Everly Brothers and Buddy Holly numbers.' BRIAN, *Rave magazine, February 1969*

Bill: 'Someone asked Lennon what kind of amp he wanted and he said, "One that plays".'

'I was training to be a teacher, but two of us went ill for the day and travelled up to London from Luton. We had to queue up outside and were afraid we'd find that our tickets were forged or something, but all went well and naturally we got in, to be greeted by the Circus get-up. Besides being pleased to see so many stars in such an informal set-up and everyone being so friendly, I was amazed to watch Mick running around Marianne Faithfull, doing all she asked him.' CYNTHIA MORGAN, *in a letter to Bill, 1982*

On the second day we finally began filming our piece around 1am. Everyone had been in the studio for nearly 14 hours so it was a tough situation. You could immediately feel the energy once we started playing, the only problem was that we kept on and on and on playing. We did endless takes. We did 'Jumpin' Jack Flash' at least three times, had six goes at 'Sympathy For The Devil' and lost count on most of the rest. We finished around 4am and all we could do was head back to the hotel, totally knackered. When Mick saw the rushes, he insisted our segment would have to be re-shot. Budgets were drawn up for the shoot, but nothing was done. It was not our finest hour.

Taj Mahal

In 1978, the Who were compiling footage for *The Kids Are Alright* and used their segment from the show, but our fans had to wait until the late 1990s to see us perform.

Circus music
'Yer Blues' (Lennon/McCartney) by Dirty Mac
'Whole Lotta Yoko' with Yoko Ono on vocals, Ivry Gitlis on violin
'Song For Jeffrey' by Jethro Tull
'A Quick One, While He's Away' by the Who
'Leaving Trunk', 'Corrina Corrina' and 'Ain't That A Lot Of Love' by Taj
    Mahal (in rehearsal only)
'Something Better' by Marianne Faithful
The Rolling Stones rehearsed 'Route 66', 'Confessin' The Blues', 'Walkin'
    Blues' and 'Love In Vain'. They filmed 'Jumpin' Jack Flash',
    'Parachute Woman', 'No Expectations', 'You Can't Always Get What
    You Want', 'Sympathy For The Devil' and 'Salt Of The Earth'.

The album and video were finally released in 1996.

69
January - December

The Sky Is Crying

Mick, Keith, an Angel and about 40 fans out of a crowd of around 500,000 at Altamont, 6 December, 1968.

That's The Way God Planned It

We began 1969 on holiday. Charlie and I were both in England, while Mick, Keith, Marianne and Anita had flown to Lima in Peru a week after the *Rock'n'Roll Circus*. Brian and Suki had gone to Kandy in Ceylon where they were initially refused a hotel room owing to Brian's scruffy appearance. Everything turned out fine when Brian produced money and it was revealed he was a pop star.

WHILE THEY WERE THERE they visited Arthur C Clarke, author of *2001: A Space Odyssey*. Mick, Keith and their ladies saw in the New Year in Brazil. In early 1969, there was much press speculation about our US tour which was then scheduled to begin in late March and run to early May. To help clarify the situation surrounding Brian, Jo Bergman had written to Michael Havers, in early December. She told him we planned to begin in South America in February and then tour the USA before visiting Japan, Hong Kong, Bangkok and India:

'I would like to emphasise that the Stones are a musically integrated group. They have never performed when one of the Stones has been unable to appear [this was not entirely true, of course]. This projected world tour is being undertaken not only for the financial consideration, but more importantly for the chance it affords, most noticeably, the American public, to see the Stones. I would be very grateful if you could let me know when the Appeal will take place, as it will be necessary to inform the American Embassy as soon as possible of our intention to apply for a visa for Brian.'

While all this pointed to the fact that we were about to reconquer the world, things are not always as they seemed:

'I feel I'm old enough to get out of the group scene and go into something completely different. If we step out of line, whatever we do, we get pages of space in the newspapers, the national press, but if we spent weeks perfecting an LP, we'd be lucky if any national paper even bothers to mention it.' MICK, *in Teenbeat 1969 Annual*

Mick was hedging his bets at that time. If *Beggars Banquet* had failed to cut it then he was considering

'The Stones would, of necessity, have was not permitted to perform on

his solo options. He had, after all, worked on *Performance*, both as an actor and as composer: 1969 was going to be an important year for us.

Brian's appeal

Before Brian got back from Ceylon, Michael Havers was in court appealing against the conviction. The appeal was thrown out. This was a huge problem for Brian. A US visa was all but out of the question. For the rest of us, money was a continuing source of worry, albeit to varying degrees. Our UK office continued to telex and call Klein, seeking funds.

We were being hounded for back taxes and even comparatively small bills went unpaid. Tom Wilkes, the designer of *Beggars Banquet*, had to cable us asking for his six-month-old bill to be paid, while Tony Visconti wrote and asked for his fees for the *Circus*. Allen Klein took over the running of Apple, much to Paul McCartney's dismay.

On 10 February, we were back at Olympic – everyone but Brian, who was still in Ceylon. He got home a few days later and was soon a regular at the sessions. With no solution to Brian's visa problems, our tour plans were put on hold. In saying that, the logistics of touring were becoming a huge undertaking – we were more like a corporation than a group. I told *Top Pops* magazine that we hoped to be touring by the end of the year. This would give us time to sort out both the practical issues and, hopefully, Brian. In the short term, there was the possibility of a show in Rome, organised by our old friend Stash. The venue was to be the Coliseum.

A smaller project was on my mind. I had decided to redecorate Gedding Hall. I got designer David Hicks to come and give us his ideas. He did, along with an estimate of over £5,000 – just for curtains and carpets. As I had an overdraft of almost £8,000 at the time, I politely declined. Astrid and I did it ourselves. Later I did have a designer do some work for us. At the same time, Mick was having a survey done, with a view to putting a lake into the grounds of Stargroves.

I was driving up and down to Olympic Studios from Gedding, in Suffolk, as songs like 'Let it Bleed' and 'Midnight Rambler' were beginning to come together. We also added the choir to 'You Can't Always Get What You Want' on 15 March. Three days later, Brian was back at the Priory

Producer/arranger Jack Nitzsche and Mick in the studio on 15 March, 1969

clinic in Richmond. His relationship with Suki was on the wane and by April he was seeing a Swedish student and model called Anna Wohlin. As well as working at Olympic, we were using our Bermondsey rehearsal studio to work on material. We also considered a re-shoot of our *Circus* segment. The problem was production company Colourtel had not been paid. Once more, a telex was dispatched by Fred Trowbridge to Ronnie Schneider:

Colourtel telephoned me this morning and want an immediate answer to the following:
1. *Has the money been wired to Colourtel yet? Answer yes or no.*
2. *They will not consider working on the re-shoot unless they have money for the original show and money in advance for the re-shoot.*

We got a solicitor's letter from Colourtel saying they were going to take us to court. This hand-to-mouth financial existence was a major strain on the people who worked in the office. While we band members were affected through the fluctuations in our personal finances the office faced a relentless barrage from creditors. It was frustrating for us to always seem to be asking for our own money.

Brian's behaviour was becoming ever more irresponsible. In March, he borrowed the group car, a Jaguar, and went shopping in Pimlico Road.

The car was towed away by the police, so he just hired a chauffeur car and returned to Cotchford Farm. Two months later, he was out on his motorcycle and crashed into the window of a shop near Cotchford. He was admitted to hospital under an assumed name to avoid publicity.

Apple, pear and jam

We were also planning the release of a second greatest hits package, in the third week of May. Before that, I had to appear in court for a preliminary hearing over my divorce from Diane. The night of the hearing we worked on a song with an appropriate title – 'Let It Loose'. It was cut on vinyl three years later.

Two nights later, we met up with guitarist Ry Cooder and spent the evening jamming, except Keith who was not around. Many of the tracks we cut, 'Blow With Ry' and 'Highland Gig', ended up on an album that came out in January 1972, called *Jamming With Edward*. It featured the brilliant piano of Nicky Hopkins, although the album was to be rather less outstanding.

We even cut one of my songs. It was a boogie blues with the working title 'Lyle Street Lucie', that later turned up on an album of bits and pieces put together by Klein. It was renamed 'Downtown Suzie'.

A Hooker in Bishop's Stortford

Bill was blown away when he went to see one of his heroes play near his new home: 'I went to see John Lee Hooker on 3 March, a few miles south of Gedding, at Bishop's Stortford. We chatted backstage and I took pictures from the side of the stage. He was an amazing performer, just him and his guitar. He stood there with his chin pushed out, stamping his foot in rhythm – he looked like a god.'

to cancel this tour if Brian Jones stage with them.' JO BERGMAN, *Stones office*

Mick Taylor

The man who would replace Brian Jones was born Michael Kevin Taylor in Welwyn Garden City, Hertfordshire, on Saturday 17 January, 1949. His father, Lionel Taylor, was an aircraft worker and his mother's name was Marilyn. He had a sister of the same name.

In September 1959, he started at Onslow Secondary Modern School in Hatfield, Herts. At the age of 12, he taught himself to play guitar. He left school in 1963 and started work for a local firm as a commercial artist and also laboured in a paint factory. He joined a local Welwyn group called the Gods, who included Greg Lake — of Emerson, Lake and Palmer fame — and others who formed Uriah Heep.

Taylor saw John Mayall's Bluesbreakers and sat in with them when lead guitarist Eric Clapton failed to turn up. He joined full time to fill Peter Green's place.

As a Bluesbreaker, Mick visited every country in Europe and lived with Mayall in America. He was featured on three Mayall albums — *Crusade, Bare Wires* and *Blues From Laurel Canyon*. Still startlingly young, he parted company with John Mayall in early 1969 to pursue his own career.

Mick Taylor plays Amsterdam, 8 November, 1967.

'*The Rolling Stones may launch their own Pear label next February. Their current recording contract with Decca will have terminated and they would follow the pattern of the Beatles and Apple.*' NME, *May 1969*

In early May, members of the Beatles and Stones got together with Billy Preston, who was recording a single for Apple at Trident Studios in London. George Harrison produced 'That's The Way God Planned It' with Keith on bass, Eric Clapton and George Harrison on guitars and Ginger Baker on drums. Billy went on to play organ with us in the 1970s.

On the home front, Keith had been looking for a London pad and decided to buy 3 Cheyne Walk for £55,000. He was to be Mick's new neighbour. We also started work on a new song, 'Honky Tonk Women'.

Then just as things appeared to be going smoothly, Marianne and Mick were busted. He was leaving his place in Cheyne Walk for the studio on 28 May and met five policemen and two police dogs (Yogi and Fred) coming the other way. They had been on watch for 90 minutes. As Mick got into his car at 7.45pm, they stopped him and said they had a search warrant. Mick turned and dashed to the house.

The police heard him shout, 'Marianne, Marianne, don't open the door. It's the police. They are after the weed,' as he raced down the basement steps. Christopher Gibbs, who was also there, heard Mick questioning the validity of the police's warrant.

The police got in to find a substance in a cigarette box on a table in the lounge. Asked what it was Mick replied, 'I don't think I had better answer that.' It was the remains of cannabis resin.

On the fourth floor, they found a bureau with its roller lid open. Yogi went straight to it and stood with his paws on the edge of the drawers. In one of them, the officer later said, he found a brown substance wrapped in silver paper. Marianne was weeping.

'Have they found it, have they found it?' she sobbed. Regaining her composure, Marianne said, 'Mick will answer for me. I am not saying anything.' After 45 minutes, the couple were arrested and taken to Chelsea

police station. They were charged and summoned to appear at Marlborough Street Magistrates' Court the next morning. At the studio later that day, we finished 'You Can't Always Get What You Want' – life is full of irony… Mick and Marianne were remanded on bail of £50 each until 23 June.

Goodbye Brian

Matters were also coming to a head over Brian. Things could no longer go on the way they were. Brian was no longer a musically integral part of the band. He was unhappy with his role within the band, nor could we realistically tour America with him given his problems with US immigration. In view of our upcoming shows, we needed a solution. Stu, as usual came up trumps, and recommended Mick Taylor as a replacement. Mick phoned him and told him that Brian was thinking of leaving and invited him to come to the recording session in Barnes that evening. So it was that Michael Kevin Taylor arrived at Olympic on 31 May, 1969. He was about to become a Rolling Stone.

We worked on 'Live With Me' that night and had another go at 'Honky Tonk Women' the following day. This time it gelled. We finished it off on Charlie's 28th birthday.

In the early hours of 7 June, on their way home to Redlands from Olympic, Keith and Anita crashed on a bend of the A286 near Chichester, eight miles from Redlands. The Mercedes was later written off, but Keith escaped unhurt. Anita broke her collarbone and was taken to the aptly-named St Richard's hospital in Chichester. She was soon allowed home to Redlands. Lucky old Keith had got away with it again.

Mick and Marianne and some friends went to Hyde Park for a free concert given by Blind Faith in front of 150,000 fans. Eric Clapton, Ginger Baker, Stevie Winwood and Rick Greech played 'Under My Thumb' as Mick and Marianne watched.

In the meantime, Leslie Perrin had sent an invitation to the press to meet with Mick on 19 June to talk about our future plans. There was no doubt that we would need to make an announcement about Brian, as by now rumours were rife. On Sunday 8 June, Mick, Charlie and Keith spent the afternoon mixing at Olympic.

The photoshoot, right, for the 'Honky Tonk Women' sleeve took place at a strip club called Gigi – Mick Taylor played the barman.

I wasn't really needed so I saved myself the five-hour round-trip and stayed at home in Gedding. During the afternoon, they told me they had talked about Brian and what to do. Brian had probably phoned as he had been called at home and been forced to deny he was leaving the band. Somewhat on the spur of the moment they decided to go and see him. They got to Cotchford Farm in about 75 minutes and had what they all said was a friendly, but very difficult, half-hour talk with Brian.

He knew that he would be barred from America. It was also questionable whether his body could stand up to the strain of a tour. There was another simple truth. Brian had moved away from us musically, or we had from him. He was contributing less and less in the studio and it was highly doubtful as to whether Brian could really contribute on stage anymore. His blues-based style was not where we were at any longer. We were a fully-fledged rock band, and rock'n'roll was not Brian. Mick, Keith and Charlie agreed that Brian should make a statement and that we should all stick to the story. Later in the evening, it was announced that Brian had left the Stones. His place was to be taken by Mick Taylor.

Taylor-made

On 11 June, we did a whole mass of interviews at the office and the following day, we did a photo session with Ethan Russell. We needed

Brian at Cotchford Farm

Mick Taylor and the Stones in Hyde Park on 13 June, 1969

'I no longer see eye to eye with the others over the discs we are cutting. We no longer communicate musically. The Stones' music is not to my taste anymore. I have a desire to play my own brand of music rather than that of others, no matter how much I appreciate their musical concepts. The only solution is to go our separate ways, but we shall still remain friends. I love those fellows.' **BRIAN,** *on leaving the Stones*

new images of the band with Mick Taylor for use on our upcoming single.

Mick had a meeting with a promotions company called Blackhill about putting on a free Stones concert in London. On Friday 13 June, at the bandstand in Hyde Park, there was a hastily-convened press call to introduce Mick T. to the world. We also announced that we would be doing the free show in Hyde Park within a month.

The press was greeted by a slightly shorter-haired Mick. He had it cut for his starring role in the film *Ned Kelly*, about the notorious 19th-century Australian outlaw. It was not short enough and on 17 June it was cut again. Straight afterwards, he went to Wig Creations to have a wig fitted, a couple of weeks before the Hyde Park concert.

The following week, while we were at Olympic, Brian came to the studio and we talked about the future. As a band, we knew more about what we were doing and, although Brian was less clear, he was nevertheless excited about his own plans.

A new Korner

Two days later, Brian hired a chauffeur-driven car to take Alexis Korner and his family from Bayswater to Cotchford Farm. They were going to spend the weekend with Brian and Anna, who had now 'taken over' from Suki

Mick and Marianne
at court

as the girlfriend. Brian talked of joining Alexis Korner's New Church band, but Alexis encouraged him to form his own band. Alexis was right – Brian needed to regain his confidence and become a leader again.

On Monday 23 June, Mick and Marianne went to Marlborough Street Magistrates' Court for their second brief appearance. Michael Havers was there to defend them. He explained they had a contract to film in Australia, where Marianne was co-starring as Ned's sister. He requested a formal remand until 29 September. The £50 bail was continued.

Afterwards Mick joined the rest of us in the basement rehearsal facilities at Apple in Savile Row. We were also kept busy at Olympic, recording and mixing the new album. It wasn't just Mick Taylor's arrival that prompted and necessitated all this extra work. We needed to be the best that we could be. We hadn't played a full concert for over two years and while *Beggars Banquet* had done pretty well, it hadn't made No 1 on either side of the Atlantic. Being back was one thing, being back at the top was quite another.

Our two shows in Rome's Coliseum were cancelled, but that didn't stop the *Sunderland Echo* from reporting on them!

'This week saw the Stones take Rome by storm in two concerts at the city's ancient Coliseum.' SUNDERLAND ECHO, *28 June, 1967*

Three weeks after Brian left the band we were in the studio. Tuesday 1 July was a day like many others in the recent past. We were at Olympic the next day too, and that was the only thing about those two days that would be the same. On that Wednesday, Brian had been in London.

He went back to Cotchford during the afternoon in a chauffeur-driven car hired by our office. That night, shortly before midnight, I went to Olympic and met up with the others. As there wasn't much happening that I needed to stay for, I left around 2am and returned to Londonderry House, where I often stayed to avoid the long drive back to Gedding. Astrid and I got to sleep before 3am, only to be woken soon after by Charlie phoning from Olympic. He could hardly find the words to tell me. Brian was dead.

Roll Away The Stone

The evening of 2 July was humid and cloudy, the worst kind of weather for an asthma sufferer. Brian spent the early part of the evening working in his oak-beamed music room at Cotchford Farm. At around 8.30pm, Anna Wohlin and Brian were joined by 44-year-old builder Frank Thorogood and his 22-year-old nurse friend Janet Lawson.

Frank was staying in the guesthouse on the property, and Janet was staying with him. Frank was working on rebuilding a wall at the farm, recommended for the job by his friend Tom Keylock. Janet described Brian's conversation during dinner as 'garbled'.

After dinner they watched the American comedy *Laugh In* on TV. At about 10.30pm, Brian, who was complaining about the heat, suggested a swim. Janet declined and observed, 'He had been drinking. He was a bit unsteady on his feet. They were in no condition to swim. I felt strongly about this and mentioned it to both of the men. They disregarded my warning.'

Brian was wearing multi-coloured swimming trunks and Anna was in a black bikini. Frank joined them in the floodlit, blue-tiled, heated pool.

'I went to the pool to keep an eye on them. Brian had trouble getting onto the springboard, Frank helped him and he flopped into the water. The two were sluggish in the water, but I gathered they could look after themselves.' JANET LAWSON

After about 20 minutes, the two girls went into the house. Ten minutes later Frank also went indoors, for a cigarette or towel. Janet immediately went back outside, where she saw Brian at the bottom of the pool, quite motionless.

'I sensed the worst and shouted to Anna and Frank.'

Frank got Brian to the pool's edge and Anna helped drag him out. Laying Brian on his back, Janet desperately pumped a little water out of him and then massaged his heart for 15 minutes. Anna was sure he was still alive when they got him out of the water. He still had a pulse. She tried the kiss of life and Frank gave him artificial respiration, but they got no reaction.

Someone phoned for an ambulance and a local doctor. Frank called Tom Keylock in London. It was Tom's wife who phoned Olympic studios and spoke to Mick.

Ambulance men used a pump for about 30 minutes to try to revive Brian. Anna told Astrid and me that they didn't seem to take the incident seriously and were very slow in doing anything to help him. As the rest of the Stones arrived at Olympic, the police were called. When Detective Chief Inspector Ron Marshall, head of East Grinstead CID, arrived he found the emergency crew trying artificial respiration, but Brian did not respond. A local doctor was summoned, examined Brian and pronounced him dead.

At 1am, Leslie Perrin was woken with the news and headed for Cotchford. The police took statements from Frank, Anna and Janet. Brian's body was put in an ambulance and taken to the mortuary. At East Grinstead police station at 3am, Detective Chief Inspector Robert Marshall made a statement to the press. Half-an-hour later, Leslie Perrin and Tom Keylock arrived at the house.

'Brian's father and all members of the Stones have been informed and all had expressed shock,' Leslie said. Anna, who was in shock, finally went to bed at about 5am. Tom Keylock and Leslie inspected the pool. 'We found Brian's puffer [inhaler] on the side of the pool. We gave it to the police,' said Leslie. Coroner Dr Angus

Sommerville was informed of Brian's death and the the inquest was fixed for Monday 7 July.

Pat Andrews, living with Brian's son Mark in a council reception centre in south London, also heard the news.

'A newspaper woke me up at 6.30am and said to me, "We've just heard on the news, Brian's dead – now you'll be able to get some money." It didn't sink in until about 10am, when I heard it myself.' Pat was quoted as saying in the *People* on 13 July. 'I just broke down and cried. Even with all the trouble we had, I didn't wish this on him. It just does not seem fair that he's dead before he really got a chance to grow up. Now he does not have to work so hard at living.'

Janet Lawson went home to Lincolnshire. Arrangements were made for Brian's three spaniels and his Afghan hound to go to boarding kennels.

Dr Albert Sachs performed an autopsy at the Queen Victoria Hospital. He reported a death by drowning, drugs and liver degeneration. The inquest was told that Brian had natural diseases. He had pleurisy, his heart was larger than it should have been and his liver was twice the normal weight. There was no evidence of an asthma attack, though there were indications of chronic bronchial trouble.

Brian had taken a large quantity of a drug. After questioning witnesses, the coroner said, 'He would not listen. So he drowned under the influence of alcohol and drugs.' The verdict was misadventure.

In 1993, it was reported that Frank Thorogood made a deathbed confession to killing Brian. Tom Keylock, the man to whom he apparently admitted murder, later told the police that he didn't say anything.

'Today's a normal day for Brian. He always seemed to be losing out. A little bit of love might have sorted him out. I don't think death is necessarily a bad thing for Brian. He'll do better next time. I believe in reincarnation.' PETE TOWNSHEND, *Evening News, 3 July, 1969*

'He died when he was happier than he had ever been. I hope that people give him a better deal in death than they did in life.' ALEXIS KORNER, *Daily Express, 4 July, 1969*

'A lot of people used to get annoyed with him but he was smashing.' PAUL MCCARTNEY

A Free Pardon

Brian was just 27 when he died and he had lived much of his adult life in the spotlight. The temptations that money afforded were plain to see. Insecure, complicated Brian was tempted more than most – much more than I.

I am not going to play amateur psychologist and nor do I want to reopen the debate about the circumstances of Brian's death. There have been too many conspiracy theories, often started by people with a vested or mercenary interest. Others were deluded. I think now, as I did then, that it was a dreadful accident.

It's true that Mick and Keith shaped our music. And Mick and Andrew were the brains behind our success. But it was Brian with whom millions identified – and not just fans. Musicians from Dylan and Hendrix to John and Paul admired his talent. And it was Brian who gave us an edge in the image stakes.

When people think of the Stones now, Mick and Keith come to mind. Back then, it was as likely to have been Brian. He had style and, despite the way he was towards the end, he did more than anyone to glamorise hippy chic. He was probably a better natural musician than the rest of us put together – he played bloody great bottleneck guitar long before anyone else in England knew what it was.

Brian was weak, had hang-ups and at times was a pain in the arse. But he named us, we were his idea and he chose what we first played. We were Brian's band and without him our little blues outfit wouldn't have become the greatest rock'n'roll band in the world.

Keith once said to Brian, 'You'll never make 30, man,' to which Brian simply replied, 'I know.'

As the years go by, I become even more convinced that he's entitled to that free pardon. Brian Jones is a legend and his legacy is there for all to hear. While the Rolling Stones damaged all of us in some way, Brian was the only one who died.

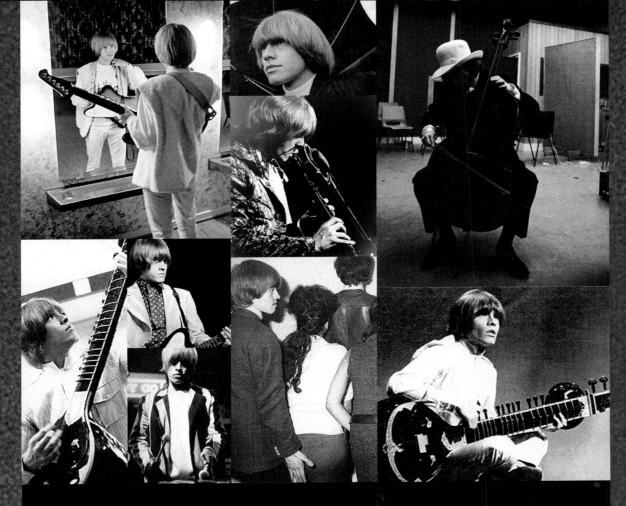

'If Keith and Mick were the mind and body of the Stones, Brian was clearly the soul.'
ROLLING STONE, *9 August, 1969*

The Stones In The Park

In the immediate aftermath of Brian's death, Astrid and I stayed up for hours – there was no way I could sleep. When somebody close to you dies, it's strange to think that you'll never see him or her again. But everything else goes on. Hard though it was, there were decisions to be made. Should we do our Hyde Park show?

I N THOSE FIRST FEW hours, Astrid and I talked of all the good times Brian and I had shared, and all we had achieved. With hindsight it's easy to see Brian's faults, and in truth we saw many of them at the time. But we all have flaws and shortcomings.

That afternoon, I met the boys at our office. Brian's death was all we could talk about. We had to go to Lime Grove Studios to record an appearance on *Top Of The Pops*. It was not our greatest performance.

Mick had spent time earlier in the day trying to find an all-white outfit to wear at his friend Prince Rupert Loewenstein's white-themed ball that night. He phoned designer Michael Fish who had just what Mick was looking for. The outfit was a Greek-inspired, voile dress. Many years later, Sammy Davis Jr told me that he had ordered the outfit and was due to collect it before it was lent to Mick. Sammy ordered three more at £89 each, in black, brown and champagne.

Stones on TV
Granada, who paid a considerable sum to Blackhill Enterprises for the exclusive rights, filmed the concert. It was first shown in the UK in September 1969.

The press was full of Brian's death. Speculation was rife that we would cancel our Hyde Park concert, but we were unanimous that it should go ahead in Brian's honour. On Friday we rehearsed at Apple between 5pm and 8pm. We couldn't do too much as Mick was suffering from laryngitis. When I got back to my hotel suite I found Anna Wohlin with Astrid. Tom Keylock had rescued her from the press and taken her to Astrid to hide, thinking that it would be easier for another Swede to take care of her.

At the same time, in Hyde Park, around 500 people were bedding down under the stars. At 11pm, there was a poignant moment as someone called for a two-minute silence to remember Brian. Everyone stood in tribute. A few people smashed up deckchairs, tore down fences and stripped branches from trees to light around 50 small fires. Several idiots brandished flaming torches and got pelted with empty beer cans by other angry fans. One went off in an ambulance with a cut head. In all, 12 people were arrested and five were charged. By morning, there were around 7,000 people in the park.

Pay to play
The free concert – organised by Blackhill Enterprises in association with our organisation – was quite expensive to mount. The cost was even higher than the £600 or so it had cost to put on Blind Faith's free concert. Blackhill reckoned they spent £3,000. One significant factor was the stage, normally three feet high. For this event, a special new 10-foot platform had to be constructed. This allowed more people to see us perform. There was also a special 10-foot dais for the amplifiers, raising them 20 feet above the ground, enabling the sound to carry further.

Terry Yason from Blackhill Enterprises said, 'I think everybody will be able to hear, but only 75,000 will be able to see.' It all seems rather quaint today, but back then it was cutting-edge stuff.

Other significant costs included the hire of caravans for backstage to be used as offices and changing rooms. Mick ordered carpet to be laid on the stage so he could dance barefoot. He wanted the stage decorated with palm trees, parakeets and special flowers. Palm trees were no problem, but parakeets were in short supply.

Beneath the stage was a first-aid centre, while in front, VIPs were allowed in a special enclosure. A hundred stewards were hired to protect the enclosure and its guests. If the weather was fine, an audience of a quarter of a million was expected.

Hippy heaven
According to police estimates, 20,000 fans were sweltering in the sunshine by 11am. Hundreds cooled off in the Serpentine lake and every ice cream and soft drink was sold. People strummed guitars and played tom-toms as thousands swarmed into the park. Beaded, bangled, bejewelled – it looked like a hippy heaven.

My son Stephen, now seven years old, arrived

'Cool it for a minute, because I would really like to say something about Brian. I don't know how to do this thing, but I'm going to try. I'm just going to say something that was written by Shelley.' **MICK**

at the Londonderry House Hotel. Our suite had been chosen as the meeting place for everyone and all anyone could speak about was Brian. Mick, still suffering from laryngitis, was very upset and found it difficult talking about his former band-mate without becoming emotional. I told Mick that there was a reason for it all and we should try to feel positive about it.

Shelley's blues

Back in the park, King Crimson's set included the anthemic '20th Century Schizoid Man'. Apparently, Crimson and Family were the only bands that captured the audience's imagination. We didn't see them as we were still at Londonderry House.

'There was a sense of occasion as we hit "Schizoid" for the thousands of British hippies and devotees of contemporary culture laid out on the grass before us in an endless ocean of colour.' IAN MCDONALD, *King Crimson*

A dark-green converted army ambulance waited at the hotel to take us to the park. Allen Klein was acting as Chief of Security and certainly looked the part. We arrived shortly after 4.15pm and slowly made our way through the throng. We sat backstage with our instruments, trying to tune up using a harmonica but had great difficulty because of the noise.

'The Stones want to play tonight for Brian.' SAM CUTLER, *compere*

We went onstage at 5.25pm to an amazing reception. I can barely describe the feelings I had, thinking how much Brian would have loved it – the hippy king with all his courtiers. The fans' warmth and affection seemed to come at us in waves. Mick intended to wear a snakeskin suit designed by Ossie Clark, but decided to wear the white dress, as it was so hot.

Mick made a brief speech, then read an extract from Percy Bysshe Shelley's 'Adonais'. Hyde Park erupted. We began with Johnny Winter's 'I'm Yours, She's Mine', blasting the air with our music as 3,500 butterflies were released from their cardboard prisons. Mick leapt into the air, performing as only he can. With that, the most famous free concert in the UK was under way. Years later I read a report by a fan who described our playing as 'ropey'. He was right. Brian's

Life, like a dome of many-coloured glass, Stains the white radiance of Eternity, Until Death tramples it to fragments.—Die, If thou wouldst be with that which thou dost seek Follow where all is fled !— . . .

death, our lack of roadwork, the introduction of a number of new songs and a lack of rehearsals all conspired against us.

We played for just under an hour and the concert ended at around 6.15pm. Afterwards, the multitude simply melted away. According to much of the press, the crowd was estimated at 250,000, or closer to 500,000, if you believed the organisers and the *Daily Telegraph*. Another legendary day was over. All in all, it was a very 'British' affair.

Park life

One of the few losers in the show was Pierre Rostand, managing director of the UK division of Chambourcy. The head of the French yogurt, cheese and desserts concern was ejected from the show for breaking Royal Park regulations by selling 10,000 pots of yogurt to fans.

A silent film of the show was made by Peter Ungerleiden and titled *Under My Thumb*. It was shown in March 1970 at the New Arts Lab in Camden.

We stopped briefly in our caravan after finishing the set and then we were all hustled into the truck and driven back to Londonderry House. We relaxed before everyone dispersed. Astrid and I spent the night in the hotel – it was low-key. When you are so closely involved in something that everyone views as important, it somehow seems to pass you by. Later, Mick and Marianne went to the Pop Proms at the Royal Albert Hall to see Chuck Berry and the Who.

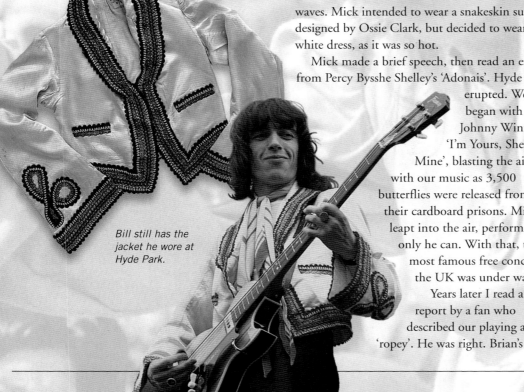

Bill still has the jacket he wore at Hyde Park.

Memories Of A Free Festival

'In the summer of 1969, I went to Europe after graduating high school. In July I was in Rome when I read that Brian had died. The paper said that the Stones were going to make their Hyde Park concert a tribute to him. My girlfriend and I packed up and left for London. We attended the Hyde Park concert and were lucky to see the stage. The atmosphere was wonderful. It was good to be there with European fans who really loved the Stones. It was a bittersweet experience.' STEPHAN SHERRICK, *in an email to Bill, 6 April, 1999*

'Blackhill told us the Stones would appear and urged us to provide 1,500 watts or more. Suddenly, the responsibility of what we were doing dawned upon me. A concert with a group as famous as the Stones. An audience estimated at 500,000. Another problem was finding on the day that we could only muster 600 watts, so we asked the groups to loan us their gear and the roadies responded magnificently. These boys knew so much about amplification that they made me feel like a novice. They humped our two-and-a-half tons and 1,500 watts of equipment into the towers quickly and efficiently. People scrambling about the stage knocked the whole mains feed out on three occasions.' CHARLIE WATKINS, *Watkins Electric Music*

'I thought it would be fun, so I decided to go without telling anybody. I took my sleeping bag and spent Friday night in Hyde Park. It wasn't worth it. I couldn't see a thing for the crowds.' COLIN GRAY, *(aged 11) from Stockton, County Durham, who hitch-hiked 230 miles to London*

Set list

'I'm Yours, She's Mine'
'Jumpin' Jack Flash'
'Mercy Mercy'
'Stray Cat Blues'
'No Expectations'
'I'm Free'
'Down Home Girl'
'Love In Vain'
'Lovin' Cup'
'Honky Tonk Women'
'Midnight Rambler'
'(I Can't Get No) Satisfaction'
'Street Fighting Man'
'Sympathy For The Devil'

'I was around 18 and from east London. We weren't Hell's Angels; we were the Forest Gate Greasers. We all liked the band, so about 10 or 12 of us turned up the night before and slept out in the park. In the morning we went up to the stage set up and asked if we could help provide security. There were other Stones security people as well, but they said sure, OK. There were some of the Hell's Angels there. There was one tall thin guy called Wild Child – at least that's what he had on his jacket. He had a Nazi helmet on and was doing a lot of shouting and strutting about, but there weren't too many of them there. I think that some of them were riding around. We had a chat and a cup of tea. We didn't get any money for it, but they gave us a seven-inch single of "Honky Tonk Women".' STEFAN GRADOFIELSKI, *a greaser*

334

‘Mick Taylor played very little lead guitar and I could barely hear Charlie or Bill, but it was a nostalgic, out-of-tune ritual that summed up a decade of pop.’ **CHRIS WELCH,** *Melody Maker, 12 July, 1969*

Support in the park
Starting at 1pm:
The Third Ear Band
King Crimson
Screw
Alexis Korner's New Church
Family
The Battered Ornaments

Ginger Johnson's African Drummers played on 'Sympathy For The Devil'

The butterflies were supplied by Brian Gardiner, a Cambridge researcher to the Unit of Invertebrates Chemical Physiology. He bred them as a hobby. He said a number of them were sterilised, but some were not. A further 500 came from World Wide Butterflies, run by Robert Gooden. He said they were all unsterilised. They cost £300.

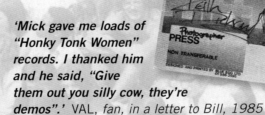

‘Mick gave me loads of "Honky Tonk Women" records. I thanked him and he said, "Give them out you silly cow, they're demos".’ VAL, *fan, in a letter to Bill, 1985*

‘In the musicians' enclosure were Paul and Linda McCartney, Eric Clapton and girlfriend Alice Ormsby-Gore, Ginger Baker, Donovan, Chris Barber, Marsha Hunt, Kenny Lynch, Stevie Winwood and Mama Cass. On the stage were Marianne and her son Nicholas, Michael Cooper and Julie Felix. Allen Klein looked after my son Stephen.’ BILL

‘It got very intense around the stage and we moved away to the other side of the lake – many did that. Mick did make some references about what was going on, asking people to cool it and calm down, but by then the Hells Angels were biking up and down the road to the side.’ PETER COLE, *fan*

Encouraged by offers of a free record for every three sacks of rubbish collected, fans cleared up 15 tons of debris and left the park cleaner than on a normal Saturday.

'HONKY TONK WOMEN'

Subtle horns, a fabulously funky guitar riff and a dream chorus heralded the Stones' 15th UK and 20th US single. Released on 4 July and first performed on stage the following day at Hyde Park, 'Honky Tonk Women' has since been a mainstay of the Stones' live shows. It's another candidate in the quintessential Stones single stakes.

Recorded
a-side 12 May–12 June, 1969
b-side 17 and 28 November, 1968, 15 March and 28 May, 1969
Studio
Olympic Studios London
Producer
Jimmy Miller
Engineer
Glyn Johns
Release date
UK Friday 4 July, 1969
Decca F 12952
US Saturday 5 July, 1969
London 45 910
Composers
Jagger/Richard
Highest chart position
UK No 1, for five weeks
US No 1, for four weeks
Personnel
Jack Nitzsche: arrangements b-side
60-voice choir
Al Kooper: piano, organ and French horn

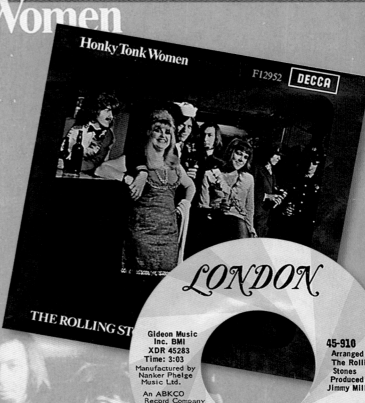

It was the band's longest running UK No 1 single, spending five weeks on top of the UK chart. It was their eighth and last UK No 1. Four weeks at the top of the US charts equalled the run enjoyed by 'Satisfaction'.

'"Honky Tonk Women" has been cut and marks the debut of new Stone Mick Taylor. He joined the group this week to replace outgoing founder member Brian, who does not appear on either side of the new release.' LESLIE PERRIN, *in a press release, June 1969*

The b-side, 'You Can't Always Get What You Want', was featured in the soundtrack of the 1983 film *The Big Chill*.

'An important single for the Stones, but a disappointing one for us. The supposedly gutsy "Honky Tonk Women" fails to make much impact and the drum and guitar sound is rather unconvincing.' MELODY MAKER, *July 1969*

'I added something to "Honky Tonk Women", but it was more or less complete when I arrived. I played the country kind of influence on the rock licks between the verses.' MICK TAYLOR, *1979*

'In the south of America we went to a ranch and wrote "Honky Tonk Women" because I was into a cowboy thing. The guitar is in open tuning – G – on that. I learned that particular tuning off Ry Cooder.' KEITH, *Rolling Stone, 19 August, 1971*

The Chelsea Drugstore on the Kings Road where Mick's prescription is filled in 'You Can't Always Get What You Want'.

Diary of a recording

'Honky Tonk Women' ran over a number of sessions which Bill noted in his diary.

Monday 12 May, 1969	First cut
Wednesday 14 May	Worked on 'Honky Tonk Women' again.
Sunday 25 May	Nicky Hopkins, piano, and brass overdubs by S Gregory and G Beadle on saxophone.
Wednesday 28 May	Girl singers, including Madeleine Bell, were recorded
Sunday 1 June	At 11pm, we had another go at recording 'Honky Tonk Women'. We tried various ways to do it, and eventually Jimmy Miller sat down at the drums and showed Charlie a rhythm. Jimmy picked up a cowbell and played it on the track. At 3.15am we got a great master. We did a rough mix, finishing at 4am. Mick Taylor was at this session.
Wednesday 4, 8, 12 June	Mixing

It was now taking the band a little longer to record than it had back when they cut 'Come On'…

'That's what it is – just instant *move your arse*.' CHARLIE, *1973*

The Pied Piper And His Lady

The morning after the concert, Astrid and I woke up at Londonderry House to news that scores of fans claimed to have seen a ghostly image of Brian on the stage. In reality, it was a life-size photograph. The *Daily Sketch* said, 'Love 'em or loathe 'em, the Stones are still the Pied Pipers of Britain's youth.' A duff note was struck by Brian's most recent chauffeur, Brian Palastanga, who was quick to sell his story to the *People*.

WHILE WE TRIED TO GET ON with life after the concert, the *People* interviewed other people and revelled in the lurid details of Brian's personal life.

Mick and Marianne left London and flew to Sydney via Los Angeles to begin filming *Ned Kelly*. As they left, they heard that 'Honky Tonk Women' had zoomed into the charts at UK No 19 after just 48 hours. In those days, things moved a little slower – today everything seems to go straight to No 1. Mick appearing as Ned Kelly was not popular. Listeners called radio stations and others signed petitions against 'a long-haired British pop star' playing their national folk hero. Mick was obviously going to have to tread carefully in Australia, especially if anyone got hold of the *Daily Sketch* from 8 July.

'Huh! Those Australians. They really are dummies! But you can bet that there will probably be one or two people protesting when I get there and I'll throw beer at them. They're so pathetic. When it comes to acting, they make out it's something special. It's not. It's just as natural as singing. You can either do it or you can't.' MICK, *Daily Sketch, 8 July, 1969*

When Mick and Marianne landed in Sydney, Mick was dressed more like the Pied Piper than Ned Kelly, wearing a maroon maxi-length coat, black-and-white checked flared suit, a white Isadora scarf, a straw hat, black field boots and an Italian leather fringe purse over his shoulder. He wound up waiting reporters by blowing them kisses.

'My first numbing impression when I saw him was that this wasn't Mick Jagger, it was Barry Humphries having us on.' PETER BOWERS, *Sydney Sun, July 1969*

Back in the UK, it was announced that Brian's funeral would be on Thursday 10 July, in Cheltenham. The family asked for the funeral to be private and the police made arrangements to deal with the large influx of fans. Anna Wohlin, who had attended the inquest on Monday, flew home to Stockholm.

I was also in court that week, to divorce Diane. Judge Willis approved the financial arrangements I entered into at the time of our separation. He asked if I had a residence large enough to accommodate Stephen and there was laughter in court when I gave details of Gedding Hall. I was given custody with agreed access for Diane. Looking back, this was remarkable, given my shoulder-length hair and the fact that I was a man. I was a member of the most notorious band Britain had ever known, members of which had been found guilty of drug abuse over the previous two years.

Tears go by

Over in Sydney, things were going badly wrong. Mick was doing an interview in his suite during which Marianne repeatedly called to him from the bedroom. At 11.30am, she staggered into the room, crying, and fell to the floor, lapsing into a coma. She was taken to St Vincent's Hospital and admitted under her real name, Evelyn Dunbar. Mick had followed the ambulance to the hospital and waited for a while before returning to the hotel. Marianne was given artificial respiration for a long time before she resumed breathing. She was moved to the intensive care ward, where the staff injected her with saline and tried to maintain her blood pressure.

Detectives from the New South Wales drug squad arrived at the hospital to inquire into Marianne's condition, but were told she couldn't be disturbed. They were told that it would be up to a week before they could interview her. Later, a hospital spokesman said her condition was serious, and she was still in a coma. It was believed that she was suffering from an overdose of the sleeping drug Amytal. Before very long, the press found out about it and began camping out at the hospital. Mick held a conference, telling the reporters that he considered Australia even more puritanical in its attitudes than other 'colonial nations' such as South Africa. He light-heartedly offered to 'ride in and shoot up Victoria's Kelly Country'.

'Marianne turns me on to good things. She has led me into music and drama and literature which I haven't read before. I turn her on to more basic things. I don't think she's taken an overdose. Certainly not. She is suffering from extreme exhaustion. She is a delicate woman and the trip here was hard. Her condition doesn't seem to be serious, but they are checking her. The Stones' drug-taking is no worse than anyone else's. It's just one of the facts of being in a rock'n'roll band.' MICK

In a radio interview, Mick discussed the church and religion, marriage and children and offered some self-criticism, saying, 'I don't like my ears. My feet are too big and I'd like to be two inches taller. If I had my life over again, I'd change what I look like.'

That evening Marianne was reported to be critically ill. It was revealed that her collapse had been due to what doctors described as a massive overdose of barbiturates. Police officers visited the Chevron Hotel and took away two containers and a number of capsules. They interviewed Mick as part of routine enquiries.

Some 36 hours later, Marianne was still in a coma and doctors believed she was likely to remain unconscious for another 48 hours, although her condition appeared to be stabilising. She was breathing with the assistance of an artificial respirator. Tests suggested she had taken several types of drugs, including a large quantity of sodium amytal and sleeping tablets. Her relationship with Mick had been tense since she miscarried and she was, after all, still only 22 years old.

Are There No Stones In Heaven?

On the morning of Thursday 10 July, Astrid and I were driven to Brian's parents' house in Cheltenham. It was intensely emotional for us to meet Brian's family. Charlie and Shirley Watts, Ian and Cynthia Stewart, Tom Keylock, ex-manager Eric Easton, and ex-girlfriend Suki Potier were also there. Linda Lawrence and Julian, the son she had with Brian, flew in from America, where she lived with the singer Donovan.

Mick and Marianne, of course, were filming in Australia. As we talked between ourselves it was very difficult to comment on much, except for the masses of floral tributes. Among them were a wreath of red roses shaped like a guitar from Brian's parents and sister Barbara, a wreath from Mick and Marianne and an eight-foot arrangement of red and yellow roses from the Stones. From our office, Jo Bergman sent a rose.

We were driven to Cheltenham Parish Church, where Brian had been confirmed and sang in the choir as a schoolboy. There were 14 cars in the cortege, four of which contained flowers. The drive through the streets of Cheltenham was, in all the sadness, a wonderful experience. Hundreds of people, some who had come to pay their respects and others who were just shopping, stood in the gently falling rain, watching the cortege pass by. Many held handkerchiefs and were openly weeping.

More than 500 people gathered at the church to say goodbye to Brian. Outside were lots of girls, dressed in black and carrying red roses. Many sobbed as the casket was carried into the church. The service, following a request from Brian's father, was simple. It took just 15 minutes. Canon Hopkins, who took the service, talked of Brian as being a rebel, which at

Attending the funeral, from left, Brian's sister Barbara, Suki Potier, his parents Louisa and Lewis and Stones' driver Tom Keylock

'We had our violent disagreements, but we never stopped loving him.' LEWIS JONES

'I hold in my hand a telegram which Mr and Mrs Jones treasure more than they can say. It was sent to them by Brian some little while ago after he had come into conflict with the law. The telegram said, "Please don't worry. Don't jump to hasty conclusions and please don't judge me too harshly." Here I believe Brian speaks to us not only for himself, but also for all his generation and I pass his words on to any who will hear of this service today. Brian was confident that whatever trouble he had landed himself in, his parents' love would remain unshaken.'

CANON HOPKINS

Suki Potier, centre *and Barbara Jones,* right, *at Brian's funeral*

Hundreds of people lined the route and filled the graveyard. Everyone stood quietly, immersed in his or her own thoughts, as the two hundred-weight, solid bronze casket, which had been flown over from New York, was lowered into the green carpeted grave. Many girls tossed their roses on top of the coffin.

The press behaved shamefully, pushing relatives and mourners out of the way and hanging over the grave, taking photos as Brian's mother held Julian close to her. We went back to Brian's parents' house and talked about him, the funeral and had all those other funny little conversations that happen at such a time. The drive back to London in the rain seemed to take a long, long time.

'I just say my prayers for him. I hope he becomes blessed. I hope he is finding peace, and I really want him to.' MICK, *in the NME, 12 July, 1969*

the time we thought was somewhat judgemental.

With the passing of the years it is easier to see how difficult it was for the older generation to contemplate the death of someone so young. Brian lived a life so different from any Canon Hopkins could or would want to imagine. There will always be a generation gap, but back then it was a yawning chasm.

After Canon Hopkins' service, we left the church for the three-mile drive to the cemetery near Prestbury.

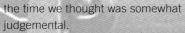

Wight And Woodstock

WOODSTOCK
MUSIC & ART FAIR
presents
AN
AQUARIAN
EXPOSITION
in
WHITE LAKE, N.Y.

3 DAYS
of PEACE
& MUSIC

AUGUST
15, 16, 17

In August 1969, there were major festivals to keep music fans happy. One was a US festival that's become so famous it's known by one word: Woodstock. Two weeks later in the UK, fans flocked to the Isle of Wight to see some of the biggest names on the scene.

Over three days in mid-August, a festival which would gain legendary status took place in upstate New York. Entitled the Woodstock Music and Art Fair, the event attracted 500,000. All roads, including the freeways, were blocked for 20 miles around the site. Despite it being declared a disaster area, the festival engendered a tribal spirit among its fans who have been referred to since as the Woodstock Generation.

Among those appearing over three days were Jimi Hendrix, Creedence Clearwater Revival, Santana, Jefferson Airplane, Crosby, Stills, Nash and Young, Richie Havens, Ten Years After, Joan Baez, the Band, the Grateful Dead, Blood, Sweat and Tears, Mountain, Canned Heat, Tim Hardin, Country Joe and the Fish, John Sebastian, Sly and the Family Stone, Johnny Winter, Ravi Shanker and the Who.

Famously, besides the music there were three deaths, two births and four miscarriages at Woodstock. Where are those two 30-somethings now?

> Of the 400,000 who attended, 320,000 left before Jimi Hendrix played 'The Star Spangled Banner'

The Isle of Wight
A major British rock festival followed just two weeks later. Held at Woodside Bay near Ryde it was called, rather appropriately,

the Isle of Wight Festival of Music. On the second day, Keith hired a yacht to take some friends to the festival from Redlands. Anita didn't want to go, having just given birth to baby Marlon. But Keith was joined by Donald Cammell, John Dunbar, Michael Cooper, 'Spanish' Tony Sanchez and Robert Fraser. They slept on the boat overnight.

On the Sunday, 29-year-old Bob Dylan appeared with the Band (Bob got £38,000 cash for his one-hour show). Among the celebrities gathered at the event were Liz Taylor, Richard Burton, Jane Fonda, Roger Vadim, John and Yoko, George Harrison and Ringo Starr (the Beatles' bass player missed it too, but Linda had just given birth to daughter Mary). Charlie and Shirley Watts also went. As Mick couldn't be there, he sent Dylan a hat and a note saying, 'I'm on some strange Australian mountain range.' This was a reference to a line in 'Outlaw Blues' from Dylan's 1965 album *Bringing It All Back Home*.

The festival drew a crowd of over 200,000. Other acts included the Who, the Moody Blues, Fat Mattress, Joe Cocker, the Bonzo Dog Band, Family, Free, the Pretty Things, Marsha Hunt and White Trash, Battered Ornaments, Aynsley Dunbar Retaliation, Blodwyn Pig, Gypsy, Blonde On Blonde, the Edgar Broughton Band, King Crimson, Ritchie Havens, Tom Paxton, Pentangle, Julie Felix, Gary Farr, Liverpool Scene, Indo Jazz Fusions and the Third Ear Band.

Keith on his way over to the Isle of Wight

Above, Bob Dylan at the Isle Of Wight; left, Joan Baez

BOB DYLAN
& THE BAND
IN CONCERT

Hail The Conquering Heroes

Just days after Brian's funeral, Mick called Stones publicist Leslie Perrin in London. He told him that Marianne was expected to recover consciousness within the next 24 hours. He then left for Melbourne to shoot the first scene of Ned Kelly with director Tony Richardson. When it became clear that Marianne was not going to be fit enough to film, her part was taken by a 20-year-old drama student, Diane Craig.

Mick filming Ned Kelly

O N MONDAY 14 JULY, Marianne's Austrian-born mother, Baroness Erisso, left London for Sydney. Mick was travelling from the set to the hospital to be at Marianne's bedside and he was there when she finally opened her eyes later that evening.

Filming continued while 'Honky Tonk Women' went to UK No 1 on Saturday 19 July, remaining there for five weeks. Anita Pallenberg announced to the press that she was expecting Keith's baby in August. A week later, Mick celebrated his 26th birthday.

The following day, Mick visited Marianne at the hospital. They spent the afternoon

Anita, Keith and baby Marlon

wandering through the grounds. He stayed for hours and resumed filming later in the day.

Looking back on this today it seems almost impossible that so much happened in those two weeks.

Baby Brando

Anita entered Kings College Hospital in Dulwich to have Keith's baby. On Sunday 10 August, they had a seven-pound, four-ounce baby son. Keith, wearing a black shirt, black velvet trousers with silver studded seams and brown snakeskin boots, picked up Anita and baby in his blue Bentley and took them home to Cheyne Walk. They named the baby Marlon, after the actor

Marlon Brando.

On the same day 'Honky Tonk Women' went to US No 1. It had already sold a million copies. A few months later, in an interview with *The Saturday Review,* both Mick and Keith admitted they hadn't wanted it to be released as a single.

Marianne left Australia with her mother on Sunday 17 August, to continue her convalescence at a Swiss sanatorium. Mick stayed on to continue shooting the film. At Captain's Flat, near Canberra, they shot 'the siege of Glenrowan' and Mick was injured for real. The replica Navy Colt revolver loaded with blanks that he was holding backfired. He was thrown to the ground and a piece of metal from the percussion cap embedded itself in the base of his right thumb. At hospital, doctors removed the metal and stitched him up. He left with his arm in a sling.

Mick puts his spin on it

During the filming, Mick said, 'I think we're all latent homosexuals. Like most men, Ned Kelly probably had affairs with women. And he had a great camaraderie with men.' It was good to know that even with Andrew well off the scene Mick hadn't lost our touch.

Back in the UK, we continued work with Jimmy Miller at Olympic. Mick

Side one
1. 'Jumpin' Jack Flash'
2. 'Mother's Little Helper'
3. '2,000 Light Years From Home'
4. 'Let's Spend the Night Together'
5. 'You'd Better Move On'
6. 'We Love You'

Side two
1. 'Street Fighting Man'
2. 'She's A Rainbow'
3. 'Ruby Tuesday'
4. 'Dandelion'
5. 'Sittin' On The Fence'
6. 'Honky Tonk Women'

US side 1
1. 'Paint It, Black'
2. 'Ruby Tuesday'
3. 'She's A Rainbow'
4. 'Jumpin' Jack Flash'
5. 'Mother's Little Helper'
6. 'Let's Spend the Night Together'

US side 2
1. 'Honky Tonk Women'
2. 'Dandelion'
3. '2,000 Light Years From Home'
4. 'Have You Seen Your Mother, Baby'
5. 'Street Fighting Man'

Cover photography
Ethan Russell

Release
UK Friday 12 September, 1969 Decca SKL/LK 501
US Saturday 13 September, 1969 London NPS 3

Highest chart position (time on chart)
UK No 2 (37 weeks)
US No 2 (16 weeks)

Not bad for a band that, according to Keith, in 1962, 'No matter what we do we'll never be up there in the hit parade. That's impossible with our sort of music. We are a kind of minority. But if we have a real go at it, really work at our material, we could perhaps get a bit of work and maybe build up a little following by persuading people to like the same things as we like.

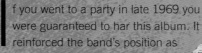

If you went to a party in late 1969 you were guaranteed to har this album. It reinforced the band's position as the purveyor of party pop and rock.

Some of Ethan Russell's outtakes from the photoshoot

'On Wednesday, 21 May I met up with the boys for an afternoon photo session with Ethan Russell at St Katharine's Dock, next to Tower Bridge. We needed a cover for our second greatest hits album.' BILL

Prince Rupert Loewenstein
Mick had met merchant banker Prince Rupert socially in 1969. As they got to know each other it was clear that the Prince's financial skills could be tremendously helpful to the Stones. The band's dissatisfaction with Klein was one thing, having someone they could trust and respect to deal with ther complex financial affairs was another. Prince Rupert proved to be the ideal solution and 30 years later he remains their financial advisor. In the early 1980s, Prince Rupert founded a group to advise other people with similar backgrounds to the Stones.

'After the coming US tour, I think we'll do some concerts in Europe. I'd very much like to do Prague – if we can get in there.' KEITH

One Russian newspaper denounced Western pop as a 'flood of cacophony, yells and giggles'.

Keith was getting into the idea of playing Eastern Europe again, despite the Cold War – it would take another 21 years. On 18 August, 1990, on the Urban Jungle Tour, we finally played Prague to an audience of 107,000.

On Tuesday 14 October, Mick's friend Prince Rupert Loewenstein sent him a memo, laying out the pros and cons of becoming tax exiles. He suggested moving to France for two years. It was the first time we had really begun to get to grip with our finances. We wanted to get control back on our side of the Atlantic. We were continuing to have difficulties in getting our hands on our

money held by Allen Klein in New York. Numerous phone calls and telexes were flying back and forth. Our London office was existing on a financial shoestring. A telex to Allen Klein in October was typical:

We still have no money. What has gone wrong over there? How does one keep the wolves from the door? Please reply as this is really desperate.

On the morning of Friday 17 October, Astrid and I met our entire entourage at London airport and flew to Los Angeles. We were heading over to the States for what was not only going to be the sixth US tour, but also our first of any kind

joined us after he arrived home from Australia on Friday 12 September, 1969. Two days later we finally announced that our US tour would begin on 26 October. With our new album almost finished, and the greatest hits package ready, London Records were gearing up for one of the largest promotions ever undertaken on a touring act. Keith attended a private viewing of the *Rock'n'Roll Circus* and Mick said, 'We really must finish the *Rock'n'Roll Circus* soon.' Mick and Marianne's court appearance was put back until 18 December, because of our US tour.

Shelter people

Glyn Johns called me and said that he was recording an album with American artist Leon Russell at Olympic. He wanted Charlie and I to work with him. Going to Olympic, we joined Stevie Winwood on guitar and Leon Russell on piano, along with producer Denny Cordell. Leon played us a few demos, so we could get the feel of his songs. The first one had key changes all the way through and Stevie and I looked at each other and said 'Fuck!'

We cut two tracks that day, including 'Roll Away The Stone' and two the next. I got to know Leon and his band really well and he paid back the favour a few years later by playing on my first two solo albums.

During the first two weeks of October, there were frequent sessions at Olympic with Jimmy Miller and assorted members of the band. In the same fortnight our second greatest hits package, *Through The Past, Darkly*, had made over $1 million in the US. It was also reported that in Poland, Hungary and Czechoslovakia our last album was fetching something like £20 on the black market – despite criticism from the press.

Charlie, Seraphina and Shirley leave London.

It was on this tour that Sam Cutler, who acted as MC, coined the phrase, 'the greatest rock'n'roll band in the world', to introduce the Stones… It certainly stuck.

Tickets for the 17-date, 23-show tour sold out in hours. So great was the demand that extra concerts were added in New York and Los Angeles. The Stones started out rehearsing in Stephen Stills' basement before moving to Warner Brothers' Studios.

'After playing every night for three or four years you miss the road.' KEITH

The Stones flew between most gigs, basing themselves in Los Angeles and New York for most of the tour. Even though they were flying they quite often went on stage late, sometimes very late. On 8 November in Inglewood, the second show didn't begin until 4am.

Ticket prices for the concerts ran from $4.50 to $7.50 (and hit a high of $8 in NYC). The Stones played to around 335,000 people and the tour grossed $1,907,180.

In one of the most famous exchanges between Mick and the press, a girl reporter asked, 'One of your biggest songs was "Satisfaction". Have you found satisfaction?' 'Sexually, yes. Financially, no. Philosophically, trying,' Mick replied.

'Jimi came to see us at Madison Square garden. He sat through the show behind Keith's amp. Not a safe place for most people.' BILL

Big sister
On the first day at Madison Square Garden, 'Just as Ike and Tina finished their set, Janis Joplin came onstage and she and Tina sang together. Incredibly exciting, even if Janis' key wasn't the same one the band was playing,' wrote Richard Robinson in *Disc*. Bill: 'She then told us she would come onstage during our performance. She was warned that if she did, we'd walk off and leave the stage to her. She forgot it.'

North America, *November 1969*

7 November State University, Fort Collins, Colorado
8 November Inglewood Forum, Los Angeles, California (two shows)
9 November Oakland Coliseum, Oakland, California (two shows)
10 November International Sports Arena, San Diego, California
11 November Coliseum, Phoenix, Arizona
13 November Moody Coliseum, Dallas, Texas
14 November University Coliseum, Auburn, Alabama
15 November University of Illinois, Champagne, Illinois (two shows)
16 November International Amphitheater, Chicago, Illinois (two shows)
20 November Inglewood Forum, Los Angeles, California
24 November Olympia Stadium, Detroit, Michigan
25 November Spectrum, Philadelphia, Pennsylvania
26 November Civic Center, Baltimore, Maryland
27 November Madison Square Garden, New York
28 November Madison Square Garden, New York (two shows)
29 November Boston Gardens, Boston, Massachusetts (two shows)
30 November International Raceway, West Palm Beach, Florida

Jimi Hendrix and Charlie, backstage

Set from:
'Jumpin' Jack Flash'
'Carol'
'Sympathy For The Devil'
'Stray Cat Blues'
'Love In Vain'
'Prodigal Son'
'You Got To Move'
'Under My Thumb'
'I'm Free'
'Midnight Rambler'
'Live With Me'
'Gimme Shelter'
'Little Queenie'
'Satisfaction'
'Honky Tonk Women'
'Street Fighting Man'

Support bands
The Stones wanted quality support bands and acts that they liked. At least two of the four artists were used at all the dates, except West Palm Beach: Terry Reid, BB King, Ike and Tina Turner and Chuck Berry.

At West Palm Beach Festival were the Moody Blues, Ten Years After, King Crimson, Spooky Tooth, the Band, Janis Joplin, Steppenwolf, the Chambers Brothers, and Iron Butterfly.

This was the first tour on which staff and guest backstage security passes were used.

The Greatest Rock'n'Roll Band In The World

On Sunday 23 November the Stones appeared on Ed Sullivan's Show, their sixth and last appearance. Ella Fitzgerald was on the show and the Stones performed 'Gimme Shelter', 'Honky Tonk Women' and 'Love In Vain'. Apparently, Mr Ed carefully viewed the movements of the Stones and advised them to avoid any suggestiveness.

Albert Goldman said, 'Mick Jagger and company are "pure Nuremberg".' He saw strong parallels between Jagger and Hitler using their art as a youth magnet.

'During our show at the International Amphitheater in Chicago we played, as we usually did, "Midnight Rambler". In the paper the next day it was mistakenly referred to as the "Midnight Rapist".' BILL

'Hysterical girls whipped off their panties and hurled them.' **THE PEOPLE**

From left, the Stones aboard their private jet; Chuck Berry and Mick; Ike and Tina with Mick backstage; BB King onstage

What the papers said...

'The Stones have succeeded in turning outrage into art. Are they really able to use all that money?' ROBERT HILBURN, *Los Angeles Times*

'Mick Jagger answered most of the questions in a polite way. Bill Wyman shouted for order. Charlie Watts looked bored, Keith Richard toyed with the single yellow earring that swung in and out of his long black hair. Someone asked Mick Taylor how he felt about replacing Brian Jones. Taylor shrugged.' BETTY FLYNN, *writing about the New York Press conference*

'It turns out that the Stones are musicians rather than monsters' AL RUDIS, *Chicago Sun Times*

'The Rolling Stones took the fans by storm, preaching male chauvinism, sex, drugs, freedom and violent revolution.' NEW YORK DAILY NEWS

'The Stones present a theatrical musical performance that has no equal in our culture.' THE NEW YORKER

CONCERTS WEST & STUDENT COALITION PRESENT ONE HISTORIC CONCERT

THE ROLLING STONES

SMU MOODY COLISEUM — NOVEMBER 13 - 8:00 P.M.
TICKETS—$7.50 $6.50 $5.50 and $4.00
TELEPHONE ORDERS - 363-9311
MAIL ORDERS to Preston Ticket Agency
P.O. Box 12000
Dallas, Texas 75225

◇ PRESTON TICKET AGENCY
◇ COGHILL-SIMMONS MUSIC STORES
◇ EXCHANGE PARK
◇ NEIMAN-MARCUS
◇ SMU-STUDENT CENTER
◇ PRESTON RECORD CENTER
◇ HOTEL TEXAS (FT. WORTH)

'You got a lot of nice things in Boston. One of them is us. Welcome to the homosexuals in the audience and all minority groups.' **MICK,** *greeting the fans at the Boston Gardens show*

for over three years. News of 'Honky Tonk Women' getting to US No 1 and strong sales of *Through The Past, Darkly* augured well.

This was Mick Taylor's first trip with the band. He and I checked into the Beverly Wilshire hotel. Mick and Keith were guests at Steve Stills' place near Laurel Canyon. Charlie and his family, along with Stu and Glyn Johns, moved into a mansion previously owned by the Du Pont family, overlooking Sunset Strip. This was to be group HQ on the West Coast.

Preparing for battle

At Charlie's house, we met tour director and nephew of Allen Klein, Ronnie Schneider, and John Jaymes, head of Young American Enterprises. Jaymes was to deal with transportation, security and public relations. Our all-star bill would include BB King, Ike and Tina Turner, Chuck Berry and UK singer Terry Reid. We planned to play for over an hour, including old songs and a few from our new album which Keith had decided to call *Let It Bleed*. We confidently expected to gross $2 million by the end of the tour, by far our biggest-grossing of our career.

Reporters, photographers, cameramen and hangers-on assembled for a press conference in the Sans Souci Room at the Beverly Wilshire. We told them that we'd entered the country with no more difficulty than J Edgar Hoover and FBI agents – the truth was that without Brian, things were easier. On 21 October, we sent a

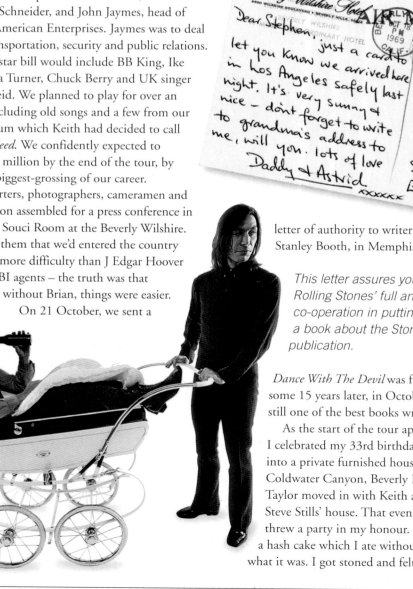

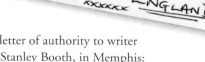

letter of authority to writer Stanley Booth, in Memphis:

This letter assures you of the Rolling Stones' full and exclusive co-operation in putting together a book about the Stones for publication.

Dance With The Devil was finally published some 15 years later, in October 1984. It is still one of the best books written about us.

As the start of the tour approached, I celebrated my 33rd birthday by moving into a private furnished house at 2101 Coldwater Canyon, Beverly Hills. Mick Taylor moved in with Keith and Mick at Steve Stills' house. That evening the Stones threw a party in my honour. Someone made a hash cake which I ate without knowing what it was. I got stoned and felt pretty awful

Postcard of the Beverley Wilshire hotel where Bill stayed and the back, sent to his son at school. Above, October press conference at Stones HQ in LA.

and panicky. I went into the bathroom and splashed my face with water, trying to get straight. Eventually, I had to leave. Stu drove Astrid and I back to our house, through the hills – really fast. We sat in the back of the car and I got very claustrophobic and wanted to jump out. Astrid kept me calm. It put me off drugs even more than ever.

Kicking the crap

After our warm-up gig in Colorado, our first proper show was at the 18,000 capacity LA Forum in Inglewood. Unfortunately, there was an ice hockey game in the afternoon and we agreed to go on after it was finished. The Forum was cleared of ice hockey fans at 4.30pm, leaving little time for us to set up. It took four hours to set up the stage and the sound system. The first of our two shows didn't start until 9pm. Terry Reid opened and was followed by BB King and then Ike and Tina

Girl by a motorcycle

On Monday 3 November, we did a photo session with Terry O'Neill at Steve Stills' house. The girl was called Angel. I met her again in May 1978 at Todd Rundgren's house in Woodstock. By then married with a daughter, she was working as Todd's housekeeper.

Turner. We finally took the stage at 11pm.

The fans that were trying to get in to see the second show met the fans trying to get out from the first show – the result was a monumental traffic jam. We got on at 4am and played a 90-minute set. Fans packed the aisles and danced on their seats and there were stage invasions during both shows. The Forum gig became the most lucrative one-night stand in pop history. We grossed $260,000, beating by $20,000 the Beatles' record for their 1966 Shea Stadium show.

Three weeks and 300,000 fans later, we made it to the International Raceway at West Palm Beach in Florida, but only just. We had the worst flight that I have ever experienced. While the fans waited for us to arrive, promoter Dave Rupp allowed part of his raceway to be torn up and burned to keep them warm. We went on at 5am and played for an hour and a half. Our next stop on the live schedule was to be in San Francisco to play a free concert. We were going to take some time out to go into the studio before then.

On Tuesday 2 December, we flew to Atlanta, Georgia, then on to Sheffield, Alabama, for three days of recording sessions at the eight-track Muscle Shoals Sound. We had heard good things about the studio and wanted to try it out for ourselves. Jimmy Miller was already there waiting for us, as were Jimmy Johnson, the engineer at the studio, and Ahmet Ertegun, producer and founder of Atlantic Records, who was also using the studio. The first night we cut Mississippi Fred McDowell's 'You Got To Move' and I sat in on electric piano during some of the numerous takes. Mick Taylor played a Fender Telecaster and Keith played a National guitar. The second night we did 'Brown Sugar' with

Stu on piano. On our last night in the studio we cut a country ballad, 'Wild Horses', with Memphis session player Jimmy Dickinson on piano.

We left Muscle Shoals for San Francisco, arriving the day after *Let It Bleed* came out in Britain. During the tour, Keith had said to a journalist, 'It's always been the Stones thing to get up on stage and kick the crap out of everything.' Well, at Altamont we nearly had the crap kicked out of us.

Ahmet Ertegun talks with Mick.

Altamont

'It was a disaster right from the start. It went wrong from the moment we left Muscle Shoals.' STU

We had been working on the idea of a free concert in the Bay Area since
our show in Oakland. Idealistically, we thought that it would be the
West Coast's Woodstock. By the time we got back to California for the
6 December concert, it had been relocated several times. Golden
Gate Park was the first choice, but City Hall would not agree.
We then chose Sears Point Raceway in Sonoma County.
Their demands would not be met by our people.

M ick and others involved in the organisation met up with Hell's Angels to discuss the security arrangments. Just 24 hours before the concert, lawyer Melvin Belli was brought in and a contract was agreed with Dick Carter of the Altamont Raceway, 50 miles east of San Francisco. It was an 80-acre plot with parking for 80,000 cars. The biggest crowd they had handled to that date was 65,000.

Numerous people were involved in the logistics, including Chip Monck (who stage-managed the Monterey and Woodstock festivals), Sam Cutler, Rock Scully, Jerry Garcia and Phil Lesh (of the Grateful Dead), Lenny Hart (from the Dead's management company), David Crosby (of Crosby, Stills, Nash and Young) and John Jaymes and Ronnie Schneider from our organisation.

'It wasn't sloppy for lack of effort, but for lack of time.'
DAVID CROSBY, *after Altamont*

A sunken area near the highway was chosen as the best place for the stage, maximising everyone's view. It was estimated that something like 250,000 fans would show up and by early evening around 5,000 people were there. Mick went to the site by helicopter to check out the scene, where he did a walkabout and talked with fans, before returning to the hotel in San Francisco. By midnight about 25,000 fans had assembled.

As Saturday dawned, it was a little above freezing on a day when everything would go wrong. The gates were opened at 7am and within 30 minutes the hills were packed with people arriving from all directions. Soon there was a 30-mile jam and drivers simply abandoned their cars and walked to the site. Doctors and psychiatrists had been hired to help with anticipated drug problems, but faced a daunting task. Extra supplies of thorizene (used to reduce the bad effects of

hallucinogenic drugs) were flown in from a nearby hospital. There were numerous bad trips as a result of yellow pills given away as 'organic' acid.

To begin with Krishna monks provided the music as helicopters shuttled performers into the site. Hell's Angels acted as security guards – probably the greatest contradiction in the whole history of rock'n'roll. The concert was due to start at around 10am but it wasn't until 1pm that Santana began playing. Trouble started almost immediately. A young guy was set upon by Hell's Angels and pulverised with punches. He fell to the ground and was kicked in the face. For an encore, the Angels beat up a couple of naked people and then leapt on a photographer, smashing the camera into his face. They set about him with pool cues. He collapsed, drenched in blood, and was taken care of by the Red Cross.

'There were bad vibes from the start. The fights started because the Hell's Angels were pushing people around. There was no provocation – the Angels started the violence. I could see a guy from the stage who had a knife and wanted to stab somebody.' CARLOS SANTANA

By the time Santana started their third song, around 40 Hell's Angels had mounted the stage carrying cases of beer. After they charged across the stage and beat up another victim, Carlos gave up. His band had managed four numbers. The unique combination of circumstances and substances seemed to make the Angels aggressive even by their own standards.

After a long delay, Jefferson Airplane took the stage, but were badly out of tune. A naked black man, spaced-out, clambered onto the stage to be beaten senseless by the Angels. As Airplane's Marty Balin tried to intervene, he was knocked out. Bass player Jack Cassidy shouted, 'Will the Angels please note that when somebody's freaking out, you don't help by kicking the shit out of him.

I'd also like to announce that Marty Balin was punched unconscious in that little comic number you just saw staged and I'd like to say…' That's all he did say: the Angels charged into the band and when they'd finished only Grace Slick was left untouched. Sam Cutler grabbed a mic and requested, that all 'unauthorised people' leave the stage immediately. The Angels didn't move – the Airplane finished playing.

Should they stay or should they go?
We didn't witness any of this first-hand, relying on reports of the violence which were coming through to our hotel. We discussed whether or not we should do the show. Keith was certainly against going. In the end, we came to the conclusion that we should get there, play and close the concert down quickly.

We were ferried to the site in helicopters. Mick Jagger and Mick Taylor were the first to arrive. We saw what appeared to be a huge brown spot – it turned out to be people. As Mick was trying to get to our backstage area, he was surrounded. Some crazy guy broke through the cordon shouting, 'I hate you!' and punched him in the mouth. Mick was shaken but not hurt.

The Flying Burrito Brothers – Gram Parsons' new band – played a set

which went off peacefully. Mick and Keith watched from the side of the stage, accompanied throughout by three or four Angels. I stayed backstage with Astrid. The area was packed with celebrities and an endless supply of groupies. It was all very weird – even by our standards.

By the time Crosby, Stills, Nash and Young were due to go on, the whole stage was covered with so many Angels that I doubt anyone in the audience could see much. Their view wasn't made any clearer by the fact that the stage was only about four feet high. Soon after CSNY started, the Angels charged the crowd, swinging pool cues at whoever was in their way. At the end of the set, stretchers were sent into the audience and bodies were passed across the stage to the Red Cross area.

The Grateful Dead were supposed to go on next, but a decision was made that we would play before them – Jerry Garcia's crew never did take the stage. It was around 4.30pm and getting dark. Dozens of fires were lit on the hillsides and people were packed together tighter than ever. Nightfall hadn't cooled the Angels. About a dozen of them ploughed through the crowd on their motorbikes and parked in front of the stage.

Sam Cutler went on the stage again and asked in vain for the area to be cleared. There were about a hundred people up there with us as we opened our set with 'Jumpin' Jack Flash', but for a while at least, the atmosphere was calm. As we went into 'Carol', there were panicked shouts of 'Fire!' The Angels hurled themselves into the crowd and beat people. After 'Sympathy For The Devil', to ease the mood, we played a slow blues instrumental

Running order
Santana
Jefferson Airplane
The Flying Burrito Brothers
Crosby, Stills, Nash and
   Young
The Rolling Stones

ROLLING STONES

FREE CONCERT

DICK CARTER'S   ALTAMONT SPEEDWAY

LIVERMORE   DECEMBER 6, 1969

300,00

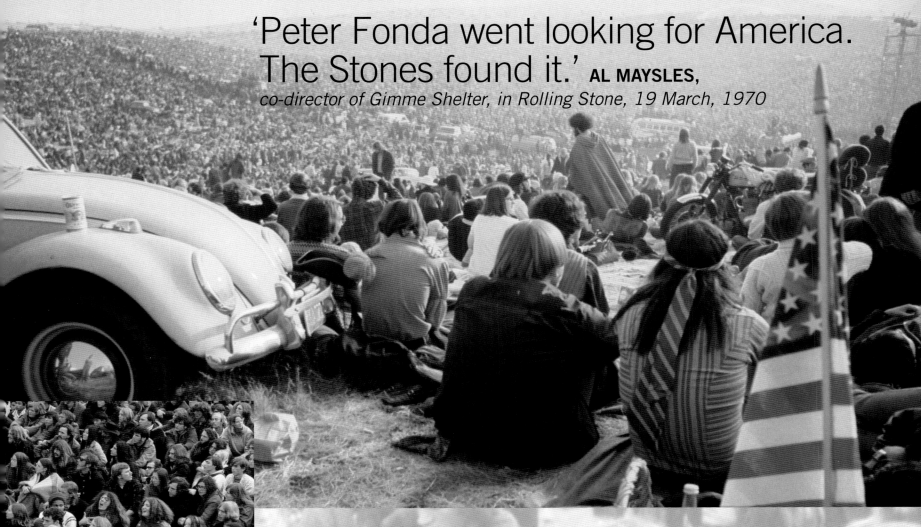

'Peter Fonda went looking for America. The Stones found it.' AL MAYSLES,

co-director of Gimme Shelter, in Rolling Stone, 19 March, 1970

before 'Stray Cat Blues', 'Love in Vain' and 'Under My Thumb'. Another fight broke out and we stopped playing. ' Why are we fighting?' asked Mick. 'We don't want to fight at all. Who wants to fight, who is it? Every other scene has been cool. We gotta stop right now. You know, if we can't there's no point.'

We restarted 'Under My Thumb' and a black guy in a green suit, near my side of the stage, got involved in a scuffle with five or six Angels. We could see very little, but sensed something serious was going down and stopped playing.

'A Hell's Angel grabbed a guy beside me by the ear and hair and yanked, thinking it was funny. He shook loose and the Hell's Angel hit him in the mouth and he fell back into the crowd. He tried to run and four Angels jumped him. He ran into the crowd, pushing people away. The Angels are hitting him and one stabbed him in the back. The kid pulled out a gun with a long barrel, like a six-shooter. He was still running. I remember this chick screaming, "Don't shoot anyone." So he didn't shoot. One of the Angels grabbed the gun and stabbed him in the back. Then they hit him – I couldn't tell if it was a knife – on the side of the head. He stumbled and fell down on his knees. The Hell's Angel grabbed his shoulders and kicked him in the face and he fell down. He rolled over, muttering, "I wasn't going to shoot you." One of the Hell's Angels said, "Why did you have a

gun?" He didn't give him time to say. He grabbed one of those cardboard garbage cans with the metal rimming, and he smashed him over the head. Five of them kicked his head in. The guy that started the whole thing, the fat guy, stood on his head and walked off. They wouldn't let us touch him for about two minutes.' A WITNESS

We could feel the fear in the crowd and we were worried ourselves, none of us had ever experienced this level of menace. Mick sounded frightened as he spoke to the crowd.

'Brothers and sisters, come on now! That means everybody just cool out. We can cool out, everybody! Everybody be cool, now. Come on. How are we doing over there? Everybody alright? Can we still collect ourselves? I don't know what happened, I couldn't see, I hope you're all right. Are you all right? Okay, let's just give ourselves another half a minute before we get our breath back. Everyone just cool down. Is there anyone there who's hurt? Okay, I think we're cool, we can groove.' MICK

Santana opening the festival

Say It with Music

Hell's Angels start on Jefferson Airplane

'Either those cats cool it, man, or we don't play. Keep it cool! Hey, if you don't cool it, you ain't gonna hear no music!' KEITH

'Fuck you!' AN ANGEL, *grabbing the mic*

A witness later reported, 'Chicks were screaming. It was all confusion. We rubbed his back to get the blood off and there was a big hole on his spine and a big hole on the side and there was a big hole in his temple. A big open slice. You could see all the way in. All of us were drenched in blood.

'We were trying to carry him to the stage, but the Hell's Angels wouldn't let us through. They knew he was going to die in a matter of minutes. It took about 15 minutes to get him behind the stage where there was a Red Cross truck.'

Robert Hiatt, the first doctor to reach the boy, whose name was later revealed to be Meredith Hunter, said: 'It was obvious he wasn't going to make it. He had very serious wounds. He had a wound in the lower back, which could have gone into the lungs, a wound in the back near the spine, which could have severed a major vessel and a fairly large wound in the left temple. There was no equipment there to treat him. He needed to be operated on immediately.'

Start your engines

On-stage, Mick was getting increasingly edgy and his voice showed it. 'We're splitting – we're splitting if those cats don't stop. I want them out of the way.' The Angels on the stage crowded round Mick and were extremely menacing. Many in the front rows began to start up their engines. From the stage, it was difficult to see what was happening. Mick pleaded: 'Please relax and sit down. If you move back and sit down, we can continue and we will continue.'

'First of all, everyone is going to get to the side of the stage, aside from the Stones. Please, everyone. We need a doctor and ambulance right away. Just sit down and keep calm and relax. We can get it together.' SAM CUTLER

'Those people were messed up on everything – dope, wine and needles. They were higher than any altitude I've ever flown at.' JAN VINSON, *helicopter pilot*

After finally managing to finish 'Under My Thumb' we played 'Brown Sugar' live for the first time ever. We just had to keep going, and all the while Mick was doing everything he could to quell the violence, knowing that if we stopped it could get even worse. We played 'Midnight Rambler' then 'Live With Me'. We'd never played music in such a hostile atmosphere before, but everyone

View from a fan

Fan Diane Dibble wrote to me with her own version of the day's events:

'Rock Scully has been telling us about the free Stones concert for weeks. In the late afternoon of 5 December, Rock calls and says they need people to help get the stage and equipment moved from Sears Point and set up at the Altamont site. Early that evening several of us head to Altamont. We "wake up" a little after 7.00am, still very stoned.

'During the day, we go back and forth from the backstage area, where we're working in the food tents, to the crowd in front of the stage. The Hell's Angels arrive and start to cause problems and we retreat backstage.

'There's no way to get out, but it's also as if there's some strange force that's keeping us there. The bands' equipment trucks are parked along the back of the stage with the back ends opening onto the stage.

'We make our way to the area near the Dead's truck just as the Stones come on. The Hell's Angels are drinking beer and dropping from Marine bottles full of electric kool aid [acid]. They're pushing everyone.

'On the stage, I'm standing behind Mick Taylor. There's a big commotion in front. The music stops and starts but – amazingly – when they manage to play, the Stones are playing *really* well.

'I have no idea what's happening in front of the stage. All I know is I don't like being where I am – even if I am on stage with the Stones.'

Some Were Born... Some Died

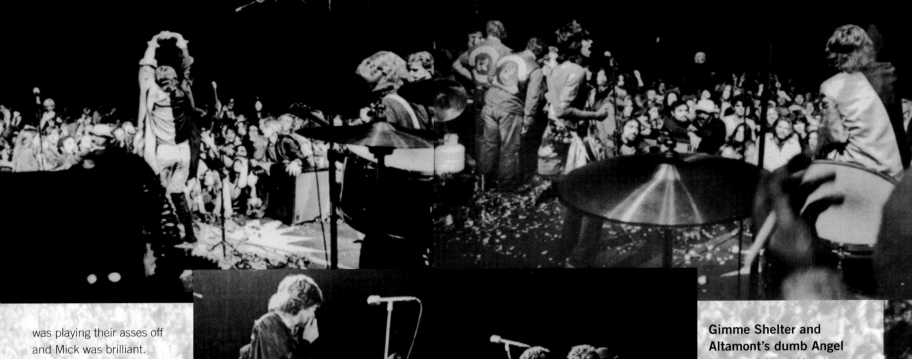

was playing their asses off and Mick was brilliant.

Next we played 'Gimme Shelter', then 'Little Queenie', which really grooved. We followed that with 'Satisfaction', during which a naked girl climbed onto the stage, and was dragged away. As 'Satisfaction' ended, helicopter pilot Jan Vinson came onstage and told us in no uncertain terms that his was the last helicopter and he was leaving, with or without us. We played 'Honky Tonk Women' and ended the show with a stupid choice – 'Street Fighting Man'.

From the stage we trudged through thick mud, hardly able to see where we were going. We all piled into the helicopter with our ladies and friends. There were about 20 of us in all, really far too many for one helicopter. I'll never understand how the pilot managed to get airborne. He took off sideways, slowly gaining altitude and flew us back to San Francisco.

'I swear I will never work a rock festival again because of the mass confusion which was dangerous to me, the machine and the crowd.' JAN VINSON, *helicopter pilot*

Altamont was as complete a disaster as anyone could have imagined. Looking back, I can only say that it was naivety that got us into the whole bloody mess and it was luck, and little else, that got us out of it.

Gimme Shelter and Altamont's dumb Angel

David and Albert Maysles, who naturally we called the Measles, filmed the entire proceedings.

'When the cops heard about it they called us,' the brothers later said. 'We thought it was our duty to show it to them. When we first looked at it, we figured we were sitting on a powder keg. We have the whole actual sequence of the killing.'

Their film was handed over to the Alameda County Court under order. It was shown in court as evidence when Hell's Angel Alan David Passaro was tried for the murder of Meredith Hunter. On 14 January, 1971, at Alameda County Superior Court, California, USA, Passaro was found not guilty. Passaro took the stand in his own defence and said he stabbed Hunter twice in self-defence. Passaro later sued the band for £200,000 for invasion of privacy.

Altamont statistics
Up to 500,000 people attended
Meredith Hunter killed
Another man, on LSD, drowned in a fast-flowing irrigation canal
Two young men sitting by a roadside bonfire killed by a hit-and-run driver
One man broke both legs and his pelvis when he leapt from a freeway overpass
Two babies born
$400,000 worth of damage

And then it was all over

Peaceful Otherwise

ROLLING STONES LET IT BLEED

DECCA

The second Jimmy Miller-produced album was the band's 10th UK and 14th US album. It was recorded during Brian's final months as a Stone, but there is precious little of him anywhere on the album. *Let It Bleed* was up against stiff opposition for chart honours, as the Beatles had released *Abbey Road* two months earlier and Led Zeppelin's second album had also just been unleashed.

The album contains two absolute classics in 'Gimme Shelter' and 'Midnight Rambler'. Both have remained staples of live shows for four decades.

'[We went from] the very basic Chicago sound of "Midnight Rambler" to the original Hank Williams-type version of "Honky Tonk Women".' KEITH

'On "Country Honk" Mick Taylor played a cheap Selmer Hawaiian guitar on his lap. I played auto-harp on "Let it Bleed" and vibes on "Monkey Man".' BILL

Around the end of October, Mick and Keith were finishing off tracks for *Let It Bleed* at Elektra Studios, Los Angeles. One night Merry Clayton was dragged out of bed at 1am to do the back-up vocals on 'Gimme Shelter'.

On another night, fiddle player Byron Berline was recorded over-dubbing 'Country Honk' on the pavement of Wilshire Boulevard, leaning against a limo, with a horn beep as his signal. Other tracks, including 'Midnight Rambler' and 'Monkey Man', were re-mixed at Elektra.

'An overwhelming record … the Stones have never done anything better.'
GREIL MARCUS, *Rolling Stone*

'This record should be played loud.' **LET IT BLEED,** *liner notes*

"'Let's have some Stones on the record player' . . . they were your very words."

РОЛЛИНГ СТОУНЗ   ПУСТЬ ЛЬЕТСЯ КРОВЬ

The back cover of the Russian release

Keith plays a National guitar

'In early August, Stu said "Bill has long been associated with his homemade bass. The rest of the group are forever trying to hide the venerable old instrument and get him to use a more sophisticated model, but he won't have it, so that's what's on record." Keith in particular was always trying to talk me into playing a Fender bass guitar, as all the great bass players he admired used them. I looked for a short-scale model with a narrow neck for my small hands. I wanted a a sound more like the upright double basses used on early blues and R&B records. My home-made bass was the only one to give a similar sound and so I stuck with it for many years.' BILL

On Radio Luxembourg, at 12.30am on 29 November, DJ Kid Jensen was playing *Let It Bleed* right through without interruption. This was an almost unheard of honour in those days.

'Far from being yet another product of Jagger's imagination, "Midnight Rambler" is in part a skilful piece of reportage. Remember when Jagger grunts about Boston, midnight, cupboards and rape? Turn to page 354 of Gerald Frank's book The Boston Strangler and you'll find that these were the exact words of Albert de Salvo's confession as he described the rape and murder of one of his victims.' NME, *March 1976*

'It was news to me too!' BILL

Cover story

On Thursday 21 August, Robert Brownjohn showed Keith sketches of the cover idea for the new album, then still to be titled – *Automatic Changer* was the alternative at the time. Keith was very receptive to the initial design and Robert planned to shoot it a week later, at a total cost of about £1,000.

'I was working then as a jobbing home economist with a food photographer who shot for commercials and magazines. I'd cook anything they needed. One day they said they wanted a cake for a Rolling Stones record cover, it was just another job at the time. They wanted it to be very over-the-top and as gaudy as I could make it.' DELIA SMITH, *cookery guru and TV presenter*

Delia Smith

ROLLING STONES   LET IT BLEED

THIS RECORD SHOULD BE PLAYED LOUD

'The crummiest cover art since *Flowers*.' **ROLLING STONE**

Recorded
Feb–October, 1969
Composers
All tracks Jagger/Richard, except where indicated
Studios
Olympic Studios London, Sunset Recorders Los Angeles, Elektra Studios Los Angeles
Producer
Jimmy Miller
Engineers
Glyn Johns and George Chkiantz
Cover photography
Don McAllester
Design
Robert Brownjohn and Victor Kahn
Release
US Saturday 29 November, 1969 London NPS 4
UK Friday 5 December, 1969 Decca SKL 5025
Highest chart position (time on chart)
UK No 1 (29 weeks)
US No 3 (19 weeks)
Additional personnel
Stu: piano
Nicky Hopkins: piano and organ
Al Kooper: piano, organ and French horn
Ry Cooder: mandolin
Dave Mason: guitar
Byron Berline: fiddle
Leon Russell: piano
Bobby Keys: saxophone
Nanette Workman, Merry Clayton, Madeline Bell: backing vocals

December

69

72

November

Goodbye
And
Bonjour

Somewhere in Europe, September 1970

The End Of The Sixties

The day after Altamont, Astrid and I flew to Stockholm for three days to stay with her family. It was the perfect antidote to a nightmare. Altamont was the end of the Swinging Sixties – the dream was over. Back in England, Mick and Marianne were up in court again and we were preparing to become tax exiles. As the music press wrote us off, we came back at them with our biggest European tour to date.

I N SAN FRANCISCO, most musicians blamed us. We didn't handle the fallout very well. Keith said, 'You can put half-a-million young English people together and they won't start killing each other.' He blamed the Grateful Dead for suggesting we had the Angels there at all.

The truth was everyone was partly to blame.

You cannot organise something of that magnitude in four days; the logistics were beyond our loosely-put-together organisation. Back then, we just got caught up in the euphoria of the whole thing. We believed we could do anything and we had something to prove, when we should have just said no, we're not doing it.

'Mick thinks he's leading some kind of workers' revolution. But how could he, living in a 40-roomed house somewhere and driving a Rolls-Royce.' JOHN PEEL, *DJ*

We needed a rethink, maybe even a new direction if we were to remain vital. We decided to do some gigs in London. The Albert Hall turned us down because of the wild scenes at our shows in September 1966. We decided to book two shows

'You could blame reds and liquor for the whole fucking mess.'

CARLOS SANTANA, *in Rolling Stone, on Altamont*

'What can a Rolling Stone do at 40? It's the saddest thing in the world to contemplate a Rolling Stone in middle age.' DOUGLAS HAYWARD, *Illustrated London News, December, 1969*

at the Saville Theatre in Shaftesbury Avenue on 14 December and two more at the Lyceum Ballroom a week later.

Not so faithfull

Mick and Marianne were back in court, charged with possession of cannabis. Their relationship was further strained by Marianne and son Nicholas' move into the Rome apartment owned by Mario Schifano, an Italian painter and film director. Marianne said she had fallen in love and vowed never to return to England.

'Mick phoned every day asking me to come back and I always said no. In the New Year I hope to return to Rome and to my Mario.' MARIANNE FAITHFULL, *on leaving Mick*

Mick and Marianne appeared at Marlborough Street Magistrates' Court on Keith's 26th birthday. Michael Havers acted as their defence QC. Pleading not guilty, the couple's defence hinged on a claim that the 173.5 grams of cannabis was planted by the police. Their case was adjourned until 26 January and although they left court together, they went their separate ways. Marianne joined Mario at her cottage in Berkshire. A few days later, Mick went to get Marianne back.

Another day in court for Mick and Marianne

According to Marianne, she left the men arguing and said to herself that whoever she woke up with would be the one she stayed with. 'I woke up with Mick.'

But it wasn't a fairytale ending, as Marianne explained. The couple visited the Earl of Warwick. 'There were footmen behind every chair and I took a couple of mandies [Mandrax, a depressant] and passed out in the soup. Mick was so humiliated by this – he had to carry me upstairs and put me to bed.' Marianne and Mick broke up for good not long after and he began an affair with the singer Marsha Hunt.

When Mick and Marianne went back to court at the end of January, he was found guilty and fined £200 with costs. Marianne was acquitted.

New decade, new bands

The media declared open season on the Stones in the first few months of 1970. The journalists had decided a new decade was the right time for new bands.

'Let's hope in 1970 we see the break up of the Beatles and Stones. Let's face it – they've had a good innings and even they must admit their whole concept is now pure dullsville.' MELODY MAKER, *10 January, 1970*

Meanwhile, Stu and set designer Chip Monck were flying all over Europe looking at venues for the biggest European tour of our career to date.

Part of our radical rethink concerned Allen Klein. Our personal tax liabilities were a major headache which hampered our planning. On 4 February, there was a meeting attended by Mick's friend Prince Rupert Loewenstein, our lawyers, accountants and tax advisers to discuss relocating the band to France in an effort to avoid high UK taxes.

It was agreed we would move out of the country in 1971 for 21 months. This

would clear up our old tax affairs, as well as untangle our complex business relationship with Klein. But there was another bombshell on Thursday 19 February. Our advisors told us that Allen Klein owned our recorded masters and publishing rights. For the first time we realised the full consequences of our original deal – Andrew Oldham had bought and sold us. Our naivety over the reduced royalty paid by him and Eric paled into insignificance.

It hit me personally, in that I had to organise an overdraft at Leopold Joseph Bank to pay my tax bill of £13,000. I also had to find £8,000 to cover my share of the mobile recording studio. With some irony, Andrew Oldham's Immediate Records announced bankruptcy in early April, while our game of transatlantic tag continued with Allen. On 17 March, Keith telexed Klein:

'When I want things done, you never do them. Please call Sir Edward Lewis [Decca UK] today and get the partnership monies together. We have not received any since January. We are due £8,000. I want some positive action immediately.'

Two months later Mick and Keith tried again:

'Your delaying tactics on assigning our rights we now regard as hostile. We will reluctantly have to start proceedings against you to get them, if you do not sign your own agreement by this evening.'

Later on that day, 11 May, a further telex from Mick ran:

'To save further trouble please give all the copyrights back to Keith and me as of 1 August, as you promised. In view of past

'How did you get the reputation as the biggest prick in the music business?' **PLAYBOY MAGAZINE,** *to Allen Klein*

The Wolf

On 5 and 6 May, Charlie, Stu, Stevie Winwood, Eric Clapton and Bill recorded at Olympic Studios with Howlin' Wolf and his guitarist Hubert Sumlin. Rolling Stones Records released *The London Howlin' Wolf Sessions* on catalogue number COC 49101 in the UK on 20 August 1971. The album was issued on the Chess label in the US.

trouble with such releases, I suggest you draw up the documents yourself and send them to me by 15 June as well. PS: Fred [Trowbridge, Stones accountant] tells me that Keith and I have to find £51,200 each for back tax demands. Please lend us dollar counter value and pay money soonest to our personal bank accounts.'

Around the same time it was revealed that Brian had debts of £191,707 when he died and assets of just £33,787.

From the beginning of the year there were a number of sessions at Olympic with Jimmy Miller. There was mixing and over-dubbing of tracks recorded on our US tour and, by June, we were cutting new tracks such as, 'Stop Breaking Down', 'Leather Jacket', 'Can't You Hear Me Knocking', 'Hey Mama', 'Sweet Virginia', 'I'm Going Down' and 'Give Me A Hamburger To Go'.

Mick turned up at one session with a bizarre telegram he had received from a promoter in Mexico. 'Dear Mr Harrison,' began the invitation to stage a 'possible performance to 48,000 feets … Please answer yes or not.'

On 24 June, Astrid and I went to the premiere of *Ned Kelly* at the London Pavilion in Piccadilly Circus. Mick Taylor was there, as were Mick's parents and other guests. Mick and the director didn't show up – the critics slammed the film.

Mick had earlier said: 'I was pleased with the part. It was what I needed to sharpen my wits and toughen me up.' Following the reviews, he said, '*Ned Kelly* was a load of shit. I only made it because I had nothing else to do.' Meanwhile, Waylon Jennings offered an alternative view in *Melody Maker:*

'Sheeit! It had the worst goddamn fight scene I've ever seen in my life. Anybody could whup his ass if that's the way he fights. Looked like they could've given him some lessons at least on how to hold his fists up. He looked like a girl, y'know.'

As easy as ABK

On the anniversary of Brian's death, we sent flowers to Cheltenham. Suki Potier put red roses on his grave. In the years following Brian's death, she moved to Hong Kong, got married and had two children, but tragedy

followed her. She and her husband were killed in a car crash in the 1980s.

Plans to form our own record label were going well. Trevor Churchill was recruited as label manager, and Marshall Chess (son of Chess brother Leonard) was general manager. Atlantic was to distribute us in America but we had no deals for the rest of the world. On 20 July, we wrote to Decca to let them know that our

Mick had been seeing the singer Marsha Hunt since the spring and sent her red roses on 23 July.

contracts would have expired by the end of the month. We asked for written confirmation and told them that Allen Klein was no longer empowered to negotiate on our behalf. We wrote to explain the situation in simple terms:

'We wish to inform you that we do not wish you or ABKCO Industries or any of its subsidiaries to be involved in any of our new recording contracts, nor will our publishing

Performance
In early August, *Performance* opened in New York (Mick with Anita in a still from the movie, *right*). The 105-minute film, now almost two years old, drew long queues for every showing. Mick had great reviews for his performance in one of the era's classic movies.

'If they have any sense of neatness, they'll get themselves killed in an air crash before they are 30.' **NIK COHN,** *on the Stones in his book Awopbopaloobop Awopbamboom, 1970*

contracts be renewed with you. We must also inform you that as of today you are no longer empowered to negotiate on our behalf.'

Playboy magazine interviewed Klein, who seemed both hurt and surprised:

'I knew Jagger had been talking to other people, but we'd been working closely for three months on a deal with Decca, so in that way it was a surprise. I guess I should have expected it. He was jealous of the Beatles. It was a question of ego – and how little time I had for the Stones. I can't really fault him for that. I told Jagger, "I was there when you needed me, what's your bitch?"'
ALLEN KLEIN, *in Playboy magazine*

On 5 August, we rehearsed in Morden for the European tour. In all, we practised 13 times in the next month, mostly between 5pm and 11pm. We held a press conference to promote the tour but Charlie and I were the only ones on time, followed by Mick T. Mick arrived an hour late and Keith never turned up at all (apparently he'd fallen downstairs and hurt his back).

'I'm not amazed that the band is still going, just amazed they get anything together. That's our claim to fame.' CHARLIE

Mick predicted our retirement again. 'I think musicians should live out of suitcases and not out of country houses. I can't see myself doing all this when I'm 30. I'll draw the line, then.' Mick would be leaving the band in August 1973, then.

Wonderful Copenhagen

After rehearsing at the Lyceum, we flew to Copenhagen on 29 August to start our European tour. We had never been better prepared.

We met up with Buddy Guy, Junior Wells and Bonnie Raitt, who were to support us. The Scandinavian leg went off fine – apart from the odd riot. Stockholm was fairly typical.

Just after we started our show, hundreds of fans left their seats, streamed over the grass and fought to climb the stage. Police and guards rushed to protect us, and there was a struggle before they pushed back the crowd. The 2,000 fans who invaded the pitch didn't settle down until the management turned on the floodlights and threatened to cancel the concert.

Clockwise from top right, Buddy Guy, Charlie and Bill, Keith on a ferry to Halsingborg on 30 August, a press conference, and Mick T on the ferry

Chip Monck and Stu spent the first six months of the year travelling Europe to nail the logistics of this tour. There was to be no repeat of the Altamont fiasco. Chip's budget came to almost $250,000 (an awful lot of money for the time). There was a travelling entourage of 51, including a stage crew of 26.

The staging was described as a new milestone in the presentation of pop music on the road. It needed two lorries and a forklift truck to move it. The set included a huge proscenium arch, supporting six rows of curtains and several banks of lights.

Over 200,000 people watched this 20-date tour of eight countries. The cost was so high that the band made no money at all.

Stu was on piano, Jim Price played trumpet and Bobby Keys was on the sax.

All 12,000 tickets for the Copenhagen show sold out in a record six hours. The previous fastest was six days for Louis Armstrong.

'News of Altamont prompted some Hell's Angels to come to the European shows. In Hamburg, I was amazed to see that one of them had a badge pinned onto his bare chest. Others seemed to be rougher than they might have been previously; riot police were at almost every venue. The worst trouble was in Berlin, where 250 youths broke through a cordon of 500 armed police to gatecrash the concert. They exploded petrol bombs, smashed cars and tore up paving stones. They came up against baton-wielding police with water cannons, tear-gas canisters, barbed wire and 25 dogs. Those who fought their way to the top floors of the hall hurled office equipment down on the police below. Every window in the hall was broken. The irony was that while Mick may have sung of "street fighting", his idea of revolution was an abstract concept.' BILL

The usual 75-minute set was:
'Jumpin' Jack Flash'
'Roll Over, Beethoven'
'Sympathy For The Devil'
'Stray Cat Blues'
'Love In Vain'
'Let It Bleed'
'Prodigal Son'
'Dead Flowers'
'Midnight Rambler'
'Live With Me'
'Let It Rock'
'Little Queenie'
'Brown Sugar'
'Honky Tonk Women'
'Street Fighting Man'

Support bands
Buddy Guy and Junior Wells
20-year-old Bonnie Raitt

Europe, *August–October 1970*

30 August Baltiska Hallen, Malmo, Sweden
2 September Olympiastadium, Helsinki, Finland
4 September Fotbollstadion, Stockholm, Sweden
6 September Liseberg Fairground, Gothenburg, Sweden
9 September Tennis Stadium, Aarhus, Denmark
12 September Forum, Copenhagen, Denmark
14 September Ernst Merck Halle, Hamburg, West Germany
16 September Deutschlandhalle, West Berlin, West Germany
18 September Building No 11, Cologne, West Germany
20 September Killesberg, Stuttgart, West Germany
22 September Palais Des Sports, Paris, France
23 September Palais Des Sports, Paris, France
24 September Palais Des Sports, Paris, France
27 September Stadthalle, Vienna, Austria
29 September Palazzo Dello Sport, Rome, Italy
1 October Palazzo Dello Sport, Rome, Italy
3 October Palais Des Sports, Lyon, France
5 October Festhalle, Frankfurt, West Germany
7 October Grugahalle, Essen, West Germany
9 October Rai Halle, Amsterdam, Holland

Boats, Planes And Cars

On the afternoon of 18 September, we heard that Jimi Hendrix had died of a drug overdose in Notting Hill, London. He was 24. Just over two weeks later on 4 October, Janis Joplin, aged 27, died of a heroin overdose in a Los Angeles Hotel. Rock was taking its toll. The film *Monterey Pop* had recently been released. It featured Otis Redding, Jimi Hendrix, Janis Joplin, and, briefly, Brian Jones among the audience. With all four dead it became something of an epitaph to a lost era. Within a year, the Doors' Jim Morrison would be dead too.

The show in Paris on 22 September was recorded on the Stones' 16-track mobile studio by Glyn Johns. It was broadcast live on Europe No 1 Radio.

In Frankfurt, Mick told the press, 'Groupies are a drag. They make life very difficult. They're in your bed when you get home. They're in your dressing room when you get to a theatre. They're trouble.'

'We landed at Leonardo Da Vinci airport, Rome, at the same time as US President Richard Nixon. He was apparently freaking because he knew that we had landed at the same time, and he was afraid to exit Air Force One. Mick took the initiative and decided to disembark first. President Nixon waited aboard his plane while all the Italian fans went nuts, and when he finally did leave, there was nobody left at the airport to greet him.' BILL

What the papers said...

'Even the bag of Anita Pallenberg's child was searched. A command from Interpol: the Rolling Stones must be searched everywhere in Europe.'
SUOSIKKI MAGAZINE, *in Finland*

'Soon after the Helsinki show opened, a Vietnam Association procession, numbering thousands of people, began to march towards the stadium, shouting slogans and demanding free admission. The 30-strong police guard was unable to resist the marching horde; the gates of the stadium were flattened and thousands poured into the arena. Once in, however, the free-loading audience behaved itself well.' RECORD MIRROR

'Coming down off the stage, Keith whispers to Mick: "Mediocre". That's the biggest bit of modesty or arrogance I ever heard.'
MELODY MAKER

'On stage at the forum, he is a demented puppet in satin suit and top hat, spinning and twisting, howling at young Danes – hands on hips and bottom wiggling, his is an almost bisexual, vulgar appeal – Mick Jagger and his swinging blue genes.'
DAILY SKETCH, *14 September, 1970*

The Times *wrote: 'Jagger gives a remarkable imitation of a junior assistant to the Marquis de Sade.'*

Below: *It took two trucks to haul them.* Below centre: *Mick takes a fan's view.* Right: *The poster designed by John Pasche.*

THE ROLLING STONES EUROPEAN TOUR 1970
A SBA PRESENTATION

FINNAIR, LUFTHANSA and HERTZ

'Lead singer Mick Jagger was as vulgar as ever. The Stones acted like real street hoodlums – but what talent.' LE MONDE

Side one
1. 'Jumpin' Jack Flash'
2. 'Carol' (Berry)
3. 'Stray Cat Blues'
4. 'Love in Vain' (Johnson)
5. 'Midnight Rambler'

Side two
1. 'Sympathy For
   The Devil'
2. 'Live With Me'
3. 'Little Queenie' (Berry)
4. 'Honky Tonk Women'
5. 'Street Fighting Man'

Recorded
Baltimore (26 November, 1969), Madison Square Garden, New York (27 and 28 November, 1969)

Composers
All songs Jagger/Richard, except where stated

Studios
The Wally Heider Mobile, January–April, 1970. Remixing and over-dubs at Olympic Sound (London) and Trident Studios (London)

Producers
The Rolling Stones, Glyn Johns and Jimmy Miller

Engineers
Glyn Johns
Andy Johns

Photography
Cover: David Bailey
Liner: Ethan Russell

Design
John Kosh and Steve Thomas Associates

Release
UK Friday 4 September, 1970 Decca SKL 5065
US Saturday 26 September, 1970
London NPS 5

Highest chart position (time on chart)
UK No 1 (15 weeks)
US No 6 (10 weeks)

The second live album of the Stones' career was their 11th UK and 15th US release. It was, without doubt, the greatest live album of the rock era and it still gives every live album a good run for its money.

Originally it was to be a double album, including tracks by BB King and Ike and Tina Turner. Mick said, 'Decca weren't interested. "Who is BB King? Who are these people?" they asked. They just didn't know who these acts were. So in the end I gave it all up 'cause it just wasn't worth carrying on with.'

'I think I bust a button on my trousers, hope they don't fall down – you don't want my trousers to fall down do ya?' asks Mick before the band eases into Chuck Berry's riffing rhythm. It had been six years since the Rolling Stones first learned Berry's 'Carol' at Studio 51 in Soho. They had included a studio version on their first album, but it never sounded better than it did live on stage in 1969.

On 8 February, Michael Berkofsky did a photo session on a motorway which starred Charlie and a donkey, but it was rejected. David Bailey re-shot it on 7 June. Designer John Kosh was paid around £1,000 for his work.

'GET YER YA-YA'S OUT!'
The Rolling Stones in concert

The original Yas Yas
Blind Boy Fuller, real name Fulton Allen was a blues singer born in North Carolina in 1908. He was not blind as a child or teenager, but became partially sighted in 1926 and fully blind when he was 20. He first recorded in July 1935, and spent a short time in prison for shooting his wife in the leg – not bad for a blind man. He recorded a song called 'Get Your Yas Yas Out' on October 29, 1938, in Columbia, South Carolina. Fuller died at the age of 32 in 1941.

What the papers said...

'The Stones have won. They've possibly changed the thinking of an entire generation.'
RECORD MIRROR, *5 September, 1970*

'In a hundred years' time, when researchers start examining the pop phenomenon, I wonder if they will understand why the Rolling Stones were a legend in their own time?' TRIBUNE MAGAZINE

'No one has ever played rock'n'roll as pure and as hard as the Rolling Stones.'
LOS ANGELES TIMES

'The best rock concert ever put on record.'
LESTER BANGS, *UK rock critic*

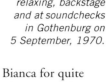

Patriot Games

After Scandinavia came Germany where riots were once again the (dis)order of the day. We also had a problem with counterfeit tickets. The move to France came a step closer and Mick started to see a new lady.

A WEEK BEFORE OUR Hamburg show, the organisers started changing all 7,500 tickets in an effort to combat skilfully produced forgeries. Mick T and I almost didn't make the show in Berlin, when East German border guards at Checkpoint Charlie on the Berlin Wall detained us. We spent almost two hours haggling to get our passports back, but they acted dumb and left us in limbo. Finally I told them in broken German that we had to catch a plane. They returned our passports immediately.

Back in England, The *Investor's Guardian* ran a story that we had 'been selling records by the million for a common-or-garden royalty level that must have accounted for a fair-sized chunk of Decca's doubled profits since 1964.' It was this that was at the heart of our dissatisfaction with our record deal. We'd been easily led in the early days but we were poised, we hoped, to swing the balance back in our favour. With everything that was going on, it was inevitable that the press would start digging deeper and before long they got a whiff of French scent.

They reported that we were planning to emigrate. Mick denied it, but they were hot on our trail. Today it is difficult to imagine why there

Checkpoint Charlie

was so much interest in what we were doing. By leaving Britain and failing to pay our taxes, we were adding disloyalty to the list of charges that could be brought against us.

'The whole move is rightly shrouded in the kind of secrecy reserved for major financial operations. Exploratory talks regarding a move to Paris began three weeks ago with France's leading financial lawyer and a close friend and adviser of the Prime Minister. The Rolling Stones fortune from records alone is estimated at $200 million. One problem the Rolling Stones face in Paris is that Mick Jagger and Keith Richards have previous drug convictions. With the present mood of the Paris police this may ensure unpleasantly close police surveillance.'
THE LONDON EVENING STANDARD

Keith, drugs and the French authorities would become something of a recurring theme.

South American señorita

Stephen came on tour with Astrid and I, but had to return to school in the UK on 21 September, 1970. While I was taking him back, the others flew on to Paris. There, Mick went to a party where he met Bianca Perez Morena De Macias. Nicaraguan-born Bianca later recalled the first encounter. 'He had an impression he was looking at himself. People love to theorise that Mick thought it would be amusing to marry his twin.'

Then 25 years old, Bianca was previously actor Michael Caine's girlfriend. 'I was with

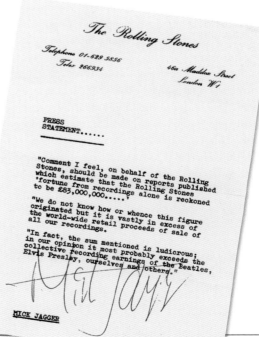

Caught on camera relaxing, backstage and at soundchecks in Gothenburg on 5 September, 1970.

Bianca for quite a long time,' he remembered. 'We enjoyed the relationship very much. She'll argue the toss until you feel you're going mad. I found her attractive, amusing and often amazing. God knows what it is she saw in me.'

I joined the band at the Georges V hotel in Paris and first saw Mick with Bianca when I got to the gig. It was quite a change. Just a month earlier Mick had said, 'I don't envisage a time when I

Mick took issue with the press over the amount the band was said to have earned.

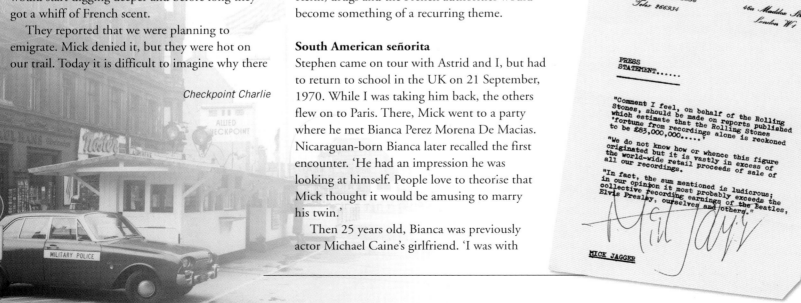

'I want to be frank. Mick wanted to achieve the ultimate in sexual experience – by making love to himself.' BIANCA PEREZ MORENA DE MACIAS

French letters

In November we were kept pretty busy recording and Mick became a father for the first time. On Wednesday 4 November, Marsha Hunt gave birth to a daughter she named Karis. Marsha had been the hottest thing in London, starring in *Hair*. There was a time when you couldn't open a magazine without seeing her picture, but Mick was with Bianca now.

My own problems were more mundane and revolved around money, or my lack of it. The Leopold Joseph bank agreed to loan me £10,000 for a period of up to six months at a rate of interest of four per cent over the bank rate per annum. They also lent money to the rest of the band, as they too were in trouble. Extricating ourselves from Klein was not easy.

Jo was putting the next part of the plan into action, busy writing to French estate agents, looking to rent five houses of character for two years in the south of France.

Towards the end of November, we took a break from recording and Mick and Bianca went on holiday to the Bahamas. Photographed together at London airport, for the first time, their relationship became public knowledge. Astrid had gone home to Sweden for a few days and I went to see Muddy Waters at the Hampstead Country Club in London. He, as usual, was brilliant and as there were no seats left I sat on the floor.

'I'm really glad someone from the Rolling Stones is here. I love them very much. If it wasn't for the Stones, none of the white kids in the States would have heard of Muddy Waters, BB King or any of 'em. Nobody knew my music in the States until they played it.'
MUDDY WATERS, *live in Hampstead*

A year to the day after Altamont, the Maysles' film premiered at the Plaza in New York. None of us needed reminding about that concert and none of us went. On a lighter note, menswear bible *The*

shall ever get married and settle down. I might have kids and I might get married but I'll never settle down. I'm not the type. I think marriage is relevant, but it must be blessed by God. I'd want my marriage to be sanctified. I'd want it blessed, I believe in God. And if I got married before God I'd think twice about splitting up. I'd want it to last.' Mick was to marry Bianca less than nine months later.

Twelve days after the tour finished in Amsterdam we were back at work recording at Stargroves with our mobile studio. Along with Andy and Jimmy we cut more tracks, including 'Red House', 'Bitch' and 'Sweet Black Angel'. Prince Rupert and Jo Bergman came to Stargroves one day to talk over our record deal; Atlantic had offered $5.7 million for six new albums over six years. RCA bid $7 million, but we felt happier with Atlantic. We discussed future tours, and the move to France early in the new year, which would secure our financial independence. Charlie was anxious to stay in Britain and he was told that if he did he would be subject to full UK taxes – 89 per cent on earnings above £15,000 per year.

The naming of labels

On Thursday 3 December, we tried to decide on a name for our new record label, to be released through Atlantic. We voted on a shortlist. Fortunately 'Pear' had dropped out of the running.

The votes were as follows: Panic 11, Low Down 10, Rolling Stones Records 8, Ruby 4, Snake 4, Meanwhile 2, Juke 1, Heaven Research 1, Red Lights 1/2, Lick 1/2 .

Mick: 1 Low Down, 2 Panic, 3 Red Lights/Lick
Keith: 1 Low Down, 2 Meanwhile, 3 Juke
Bill: 1 Panic, 2 Rolling Stones Records, 3 Low Down
Charlie: Non-voter
Mick Taylor: 1 Rolling Stones Records, 2 Panic, 3 Heaven Research
Marshall Chess: 1 Low Down, 2 Panic, 3 Ruby
Jo Bergman: 1 Ruby, 2 Snake, 3 Panic
Trevor Churchill: 1 Rolling Stones Records, 2 Snake, 3 Panic

For some strange reason, we ended up with the snappy name Rolling Stones Records. I've absolutely no idea why.

Tailor And Cutter wrote an enthusiastic piece about Mick: 'He has moved away from his former scruffy image – in fact, he is one of our more elegant popocrats.'

This was the same publication that praised Prime Minister Edward Heath and Prince Philip for their style. That Mick received the ultimate seal of sartorial approval meant the establishment was perhaps getting to like us after all.

'In the end, I'm probably going to be like Cary Grant, with a lot of old ladies writing letters to me.' MICK, *talking to Newsweek*

The *Fab 208 Annual* published just before Christmas said: 'Sooner or later, even the Rolling Stones will join the ranks of the unemployed, retire to their gilded halls and try to convince their kids that once they were hungry and homeless and happy playing their blues, storming the world, shaming the Establishment with their honesty. But when? How long can their satanic majesties keep pulling the rabbit out of the hat, keeping their fans dancing when they call the tune? It would be uncharacteristic of the Stones to simply fade away; they are more likely to fragment and fall apart after a big bang.'

In early 1971, we recorded some new tracks and mixed existing songs with Jimmy Miller, mostly at Olympic, but also at Island and Trident Studios. On Monday 4 January, *Performance* finally premiered in London, some two years after it was filmed and a full six months after its US release. Keith and Anita were there, but Mick failed to make it, as his plane was fog-bound in Paris.

'Jagger in smock, frock, sari, kaftan or whatever his ectoplasmic outer-wrapping is called, resembles the survivor of an Indian famine and fastens on his victim like a piranha fish wearing day-glo make-up.'
THE EVENING STANDARD

Two days later, Mick T's girlfriend, Rose Miller, gave birth to Chloe at St Teresa's Hospital in Wimbledon.

Stone Age rampage
We had another meeting about France in which we discussed disposing of our UK property by leasing it, either to friends or to family. We also went through plans for the rest of the year. There was a possibility we might do a short English tour in March. From mid-April, we would record in France for three or four weeks, using the mobile studio and we would mix the album in America.

A tour of Japan and Canada with a stopover in Hawaii was mentioned for the summer, with an American tour in September or October. We talked about taking Nicky Hopkins with us to France and whether we should put Bobby Keys and Jim Price on retainers. Jo sent us a memo at the end of January.

Rose Miller, Mick Taylor and baby Chloe

'We must decide immediately about doing the English tour. A very, very loose idea of money you could expect to make would be about £12,000 – this does not include deductions for agent, lighting and transport.'

In a New York court case, which had nothing to do with the Stones, Allen Klein was found guilty on 10 counts of tax offences. Quite separately, he was also effectively removed as the Beatles' business manager.

On Tuesday 9 February, Astrid and I flew to Nice for two days to look at a house Jo had found. We decided to take it. When I got back I spent time at Gedding working in our mobile studio.

Charlie came to Gedding on 19 February. It was just four days after Britain converted to decimal currency and we cut a demo of my song 'Texas Girl'. I also worked on 'The Walls Came Down' and 'Going To The River'. The Stones were finally released from London and Decca Records recording contracts.

The office had sent Decca's Dick Rowe some tapes back in January, as we were contractually obliged to produce one more single. Dick responded:

'As this is a Rolling Stones matter, you will appreciate that I shall require instructions from the Chairman before being able to specifically notify you as to whether or not we shall want to issue any of the recordings. Marcel Stellman and I have both listened to them, and one or the other of us feel that "Midnight In Hoboken", "Seaside Blues", "Brown Sugar", "You Gotta Move" and "Wild Horses" are of interest, particularly "Brown Sugar".'

This film was ten years ahead of its time. Now, you're almost ready for...

PERFORMANCE x

James Fox/Mick Jagger/Anita Pallenberg/Michele Breton in *Performance*
Written by Donald Cammell/Directed by Donald Cammell & Nicolas Roeg/Produced by Sanford Lieberson in Technicolor®
A Goodtimes Enterprises Production from Warner Bros. A Warner Communications Company Released by Columbia-Warner Distributors

'We would not recommend seeing it while tripping.' ROLLING STONE MAGAZINE, *on Performance*

Our new label manager Trevor Churchill called Dick to talk about the songs. 'I explained to Dick that we had received the tapes back with no comment and that before I sent them away to be stored, I just wanted to check whether he needed them or not. He chuckled and said that there was really nothing worthwhile on the tapes and agreed with my comment that they were unfinished titles and really only demos.'

Decca never did release another new Stones single. They made up for it by issuing material that we had neither authorised nor felt happy about. We were powerless given the intricacies of our contractual arrangements with Andrew Oldham, Eric Easton and Allen Klein. The first post-contract album Decca released was *Stone Age*, a collection of old tracks. We were so

Complete catalogue
of their records on
DECCA

Live in Wardour Street
The band filmed their appearance at the Marquee Club in Soho on 26 March, 1971.

angry that we paid for full-page, black-bordered advertisements in the British music papers.

'Beware! Message from the Stones re: Stone Age. *We didn't know this record was going to be released. It is, in our opinion, below the standard we try to keep up, both in choice of content and cover design. Signed Mick, Keith, Charlie, Bill, Mick Taylor.'*

What really pissed us off was the fact that Decca parodied the graffiti sleeve we wanted for *Beggars Banquet*. Not only did they do it badly, but they had also objected to our idea in the first place. There was bugger all we could do about it, but at least they couldn't stop us having our say. Our Decca royalties were so low it hardly mattered if it sold or not.

Our UK tour went ahead and on 4 March, Astrid and I travelled by train with some of the

Let it be
The Beatles first performed under that name on 18 August, 1960. 'Love Me Do', their first single, came out in October 1962.

On 19 January, 1971, Paul McCartney's lawyer filed for the legal dissolution of the Beatles. A sad end to a glittering career that saw them break records and produce music that has inspired musicians and fans for five decades. In 10 years, they had 27 UK or US No 1 singles. There are very few homes in Britain or America that do not have a Beatles record, or one of the thousands of cover versions of their songs.

marquee club
90, WARDOUR STREET, LONDON W.1.

'Bass goes in from your head and out through your fingers.' BILL

band from Kings Cross to Newcastle. 'We'd forgotten what towns like Middlesbrough were like,' I told an interviewer. Keith missed both

trains and was driven to Newcastle with Gram Parsons, arriving only minutes before the show.

Sent packing

Back from tour, we began packing for France. A week later, on Friday 26 March, we went to the Marquee Club to film a TV special. Keith didn't show up for about four hours. When he finally did, he looked awful. He was dirty, unshaven and very untogether. We played 'Live With Me', 'Dead Flowers', 'I've Got The Blues', 'Let It Rock', 'Midnight Rambler', 'Satisfaction', 'Bitch' and our next single, 'Brown Sugar'.

Eric Clapton, Jimmy Page, Ric Grech (who had played with Eric in Blind Faith) and Andrew

Oldham were all there, as was owner Harold Pendleton. Keith took exception to his presence and rushed to the side of the stage and swung his guitar at his head. Mick had earlier argued with Pendleton about taking the club sign down from its position above the stage.

'They're still the most fertile live group there is. They're still into songs. The music business has nothing to do with real life, whereas the Stones do.' ANDREW OLDHAM, *Marquee Club, 26 March, 1971*

Four days later we threw a farewell party at Skindles Hotel, in Maidenhead. There were about 250 of us there and we had a great time. John and Yoko came, as did David Bailey, Roger Daltrey of the Who, the Earl of Litchfield, Eric Clapton and Traffic's Dave Mason. Next day it was formally announced that we were to become the first rock 'n' roll tax exiles.

The United Kingdom, *March 1971*

Two shows everywhere, except Brighton and Leeds.
4 March City Hall, Newcastle upon Tyne, Northumberland
5 March Free Trade Hall, Manchester, Lancashire
6 March Coventry Theatre, Coventry, Warwickshire
8 March Green's Playhouse, Glasgow, Scotland
9 March Colston Hall, Bristol, Avon
10 March Big Apple, Brighton, Sussex
12 March Empire Theatre, Liverpool
13 March Refractory, Leeds University, Leeds, Yorkshire
14 March Roundhouse, Chalk Farm, London

Mick Taylor on the train and the band on stage at the Roundhouse, London

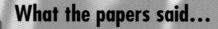

★ Glasgow

★ Newcastle upon Tyne

★ Leeds

★ Manchester
★ Liverpool

★ Coventry

LONDON ★

★ Bristol

★ Brighton

It was farewell to the UK for the band. This nine-city, 16-show mini-tour was the first nationwide dates that the Stones had undertaken since autumn 1966, over four years earlier. Demand was high, with fans in Newcastle waiting overnight for tickets – some were queuing for 16 hours, a long time to be outside in the north of England during February.

On-stage with the Stones were Bobby Keys on saxes, Jim Price on trumpet and Nicky Hopkins on piano. Sometimes Stu played keyboards too. Keith played an Ampeg guitar with a plexiglass body, a Les Paul SG and a Gibson. Mick Taylor stuck with Les Paul guitars and Bill used a Fender Mustang bass. Charlie played a Gretsch drum kit.

What the papers said...

'The Rolling Stones proved once again that they are still the best little rock'n'roll band in the land.' RECORD MIRROR

'Bill Wyman in particular looked as if he was waiting for a bus. But he didn't sound like it because he and the others played superbly.' NEWCASTLE JOURNAL, *6 March, 1971*

'The band are playing with as much guts and excitement as they ever have done, and all of them – with the exception of Mick Taylor – are now pushing 30 (though Jagger at 50 is a curiously inconceivable image).' THE SPECTATOR

'The Stones remain the masters of rock theatricality. Musically the Stones are as tight, raw and unsentimental as ever.' THE LISTENER

Set list
At Newcastle, the band's set was:
'Jumpin' Jack Flash'
'Live With Me'
'Dead Flowers'
'Stray Cat Blues'
'Love In Vain'
'Prodigal Son'
'Midnight Rambler'
'Bitch'
'Can't You Hear Me Knockin''
'Wild Horses'
'Honky Tonk Women'
'Satisfaction'
'Little Queenie'
'Brown Sugar'
'Street Fighting Man'
Encores
'Sympathy For The Devil'
'Let It Rock'

For the remainder of the tour some songs were dropped at certain shows.

Support bands
The Groundhogs
Merlin (Glasgow only)
Noir (Leeds and London only)

The Farewell Tour

'Jagger might be the last of the great white pop entertainers. Those watery eyes stared out at the audience like a fish in an aquarium tank. What we will miss particularly, if the Stones do not tour here again, is their showmanship. The Stones are a piece of social history.' FINANCIAL TIMES

Travellers' tales

After Keith's near miss in getting to Newcastle on time, travel continued to be a hairy experience – and Keith was often in the thick of it. Just about everyone flew back to London on the charter plane from Glasgow. Keith, Anita and Marlon had a puppy with them and the airline officials refused to fly until he was put in the hold. Keith wouldn't agree and the airline staff brought two policemen onboard. After much arguing, the dog was finally put in the hold.

Robert Greenfield covered the tour for *Rolling Stone* magazine: 'Mick misses the train to Bristol even though he's on the platform when it pulls out. He doesn't want to run for it. No one expects Keith, Anita, baby and dog to make trains. Along with Gram Parsons they've become a separate travelling entity.'

'In Liverpool we went on very late because Keith missed the train from London. Then the chartered jet to get him to the theatre broke down. Then the propeller aircraft that was to replace the jet also broke down. Keith, Anita and Marlon arrived an hour after we were due on stage.' BILL

'The show started 40 minutes late because a white Bentley bringing Jagger and drummer Charlie Watts from Newcastle got lost on the way.' DAILY EXPRESS

Tour economics

Typical ticket prices: £1, 85p, 75p, 65p, 50p.

The total number of people that watched the band on this tour was 34,400. Being generous, they probably averaged 75p per person, which meant they grossed £25,800. The *Weekly News* of 6 March said: 'To date, their record sales have amounted to more than £60 million. It's reckoned that this eight-day jaunt will net the group getting on for a cool half-million pounds. Being near millionaires encourages their arrogance.' It was a long way from the £60,000 predicted by Jo Bergman in January.

Not everyone failed to profit from the tour. For the London shows scalpers were selling £1 tickets for up to £10 each.

The shows at Brighton, Liverpool, Leeds and London were recorded live on the eight-track Stones mobile studio by Glyn Johns, all except London where Chris Kimsey did the honours. It was the first time Chris had such responsibility, having met the band through working at Olympic as an assistant engineer. A one-hour tape of the Leeds show was presented to Radio One's John Peel for broadcast on 30 May.

'At the Roundhouse in London, promoter John Smith had employed 25 stewards. As usual, there were many of our friends there to watch, including Dave Mason, Jim Gordon, Jim Keltner, Family, Edgar Broughton, the Faces, John Peel, Tom Donahue and my protégés Tucky Buzzard.' BILL

'Mick Jagger strutted, pranced and postured like an over-sexed circus pony. Bill Wyman wore his gravedigger's smile. The Stones were in trenchant form and Jagger was superb. He moved like a kingfisher and bellowed like a mule.' YORKSHIRE POST

Goodbye Et Bonjour

As the tour finished, the *Sun* flirted with the facts. 'A lot of the excitement was due to nostalgia and the feeling that perhaps this was the last time the group would appear on stage together. They have new heroes now. The Rolling Stones have become pop curiosities, interesting but irrelevant. The five bad boys of British pop are off to France. There, they will soak up sun and begin to chew their way through the millions they have made from their music.' They were right about us being off to France.

ON APRIL FOOL'S DAY in 1971, Astrid, Stephen and I sadly left Gedding to fly to Nice with Mick T. and Rose Miller. We were driven to the Alpes Maritimes, where we explored our new home in Grasse, the Bastide St Antoine and its gardens. It wasn't long before reporters and rain arrived – both were unwelcome.

On Saturday 3 April, Keith, Charlie and their families flew to Nice. The Watts checked into a hotel in Cannes, while Keith went to his rented home, the Villa Nellcote, in Villefranche-sur-Mer. Nellcote was surrounded by jungle-like gardens, an ideal place to ensure privacy.

Mick and Bianca flew to Paris and checked into the Plaza-Athénée Hotel. We visited Mick T and Rose at their house at Le Haut, Tignet, in Grasse. For the next few months we all socialised together – except for Mick. With Bianca being pregnant, he spent a lot of time with her in Paris.

Art house

We had dinner with Charlie, Shirley, Mick and Rose in St Paul de Vence at a famous restaurant called La Colombe d'Or. On the walls were paintings by Picasso, Matisse, Léger and Braque, who had lived in the area early in the century and would pay their food and drink bills with works of art. Little did I know this would become my local in future years.

By 7 April, our effects had still not arrived from England, but Charlie and Shirley left for their rented house at La Borie in Thoiras, near Arles. Back home the band made its first appearance of the 1970s on *Top Of The Pops*. They showed 'Brown Sugar', which we had recorded back in March. The other acts on the show were the Fantastics, Guy Fletcher, Waldo de Los Rios, Bruce Ruffin, Diana Ross, and the Groundhogs. We didn't get to see the broadcast in France – this was decades before satellite TV.

To celebrate the release of 'Brown Sugar' in the UK, we held a reception at the international yacht club in Cannes. It was the first release on our own label. We all drove to Cannes from our rented homes. Atlantic boss Ahmet Ertegun, record executive Eddie Barclay, Steve Stills and Bobby Keys were there too. The evening was only marred by a photographer who kept bugging Mick. Mick finally snapped and threw a glass of wine in his face. We went back to my place: Steve, Charlie, Keith and Anita, Bobby and Judy, Ahmet and friends all came along and, in the spirit of rock'n'roll, we stayed up all night.

A week after our new single came out, *Sticky Fingers* hit the stores.

'BROWN SUGAR'

Nasty, rampant and raw, 'Brown Sugar' is everything that's best about the Stones. The first release on their own label was a sure-fire hit. In recent years, Mick has said that he would probably censor his lyrics of slavery and young black girls if he were writing it now. It's a good job he didn't 30-something years ago. It became the 16th British single release and the 21st in America.

The single was kept off the UK No 1 spot by Dawn's 'Knock Three Times'. However, it became the band's second consecutive US chart topper, a feat they hadn't managed since 'Get Off Of My Cloud' followed 'Satisfaction' back in 1965.

'Mick came up with the song while filming in Australia. It was Mick's riff rather than, as you might well assume, something by Keith. Inspired by the music of Freddy Cannon, Mick originally called his track "Black Pussy" before deciding to give it a more sensible title. The lyrics were partially inspired by a black backing singer we knew in LA called Claudia Linnear.'
BILL

On 18 December 1970, a session at Olympic turned into a birthday celebration for Keith. A new version of 'Brown Sugar' was cut, with Al Kooper on piano and Eric Clapton playing lead. Keith wanted to use it because it was a new version. Having listened again to the Muscle Shoals version, he decided that there was something special about the feel of it – 'Charlie really filled the sound and it was so easy to cut down there, ' said Keith.

What the papers said...

'They finish "Under My Thumb", then get into a new song they've never performed in public before: "Brown Sugar". It goes well.' ROLLING STONE, *on the song's first airing at Altamont*

'Mick chortles with considerable enthusiasm and the guitars chug nicely out of tune, "Bitch" is probably the stand-out track.' MELODY MAKER, *17 April, 1971*

The first 20,000 copies of the UK single came in a picture sleeve designed by Peter Graves, who also did the RSR label.

Recorded
a-side 3 December, 1969 (over-dubs August 1970)
'Bitch' October 1970
'Let it Rock' 13 March, 1971
Locations
a-side Muscle Shoals
'Bitch' Stargroves
'Let it Rock'
Leeds University
Producer
Jimmy Miller
Engineers
Jimmy Johnson at Muscle Shoals
Glyn and Andy Johns
Release
UK Friday 16 April, 1971
RS 19100
US Saturday 17 April, 1971
RS 19100
Composers
All tracks Jagger/Richard except 'Let It Rock' Berry
Highest chart position
UK No 2
US No 1, for two weeks
Weeks on chart
UK 13 weeks
US 12 weeks
a-side personnel
Charlie: drums
Bill: bass
Keith: acoustic and electric guitar and harmony vocals
Mick Taylor: electric guitar
Mick: vocals, castanets and maracas
Stu: piano
Bobby Keys: saxophone

'...and everyone else who had the patience to sit thru this for two million hours.'
STICKY FINGERS, *liner notes*

Kinney Record Group
Special single release
To be released on 16th April 1971 RS 19100

The Rolling Stones

Brown Sugar
Bitch
Let it rock

Suggested retail price 50p

Available from CBS Depot
11/15 William Road London NW1
Telephone 01-388 1071

Kinney Record Group
69 New Oxford Street, London WC1
Telephone 01-836 9381

Arguably the Stones' most successful album, this was their 13th in the UK and the sixth to top the UK charts. More significantly for the future, it was their second US No 1 album – *Out Of Our Heads* had spent three weeks at the top in 1965. Almost two years elapsed between recording the earliest material and the string over-dubs, which completed this 16th US album at London's Trident Sound in January 1971.

'*During November 1970, there were seven recording sessions at Stargroves using the mobile with engineer Andy or Glyn Johns and Jimmy Miller. These were usually held between 9pm and 7am. On 2 November we cut "Moonlight Mile" without Keith – he never turned up. Other tracks included "Sway".*' BILL

Above right: *The insert to prevent the zip scratching the record*
Above: *The back cover*

'Fame has spread from Mick Jagger's lips to his zips!' **NME**

The Rolling Stones new album ... Sticky Fingers

The Russian version of Sticky Fingers *featured a female model.*

MIRAGE MUSIC LIMITED

60p

Kinney Record Group
Special album release
To be released on 23rd April 1971. COC 59100

Side One Brown Sugar-Sway-Wild horses-Can't you hear me knocking-You gotta move
Side Two Bitch-I got the blues-Sister morphine-Dead flowers-Moonlight mile

Suggested retail price £2.25

Available from CBS Depot
11/15 William Road, London NW1
Telephone 01-388 1071

Kinney Record Group
69 New Oxford Street, London WC1
Telephone 01-836 9381

Cover story

For the band's first record on Atlantic they certainly stretched the collateral with the cover art. Mick had asked Andy Warhol to come up with a design even before the album had its name. With the real zip on the original LP cover, it represented a logistical problem to protect the delicate vinyl from the metal of the zip. To help alleviate any problems there was a cardboard insert that featured a young man in his underwear.

The Stones paid Andy Warhol £15,000 to design the cover. As Bill recalls, the man in the denim jeans is Andy's friend Corey Tippin. Recently, Glenn O'Brian, who worked as one of Warhol's assistants, claimed that Jed Johnson was the front-cover model, while Glenn himself is wearing the underwear.

The zip cover was banned by Franco's dictatorship for being obscene. The substitute cover (below) was seen as more acceptable by the Spanish authorities!

What the papers said...

'As a record store attraction the album is positively too dreadful to ignore. That can mean only one thing: the return of Satan's jesters, otherwise known as the Rolling Stones. Sticky Fingers may well plunge the Stones into a controversy over rock lyrics now raging between the Federal Government and American radio stations.' TIME MAGAZINE

'My God! The Rolling Stones, as the 1960s drew to a close, were not only still alive, but were kicking the shit out of everything else being done in rock music. Finally, after a long wait, Sticky Fingers came out. It is the latest beautiful chapter in the continuing story of the greatest rock group in the world.' ROLLING STONE MAGAZINE

Singapore sling

The Ministry of Culture's Controller of Undesirable Publications in Singapore sent a Letter to Cosdel, Atlantic's distributor there, saying, 'I am to inform you that the above named record is deemed to be objectionable and may not be distributed in Singapore. You are therefore requested to surrender all copies of the record to this office for detention, as soon as possible.'

Zipped up

A digitally remastered CD edition of *Sticky Fingers* was released in the early 1990s. It included a sleeve complete with a real miniature zip, less than two inches long.

Exiles

The exiles settled in France. Mick got married to Bianca and we began to record a new album. But progress over the following 12 months would prove to be frustratingly slow, not least because of a deepening drug problem in the band. We split our time between France and LA and attempted to resolve the situation with Allen Klein.

ON THE AFTERNOON OF Wednesday 5 May, I picked up Mick T and went over to Keith's house. Bobby Keys was already there; it was our first rehearsal in France, the first of many. Mick told us that he and Bianca were getting married and the following day he got a special marriage licence without having the banns posted. With the date set for 12 May, Mick phoned the day before and invited us to the reception. Astrid and Rose bought a tandem bicycle as a wedding present. The civil ceremony went ahead 45 minutes late. Keith, the best man, turned up in black braided tights and green combat jacket and was only just allowed into the building.

Mick and Bianca went in his white Bentley to the blessing in the 17th-century Catholic chapel of St Anne overlooking St Tropez bay. A medley of themes from the film *Love Story* was played at Bianca's request. The reception was at a little theatre alongside the Café des Arts in St Tropez.

We drove to the reception with Charlie, Shirley, Mick T and Rose. Bianca was wearing a small open bolero top. By rather sad contrast, earlier that morning Marianne Faithfull had been arrested for drunk and disorderly conduct in Paddington, London and she was fined £1.

Admittance to the reception was granted to

'The devil certainly looks after his own.' KEITH, *on Mick's wedding to Bianca*

The guest list
Mick chartered a Dan-Air Comet to bring his friends, family and associates from London, including Eva and Basil Jagger, Paul and Linda McCartney and their children, Ringo and Maureen Starr, Nathalie Delon, Doris Troy, Leslie Perrin, Roger Vadim, Patrick Lichfield, Bobby Keys, Nicky and Linda Hopkins, the Loewensteins, Eric Clapton and Alice Ormsby-Gore, Ronnie Lane, Ian McLagan, Ronnie Wood, Kenney Jones, Marshall Chess, Jimmy Miller, Donald Cammell, Glyn Johns, Stephen Stills and PP Arnold.

'We all met at the plane. If it had gone down, there would be no music business. Ringo and Paul were on it, sitting at opposite ends as they weren't talking then. We all piled on to three coaches to take us to St Tropez.'
ANNA MENZIES, *Stones office*

Airplane seats were removed to make more room for a PA system and amps.

Left: *The Villa Nellcote was decadent perfection for Keith and the Stones.* Right: *The band's mobile studio got stuck in a narrow road near the house.*

'It's a pretty good house; we're doing our best to fill it with kids and rock'n'roll.'
KEITH

those who wore specially-distributed green or cerise badges saying 'Turn On To Tony – Tony Blackburn'. Astrid and I left in the early hours with Charlie and Shirley, and went back to our house.

The Comet flew Mick's guests back to London. He chartered a 97-foot yacht to cruise the French and Italian Riviera on his honeymoon, but they were pursued by paparazzi. He and Bianca retreated to an isolated chateau, accessible only by sea, to escape the photographers. They returned to St Tropez at the end of May.

Honky chateau

While Mick was away, Keith got into a spot of bother with the law when his car was in a collision with another containing two Italian tourists. Keith got into a furious row and demanded immediate compensation in dollars. They refused and the argument escalated into a fight. Keith had to go to court in Nice, where he was accused of injuring a French port official, Jacques Raymond. He and Keith presented medical certificates proving that they had been injured. Keith was charged with assault and battery and was told he would go to trial. The charge was withdrawn after Keith went to the magistrate's office and apologised – but the French police had marked Keith's card.

On 26 May, with Mick still away, Astrid and I, John Walker (formerly of the Walker Brothers) and his girlfriend Julie went to Strawberry Studios, at the Château d'Heuroville, near Paris (immortalised in Elton John's album *Honky Chateau*). I was producing John Walker's album, and we spent a week at the studio. While we were there we celebrated as both *Sticky Fingers* and 'Brown Sugar' made No 1 in America.

Most people at home thought we were on one long holiday, none more so than Keith's friends. Many went to stay at Nellcote and one particular guest, who claimed to be a racing driver, arrived with his two kids aged six and eight. Almost as soon as they got there he told the kids to take off their shirts. Taped to their backs were bags of white powder. Keith was disgusted that anyone could use

A cable from Marshall Chess proclaimed the success of the Stones' latest album in the US.

'WILD HORSES'

Recorded
a-side 4 December, 1969
(over-dubs 17 February and
August 1970)
b-side November 1970
Studios
a-side Muscle Shoals and
Olympic Studios
b-side Stargroves and
Olympic Studios
Producer
Jimmy Miller
Engineers
Jimmy Johnson at
Muscle Shoals
Glyn and Andy Johns
Release
US Tuesday 12 June, 1971
RS 19101
Composers
Jagger/Richard
Highest chart position
US No 28
Weeks on chart
US 8 weeks
Additional personnel
Jim Dickinson: piano

This US-only release was the band's 22nd single in the States. Its relatively poor chart showing was, in part, a reflection of the times. The move away from singles was in full swing and albums were the thing.

Marlon Richards watches daddy at the piano in France.

Keith came up with the line 'wild horses wouldn't drag me away' about having to leave Anita and baby Marlon to go on tour. Mick finished the lyrics during the difficulties he was having with Marianne, so it got slightly confused.

Mick Taylor played a 12-string and Keith soloed on 'Wild Horses'. Wonderful Taylor guitar pervades 'Sway' – on which Keith didn't play.

their kids in such a way.

We all spent the best part of a month looking for somewhere to record. By the time our mobile studio arrived on 7 June, after a four-day drive from London, we had decided to use Keith's home. The basement was our makeshift studio, from which cables ran to the mobile parked outside. Another advantage of using Nellcote was that we could guarantee Keith would be there… But even then he held up work, albeit not deliberately. Shortly after the mobile arrived, he went Go-Karting, fell off and tore all the skin from his back. It looked bad and hurt worse.

I used the downtime to commandeer the mobile and record with John Walker. Keith soon recovered and ended up playing on one track. From then on we worked every night, usually from 8pm to 3am, until the end of June, although not everyone turned up each night. This was, for me, one of the major frustrations of this whole period. For our previous two albums we had worked well, been pretty disciplined and listened to producer Jimmy Miller. At Nellcote things were very different and it took me a while to understand why.

Two weeks after 'Wild Horses' came out in America, Decca released a new single from the collection of our material that they had amassed over the years. 'Street Fighting Man' was our 21st release, made UK No 21 and had been recorded three years earlier. Still, that's what happens when you have no control over your own catalogue.

The basement band

On Tuesday 6 July, we finally got around to recording with Andy Johns and Jimmy Miller at Nellcote. For two weeks we recorded jam sessions and most of those nights were dull and boring. Recording in Keith's basement had not turned out to be a guarantee of his presence. Sometimes he wouldn't come downstairs at all.

Keith was getting out of it a lot and in retaliation Mick wouldn't turn up some nights. The principal spectators at these games were me, Charlie and Mick T. Stu, who was with us in France, was equally frustrated and his 33rd birthday on 17 July was probably one of the least memorable for him.

In the middle of this craziness we met Prince Rupert to resolve not just the Allen Klein situation but also our ongoing problems with Andrew Oldham and Eric Easton. We had been taking legal advice for some time and on Friday 23 July, a High Court writ was filed against Andrew and Eric by lawyers on behalf of the original Stones and Brian Jones' estate. We alleged their secret deal with Decca Records in 1963 deprived us of record royalties. Our six per cent share out of a total of 14 per cent that Eric and Andrew received for the deal they signed on behalf of Impact was unfair

For good measure, we sued Allen Klein for $29 million, alleging he failed to represent our best financial interests. We'd believed we ran our company, when in truth it was controlled by Klein. Our transatlantic telex bills were a testament to that.

A week later, Mick and Bianca flew to London, where Mick announced she was expecting their baby in September. They holidayed in Dublin with the Guinness family. This further frustrated our recording process and Marshall Chess told me, 'In talking to Charlie, Mick Taylor and Keith, I get the feeling that things are really moving at a slow pace. I am very concerned with this.'

Sound engineer Andy Johns at Nellcote

It was certainly bizarre at Nellcote; it made *Satanic Majesties* seem organised. Andy Johns had to try to record guitar over-dubs while people were eating in the kitchen. It was like making one of those 1960s party records in which everyone felt they should be involved. This chaos was not eased by Keith and Anita's lifestyle, which was becoming increasingly chaotic.

It was obvious drugs were at the centre of the problem – whatever people tell you about the creative relationship between hard drugs and the making of rock'n'roll records, forget it. Believe you me, they are much more a hindrance than a help. There were always other people at the villa, assorted hangers-on as well as those who needed to be there. Ahmet Ertegun was anxious to hear what we were getting down on

In September, the very first badges of the Stones tongue logo were produced for promotion.

tape, as was Marshall Chess. Our deal with Atlantic was lucrative, but we had to deliver and at times it felt like we would never get anything finished.

At the club
To get away for a while, I hired a yacht and took a five-day holiday in early September. Keith worked on a song called 'Happy' while I was away and it was very good. When I got back we listened to two tracks recorded earlier and I immediately realised that Keith had taken it upon himself to re-record my bass part on both tracks – I thought they sounded terrible and I told him so. Finding my outburst very funny, both Keith and Jimmy started to take the piss. I went home really angry and, falling into the same trap as everyone else, didn't go back the next day. It was becoming clear that Jimmy, Andy, Bobby

and Mick T were also involved with hard drugs. I felt like I wasn't in the club – not that I wanted to join.

One day Keith was watching TV at Nellcote when it was burgled. It was just after I'd returned, and the thieves stole nine guitars without Keith hearing a thing. The haul included Albert King's old Gibson Flying Arrow (which Keith used at Hyde Park), my Fender Mustang Bass and Bobby's baritone sax.

To try and keep myself busy and relieve the frustration I continued working with John Walker. We went back to the Château d'Heuroville in late September but John was drinking masses of whisky and was unable to get his singing together. It was as though disaster was following me around. Mick was very worried about Keith. We talked about the situation without ever really coming up with a plan. All we could do was to try and keep going, hoping that it would come together amid the chaos.

'I do not want you to become bogged down in a depressing situation that would inhibit your musical creativity.' **MARSHALL CHESS,** *to Bill on recording*

Below: *Bill had bought a rabbit as a present for the kids*
Page 386: top, *Keith serenades Mick and Gram Parsons and,* below, *recording in the basement studio*
Page 387: top, *Keith in the drawing room and,* below, *Bill in the basement*

Mick himself was away with Bianca for long periods and recording ground to a halt. Astrid and I decided to go to LA at the end of September. We checked into the Beverly Wilshire hotel and later we attended Tucky Buzzard's first night at the Whisky A Go-Go.

The band had evolved from my old protégés the End and it was good to see them getting some of the recognition I felt they deserved. According to guitarist Terry Taylor the gig took a strange turn. 'At the moment we started playing the doorman had a heart attack and died…' Two days later, the band and I met at Capitol Records to discuss the album I had been producing for them. We settled on a name for it – *Warm Slash* – the back cover shot was me having a pee.

We also saw the Ike and Tina Turner show in LA. Backstage, Tina told me that it was thanks to the Stones that their careers had worked out so well. I also went to the Ash Grove, where I once again saw John Lee Hooker perform; he was just as good as always.

Life beyond LA

From LA, we went to Miami and stayed with Allen Klein's nephew, Ronnie Schneider. Steve Stills dropped by and asked if I would play bass at a session that night for his band Manassas. Their bass player Fuzzy Samuels was stuck in England. The session at Criteria included drummer Dallas

Taylor, Chris Hillman on guitar and the rest of Manassas. Once again drugs got in the way. There was lots of coke being done and the band sounded terrible. I was the only straight one there and ended up trying to produce the session.

Next evening, 7 October, engineers Howie and Ronnie Albert did the session, which was much better. We cut two good tracks. The following night we cut 'Rock'n'Roll Crazies' and 'Cuban Bluegrass'. We also did 'Love Gangster' – which I co-wrote – and it ended up on the Manassas double album.

Back in France in mid-October, Andy and Jimmy were still doing their best to keep things moving along. There was hardly a day when someone wasn't missing. Keith was becoming even less communicative. Where he was always so

decisive and to the point, he was now vague and withdrawn. Mick had an excuse for not being around as Bianca's baby was due at any moment.

When she gave birth in Paris on 21 October, Bianca's beautiful six-pound and 10 ounces baby girl was named Jade.

'Mick thinks the time has come to settle down a bit. Mick has always been a fairly ordinary man really.'

EVA JAGGER, *on her son's new role as a father*

Keeping up appearances

Andy and Jimmy prepared rough mixes of as many tracks as possible for Atlantic. But one night disaster nearly struck when there was a fire at Keith's house. His staff quickly dealt with the situation. Keith's chauffeur said he broke down the bedroom door to find Keith and Anita lying on the bed, naked, with the mattress in flames around them. His first thought was that they were overcome with smoke, but they were completely out of it.

Pills, hash and the occasional mind-expanding drug were one thing – but they were on the slippery slope.

Over the course of the next month, we discussed what we should do. We decided to decamp to Los Angeles to finish the album. On 29 November, Mick, Keith, Mick T and their families, Jimmy and Andy all flew to LA. Anita was pregnant, so Keith knew he needed to get

things under control.

Astrid and I followed on later. Ahmet Ertegun regularly visited our mixing and over-dubbing sessions, keen to check on his investment. When I wasn't with the Stones at Sunset Sound, I was finishing John Walker's album.

Mick T and Rose employed Janie Villiers as their cook. As a newcomer to our gang she was able to see things a little more clearly. In some ways we had all grown accustomed to the madness. Mick T, Rose and one-year-old Chloe lived in a little ranch house in Stone Canyon, across the street from Keith and Anita. Janie was impressed by Keith and would take meals over to his house. She was shocked at first, later saying, 'He answered the door, wild-eyed, his hair tousled and his trousers halfway down his bottom. "Who are you?" he asked, eyeing me suspiciously. It took some effort not to drop my casserole and run. I thought at first he was exactly like his image – the scruffy, wild Rolling Stone who took drugs and didn't care a hoot about appearances. Keith, to my astonishment, turned out to be the warmest and kindest Stone of them all.' She described Keith's rented house as 'a cosy, warm home full of laughter and strewn with three-year-old Marlon's toys.'

Besides looking after baby Chloe, Janie also looked after Jade for Mick and Bianca who were renting a huge 30-room mansion a short drive away. Astrid and I were staying at a hotel and Charlie and Shirley were back at home in France.

Child of the revolution

Mark Bolan of T-Rex visited the Stones' 1971 sessions in LA. The flamboyant star caused quite a stir when he kissed Mick on the mouth.

Bass + business = Bill

Astrid and I flew home to France before Christmas, spending the holiday with Charlie and Shirley. Three days later the mobile studio left Nellcote to return to London. Its exile was over. Ours was far from at an end and we needed to handle our increasingly complex business affairs more effectively. Prince Rupert wrote to Mick:

'I hope to be in a position to make clear recommendations for future procedure. This will include a monthly financial review of your budget and expenditure which would be sent to all of you, preceding a regular monthly meeting which could be attended by such of you as wished to attend. As a standard practice, I gather that Bill would be quite happy to act for all of you and attend this meeting regularly on your behalf. Since he has a good and accurate feel for figures, this could well be a good idea.'

Mick, Keith and Mick T remained in LA in early 1972. While they mixed the album, Charlie and I stayed in France. I found a new house to rent near Vence. Over in LA, it was far from all work and no play. Keith and blues man Dr John found time

to sit in with Chuck Berry on stage.

'Berry was awful. Keith managed to sneak in a few little guitar riffs, but Chuck eventually threw everyone off the stage,' said Dr John.

'A couple of guys were a little loud – they were playing a second guitar over and above the solo and between the lyrics. So I did my usual bit, "Slow down, man!" Stretched out my hands, palms down, to lower the volume. But I got no decrease, so I went and whispered to them to turn down. Nothing! And the next song was louder still. I thought, "If you're going to play with me – play *with* me. Not against me." Next song was so loud that I stopped. Then they left. When I came off, my secretary told me it was Keith. I really didn't recognise him 'cos he had a hat right down over his face. If I'd known it was them I might have suffered it through, 'cos I love them. They've even recorded some of my numbers.' CHUCK BERRY

The next night Dr John took Mick to see Bobby Bland at a soul club in Watts, where Mick sang with Bobby. Mick spoke to *Rolling Stone* about the new album: 'We've just been screwing around. It's

nice to be here, somewhere where you can get to some music. We haven't really finished, we're about halfway through.'

Towards the end of January I returned to LA. Mick had told Charlie they had mixed 10 tracks in eight weeks and had 10 more to do. When I got to LA, I discovered Marshall Chess thought the tracks sounded good, but might need remixing (this was a frightening thought). Mick told me 13 tracks were now finished and were all sounding fine. Keith, who seemed to be much better, didn't make the meeting but called me to say that he hoped to finish up within the next two weeks.

Badges have been produced in many different forms since the logo was introduced.

End of the line for Klein

By early February, I was back in France and I phoned Ronnie Schneider. He suggested that the Stones should meet Klein to resolve our affairs with him. Allen phoned Mick the next day to request a settlement. Charlie and I returned to LA in late February, by which time there had been more meetings about Klein, mostly attended by Mick, our lawyers and Prince Rupert Loewenstein.

'I have the ability to think like a thief.'

ALLEN KLEIN, *in Melody Maker*

Having read the *Melody Maker* it was clear that things did not bode well.

Early in March 1972, June Shelley, who used to be married to the folk singer Ramblin' Jack Elliot and worked for us in France, met with our French lawyers. They told June that Keith's life in France would not be easy, as people who had worked at Nellcote had spilled the beans to the police about the drugs used at the house. Over the next couple of weeks Keith and Anita reached the crossroads. Keith was still worried about the effects of their continuing heroin intake. He also knew that he needed to get things sorted out if he was to return to France, which was for now his home. If they continued to follow the same path, then home might not be where he wanted it to be. Keith decided to fly to Switzerland with Anita and Marlon to get help.

Swiss cure

On Sunday 26 March, June Shelley flew to Dr Denber's clinic in Vevey, Switzerland, to get Keith settled on his arrival. From their hotel, Keith was taken to the clinic by ambulance. The next day our lawyer Mr Rivet passed on to me the disturbing news of how bad Keith was. June said Keith was now unconscious and in the clinic. Dave, his driver, had quit after having delivered Keith's car. I called Mick T and Charlie.

'Bill said, "If there's anything I can do to help Keith or you, June, don't hesitate. I'll come up there." I was overwhelmed by his kind gesture. But I explained that so far the story had not leaked into the press – with another Stone around, our luck might not hold.' JUNE SHELLEY, *of the Stones' French staff*

Anita and Keith were not the only worry. We all knew that Mick T had

dallied with the hard stuff, but we didn't realise that his situation had left him very depressed.

'I began to find little screwed-up notes written around the villa,' said Janie Villiers. 'They'd say, "I don't want to be in the Rolling Stones any more" or, worse, notes which made me feel even his life

might be at risk. Sometimes, Mick would talk to me about his fears, saying, "I'm so lonely. I never meet anyone any more."'

Mick Taylor even rang me and suggested that he, Charlie and I should record some of our own music, I told him to forget it. On Saturday 1 April, June called to say that Keith was fine and would call us in a few days time. 'He looks much better. Though he's still sedated and a bit groggy, he was allowed to go out into the hall for a cigarette, and to mingle with the other patients.'

Keith wrote from Switzerland to thank me for offering to help, also saying how good he thought Astrid was for me. He thought he and I should write together more often. 'PS: All this is written under heavy sedation,' he added, 'as you can probably tell by the wobble.'

Within a couple of days, Anita began her course of treatment. As if all this wasn't enough, the situation with Klein was coming to a head. I flew to New York to give a deposition to the Supreme Court. My stint lasted four days.

I returned to England with Astrid for a short holiday at Gedding. It was good to be back in my real home.

TUMBLING DICE'

The band's 23rd in the US and 17th in the UK was the only track on *Exile On Main St* that could be considered a lead-off single. It is the total antithesis to the hard-edged rock of 'Jack Flash', 'Honky Tonk Women' and 'Brown Sugar', but representative of the free-wheeling feel of *Exile.* It's remained a perennial live favourite.

The track was originally called 'Good Time Woman' when Keith wrote the groove. It evolved into 'Tumbling Dice' once Mick began working on the lyrics and added his vocals.

'I know we had a hundred reels of tape on the basic track. That was a good song, but it was really like pulling teeth. It just went on and on.' ANDY JOHNS

'On 3 August we worked on "Good Time Woman" and when I arrived the following day I found Mick Taylor playing bass. I hung around until 3am, then left.' BILL

Although the b-side is called 'Sweet Black Angel' on the single release, it is simply referred to as 'Black Angel' on the cover of *Exile on Main St.*

'"Sweet Black Angel" is about [political activist] Angela Davis.' MICK, *May 1971*

What the papers said...

'Unison guitars from Keith and Mick Taylor, rather than double-tracking, lead us out and down the hole in the middle. By that time, hypnosis has set in and you are cursing the fact that the single doesn't last six minutes longer.' DISC, *15 April, 1972*

'It's impossible to see their names on a label and not undergo inner convulsions in which joy, mirth, tears, nostalgia and deep emotion are inevitably interwoven.' MELODY MAKER, *15 April, 1972*

Cover art

It may not be a picture sleeve as we know it, but it certainly took packaging to a new and more creative level. *Sounds* had described 'Sweet Black Angel' as 'pretty'. The sleeve was far from that, but it was pretty effective.

Recorded
a-side March 1970–December 1971
b-side October 1970–December 1971
Studios
Stargroves and Olympic Studios, Rolling Stones Mobile, Villa Nellcote
Producer
Jimmy Miller
Engineers
Glyn Johns, Andy Johns and Joe Zagarino
Release
UK Friday 21 April, 1972 RS 19103
US Saturday 15 April, 1972 RS 19103
Composers
Jagger/Richard
Highest chart position
UK No 5
US No 7
Weeks on chart
UK 8 weeks
US 10 weeks
A-side personnel
Charlie and Jimmy Miller: drums
Mick Taylor: bass guitar, rhythm guitar
Mick: lead and background vocals
Keith: solo guitar, harmony and background vocals
Clydie King and Venetta Field: background vocals
Nicky Hopkins: piano
Bobby Keys: saxophone
B-side personnel
Keith: acoustic guitar, harmony vocals
Mick: lead vocal, harmonica
Richard 'Didymus' Washington: marimbas
Jimmy Miller: percussion

Settling Cracks

When Keith and Anita's baby was born, she was thankfully a perfect, healthy baby girl. Our focus returned to more mundane matters associated with running our business – the Rolling Stones.

TWO DAYS AFTER 'TUMBLING DICE' came out, Anita gave birth to a baby girl that she and Keith named Dandelion – she would later be called Angela.

'Anita went into labour several weeks earlier than expected. Fortunately, she had a very easy time giving birth.' JUNE SHELLEY, *Stones French staff*

As always bad news seems to follow good. We heard that Klein was trying to stop our new album being released. Our US lawyer, Peter Parcher, phoned to tell me Prince Rupert was in New York talking over the settlement with Klein and his lawyers. Crazy as it seems, I went to the Stones UK office and started to go through Fred Trowbridge's files. The accountant had left us and the band's affairs were in a real mess. I found many cheques not paid in and unused air tickets not returned for credit. There were errors everywhere.

On Monday 1 May, I had a phone call from our UK solicitor, Paddy Grafton Green, telling me that I was not to go back to France, because the Nice police wanted to question me about Keith's involvement with drugs. In Paris, Mick and

Bianca marched in support of US political activist Angela Davis at a rally that began in the Place de la Bastille.

A day later, June phoned from France to confirm that the French police wanted to question Mick and me. While Mick flew to New York, I was told to stay away from France for two weeks. I had plenty to do in London trying to sort out the mess that our accounts were in. I was also working with Alan Dunn from our office, who was in New York working on the logistics of our next American tour.

Mick was arranging the final details of our settlement with Allen Klein. On Friday 5 May, Mick phoned me in the early morning and filled me in on the details. They were not that good for Charlie and me. Over several hours of conversation, Mick told me that our lawyers and accountants thought that Klein owed us a minimum of $17 million and maybe more. If we went ahead with a lawsuit, all our money would be tied up and it could take two years or more to resolve.

Our people wanted to be rid of Klein and settle for $2 million, which was $1 million for Mick and Keith's songwriting and publishing and $1 million shared between each of the original Stones and Brian Jones' estate. Legal costs were to be split equally five ways, which was totally unfair. Charlie and I would end up with about $160,000 each. I told

Pickett line
On Friday 5 May, 1972, Bill and Charlie met up with Wilson Pickett (pictured between the Stones). Mick was in New York sorting out Allen Klein.

Publicity postcards to promote the new tour

Charlie how dissatisfied I was with the deal. I tried to convince him that we should stick together and get a better one. In the evening I spoke to Prince Rupert and again argued for better terms for us. The more I thought about it the worse the deal seemed for Charlie and me. It would be crazy to sign on those terms. Charlie finally agreed and I then went back and put in a counter-offer to Prince Rupert.

It's a deal
In the morning I phoned Peter Parcher in New York and he said my counter-offer had been accepted. Later, Prince Rupert called and gave me details of the settlement, which was $160,000 each from Klein and – for me and Charlie – an extra $50,000 to be paid to each of us by Mick and Keith. I felt a little more satisfied.

Keith was at the Hotel des

Trois, Vevey, just outside Geneva on Wednesday 10 May, when the press release on our settlement was issued.

'Joint statement by the Rolling Stones and ABKCO Industries Inc and Allen Klein: the Rolling Stones and ABKCO Industries Inc and Allen Klein announce settlement of all outstanding differences to the satisfaction of all parties. Further, the Rolling Stones have assigned their claims against Eric Easton to ABKCO Industries Inc and will cooperate with ABKCO in that action. Both Allen Klein and the Rolling Stones wish it to be made clear that ABKCO no longer act as business managers for the Rolling Stones. In a personal quote from his office at 1700 Broadway, New York, Mr Allen Klein said, "Law suits are like wars – no one wins."'

The following Friday, 12 May, Astrid and I flew to Geneva and were met by Stu and June. When we checked into the hotel in Montreux, we bumped into Marshall Chess and a Keith Richards who looked so much better. It was a great relief. Charlie arrived and we had dinner together, then Mick and Bianca flew in from London.

All of us spent a week rehearsing at the Rialto Cinema in Montreux, sessions running until 4am. The police came several times to investigate complaints about the noise level. During the late afternoon, we met a couple of times to go over our Klein settlement and other business aspects of the forthcoming US tour. We had all decided to open Swiss bank accounts to take the money we were due to be paid by Klein on 1 July. Keith and Charlie got me to oversee their personal finances as well as some aspects of the tour.

On Saturday 20 May, we all flew back to London. News of the tour was good: Los Angeles had sold out as soon as tickets went on sale. On Wednesday, we all met at the US Embassy to get our work permits – first enduring a lecture like schoolboys from an elderly American lady. That afternoon, Astrid and I flew to Los Angeles. Our new album was in the shops in the UK and had come out two days earlier in America. Things were looking positive. We had settled with Klein, we were back on the road and advance orders for the LP were so good that we had already been awarded a gold record. We were back on track. The next day the rest of the band flew to Los Angeles.

An airport somewhere in America

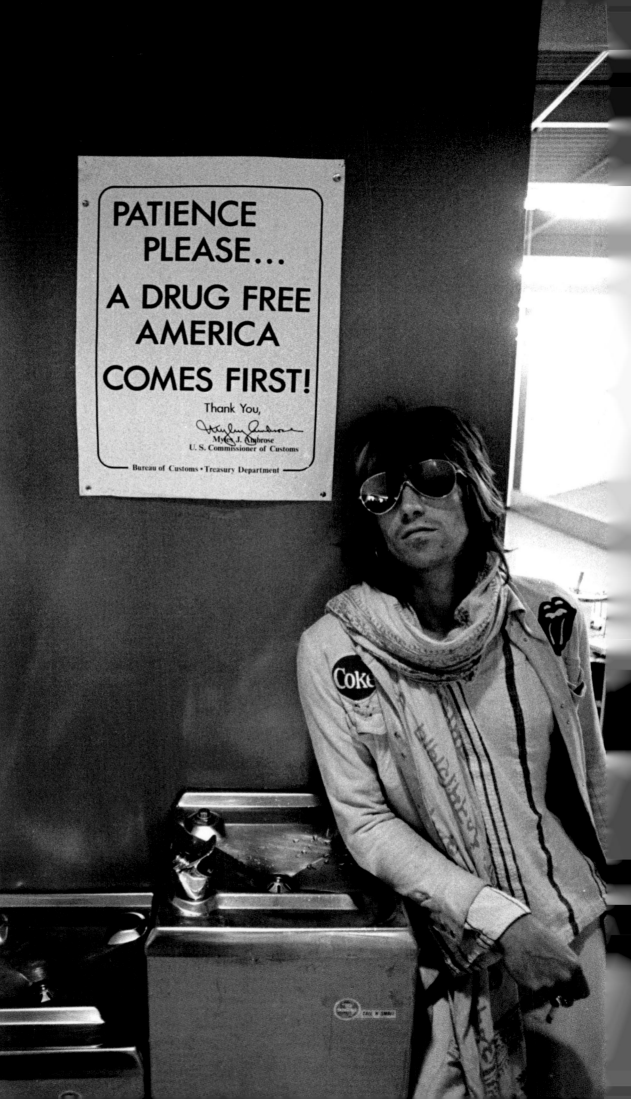

Cover concept

Back in early November 1970, Marshall Chess had written to the band:

'Hopefully, Man Ray will have seen you and will have come up with some ideas for a cover before you leave for America. Mick told me he conveniently changed his price from $1,000, which he had quoted me, to $5,000 for the Stones album cover. It was obvious that he found out from some people that he could probably get more money from the Rolling Stones.'

Three weeks later Mick told the *NME*, 'Sufficient material has been recorded for a double album. The working title is *Tropical Disease*.' John Van Hamersveld and Norman Seiff were chosen to design and Robert Frank took the pictures in LA. The album came with a set of 12 postcards. Bill did not attend the photo session and his face was superimposed over a stand-in.

The label for a four-track promo disc that went out to New Musical Express *featuring 'M Jagger with piano accompaniment'*.

For many people, this is the quintessential Stones album, the very antithesis of everything Beatles and proof of the genius of Keith Richards. For others, it's a shambling album that perfectly evokes the atmosphere in which it was made and in no way reflects what made the Stones the GRNRBITW. Whatever your view, it ranks up there with the greatest rock albums of all time. In Bill's words, 'It was a good result from very difficult circumstances.'

What the papers said...

'The Rolling Stones have a talent for survival. They've been a monster success for almost a decade. But I've an awful feeling it won't last much longer. With their new double album they seem to have reached a dead end.' KEN FOLLETT, *world-famous author, then a young reporter for the South Wales Echo*

'A tremendous set which skilfully uses all the accepted musical mechanics of rock'n'roll.' NME, *20 May*

'An album that might take a few listens but is rich with Stones power and movement.' SOUNDS, *27 May*

German promo poster

Anyone will tell you that this, the 17th US and 14th UK album, was recorded in France at Keith's house, as indeed much of it was. But by the time the Stones arrived in France, they already had seven tracks well under way, including 'Tumbling Dice', 'Black Angel', 'Stop Breaking Down' and 'Shine The Light'. Many of Mick's vocals were done at Sunset Sound once the band had decamped to LA.

'On Friday 14 April, I got an advance copy of Exile On Main St *from the Stones office. I pointed out many errors on the credits. Bill Plummer was down as bassist on 'All Down The Line' and Mick Taylor bassist on 'Shine A Light', when I played bass on both of these tracks.'* BILL

'We cut at least 30 tracks in France. Mick was close to becoming a father and kept skipping off to Paris to see Bianca, which left Keith to lay down the rhythm riffs. On many of the tracks, Mick came in later. It was mid-summer on the Riviera when we cut most of the album and very humid and very hot working in the basement studio. Guitars didn't stay in tune and it was often difficult to get a really good drum sound. Many of the actual songs came quite late on. We had an awful lot of rhythm tracks with no songs written to them.'
JIMMY MILLER, *Rainbow magazine, 1972*

'Mick and Keith liked a few of my songs and we gotta lotta kicks outta just sitting around playing together. All I did was sing and pick with the Stones.'
GRAM PARSONS, *Melody Maker, 12 May, 1973*

'The trouble is that people expect too much from bands like us.' **KEITH**, *NME, April 1971*

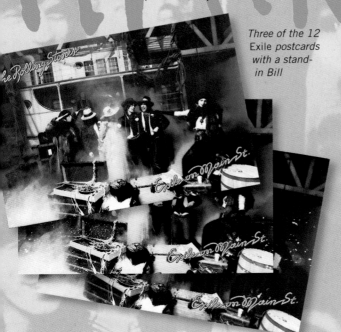

Three of the 12 Exile postcards with a stand-in Bill

'Mick and Keith work out something that's very rough and very basic. There's very little substance to the number in the beginning, which leaves ample room for us all to work out a new chord sequence or put in a middle eight. Keith might have something on his mind about a track, but he might not be there when some of us are sitting around playing with it. I might be playing electric piano, Taylor will be playing bass and Charlie's seated at his drums. We'll just be kinda messing about when all of a sudden Bobby Keys starts blowing away until we all get into some kind of riff. Keith will then turn up, start playing and come in with a country or blues-type thing and adapt it to fit this format. I'd say that three-quarters of the numbers haven't got any words during these initial stages. So if Mick or Keith haven't got the lyrics together for a particular song, it's put aside.' BILL

'It's difficult to define limits about who wrote what. Even if I write something on my own, Charlie might change it more than anyone by changing the beat. I'd have to sing it differently, which might mean changing the words. Keith never has any songs done, ever. That's our big argument, dear – I always want the songs finished, 'cause I have to sing them. It's all right for the band to work on a riff, but it ain't no fun for me.' MICK

Additional personnel
Bill Plummer: bass, 'Rip This Joint' and 'Turd On The Run'
Al Perkins: pedal steel guitar, 'Torn And Frayed'
Billy Preston: piano and organ, 'Shine A Light'
Richard Washington: marimba, 'Black Angel'
Nicky Hopkins and Stu: piano
Bobby Keys: saxophone
Jim Price: trumpet and organ, 'Torn And Frayed'
Jimmy Miller: drums and percussion
Gram Parsons, Clydie King, Joe Green, Venetta Field, Tamiya Lynn, Shirley Goodman, Dr John, Joe Green, Kathi McDonald and Jesse Kirkland: backing vocals

Side one
1. 'Rocks Off'
2. 'Rip This Joint'
3. 'Shake Your Hips' (Moore)
4. 'Casino Boogie'
5. 'Tumbling Dice'
Side two
1. 'Sweet Virginia'
2. 'Torn And Frayed'
3. 'Black Angel'
4. 'Loving Cup'
Side three
1. 'Happy'
2. 'Turd On The Run'
3. 'Ventilator Blues' (Jagger/Richard/Taylor)
4. 'Just Wanna See His Face'
5. 'Let It Loose'
Side four
1. 'All Down The Line'
2. 'Stop Breaking Down' (Johnson)
3. 'Shine A Light'
4. 'Soul Survivor'
Recorded
March 1970–February 1971
Composers
All tracks Jagger/Richard, except where indicated
Locations
Stargroves (Berkshire)
Olympic Studios (London)
Villa Nellcote (France)
Sunset Sound (Los Angeles)
Producer
Jimmy Miller
Engineers
Andy Johns, Glyn Johns and Joe Zagarino
Cover concept and photography
Robert Frank
Design
John Van Hamersveld and Norman Seiff
Release
US Monday 22 May, 1972
Rolling Stones Records
COC 2 2900
UK Friday 26 May, 1972
Rolling Stones Records
COC 69100
Highest chart position
US No 1, for one week
UK No 1, for four weeks
Time on chart
US 17 weeks
UK 16 weeks

The Return Of The Exiles

Every city on the tour sold out and *Exile* was headed for the top of the US chart. Things were looking good. You couldn't turn on a rock station in California without hearing us – it was saturation marketing.

'In Los Angeles, it's been declared Rolling Stones hour, day or week depending on which radio station you listen to. It's Stones, Stones, Stones.' EMPEROR ROSKO, *BBC Radio One, 1972*

We WERE INTRODUCING a lot of new material from *Exile* on tour, so we rehearsed for four days at the Warner Brothers Studios with Jim Price, Bobby Keys and Nicky Hopkins.

Denied permission to fly into Canadian airspace on Saturday 3 June, we chartered an Electra turboprop from McCulloch Oil to fly from LA to a small suburban airport in Washington state. Then from there, six black Cadillacs drove us to the Georgian Towers hotel in Vancouver.

A ticketless crowd of 2,000 outside the Pacific Coliseum hurled firebombs, stones and battled police, but there was no trouble inside. Stevie Wonder and Wonderlove opened for us at 8.30pm and we played for an hour and 40 minutes to a sell-out crowd. We tried out some songs that in the end didn't stay in the set for the rest of the tour.

Bacchanal rock

Next came Seattle, then San Francisco. The Winterland shows had 16,000 capacity and requests for 100,000 tickets. The barter price for a $5 ticket was an ounce of grass, a quarter of an ounce of hash or $50 cash. KSAN Radio ran a competition, asking listeners what they would do to get a pair of tickets to see the Stones. The winner said, 'I would shave off all the hair on my body and smoke it.' In Chicago, the price for a $6.50 ticket was

$70 and in New York it was $100. Backstage in San Francisco was John Lee Hooker – it was great to see him again. Stanley Booth, who wrote about our 1969 tour, was also there. I tackled him about my scrapbooks that he'd borrowed to write his book. He promised to return them to me. I finally got them back in 1982.

As we boarded our charter flight to LA, a lady in hotpants talked her way onto the aircraft and sidled up to Mick. She pulled a sheaf of papers out of her bag and said, 'I am hereby serving you Michael Philip Jagger, with the following subpoenas.' Among them was one claiming £328,500 damages for farmland trampled by fans at Altamont: the nightmare was back.

Suddenly, she ran down the steps from the plane, shouting and screaming that Mick had slapped her face. Keith stood on top of the

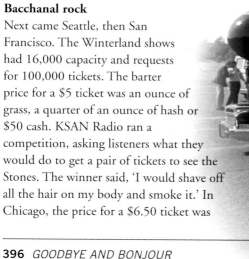

Cadillacs took the band from their plane into Canada.

steps and threw her papers in the air. Within a minute the doors shut and we taxied for take-off. Three years later, all the charges against the band were dropped.

In LA, 4,500 tickets for the Hollywood Palladium sold out fast – 120,000 fans applied by mail. Our second show in the LA area was in Long Beach. At the aftershow party, Stevie Wonder played and Screaming Lord Sutch was there; it was all a very long way from the Ealing Club. The biggest dates in the LA area were at the Forum where we played to 37,000 people at two shows.

'They could play three months in San Francisco and probably six in New York and sell out every seat.' BILL GRAHAM, *tour promoter*

Bill Graham arranged a backstage dinner, complete with towels and toilet-seat covers sporting the tongue logo. Jack Nicholson, Goldie Hawn and Tina Turner were among countless guests. The crowd just wouldn't let us leave the second show. 'I think they like us,' said Mick. As we went back on stage the building erupted to 'Honky Tonk Women'.

Our last show in California was on Tuesday 13 June in San Diego. Mick wore a purple silk

'Outrageous. Picaresque. Jaunty. Flagitious. Taunting, teasing, tempting. An hour-and-a-half of bad influence on your daughter and exquisite bacchanal rock from the one and only Mick Jagger and his band of plug-uglies.'

MERI REAGLE, *Tucson Citizen*

jumpsuit, a blue denim jacket, a blue neck-scarf, a red sash round his waist and white shoes. He had rhinestone bracelets on each wrist, red sparkly eye paint and gold glitter in his hair – his usual stage get-up on this tour.

Tucson Citizen journalist Meri Reagle wrote, 'Charlie Watts sits toad-stoic atop his Gretsch drums. Mick Taylor stands oddly tall and pretty, Bill Wyman stands frozen in Tussaud wax, Keith Richards bounces around like the living dead, and Jagger is a bird – rooster, cockatoo, jay. Ohmygosh.' Do you think she liked us?

After San Diego we played Albuquerque, then Denver. Astrid and I took a day off in Boulder, where we met up with Steve Stills and the Manassas band. We drove to the Caribou ranch in the mountains where they were recording. Back in Denver, we went to a party at the house of promoter Barry Fey. In Keith's hotel suite, he and Steve Stills got into an argument about nothing and drew knives, but it was all front and the whole thing fizzled out.

Rehearsing in LA on 1 June, 1972

After playing in St Paul in Minnesota we headed to Chicago for three shows.

'The band seems to be having a good time. Mick Taylor is smiling and relaxed in a spangled version of the tongue t-shirt. Bill Wyman, in a yellow suit, kicks joints to the back of the stage and out of the way as fans throw them. Mick pours a bowl of water over the crowd. He grabs two bowls of rose petals from a stagehand, mashes them to his face, then tosses them to the crowd, followed by the bowl. It hits someone in the head in the 15th row. There is an instant scramble for the bowl. The music stops and the lights blink out. The Rolling Stones are gone.' J ROBERT TEBBEL, *the Minnesota Daily*

All I can really remember about the St Paul gig is how hot it was – even I sweated. Charlie had trouble holding his sticks and Bobby Keys' shirt was transparent when he came off stage.

In Chicago we were driven to the Playboy Mansion. Hugh Hefner had invited us to stay. We watched *Is There Sex After Death?* on Hefner's cinema screen, followed by a movie made in 1959 by Robert Frank. He was travelling with us and filming the tour.

I spent the next afternoon playing table tennis with trumpet player Jim Price, Mick T and luggage man Willie Vacarr. I beat everyone, but Willie got his own back when we switched to pool; he repeatedly won, playing one-handed. We did a great show that evening. I gave my best performance in ages, but it was so hot again.

North America, *June–July 1972*

3 June Pacific Coliseum, Vancouver, British Columbia, Canada
4 June Seattle Center Coliseum, Seattle, Washington (two shows)
6 June Winterland, San Francisco, California (two shows)
8 June Winterland, San Francisco, California (two shows)
9 June Hollywood Palladium, Los Angeles, California
10 June Pacific Terrace Center, Long Beach, California
11 June Inglewood Forum, Los Angeles, California (two shows)
13 June International Sports Arena, San Diego, California
14 June Community Center, Tucson, Arizona
15 June University Of New Mexico, Albuquerque, New Mexico
16 June Coliseum, Denver, Colorado (two shows)
18 June Metropolitan Sports Center, St Paul, Minnesota
19 June International Amphitheater, Chicago, Illinois
20 June International Amphitheater, Chicago, Illinois (two shows)
22 June Municipal Auditorium, Kansas City, Missouri
24 June Tarrant County Convention Center Arena, Fort Worth, Texas (two shows)
25 June Hofheinz Pavilion, Houston, Texas (two shows)
27 June Municipal Auditorium, Mobile, Alabama
28 June University Of Alabama, Tuscaloosa, Alabama
29 June Municipal Auditorium, Nashville, Tennessee
4 July Robert F Kennedy Stadium, Washington, DC
5 July Scope, Norfolk, Virginia
6 July Coliseum, Charlotte, North Carolina
7 July Civic Arena, Knoxville, Tennessee
9 July Kiel Auditorium, St Louis, Missouri (two shows)
11 July Rubber Bowl, Akron, Ohio
12 July Convention Center, Indianapolis, Indiana
13 July Cobo Hall, Detroit, Michigan
14 July Cobo Hall, Detroit, Michigan
15 July Maple Leaf Gardens, Toronto, Canada (two shows)
17 July Forum, Montreal, Quebec, Canada
18 July Boston Gardens, Boston, Massachusetts
19 July Boston Gardens, Boston, Massachusetts
20 July Spectrum, Philadelphia, Pennsylvania
21 July Spectrum, Philadelphia, Pennsylvania (two shows)
22 July Civic Arena, Pittsburgh, Pennsylvania
24 July Madison Square Garden, New York
25 July Madison Square Garden, New York (two shows)
26 July Madison Square Garden, New York

The Stones played to almost 750,000 people on their seventh North American tour and could have played to several million, such was the demand to see them. As *Life* magazine pointed out, 'They had earned some of the worst press clippings since Mussolini and have become one of the most visually and musically stunning ensembles in any form of music.' The tour grossed $4 million from 51 shows at 32 venues, making it the richest rock tour in history.

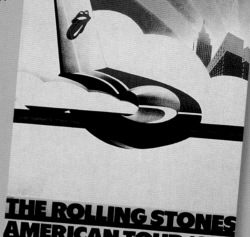

'Chip Monck is responsible for the lighting and stage production that makes this tour different from any other. A 16-by-40-foot mirror will be hung above the Stones, in front of the stage. Six large spotlights are then focused up from the back of the stage. In one fell swoop, the Stones get backlit and spotlit in front. At each side of the Stones will be hydraulic lifts filled with Tychobrahe speakers. Each hydraulic weighs 10,000 pounds fully loaded, and cranks up to a height of 18 feet. The sound will spread evenly in large arenas.' ROBERT GREENFIELD, *Rolling Stone magazine*

The stage floor was made up of six white panels on which a giant double serpent had been painted in green and yellow.

'It gets up to 140 degrees onstage. If we turned everything on full it would get hotter. There are 64,000 watts of light and eight Super Troupers. You could cook people with the heat.' CHIP MONCK, *Melody Maker*

Set list
A typical night featured:
'Brown Sugar'
'Rocks Off'
'Gimme Shelter'
'Bitch'
'Tumbling Dice'
'Happy'
'Sweet Virginia'
'You Can't Always Get What You Want'
'Love In Vain'
'Midnight Rambler'
'All Down The Line'
'Bye Bye Johnny'
'Rip This Joint'
'Jumpin' Jack Flash'
'Street Fighting Man'
Encore (sometimes!)
'Honky Tonk Women'

On some nights, fans heard:
'Loving Cup', 'Torn And Frayed', 'Dead Flowers', 'Sweet Black Angel', 'Johnny B Goode' and 'Don't Lie To Me'.

American Tour 1972

Diary extracts

1. Seattle The Stevie Wonder Band opened for us and then we went onstage and played to a crowd of 14,000. Keith had lots of trouble with his guitars and amps.

2. San Francisco Backstage were Neil Young, Jerry Garcia, and most of Grateful Dead and Jefferson Airplane. We played to 4,000 fans. The show was very good. Mime artist Robert Shields appeared during intermission at both shows.

3. Los Angeles At the Hollywood Palladium, we went on at 9.30pm and played to about 5,000 fans. It went off well, but I had a bad night. We did an encore of 'Honky Tonk Women'. The gross was $29,250.

4. Albuquerque We played to 15,000 fans. Mick wore a purple and silver outfit, purple eye shadow, two pink stars pasted to each temple just behind the eyes and glitter in his hair. We gave a reasonable performance to a good crowd, finishing just after 10.30pm.

5. Houston The evening show was filmed and recorded live by Andy Johns and the Record Plant 16Tk Mobile Recording Unit.

Tuscaloosa After the show, Keith and Bobby Keys stayed the night and partied with the Stevie Wonder band. The rest of us flew out in very stormy weather and watched fantastic lightning most of the way to Nashville. We checked into a local hotel and then went to dinner at Mario's Italian Restaurant. They had an awful violin player going from table to table, who we paid — not to play.

6. Norfolk We went onstage at 9.30pm and played to 11,728 fans. It was a really good performance and very enjoyable. Police reported 15 arrests [pretty much the average number for the tour].

7. St Louis It was a bad show for me; I had three amps break down. The sound was horrible.

8. Detroit A sell-out crowd of 12,000. It was a very good show, and the audience was really great. We did an encore of 'Uptight' and 'Satisfaction' with Stevie Wonder's band.

9. Pittsburgh We broke the Jackson Five attendance record with a crowd of 13,911. We went on to a rather reserved audience. Even so, about 70 people were arrested.

10. New York Bob Dylan was in the audience. We went onstage at 9.37pm, and performed to a great crowd, but Keith played far too loudly.

Accompanying us for some of the tour is Truman Capote, who has been commissioned to write for *Rolling Stone*. Also along for the ride is Terry Southern [the writer of *Dr Strangelove*] who is writing for the *Saturday Review*.

Tour entourage

Rolling Stones plus girlfriends and wives:

Ian Stewart *road manager*
Peter Rudge *tour manager*
Jim Price *trumpet*
Bobby Keys *saxophone*
Nicky Hopkins *piano*
Marshall Chess *Rolling Stones Records*
Martin Rothman *tour accountant*
Jo Bergman *secretary*
Alan Dunn *logistics*
Leroy Leonard and Stan Moore *Security*
Ted Newman Jones *guitar tuner*
Rich Mandella *amp tech*
Steve Goekee *make-up*
Larry Badgely *doctor*
Willie Vacarr *baggage*
Gary Stromberg *publicity*
Robert Frank *film cameraman*
Danny Seymour *film sound*
Chip Monck *stage and lighting*
Don Watson *advance man*

June dates   July dates

'I feel a bit like Montgomery before El Alamein – it's not like a rock'n'roll tour, more like a military assault.' **PETER RUDGE,** *tour manager*

Bunnies, Bombs, Busts And A Princess

Our American tour was proving to be incredibly successful. We were toasted by everyone from Hugh Hefner and his Bunnies to Tennessee Williams and Truman Capote. The trip was amazing in more ways than one.

Hefner's beauties – Mercy Bunny not pictured

THERE WERE PLAYBOY BUNNIES everywhere when we arrived back at Hugh Hefner's mansion after the first night, and everyone got drunk. Charlie couldn't deal with it and went to stay at a hotel.

It wasn't long before people ended up in the sauna with Bunnies. Mick got very well acquainted with a girl called Mercy. I, on the other hand, got stuck playing backgammon with Hugh, which he won 5–3. Stevie Wonder came over with some friends and played and Phil Upchurch provided some great bass.

After we left, the Micks and Keith made fun of Charlie and I for not taking advantage of the Bunnies. We were just relieved that we hadn't caught anything.

In Kansas, we met Princess Lee Radziwill, Jackie Kennedy's sister, who came along with Truman Capote. It wasn't a good show. My amp broke down and Keith's guitars were out of tune. I think everyone was pretty washed out after four days at the Hefner mansion.

'It's not much of a way to see the country, is it? All you care about is how good the bed is and can you get something to eat after the show.' CHARLIE, *en route to Dallas*

To everyone out front it seems so glamorous and exciting, but for the main part it's just a job. It's not most people's idea of a job, but it is still a job. And before anyone asks about the Playboy mansion, it was one perk this Perks avoided. In truth, I couldn't get up to anything because Astrid was with me.

Next day in Dallas, we saw the other side of the touring coin. We decided to change around the set list and booked Sunset Sound Studios to rehearse. We ordered some refreshments in the hotel first and it took two hours to get a cup of tea and another hour for a sandwich. We were supposed to leave at 4pm, but didn't actually get out until gone 8pm. It was a waste of five hours at the studio. Even the jamming was pretty bad.

'I have never been on anything like this. I have been on trips with extraordinary people before, but this totally excludes the outside world. Never to know what city you are in – I cannot get used to it.' ROBERT FRANK, *film-maker, on shooting the band in Dallas*

All of us had our little rituals to make life on the road more bearable. Keith's favourite trick was to drape the lights in his room with scarves, making it look like a gypsy encampment, as someone

described it. Life on the road is a form of madness: you just have to try to stop it getting to you.

We headed south to Houston where Bianca arrived to join Mick for 10 days. We moved on to New Orleans for a day off and I had a great dinner with Charlie, Mick T, Ahmet, Peter Rudge and Truman Capote. Later we went to an old, barn-like recording studio for a party organised by Ahmet. We were entertained by the blind guitarist Snooks Eaglin, R&B pioneer Professor Longhair and the legendary Roosevelt Sykes, a 66-year-old pre-war master of blues piano.

Independence, sexism and the Stones

One of our smallest audiences was in Nashville, the home of country music, where we played a sell-out show to fewer than 10,000 people. Duck Dunn, the brilliant bassist with Booker T and the MGs, came backstage with his wife June. He invited Astrid and I to spend the Fourth of July weekend at their home in Memphis.

We had a fantastic time, relaxing and living like normal people. There was a barbecue in the garden and we played music with Duck's friend Don Nix, who produced guitarists Freddie and Albert King and performed in his own right.

At the Mid-South Coliseum, where the Stones had played in November

'Chicago was quite somethin', stayin' at the mansion and all, which I liked. Hefner was nice to us. It would take hours for me to tell you all of the craziness that went on there.' MICK

Left: Truman Capote, Princess Lee Radziwill and Norman Mailer. Above: Roosevelt Sykes

1965, we went to see a show with BB King, Isaac Hayes and Rufus Thomas. I hadn't seen BB King since he toured with us in 1969.

The band had been to the Virgin Islands for the weekend. We reunited in a hot and humid Miami, checking into the Thunderbird Motel. Then it was off to Criteria Studios, where we worked on a new song until 5am, but it came to nothing. We went back the next day to produce more of the same. Washington was our next gig, where Men Struggling To Smash Sexism were handing out leaflets entitled 'The Stones And Cock Rock'.

'If you are male, this concert is yours. The music you will hear tonight is written for your head. It will talk to you about your woman, how good it is to have her under your thumb. Men will play hard, driving music that will turn you on, hype you up, get you ready for action – like that at Altamont. The Stones are tough men – hard and powerful. They're the kind of men we're supposed to imitate, never crying, always strong. In Vietnam, our brothers have killed and raped millions of people in the name of this ideal. We resent the image the Stones present to males. If you are female, you don't need this leaflet to tell you where to fit in. If you choose to fight, to smash the sexist society that has been constructed to oppress you – tonight, here and every day, throughout America – we will attack sexism and support your struggle.'

I don't think they recruited many people.

A few days later we had a break in St Louis before two shows at the Kiel Auditorium. We viewed the rushes of Robert Frank's film, along with some footage that Mick shot with a 16mm camera. The next day we were to play in Akron, Ohio, at the Rubber Bowl, but before we got there a home-made bomb exploded in the early hours of the morning.

45rpm
Excerpt from 'Exile on Main Street'
COC69100
FOR RADIO PLAY ONLY
Promotion copy- not for sale

HAPPY (3.00)
(Jagger/Richard)
THE ROLLING STONES
Essex Music Int.
SAM 4

'Happy' and 'All Down The Line'
On Saturday 28 June, 1972, the Stones released their 24th US single, 'Happy' with b-side 'All Down The Line' (It was Rolling Stones Records catalogue number RLS 19104). Issued in a colour sleeve, it got to US No 22 and stayed in the chart for eight weeks.

dates on the tour.

After our show in Toronto the *Globe and Mail* ran a piece that summed up where they thought we were at.

'They are the biggest draw in the history of mankind.' BILL GRAHAM, *promoter*

'A bomb damaged the stage slightly, tore a one-and-a-half-foot hole in the turf and slightly hurt four young men sleeping on top of the stage. The explosion caused $1,000 damage to a closed-circuit camera.' AKRON BEACON JOURNAL

The show in Akron went off fine, even if I did manage to blow another amp with the very first note I played.

Until Detroit, we had not included 'Satisfaction' in our set. As an encore, Stevie Wonder and his band joined the Stones and all 20 of us played it and Stevie's hit 'Uptight'.

From then on we did 'Satisfaction' at most

'The Stones offer meticulously-structured theatre – the theatre of rock'n'roll. It's a strange mix, part-Oscar Wilde, part-Las Vegas, part-Little Richard, part-Punch and Judy, part-travelling medicine show – black medicine, that is. The genius of the Stones is to pull it together. The Stones structured the act to a finale that, in retrospect, is hard to believe. The crowd was blowing its mind with the excitement of it all. Then suddenly it ended.' GLOBE AND MAIL, *Toronto*

On the morning of our Montreal show, French-Canadian separatists

detonated a bomb beneath a lorry-load of equipment outside the venue. Nobody was hurt, but windows were broken. When we found out, Mick got pretty agitated. 'I don't want to go on tonight,' he said. 'After that, I don't want to go on. Yeah, this time, I'm scared. If someone did that, then obviously something's going on. You know, there's been a lot of talk about it, but this is the only time anything's happened. I won't be very good because of that.'

Stevie Wonder had another commitment so our support act in Montreal was Martha and the Vandellas. There was no further trouble as we played to the audience of 19,000, other than Mick having to avoid a flying bottle.

On Tuesday 18 July, Stu had his 34th birthday. By way of celebration, our plane made two attempts to take off, but eventually taxied back to the terminal. After two hours they fixed it and we took off for Boston. Our destination airport was closed due to fog and we diverted to Green Airport in Warwick, Rhode Island.

All was fine as we went through customs and we were getting ready to leave when a photographer for the *Providence Journal-Bulletin* arrived in the customs area and tried to take photos of us. Our security tried to stop him

and Keith eventually hit him, quite lightly, around the legs with his belt. The situation rapidly deteriorated and we were detained in the customs area until the police arrived. They took the photographer's side and arrested Mick, Keith, Marshall Chess, Robert Frank and security man, Stan Moore. The problem was we were due on stage in under an hour.

The rest of us were driven the 60 miles to Boston in buses. When we arrived at the Boston Garden, Stevie had doubled the length of his set. By 10.30pm, the audience was restless and Mayor Kevin White, who was at the show, wound up calling Governor Clayborn Pell of Rhode Island to tell him how serious the situation was.

At a special session of Rhode Island District Court, the rest of the band pleaded not guilty and were released on bail of $3,000. They were driven to Boston with a police motorcycle escort. When he knew they were en route the Mayor went on stage to tell the fans.

'…Now I've got one final question to ask and this is the question. I'm leaving and the Stones are coming. Can you go home quietly for me and this city?' KEVIN WHITE, *Boston Mayor*

'The Stones were magnificent, still superbly capable of thrashing out the best music currently available. The horns helped, but it was Mick Taylor who played a lead guitar which burned your ears off.'
THE VILLAGE VOICE

We finally got on stage at 12.48am, more than three hours late. The next day was taken up with endless meetings about the incident. After another good show at Boston Gardens, we went to dinner at a Hungarian restaurant, after which Keith went to see Bobby Womack at the Sugar Shack in another part of town.

School's out

Stephen flew in to Philadelphia to join me. Two days and three shows later, we travelled to Pittsburgh on our charter plane. Most of these flights were pretty ordinary. People caught up on sleep, chatted, played cards or read. This flight was the exception. In the back of the plane, Larry Badgely, the tour doctor, Willie the baggage man, and two girls had another way of passing the time. As the *Sunday People* put it, 'They stripped and plunged into a wild, uninhibited sequence of sexual athletics.' I'm not quite sure it was as colourful as that, but they were encouraged by Robert Frank filming and someone who started drumming to provide an improvised rhythm for the proceedings. Astrid and I stayed up the front of the plane, keeping Stephen occupied. I had to be content with verbal reports.

When we reached New York, I checked into the St Regis Hotel as Lord Gedding. Keith (Count Ziggenpuss) booked into the Carlisle Hotel, while Mick Jagger (Mr Shelley) and Mick T (Mr Romanoff) checked into the Pierre Hotel. During our stay, all five of us had a heavily armed plain-clothes policeman sitting in each of our suites, 24

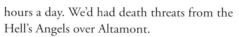

hours a day. We'd had death threats from the Hell's Angels over Altamont.

Mick and Bianca spent a day with Princess Lee Radziwill at her home in Southampton, Long Island. The following show at Madison Square Garden was like a homecoming. Having played New York on every tour, it was good to be back. *Disc* magazine reported: 'Jagger picked up a silver bowl filled with water and sprinkled the water – baptized, if you will – over the front few rows, and then poured the rest over his head.

He leapt on the piano stool with Nicky Hopkins and then jumped up and down.' We played three nights with a matinee on the middle day. Bob Dylan came to our first show and also to the party afterwards.

Before Tuesday's matinee, Dick Cavatt interviewed Mick and I for his TV show. I was smoking a joint during the interview and the whole thing got rather silly. Dick Cavatt asked if I was a chain smoker. I said I wasn't, but he persisted, 'Do you smoke very much?'

'No,' I responded.

Dick said, 'You're burning the filter there.'

'No, I'm not.'

Stevie Wonder and his band supporting the Stones on their US tour of early summer 1972.

Mick celebrates his 29th birthday on-stage in New York.

'Well, one of us is right.'

I admitted, 'It looks like I'm burning the filter.'

Birthday boy

Our last night in New York was also Mick's 29th birthday. We played a great show, to a fantastic audience. The Princess was back, along with Tennessee Williams, Andy Warhol and Bette Midler. We celebrated Mick's birthday on-stage with cakes, balloons and cream pies, which inevitably got thrown. As Mick tossed rose petals into the audience, he discovered our PR guy Gary Stromberg had put pieces of raw liver among the blooms. Back at the St Regis, we went to the ballroom for another party arranged by Ahmet Ertegun. Everyone was there – Bob Dylan, Ben E King, Andy Warhol, Woody Allen, Diane Keaton, Zsa Zsa Gabor, Lorna Luft, Robert de Rothschild, Stevie Wonder, Carly Simon and Candy Darling to name just a few. Count Basie and the Muddy Waters Band played and Mick and Stevie Wonder jammed with Muddy. There was a big cake from which one of Andy Warhol's naked protégés appeared. We got to bed at 9am, totally missing an eclipse of the moon.

The Stones vs Gandhi

The tour had been a resounding success in every respect. Peter Rudge told *Billboard*, 'There was a 100 per cent gross, due to advance sell-outs for every concert. The Rolling Stones took between

60 and 70 per cent of that amount, but that was a gross figure. All expenses came out of the Stones' earnings. And they spent a lot of money to put on good shows everywhere.'

Promoter Bill Graham said, 'New York is New York. Till you do it there it hasn't happened. They could have sold the Garden out for a year. They are the biggest draw in the history of mankind. Only one other guy ever came close: Gandhi.'

In summing up the tour, Marshall Chess said: 'When 35 chicks come to fuck the Stones, and there are only five Stones, that leaves 30 chicks, so anyone close to the tour gets one. It's part of the ritual, and it's easy to get sucked in.'

The *Hollywood Reporter* wrote that at least one person was glad we'd left. 'A top Hollywood composer–conductor is still seething because his teenage daughter was the travelling companion of Keith Richard of the Rolling Stones during the Stones' 30-city tour of the US and Canada.' Hopefully, Quincy got over it.

'This tour is going to go down as the rock'n'roll tour of all time".' ROY HOLLINGWORTH, *Melody Maker, 29 July, 1972*

Back to business
I received a letter from our tax adviser, warning that if any of us returned to become resident in the UK between April 1972 and 1973, we would have an enormous tax liability. We would certainly become bankrupt if we did. Keith's battle with the

police in France was coming to a head: Prince Rupert wrote saying that Mick, Charlie and I needed to meet with our French lawyer to provide evidence the French were seeking about Keith's activities at Nellcote. We discussed all this at a meeting on the Thursday after the tour finished. If Keith couldn't live in France, it narrowed the options.

After a short holiday with my brother Paul in Bermuda, we returned to France on 5 August. Keith and Anita moved to the Chalet Leterrent, Gryon, Switzerland. Mick and Bianca decided to spend some time in Ireland at the Earl of Gowrie's home.

A month later, Astrid and I went back to Gedding for a break. When we flew back to Nice customs gave us a thorough going-over. They detained us while June Shelley brought us tea, and tried to contact our French lawyers. I was treated like a criminal, and frog-marched across the airport when I wanted to have a pee. They finally released us after about four hours.

In the middle of October, I went to London to do some over-dubs on tracks recorded during the American tour. Only Charlie and Mick were there and I did a bass overdub on 'Tumbling Dice'. Some of the Faces arrived and we tried to do a version of 'Silent Night' with Stu on piano, which turned into a farce.

Charlie gave me a great primitive painting of a

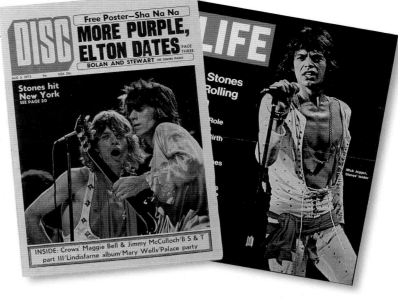

foxhunt, as thanks for my help over Klein. A few days later Andy Johns and I mixed 'Brown Sugar', then Mick, Bobby Keys, Bonnie Bramlett and Glyn Johns arrived. I borrowed a bass from the Who's Pete Townshend, who was in the next studio, and did an over-dub on 'Rip This Joint'.

Judgement day
On 1 November, I sat down with Charlie, Paddy Grafton Green and two French lawyers in Vence. Numerous meetings had taken place during the last month but now we were to meet a judge in Nice. We were individually questioned in his chambers. I went in first for almost an hour. It was easier than I had expected it to be. The Micks returned to London while Charlie and I stayed in France. The next morning, Mick phoned to warn us to be prepared to leave France at very short notice – the judge was proving to be very stubborn.

He and Mick T flew to Ireland, as there was still a need to stay out of England for tax purposes. It was amazing: we were doing all this running around and worrying because of Keith and Anita. Sometimes, being in the Stones was a very one-sided affair. We had a commitment to Atlantic to produce another album and agreed to record in Jamaica. At least Keith would not be hassled there.

'In contrast to the brash Jagger was Bill Wyman, whose only movement came when he breathed.'
TOM SQUITIERI, *The New Kensington Dispatch, Pittsburgh, July 1972*

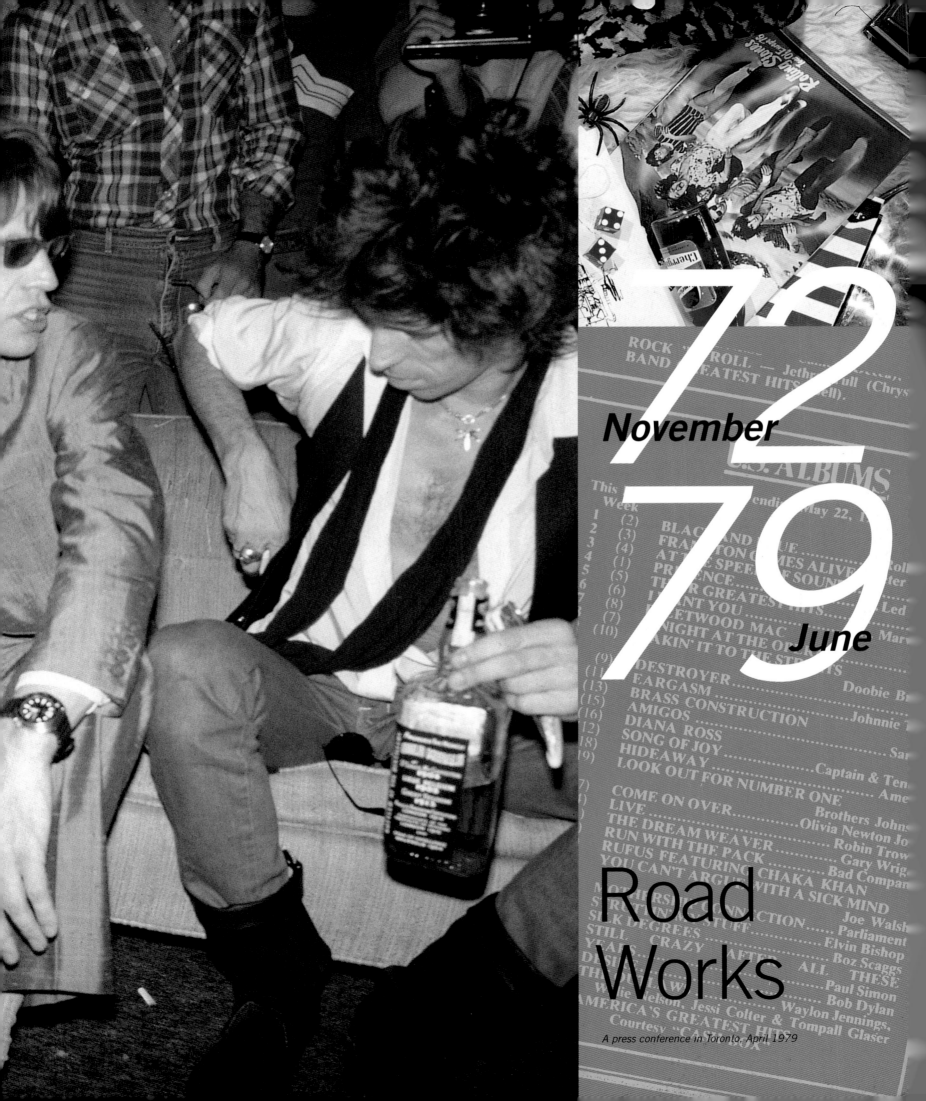

November
72
79
June

Road
Works

A press conference in Toronto, April 1979

Kingston To Kings Cross

We were ready to record in Jamaica, but the spectre of Keith's drug problem in France was very much on our minds. It wasn't just something that affected Keith – it affected our ability to tour, our whole way of life.

ON THURSDAY 23 NOVEMBER, Astrid and I flew from London to Jamaica. We checked into the Spanish-style Terra Nova hotel, formerly the home of Island Records founder Chris Blackwell. We recorded for a week at Byron Lee's Dynamic Sounds studio in Kingston. When I arrived, I was surprised to see a big black guy with a shotgun sitting on a chair outside – security, Jamaican-style.

We worked on 'Angie' and another song with the working title 'Star Fucker'. But all too soon, our attention shifted from recording to Keith's French situation, a problem that was increasingly our problem.

This song is about you
At the end of November Carly Simon's 'You're So Vain' came out in the UK. There has always been speculation that the song is about Mick – he sang backing vocals but the subject is actor Warren Beatty.

On 1 December, we met with our lawyer and decided that the band, with the exception of Keith, should return to France the following day to meet with the judge handling the case. Keith could not set foot in France without being arrested. There was a chance they might arrest us, as we too had been implicated by informants. Nevertheless, Charlie, Mick Jagger, Mick Taylor and I flew to London, where Prince Rupert, Paddy Grafton Green, Bianca and, from the Stones office, Alan Dunn met us. We flew by executive jet to Paris. Mick and Bianca went to see a Parisian lawyer, while the rest of us flew on to Nice. Mick came the next day.

On Monday 4 December, we went to the judge's chambers in Nice, where everything went far better than any of us had hoped. The police witnesses denied everything and insisted that they were made to sign false statements. While this put us in the clear, it still left Keith with a major problem. We returned to Jamaica as the public prosecutor in Nice issued arrest warrants for Keith and Anita on charges of drug trafficking. One rumour had it that they could get the charge reduced to one of straightforward drug usage if they gave themselves up. Leslie Perrin called Keith while we flew back to Jamaica to tell him the news.

Press-ing problems

The UK press wrote that we were all on heroin charges in France: 'Police said that Mick Jagger and three other members of the Rolling Stones have been charged with illegal use of heroin and other narcotics,' reported *The Times*. 'The charges were made out before they went on a tour of the US this summer but were kept secret. Three young Frenchmen, who police said provided 50 grams of heroin to the Stones and their entourage each week during the spring and summer of last year, were also arrested and present at the hearing.'

Leslie worked out a damage limitation strategy in England, briefing friendly journalists. I was

Earthquake in Nicaragua
Astrid and Bill were at home in France on Christmas Eve when they heard about a serious earthquake in Nicaragua. With 18,000 reported dead, Bianca was in shock, as Managua, her mother's hometown, was devastated. Mick and Bianca flew to Kingston the day after Christmas and heard her mother was safe. Mick and Bianca arrived in Managua the next day with 2,000 typhoid injections and other medical supplies.

worried about Stephen's reaction and phoned Paddy to ask him to explain everything to the school. It was better that the teachers heard it from a lawyer. Leslie Perrin issued a statement on our behalf.

'Arrest warrants have been issued in respect of Rolling Stone Keith Richards and his German actress friend Anita Pallenberg. Keith Richards said, "The first I heard of the warrant for my arrest was when I read it in the newspapers here (Jamaica) this morning."'

The threat of cancellation hung over the tours of Japan and of the Far East, planned for the New Year. We heard we might be able to hang on to our Australian tour. Keith defended himself in the media. 'If you really suss the story you'll read that they retracted any heroin charges whatsoever,' he said. 'There is an arrest warrant out for me, but they don't say what for. And I don't know what it's for… We can't find out who made the statement about the heroin thing. It could have been pulled out of the sky. At the moment I know they've got a warrant out for questioning and I don't know if I'm going to go back and be questioned. It's all a bunch of political bullshit. It's always somebody trying to get promoted. I have a feeling that the French are trying to show the Americans that they are doing something about the drug problem. But rather than actually doing something about it, they bust a big name. The only thing I resent is that they try and drag my old lady into it. I find that particularly distasteful.' But perhaps Keith also meant that he was worried about how this whole thing had affected the rest of us.

The Stones filled Australian papers as much as they did back home in the UK.

Banned in the USA

Recording in Kingston continued until 13 December, but with few usable results. The atmosphere just wasn't right. I flew to Nassau with Mick Taylor and his partner Rose. She told me that Mick T was seriously thinking of leaving the Stones and joining Free.

Mick and Bianca returned to Jamaica on 4 January and Peter Rudge, our tour manager, called us to say that both Australia and the US had now refused work permits, meaning the whole tour was off. Mick and Keith decided we should do a benefit concert for the earthquake victims, for which we hoped Keith would be granted a visa. A few days later the Australian Immigration Minister lifted their ban and, with a work permit quickly secured for Keith, our US promoter Bill Graham announced that we would perform a benefit concert in Los Angeles on 18 January. There was a mad scramble for seats as 18,000 or more tickets were gobbled up in a matter of hours.

Our tour of Japan looked doubtful, but we hadn't given up on it. Mick went to the Japanese Consulate and was told he would not be granted a visa because of the drug bust and because he was 'too famous'.

SIR Mick

On 16 January, we spent three days at Studio Instrument Rentals (SIR) in Hollywood, but took time out to celebrate Mick T's 25th birthday. Backstage at the Forum, the Nicaraguan Ambassador presented Mick with a plaque, thanking us for our contribution to the fund. We followed comedians Cheech and Chong, and Santana onstage. We played for 100 minutes. Everyone enjoyed the show, but I felt we were nowhere near our best. We played old numbers like 'Route 66', 'It's All Over Now', 'No

Expectations' and 'Stray Cat Blues', in addition to songs performed on our last tour. We grossed $516,810 and Mick and Bianca later went to Washington to present the fund with a cheque for $350,000, the proceeds after the concert's expenses had been deducted. We also heard that our French legal bills totalled $58,690. It was split six ways, Anita's being the sixth share.

Two days later, we flew to Hawaii to start what remained of our Pacific tour. The shows were all sold out and it was a great time of year to be visiting Honolulu. We went back to LA and recorded some more at Village Sound Studios with engineer Baker Bigsby and producer Jimmy Miller. The tapes that we brought from Jamaica were marked Muddy Waters and everyone was sworn to secrecy to prevent us getting bootlegged – which was an all-too-frequent occurrence.

On Tuesday 6 February, we flew to Sydney and stayed at the Kingsgate Hotel in the Kings Cross area of the city, using the names of famous racing cyclists – Charlie was Eddie

Merckx. For the rest of the tour we used the names of famous cricketers as pseudonyms. Our shows in Auckland and Australia went down well with the audience, although I think our playing on some dates was a little suspect. The weather was often our biggest problem.

In Brisbane, we had to delay going on stage because the rain was so bad. Our first show in Melbourne was exactly the opposite: the temperature was 97 degrees Fahrenheit and it was almost too hot to play. Apart from minor skirmishes between fans and police, almost everywhere we played was good.

We did nearly get in a spot of bother when some cannabis was found on our crew plane. The Deputy Premier, Sir Gordon Chalk, got pretty upset when someone suggested that we had said the police planted the stuff, 'If this is the attitude of the Rolling Stones then I think that the sooner they leave Queensland the better it will be for the State.'

Our last shows were at the Royal Randwick racecourse in Sydney. We were driven from the backstage area to the stage in an open coach pulled by four white horses. When we finished playing, we were showered with multi-coloured ping-pong balls from above. Fireworks followed as 'Land Of Hope And Glory' played on the PA. Mick flew to Jamaica for a holiday on Cary Island in Ocho Rios, while Mick T flew to Hong Kong for a break. Charlie went home to France and Keith returned to Switzerland. Astrid and I flew to LA, via Hawaii, with Stu. The Customs gave me a real going-over. I was taken to a room, where I insisted that an independent witness was with me. They gave me a complete body search and found nothing. I think they worked on the principle of guilt by association.

At the end of the tour in Australia, Bill and Astrid sent Stephen a postcard made of bark.

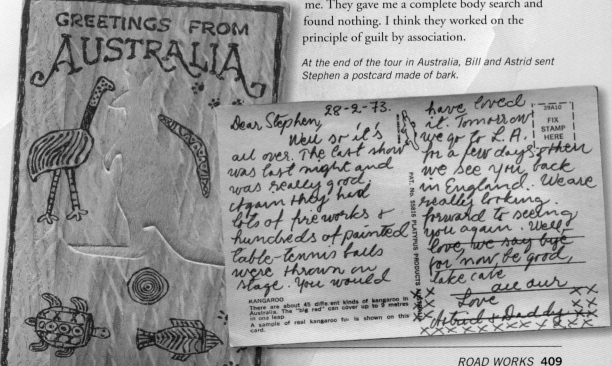

A U S T R A L I A

WA
NT
QLD
SA
NSW
VIC
TAS

Perth
Adelaide
Melbourne
Sydney
Brisbane

▼ Honolulu, Hawaii, 4900 miles (7900 km) northeast of Australia

Auckland

NEW ZEALAND

The Pacific, *January–February 1973*

21 January Honolulu International Center, Honolulu, Hawaii
22 January Honolulu International Center, Honolulu, Hawaii (two shows)
11 February Western Springs Stadium, Auckland, New Zealand
14 February Milton Park Tennis Courts, Brisbane, Australia
17 February Kooyong Tennis Courts, Melbourne, Australia (two shows)
18 February Kooyong Tennis Courts, Melbourne, Australia (matinee)
20 February Memorial Park Drive, Adelaide, Australia
21 February Memorial Park Drive, Adelaide, Australia
24 February Subiaco Oval, Western Australia Cricket Ground, Perth, Australia
26 February Royal Randwick Racecourse, Sydney, Australia
27 February Royal Randwick Racecourse, Sydney, Australia

Crowds
Honolulu	25,500
New Zealand	31,500
Australia	128,500
Total	**185,500**

The third tour Down Under included shows in Hawaii. The band was also originally scheduled to play five shows at the Budokan in Tokyo and two in Hong Kong.

According to Bill, this was far from the best tour of the Stones' career. Their playing was sometimes sloppy and they also had niggling technical problems. The trauma of the past few months had taken its toll on the band's performances.

'Response to the Stones' act was good, but not brilliant… But nobody will forget they've seen the rock'n'roll band of all rock'n'roll bands.'
THE SYDNEY SUN

On this trip the musicians travelled under cricketing pseudonyms. Mick was WG Grace, Keith was Freddie Truman, Charlie was Trevor Bailey, Bill was Len Hutton, Mick Taylor was Peter May, Bobby Keys was Jack Hobbs, Jim Price was Herbert Sutcliffe and Nicky Hopkins went under the name Tony Lock. Peter Rudge and Alan Dunn opted for British prime ministers. Peter was Ted Heath and Alan called himself Harold Wilson.

'Peter Rudge? He was a Hitler, screaming and shouting at everyone, but the tours were good.'
ANNA MENZIES, *Stones Office*

Set list
'Brown Sugar'
'Bitch'
'Rocks Off'
'Gimme Shelter'
'It's All Over Now'
'Happy'
'Tumbling Dice'
'Sweet Virginia'
'Dead Flowers'
'You Can't Always Get What You Want'
'All Down The Line'
'Midnight Rambler'
'Live With Me'
'Rip This Joint'
'Jumpin' Jack Flash'
'Street Fighting Man'

As the tour progressed 'Love In Vain', 'Honky Tonk Women', 'Bye Bye Johnny' and 'Little Queenie' appeared in the set, usually at the expense of 'It's All Over Now', 'Dead Flowers' and 'Live With Me'.

Support bands
ZZ Top in Honolulu, Itambu in Auckland, Headband in Sydney, Chain and Madder Lake in Melbourne

Cricket Anyone?
Hawaii And Australasia

1973

What the papers said...

'The Stones, still unquestionably the world's No 1 rock band. White carnations covered the stage. There were 1,500 pigeons launched to herald the Stones' entry.' RECORD MIRROR

'Bedclothes used by the Rolling Stones pop group at an Auckland hotel raised $1,329 at a charity auction. The top price of $200 dollars each was paid for four sheets, billed as having been on the bed of the group leader, Mick Jagger. They went to buyers who said they planned to make them into shirts and handkerchiefs and promised any profits for Boystown, a police and community club. A girl paid $19 for a Jagger pillowslip.' AUCKLAND COURIER-MAIL

'Jagger is the perfect pop star, the perfect entertainer. Keith Richards, even more evil than before, is still the prancing gypsy. Mick Taylor stands back. Musically, he is the highlight of the band.' ADELAIDE NEWS

Backstage drinks rider

In the early days of the Stones, a coke or a beer would have done the trick. By the 1970s, everyone had his own favourite tipple on tap.

The general rider featured Champagne (Dom Perignon, Moët and Chandon, Krug) and beer. Mick went for Jack Daniels Black, beer, Wild Turkey. Keith had Cuervo Gold Tequila, orange juice and Grenadine. Bill's choice was vodka, 7-Up and lemonade. Mick T went for Courvoisier cognac, bourbon and Coke, and Kahlua. Bobby Keys was another for the Jack Daniels Black, as was Jim Price. Nicky Hopkins enjoyed a drop of Johnnie Walker with coke. Charlie's request was simple: everything.

Go-set magazine reported, 'During a reception, the Stones got the chance to meet art director Ian McCausland, who designed the poster for their 1973 tour in Australia.'

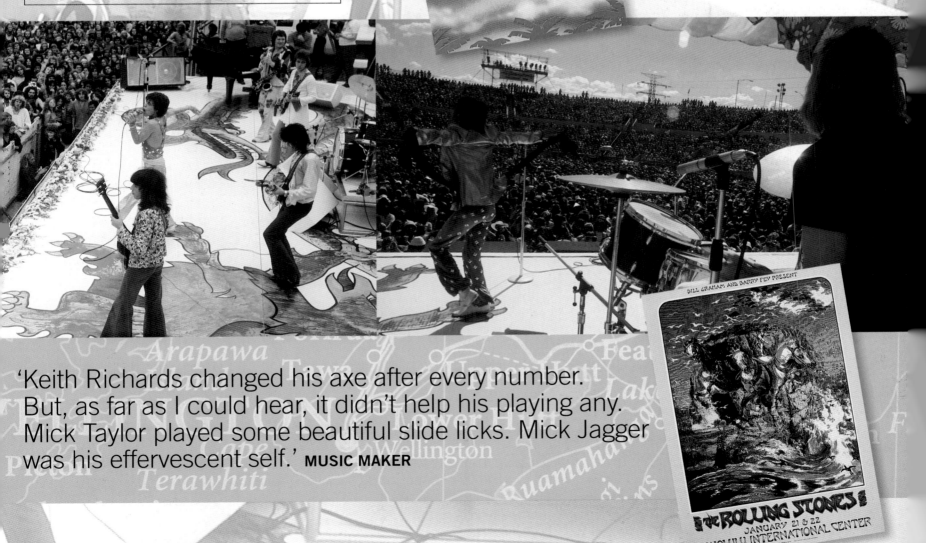

'Keith Richards changed his axe after every number. But, as far as I could hear, it didn't help his playing any. Mick Taylor played some beautiful slide licks. Mick Jagger was his effervescent self.' **MUSIC MAKER**

Cockroaches

We got back to France in early March and had some time to ourselves, the first period in quite a while that I had relaxed. When we got back to recording, it started slowly, a feature that would become a habit over the coming years. A certain Mr Ronnie Wood would become a part of our scene.

MARSHALL CHESS WROTE to outline plans for completing the album in LA during April. We also found out we would be able to tour in the UK later in the year without jeopardising our tax position.

I decided to buy some land in Vence and build my own house. It was a fantastic spot with great views all the way to the Mediterranean.

There was a long delay before getting down to recording. We finally began on Monday 7 May at Olympic. We were booked in as 'the Cockroaches' to avoid arousing any interest. We cut a couple of tracks, tried new ones that failed and worked on improving others, mostly without success.

Mick, in a rash moment, had agreed to pose for the centre-spread picture of *Cosmopolitan* magazine. Manhattan photographer Francesco Scavullo was going to shoot him nude, but in the end Mick backed out. Soon after this he went to look at the island

On Friday 8 June, the band each received a jumper with a goat's head design to mark the 10th anniversary of 'Come On'.

of Gigha, off the coast of Scotland, but his offer to buy it was refused.

'Rumours circulating this week, suggesting that Keith Richards is leaving the Stones were vehemently denied by Mick Jagger. The story seems to have emanated from LA, where Nicky Hopkins reportedly told a US rock writer that Richards had been ousted by Jagger, who was seeking Ronnie Wood of the Faces as a replacement.' NME, June 1973

It was more a case of two and two making five. On Tuesday 24 July, Mick and Keith went to Ronnie Wood's house, the Wick in Richmond, and recorded a version of 'It's Only Rock'n'Roll'. Woody and fellow Faces Kenney Jones and Ian McLagan were on the track. Before long, there were stories that the Stones and the Faces were going to join forces (minus Rod Stewart).

Bust and busted

Anita flew into London in June, having been busted for drugs in Jamaica, a feat that took some doing.

'Anita spent three days in jail. We bailed her out with $600 and were told to keep out, not for good, but for a while.' KEITH

Two weeks later I woke up to the news that Keith had been busted again, this time in London. The police raided his house in Cheyne Walk and found Keith and Anita in their four-poster bed. Their friend Stash was in another bedroom. They not only found drugs, but also a Smith and Wesson revolver in a holster in Keith's bedside cabinet. For good measure, a shortened shotgun was also found on the ground floor. All in all, the bust of all busts. I called Charlie and Mick, who was staying at the Savoy Hotel in London. Mick said he couldn't believe it but, in truth, we all could. Keith, despite the treatments, was back on drugs.

In the land of prog
Pink Floyd's *Dark Side Of The Moon* came out in March 1973. Never had albums been so complex, so conceptual or so long. This was a growing fashion in the 1970s, away from the three-minute single and towards the double-sided albums favoured by Genesis, Yes and other leviathans of the progressive rock movement.

We were all sad and disappointed by what was happening to him. All three were freed on bail. Keith and Anita were allowed to keep their passports, but Stash had his taken away.

We shot promo films for 'Angie', 'Silver Train' and 'Dancing With Mr D', after waiting three hours for Keith to arrive. I know most people think Keith's attitude is the epitome of rock'n'roll cool, but it's very difficult to stay cool when you have spent as many hours as we have

'Social historians in the future may be able to draw the ironic conclusion that Mick Jagger and his friends were the ultimate weapons in the hands of the Establishment – high priests of a new religion which, this time, really was the opium of the masses.'
DAILY MAIL, *24 July 1973, on Stones tour*

Keith and Anita on their way to court in 1973

hanging about. Charlie put it best when he was interviewed in the 80s for the 'Rewind' video compilation. He was asked what it had been like playing drums with the Stones. "Five years of working, twenty years of hanging around."

Mick turned 30 at the end of July, just days before Redlands caught fire – and not for the first time that year. A couple of months earlier there had been a chimney blaze, but this time it was more serious. The thatched roof burned and all Keith could do was watch. Fortunately the fire brigade got it under control quickly, but not before a fair amount of damage was done. We never found out how it started.

A week later the tickets went on sale for the UK leg of our tour of Europe, the demand was amazing. Fans waited in line for days – in Newcastle alone, the queue was a mile long. An extra show was added in London to satisfy the demand.

On Sunday 19 August, I flew with Mick Taylor to Amsterdam to

Left, *Woody at home in the Wick, Richmond, and,* above, *Keith and Anita argue while Redlands burns.*

start rehearsals at De Doelen Hall in Rotterdam. Keith didn't show for the first night, but we then rehearsed for 10 consecutive nights, until 30 August. We were very nearly without Bobby Keys on the tour, as the day before rehearsals ended, he drove his new E-Type Jaguar into a canal and was lucky to get out alive.

The tour began as our new single and album arrived in the shops, perfectly timed to generate maximum sales.

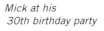

Mick at his 30th birthday party

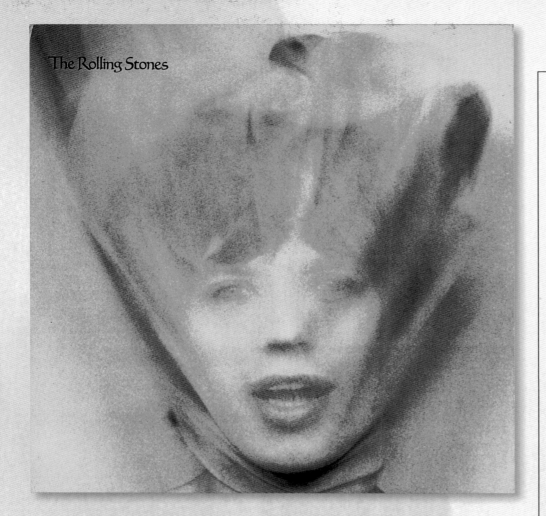

The Rolling Stones

Cover story

'Mid-way through May we did a photo session for the new album with Hipgnosis, at Floral Hall studios in Covent Garden (what is now the main market place).' BILL

'The shoot was organised for 1pm and Mick and Keith turned up about 5pm and Keith was in a very bolshy mood. Storm Thorgerson and I had outlined the concept to the Stones and they were all enthusiastic – especially Mick. They were all to be centaurs and minotaurs prancing about in the photo in an Arcadian landscape, like the young bucks they were. Right up Mick's street.' AUBREY POWELL, *Hipgnosis*

'On Wednesday 6 June, we did a photo shoot at David Bailey's house in Gloucester Avenue, northwest London, for the new album cover.' BILL

Whether or not it was the cover that made the difference, *Goats Head Soup* did become the fourth largest selling album of the band's career. It has sold well over three million copies in America alone.

The 14th UK and 18th US album became the Stones' fifth consecutive authorised release to top the UK album chart and the third in America. Topping the US charts for four weeks, it mirrored the performance of both *Exile On Main St* and *Sticky Fingers*. More than anything else, it proved the Stones were as popular as they had ever been.

Above, *the inner sleeve,* left, *the back cover and,* below, *a promotional can of soup*

'Star Star'

When the band played the original of 'Star Star' to Ahmet Ertegun it was called 'Starfucker'. He was not amused; at least, not when he thought about it. The song is about a highly active groupie and contains the sort of language that might shock a few people today – back in 1973 it was outrageous. The lyrics were prime material for lawyers, and keeping the title would have guaranteed a sales ban in the US. Even with the title change, the BBC wouldn't broadcast the song on radio.

'Atlantic Records have given us a lot of trouble over "Starfucker" for all the wrong reasons – I mean, they even got down to saying that Steve McQueen would pass an injunction against the song because of the line about him. So we just sent a tape of the song to him and of course he okayed it. It was just a hassle though. Obstacles put in our way.' KEITH, *1973*

'I suppose we ask for it if we record things like that. Christ, I don't do these things intentionally. I just wrote it... That's real, and if girls can do that, I can certainly write about it, because it's what I see.' MICK, *1978*

Recording at Dynamic Sound

'The first half hour of the Stones' sessions was exciting, then the repetition of numbers and false starts became tiresome. In the small room were about a dozen guitars, mostly Gibson and Fender, a Yamaha piano, small amps, a small PA and Charlie's Gretsch drum kit. The bass drum mic was propped up by a brick and a pillow. The Stones warmed up with a 12-bar blues with Ian Stewart adding tasty licks. Wyman plodded along on a small Fender Mustang bass, which suits his small hands. Watts and Wyman might not even look at one another, but they'd change the accent of the rhythm simultaneously.' DANNY HOLLOWAY, NME, 23 December, 1972

'They came here (LA) to see just how much they had accomplished in Jamaica. They weren't sure about the sound. We experimented with their sounds as far as texture and tone control were concerned to see if there could be some harmonious blend made from those Jamaican tapes.' BAKER BIGSBY, Engineer, in Record Mirror, 17 March, 1973

'We would be driven to Byron Lee's studio through downtown Kingston. Two large, double gates guarded by the man with the shotgun would open and let us in and then close behind us. Studio A was a low building, little bigger than an out-house. Inside was an eight-track recorder and the room where we recorded. Someone described it as "just this side of claustrophobic", they were right.' BILL

Angie
The Rolling Stones
Silver Train

'ANGIE'

The band's seventh US No 1 was their 25th US and 18th UK single. Its inspiration was Angie, then wife of David Bowie.

Recorded
November 1972 and June 1973
Studios
Dynamic Sound, Jamaica
Island Studios, London
Producer
Jimmy Miller
Engineer
Andy Johns
Release
UK Friday 17 August, 1973
RS 19105
US Tuesday 28 August, 1973 RS 19105
Composers
Jagger/Richard
Highest chart position
UK No 5
US No 1
Weeks on chart
UK 10 weeks
US 16 weeks
Additional personnel
Nicky Hopkins: piano

'David Bowie and Jagger danced together and sprawled about on each other's laps at the party while wives Bianca and Angie did likewise.' DISC MAGAZINE, 3 July, 1973

'This is positively the most depressing task I've had to undertake as a rock writer. This single is a dire mistake on as many levels as you care to mention. "Angie" is atrocious.' NICK KENT, New Musical Express

Recording and mixing

Dynamic Sound Studios
23 November, 1 December, 6 December, 14 December, 1972

Village Recorders
27 January, 30 January, 1973

Olympic Studios
7 May, 17 May, 1973

Island Studios
28 May, 8 June, 1973

Olympic Studios
Mixing: 6 July, 9 July, 1973

Side one
1. 'Dancing with Mr D'
2. '100 Years Ago'
3. 'Coming Down Again'
4. 'Doo Doo Doo Doo Doo (Heartbreaker)'
5. 'Angie'
Side two
1. 'Silver Train'
2. 'Hide Your Love'
3. 'Winter'
4. 'Can You Hear The Music'
5. 'Star Star'
Recorded
November 1972–July 1973
Composers
All songs Jagger/Richard
Studios
Dynamic Sound Studios, Kingston, Jamaica
Village Recorders, Los Angeles
Olympic Studios, London
Island Studios, London
Producer
Jimmy Miller
Engineers
Andy Johns, Bob Fraboni, Baker Bigsby, Howard Kilgour and Carlton Lee
Cover photography and design
David Bailey
Release
UK 31 August, 1973
Rolling Stones Records
COC 59101
US 12 September 1973
Rolling Stones Records
COC 59101
Highest chart position (time on chart)
UK No 1 (14 weeks)
US No 1 (19 weeks)
Additional personnel
Nicky Hopkins and Stu: piano 'Silver Train', 'Star Star'
Billy Preston: clavinet
Bobby Keys, Jim Price and Jim Horn: saxophone
Chuck Findley: trumpet
Rebop: congas
Jimmy Miller, Pascal and Ray Cooper: percussion
Nick Harrison: string arrangements 'Angie', 'Winter'

A total of 307,700 people watched the Stones on this 21-city tour of eight countries, the biggest European tour of their career so far. The Stones did not play in France, given Keith's problems with the authorities.

The band's pseudonyms were Mr Groves (Mick), Mr Dino (Keith), Mr Parker (Charlie), Mr C Palace (Bill), Mr Terrace (Mick Taylor) and Mr Wilshire (Bobby Keys) John Pasche designed the tour poster, which was also made into promotional stickers; these were given away with every ticket sold. Additional musicians were Billy Preston (piano, organ, clavinet), Bobby Keys (saxophone), Trevor Lawrence (saxophone) and Steve Madaio (trumpet and trombone). Billy Preston's band, the God Squad, was main support. On many European dates, Kracker, produced by Jimmy Miller, for Rolling Stones Records, opened the show.

The United Kingdom/Europe,
September–October 1973

1 September Stadthalle, Vienna, Austria
3 September Eisstadion, Mannheim, West Germany
4 September Sporthalle, Cologne, West Germany (two shows)
7 September Empire Pool, Wembley, London
8 September Empire Pool, Wembley, London (two shows)
9 September Empire Pool, Wembley, London
11 September King's Hall, Belle Vue, Manchester, Lancashire
12 September King's Hall, Belle Vue, Manchester, Lancashire
13 September City Hall, Newcastle upon Tyne, Northumberland (two shows)
16 September Apollo Theatre, Glasgow, Scotland
17 September Apollo Theatre, Glasgow, Scotland
19 September Odeon Theatre, Birmingham, Warwickshire (two shows)
23 September Olympiahalle, Innsbruck, Austria
25 September Festhalle, Berne, Switzerland
26 September Festhalle, Berne, Switzerland (two shows)
28 September Olympiahalle, Munich, West Germany (two shows)
30 September Festhalle, Frankfurt, West Germany (two shows)
2 October Ernst Merck Halle, Hamburg, West Germany (two shows)
4 October Bejlby Risskorhallen, Aarhus, Denmark (two shows)
6 October Scandinavium Stadium, Gothenburg, Sweden (two shows)
7 October Brøndby Hallen, Copenhagen, Denmark (two shows)
9 October Gruga-Halle, Essen, West Germany
10 October Gruga-Halle, Essen, West Germany
11 October Gruga-Halle, Essen, West Germany
13 October Ahoy Halle, Rotterdam, Holland
14 October Ahoy Halle, Rotterdam, Holland (two shows)
15 October Palais de Sport, Antwerp, Belgium
17 October Forest Nationale, Brussels, Belgium (two shows)
19 October Deutschlandhalle, West Berlin, West Germany

'Touts were asking £40 for tickets priced at £2.20 for the Rolling Stones at Wembley.' **EVENING NEWS**

Economic crisis
On 17 October, oil-producing states increased their prices by 70 per cent, a move that sent shivers through the Western world. It was to herald a period of major economic difficulties, one in which Britain would be put on to a three-day working week, due also to a coal miners' overtime ban. The shadow chancellor told the government that he should tax the rich rather than slash public services — but Mick and Keith were already tax exiles. As the crisis took hold, many acts stopped touring.

Set list
Taken from the following:
'Brown Sugar'
'Gimme Shelter'
'Happy'
'Tumbling Dice'
'Rip This Joint'
'100 Years'
'Star Star'
'Angie'
'You Can't Always Get What You Want'
'Dancing With Mr D'
'Doo Doo Doo Doo Doo (Heartbreaker)'
'Midnight Rambler'
'Sweet Virginia'
'Silver Train'
'Honky Tonk Women'
'All Down The Line'
'Jumpin' Jack Flash'
'Street Fighting Man'

Money matters
The accounts for the European tour 1973:
Gross receipts: £388,815.10p
Expenses: £138,674.53p

Profit: £250,140.57p

Ol' Blue Eyes Is Back

'Bianca Jagger storms in, strikes the wall with her cane and demands that everyone leave because she wants to be made up "like Diana Ross" to go on stage and dance with Billy Preston. Mick Taylor has donned a huge, ginger, steel wool Afro wig in readiness for his jam with the Preston band. On stage, Taylor lets loose with the most searing guitar work I've witnessed in an age, building up riffs meticulously, pulling surprises and spinning guitar-lines like fireworks over Preston's keyboard dynamics. And, yes, Bianca Jagger does appear, strutting an effete boogaloo, floating her peerlessly white teeth while Preston bumps and grinds behind his portable synthesizer. Off-stage, Keith Richard, has one hand around the waist of an almost obscenely beautiful girl (German model/film-star Uschi Obermeier), while the other constantly drags itself through his ratted hair.' NICK KENT, New Musical Express

'Three Russian "spies" watched the Rolling Stones perform at a Vienna rock concert. Their assignment: to report back to Moscow's Ministry of Culture on whether Mick Jagger and his group can appear in Russia later this year. If the Stones get the all-clear, they would be the first rock band to appear in Moscow. Their German promoter, Joachim Lieben, is planning two other Iron Curtain shows in Prague and Warsaw.' NEWS OF THE WORLD

IT'S THE ROLLING STONES 1973 EUROPEAN TOUR!

'Mick Jagger should have distributed cyanide capsules to the audience. Nothing, absolutely nothing could ever follow a show like that.' **NEW MUSICAL EXPRESS**

Champagne And Sex

Billy Preston and Mick
at Blenheim Palace

Having kicked off the European tour with a full house at Vienna's Stadthalle it continued that way for the next seven weeks. Back in Britain for our UK shows there was a press reception at Blenheim Palace, near Oxford, Winston Churchill's birthplace. Keith was dogged by court cases over the next few months, while I was busy recording the first-ever solo Stone album.

AT THE BLENHEIM PALACE press launch, there were fire-eaters, sword-swallowers, people dressed as puppets, a string quartet and a fortune teller.

It was very much a period rock'n'roll event. Some 500 bottles of champagne were drunk. The party cost Rolling Stones Records (ie us) £10,000.

Someone sent me a letter later that I thought summed it all up perfectly:

'Charlie Watts, his face bearing the glazed stare of a man who had read too many copies of Downbeat *magazine, was dressed like an extra from* Young Winston. *He seemed to be under the constant illusion that he was at the wrong party.'*

Our first show in London was great. After three years, it was good to be back, even *The Times* said so: 'The Rolling Stones played with such energy in a stage show of expertise seldom known in Britain that any group who wishes to challenge these one-time rebels of the early 1960s will be hard put to do it.'

By the time we reached Frankfurt, our well-oiled machine was in overdrive – Bobby Keys in particular. Back at the hotel, he got well acquainted with a groupie and ordered 28 bottles of Dom Perignon Champagne from room service.

He filled the bath, into which they both clambered, and proceeded to try and drink the lot. He didn't turn up for several days.

Mick flew to Hamburg in Ahmet Ertegun's private plane early in the morning. The rest of us waited in a hotel suite until 6pm for the plane to come back. Keith started getting mad and began throwing his knife across the room into lampshades, cutting them to ribbons. He cut out a print from a frame on the wall and put it in his bag. Discovering another picture – of the Queen – he added tits, a cock and balls and fitted it into the empty frame on the wall. We finally heard that air traffic control were on strike, and the plane wouldn't be coming back for us. We all trooped off to the railway station, and caught the train to Hamburg.

Like a candle in the wind

In Copenhagen, we attended a press conference staged at the Eden, a porno club. After the interviews, the club put on a show just for us. It was pretty boring, featuring lighted candles up the girls' bums and similar stunts, but we had lots of laughs.

Two days later, I was lucky to make our own show when I accidentally took a couple of Valium instead of appetite pills.

On a more serious note, Keith's French case came before the judge at the Court of Grand Inctance in Nice some three days before the end of the tour. Keith and Anita were found guilty of use, supply and trafficking of cannabis and they both received a one-year suspended sentence and a fine in their absence. Bobby Keys got a four-month suspended sentence and was fined FF1,000.

The gigs that never were
The Stones planned to do shows at the castles of Cardiff and Pembroke in Wales, which were then cancelled for various reasons. Bill: 'The poster for these concerts is now a collector's item – beware of forgeries!'

'Seeing the Stones is not just seeing a band but watching history in action.' COLIN STEWART, *Mail on Sunday, September 1973*

That night we were in Antwerp, playing the Palais de Sport to 15,000 fans.

And then it was all over, well almost. This particular round of sex'n'drugs'n'rock'n'roll actually ended in West Berlin on 19 October.

'There were strippers and two naked young ladies doing interesting things with mics and candles. One of these had served topless behind the bar in the "hospitality room" during the concert. It was a fitting end to one of the tours of all time.' ROSIE HORIDE, *Disc, on the end-of-tour party*

I celebrated my 37th birthday five days later, as Keith was having a special day of a different kind. He, Anita and Stash were in London, appearing at court in Marlborough Street. The magistrate accepted the defence argument that the drugs found in Keith's house were nothing to do with him and there was nothing sinister in his having the guns. He was fined £125 on the firearm charges and £80 on the drugs charges. The prosecution dropped all charges against Anita, except for the possession of 25 Mandrax tablets. She was conditionally discharged for a year. Stash elected trial by jury on a cannabis charge.

'Dope plays a very small part in my life. I am really not interested in it. Before the kids arrived, I tried other drugs. But I've never been strung out on any of those,' Keith told the *Evening News*.

Keith's continuing flirtation with flames culminated in him and Anita setting fire to their bedroom at the Londonderry House Hotel. We were immediately banned. I was due in London the next day – I had to stay elsewhere.

Tales of the Arabian slippers
We went to Munich, Germany, in November to work at the Musicland Studios with Andy Johns. Mick Taylor came down with a mystery illness and didn't arrive. The Faces' Ronnie Wood came along and played on one of the tracks.

When we finished in Munich, Astrid and I went on to Los Angeles so that I could begin working on my own tracks. There was no way my songs were ever going to be on a Stones album so going solo was the only alternative.

I began working at Electra Studios with Ronnie and Howie Albert, whom I met at Steve Stills'

Life between shows
Far left: Stu driving in Munich. *Left and centre row*: Keith and Charlie with Shirley and Seraphina on the coach near Newcastle, 13 September. *Bottom row*, crew, Bobby Keys, Bill and Laurence Myers, Bobby Keys and wife on the train in Germany.

'Keith Richards to me is everything, visually, that rock'n'roll is about. The clothes, the teeth… everything.'
IAN HUNTER, *of Mott the Hoople, NME, January 1974*

sessions. We couldn't get a good sound, so I switched to Ike Turner's Bolic Sound Studios, in Inglewood. Ike turned up when I was jamming with organist Jimmy Smith. For some reason, he wandered about the studio in a dressing gown and Arabian slippers with turned-up toes. We finished on 14 December and had a great party to wrap it up. Leon Russell, Dave Mason, Todd Rundgren, Claudia Linnear, Dallas Taylor, Joe Lala and

'DOO DOO DOO DOO DOO (HEARTBREAKER)'
On Wednesday 19 December, 1973, Rolling Stones Records released the 26th US single. 'Doo Doo Doo Doo Doo (Heartbreaker)' was backed by 'Dancing With Mr D' as RS 19109. It got to US No 15 and spent 11 weeks in the charts.

Danny Kortchmar (some of whom played on the record) were there.

I went on to another party and John Lennon was there with his girlfriend May Pang (it was during his lost weekend). I hadn't seen John in a long while and we talked for ages. He said he'd love to go on the road with Charlie and me.

Jam packed
Four days later, Keith was 30 – a turning point for many, it seemed to pass Keith by. The court of appeal at Aix-en-Provence soon marked the year by upholding his conviction. He and Bobby Keys were barred from French territory for two years.

'The Rolling Stones lasting 20, 30 years – what a stupid idea that would be. Nobody lasts that long.' LESTER BANGS, *in Creem, December 1973*

I returned to the US in mid-January 1974, having spent time at home in France. I recorded at Criteria Studios in Miami with the Alberts. Mick and Bianca, meanwhile, watched cricket in Trinidad.

'Personally, I don't really like talking about those [old] days – firstly, because I don't remember too well and, secondly, because I seem to tell the story differently each time.' MICK, *9 February, 1974*

In Munich, we worked on 'It's Only Rock'n'Roll', 'Time Waits For No One', 'Everyone Wants To Be My Friend' and 'Labour Swing'. I continued my own sessions in Miami and from there I went to Los Angeles. Mick and I got together at the Record Plant for a jam with John Lennon, Harry Nilsson, Jack Bruce, Jesse Ed Davis, Jim Keltner, Bobby Keys and Danny Kortchmar. A promising line-up, it was actually a fiasco. There were three drummers and two bass players and I just listened in. Sometimes those impromptu get-togethers sound a lot more interesting than they really are – jamming takes practice.

Solictor Paddy Grafton Green advised us that we should remain out of the UK for the next tax year. While I would have preferred to be in England, my new house in Vence was coming along nicely. Early in April, Georgio Gomelsky,

Take your seats
Ladies and Gentlemen, The Rolling Stones, a film of the 1972 US tour, premiered on Sunday 14 April, 1974, at the Ziegfeld Theater in New York, before having a run in Houston, Texas. Edited to two hours from over 30 hours of footage, the film had "quadraphonic" sound and used a bigger PA than normally found in cinemas.

Side one
1. 'I Wanna Get Me A Gun'
2. 'Crazy Woman'
3. 'Pussy'
4. 'Mighty Fine Time'
5. 'Monkey Grip Glue'

Side two
1. 'What A Blow'
2. 'White Lightnin''
3. 'I'll Pull You Thro''
4. 'It's A Wonder'

Recorded
December 1973–
February 1974

Studios
Bolic Sound Studios,
Los Angeles
Elektra Studios,
Los Angeles
Criteria Studios, Miami

Producer
Bill Wyman

Engineers
Ronnie and Howie Albert

Release
UK/US 13 May, 1974
Rolling Stones Records
COC 79100

Additional personnel
Dr John: piano
Dallas Taylor: drums
Byron Berline: fiddle
Leon Russell: piano
Lowell George: guitar
Joe Lala: percussion
Danny Kortchmar: guitar

On Monday 13 May, 1974, Rolling Stones Records released Bill's long player in the UK and US. It was the first solo album by a Rolling Stone.

'Bill Wyman is here with a portfolio of nine songs, most of which are so bloody commercial it makes you wonder why the hell his writing ability hasn't been utilised before. Wyman once and for all puts paid to the theory that he's just a poker-faced mute.' NME

'Bill has long been considered one of the finest rock bassists in the world and his lines are classic. This is powerful, dynamic and an impressive step for the artist.' CASHBOX

'Monkey Grip is easily the best thing to have appeared on RSR.' SOUNDS

Singles
UK: 'Monkey Grip Glue' and 'What A Blow'
    Friday 7 June, 1974, Rolling Stones Records RS 19112
US: 'White Lightnin'' and 'Monkey Grip Glue'
    Saturday 13 July, 1974, Atlantic RS 19110
UK: 'White Lightnin'' and 'Pussy'
    Friday 15 November, 1974, RS Records RS 19115

'Monkey Grip… was my rhyming slang.' BILL, *on naming his first solo album*

who was now living in Valbonne, visited. We talked about old times, including the old film he shot of us in Richmond back in early 1963. He had no idea where it was.

Marx man
I spent 7 May in New York promoting my new album. Doing the same in LA, I went to the launch party of Led Zeppelin's Swan Song label with former *Ready Steady Go!* man Michael Aldred. Along with Jimmy Page, Robert Plant, John Bonham and Peter Grant were Alice Cooper and Bryan Ferry; best of all I got to meet Groucho Marx, then aged 84. The next day we went with the Led Zeppelin guys to see one of my heroes, Elvis Presley, in concert at the Los Angeles Forum. It was a good show to begin with: James Burton was on guitar, and played great. As the show went on, Elvis got lazier. Afterwards we were asked if we wanted to go backstage to meet him. Everyone else did but I declined. Sometimes your heroes are more heroic from out front.

Top, *Dr John, Peter Grant, Bill and Astrid,* below, *Bill and Jimmy Page celebrate the launch of the Swan Song label.*

Elegantly Wasted

In mid-May, I returned to England after my US promotional tour. Keith and Woody had a new project that they were working on. I, too, had plenty of interests outside the Stones to keep me occupied.

LATER, ON THE DAY of my return, we had a band meeting to sort out tax, the old Stones partnership accounts and Allen Klein, about whom there still remained unresolved issues. We discussed touring America the following spring. There were concerns about Keith obtaining a work permit and we agreed that the lawyers would work on his visa. We were off the road until then.

While in England, Keith spent a lot of time hanging out with Ronnie Wood. They worked together on a project called the New Barbarians.

'A typically jaundiced comment from Ian Stewart – who's only down 'ere anyway because Keith needed his amp – "This band needs a leader," he mutters, casting a disparaging glance at the activity, or lack of it. Stu stares dolefully at the stage again. Woody, Richards and McLagan make a hasty exit to the toilets to return five minutes later in an even more agitated frame.' NICK KENT, *in the NME*

Keith went shopping for clothes in the Kings Road. He found some rhinestone-encrusted jeans at Peter Golding's shop, Ace, and tried them on, or attempted to. Nick Kent was on hand to record his efforts: 'He struggles manfully first to locate and then to undo the button on his own trousers. Several minutes of this frustrating activity pass without success. Even the transcendental time-sense of the World's Most Elegantly Wasted Human Being becomes acquainted with the realisation that little is being accomplished here. "Oh, lissen, man, I'll take the fings on spec." And with that, our hero rides, lolling meditatively, into the sunset. From this, living legends are made.' I had witnessed many such scenes myself, although none involved trousers.

We were in the UK in June with Michael Lindsay Hogg, shooting videos for 'Ain't Too Proud To Beg' and 'Fingerprint File'. We filmed 'It's Only Rock'n'Roll' wearing sailor suits in a tent which was filled with a sea of foam during the course of the song. The next day, Charlie was 33. I don't suppose Charlie, in fact least of all Charlie, expected to be drumming in a film getting covered with foam while Mick sang 'It's only rock and roll but I like it' when he was this aged.

Smokin' and drinkin'

Dallas Taylor, drummer with Crosby, Stills, Nash and Young, came to stay with me in France at the end of June. He and Tucky Buzzard's Terry Taylor made up the rhythm section that I'd been asked to put together to perform with Muddy Waters, Buddy Guy, Junior Wells and Pinetop Perkins at the Montreux Jazz Festival. We rehearsed briefly with Muddy, Junior and Buddy. When we finished Buddy and Junior said they didn't like their backing group and would be back them on their spot.

We ran through three numbers and ended up playing a 75-minute set that evening. It was great fun and I think we did a good job, too.

Smokin' Bill Wyman
Buddy Guy and Bill's performance at Montreux was later released as *Drinkin' TNT and Smokin' Dynamite.*

After the interval we backed Muddy and it went off really well, with many encores.

Charlie and Shirley came over to see us in August. I was surprised when Charlie walked in with his hair almost shaved off. That's typical Charlie, not different for the sake of it, but because that's how he wants to be.

Ronnie Wood's *I've Got My Own Album To Do* came out in September. It featured Keith singing, playing guitar and piano and Mick T provided some bass and guitar.

In mid-July, New Barbarians Keith, Woody, Ian McLagan, Willie Weeks and Andy Newmark played at the Gaumont State Theatre in Kilburn.

'Keith came round to the house for a drink and ended up staying for a month. Wore the ass out of all my pants and tore my jacket too.' WOODY

Keith spent most of September in Switzerland. The following month he was interviewed by the *NME* and came out with one of his most bizarre quotes – and he, like all of us, has given a few... He had, he said, gone to Switzerland

to ski – I find it impossible to imagine, too! 'I'm changing my image,' he added. 'I've arranged for a whole series of dental appointments in Switzerland. I originally lost my teeth in a fight and recently I've decided to have them all reclaimed.'

'Keith Richards gets gum job – thousands slain in tooth avalanche.' NICK KENT, *in the NME, 19 October, 1974*

I celebrated my 38th birthday with French poet André Verdet. We visited the home of artist César, who cooked us lunch. After food, we sat in the garden in the sun and had a wonderful day. Being a nearly middle-aged Stone was not too bad.

'Rock'n'roll is an adolescent medium. When you don't feel like an adolescent, you stop. I still feel like an adolescent three days a week.'
MICK, *BBC Radio One, 31 August, 1974*

'IT'S ONLY ROCK'N'ROLL'

> It's Only Rock'n'Roll
> The Rolling Stones
> Through The Lonely Nights

Recorded
a-side 24 July, 1973 and February 1974
b-side November 1972
Studios
a-side 24 July, 1973 Ronnie Wood's home studio, February 1974 Musicland, Munich
b-side Dynamic Sound, Jamaica
Producers
a-side The Glimmer Twins
b-side Jimmy Miller
Engineers
a-side Keith Harwood
b-side Andy Johns
Release
UK Friday 26 July, 1974
RS 19114
US Saturday 27 July, 1974
RS 19301
Composers
Jagger/Richard
Highest chart position
UK No 10
US No 16
Weeks on chart
UK 7 weeks
US 10 weeks

The 27th US and 19th UK single came out a month before the parent album. It was, at that point, the least successful first single from any Stones album on either side of the Atlantic.

'The original version done at Woody's house featured Mick and Ronnie Wood on guitars, Willie Weeks on bass and Kenney Jones on drums. We went on to record over-dubs at Musicland in Munich.' BILL

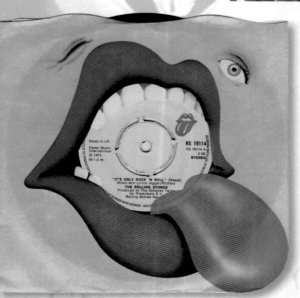

'I doubt whether you'll find an album more eminently rewarding this year. And, yes, you can dance to it.' **NME**, *12 October, 1974*

Under the influence
'Ain't Too Proud To Beg' had been a hit for the Temptations in 1966, topping the US R&B chart.

Studios
14–25 November, 1973, 20 February–3 March, 1974 (Musicland, Munich), 12 April–2 May, 1974 (Stargroves, Berkshire), 4 May–27 May, 1974 (Island Studios, London)

Tracks and composers
All songs Jagger/Richard, except where indicated

Producers
The Glimmer Twins

Engineers
Andy Johns
Keith Harwood
George Chkiantz

Design and painting
Guy Peelaert

Release
US Wednesday 16 October, 1974 Rolling Stones Records COC 79101
UK Friday 18 October, 1974 Rolling Stones Records COC 59103

Highest chart position (time on chart)
US No 1 (11 weeks)
UK No 2 (9 weeks)

Additional personnel
Nicky Hopkins, Billy Preston and Stu: piano 'It's Only Rock'n'Roll', 'Dance Little Sister' and 'Short And Curlies'
Billy Preston: clavinet
Ray Cooper: percussion
Charlie Joly Kunjappu: tabla

The release of the 15th UK album was signalled by a graffiti campaign throughout London. It had come out a week earlier in America and took two months to reach the top of the US album charts, where it stayed for just a week. The Bay City Rollers and Rod Stewart kept it from the top in the UK.

On 8 March 1975, the NME voted the cover the best designed album of 1974.

'Mick Taylor was involved in the actual composition of "Time Waits For No-One", even though the writing credits will go to Jagger and Richards, as ever. It also turns out that Taylor has made creative inserts into other tracks like "Till The Next Goodbye" and "If You Really Want To Be My Friend". Still no credit.'
NICK KENT, *NME*

"It's only Rock'n Roll." It's only the Rolling Stones new record. It's only on

Album NºCOC 59103
DISTRIBUTED BY ATLANTIC

'His brilliant playing embellished and improved upon much of what we produced.'
BILL, *on Mick Taylor*

Ending And Beginning

A few days after my birthday in October 1974, I flew to Geneva to join Prince Rupert, Mick and Charlie at the Hotel des Bergues. Keith and Mick T were at the Hotel President. We had grand plans – but our line-up was about to change.

W E DISCUSSED PLANS FOR the following 18 months, including the possibility of hosting a TV series in the new year, a world tour with accompanying film, four albums, TV shows and a book. During day one of discussions, Mick T got into a real huff and returned to London. He was fed up with what he saw as a lack of recognition for his input.

A month later, Anna Menzies called me from our office. 'Mick Taylor phoned me to say he is leaving the band,' she said. 'I said that perhaps he should tell you – I think he wanted me to do it.'

I phoned Mick T, who was adamant about leaving. His departure was inevitable. He joined when he was young and did a lot of growing up in the following five-and-a-half years. He contributed enormously to the 'golden Stone age' and his brilliant playing embellished and

overdose. By the third night, we decided that if Keith didn't arrive, we would all return to London. Eventually, he turned up.

For the next six days we worked solidly and got some promising stuff done, including 'Something Good', 'Cable From My Baby,' 'Fool To Cry', 'Crazy Mama' and 'Cherry Oh Baby'.

Semi-pro band seeks guitarist
The press soon began speculating on Mick T's replacement. Among the contenders were Ronnie Wood, Mick Ronson (formerly David Bowie's lead guitarist) and Paul Kossoff, from Free.

'Ron Wood 8-1, Jeff Beck 17-1, Bobby Tench (a dark horse) 20-1, Dr Feelgood's Wilco Johnson 50-1 and Hank Marvin 3-1 on.' NME, *tipping the candidates*

The new Face
Ronald David Wood was born at Uxbridge, Middlesex, into a working-class family on 1 June, 1947. Woody had two older brothers, Arthur (Art), who played with Alexis Korner and had his own group, the Artwoods. Edward (Ted) born in 1939 was once a member of the Temperance Seven. Immediately before joining the Stones, Woody had been in the Faces with Rod Stewart. He had started his career with a local West Drayton group called the Thunderbirds who had recorded in 1964 as the Birds. When they split in 1966 he joined the Creation and then he played bass for the Jeff Beck Group, which included Rod Stewart.

'We are all most sorry that he is going and wish him great success and much happiness. No doubt we can find a brilliant six-foot three-inch blond guitarist who can do his own make-up.' MICK

improved much of what we produced. He chose early December to leave because he didn't want to join the rest of us to record another album.

Munich glad to be back
One guitarist down, on 6 December, we went ahead with the sessions in Musicland, Munich – sort of. Keith and Nicky Hopkins didn't turn up on the first night and I sat in the hotel cocktail lounge, discussing guitarist candidates with Mick. The next night Mick, Charlie and I jammed for a while before Nicky Hopkins arrived. We did nothing constructive. Back at the hotel, Nicky passed out in the hotel corridor from an accidental

As the year ended, I went on holiday to Bermuda and Keith joined Rod Stewart on stage in Kilburn for the last show of the Faces' tour. *It's Only Rock'n'Roll* was voted second-best album of the year by the *NME*, which I can't help thinking exaggerated its worth. 1975 was going to be a new year in more ways than one.

Charlie and Stu

Mick Ronson

Hank Marvin

NO BEGGING
On Thursday 31 October, 1975, 'Ain't Too Proud To Beg', backed with 'Dance Little Sister', was the 27th US single to be released. Rolling Stones Records RS 19302 made US No 17.

Mark III

On Wednesday 22 January, 1975, Mick, Keith, Charlie and I along with Billy Preston went to Rotterdam to try out guitarists. On the first two nights, blues guitarist Rory Gallagher jammed with us. A few days later, Jeff Beck spent 48 hours with us and, in early February, respected session player Wayne Perkins came for a day.

When we had finished, the mobile studio went to Gedding and I went too. We planned to put out a set of old and rare Stones recordings, with the working title *The Black Box*. From 10 February, engineer Mick McKenna and I

we still had not made our minds up on a replacement. Towards the end of the month, we returned to Musicland with guitarists Wayne Perkins and Harvey Mandel.

Somewhat appropriately, Ronnie Wood arrived on 1 April. While he was away, the police raided his home in Richmond and discovered cocaine, along with Woody's wife Krissie and a girl named Audrey Burgon. Both women were arrested – the curse of the Stones struck again. To add spice to the story, as far as a certain section of the press was concerned, it was alleged that Krissie and Audrey were naked in bed together.

for Keith and a great guy too. As with so much in life, it's all about chemistry.

Ronnie was staying in LA with Gerry Beckley, a member of America. Dewey Bunnell, also in America, was there too. 'Woody was staying at my old home on Flicker Way in the Hollywood Hills,' recalled Gerry. 'He got a call from the Stones office, he hangs up the phone and says, "Dewey! I'm a Rolling Stone!"' The rest of the world heard in a press statement issued on 14 April:

'Dewey! I'm a Rolling Stone!'

WOODY, *to friend Dewey Bunnell of America*

worked together for 19 days, listening to and editing our old tapes. I went to Olympic early in March and cut masters with Keith Harwood.

Despite the fact that Mick jammed at the Record Plant in LA with Woody and some of Wings in mid-March,

The jury failed to reach a verdict at their trial in July, and Krissie was found not guilty at the retrial in April 1976. There was no doubt once he'd played with us that Woody would be the one, although it was initially on a temporary basis. He may not be the greatest guitarist in the world but he is a perfect foil

'It is confirmed by Mick Jagger that Ronnie Wood, lead guitarist with the Faces, will be accompanying the Rolling Stones when they undertake a tour of North and South America, which

is due to start in June. Although this arrangement is in no way permanent, Mick says he and the rest of the Stones are looking forward to Ronnie playing with the group.'

On Saturday 26 April, we flew to New York. Mick and Charlie stayed at the Plaza Hotel and Keith and I checked in at the Pierre Hotel. Our pseudonyms for this trip were cars; Mick (Michael Benz), Keith (Keith Bentley), Charlie (Charlie Ford), me (Bill Austin), Woody (Ronnie Morris) and Billy Preston (Billy Hillman). We rehearsed and then went to 12th Street and 5th Avenue to board a flatbed truck.

Keep on truckin': The Stones publicise their US tour from the back of a truck in New York on 1 May, 1975.

We performed live all the way to the Feathers restaurant, where the press was waiting. The truck rumbled on to Washington Square Arch, with us still playing. There were shades of Andrew Oldham's Chicago traffic island stunt of June 1964.

On Friday 2 May, Bianca celebrated her 30th birthday and we rehearsed at Andy Warhol's House, in Montauk, Long Island – Mick didn't make it. Eighteen days later we flew to Newburg, New York State, where our stage set was assembled in an aircraft hangar. After five days in Newburg, we flew back to Montauk for a few more days, before returning to Newburg to board our chartered Boeing 720, the *Starship*. We were off to New Orleans to begin our most ambitious tour of North America.

We took the stage at Louisiana State University in Baton Rouge for the first of our two shows that day to the strains of Aaron Copland's *Fanfare For The Common Man*. It was Woody's 28th birthday.

Keith and Ronnie at Montauk, Andy Warhol's house in Long Island

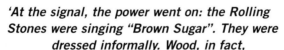

'At the signal, the power went on: the Rolling Stones were singing "Brown Sugar". They were dressed informally. Wood, in fact, was the only Stone who looked the least bit glittery. As "Brown Sugar" ended, Jagger threw leaflets into the crowd with information about the first Stones tour since 1972.' CREEM MAGAZINE

The Stones' previous US tour three years earlier had been big, but the 1975 tour was *very* big. They played to over a million people at 45 shows in 26 cities in 21 states (plus DC and Canada). It grossed in excess of $10 million, a far cry from the first tour that opened in San Bernardino 11 years previously. It was as if Mick and Keith reaching 30 had somehow turned the band into rock royalty.

ROLLING STONES
TOUR OF THE AMERICAS '75

North America, *June–August 1975*

1 June Louisiana State University, Baton Rouge, Louisiana (two shows)

3–4 June Hemisfair Plaza Arena, San Antonio, Texas

6 June Arrowhead Stadium, Kansas City, Missouri

8 June County Stadium, Milwaukee, Wisconsin

9 June Civic Center, St Paul, Minnesota

11–12 June Boston Gardens, Boston, Massachusetts

14 June Municipal Stadium, Cleveland, Ohio

15 June Buffalo, Memorial Auditorium, New York

17–18 June Maple Leaf Gardens, Toronto, Canada

22–27 June Madison Square Gardens, New York

29–30 June Spectrum, Philadelphia, Pennsylvania

1–2 July Capitol Center, Washington, DC

4 July Memorial Stadium, Memphis, Tennessee

6 July Cotton Bowl, Dallas, Texas

9–13 July Inglewood Forum, Los Angeles, California

15–16 July Cow Palace, San Francisco, California

18 July Center Coliseum, Seattle, Washington

20 July Hughes Stadium, Fort Collins, Colorado

23–24 July Chicago Stadium, Chicago, Illinois

26 July Indiana University, Bloomington, Indiana

27–28 July Cobo Hall, Detroit, Michigan

30 July Omni Coliseum, Atlanta, Georgia

31 July Coliseum, Greensboro, North Carolina

2 August Gator Bowl, Jacksonville, Florida

4 August Freedom Hall, Louisville, Kentucky

6 August Hampton Coliseum, Hampton Roads, Virginia

8 August Rich Stadium, Buffalo, New York

Hey Preston
Billy Preston (organ and piano) and Ollie E Brown (percussion), from Stevie Wonder's band, were additional musicians. Billy did two of his own songs as part of the Stones set – 'That's Life' and 'Outa Space'.

Getting it up
Robin Wagner designed the 10-ton stage set in the shape of a lotus flower with five petals that went out into the audience. A more sophisticated version was used at the larger venues, where the petals were raised and lowered hydraulically. There were over 300 lights, which was a record for any band up until this point.

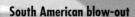

'Mick burst back into the limelight – sitting astride a giant penis. The 20-foot-high sex symbol appeared through a hole in the stage. Mick circled the huge phallus and finally straddled it before it sank from sight. Eight tons of speakers blasted out a sound that could be heard two miles away. They took an 11-minute encore before they were allowed to finish.'
DAILY MIRROR

South American blow-out
The Stones planned to continue on to play South America for the very first time – with this in mind the tour was called the 'Tour Of The Americas'. The scheduled South American dates were to be: four shows: National Auditorium, Mexico City, 7–10 August; four shows: Maracanzinho, Rio De Janeiro, Brazil 14–17 August; four shows: Convention Hall, Sao Paulo, Brazil, 19–24 August; four shows: El Poliedro, Caracas, Venezuela, 28–31 August. It would be another 20 years before the Stones finally visited South America.

Set list
Played most nights:
'Honky Tonk Women'
'All Down The Line'
'If You Can't Rock Me'
'Get Off Of My Cloud'
'You Gotta Move'
'Ain't Too Proud To Beg'
'Star Star'
'Gimme Shelter'
'You Can't Always Get What You Want'
'Happy'
'Tumbling Dice'
'Fingerprint File'
'Angie'
'That's Life'
'Outa Space'
'Brown Sugar'
'It's Only Rock'n'Roll'
'Jumpin' Jack Flash'
'Rip This Joint'
'Street Fighting Man'
'Midnight Rambler'

Two or three from the following:
'Sure The One You Need'
'Wild Horses'
'Doo Doo Doo Doo Doo'
'Sympathy For The Devil'
'Rocks Off'
'Luxury'
'Dance Little Sister'

Pomp Rock

Paper view...

'Jagger wore lipstick and 18 pounds of eye shadow. Jagger is past 30 now and beginning to acquire the classic haggard, overtired look of English rock'n'rollers.' WASHINGTON POST

'They arrive to cheers of adulation that only the Caesars must have known. For a moment the Stones concert seems like a scene out of Ben Hur.' MIAMI HERALD

'It was the largest musical audience ever to assemble there, and only just missed the all-comers record. That stands at 57,000, set in 1963 by a Jehovah's Witnesses revival meeting.' RECORD MIRROR, on Milwaukee, Wisconsin, show

'The Stones certainly more than satisfied. In another three years the boys all will be in their mid-30s – a bit long of tooth for the roles they play on stage.' CHICAGO DAILY NEWS

'At the Municipal Stadium in Cleveland, Ohio, 82,800 Fans watched and paid $840,000 for the privilege. The Rolling Stones set attendance records for a rock band in a controlled seating environment.' CASHBOX MAGAZINE

'At one point Keith Richards lost his guitar cable twice in the span of five minutes. First, he got distracted from the piece, walked over to his amps, fiddled around for a bit, decided to have a smoke, tuned up, walked out front, lost the guitar cable, went back, plugged in, fiddled with the amp dials some more, walked out, lost the cable again, plugged it back in, was ready to play, but the song had just come to a close. He smiled, slightly embarrassed.' MELODY MAKER

Support bands

The Meters and J Geils Band played at many venues — not usually the same ones. Other support bands were: the Gap Band, Rufus, Montrose, the Crusaders, Joe Vitale's Madmen, Trapeze, Tower of Power, Ethnic, Procession, Mighty Clouds of Joy, Charlie Daniels Band, Atlanta Rhythm Section, Commodores, Outlaws, Bobby Womack, the Eagles, Furry Lewis and a 100-piece steel band in NYC.

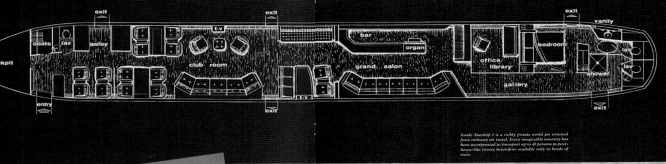

Inside Starship 1 is a richly private world far removed from ordinary air travel. Every imaginable amenity has been incorporated to transport up to 40 persons in penthouse-like luxury heretofore available only to heads of state.

The Starship *was the only way to tour back in the mid-1970s, offering privacy and total luxury.*

'When I consider it coolly, I think it's more than possible that they've peaked. I wonder what I'll think of them in 1978?' **PHILADELPHIA INQUIRER,** *1975*

National Stars

We seemed to break records everywhere we played in the States, a far cry from our first tour. I continued to get called 'the static Stone' and other epithets referring to the fact that I didn't leap about. What was amazing to me was to stand on stage and study the audience who seemed transported into a world created by us and them. It was one of the best things about playing live.

'Mick Jagger should come to America more often, because it does us good to look at ourselves squarely in the eye and see where we have failed.'
THE NATIONAL STAR, *1975*

AS I SAID TO THE PRESS at the time, 'I just get right into whatever's happening in the audience – things that happen between people in the audience, reactions to what Mick does. I think that's really interesting, it's a lot of fun. Especially if the audience is aware of me watching them, then some funny things happen. But the rest of the band aren't aware of that.' More than 25 years on, it's no different.

Throughout our tour, there were dozens of people there every night, most of whom we were very happy to see. George Harrison came to one of the Forum shows, a reminder of how far we'd come from the time the Beatles saw us at the Station Hotel in Richmond. Eric Clapton played on the encore one night in Madison Square Garden and Carlos Santana played 'Sympathy For The Devil' with us on another occasion.

Elton John took our hospitality a bit far in Fort Collins, Colorado.

He was supposed to play on 'Honky Tonk Women', our opening number. To the surprise of everyone – not least us – he remained on stage for the next 10 songs.

Not everyone in America was glad we were back. A Mr Dunleavy wrote in the *National Star,* 'Where have we gone wrong that our 12- and 13-year old daughters are making him [Mick] a millionaire – yet again? Where have we failed that this pimply-faced disciple of dirt is a

Remember the Alamo
'On Wednesday 4 June, we did a photo session at the Alamo for the *Daily Mirror*,' said Bill. 'Keith wanted to wear the coon-skin hat that I chose – he was not amused!'

rootin', tootin' hero to our teenage kids? We have this pale-faced foreigner, this Englishman, getting $10 a seat from our kids to see him perform. And what do they see? They are blitzkrieged by a tightly packaged excess of four-letter words and tacky smut.'

Road trip

A more damaging blot appeared on our horizon when Keith again got himself into trouble. He, Woody, Jim Callaghan (our security man) and Freddie Sessler (a longstanding, fairly dubious friend of Keith's from New York) decided to rent a car and drive to Dallas while the rest of us flew.

They had stopped in a gas station in Fordyce, Arkansas, for a late lunch, when the police searched the car and found a knife and drugs. All four occupants of the car were handcuffed and taken to jail at Fort Ash, where the substance was

analysed. Eventually they were freed. Keith's bail was set at $160 and he was charged with reckless driving and possessing an offensive weapon. Keith had to return to Fort Ash on 1 August. Sessler was charged with possessing an unidentified drug and was released on $5,000 bail. They chartered a plane and joined us in Dallas. Keith was cleared of the knife charge.

Honouring the Wolf

I got a reminder of that tour in 2001 while in Memphis for the launch of my book *Blues Odyssey*. When I went to visit blues enthusiast Sherman

Bill and Woody join David Bowie to celebrate Peter Sellers' birthday in LA.

Cooper at his farm near Como, Mississippi, he told me of seeing us in Memphis on 4 July, 1975. His sister – who was a nurse – bandaged Sherman's leg as if it was broken and pushed him to the very front of the stage in a wheelchair. 'I had the best damn view of anyone there,' he told me.

One of the all-time tour highlights was being able to get Howlin' Wolf to come to one of our shows in 1975. He and his wife Lil were in Chicago with Buddy Guy and Junior Wells. I sent a limo to pick them up and they visited us backstage before the show. When he took his seat, the spotlight picked him up. The whole audience rose to their feet and cheered wildly. I was watching from the side of the stage and felt very proud for Wolf.

Lil invited us all over the next evening for dinner at their house. I was the only band member who went and I was so glad that I did. Wolf is one of the only people I have met who deserved to be called a legend (I think Muddy did too). He was one of the great men of 20th century music. Sadly, he died less than a year after the tour, on Saturday 10 January, 1976, at the age of 66.

Side one
1. 'Brown Sugar'
2. 'Tumbling Dice'
3. 'Happy'
4. 'Dance Little Sister'
5. 'Wild Horses'
Side two
1. 'Angie'
2. 'Bitch'
3. 'It's Only Rock'n'Roll'
4. 'Doo Doo Doo Doo Doo (Heartbreaker)'
5. 'Rip This Joint'
Release
US May 31, 1975
UK June 13, 1975
US/UK highest chart position
US No 6 (9 weeks)
UK No 14 (12 weeks)

To accompany the tour, Rolling Stones Records released the band's 20th official US album. *Made In The Shade* was a greatest hits package, which became the band's 16th UK release.

'To capitalise on the tour, ABKCO and Decca released **Metamorphosis,** *an album of early tracks that had not been issued. It even included one of my songs, "Downtown Suzie"! It made UK No 45, but got to US No 8, such was the American demand for all things Stones.'* BILL

'This week the Rolling Stones surpassed the Beatles with their total number of Top 10 albums. **Made In The Shade** *and* **Metamorphosis** *bring the Stones' total to 22, compared to 21 for their one-time rivals. The Stones have benefited from an extra five years since the Beatles broke up. At this point in 1970, the Beatles had 19 Top 10 LPs, compared to only 13 for the Stones.'* BILLBOARD, *12 July, 1975*

I took time off at the end of the tour to travel with Astrid and Stephen and visit friends in New York, Miami, and LA. There I stayed with Gary Kellgren, who worked with me in the studio.

On Monday 25 August, the pair of us flew to San Francisco to record sessions at the Record Plant Studios in Sausalito. We were assisted by Leon Russell, Jim Keltner, Van Morrison, Sly Stone, the Tower of Power, Eagles guitarist Joe Walsh, Joe Vitale and Dallas Taylor. Over six nights, we cut masters of 'Joyous Sound' (Van Morrison), 'Every Sixty Seconds', 'I'm Gonna Move' and a demo of 'Countrified Girl'.

Mick was working on his own solo ideas at Thunder Sound Recording Studios in Toronto. In the meantime I returned to LA, where I was visited by Al Kooper and his girlfriend on 2 September. Keith Moon and girlfriend Annette Walter-Lax invited us to Peter Sellers' birthday party, where Hugh Hefner, Peter Cook, Marty Feldman, Henry Mancini and Tony Curtis were among the guests. I jammed on a stage in Sellers' house with Ronnie Wood, Keith Moon, drummer Nigel Olsson, Joe Cocker, guitarist Danny Kortchmar, Jesse Ed Davis, David Bowie and Bobby Keys. But it was hopeless – we couldn't get one song together between us.

I recorded some more in LA and flew back to France. Charlie had also returned to France after the tour, but was called to England when his house, Peckhams, was burgled. The haul included 17 antique revolvers and 10 rifles, but the culprits were caught and Charlie recovered some of his valuable American Civil War pieces.

Get out and stay out

There was renewed debate in the press about our status as tax exiles. Some of the media thought it would be better if we were encouraged to stay in Britain by a reduction in tax. On the other hand, Labour MP Robert Kilroy-Silk declared,

'Pop stars and other celebrities who leave the UK for tax reasons should be stripped of their British citizenship.'

A bizarre story hit the US press in October. According to *The Chicago Sunday Times*, 'Three American promoters who arrived in Santiago, Chile, on Monday say they are here to set up a mammoth three-day rock concert on remote Easter Island at which the Rolling Stones will make their last appearance as a group. Rolling Stones spokesman Peter Rudge denied that an Easter Island concert was being planned and that the group was going to disband.' Bizarrely, just a week earlier, André Verdet had taken me to the house of the artist Arman, where we spent an afternoon talking about Easter Island.

On Friday 24 October, I celebrated my 39th birthday. The others were in Montreux, working at Mountain studios. They over-dubbed and added vocals on tracks that we cut in Munich, but I was not needed. Busy with my own material, I returned to Sausalito and cut a bunch of new songs. I finished up for a week in LA before flying to Geneva on 26 November to meet with the rest of the band. Stu met us and drove us to Montreux, where we checked into Suite 411 at the Palace Hotel. Later there was a meeting between Mick, Charlie, Prince Rupert, Paddy Grafton Green and I; Keith never made it. Among the things we decided was a UK and European tour for summer 1976, our first there for almost three years.

'Damning rock music for its "appeal to the flesh", a Baptist church in Tallahassee, Florida, has begun a campaign to put records by Elton John, the Rolling Stones and other stars to the torch. Records worth a total of more than £1,000 were tossed on to a bonfire this week. Reverend Charles Boykin, associate pastor and youth director at the Lakewood Baptist church, said he had seen statistics which showed that "of a thousand girls who became pregnant out of wedlock, 984 committed fornication while rock music was being played." He said he couldn't remember the source of the statistics.' LEICESTER MERCURY

Bill's second solo album was released on Saturday 28 February. Stone Alone (COC79103) came out on Rolling Stones Records.

In early December I did a photo session with Bill King in a New York studio for my new album cover. My working title was *Don't Hold It, Eat It,* but I dreamt a different title the night before the album was finalised. I remember thinking in the dream, 'Oh God, the record company printed it up wrong,' because the title was *Stone Alone*. I woke up and decided the alternative actually fitted perfectly.

Mick and Bianca went to Rio de Janeiro for Christmas, and after the holiday they flew to New York to look for an apartment. Mick had once vowed never to live in the US, but as a tax exile he had no choice. New York was the perfect choice as it offered easy access to London and Europe.

Left, *Bill and Stephen at Gedding in 1975 and,* right, *a promotional video for* Stone Alone *shot at the end of the year.*

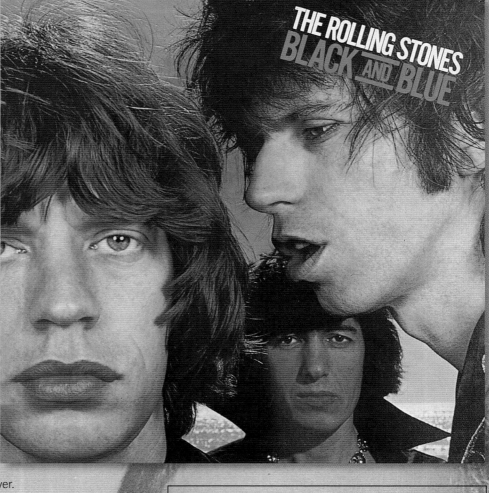

THE ROLLING STONES BLACK AND BLUE

Side one
1. 'Hot Stuff'
2. 'Hand Of Fate'
3. 'Cherry Oh Baby'
   (Donaldson)
4. 'Memory Motel'

Side two
1. 'Hey Negrita'
2. 'Melody'
3. 'Fool To Cry'
4. 'Crazy Mama'

Location
Jan, Feb, '75 (Stones Mobile, Rotterdam), Mar, Apr, Dec, '75 (Musicland, Munich), Oct, '75 (Mountain Recording, Montreux), Jan, Feb, '76 (Atlantic Studios, New York)

Tracks and composers
All tracks Jagger/Richards, except where indicated

Producers
The Glimmer Twins

Engineers
Keith Harwood, Lew Hahn and Glyn Johns

Cover photography
Hiro

Cover design
Bea Feitler

US/UK release
US Thursday 15 Apr, '76
Rolling Stones Records
COC 79104
UK Friday 23 Apr, '76
Rolling Stones Records
COC 59106

**US/UK highest chart position
(time on US/UK chart)**
US No 1 (14 weeks)
UK No 2 (14 weeks)

Additional personnel
Harvey Mandel and Wayne Perkins: guitar
Billy Preston and Nicky Hopkins: synthesiser, piano and organ
Arif Mardin: horn arrangements
Ollie Brown: percussion

The 21st US and 17th UK album has the distinction of having the fewest tracks of any Stones release. It's more about groove than tunes and the standout songs are ballads. The album has less to do with rock'n'roll than anything else the band recorded.

This was the first Rolling Stones album to feature Ronnie Wood. It also had contributions from Stones try-outs Harvey Mandel and Wayne Perkins, who each played on several tracks. Harvey came out of the Chicago blues scene. He joined Canned Heat in 1969, worked with John Mayall and recorded solo albums. Wayne, from Birmingham, Alabama, was a noted session player.

Under the influence

Eric Donaldson's reggae song 'Cherry Oh Baby' won the Jamaican Festival Song competition in 1971. Issued as a single, it became a local hit and was heard by the Stones while they were recording in Jamaica.

'A Billy Preston riff inspired "Melody". I covered this track on the Rhythm Kings's album Struttin' Our Stuff *in 1997. "Hey Negrita" came from a Woody riff.'* BILL

Fool To Cry

On Thursday 8 April 1976, 'Hot Stuff', backed by 'Fool To Cry', was issued in the US as Rolling Stones Records RS 19304. 'Fool To Cry' became the a-side and hit US No 10. It spent 15 weeks on the chart. 'Hot Stuff' made US No 49. 'Fool To Cry', with 'Crazy Mama', came out in the UK on Friday 16 April (RS 19121). It peaked at UK No 6 and was in the charts for 10 weeks.

'In 1973, jazz and blues singer Helen Humes won the "Hot Club of France Award" for the best album. The title was Black And Blue.*'* BILL

'God – if I commit suicide, I'm gonna miss the next Stones album.' PATTI SMITH, *NME*

Death of a sound engineer

On 16 September, 1976, Keith Harwood and Mick McKenna (who was the Stones' mobile engineer) were on their way home from Stargroves in the early hours of the morning when they were involved in a car crash. Sadly, Harwood was killed and McKenna was taken to hospital with two broken legs.

National Lampoon spoofed the Stones.

THE "MATCH THE COUPLES" GAME.

PLEASE MAKE YOUR SELECTIONS FOR OUR NEW
"COUPLES GAME" BY FILLING IN THE EMPTY
BOXES WITH THE MATCHING LETTERS BELOW.

LADY PUBLICITY.	A	IAN STEWART.	☐
LADY ACCOUNTANT.	B	ALAN DUNN.	☐
LADY SECRETARY.	C	MIKE CROWLEY.	☐
LADY MAKE-UP.	D	PHIL CARSON.	☐
LADY OUTSIDER.	E	BILL ZYSBLAT.	☐
LADY NEW YORK.	F	FRANK FOY.	☐

ALL ENTRIES MUST BE HANDED IN TO PAUL
WASSERMAN BEFORE CONCERT TIME THURSDAY.
THE WINNER WILL RECEIVE "A WINE + DINE"
DINNER FOR ONE.
(N.B. ONLY SEALED ENVELOPES ACCEPTED).

*Place your bets: who will end up with
who on tour?*

Homespun Wisdom?

Anita had a baby in Geneva on Friday
26 March. The couple named the boy Tara
after the late Guinness heir and friend of
Keith. A new Stones tour was announced,
provoking huge demand for tickets, if
not quite the level of interest claimed
by the promoter.

*Bianca and Mick
dining on 2 May*

Rolling with Mr Richards

One night we were
in the bar and Keith
treated a journalist
to his homespun
philosophies on life as
Keith Richards. 'You
should stay up for four
days and nights,' he
said. 'Time turns itself
upside down.'

HARVEY GOLDSMITH claimed that over one million postal ticket applications had been received for our shows at London's Earl's Court. This equated to 67 sell-out shows. He made this announcement on 1 April, so it's probably fair to say he exaggerated just a little. In the end we added three extra London shows to the three we were going to play. Rehearsals were planned at a private house in the South of France, near Cannes. As Keith could finally get back into the country, there was nothing to stop us.

They were supposed to start on Sunday 11 April. Woody flew into Nice and then slept all day. The rehearsal was moved back 24 hours, but Keith and Billy Preston still hadn't arrived and the others were playing tennis. The pattern continued for the next week, as Keith still hadn't arrived. We did manage to work through some material with just the four of us, but it kind of defeated the object of rehearsing.

Eventually, on Monday 19 April, Keith turned up with Marlon, and the band finally got together later that day, but it was still very disorganised – and further rehearsals continued that way until 24 April. We flew to Frankfurt (except Keith, who drove in his Rolls with Woody) to begin the tour. In Brussels, I shocked everyone when I did a little dance onstage with Billy Preston during the set. The next day we flew to London in Ahmet's plane and customs gave us a real going-over. When we got there, Mick heard from Bianca that she had spent almost £30,000 buying six antique paintings and a sofa at a Christie's sale in Ireland.

A couple of nights later, at the Apollo Theatre in Glasgow, we went onstage to play a show which soon turned into a disaster. Billy Preston went overboard with his volume and I nearly gave up. The sound became physically painful – almost unbearable. For several hours after the show, everyone got involved in terrible rows. It proved useful in some ways, as we certainly played better as the tour went on.

*'It is 5am and the last
of the Rolling Stones arrives. "I feel,"
says Keith Richards, bleary eyes set
deep in what look like pools of mascara,
"like the man from the moon." They had
arrived at 3.20am. "Where's the welcoming
party?" they ask waiting European promoter
Fritz Rau. "The welcoming party," he says,
"has been waiting to welcome you since
7.30pm last night."'* GARTH PEARCE,
in the Daily Express

Forty-one shows in 22 cities in nine countries to 554,000 people meant that this tour easily eclipsed the European tour three years earlier. It was also the first time that the Stones had ever played live in Yugoslavia and Spain. There was also a return to France following Keith's two year ban.

As was customary, the band had pseudonyms: Patrick Moore (Woody), Arthur Ashe (Mick), James Burke (Billy Preston), Peter West (Charlie), Percy Thrower (Keith) and Robin Day (Bill). Ollie Brown went under his own name.

Personnel: Chuch Magee and Ted Newman Jones (Woody and Keith's guitar techs), Jennie Collen-Smith (press), Stu, Sally Arnold (Peter Rudge's secretary), Jill Koerner (secretary), Jim Callaghan, Bob Bender, Bob Poweski, Stanley Orlen (security), Peter Rudge (tour manager), Alan Dunn (logistics), Jay Jensen (make-up), Phil Carson (Atlantic Records), Bill Zysblat (accounts), Debbie Freis (accounts secretary), Mike Crowley, Frank Foy and Paul Wasserman (US press) and Paul Dunn (baggage).

The United Kingdom/Europe,
April–June 1976

28–29 April Festhalle, Frankfurt, West Germany
30 April Münsterland Halle, Münster, West Germany (two shows)
2 May Ostseehalle, Kiel, West Germany
3 May Deutschlandhalle, West Berlin, West Germany
4 May Stadthalle, Bremen, West Germany
6–7 May Foret Nationale, Brussels, Belgium
10–12 May Apollo Theatre, Glasgow, Scotland
14–15 May Granby Hall, Leicester, Leicestershire
17–18 May New Bingley Hall, Stafford, Staffordshire
21, 22, 23, 25, 26, 27 May Earls Court, London
29–30 May Zuider Park, The Hague, Holland
1 June Westfalenhalle, Dortmund, West Germany
2 June Sporthalle, Cologne, West Germany (two shows)
4–7 June Aux Abattoires, Paris, France
9 June Palais des Sport, Lyon, France
11 June Plaza de Toros Las Arenas, Barcelona, Spain
13 June Parc des Sports de l'Ouest, Nice, France
15 June Hallenstadion, Zurich, Switzerland
16–17 June Olympiahalle, Munich, West Germany
19 June Neckarstadion, Stuttgart, West Germany
21–22 June Dom Sportova Hall, Zagreb, Yugoslavia
23 June Stadthalle, Vienna, Austria

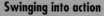

Swinging into action

The vast stage cost £150,000 and took a team of 14 to build at each venue. A bank of 300 lights weighing 16 tons was suspended 30 feet above the stage and a mirror — 25 feet by 6 feet — was turned at an angle towards the stage, hovering some 20 feet away. It took eight hours to get the set down. 'The lighting was spectacular and so were some of the special effects,' reported the *Guardian* in the UK. 'Jagger being swung on a rope far out across the audience was exciting, though it was clearly disappointing for him that the enormous inflated phallus that emerged during "Starfucker" was quite so limp. He's still unique.'

Set list

'Honky Tonk Women'
'If You Can't Rock Me'
'Get Off Of My Cloud'
'Hand Of Fate'
'Hey Negrita'
'Ain't Too Proud To Beg'
'Fool To Cry'
'Hot Stuff'
'Star Star'
'Cherry Oh Baby'
'Angie'
'You Gotta Move'
'You Can't Always Get What You Want'
'Happy'
'Tumbling Dice'
'Nothing From Nothing' – *Billy Preston spot*
'Outa Space'– *Billy Preston spot*
'Midnight Rambler'
'It's Only Rock'n'Roll'
'Brown Sugar'
'Jumpin' Jack Flash'
'Street Fighting Man'

'All Down The Line' was played at Festhalle, Frankfurt and 'Sympathy For The Devil' on 21 May at Earls Court London.

Support bands

The Meters played every gig. Kokomo and Robin Trower played in The Hague. John Miles played in Paris, Lyon, Barcelona and Nice. Little Feat played in Stuttgart.

Patrick, Peter, Percy, Arthur and Robin

'Tour manager Peter Rudge says of Jagger: "If the salt water in his dressing room isn't there, he gets hysterical. He phoned me at 6am the other morning to tell me the colour of the shadow on Charlie Watts' eyes was wrong."' DAILY MAIL

'It was a vision of hell that only Dante could enjoy.' JEWISH CHRONICLE

Rock royalty
On Sunday 23 May, 1976, Princess Margaret came to the Stones' Earls Court show. Bill: 'When she arrived backstage to meet us, I was in the toilet. I only just got back in time to be introduced.' After the show, Ahmet Ertegun threw a party at Sotheby's and Princess Margaret, Caroline Kennedy, Van Morrison and Jim Capaldi (ex-Traffic) were among the guests.

'Jo [Howard] first saw the Stones at one of those Earls Court Shows and only stayed for 30 minutes because she didn't like us.'
WOODY, *who later married Jo*

'Guitarist Ronnie Wood looked like a 40-fags-a-day Brillo pad.' LEICESTER CHRONICLE AND ECHO

'If you took an electric drill or a pile driver, tuned it so that it sounded a note, amplified it a hundred times and then played it over a public square, it would sound to the people forced to live nearby much as this concert sounded to me.' **YEHUDI MENUHIN**, *violinist, on the Earls Court gig*

Courting Disaster

Over the next couple of years, Keith had to cope with a series of personal problems that caused severe strain. Recording was becoming much more of a chore with all the uncertainty and Mick's personal life was getting a little complicated.

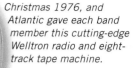

Christmas 1976, and Atlantic gave each band member this cutting-edge Welltron radio and eight-track tape machine.

JUST BEFORE we played in London in May 1976, trouble once again found Keith. He was on his way home at about 5am when he crashed his Bentley near Newport Pagnell. He fell asleep at the wheel, the car left the M1, went through a barrier and ended up in a field. The car was badly damaged, but Keith was not hurt. A passing motorist called the police and Keith was taken to their interview office at Newport Pagnell service station. In the pocket of his pink jacket there was a piece of paper wrapped around another, stained, fragment. 'We all wear each other's stage clothes,' Keith told the officers. 'It could belong to anyone. I don't even know what it is.' In his Bentley was a silver chain with a horn, a knife and a tube about the size of a cigarette. 'I don't know who it belongs to. The car is used by so many members of the group. It's certainly not mine.' They charged him on suspicion of being in possession of drugs and released him.

Baby heartbreak

Just two weeks after the car crash, Keith had some terrible news. Anita phoned to say their baby had died of a flu virus in a Geneva hospital. He was just 10 weeks old. Despite the tragedy, we still played that night and Anita arrived the next day. We all felt for Keith and Anita over the baby's death. The pain of losing his baby certainly didn't make things easy for

Keith. While I'm not making excuses for what Keith did, I think any one of us would have reacted in a dramatic way to such a tragedy.

After the following show, a guy burst into the backstage area brandishing a pistol, causing some excitement before he was caught. Everyone was remarkably calm during this incident and we never found out what it was all about.

After our Lyon gig, Stu, Astrid and I drove in my Citroen Maserati to Vence. At the tollgate at Fréjus, police armed with machine guns stopped us. They asked me if I was Keith and only allowed me to continue after I showed them my passport. As soon as we got to the house we phoned back to Lyon and told Keith what the police were up to.

After the two-month tour, we had most of the summer off. I spent time at home in France. Mick and Bianca were around for the early part of July and Woody and Krissie came to stay for a

Bianca and Andy Warhol at Mick's 33rd birthday

week. Mick celebrated his 33rd birthday with a party at Andy Warhol's house in Long Island. Mick also took his father to Montreal for the Olympic Games that summer.

Back home at Stargroves, Mick entertained members of the Basingstoke District Council in an effort to obtain planning permission for a recording studio.

As we were to play at Knebworth on the August bank holiday weekend, the papers were full of stories about us. The *South Shields Gazette* had a particularly inaccurate piece. They carried a photo of Mick and Keith with the caption 'Rolling Stones Mick Jagger and Brian Jones – on the Knebworth bill next Saturday.'

Court without trousers

Keith made several court appearances over the summer and on 6 October he answered the charges arising from his M1 crash. Keith arrived at court more than two hours late, after his lawyer had called to say Keith had no trousers to wear.

In court, Keith said his son Marlon had German measles and he was late because the child's health came first. The magistrate rejected this and insisted the true story should be revealed to the press – Keith's laundry had arrived minus the trousers and the magistrate said it struck her as quite extraordinary that any gentleman of Keith's stature should have only one pair of trousers.

Keith elected to go for trial on separate charges of possessing cocaine and LSD. While this dragged on, we learned that the US Drugs Enforcement Administration (DEA) had asked Thames Valley police to keep them informed of events. It made planning very difficult and it was about to get worse.

Mick's problems, meanwhile, were all related to the press, who insisted on publishing details of his and Bianca's life together. Not that Mick didn't fuel the situation. He was spotted with Woody at the Roxy in LA when JJ Cale played. Apparently

KNEBWORTH FAIR

Knebworth Park overflows with Rolling Stones fans, many of whom thought it would be the band's last gig. Bill took this picture from the helicopter as he arrived.

Running order

Don Harrison Band
Hot Tuna
Todd Rundgren's Utopia
Lynyrd Skynyrd
10cc
The Stones
Compere: Capital Radio's Nicky Horne

Set list

'Satisfaction'
'Ain't Too Proud To Beg'
'If You Can't Rock Me'
'Get Off Of My Cloud'
'Hand Of Fate'
'Around And Around'
'Little Red Rooster'
'Stray Cat Blues'
'Hey Negrita'
'Hot Stuff'
'Fool To Cry'
'Star Star'
'Let's Spend The Night Together'
'You Gotta Move'
'You Can't Always Get What You Want'
'Dead Flowers'
'Route 66'
'Wild Horses'
'Honky Tonk Women'
'Tumbling Dice'
'Happy'
   Billy Preston spot
   'Nothing From Nothing'
   'Party'
'Midnight Rambler'
'It's Only Rock'n'Roll'
'Brown Sugar'
'Rip This Joint'
'Jumpin' Jack Flash'
'Street Fighting Man'

O n Saturday 21 August, the Stones went to Knebworth Park in Hertfordshire to play their biggest UK show since Hyde Park. It should have been by far their most lucrative gig.

Tickets were priced at £4.50 and it was estimated that the crowd numbered between 150,000 and 200,000. The Stones went on stage four hours late as someone pulled some cables at the last minute.

The day turned sour when it came to being paid. They were on a percentage of the gate and were told by the promoter that there were less people than had been estimated. There were 110,000 pre-sales and 30,000 tickets sold on the day. Later, promoter Fred Bannister said less than 100,000 tickets had been sold.

'The outcome was that we never received a penny for the gig and we paid Billy Preston £500 and Ollie Brown £200.' BILL

A pre-show Champagne party was attended by Jack Nicholson, Dave Gilmour, Jim Capaldi, John Paul Getty III, one-time Mamas and the Papas member John Philips, Ian McLagan, Leslie Perrin, Van Morrison, Judy Garland's daughter Lorna Luft, and Paul and Linda McCartney. The Stones finally took the stage at 11.30pm and played until after 2am.

'It was the longest show we had ever played and included many of our old songs.' BILL

'Charlie Watts looked very neat and as like Bertrand Russell as ever. One's feet were with him and one's pulse with Bill Wyman.' THE LISTENER

'Jagger was down to his last stitch, a flashy pair of tights and raving rather like a gay Richard III. Ah well, it's only rock'n'roll.' DAILY MIRROR

the two were with four young ladies. He also spent a lot of time with Linda Ronstadt.

Looking for a deal

Three weeks after my 40th birthday, I flew to London and met with the others to talk over our new record deal. We met with Polydor and with Atlantic's Ahmet Ertegun.

Mick and Bianca went to Mustique to attend aristocrat Colin Tennant's 50th birthday. Among the 150 guests was Princess Margaret.

Keith was back in court on Monday 10 January, 1977. This time he arrived at Aylesbury Crown Court 20 minutes early and denied having drugs in his car, pleading not guilty. Sir Peter Rawlinson QC, a former Attorney General, defended him while Mick watched from the balcony.

Keith maintained his story about grabbing someone else's clothes and Alan Dunn and Stu gave evidence to the court

Keith at court in 1977

of the numerous gifts and objects showered onto the stage. On the third day Keith was found not guilty of possessing a smudge of LSD but guilty of possessing cocaine. The judge said he did not feel the conviction merited imprisonment – even though Keith had been found guilty of previous drug offences. Keith was fined £750 with £250 costs. There seemed to be nothing that could slow him down.

'We'll always be able to play somewhere. The State Department takes a much more adult point of view. America doesn't hinge on this case. Decisions are made on a much wider plain.' KEITH

On 16 February, 1977, we signed a deal with Atlantic for the US and Canada and EMI for the rest of the world. Mick was feeling patriotic.

'In this jubilee year I feel it is only fitting that we should sign with a British company.'

I flew to Toronto some days later and checked into the Harbour Castle hotel. We were to be recorded live at a small club in the city. I went to Mick's room and joined Woody, Ollie Brown and Alan Dunn – but not our other guitarist.

We did a series of rehearsals, the first three of which Keith and Billy Preston didn't attend. When he, Anita and Marlon finally flew in from London, Anita was stopped at customs. They discovered 10 grams of hashish. She was charged with possessing the hashish and a small quantity of heroin. When they got to the hotel Keith went straight off to bed and slept until the early hours. He arrived at rehearsal about 4.30am, but it wasn't a very productive session.

The Toronto bust

On Sunday 27 February, at 4.30pm, four drug squad officers swooped on the suite registered to one 'Mr K Redland'. They found Anita awake and Keith in bed. In a pouch on the bedside table there was an ounce of high-quality heroin. Keith and Anita were both arrested and had their passports confiscated before being released on bail. We learned that Keith had been charged with possessing heroin for the purposes of trafficking. It carried a life sentence. Even if he elected to go for trial by jury on a lesser charge, he could find himself in prison for seven years. Everyone was stunned at the news.

Tour manager Peter Rudge was trying to keep the press at bay and we met to talk things over. The following day, we vowed to carry on as planned. After the meeting, Woody and I found Keith in a bad way, throwing up and having a terrible time. To help him, we both went out and scored some heroin for him: it was the only thing to do to help Keith through the agony of withdrawal. Mick then flew to New York, saying that Jade was ill.

On Friday 4 March, Anita appeared in court to plead guilty to possession of heroin and hashish. Later that day our US publicist Paul Wasserman sat with her to watch the proceedings on the

early evening news: 'The whole thing was very upsetting for Anita,' he said.

Around 4.30pm, we went to the 300-seat El Mocambe Club for a soundcheck. In a bid to avoid advance publicity, we were taking over two nights from the Canadian group April Wine.

When we went back to play the gig, Mick took Margaret Trudeau in his limo. She had just parted from Canadian Prime Minister Pierre Trudeau and was very happy to be hanging out with us.

She probably hadn't fully thought through the consequences of her actions, as she ended up, in her own words, 'Branded: a promiscuous, irresponsible wife, prepared to go to any lengths to escape her husband.'

Musically, our opening night at the El Mocambe was not good. We were all very loose and the first half was far from tight. The second part went very much better and, overall, we had a good time. We played many of the songs from the Knebworth set, including a lot of the old numbers. By the second night, word had got around and it was very difficult to get in. Our playing was much improved and Eddie Kramer, who used to work at Olympic Studios, recorded the whole thing. The next

'Nothing is the end of this band. We'll always be able to play somewhere. We're a determined group of lads. Nothing short of nuclear weapons are gonna put this lot out of action.'
KEITH, *January 1977*

No Stones in 1977

Somebody forgot to tell the Rolling Stones they were supposed to have been swept away by the punk revolution. Sex Pistols' hysteria reached a height with their riposte to the Jubilee, 'God Save The Queen'. A new generation of bands was coming to the fore and the Clash sang, 'No Elvis, Beatles or the Stones in 1977'. These young guns owed more to the 1960s than they let on to their fans and the Stones need not have worried — if, indeed, they ever did. 'They're a bit limited,' declared Keith in the *Daily Mirror* that October. 'They don't have the stamina to be real rock stars.'

day we listened to the tapes, trying to relax before Keith appeared in court the next day.

Keith on remand

Just after 2pm, Keith went to the Old City Hall Court in Toronto for a three-minute appearance. On his way into court, he was grabbed by the hair by a man identified as a freelance photographer for a leftist publication, who called him 'limey' and 'junkie bastard'. It really shook Keith up.

During his court appearance, Keith was remanded until 14 March, 1977, on bail of $1,000. He was later informed of a second charge. The Mounties claimed that they had seized one fifth of an ounce of cocaine.

At the same time, the police were making things very hot for the rest of us. Mick, Woody and Peter Rudge decided to leave for New York without telling us. I was furious. Mick said we should get together in New York for the album photo and studio work, without Keith.

To keep ourselves occupied, Keith, Charlie and I went to the studio and worked on over-dubs. Having said he was staying, Charlie flew to New York on 9 March. I followed with Astrid two days later. There was nothing else of use that we could really do. At the trial on 14 March, Anita got off with two small fines. Keith's trial date was set for 27 June. We all met at Mick's place in New York and discussed the future of the band for several hours. It was all rather inconclusive as none of us really wanted to contemplate the worst.

At Atlantic, we haggled over the last details of our contract, despite the cloud over the whole proceedings.

The only way to help Keith was to get him off the heroin, the only question was how. Jane Rose travelled from our office to inspect the Stevens Psychiatric Centre, on Sutton Place South, New Jersey, which we'd heard was a good clinic. Charlie and I returned to France, while Keith and family flew to New Jersey.

The Wyman 1977 album
From *left*, Bill with Prince Rupert in February, Margaret Trudeau in March and Muddy Waters in July.

News of the blues

Our lawyers were in court at the same time. They were attempting to prevent the *News of the World* publishing pictures from Robert Frank's *Cocksucker Blues*, the film of the 1972 tour. 'Spanish' Tony Sanchez, who claimed he was Keith's personal assistant and bodyguard, had showed the film to the paper. We withdrew our case a couple of months later and paid their legal costs.

The Keith question

On Wednesday 11 May, Prince Rupert called to say he was very worried about Keith. I phoned Charlie and we agreed to go to New York to help if needed. Mick was asked a couple of days later if we would split up should Keith be imprisoned. 'We wouldn't if Keith was only in jail for a month or two,' he answered, 'but if he were in jail for a long period of time, I suppose we'd have to.'

At the end of June, the month in which Woody was 30 and Charlie hit 36, Keith was due back in court in Toronto. He failed to appear and his lawyer told the court he was taking a cure for addiction. His case was adjourned until 2 December.

Lester Bangs wrote about Keith in *NME* at the time: 'The rich are different from you and me.

I have friends who are dead because they didn't know that difference and that's not Keith's fault, but it doesn't make me care about what happens to him. The thing that offends me is not that Keith is an addict but that he played exactly one lead guitar solo on *Black And Blue* and that album cost five dollars. Even Keith should appreciate that five dollars buys a nickel bag. I've got friends who need that five dollars. If that logic seems askew, write it off to a drug culture that he perpetuates by making it seem glamorous to appear half-dead. People consider him to be Mr Rock'n'Roll, but if your last shred of charisma is a guy who doesn't play much any more, who seems half-dead by his own choice, then who the hell cares about the Rolling Stones or rock'n'roll?'

'Sometimes, people who are outside a situation see things with greater clarity than those who are stuck in the middle. I can tell you, I cared about Keith, and not just as a work colleague. We had been through so much in the previous 13 years, conquered the world, shared in an adventure the likes of which mere words cannot do justice to. But it was true, Keith didn't have to live by the rules of normal society. Money afforded him that luxury, if

'We can't wait five years. In five years we won't be touring at all – not much, anyway.' **MICK,** *speculating on Keith going to prison*

Side one
1. 'Intro (Fanfare For The Common Man)
2. 'Honky Tonk Women'
3. 'If You Can't Rock Me'
4. 'Get Off Of My Cloud'
5. 'Happy'

Side two
1. 'Hot Stuff'
2. 'Star Star'
3. 'Tumbling Dice'
4. 'Fingerprint File'
5. 'You Gotta Move' (McDowell)

Side three
1. 'You Can't Always Get What You Want'
2. 'Mannish Boy' (Morganfield)
3. 'Crackin' Up' (McDaniel)
4. 'Little Red Rooster' (Dixon)
5. 'Around And Around'

Side four
1. 'It's Only Rock'n'Roll'
2. 'Brown Sugar'
3. 'Jumpin' Jack Flash'
4. 'Sympathy For The Devil'

Recorded
Paris, London, Toronto and Los Angeles 1975–1977

Producers
The Glimmer Twins

Engineers
Keith Harwood, Andy Johns and Eddie Kramer

Cover painting and design
Andy Warhol

Release
UK Friday 16 September 1977 Rolling Stones Records COC 89101
US Thursday 15 September, 1977 Rolling Stones Records COC 29001

Highest chart position (time on chart)
UK No 3 (8 weeks)
US No 5 (7 weeks)

This live double album featured songs recorded over a two-year period, the most recent of which were captured at the tiny El Mocambe club in Canada. The album went top five in both Britain and America.

'I told Jerry I thought Mick had ruined the Love You Live cover I did for them by writing all over it – it's his handwriting and he wrote so big. The kids who buy the album would have a good piece of art if he hadn't spoiled it.' ANDY WARHOL, from his diaries

Left, Warhol's design, right, Stones in concert, May 1976

indeed it is a luxury. But when all is said and done, it's Keith's life. He makes choices and does what he wants. What was irritating for the rest of us was the way his drug-taking was getting in the way of making music. Keith would also say he expects no one to follow his example. But Keith is an icon and people set out to glamorise his life. Then again, if you say that his lifestyle works because it hasn't actually killed him, all well and good.' BILL

And the living's easy

I spent the summer at home in France. Mick seemed to be everywhere, if you read the papers. He spent some of the time trying to save his relationship with Bianca, but they were very much on the slippery slope. Both were enjoying the company of others. It was shortly after that they split up for good.

On Wednesday 14 September, we were at the Marquee club for a press reception for the launch of our live album, although Keith was still in New Jersey. Two days later, Astrid and I went to dinner at Tramp, joining Ringo, the Who's Keith Moon and his girlfriend Annette. They persuaded us to go back with them to the Royal Garden Hotel. I caught a baby mouse in the corridor, prompting Keith to order a tray of assorted cheeses from room service. He played me some amazingly good demos, which Pete Townshend had made for the Who.

In the third weekend of September, we promoted the new album in New York. Charlie and I went to Mick's house for the photo session and found him and Woody asleep. They finally got up at 1.30pm, when Keith arrived. He was looking much thinner.

Time for tea

In the second week of October, we began recording at Pathé Marconi studios in Paris. We celebrated my 41st birthday at a restaurant and Mick arrived with a beautiful American girl – Jerry Hall.

Bill's house in Vence, France

Jerry later told me how she and Mick had got together. 'I saw him for the first time on-stage in London in May 1976. I was going out with Brian Ferry at the time and we went backstage after the show, and later to Mick's suite at the Ritz hotel. When I saw him on stage, I was mesmerised by how high he could jump! When I was introduced to Mick, he was wearing a silk dressing gown and my first impressions were how androgynous he was, and that he was both vulnerable and interesting. From then on I met him a number of times – he just kept turning up. I admit I was interested in him but at the same time I was loyal to Brian and kept a proper distance from him. The following summer, while Brian was on tour in Japan he had an affair with another model. I went to a dinner party in New York and Mick was

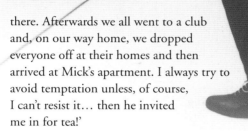

The Stones in New York

'I always try to avoid temptation unless, of course, I can't resist it… then he invited me in for tea!' JERRY HALL

Mick and Jerry, 9 May, 1978

there. Afterwards we all went to a club and, on our way home, we dropped everyone off at their homes and then arrived at Mick's apartment. I always try to avoid temptation unless, of course, I can't resist it… then he invited me in for tea!'

We recorded until the end of November – much of the time it was frustrating. Keith wouldn't turn up when we did, and when he wanted to work he'd call us all in. One night at 5am, Woody rang to say all of them apart from Mick were going to cut Chuck Berry's 'Run Run Rudolph' as a Christmas single for Keith. They wanted me to go, but that time I just said no.

Keith, Kimsey and Krissie
We took a break from recording so Keith could

get back to Canada to appear in court. Refuting the trafficking charge, Keith's lawyer showed the court a letter from a bank stating that Keith had spent more than £200,000 in 1977 on living expenses. So why, the lawyer asked, would he need to traffic? The case was put back to February 1978. We reconvened on 9 December, 1977, in Paris, recording 'I Can't Help It', 'Just My Imagination', 'Everlasting Is My Love', 'Muck Spreading Dub' and 'Black Limousine'. Mick spent Christmas with Jerry Hall at the Savoy Hotel in London and New Year in Barbados. By then, Bianca had gone back to New York.

During the middle of January 1978, we returned to Paris, with Chris Kimsey engineering. Over the next month, we cut 'Some Girls', 'Lies' and 'Girl With The Faraway Eyes'.

Early the following month, Woody's wife Krissie filed for divorce. Ronnie was seeing model Jo Howard, who was in Paris for much of our recording. By May, Bianca had also started divorce proceedings. Rather inappropriately, given its title, our single 'Miss You' came out on 20 May in America.

While out with Jerry in 1978, Mick gets into an altercation with a photographer… and loses.

'MISS YOU'

Recorded
a-side December 1977
b-side January 1978
Studio
Pathe Marconi Studios,
Paris
Producers
The Glimmer Twins
Engineer
Chris Kimsey
Release
UK 26 May, 1978
RS EMI 2802
US 10 May, 1978
RS 19307
Composers
Jagger/Richards
Highest chart position
UK No 3
US No 1
Weeks on chart
UK 7 weeks
US 20 weeks
Additional personnel
Mel Collins: saxophone
Sugar Blue: harmonica
Ian McLagan: piano

Faced with the twin onslaught of punk and disco, there were some who were ready to write the Stones off in early 1978. Mick and Keith had the perfect response to the critics with their own brand of disco sass. 'Miss You' spent longer on the US charts than any of the band's 29 previous releases. It was also the band's last chart-topping US 45.

The single was mixed in New York by Bob Clearmountain at Power Station Studios. He also remixed a 12-inch, 8-minute disco version of 'Miss You'. This was the first official Stones 12-inch. Some were issued on gaudy pink vinyl.

'The idea for the bass lines came from Billy Preston. We'd cut a rough demo a year earlier after a recording session. I'd already gone home and Billy picked up my old bass when they started running through that song. When we finally came to do the tune the boys said, "Why don't you work around Billy's idea?" I listened to it, heard that basic run and took it from there. It took some polishing, but the basic idea was Billy's.' BILL

On Saturday 10 June, the Stones played the first night of their 1978 US tour at Lakeland Civic Center in Orlando, Florida, to 9,917 people. It was the first time 'Miss You' was played live – but certainly not the last. It was a staple of live shows throughout the next 20 years. In 1998, Mick licked the toes of one of the backing singers while performing it. The song was dropped in the No Security tour in 1999.

There was a fundraising concert in New York on 20 October, 2001, for the families of public service workers killed in the 11 September attack on the World Trade Center. Keith joined Mick for two songs, including 'Miss You'.

'Tuesday 2 May, 1978, was Bianca's 33rd birthday. From 12.30pm to 1am we shot promo videos with director Michael Lindsay-Hogg for "Miss You", "Respectable" and "Far Away Eyes" while Michael Putnam took photos. At 2am, we went to Studio 54 for Bianca's birthday party. Among the guests were Ryan O'Neal, Truman Capote, Liza Minelli and David Frost. The next evening, Astrid and I flew home to Nice.' BILL

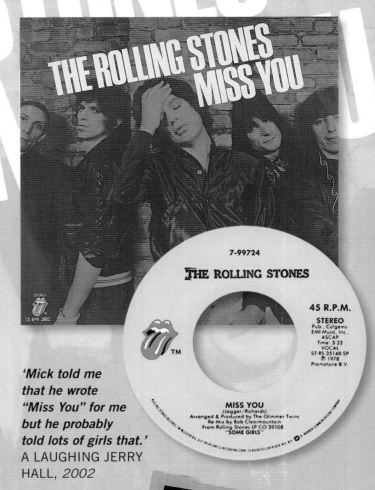

7-99724
THE ROLLING STONES

45 R.P.M.
STEREO
Pub., Colgems-
EMI Music, Inc.,
ASCAP
Time: 3:33
VOCAL
ST-RS-35148-SP
℗ 1978
Promotone B.V.

MISS YOU
(Jagger/Richards)
Arranged & Produced by The Glimmer Twins
Re-Mix by Bob Clearmountain
From Rolling Stones LP CO 39108
"SOME GIRLS"

'Mick told me that he wrote "Miss You" for me but he probably told lots of girls that.'
A LAUGHING JERRY HALL, *2002*

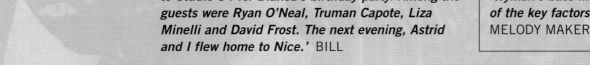

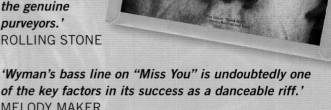

What the papers said...

'Disco, but they play it with more aggression than the genuine purveyors.'
ROLLING STONE

'Wyman's bass line on "Miss You" is undoubtedly one of the key factors in its success as a danceable riff.'
MELODY MAKER

'...the haunting, four-to-the floor groove of "Miss You".' **Q MAGAZINE**

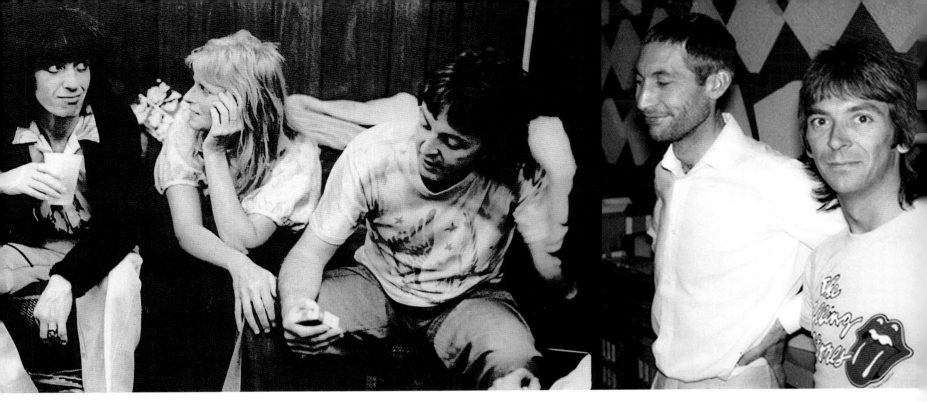

Some Macs And Some Girls

Charlie, Astrid and I travelled to Woodstock to rehearse for our upcoming US tour. Mick was already there with Jerry Hall and Keith was in the other studio playing with the Peter Tosh Band. I was to stay at the house of songwriter/producer Todd Rundgren.

Linda and Paul McCartney backstage in New York and, above, Charlie with another Mac – Ian McLagan

A S WE WERE LEAVING for Todd's place, Woody arrived, looking far from his best, and two days later, Keith abandoned the rehearsals to get a new US visa in Paris. Keith's timing has always been restricted to his guitar playing.

He even managed to miss the plane back the following day. We finally began on Saturday 27 May, 1978 and continued for 13 days. One night we managed a very good version of Chuck Berry's 'Beautiful Delilah' and on another, we played loads of Eddie Cochran songs. More often than not, we just jammed.

Meanwhile, back at Todd's place, I was getting acquainted with the technological age. Todd had a home computer – one of the first Apple Macs. I was suitable impressed with it and followed his advice to get one. All my diaries and this whole book were written on a Mac.

You can't get the staff

We flew from Newark to Orlando to spend two days rehearsing at the venue. Mick got very stressed. The crew was all so disorganised and the frustration was really beginning to show. Keith got

mad too, when he heard that his friend Freddie Sessler had been busted on his way over to Orlando. The police let Freddie off and he went straight back to New York.

Two days before our tour kicked off, Ian McLagan was drafted in on keyboards. Our first date in Orlando was something of a warm-up gig. We were billed as 'The Great Southeast Stoned-out Wrestling Champs' but it was not great. Once we got into our stride we played some brilliant shows.

Backstage was, as usual, a zoo. In some places, there were so many friends, it was difficult to get away and actually play. In New York, Paul and Linda McCartney came backstage and later joined me at my hotel. We sat around listening to music and chatted. The conversation got around to the fact that I carried a video recorder with me on tour to tape things off the TV. I played videos of early Beatles' shows from the

Keith backstage at Soldier Field with Willie Dixon

mid-1960s, which Paul himself had never seen.

After the show at Soldier Field in Chicago, we went to see Muddy Waters and Willie Dixon at a local club. Mick, Keith and Woody joined Muddy to play 'Mannish Boy', 'Long Distance Call' and 'Got My Mojo Working'.

To accompany the tour, our new album *Some Girls* came out the day we played JFK Stadium in Philadelphia to over 90,000 fans. 'Miss You' had already been on the radio for almost a month and we were definitely back with a vengeance. Not that I thought we'd really been away, although some critics thought we were on our way… out.

THE ROLLING STONES

'American black rights leader Reverend Jesse Jackson described the title song of the group's latest album Some Girls as "vulgar and obscene". It was also "an insult to coloured people". Mr Jackson said he would be meeting singer Mick Jagger and representatives of Atlantic Records about his complaint. "We do not want to act like censors," he said, "but we feel that Mick Jagger has a social responsibility."' DAILY EXPRESS, *22 September, 1978*

Engineer Barry Sage's original list of mic to recording desk cables

The 23rd US and 19th UK album was a massive seller, particularly in America, where the tour and the three singles helped to push it to No 1 and keep it on the chart for 32 weeks – the longest run of a regular Stones album since *Sticky Fingers* in 1971. It also spent 25 weeks on the UK chart.

THE NATIONAL ACADEMY
OF
RECORDING ARTS AND SCIENCES
presents this certificate to
ROLLING STONES
in recognition of
NOMINATION
for the
ALBUM OF THE YEAR
"SOME GIRLS"
for the awards period
1978

In 1978, Some Girls was nominated for a Grammy.

Cover story
Mick gave American designer Peter Corriston the original concept when he told him the album would be called *Lies*. Peter was inspired by wig ads from black magazines of the 1960s.

'Famous ladies Raquel Welch and Lucille Ball were furious when they discovered their pictures were on the sleeve of the Rolling Stones' latest album Some Girls. Lucille is one of the richest women in America and the thought of paying her suitable damages quickly persuaded record company chiefs to withdraw the album. A spokesman for the Rolling Stones said: "We understand the two ladies claimed that the photographs had humiliated them."'
DAILY MIRROR

Some singles

'Miss You' (see page 446)

Monday 28 August, 1978
31st US single
RS 19309
'Beast Of Burden' and 'When
The Whip Comes Down'
US No 8, 13 weeks on chart

Friday 22 September, 1978
22nd UK single
EMI.2861
'Respectable' and 'When The
Whip Comes Down'
UK No 23 (the first official
release not to make the UK Top
20 since 'Come On' in 1963)

Wednesday 29 November, 1978
32nd US single
RS 19310
'Shattered' with 'Everything's
Turning To Gold'
US No 31 (the least successful
official single since 'Street
Fighting Man' in 1968)

*Left, a promo single
of 'Before They Make
Me Run'*

*Recording Some Girls
at Pathé Marconi in
Paris, with, bottom,
a signed Polaroid
picture for assistant
engineer Barry Sage*

Side one
1. 'Miss You'
2. 'When The Whip
   Comes Down'
3. 'Just My Imagination'
   (Whitfield/Strong)
4. 'Some Girls'
5. 'Lies'
Side two
1. 'Far Away Eyes'
2. 'Respectable'
3. 'Before They Make Me
   Run'
4. 'Beast Of Burden'
5. 'Shattered'
Recorded
7 Oct, 1977–
22 February, 1978
Composers
All tracks Jagger/Richards
except where indicated
Studio
Pathé Marconi, Paris
Producers
The Glimmer Twins
Engineer
Chris Kimsey
Sleeve design
Peter Corriston
Release
UK Friday 16 June, 1978
Rolling Stones Records
CUN 39108
US Saturday 17 June,
1978 Rolling Stones
Records COC 39108
**Highest chart position
(time on chart)**
UK No 2 (25 weeks)
US No 1 (32 weeks)
Additional personnel
Ian McLagan:
piano and organ
Sugar Blue: harmonica
Mel Collins: saxophone

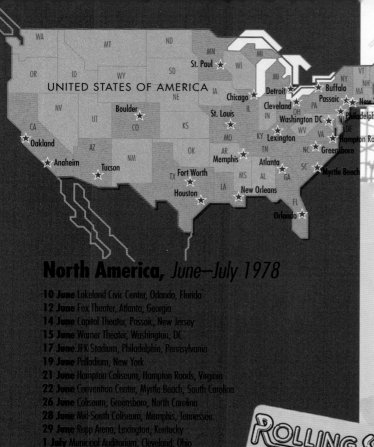

North America, *June–July 1978*

10 June Lakeland Civic Center, Orlando, Florida
12 June Fox Theater, Atlanta, Georgia
14 June Capitol Theater, Passaic, New Jersey
15 June Warner Theater, Washington, DC
17 June JFK Stadium, Philadelphia, Pennsylvania
19 June Palladium, New York
21 June Hampton Coliseum, Hampton Roads, Virginia
22 June Convention Center, Myrtle Beach, South Carolina
26 June Coliseum, Greensboro, North Carolina
28 June Mid-South Coliseum, Memphis, Tennessee
29 June Rupp Arena, Lexington, Kentucky
1 July Municipal Auditorium, Cleveland, Ohio
4 July Rich Stadium, Buffalo, New York
6 July Masonic Auditorium, Detroit, Michigan
8 July Soldier Field, Chicago, Illinois
10 July Civic Center, St. Paul, Minnesota
11 July Kiel Opera House, St. Louis, Missouri
13 July Superdome, New Orleans, Louisiana
16 July Folsom Field Arena, Boulder, Colorado
18 July Will Rogers Auditorium, Tarrant County, Fort Worth, Texas
19 July Sam Houston Coliseum, Houston, Texas
21 July Community Center Arena, Tucson, Arizona
23 July Anaheim Stadium, Anaheim, California
24 July Anaheim Stadium, Anaheim, California
26 July Oakland Coliseum, Oakland, California

This was a shorter tour than the band's last American extravaganza. It ran over seven weeks and they played to 767,189 people at 25 shows in 24 cities. It was a different type of tour in that the Stones played both stadiums and small theatres.

The Stones' audiences ranged from just 2,000 at the Warner Theater in Washington, DC to 91,000 at the JFK Stadium in Philadelphia. It was also a far simpler show, with the band relying more on their playing and less on their stage set and their costumes.

'No flash, no gimmicks, just rock'n'roll.' BILLBOARD

'Jagger gave everything from sex to violence in the best show I can recall from the Stones since Richmond Jazz Festival in 1963. The Stones' rhythm section has definitely perked up and modernised.' CHRIS WELCH, Melody Maker

'At the end of the show at the Civic Center in St Paul, I ran off the stage the wrong way and fell through the curtain at the back of the stage, landing on the concrete seven feet below. I hit my head and cut it a bit, hit my shoulder, arm, wrist and hand and was knocked out. I was taken to the local emergency hospital and admitted for the night. For much of the rest of the tour, I played bass with my fingers strapped up. In the end I got quite used to it.' BILL

At three of the shows the band grossed over $1 million, the first million-plus gates in the history of rock music.

Set list
The regular set was:
'Let It Rock'
'All Down The Line'
'Honky Tonk Women'
'Star Star'
'When The Whip Comes Down'
'Miss You'
'Lies'
'Beast Of Burden'
'Just My Imagination'
'Respectable'
'Far Away Eyes'
'Love In Vain'
'Shattered'
'Tumbling Dice'
'Happy'
'Sweet Little Sixteen'
'Brown Sugar,'
'Jumpin' Jack Flash'

Occasional numbers:
'Some Girls'
'Johnny B Goode'
'Fool To Cry'
'Memory Motel'
'Get Off Of My Cloud'
'It's Only Rock'n'Roll'
'Street Fighting Man'

Keeping It Simple – The US Tour

What the papers said...

You'd think that it had all been said, and in truth it had, but some reporters still managed to find a new twist.

'For the last 14 years Mick Jagger has been singing rock'n'roll for the Rolling Stones. He is a camping, vamping James Dean up top. Down below, he is gyrating androgyny, outfitted in leather pants whose elastic grabs his groin with obscenely bulging effect; a prancing, high-stepping leprechaun; a vulgar fellow given to fondling himself in public; the greatest rock'n'roll singer going. Eighteen songs and a 90-minute performance did nothing to dispel the myth perpetuated over a generation-and-a-half that Their Satanic Majesties can whip up a crowd like nobody else going.' DAVID NEWTON, *Greensboro Daily News*

Support bands
The Peter Tosh Band played at over half the gigs and Etta James played seven.

Elsewhere, support came from:
Henry Paul Band
Patti Smith
Foreigner
Furry Lewis
Eddie Money
Kansas
April Wine
Journey
Atlanta Rhythm Section
Southside Johnny and the
    Asbury Jukes
Van Halen
The Doobie Brothers
Doug Kershaw
The Outlaws
Santana

Special guests
Ian McLagan (below with Charlie) came in for Billy Preston on piano and organ. Stu also played piano on some numbers. Eddie Money played saxophone on 'Miss You' when supporting the band. Bobby Keys played saxophone and Nicky Hopkins piano in LA, and Linda Ronstadt sang 'Tumbling Dice' with Mick in Tucson. Doug Kershaw played fiddle on 'Far Away Eyes' when supporting.

'You have to tour. That's really when a band is a band. You have to go back on the road and like it.'

BILL, *Miami Herald, 11 June*

Barbarians At The Gates

The day after the tour ended we heard the sad news that our PR man Leslie Perrin had died in a Surrey hospital, aged 57. Leslie had been on the front line, dealing with our press for 10 years during some of our worst nightmares. We talked about him when we met to work out whether to stay on and record right then or come back later. In the end we decided to return in August.

I GOT BACK TO LA and went to Wally Heider's studios, the old RCA place we used in the 1960s, a month later on 23 August at 3am. Chris Kimsey, Mick and Charlie were there, Woody came an hour later and Keith turned up at 6am.

We ran through old and new material. Mac and Stu played keyboards and we finished at 11am. This was the pattern for the next two weeks. Drummer Jim Keltner would come in some nights and we did manage to cut some good numbers, but not many. Jo came with Woody a couple of times but mostly slept, as she was heavily pregnant.

The best thing that happened for me was when Stephen called from Gedding to say he'd passed

all 10 of his O-levels. The worst moment was when we heard that Keith Moon had died in London on 7 September, just as our last session finished. Charlie and I flew home for the funeral. Keith was a great mate and a friend to all the Stones – loony, yes, but lovely too.

Two weeks later Woody and Jo had a baby girl named Leah. A week afterwards, we flew to New York to appear on *Saturday Night Live*. We were all staying at the Essex House hotel, booked in as Michael Phillips (Mick), Thomas Crapper (Keith), Norris Thermidor (Woody), William Travis (Bill) and Mr Watts (Charlie) – what does that tell you about each of us? We rehearsed, host John Belushi singing on some of the numbers, as we played 'Respectable', 'Beast Of Burden', 'Shattered' and 'Summer Romance'. We were also involved in little skits, but they cut out quite a lot as they were running late. Unfortunately, it included the parts that Keith and I were in.

Legal service

The day before my birthday, Keith was back in court in Toronto. He pleaded guilty to possession of heroin but the more serious charge of trafficking in the drug was withdrawn. This plea bargain deal had been going on behind the scenes for some time and it was to everyone's relief, most of all Keith's, when it was accepted. In defence of Keith, his lawyer likened him to Van Gogh, Aldous Huxley, Dylan Thomas, F Scott Fitzgerald and Billie

Bill and Charlie talking with Roger Daltrey at Keith Moon's funeral

Holiday, which did the trick. The following day, Keith was ordered to play a special concert for the blind in Toronto and given a one-year probation order. Alan Dunn, who handled tour logistics, phoned and told me the news. On Tuesday 12 December, Keith released a solo record, his version of Chuck Berry's hit 'Run Rudolph Run'. It failed to chart whereas Boney M's more traditional approach to Christmas, 'Mary's Boy Child', made UK No 1. Six days later, Keith was 35.

After Christmas we decided to record some more, this time at Compass Point in the Bahamas. We were all there ready on the Monday – 22 January, 1979 – but Keith didn't arrive until the Friday. On Thursday, Keith's new girlfriend, Danish-born Lily Wenglass, arrived. They had been seeing each other for a short while as things between him and Anita had deteriorated. He met her on our previous US tour through Jo, Woody's girlfriend. We recorded until 4 February, cutting a whole mass of different tracks, none of

Keith alone
Keith's single was released in Japan with his cover of Jimmy Cliff's 'The Harder They Come' as the a-side. 'Run Rudolph Run' was the b-side.

which were good. Some days the atmosphere in the studio was great, but both Woody and Keith were in bad shape from an excess of partying.

Our recording was interrupted on 6 February by a real-life drama. Alan Dunn and girlfriend Ramona Herman went missing in an eight-foot dinghy (they had been diving 400 yards off the reef). Stu, Mick, Astrid, security man Bob Bender and I spent two-and-a-half days going out in rescue aircraft to look for them. I was manning the phones when we got the call that they had been picked up safe, suffering from exposure and dehydration. Everyone was so relieved. It was strange dealing with something like that; it's the sort of thing you read about, never ever expecting to be involved in yourself.

The recording went from bad to worse. Keith, who by the Friday had not slept for four days, had annoyed Mick so much that Mick refused to come to the studio, saying Keith was 'so out of it that nothing had been done'. On Monday 12 February, Mick, Charlie and Ronnie flew home. The next day Keith and Lil wanted to have dinner with us, but we avoided them. Keith said it was crazy that everyone had left when it was all going so well (he had to have been joking!).

Two months later I spoke to Mick at length about recording and the fact that Woody was going to tour with his own band and Keith was probably going with him. While he was in good spirits, I think Mick felt slightly betrayed. Three weeks went by and Keith called from our New York office saying he'd got me an acoustic bass and he was having it shipped to France. He also asked if I'd like to do the Toronto show for the blind as the others had agreed.

We did two shows at the Oshawa Civic Auditorium in Toronto. At the afternoon show the New Barbarians, Keith and Woody's band, which included Stanley Clarke (bass), the Meters' Joseph Modelliste (drums), Ian McLagan (keyboards) and Bobby Keys (tenor sax), played for an hour and were far too loud. We went on and also played for an hour to 4,900 fans, who were incredibly

enthusiastic. Our set included 'Johnny B Goode', 'Beast Of Burden', 'Shattered', 'Miss You', 'Just My Imagination', 'When The Whip Comes Down' and 'Jumpin' Jack Flash'. By the evening the Barbarians had calmed down and sounded so much better. On Monday, Charlie came to my room and chatted for an hour. He hadn't slept since his arrival and had gone shopping. He had seen a suit he liked in a shop window but it was closed. To kill some time he went to an Indian restaurant but fell asleep at the table for three

hours. Finally the restaurant owner called the police and they were the ones who woke Charlie up. They assumed Charlie was out of it but, finding he wasn't, they let him go. A Charlie moment.

Barbarians on the march

Woody and Keith flew out that same day to begin their tour in Ann Arbor, Michigan. On Thursday 3 May, Mick went to the High Court and attended a private hearing before a family division judge regarding his divorce from Bianca. Two weeks later, Mick asked if he could come and stay with me for a week for the Monaco Grand Prix.

Astrid was away in Los Angeles and on 21 May, the day Keith and Ronnie played their last tour date, I went to artist Marc Chagall's house near Vence. I managed to get about 20 photos of Chagall and his wife Vava in their garden. I also took photos of his paintings inside the house. It was wonderful therapy.

Time Waits For No One was an anthology album covering 1971 to 1977 and came out in June 1979.

On Friday 1 June, Woody celebrated his 32nd birthday. Mick and Jerry had left my place after their Grand Prix week and we released our 20th UK album, an anthology entitled *Time Waits For No One*. In many ways, it had waited for us throughout the 1970s. As the decade drew to a close, it was impossible not to contemplate the future.

June **79**

Until Forever

02

Still Rolling

Wembley Stadium, London, 25 August, 1990.
Bill's last on-stage appearance with the band.

Media Matters

We were back in Paris on 25 June, 1979, to begin a new round of sessions for our next album. We recorded throughout July and August. Arguments, sickness, lateness and other frustrations meant that these were not the most memorable of times. We failed to produce much of quality. The really remarkable things happened outside the studio.

MICK HAD TO BREAK OFF a few times to head back to London to be in court for his divorce from Bianca. I went to a party on 10 July and met a beautiful American model named Suzanne Accosta to whom I was instantly attracted.

Astrid was away in Los Angeles and we were having problems in our relationship. We had been for some time. Astrid met a man in LA and started a relationship. She told me that she wanted to live

Suzanne Accosta

there. I spent some time with Suzanne in France and by early March she decided to return to the US – but our paths would cross again many times.

A month into recording, there was a tragedy at Keith's house in South Salem. A 17-year-old guy, who was working as an odd-job man for Anita, shot himself in the head while playing Russian roulette with a pistol. Apparently, he and Anita had been watching TV together.

The case inevitably received a great deal of media attention with its connections to Keith. The press pilloried Anita, both for her behaviour and for her appearance, but she was thankfully cleared of any wrong-doing by a court in November 1979. The episode destroyed any last shred of a relationship between Anita and Keith.

'This was the astonishing figure of Rolling Stones girl Anita Pallenberg. Looking strained and paunchy, she emerged from three days in hiding, following the mysterious death of a boy in her bedroom.'
DAILY MAIL

It's true Anita and I weren't close, but it's a great shame that anyone had to end up involved in such a mess.

Rock star demo
On 11 August, the New Barbarians, featuring Woody and Keith, supported Led Zeppelin at a Knebworth concert. They returned to finish our Stones sessions on 30 August. Two days later, I flew to Las Vegas to appear with an all-star band at the Jerry Lewis telethon. We played the following

Chris Kimsey

night, when Ringo Starr, Dave Mason and Kiki Dee joined me along with some of Todd Rundgren's band.

On 16 September, all of the Stones returned to the Pathé Marconi Studios in Paris with Chris Kimsey, where we recorded until the middle of October. Mick and Keith went back in November to work on the mixing, but had a disagreement. The two of them packed up until 9 December, when they patched things up and returned to work at Electric Lady Studios, New York.

Ten days later, I started work in my home studio in Vence, recording a demo of a song I called '(Si Si) Je Suis Un Rock Star', inspired by meeting Suzanne. Little did I know it was to be the first hit single to be recorded by a solo Stone.

The Barbarians and the Zeppelin
In August 1979, the New Barbarians appeared with Led Zeppelin at Knebworth Park. It was the last time Zeppelin played – just over a year later, following the death of drummer John Bonham, the band would split.

Not leaving yet

In mid-February. I had a call from Keith Altham (a veteran of the music press who handled our PR) about doing an interview for the *Daily Express*. It was just a regular request, nothing special. I did it by phone from Vence and at one point David Wigg, the reporter, asked me how long the Stones were going to last. I told him 'a couple of years', which was what all of us generally answered to that question. By the time his article appeared, a few days later, my comments had been sensationalised – I was leaving the Stones by the end of 1982. The story appeared quite regularly in various publications. It even appears in books about the Stones written fairly recently – they say I was considering leaving the Stones at that point... untrue.

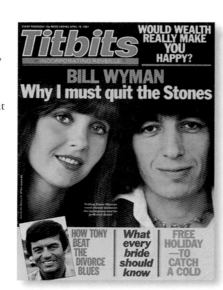

Astrid and Bill front another magazine in which he had to deny he was leaving the band.

Woody in trouble

Two days after the *Express* story came out, Woody and Jo were arrested for drug possession in St Maarten in the Caribbean. They were deported to America after five days in jail.

'He looked really beat, like a typical drug user'. POLICEMAN, *on arresting Ronnie Wood*

Two weeks later, I received a cassette of different mixes that Mick and Keith had done for the album during their marathon sessions at Electric Lady in New York. The mixing took longer than the album had done to record.

Bill with Earl McGrath

At the end of March, Charlie and I did a photo session for the album in New York. When we got there, we met at the apartment of Earl McGrath, general manager of Rolling Stones Records. Mick and Keith were there and the meeting mainly consisted of them yelling at each other about the album tracks – they couldn't decide on what to use, or whose mixes were best.

I went to Electric Lady and listened to all the new mixes. While I loved some, others disappointed me. We moved on to the Abromowitz Studio on East 92nd Street for a photo shoot with Annie Liebovitz. On Friday 28 March, we did a further session at Thermaograph Videos. I flew to LA to try and patch up my flagging relationship with Astrid.

Back home in early April, I settled at Shipton Manor Studios in Oxfordshire to record some new songs and recut 'Si Si'. I also had meetings about doing the soundtrack of a new movie called *Green Ice*. I agreed to work on it in the autumn.

A computer?

Back with the Stones, *Emotional Rescue* was released that summer and we were all needed in London for the launch. On 23 June, ready to start work, I found that Keith – for some unknown reason – had flown back to New York and Woody had decided not to come at all. One of our staff members, Alan Dunn, phoned and said that the scheduled press party had been cancelled. It was left to Mick, Charlie and I to handle all the interviews. Charlie got pissed off at this and left for home, saying he would see us in New York on Wednesday.

We finally met up on Friday, by which point Keith had played me further mixes he'd done for the album. We were interviewed by the American press at Danceteria, a club at 252 West 37th Street.

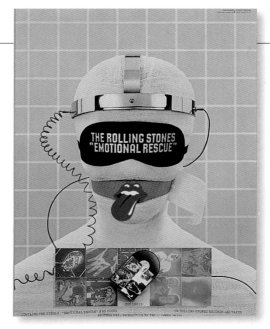

In-store poster for Emotional Rescue

'The truth of the matter is that Mick is having a sex-change operation and the rest of the group don't want to play with a girl.' KEITH ALTHAM, *to a journalist*

While I was in New York, I ordered a new Apple computer. Earl McGrath volunteered to pay for it out of band money for recording the Stones' history. Prince Rupert and Mick rejected the idea, saying that computers would never take off. I paid for it myself. We spent a few more days in New York, working on videos for the singles 'Emotional Rescue' and 'She's So Cold'. After that, Astrid and I returned home to France, where I spent much of the summer.

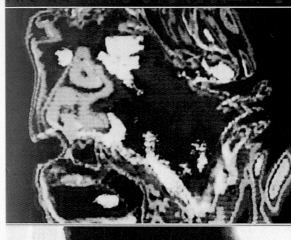

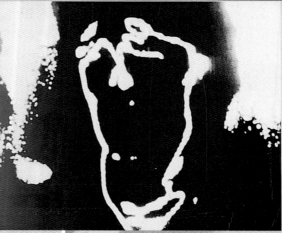

The 20th UK and 24th US album was the first since 1973's *Goats Head Soup* to top the album charts on both sides of the Atlantic. Given its lengthy and convoluted gestation, it was somewhat surprising to see it at US No 1 for seven weeks – longer than any of the other albums in the band's 16-year US career.

The conflict between Mick and Keith revolved around the musical direction of the group. It can be paraphrased as Keith – guitars, Mick – dance. According to Keith, Mick listened to too many bad records and was too interested in calculating how the 'market' was. Mick wanted hits, Keith couldn't give a…

'Claudine'

Claudine Longet was a French singer who married Andy Williams in 1961. They divorced in 1975. A year later she allegedly shot and killed her lover, a skier, in Aspen, Colorado. Her lawyer, who she married in 1986, successfully defended her and she was found guilty of criminal negligence as she maintained the gun had gone off accidentally. Keith's song about her was deemed too explicit for release.

Take two

There were a number of alternate tracks before the running order was finalised. Songs in *italics* didn't make the final album.
March 'Down In The Hole', 'Stuck In The Cold', *'Claudine'*, *'We Had It All'*, *'You Left Me'*, 'Indian Girl', *'I Think I'm Going Mad'*, 'Let Me Go', 'Emotional Rescue', 'Send It To Me', 'Summer Romance', 'Where The Boys Go', *'Ain't No Use'*, 'Dance'.
May 'Indian Girl', 'Emotional Rescue', *'Ain't No Use In Crying'*, *'Claudine'*, *'I Think I'm Going Mad'*, 'Let Me Go', 'Where The Boys Go' *'Neighbours'*, 'Summer Romance', 'Down In The Hole', 'Stuck In The Cold'.

When the acetates were sent out in early June, 'Dance' was track three and 'Summer Romance' was the opener.

Emotional Rescue
The Rolling Stones
Down In The Hole

Released
UK Friday 20 June, 1980
RS 105
US Monday 23 June, 1980
RS 20001
Highest chart positions
UK No 9
US No 3
Weeks on chart
UK 8 weeks
US 19 weeks

'EMOTIONAL RESCUE'

"'Emotional Rescue" was me and Charlie and Woody. It was towards the end of the sessions and I don't think Bill or Keith were there. We'd done it before, all together actually, in Nassau.' MICK, *1980*

'She's So Cold' / 'Send It To Me'
34th US single RS 21001, 24th UK single RS 106
Released US 10 September, UK 22 September, 1980
Highest chart position US No 26, UK No 33
Time on chart US 13 weeks, UK 6 weeks

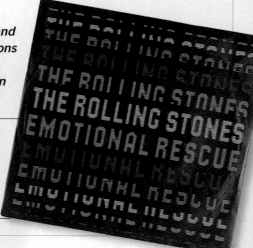

Cover Story II

ROLLING STONE
THE RETURN OF THE ROLLING STONES
The Stones Make the Great Comeback of Their Career
A SPECIAL PREVIEW OF THEIR NEW ALBUM
CREAM BREAKS UP

POP MUSIC
LES STONES, C'EST L
RAZ DE MAREE

NEW MUSICAL EXPRESS
Greatest Hits

Time Out

THE ROLLING STONES
paroles et images

BEST
STONES

1/UN STONE SOLITAIRE
Bill Wyman parle

SCHWEIZER ILLUSTRIERTE
sie + er
Das Schulbus-Drama

Trouser Press
ROLLING STONES
SECOND THAT EMOTION

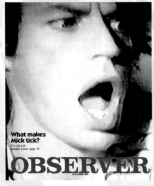

What makes Mick tick?
OBSERVER

WOMAN'S OWN
LIVING WITH MICK JAGGER

CREEM SPECIAL EDITION
THE ROLLING STONES
MICK JAGGER   KEITH RICHARDS
BILL WYMAN & CHARLIE WATTS

Music Express

stern
Die Rolling Stones privat
Vorsicht Lebensgefahr!

BEST
JAGGER: l'interview exclusive

Moviegoer
MICK JAGGER
Rockin' and Reelin'
Plus: Cheech and Chong

PLAYGIRL
MICK JAGGER
NUDE SPREAD
PICTORIAL

SUNDAY EXPRESS magazine
BEGINS TODAY:
JAGGER AT 40
THE MAKING OF A LEGEND

LIFE
LIVE AID
MOUNT ST. HELENS

OBSERVER
JAGGER'S EDGE
EXCLUSIVE INTERVIEW

GUITAR WORLD
KEITH RICHARDS
Satisfaction!

M MUSIKKUUTISET 6/89
LIVE AT LAST
ROLLING STONES

SUNDAY MIRROR MAGAZINE
THE LETHAL CHARMS OF PATSY KENSIT
JERRY, JADE, THE STONES & ME BY MICK JAGGER

Rolling Stone
The Rolling Stones

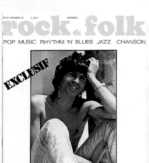

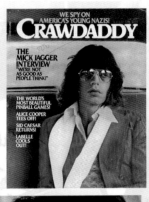

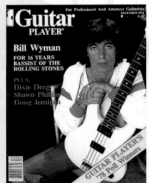

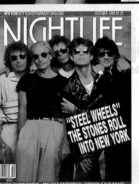

Movies And Suckers

I branched out into recording soundtracks, as our immediate working future looked bleak. We were all concentrating on our own projects and personal lives, and the Rolling Stones seemed to be taking a back seat. Mick and Keith could not agree on anything without a fight.

Rocket 88
In March 1981, Stu and Charlie's band Rocket 88 released their eponymous album on Atlantic Records (K50776). It featured Alexis Korner and Jack Bruce, Charlie's old mates from his Blues Incorporated days.

ON 5 NOVEMBER, MICK and Bianca's divorce settlement was finalised and five days later I began recording the soundtrack for *Green Ice* at Jimmy Page's Sol Studio in Cookham.

For much of the next six weeks I worked there and Jimmy often dropped by. George Harrison lived locally and was another frequent visitor. Mick was in Paris at the Pathé Marconi studios working with Chris Kimsey on Stones tracks, some of which appeared on *Sucking In The Seventies*. Charlie was there for a few days and Woody too; Keith didn't make it. Most days at Sol, I finished up in the early hours, but as I was staying there, it wasn't far to go to bed. On 9 December, 1980, we stopped at about 1am and I got to bed at 3.30am. Just 25 minutes later, John Lennon was shot dead in New York. I was called the next morning with the news. I felt a great sense of loss like everyone else who knew John, either personally or through his music.

After work finished in Paris, Mick went to Peru to star in Werner Hertzog's film *Fitzcarraldo*, a project that he was never to complete.

Alan Dunn called to say he was off to Peru to join Mick, adding that there had been talk of a possible summer tour in the US and an autumn tour in Australia. In late January, 1981, I met with Prince Rupert and Paddy Grafton Green. Much of the talk was of the widening rift between Mick and Keith. They seemed to feel it was irreparable, yet nevertheless we spoke about a US tour in the summer – maybe it would be our swan song. One good piece of news was the fact that we won our tax case. They'd accepted that the money we had from Klein consisted of loans and that there was no tax to pay.

Chez Chagall
I was back in France for most of February and March 1981, spending a good deal of time with Chagall. He even took me up to his *atelier* (workroom). It seemed a very personal and secretive place seldom revealed to outsiders. It was full of wonderful, unfinished paintings.

In March, Charlie drummed on Woody's solo LP in Los Angeles. Keith was in New York and, apart from playing with guitarist Matt Murphy (who had appeared in *The Blues Brothers*) and his band, he spent most of the time at home with a stunning girl named Patti Hanson: they had been living together for a while.

Two days after Patti's 24th birthday, Art Collins from our New York office called and said that Mick and Keith were there. Tensions had thankfully eased and a US tour seemed more likely.

Astrid and I had a holiday in Marrakesh and I called Keith in New York when I got back to Vence. He was fine and we chatted about the upcoming US tour and rehearsals, and the possibility of cutting new tracks to finish the album.

Both Keith and Mick had New York apartments, Woody was living in Los Angeles, and Charlie lived in Gloucestershire, England. Keith told me Charlie was staying with Mick, but he was in bed sick with the flu.

Green Ice premiered on Thursday 21 May in London and was panned by the critics, although some nice things were said about my music. As it was my first attempt at scoring a film, I was very pleased. The next day I got a telegram from Keith, as did Woody:

'Want you here Wednesday 17 May. If not, don't come.
'PS: If you want to be on the album cover, be here Monday 25 May.'

I called Mick and agreed that we should all get to New York on 26 May – and then Keith failed to show up. He was at his friend Freddie Sessler's house in Florida. The next few days were comical. No-one knew what was going on, as Keith was still in Florida.

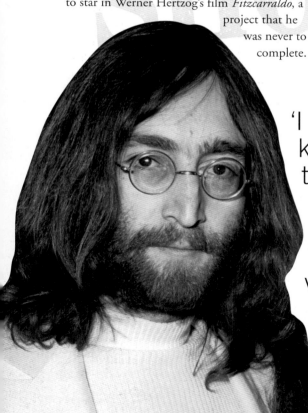

'I was really shocked, I don't know what to say really. It's the same thing as when I heard about Keith Moon and Brian Jones. It's not believable at first – it's very disappointing and very upsetting.' **BILL,** *on the day of John Lennon's murder*

Bill composed the music for the film Green Ice

THE ROLLING STONES
SUCKING IN THE SEVENTIES
THE ROLLING STONES
SUCKING IN THE SEVENTIES
THE ROLLING STONES
SUCKING IN THE SEVENTIES
THE ROLLING STONES
SUCKING IN THE SEVENTIES

Side one
1. 'Shattered'
2. 'Everything Is Turning To Gold'
3. 'Hot Stuff'
4. 'Time Waits For No One'
5. 'Fool To Cry'

Side two
1. 'Mannish Boy'
2. 'When The Whip Comes Down'
3. 'If I Was A Dancer'
4. 'Crazy Mama'
5. 'Beast Of Burden'

US/UK release
US 21 Mar, '81
RS COC 16028
UK 9 Mar, '81
CUN 39112

US/UK highest chart position
(time on US/UK chart)
US No 15 (six weeks)

This compilation of rarities, remixes and live tracks became the first Stones-sanctioned album release to fail to chart in the UK. In the US it also became the worst-performing official LP of the band's career.

'That's just going along with record company demands and what's written in the contract.' KEITH, on Sucking In The Seventies, May 1981

I went over to Mick's apartment on Friday, where he, Charlie and I listened to the new album. It sounded great, although Mick still had to remix three tracks. Around 3.45am, Woody arrived, but didn't look too good – Charlie got very drunk and insisted he wasn't going on tour.

Monday 1 June and Keith was still in Florida, despite his daily promises to fly to New York. In the late afternoon, Mick and Charlie visited my hotel and we discussed the future of the Stones. We talked about the album and the tour in some detail, and of Keith's non-appearance. It was all very disturbing.

By the Friday, I had decided enough was enough and flew back to London. Charlie phoned from New York a few days later. He'd been drinking and insisted we were finished, that there would be no tour. Failing to get hold of Mick, I spent a few days contemplating my future.

Woodwork and dentistry
Towards the end of June, everyone was calmer and I was back in New York to shoot a video with the rest of the band. We filmed five songs in three days with Michael Lindsay Hogg and everyone was in good spirits – a major turnaround in less than a month. On the last day of filming, we met to talk over the tour. Prince Rupert suggested we rehearse for a couple of weeks. We also talked about Woody and what to do if he couldn't clean up his act.

We all met with Woody and told him he had to clean up, offering him $500,000 to do the tour; Woody agreed. At the end of the meeting, Keith gave me a very nice set of cards, drawn by Robert Crumb, depicting old blues artists with brief histories on the back.

Back in England, I was busy promoting 'Si Si' on *Top Of The Pops* and in the press. I was due to fly back to New

Charlie by Bill

The June video shoot in New York, directed by Michael Lindsay Hogg

BLIND LEMON JEFFERSON

SON HOUSE

SLEEPY JOHN ESTES

Some of the cards Keith gave Bill

York to begin our two-week rehearsal, but was delayed by a very bad toothache, requiring several visits to the dentist. The others began rehearsing on 14 July. When I joined them after a two-day delay, we fell into our usual routine of starting late and Keith failing to turn up some nights. Charlie was still unhappy about touring and spoke to me one night about pulling out. Woody was still not alright and Mick asked me to talk to him to try and get him to focus a little more. The rehearsals lasted 10 days, as Mick was off to India on holiday. Two days later he was 38. Three weeks after that, our new album was out in America, just a year after *Emotional Rescue*.

'(SI SI) JE SUIS UN ROCK STAR'

On Friday 3 July, Bill's '(Si Si) Je Suis Un Rock Star' and 'Rio de Janeiro' (A&M Records AMS 8144) came out in the UK. Terry Taylor played guitar and Bruce Rowland drums. Bill played all other instruments and sang. The b-side had Stray Cat, 'Slim' Jim Phantom on drums. It hit UK No 14. It also did very well around the world, making the Top 20 in many countries.

'If it isn't a smash, I'll brush the steps of St Paul's Cathedral with a toothbrush.'
SIMON BATES, *DJ, Radio One*

'I used to be a choir boy in Westminster Abbey – a soloist – then my voice broke. That was my first training in showbiz. "Sorry, son, we can't use you anymore."'
KEITH, *May 1981*

ROLLING STONES TATTOO YOU

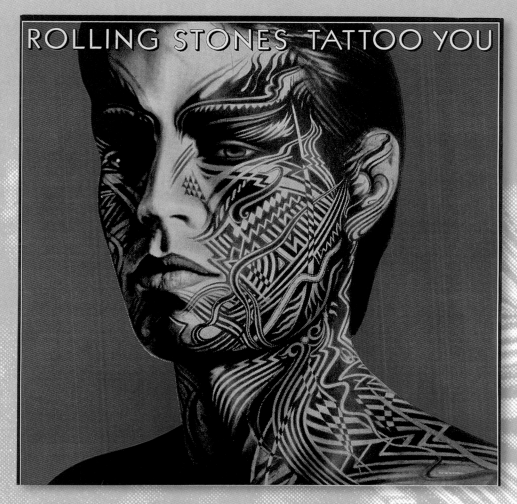

THE ROLLING STONES
WAITING ON A FRIEND

Singles
'Waiting On A Friend' backed with
'Little T&A'
26th UK single RS 109
36th US single RS 21004
Release date
UK Friday 27 November, 1980
US Tuesday 17 November, 1980
Highest chart position
UK No 50, 6 weeks
US No 13, 15 weeks

'Hang Fire' backed with
'Neighbours', the 37th US single
Release date
Thursday 4 March
6th US single RS 21300
Highest chart position
US No 20, 11 weeks

Side one
1. 'Start Me Up'
2. 'Hang Fire'
3. 'Slave'
4. 'Little T&A'
5. 'Black Limousine'
   Jagger/Richards/Wood
6. 'Neighbours'
Side two
1. 'Worried About You'
2. 'Tops'
3. 'Heaven'
4. 'No Use In Crying'
5. 'Waiting On A Friend'
Studios
Compass Point Studios,
Bahamas, 23 January–
12 February, 1979;
Pathé Marconi, Paris,
27 June–8 October,
1979; October–
November, 1980; Electric
Lady, New York
November–December
1979; Atlantic Studios,
New York April–June,
1981
Composers
All tracks Jagger/Richards
except where indicated
Production
The Glimmer Twins:
producers
Chris Kimsey: associate
producer
Engineer
Chris Kimsey
Barry Sage (assistant)
Release
US 18 Aug. '80
Rolling Stones Records
CUNS 39114
UK 28 Aug. '80
Rolling Stones Records
COC 16052
**Highest chart position
(time on chart)**
US No 1 (30 weeks)
UK No 2 (29 weeks)
Additional personnel
Pete Townshend:
guitar on 'Slave'

The 22nd UK and 26th US album was the last by the Rolling Stones to top the US charts. It held the US No 1 position on the charts for nine weeks. It was a curious album in that it had been recorded over a period of three years and on the face of it some of it was made up of leftovers from *Emotional Rescue*.

'A lot of the stuff on Tattoo You *was only half-formed during* Emotional Rescue *and we've been working on it since. We recut a couple of tracks at the end of last year. Some of these songs were begun during* Emotional Rescue *and some at points in between. We did some sessions in Nassau, early in 1979, there might be a couple from there as well.'* KEITH, May 1981

Start Me Up
The Rolling Stones
No Use Crying

'START ME UP'

THE ROLLING STONES
START ME UP

Released
UK Friday 14 August, 1981
RS 108
US Thursday 6 August,
1981
RS 21003
Highest chart position
UK No 7
US No 2
Weeks on chart
UK 9 weeks
US 24 weeks

This was the Stones last big single in America, as well as being the last to go Top 10 on both sides of the Atlantic. It was the 35th US single and the 25th in the UK.

Microsoft launched Windows 95 in August 1995 to the accompaniment of 'Start Me Up'. They paid an undisclosed fee for the song to highlight the ease-of-use of the 'start menu' in Windows, and in the process instilled a bit of rock'n'roll glamour into the world of computers.

Taking The Longview

In early August, Keith called from New York to talk about who should play keyboards on the tour. He said everyone was up for Ian McLagan and added that he didn't think we needed horns this time. I agreed. We originally planned to rehearse at Woodstock, but were recommended a farm which housed studio and rehearsal facilities. Keith had seen it and thought it was good.

Longview views
Above: Warm up gig billed as Blue Sunday and the Cockroaches. *Right:* Bill's pictures taken at rehearsals and around the farm.

K EITH TOLD ME HE had to go to Rome to get a new US visa in mid-August but that he would be back in time to rehearse.

Astrid and I arrived at Longview Farm on 18 August to join Charlie and Mick, who were already there. Keith and Woody arrived two days later to start the five weeks of rehearsals.

We had a new piano player, David Sancious, but he only stayed a couple of days. It wasn't that he was bad, he just didn't fit in. He was also the cause of an almighty row between Mick and Keith, as a result of which they eventually agreed to try out Chuck Leavell, who used to be in the Allman Brothers' band.

The first week was chaotic and, with another four weeks in hand, there wasn't much sense of urgency. On Wednesday 26 August, Mick and Alan Dunn flew from Worcester to Philadelphia to announce the tour to the media. Nobody else from the band went along. Charlie hadn't been to bed the previous night – staying up had become a bit of a habit for him. While Mick was away in the afternoon, Keith fell up the wooden steps outside our room, injuring his ankle. He was nursed by a crowd of people on a camp bed on the lawn, but fears of a break soon subsided.

For a couple of days after that, Woody didn't turn up at rehearsals, which as normal started around 11pm and ran through until around 6am. Keith got really angry with him and they ended up having a fight. Jim Callaghan, our security guy, had to separate the two. My diary entry of 28 August reminds me how bad it was:

We rehearsed until about 1.25am and then Keith and Woody wanted to break for five minutes (which was one hour). They eventually got back about 2.30am. Mick had crashed for a while and they got him up again at 3am, but he had almost lost his voice and couldn't really sing. From then on, the rehearsal deteriorated into a farce. Keith and Woody were so out of it that they couldn't even play one song between them. Even Charlie was all over the place – speeding and over-playing. Mick left at 5am, Keith at 5.30am. I finally left at 5.45am and went straight to bed, wondering how the hell we are going to manage on the road, if things don't change.

We worked with Chuck Leavell for a few days but decided to go back to our first choice, Ian McLagan. Chuck was great, but we just felt more comfortable with Mac, having worked with him before.

By mid-September, things hadn't improved. There were frequent arguments and many absences from the guitar section of the band. The prospect of a gig at a small club the next evening was far from appealing. We were to play a warm-up show at Sir Morgan's Cove Bar in Worcester, billed as Blue Sunday and the Cockroaches. It wasn't a big secret – everyone for miles around seemed to know. We ended up playing for 90 minutes and, though we made lots of mistakes between us, it went off well.

From then on we thought that things would steadily improve. But Mick got flu, missed quite a few rehearsals and we cancelled another warm-up gig in Boston after political pressure from the local council, despite the fact that Mick was back by then. We finished up in Longview on 24 September.

'PS: Don't forget your passports, foreign currency, inoculations and remember – airport dogs smell stronger than farm dogs!'
ROLLING STONES DAILY REHEARSAL NEWSLETTER, *24 September, 1981*

We arrived in Philadelphia at 4.15pm and took three vans straight to JFK Stadium to view the stage. It looked great. At 7.05am, the gates of the stadium opened and thousands of cheering fans dashed inside. It was estimated that up to 30,000 people had spent a chilly night on the grounds around the stadium waiting to grab the best seats. Around 1.45pm we drove to the venue. Another tour was just about to get underway.

God loves the Stones
A Rolling Stones press release of 6 September said, 'When Bill Wyman was passing a church in North Brookfield, Massachusetts, he discovered that the devil's favourite rock group was being wished well by the local church.' Bill was quoted, 'The Rolling Stones are true professionals, so we have no doubt that we will make it through this tour on our own speed. But it's always nice to have a little help from above.'

Playing to 2,195,071 people at 50 shows in 28 cities in 20 States and Washington DC the Stones grossed $36,147,799. It was a very big tour, one that eclipsed every other that the Stones had undertaken. Put into perspective, they played to more people at many individual dates on this tour than they played to on both their first US tours put together!

'When we go on tour it's really like an army on the move. We have about eight or 10 semi-trucks, about sixty crew who build and break down the stage, and there are about 60 people that go with you on a private plane – secretaries, publicist, photographer, doctor, etc., and you've got to hotel them and move them about the country. It's an enormous logistical problem.' BILL, *Michael Parkinson BBC TV show, February 1982*

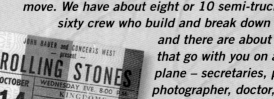

North America, *September–December 1981*

25–26 September JFK Stadium, Philadelphia, Pennsylvania
27 September Rich Stadium, Buffalo, New York
1 October Metro Center, Rockford, Illinois
3–4 October University of Colorado, Folsom Field, Boulder, Colorado
7 October Murphy Stadium, San Diego, California
9–11 October Memorial Coliseum, Los Angeles, California
14–15 October Kingdome, Seattle, Washington
17–18 October Candlestick Park, San Francisco, California
24–25 October Tangerine Bowl, Orlando, Florida
26 October Fox Theater, Atlanta, Georgia
28–29 October J Murphy Astrodome, Houston, Texas
31 October–1 November Cotton Bowl, State Fair Grounds, Dallas, Texas
3 November Freedom Hall, Louisville, Kentucky
5–7 November Brendan Byrne Arena, Meadowlands, East Rutherford, New Jersey
9–10 November Civic Center, Hartford, Connecticut
12–13 November Madison Square Garden, New York
16–17 November Richfield Coliseum, Cleveland, Ohio
19 November Checkerdome, St Louis, Missouri
20 November Unidome, Cedar Falls, Iowa
21 November Civic Center, St Paul, Minnesota
23–25 November Rosement Horizon, Chicago, Illinois
27–28 November Carrierdome, Syracuse, New York
30 November–1 December Silverdome, Pontiac, Michigan
5 December Superdome, New Orleans, Louisiana
7–9 December Capitol Center, Washington, DC
11 December Rupp Arena, Lexington, Kentucky
13 December Sun Devil Stadium, Phoenix, Arizona
14–15 December Kemper Arena, Kansas City, Missouri
18–19 December Hampton Coliseum, Hampton Roads, Virginia

Stagecraft

The outdoor stage and sets for the Rolling Stones American Tour '81 were the largest ever built for a live concert at that point. The stage was 64 feet across, with wings 80 feet wide on each side, and a roof anywhere between 20 and 30 feet high. The artwork for the large scrims comes from original paintings by Japanese artist Kazuhide Yamazaki. The set was 224 feet across, with an additional 150 feet of silk strips fanning out from each side. In its entirety, the set measured larger across than two football field lengths. (The smaller set – destroyed in Buffalo by high winds – was only about 20 feet shorter.) The artwork design was finalised on 6 September, 1981. After all contractual

Set list
Usually ran two hours or more.

'Under My Thumb'
'When The Whip Comes Down'
'Neighbours'
'Just My Imagination'
'Shattered'
'Let's Spend The Night Together'
'Black Limousine'
'She's So Cold'
'Time Is On My Side'
'Beast Of Burden'
'Waiting On A Friend'
'Let It Bleed'
'You Can't Always Get What You Want'
'Tops'
'Tumbling Dice'
'Hang Fire'
'All Down The Line'
'Let Me Go'
'Little T & A'
'Start Me Up'
'Miss You'
'Honky Tonk Women'
'Brown Sugar'
'Jumpin' Jack Flash'
'Street Fighting Man'
'Satisfaction'

On some shows 'Down The Road Apiece', 'Twenty Flight Rock' and 'Star Star' were played. Later in the tour, 'Going To A Go Go' was added too.

Manoeuvres

Additional musicians
Ian McLagan: keyboards and backing vocals
Stu: piano
After the first three shows it was decided that horns were needed
Lee Allen: sax (1–4 October)
Ernie Watts: sax (rest of tour)

Support bands
George Thorogood and the Destroyers played at roughly 20 per cent of the gigs. Other support acts included: the J Geils Band, Heart, Journey, Greg Kihn Band, Van Halen, Henry Paul Band, Stray Cats, Fabulous Thunderbirds, the Neville Brothers, Tina Turner, Garland Jeffries, Screaming Jay Hawkins, Etta James, Lamont Cranston, Molly Hatchet, ZZ Top, Iggy Pop, Santana, Bobby Womack, Meters, Joe Ely, and Prince.

Prince had just two hits by the time he opened the Stones' show in Los Angeles, and wearing just a pair of black bikini bottoms he was pelted with beer cans.

15 days – just in time for the opening shows in Philadelphia and Buffalo.

There were 10,000 square feet of cloth in the painted scrims of the set, including the backdrop and curtains. It was estimated that the amount of cloth used in the set would be enough to outfit three clipper ships with full sails. Eight large semi-trucks were used to transport the stage, set and structural materials.

arrangements were agreed, sewing of the scrim cloth was started on 11 September, and the painting of the cloth began immediately thereafter. At the same time, construction began on the stage and the steel structures, custom-built to fit the unique shape of the set's artwork.

Approximately 35 people at FM Productions in San Francisco worked 24-hour shifts and both outdoor sets were completed in approximately

'I can't go on pretending to be eighteen much longer.'
MICK, *at the start of the tour*

Extracts from Bill's diary

Philadelphia, Pennsylvania:
We went on at 4pm and played to 90,000 fans, and it was great for our first show. Mick kept telling me that I was booming all over the stage, when it was the bass drum. Keith called me and said the show was great. He'd talked to Mick about shouting at me on stage, and told Mick to apologise. Mick called and came down to see me and went out of his way to apologise.

Rockford, Michigan:
We watched the opening act – A&M's five-girl group the Go-Go's, who had a Top 30 single on the charts. After their set, Charlie and I went and said hello, and they took photos.

Los Angeles, California:
We went to three street sites, and they shot me walking and running for clips to go into the main taping on Saturday afternoon for the promo film of 'Come Back Suzanne' (a song I'd written because Suzanne wouldn't come back!). I saw one of Suzanne Accosta's posters for Ryan O'Neil's new film in town. At 4.30pm I called Suzanne and gave her tickets for the show.

At 3.30pm we finally left in the van with Mick and Charlie. As we got near the stadium, Mick stopped the van a few times, and asked the ticket touts their prices — nobody recognised him. I got Peter O'Toole backstage and I put him safely in the wings to watch. He said he doesn't get the instant adulation with his art, like we do. He said 'It was like the entry of the gladiators into Rome'. He was very moved by the experience.

Backstage we met Tina Turner, Jack Nietzsche, Bob Dylan and Clydie King, Jack Nicholson, Lou Adler, Britt Ekland, Harry Dean Stanton, the Stray Cats, Roger Taylor of Queen, and many more.

Orlando, Florida:
Saturday 24 October I celebrated my 45th birthday. When we arrived backstage, I found the whole place decorated with 'Happy Birthday', and three parrots in cages. Guests included: Keith Altham, Stu's son Giles, Jade and Marlon. We ate food, and I had a nice birthday cake from the promoter. Then a singing telegram girl and a belly dancer arrived, which was embarrassing, but funny. We went onstage at 2.30pm and played to 60,000 for two hours, in a very hot and humid atmosphere. A plane started flying around with 'Happy Birthday Bill', from Freddie Sessler and friends. After the introductions, Mick got the crowd to sing 'Happy Birthday', which was really something. Bobby Keys was here and played on the show with us.

East Rutherford, New Jersey:
At 10.15pm we went onstage and played for two hours to 19,000 fans. We put 'Twenty Flight Rock' back in and dropped 'Down The Road Apiece'. During the show Ronnie jumped on Mick's back. Mick threw him over the top, not knowing who it was, and it almost

stopped the show, as we were all laughing so much. We left and returned to the hotel in vans, arriving at 1.45am. John McEnroe and girlfriend arrived, and John asked me how to play bass, so I borrowed Keith's acoustic guitar, and showed him a few things. Then Vitas Gerulaitis and Katherine Guinness arrived with Andy Warhol. We played music and chatted until everyone left at 4.30am.

Hartford, Connecticut:
We were scheduled to leave at 4pm. We sat around until 6pm, when Keith, Woody and Mac finally arrived. We drove to the venue. Then Keith, Charlie, Woody and I listened to a lot of unused tracks. Keith said we had enough in the can for another album, without cutting any new songs, which I thought was debatable.

Chicago, Illinois:
We went onstage at 10.30pm and played our usual show to 17,000 fans. We played well and the audience was fantastic again – I really enjoyed it. We returned to the hotel by van, arriving at 1am. We left at 2.15am and went to a party that had been arranged for the crew at 'Park West'. Everyone was there. Mick and Woody were serving drinks, and Jerry and Patti were waitresses. There was a succession of strippers onstage, then the Neville Brothers got up and played for a while.

Phoenix, Arizona:
We went onstage at 4.30pm and played our usual set to 77,000 fans. I wore my steel blue Nike suit. We played a very good show in the sun to a good audience. During 'Honky Tonk Women' the Saloon Girls and the band's girlfriends came onstage from the wings and paraded. We left to a wonderful firework display, which was probably the best one on the tour.

Kansas City, Missouri:
We went onstage and played to 17,670 fans. We did our usual set. I regarded this as our worst show of the tour. Mick Taylor came onstage and played with us for most of the show, and all that could be heard were guitars. I had awful problems with my equipment, not being able to hear it at all. The audience were quite good considering.

Hampton Roads, Virginia:
Backstage I was regularly taken for Keith, Woody once, and asked if I was the sax player by one girl. Woody arrived with Ronnie Lane, who's not well and suffering from MS. We went onstage just before 10.30pm, and played a really good set. I enjoyed it after 30mins, when my sound came together. We relaxed backstage for a while, then had a party with cakes for Keith and Bobby Keys' birthdays yesterday.

Top: *Bill, Bob Dylan and Harry Dean Stanton*
Middle: *Bill and Tina Turner*
Bottom: *Bill, Charlie and the Stray Cats*

I SURVIVED
The Rolling Stones
U. S. A. TOUR 1981

'Rich Cliffard' and Bill

Bali Hi

The tour was a great success both musically and financially, but it wasn't without its problems. We had a lot of arguments and fights during the three months on the road.

THE LENGTH OF THE TOUR was probably one reason why; we had never toured for so long. We had frequent arguments about filming some of the gigs.

For a while, Keith and Mick were at complete loggerheads, with Mick unable to comprehend why Keith wouldn't compromise. I was very much against the proposals to shoot a 'satellite special', particularly as Mick and Prince Rupert seemed intent on arranging things without involving the rest of us. Mick was also drinking a lot, which didn't help. It got so bad that Charlie even hit Mick one night. When it was time to head home at the end of the tour, there were the usual mixed emotions and a round of goodbyes. Just before Astrid and I left, we popped into Keith's room. Patti and he were soon to be moving to a new apartment and Keith had been pinching room

The crew count takings on what was touted as the last tour.

service cutlery and crockery throughout the tour. The best thing about staying in nice hotels were the 'take-aways'. Finally, it was off to the airport and home. Life on the road... I finished as a French resident in December 1981 and went back to England in January 1982 to work at Sol studios on my own stuff and to produce the Stray Cats. After that I went on holiday to Hawaii, Australia, Bali and Japan. I say 'holiday' but I was also promoting 'Come Back Suzanne' and my third solo album everywhere I went. It seemed to help them do well in the charts.

While in Australia I did quite a bit of TV, and on one show I had to introduce Cliff Richard. I made a Freudian slip and called him Rich Cliffard. Around the same time Keith and Woody played with Chuck Berry in New York and Chuck, ever the man on the ball, introduced Woody as Keith!

While I was still in Australia, visiting Ayers Rock and Alice Springs, Stu called me and said our planned European tour would run from the end of May to mid-July. Mick wanted to rehearse for four or five weeks. I heard a few days later that Keith wanted to rehearse for just a week. Stu also told me that Mick and Keith were in a studio in New York listening to live tapes from the US tour. Mick wanted to record old songs in the studio and

Left: *Prince Rupert*

over-dub the audience, which didn't seem like a very good idea. Mick phoned me when I got to Bali to tell me he wasn't keen on a European tour, as there was no money in it for us, but the rest of the band wanted to do it. I said that I wanted to do it too, then asked him about the live album. He told me that it was practically finished, saying there was no more for me to do on it.

From Bali, we travelled to Japan and had a great time, being made welcome wherever we visited. After we got back we went to France and started packing, as I was finally moving back to England. I had bought a house in Mulberry Walk, Chelsea, to use as a London base. Two weeks later, on 7 May, we began rehearsing for the European tour at Shepperton studios. Prince Rupert estimated we would earn $500,000 each from the tour, a lot better than the break-even that had been talked about.

Rehearsals ran their familiar pattern; we would start sometime after 9pm and work right through until dawn. Several nights Stu ran me home in the van; it was like the old days. On 10 May, Keith met his father at Redlands. It was their first meeting in 20 years. Ten days later, he brought him along to rehearsals. Our last session was on 24 May – two days later we flew to Aberdeen for the first night of our tour.

The United Kingdom/Europe,
May–July 1982

26 May Capital Theatre, Aberdeen, Scotland
27 May Apollo Theatre, Glasgow, Scotland
28 May Green's Playhouse Theatre, Edinburgh, Scotland
31 May 100 Club, London
2, 4–5 June Feyenoord Football Stadium, Rotterdam, Holland
6–7 June Niedersachsen Stadion, Hannover, West Germany
8 June Waldbuhne, West Berlin, West Germany
11 June Olympia Stadium, Munich, West Germany
13–14 June Hippodrome D'Auteuil, Paris, France
16 June Stade Du Gerland, Lyon, France
19–20 June Ullevi, Gothenburg, Sweden
23 June St James Park, Newcastle upon Tyne, Northumberland
25–26 June Wembley Stadium, Wembley, London
27 June Ashton Gate, Bristol, Gloucestershire
29–30 June Festhalle, Frankfurt, West Germany
1 July Festhalle, Frankfurt, West Germany
3 July Praterstadion, Vienna, Austria
4–5 July Mungersdorfer Stadium, Cologne, West Germany
7, 9 July Estadio Vincente Calderon, Madrid, Spain
11–12 July Stadio Communale, Turin, Italy
15 July St Jakob Football Stadium, Basel, Switzerland
17 July Stadio San Paolo, Naples, Italy
20 July Parc Des Sports De L'Ouest, Nice, France
24 July Slane Castle, Dublin, Ireland
25 July Roundhay Park Arena, Leeds, Yorkshire

It had been six years since the Stones toured the UK and Europe and there was a huge demand for tickets. Over 35 gigs in 23 cities in 10 countries in front of 1,665,560 people – almost three times as many people as 1976. The switch to outdoor venues boosted the crowds. It was a rerun of 1981's US tour, with a virtually identical set.

Bill's diary extracts

27 May Glasgow, Scotland:
After the show went by coach to the Peebles Hydro Hotel. At 2.30am I went to the restaurant and joined Chuck and Charlie and had dinner. Some of us played pool in the games room. At 4am, Keith arrived. Everyone else left and we played until 7.30am; I beat him at every game. At 7.15am, we met Charlie wandering about the corridors of the hotel.

4 June Rotterdam, Holland:
We went onstage at 8.30pm to a crowd of 50,000. The band played great, while Hell's Angels fought in the front until Bill Graham and the security doused them with hoses.

8 June Paris, France:
After the show, we all went to dinner at the Elysée Matignon. Serge Gainsbourg joined us and began mixing cocktails from Tequila and pink Champagne. We went downstairs and joined Mick and Jerry. Roman Polanski was there too.

21 June Newcastle, England:
We went onstage at 7.30pm. The show was in the open air and it was freezing. I

Set list
'Under My Thumb'
'Twenty Flight Rock'
'Let It Bleed'
'Shattered'
'Beast Of Burden'
'Let Me Go'
'When The Whip Comes Down'
'Time Is On My Side'
'Black Limousine'
'Let's Spend The Night Together'
'Just My Imagination'
'Neighbours'
'Little T And A'
'Brown Sugar'
'You Can't Always Get What You Want'
'Tumbling Dice'
'Going To A Go-Go'
'Honky Tonk Women'
'Start Me Up'
'Miss You'
'Jumpin' Jack Flash'
'Satisfaction'

'Hang Fire', 'Sweet Little Rock', 'She's So Cold', 'Roller' and 'Chantilly Lace' were played at some shows. 'Let it Bleed' was dropped.

The Stones played 'Mona' at the 100 Club. From Madrid onwards, 'Angie' was performed most nights. At the 100 Club, in London, the Stones played to 350 people as Diz and the Doormen.

European Demands

was wrapped up in a scarf because of my bronchitis. Our breath was frosty in the air. The crew got me hot teas and brought the band buckets of hot water backstage to warm our hands after every third number. It drizzled on and off too, but the crowd were fabulous, although there were lots of fights near the front.

25 June London, England:
I went to Morton's in Berkeley Square, where I met up with Sting at noon. We attended the Music Therapy Charity lunch at the Intercontinental Hotel, London, where I accepted the life achievement award on behalf of the Stones and gave a brief speech.

3 July Vienna, Austria:
At 4pm I left by van with Bob Bender and Marlon. When we arrived at the stadium, the driver went a bit mad with kids running all over the place. He sped up and hit a guy, who ran across the road without looking. The guy looked pretty bad in the road, and we were there 20 minutes. The windscreen was smashed in, and the driver was out of his head with shock. Then ambulances arrived to look after the guy. The vans bringing Keith, Woody, Charlie and the entourage arrived, and we switched to theirs and got into the venue. Backstage, I tried taking my mind off it and played table tennis. We heard later that the fan had a fractured skull, then later still that he wasn't too bad.

12 July Turin, Italy:
At 6pm Stu called to congratulate me on the 20th Anniversary of the band — thinking I was at that first gig at the Marquee. He said that Mick Avory played the drums that day. I said that I wasn't there, and he apologised for forgetting. Ironically we did what I thought was one of the worst shows of the tour. The tempos were all wrong, and the sound was atrocious. I hated it. It was probably more like the Marquee show.

15 July Nice, France:
At 2pm I left Vence with Chuck and went to Nice Airport in the Citroën Maserati. We arrived at 2.30pm and waited by the garage for our bus. At 3.15pm we were still waiting. I called Astrid at home to see if she'd heard anything. She checked with Alan, who said that everyone was waiting for Keith.. The bus finally arrived at 3.45pm, and we all boarded the charter 707.

17 July Naples, Italy:
After the show we drove to the airport, but were delayed, as they couldn't start No 3 engine. After some hours they found that we couldn't leave, and so Bill Graham and Alan got to work trying to hire another plane. At 4am, after Bobby Keys had freaked out, a small six-seater Lear Jet arrived. Charlie was boarding with Seraphina and her friend, and we decided to let Keith, Patti and security take the three other seats. Keith argued that the band should go, so Charlie had a row with him and got off. Keith then boarded with Patti, his dad, Joe from security, Bobby Keys and his brother, and flew to Nice (so much for his thing about the band going). We decided to go back with Charlie on the second trip.

EUROPE 82

To each and every member of our team—who helped this travelling circus accomplish the seemingly impossible— our heartfelt gratitude.
THE ROLLING STONES

'Jerry was celebrating her 26th birthday and we sent her flowers. Charlie came by, and Jerry popped in to show us antique earrings that Mick had bought her. At 11.45pm, we went to a restaurant where Bill Graham's sister worked and had a party for Jerry's birthday. Keith, Woody, Peter Wolf and two others sang "Sea Of Love" to us, off-mic, and it was very good.' **BILL'S DIARY,** *2 July, Vienna*

The Wilderness Years

If Winston Churchill could have his Wilderness Years then so could the Stones. Changing attitudes and changing times meant that we needed to rethink our situation. After nearly 20 years together – an unprecedented time for a rock band – there were tensions and difficulties that needed to be resolved.

BACK IN LONDON after two months on the road, I got to work on my diaries. That morning in the *Daily Mail* they speculated that it was our last tour. I wondered if they might be right.

The band had discussed playing in Australia and the Far East. Having completed two hugely successful tours there was no reason why we couldn't go on – but you never know...

We attended a private screening of the 1981 tour film shot by Hal Ashby. The band came back to my place in Chelsea, for the first dinner party in my new home. They were joined by Robin Williams, Simon Kirk, Eric Idle, Miranda Guinness and Christopher Reeve.

Robin brought a case of Champagne and everyone was very well behaved. We later had a great laugh watching Tony Hancock videos.

August was a holiday, until Mick decided he wanted to over-dub the tour film. He told me to fly back from Vence which, for the sake of peace, I did.

Hot in West Wittering

In September, Redlands caught fire again. Keith was in America and only the housekeeper was at home – tremendous damage was caused.

In November, I met with Prince Rupert, and Russell Ash of publishers Weidenfeld and Nicolson. We discussed a book that I wanted to write on the Stones and one that Mick wanted to do.

'*Mick Jagger is at last ready to tell all in an official biography. And one writer who has been approached by the Rolling Stone is astonishingly Anthony Holden, former features editor of the* Times, *and biographer of Prince Charles.*'
EVENING STANDARD, *November 1982*

Meanwhile, Keith – who had been holidaying in Barbados with Patti – returned to London and went on to Paris, from where he called me at 5am to say that he and Patti were going to get married in the New Year. I saw him in December, when we all met up in Paris for several weeks of recording.

During the second week at Pathé Marconi we went to the Ritz hotel with Prince Rupert. We agreed to release a studio album in the summer of 1983 and discussed a compilation that would

Side one
1. 'Take the 'A' Train' (Ellington)
2. 'Under My Thumb'
3. 'Let's Spend The Night Together'
4. 'Shattered'
5. 'Twenty Flight Rock'
6. 'Going To A Go-Go'

Side two
1. 'Let Me Go'
2. 'Time Is On My Side'
3. 'Just My Imagination (Running Away With Me)'
4. 'Start Me Up'
5. 'Satisfaction'
6. 'Outro: Star Spangled Banner' (Hendrix)

Producers
The Glimmer Twins
Cover art
Kazushige Yamazaki
US No 5
UK No 4

As a live album it pales against *Get Yer Ya-Yas Out* and doesn't come close to *Love You Live*. It is best remembered as the 27th US and 23rd UK release, and not a lot else.

ROLLING STONES "STILL LIFE"

require Prince Rupert talking with Klein. A tour of Japan and the Far East in the spring of 1984 and US dates that summer were also proposed.

We had a 39th birthday dinner for Keith at the Julien Restaurant in St Denis. We finished recording the next day, and Mick and Jerry were Mustique-bound – as Mr and Mrs Vincent. Charlie and I flew home to England and Keith and Patti returned to New York.

Mick appeared in an early 1980's film of the Mikado.

'I will wear white and the ceremony will be in a church where the Stones will stage a concert for 200 guests. We'll fix a date in January – all we need is a church big enough.' PATTI HANSEN, *Heathrow airport, December, 1982*

In January, I began work with Astrid on a film project called *Digital Dreams.* It included Charlie and Shirley, actor Richard O'Brien, comedian Stanley Unwin and James Coburn. We even filmed at Patrick Moore's house in Selsey, Sussex. I missed the New York launch of *Let's Spend The Night Together* at Tavern On The Green.

The Stones regrouped at the end of January in Paris with Chris Kimsey to work on the new tracks. While recording went smoothly, outside work, my relationship with Astrid had gone downhill. Astrid had become hooked on drugs and been in rehab herself on a number of occasions, all without success. The drugs and my constant womanising had damaged our relationship to the point where we were now talking of separating permanently. We had to finish *Digital Dreams,* which meant we spent hours arguing on the telephone, me in Paris, her in London. The band finished

recording in mid-March and I returned to London to complete *Digital Dreams* and work on the soundtrack.

Within a month, Astrid and I had split for good. I tried to remember the good times during our 16 years together, rather than our difficulties.

Back to the Marquee

At the end of April, Alexis Korner, Charlie, Stu and I rehearsed at the Half Moon Pub in Putney for the Marquee's 25th anniversary. Our old mate Georgie Fame joined us along with a great horn section and we played at the Marquee on 28 and 29 April. Among the songs we performed was 'Hoochie Coochie Man'. The following day Muddy Waters died in Chicago.

I was also producing my old friend Terry Taylor's band, Sons Of Heroes, at Sol. Together

Clockwise from top, at the Marquee in April 1983: Bill, Alexis, Charlie; Stu; Alexis and Bill

Pat Andrews in January 1983, with Mark, her son by Brian Jones

with *Digital Dreams,* it took up most of the following months. Keith and Mick were in Nassau and New York, mixing and over-dubbing tracks for our next album.

Stu celebrated his 45th birthday in July and eight days later Mick was 40. I next saw the others in Paris about a month later when we all got together to sign a new recording contract with Sony Records. Combined sales of 10 million copies of *Emotional Rescue* and *Tattoo You* meant we were still a good bet.

'The Rolling Stones have just signed the biggest money deal in pop history. They will make four albums on the CBS label for a staggering £28 million. The contract was signed in Paris because of tax laws.' DAILY STAR, *27 August, 1983*

Glyn Johns involved Charlie and I in a charity concert supporting ARMS (Action for Research into Multiple Sclerosis). We played our first show at London's Royal Albert Hall on 20 September. There were various different band permutations – Eric Clapton, Steve Winwood, drummer Kenney Jones, Andy Fairweather-Low on guitar, Chris Stainton on keyboards and Ray Cooper and

Pathé Marconi sessions
In December 1982, the Stones worked on 'She Was Hot', 'Can't Find Love', 'Heartbeat', 'Cooking Up', 'Wanna Hold You' 'Keep It Cool (Pt 1 and 2)', 'Pink Pick', 'Eliza Upchink', 'Dogshit', 'Pullover', 'Stiff', 'The Golden Mile', 'Show Me A Woman', 'Mellobar', 'In Your Hand', 'Hideaway', 'Run And Take', 'Dance Mr K', 'All The Way Down', 'Munich Hilton', 'Christine', 'Christmas Issue' and 'Identification'.

'Muddy Waters was very dignified. He was funny, so charming and always listened to people.' BILL

Side one
1. 'Undercover Of The Night'
2. 'She Was Hot'
3. 'Tie You Up (The Pain Of Love)'
4. 'Wanna Hold You'
5. 'Feel On Baby'

Side two
1. 'Too Much Blood'
2. 'Pretty Beat Up'
3. 'Too Tough'
4. 'All The Way Down'
5. 'It Must Be Hell'

Studio
Pathé Marconi Paris and The Hit Factory New York

UK/US release
November 7, 1983

Composers
Jagger/Richards except Track 2 side 2 Jagger/Richards/Wood

Producer
The Glimmer Twins and Chris Kimsey (engineer)

The album was recorded between November 1982 and August 1983 and became the 28th US and 24th UK release. It made No.3 in Britain and No.4 in America. Sales of the album in America have topped a million and made it the 19th best-selling album of the band's career.

Simon Philips playing percussion. For the encore Jimmy Page, Jeff Beck and Ronnie Lane joined us. On the second night, we played for the Prince's Trust and were presented to Prince Charles and Lady Diana.

'The aristocracy of rock claimed the Albert Hall as their own last week, to present the show of a decade.' THE MAIL ON SUNDAY, *25 September, 1983*

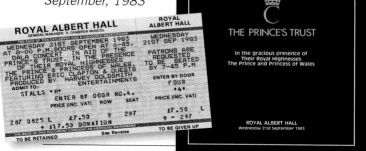

At the end of November we took the ARMS project to America, doing shows in Dallas, San Francisco, Los Angeles, and New York, where Woody joined us. Joe Cocker played with us in America, as Steve Winwood had other commitments. It was great fun to play with these guys and we felt we did a good job in raising awareness of this crippling disease.

A few weeks later, Keith and Patti got married in Cabo San Lucas, Mexico, on Keith's 40th birthday. Mick was the best man.

1984

The year started very badly when Alexis Korner died in London on New Year's Day. I was glad I had gone to see him in hospital a few weeks before he died. Without Alexis, it is arguable that there would be no Rolling Stones. He was not

'Without Alexis, it is arguable that there would be no Rolling Stones.' BILL

one of the great musicians, but was a great guy, a catalyst and an inspiration to many. In mid-January, we convened in Mexico to film a video for 'She Was Hot'. It was later banned by MTV for the scene in which, at the sight of dancer Anita Morris, all the buttons on our trousers burst.

Over lunch one day, I had the idea of collating our videos and calling the package *Rewind* so we could promote it alongside the greatest hits album of the same name. I immediately called our offices in London and New York to tell them about it. They were very enthusiastic and I developed the idea further. I shot links to go between the videos, and at the last minute Mick helped me. It proved to be very successful.

During February, I went to the Rock Awards to present a posthumous award to Alexis. It was there that I met teenager Mandy Smith – my involvement with her would kick off another Rolling Stones rollercoaster ride with the media.

Bill and Jo Wood on a videoshoot in Mexico City

Only this time, it would be me at the centre of the controversy.

Mandy and I started seeing each other regularly, keeping our relationship secret from the press, but not from the other members of the band. We went to Tramp one night with Keith and Patti and had a great time. Days later, Mick

ARMS (Action for Research into Multiple Sclerosis)

Inspiration for the ARMS project was Ronnie Lane. Ronnie had played bass with the Small Faces in the 60s, one of the era's great bands. He, along with Woody, was then in the Faces. After the Faces split he formed his own band, Slim Chance. MS forced him to virtually retire from music in the 80s. He lost his battle with the disease in 1997, a sad loss of one of the great characters.

and Jerry had their first child together. Elizabeth Scarlett was born in New York on 2 March.

Deserter songs

In late June, Mick, Charlie, Keith and I met with Prince Rupert to go over our plans, which were somewhat revised, as Mick had been working on his own solo album in Nassau for six weeks. He had, rather bizarrely, recorded with Michael Jackson and the Jacksons. Their single was released two days after our band-meeting.

In early October, the others got together in New York to talk about the new album. Keith was still annoyed with Mick for working on solo material when the Stones had committed to an album in early 1985. It almost came to blows; Charlie told me later, and Shirley confirmed, that Keith wanted to hit Mick.

I spent the rest of 1984 concentrating on my own solo project, Willie and the Poor Boys. I was working with good mates like Chris Rea, Andy Fairweather-Low and Terry Taylor.

The Paris tapes

Woody and Jo got married on 2 January, 1985, in Gerrards Cross, Buckinghamshire. Mandy and Peter Frampton came with me and there were loads of old friends, including Sabrina Guinness, Peter and Wendy Asher, Jeff Beck, Peter Cook, Ringo and Barbara Bach, Rod Stewart and Kelly Emberg. Mick didn't make it but Charlie was

there, as was Keith, who spotted John Blake, a journalist he particularly disliked.

'Ah! Mr Blake, I've got a small bone to pick with you after this photo.'
KEITH, *to John Blake*

John Blake went purple and disappeared shortly after the photos were taken. None of us liked him.

A few days later, Mick called from Paris about our upcoming sessions, and a week later his solo single, 'Just Another Night', was released and got to UK No 32. It fared much better in the US and almost made the Top 10, I was very pleased for Mick.

Two weeks later, we returned to Paris with a

Side one
1. 'Miss You'
2. 'Brown Sugar'
3. 'Undercover Of The Night'
4. 'Start Me Up'
5. 'Tumbling Dice'
6. 'Hang Fire'

Side two
1. 'It's Only Rock'n' Roll (But I Like It)'
2. 'Emotional Rescue'
3. 'Beast Of Burden'
4. 'Fool To Cry'
5. 'Waiting On A Friend'
6. 'Angie'
7. 'Doo Doo Doo Doo Doo (Heartbreaker)'

The band's 25th UK and 29th US album was largely unsuccessful in the States. American sales have since been boosted to over 500,000 by CD issues. This greatest hits package covered the period 1971 to 1984 and it made UK No 23 and US No 86.

When I'm driving in my car...

One totally non-musical result of the Stones' June 1984 meeting was the list Alan Dunn came up with when he was asked to log the band members' vehicles.

Mick Mercedes 300 SEL, Range Rover, Bentley, Ferrari Daytona, Ferrari 400L, Cadillac, Renault 16TS, Honda motorbike, BSA motorbike and Vespa bike

Keith Bentley S3, Ferrari Dino, Ferrari 400L, Jaguar E Type, Pontiac, Citroen, Jaguar XJS, Range Rover, BSA motorbike and Vespa bike

Bill Mercedes 500 SEL, Mercedes 250 CE, Ferrari 400L, Citroen Maserati, Ford Cortina, tractor and Vespa bike

Charlie Jaguar, Porsche 928, Range Rover, Citroen Maserati, Peugeot 305, horsemaster box and Vespa bike

new engineer, David Jerden. The first session was on 22 January and the first recording was, appropriately, a 12-bar blues. This was the start of a marathon set of sessions that would see us record 242 tapes over the next five months. It was a far cry from those 'three hours, cut two tracks and go and do a gig' days of 20 years earlier.

Mick and Keith were not quite at each other's throats as has been suggested by some people, but at times it was tense. Keith gave Mick the name Brenda, after he saw a book by one Brenda Jagger. It was Keith's dig at Mick for doing his own work in preference to our thing. To cap it all, Charlie went on a bender. Seraphina's 17th birthday was on 18 March, the day Keith and Patti had a baby girl, Theodora, in New York. We had taken a break from recording so Keith could be at home. Six months later Mick and Jerry had his first son: they named him James Leroy.

Woody's wedding

Live Aid

On 22 May, we spoke about the proposed Live Aid show. Due to our recording commitments we decided that we couldn't do it, which was a disappointment. Producer Steve Lillywhite, who had been with us for a while, was getting rough mixes together. While we were in Paris, Bob Geldof called me again about us doing Live Aid and even flew over to Paris to try and persuade us, but we still thought we had too much to do in the studio. Mick ended up recording 'Dancing In The Street' with David Bowie (the proceeds of which went to Live Aid) and making a video, when recording somewhat unexpectedly ended. At the last minute Mick said he would do Live Aid with our old friend Tina Turner and Woody and Keith decided to do a set with Bob Dylan. Charlie and I were both back in London and would have loved to have been there if it had worked out.

A few days after Live Aid, the marathon task of

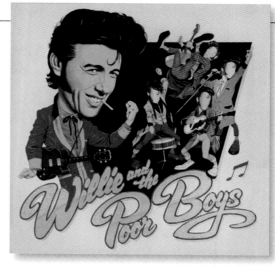

Teddy boy Bill got back to his roots with the Poor Boys, released in 1985.

mixing our album began in New York. At the end of the month I flew over to do some photos for the album. Everyone was there, except Charlie, and we all went to Mick's 42nd birthday at the Palladium. Two weeks later, the pictures of Mandy and I were in the press – it was the start of a difficult time in my life and a situation that was entirely of my own making.

Mixing continued as Mick, Keith and Steve Lillywhite worked with numerous different session players on the tracks that we had cut in Paris.

Steve Lillywhite

The Paris sessions, January – June 1985

The Stones began these sessions playing all sorts of things, mostly old songs they knew and liked, in order to inspire themselves. Bill: 'We did literally hundreds of old songs and you'll probably be amazed as to what some of them were.'

Covers

Chuck Berry: 'Betty Jean', 'Carol'
Howlin' Wolf: 'Spoonful', 'Moaning In The Moonlight'
Fats Domino: 'Blue Monday', 'I'm Ready'
The Supremes: 'Stop In The Name Of Love'
Buddy Holly: 'It's So Easy', 'True Love Ways'
Santo and Johnny: 'Sleepwalk'
The Everly Bros: 'Claudette'
Hank Williams: 'Your Cheating Heart'
Elvis Presley: 'Don't Be Cruel'
George Jones: 'Burn Your Playhouse Down'
Hoagy Carmichael: 'The Nearness Of You'
Bobby Darin: 'Splish Splash'
Elmore James: 'Dust My Broom'
Sam Cooke: 'Soothe Me'
Muddy Waters: 'Louisiana'
Ricky Nelson: 'Hello Mary Lou'
The Ventures: 'Perfidia'
The Shirelles: 'Putty In Your Hands'
The Beatles: 'Bungalow Bill'

Originals

Keith
'Had It With You'
'I Don't Wanna Hurt You?'
'I Got A Hard-on For You Baby'
'My Kind Of Rubbish'
'Baby You're Too Much For Me'
'One More From The Body' (45mins)
'Dirty Work'
'Knock Your Teeth Out One By One'
'Talk Is Cheap'
'If I Don't Have You'
'What Am I Supposed To Do'
'Why Do You Treat Me Like A Fool'
'What You Gonna Tell Your Boyfriend'

Mick
'In Love'
'The Darker Side Of Me?'
'Nobody's Perfect'
'I Need Your Love?'
'Strictly Memphis'

Woody
'Hard To Carry On?'
'Right Now'
'Golden Opportunity'

'Keith's titles give you an indication of the mood of the moment.' BILL

This way to the drum kit: Charlie shown how to get there in June 1986.

In mid-November, Charlie had his first gig with his Big Band at London's Ronnie Scott's club. It was a sign of Charlie's recovery – he was back with his beloved jazz. It was also a timely antidote to his frustrations at playing on the Paris sessions.

Stu, who had also found Paris a nightmare, was doing his own thing, as he often did between Stones work. He played piano with lots of bands, beating out that boogie rhythm and performing his beloved blues.

right not to tour. We were not in good shape as a band, the new music was far from our best. Our hearts weren't in it and nor was Mick's – and he had to front us.

Two weeks later, everyone was in London for a memorial show for Stu at the 100 Club. It was a great night and we played lots of old stuff in his honour. Cynthia, Stu's ex-wife, was there with their son Giles, along with PP Arnold, Gered Mankowitz, Glyn Johns, Chuck Leavell, Bill Graham and Kenney Jones. We were joined on stage by Simon Kirke, Jeff Beck, Eric Clapton, Jack Bruce and Pete Townshend.

award and said, 'Where's the wheels? It's got no wheels on it.' In the first week of May, we shot a video for 'One Hit To The Body' at Elstree Studios. Keith had flown in to London in time to catch Charlie's Big Band show at Ronnie Scott's club.

Mick prancing in the street with David Bowie.

A few days later I went to Keith's house in Cheyne Walk to see a rough cut. Woody was

'The man of a thousand prances.' WOODY ON MICK, *May 6, Paris*

The sixth Stone

On 11 December, Stu played with Rocket 88 at the Old Vic Tavern in Nottingham. Next evening, he went to a Harley Street specialist for a heart scan. Just after having it, he died of a heart attack in the waiting room, at the age of 47. His humour, loyalty to the band and friendship with all of us were irreplaceable.

At the end of January, Keith and Woody attended the CBS Convention in Fort Lauderdale, Florida. We then all met up in New York to shoot a video for 'Harlem Shuffle'. Keith was very anxious to tour but he and Mick were at odds over the idea.

'I ain't gahn on nah fakkin' rawd.' MICK, *on touring, according to Keith*

Two days later, Mick called me to talk about Keith and what he saw as his problems. It was all so frustrating for me sometimes. However, Mick was

Gimme Grammy

Two days later, we were at Kensington Roof Gardens to receive a Grammy Award, which Eric Clapton presented. Charlie took one look at the

there and, while we talked about many things, Keith was resigned to us not touring in the foreseeable future. I was busy on my own projects, playing at Wembley Stadium with Woody, Mac,

Video shoot in New York

Boogie With Stu

It was on 2 December, 1962, that I first met Stu at the Red Lion pub in Sutton. He was the most decent to me at my first rehearsal. In 23 years, Stu did me countless favours and made me laugh when times got rough.

The sayings of Stu could fill a book by themselves. My favourite came when he walked into a backstage area and ordered us about in front of the assembled celebrities.

'Alright, my little shower of shit, you three-chord wonders, you're on!' STU

'I said, "I always wondered why you didn't play on 'Wild Horses'?" Stu laughed and said, "I don't play minor chords. When I'm on stage with the Stones and a minor chord comes along, I lift me hands in protest." He was a boogie-woogie piano player and there was something offensive about minor chords. "Wild Horses" begins with one and he didn't bother to play it. And by the grace of that accent gave me a career! "I lift me hands in protest..."' JIM DICKINSON, *producer and session player*

Stu was our conscience. Without him, it would have been hard. All of us went to Stu's funeral; Eric Clapton and Jeff Beck were just two of the many people from the world of music who were there to honour a man that everyone liked. There was certainly nothing minor about the golf-loving, boogie-woogie playing Ian Stewart, whose bulging back pocket was always full of spanners, keys, screwdrivers and his wallet.

'Very few people realised how important he was to the Stones. He was the glue that held the whole thing together.' KEITH

'If Mick tours without this band, I'll slit his throat.' KEITH

Kenney Jones and Ronnie Lane as part of the Faces at Rod Stewart's show. Later I went to Rod's after-show party. I was refused entry, so I went to Tramp instead.

In July, Woody played with Dylan, a few days before Keith and Patti had a baby girl, Alexandra Nicole, in New York. Woody and Jo also moved back to the UK, buying a house in Wimbledon.

Less than a week later, my world was shaken to its foundations when the *News Of The World* carried a story about my relationship with Mandy, in which it revealed how old she was when we met. By this time we had actually been broken up for a few months and it appears that Mandy was put up to telling her story by some people she had met. They saw it as a way to earn some quick money. For the next three months, the papers were full of the tale, with everyone offering their 'version' of events.

I celebrated my 50th birthday in October having been in France for most of August and September. I was kept busy with my idea for a themed restaurant using my collection of Stones memorabilia. I also started talking to music journalist Ray Coleman, who had known us since the 1960s, about working on my autobiography.

Keith was in America, working with Chuck Berry as musical director on a movie called *Hail Hail Rock'n'Roll*. I gather it was a fairly nerve-wracking experience, but then being around Chuck usually was. I saw Charlie in England before he toured America at the end of the year with his Big Band.

In January 1987, Keith inducted Aretha Franklin into the Rock'n'Roll Hall Of Fame. He jammed onstage with Chuck Berry, Bo Diddley, Sting and Bruce Springsteen. Mick was at Blue Wave Studios in Barbados working on a solo

The 30th US and 26th UK album was not vintage stuff. It was an average recording created from

below-average working conditions. Its chart performance in America was boosted by 'Harlem Shuffle' (a hit for Bob and Earl in 1963), which made UK No 5 in the singles chart.

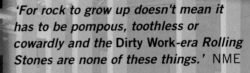

'For rock to grow up doesn't mean it has to be pompous, toothless or cowardly and the Dirty Work-era Rolling Stones are none of these things.' NME

'This album is dedicated to Ian Stewart. Thanks Stu, for 25 years of boogie-woogie.' ALBUM LINER NOTES

Side one
1. 'One Hit (To The Body)' (Jagger/Richards/Wood)
2. 'Fight' (Jagger/Richards/Wood)
3. 'Harlem Shuffle' (Relf/Nelson)
4. 'Hold Back'
5. 'Too Rude' (Roberts)

Side two
1. 'Winning Ugly'
2. 'Back To Zero'
3. 'Dirty Work' (Jagger/Richards/Wood)
4. 'Had It With You' (Jagger/Richards/Wood)
5. 'Sleep Tonight'

Studios
Jan – Jun, 1985 (Pathé Marconi, Paris)
Jul – Oct, 1985 (RPM, New York)

Composers
All tracks Jagger/Richards except where indicated

Producers
The Glimmer Twins

Associate producer
Steve Lillywhite

Engineer
David Jerden

UK/US release
UK Monday 24 Mar, 1986 Rolling Stones Records CBS 86321
US Monday 24 Mar, 1986 Rolling Stones Records CBS 86321

UK/US highest chart position (time on UK/US chart)
UK No 4 (10 weeks)
US No 4 (15 weeks)

Session musicians
Jimmy Page, Bobby Womack: guitars
Bobby Womack, Don Covay, Patti Scialfa, Tom Waits, Jimmy Cliff, Kirsty MacColl, Janice Pendarvis, Dollette McDonald: background vocals
Chuck Leavell: keyboards
Ivan Neville: bass

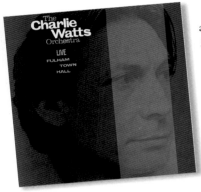

album with Dave Stewart of the Eurythmics. Mick returned to New York to mix and over-dub at Right Track Studios with Jeff Beck, keyboard player Greg Philingaines and saxophonist David Sanborn. By late March Keith, too, decided to go solo and started work on demos for an album. At Studio 900, he and Steve Jordan wrote and recorded about 40 tracks – in Keith's usual organic fashion.

Back in Britain, I worked on a project we dubbed AIMS (Ambitions, Ideas, Motivation and Success) using the Stones mobile. It was a programme designed to give young, unknown bands a chance to record. I spent a great deal of time during 1987 working on this. I also met Prince Rupert to tell him all about my restaurant idea. Woody was at home much of the time, but hosted a TV show in Italy that I put him onto.

Anyone for cricket?

I played my first charity cricket matches that summer, something from which I would derive a huge amount of pleasure over the next decade, often playing with Eric Clapton's team. Charlie was back in America working with his orchestra and probably having his best time in years.

I saw Charlie and Woody for the first time in ages when we all went to Mick's birthday party on Sunday 26 July. I was busy in my home studio working on music for Dario Argento's film *Opera*.

Keith went into the studio in Montréal to work on his solo album and two weeks after that Mick's single 'Let's Work' was released, from his *Primitive Cool* album.

Woody had an exhibition of his paintings at Katharine Hamnett's CCA Gallery in Fulham. I went along to a preview and Woody told me he was going to be touring with Bo Diddley in November.

'Ronnie's a great mixture of talent and bullshit.' KEITH

Family Affair

We hardly saw each other throughout 1988 and spoke only infrequently on the telephone. Mick called me in January, two days before he was due to attend the Rock'n'Roll Hall Of Fame ceremony to induct the Beatles. He wanted to know how I felt about touring. Keith and Mick's relationship was as strained as it had ever been and Mick was talking about his solo project. He told me that Keith was still working on his own solo album in New York.

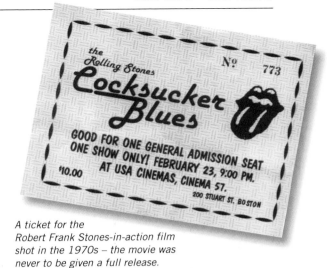

A ticket for the Robert Frank Stones-in-action film shot in the 1970s – the movie was never to be given a full release.

A FEW DAYS AFTER THE Rock'n'Roll Hall Of Fame show, Mick sang with guitarist Joe Satriani at New York's Bottom Line club. Mick was thinking about touring with Joe in Japan. Rehearsals started in February.

I was busy working on a show to support the AIMS project at the Royal Albert Hall in London and Woody agreed to appear as part of the all-star band along with Phil Collins, Kenney Jones, Ray Cooper, Simon Kirke, Eddie Grant, Jeff Beck and Chrissie Hynde. A week before the show, I went to the premiere of *Hail Hail Rock'n'Roll* in London. Chuck Berry, John Entwistle and Jeff Beck were there, but not Keith, who was in New York.

In March, Charlie called to enquire about the likelihood of touring, but it seemed like it wasn't going to happen. The same day, in Boston, *Cocksucker Blues* got a showing at the Beacon Theater. It was discreetly titled *CS Blues* and most of the really over-the-top bits were edited out.

Big in Japan

While Keith was recording in Memphis, Mick was rehearsing in New York for his Japanese tour. Woody was playing with Bo Diddley on further dates of the Gunslinger tour. By the time Mick played his first night on 15 March at the Castle Hall in Osaka, Keith had begun recording in Bermuda. He then switched to Air Studios in Montserrat.

After Mick had finished playing in Japan, he faced an American lawsuit from a musician who claimed that Mick had plagiarised a song for his solo album. Mick won the case.

On 18 May, all of us met at the Savoy Hotel in London with Prince Rupert to discuss our future. With Mick and Keith's solo activities, it was fairly easy to conclude we weren't touring for the remainder of the year. The question of what the Stones should do was kind of shelved, although we decided we might record in early 1989 and tour on the back of the resulting album.

For the next phase of Mick's solo tour, he

The Hail Hail Rock'n'Roll *premiere: guitar legend Jeff Beck, Chuck Berry, Bill and the late Who bassist John Entwistle*

began rehearsing in July before continuing in San Francisco in late August. Having finished his solo album, Keith was shooting a video for a single, 'Take It So Hard'. On 23 August, Mick and Keith met in New York to try and iron out some of their differences. With both of them about to tour, their minds were not focused on the future of the Stones.

Mick's first Australian show was a warm-up gig on 17 September in Sydney. His band was billed as the Brothers Of Sodom. Three days later he played in Brisbane,

Ron'n'Bo
Two generations of guitar heroes on the Gunslinger tour album, released in April 1988. Woody did the cover art.

Ambition, Ideas, Motivation and Success
Clockwise from top left: Eddie Grant, Terence Trent d'Arby and Woody perform at the AIMS concert at the Albert Hall. Bill gets a backstage cuddle from Ian Dury.

'If Keith Richards didn't exist, rock'n'roll would have to invent him.' CHATELAINE MAGAZINE

where the vast majority of his set was made up of Stones songs, including 'Honky Tonk Women', 'Miss You', 'Tumbling Dice', 'Ruby Tuesday', 'Gimme Shelter', 'Brown Sugar', 'It's Only Rock'n'Roll' and 'Jumpin' Jack Flash'.

Both solo albums came out in September. Mick's *Primitive Cool* album made UK No 26 and US No 41. Keith's *Talk Is Cheap* hit UK No 37 and US No 24. Although they were fairly equal in the charts, Keith's probably sold more.

Return of the human riff

Talk Is Cheap was described by *Q Magazine* as 'The swaggering return of Sir Keith Richards'. As Mick finished his tour in Indonesia and New Zealand, Keith Richards and the X-Pensive Winos hit the road. Steve Jordan, who wrote much of the album with Keith, was in the line-up and – apart from just a couple of Stones songs – the set was almost entirely Keith's solo material.

Keith's tour finished the day before his 45th birthday and he met with Mick in Barbados, firstly to make sure they had the motivation to work together and then to write songs for a new album. They flew to New York on 18 January, 1989, as the Stones were inducted into the Rock'n'Roll Hall Of Fame. Charlie and I didn't attend but Mick T and Woody joined Mick and

Keith to accept the award. There was also a band meeting in New York at which they discussed my proposal to tour but not to do the album. The answer came back that it was all or nothing which, with hindsight, was the correct thing to do.

In the second week of February, Mick called from Barbados to arrange rehearsals. I flew there on 9 March and we got together at Eddy Grant's Blue Wave studio. Eddy had been in the '60s band the Equals and had solo hits too. We rehearsed from early evening most nights, which was better than starting past midnight as we had often done in the past.

After almost two weeks, we took a break and Woody, Jo and I went to stay in Antigua at the Blue Water Beach Hotel. Mandy and I had started seeing one another again and we agreed on the phone that we should get engaged. She didn't want to wait, saying, 'Let's just get married as soon as you get back to the UK in the summer.' The only problem was that she told everyone, including her record company. Within hours, the UK media knew of our intentions and the press were heading for Montserrat. We were moving from Barbados to Montserrat to begin recording at George Martin's Air Studios on the island.

When Keith got back from New York on Friday 31 March, we met to discuss how to deal with the press. It was decided that I should fly to

Antigua to head them off. I spent 1 and 2 April doing just that, before getting back to Montserrat.

We recorded until 2 May, when I went back to London to organise my wedding to Mandy – 2 June was set as the date. Luckily, Karen Kearne, who had worked for me for about seven years, was there to ensure all the planning ran smoothly. She had also been working on the 9 May opening of my restaurant, Sticky Fingers. At the same time, we started to mix the new album at the Stones' old stomping ground, Olympic Studios. At the end of May, Keith

Howzat!

Bill's love of cricket got him involved with Eric Clapton's team and later he had his own 'charity cricket team'. Raising lots of money for good causes was a bonus as the games were always good fun and involved others from the world of music, sport and entertainment. At a match at the Oval, Bill bowled a 'hat trick', dismissing three people in three balls. It was shown on TV and was the first televised hat trick at the Oval.

Bill and Mandy on their wedding day and, right, at the blessing four days later with Jo Wood, Shirley Watts, Patti Hansen (without hat), Jerry Hall, Keith, Woody, Mick and Charlie

was presented with a Living Legend award – an entirely appropriate honour – at the International Rock Awards in New York.

Prelude and Feud

Mandy and I were married at a registry office and had our wedding breakfast in Bury St Edmunds. That night we appeared on Terry Wogan's show.

'If I'd known getting married was this easy, I'd have done it long ago. This is the first time I've worn a suit in 25 years. I feel like George Raft.' BILL, *to Terry Wogan*

Four days later we had a blessing in London. All the Stones came. It was a long time since a social occasion had brought us together. I certainly

The Steel Wheels start rolling in New York, at a Grand Central Station press conference.

appreciated it. Two days later, Mandy and I left for our honeymoon in Vence, which was a nightmare. Woody and Jo were also in France as we were promoting the upcoming tour. To be honest, it was something of a lifesaver having Woody around.

On 9 July, I joined the other Stones in New York and two days later we all went on a train to Grand Central Station for a press conference to announce the Steels Wheels tour. It was our first tour of America in eight years, the longest gap in our careers. The following day we drove

to Southbury, Connecticut, where we would spend the next month rehearsing. The secret location was a private girls' school called Wykeham Rise. As rehearsals concluded, we shot a video for 'Mixed Emotions' in the rehearsal room. It was to be the first single from the new album.

We played a warm-up gig on 12 August at Toad's Place, in Newhaven, Connecticut. We spent an hour going through some of our new numbers as well as our old standards in front of 700 people. The following day we went to Garden City, where we were to spend the next couple of weeks rehearsing and doing the technical run-through at the Nassau Coliseum. When Charlie and I arrived, Mick was already there and we were all amazed at the enormous Steel Wheels stage.

At Wykeham Rise: Bill's two bass guitars are front left

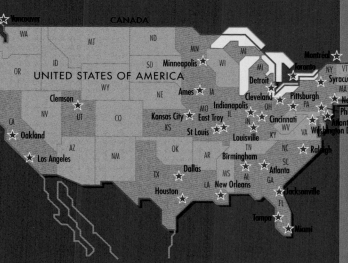

UNITED STATES OF AMERICA
CANADA

It was massive. The set, the money, the touring party, the merchandise, the sponsorship deal and the set list took the Stones to another level. At the end of 1989, *Variety* magazine reported that the band had secured 10 per cent of every dollar spent on seeing rock shows in the US.

In all, the Stones played to 3,010,094 people, grossing $98 million for performing the two-hour show. Sales of merchandise and TV and radio deals took the band's gross to £125 million for around five months' work. Ticket prices were $30 plus, and the tour programme cost $14.

Rolling Stone magazine said 'Steel Wheels Spawns New Deals' – and it certainly did. Budweiser paid £3.7 million for the exclusive rights to sponsor the tour. As part of the deal, the Stones had to do a 'meet and greet' for various VIPs backstage before the shows.

While the gross was high, the costs of keeping this massive tour on the road were enormous.

'In Philadelphia, Living Colour opened for us. We went on at 9.30pm in front of 55,000 people. Photographers, including Richard Young and Dave Bennett, were in the front for the first four songs. We played "Start Me Up", "Bitch", and "Shattered", during which, Keith came over to me and asked, "Everything alright?" I replied "Yeah!". Then there was a complete power failure of the amps, stage lights and monitors. We went off the stage. We returned 10 minutes later to complete the set.' BILL

Set list

At the opening show of the tour in Philadelphia, the band played:
'Start Me Up'
'Bitch'
'Shattered'
'Sad Sad Sad'
'Undercover Of The Night'
'Harlem Shuffle'
'Tumbling Dice'
'Miss You'
'Ruby Tuesday'
'Play With Fire'
'Dead Flowers'
'One Hit To The Body'
'Mixed Emotions'
'Honky Tonk Women'
'Rock And A Hard Place'
'Midnight Rambler'
'You Can't Always Get What You Want'
'Little Red Rooster'
'Before They Make Me Run'
'Happy'
'Paint It, Black'
'2000 Light Years From Home'
'Sympathy For The Devil'
'Gimme Shelter'
'It's Only Rock'n'Roll'
'Brown Sugar'

'Satisfaction'
'Jumpin' Jack Flash' (encore)
The set remained largely unchanged throughout the tour, but 'Shattered' was dropped after the first night.

With Matt Clifford on keyboards, it was the most tightly choreographed of any Stones tour to that point.

Steel Wheels

1989

Reportage...

After three decades it was amazing that the headline writers could come up with some new angles. Even *The Times* in London proclaimed, 'They are all older than the vice-president of the United States.'

'Mick Jogger! He Even Runs Three Miles Backwards To Get In Shape For US Tour.' PIERS MORGAN, *in the Sun*, 31 August, 1989

'Rolling Back The Years. Wrinklies Are A Wow.' PIERS MORGAN, *in the Sun*, 2 September, 1989

'Rock Rolls On: Ageing Stars Strut Their Staying Power.' TIME MAGAZINE, 4 September, 1989

'It's Only Rock And Roll – But They Like It.' PITTSBURGH POST-GAZETTE, 7 September, 1989

'Lock Up Your Grandmothers! Ooh-Er, Missus... It's The Rolling Stones!' Q MAGAZINE, October 1989

'Stones. Never Too Old To Rock And Roll.' NEW YORK NEWSDAY, 11 October, 1989

'What'll They Do With All That Money?' FORBES, October 1989

'Still Devilish After All These Years.' SAN FRANCISCO CHRONICLE, 4 November, 1989

'Time Is On Their Side.' MONTREAL GAZETTE, 13 December, 1989

'Their Rockin' Uncorrupted By Money Or Age.' PEOPLE MAGAZINE, 18 December, 1989

Additional Musicians

Bobby Keys: saxophone
Chuck Leavell: keyboards
Matt Clifford: keyboards
Lisa Fischer: backing vocals
Bernard Fowler: backing vocals
Cindi Mizelle: backing vocals
The Uptown Horns
Arno Hecht: tenor saxophone
Bob Funk: trombone
Crispin Cioe: alto saxophone
Paul Littereal: trumpet

Stage set or cityscape

Mark Fisher's apocalyptic vision of urban decay was the inspiration for the Steel Wheels Tour set design, which in turn was inspired by the writing of William Gibson. The huge construction was the largest touring stage ever built. It took 80 trucks to move it from city to city and needed a crew of 200 people to build it, along with 150 hired hands at each location. Patrick Woodroffe's lighting added immeasurably to the overall effect of Mark Fisher's vision.

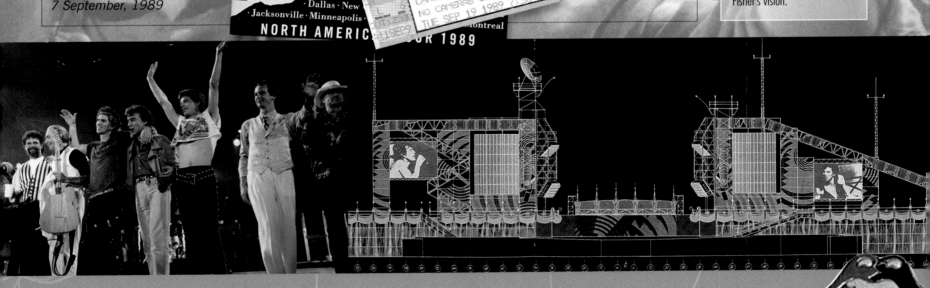

'All this vast amount of money is generated by sitting down with this little wooden instrument.'

KEITH, *January 1990*

1. 'Sad Sad Sad'
2. 'Mixed Emotions'
3. 'Terrifying'
4. 'Hold On To Your Hat'
5. 'Hearts For Sale'
6. 'Blinded By Love'
7. 'Rock And A Hard Place'
8. 'Can't Be Seen'
9. 'Almost Hear You Sigh' (Jagger/Jordan/Richards)
10. 'Continental Drift'
11. 'Break The Spell'
12. 'Slipping Away'

Studios
Air Studios, Montserrat
Olympic Studios, London
Composers
All tracks Jagger/Richards except where indicated
Producers
The Glimmer Twins and Chris Kimsey
Engineer
Christopher Marc Potter
Design
Karl Hyde and Rick Smith
UK/US release
29 September, 1989
CBS 465752 1
UK/US highest chart position (time on UK/US chart)
US No 3
UK No 2
Additional personnel
Phil Beer: fiddle, mandolin
Simon Clarke, Tim Sanders and Paul Spong: brass
Roddy Corimer: trumpet, brass
Kick Horns: horn, brass
Matt Clifford: keyboards, piano and clavinet
Bernard Fowler, Sarah Dash and Lisa Fisher: background vocals
Luis Jardim: percussion
Chuck Leavell: organ, piano, keyboards

A lot was riding on the band's 30th American and 26th UK release, not least a tour. It did the job and while it is not a classic Stones album it did generate good sales and get radio airplay. 'Mixed Emotions', 'Rock And A Hard Place' and 'Almost Hear You Sigh' were all released as singles. In the US, sales of *Steel Wheels* have topped the two million mark, making it the eighth best-selling album of the band's career.

Mick and Keith, along with Woody, made a trip to Morocco to record the Master Musicians of Joujouka that Brian had recorded back in the late 1960s. They used them on the track that Mick wrote, 'Continental Drift'.

'Steel Wheels is a self-styled reunion album. It often feels as if they sat down and decided exactly what their audience wanted from a Stones album, and they deliver a record that gives the people what they want.'
ALL MUSIC GUIDE

Mixed Emotions
The Rolling Stones
Fancy Man Blues

Released
Thursday 17 August, 1989
Highest UK/US chart positions (time on chart)
UK No 36 (5 weeks)
US No 5 (12 weeks)

Rolling in money
These six limited edition solid silver coins of the Stones were issued in a presentation box to coincide with the release of *Steel Wheels*.

Wheels Of Steel

Apart from a more programmed feel to our music on the Steel Wheels Tour, the other major change was that we regularly soundchecked before gigs. It meant that we were often at the stadium for longer and backstage took on the appearance of a Bedouin encampment – albeit an upmarket one – with all the trailers and portable buildings. There were loads of guests, along with wives, girlfriends, friends and families. Mandy was having treatment at a clinic for her allergy problems, which meant I spent most of the time alone on tour.

A Japanese plaque to mark Steel Wheels, dated February 1989.

AS USUAL, CANADA proved difficult for Keith. The customs people gave his bags an intensive search, and they confiscated a small knife.

The officer told Keith that he would give him a receipt for the knife. Keith said, 'Does that mean that I can collect it when I leave the country?' The officer replied in the negative. Keith said, 'Then why the receipt, man? Have it on me. It's a gift!'

It was a gruelling tour and at times relationships were strained. There were arguments over the upcoming European tour and we were angry that others seemed to be making too much money out of our activities. While there was nothing new in that, it was the size of the percentages that annoyed us. In truth, we had probably been ripped off far worse in the past. It was just that we were much more aware of the business side

of the band than we ever had been.

In Washington, we had a meeting with Prince Rupert and Keith got really angry when we were told the budget for our

Bill on the tour plane, and backstage with Johnny Johnson

next video was $450,000. Things really were out of all proportion.

I was also having an increasing amount of bad press about Mandy and me being apart. The newspapers, starved of the truth, made up stories.

'Bill Wyman and his teenage wife Mandy Smith have been reunited for the first time in months and appear to be making up lost time in passionate style. Mrs Wyman looks glowing and glorious. Mr Wyman looks

absolutely exhausted. He's sent someone from the hotel out to buy him a bottle of super vitamins.' NEWSPAPER REPORT

Mandy never came to the US throughout the whole tour. Stephen and my Mum and Dad flew into New York for my birthday and came to the show. Afterwards, the rest of the band had organised and paid for a party, to cheer me up. It was a lovely gesture.

Dad had not been very well and it was great that he was able to be there. However, soon after, he was admitted to hospital.

Sadness in Japan

After the tour, we returned home for Christmas, before our thoughts turned to the Japanese leg of the Steel Wheels Tour. I delayed my departure from Vence to Tokyo when my Dad took a turn for the worse in early February 1990. My Mum told me that she was expecting the worst, which made it very difficult

A life in pictures
Bill helped with the publication of a book of Michael Cooper's photographs, launched at Earl McGrath's gallery in LA, with Woody, Eric Clapton and Graham Nash. Michael committed suicide in 1973. Bill: 'Some of the 70,000 pictures he took grace this book. They are a wonderful insider's look at our early days.'

'If this is a social call and you're here on vacation, that's fine. If you're here to discuss how much money you're going to dredge from the European tour next year, then you can fuck off.' **KEITH,** *to a Stones finance man*

for me to leave to work with the band. After arriving in Japan, on 12 February, I called several times each day to find out how Dad was. He did rally slightly, but he died on 20 February. With the time change, I heard at 7am Tokyo time and that night I had to play a show, which was tough. During the day, people from the tour called and came by to offer me support. Arnold and Alan Dunn were, as usual, very supportive, as was Charlie. Mick wrote me a very nice letter.

We decided as a family to postpone the funeral until I got home from Japan. In the following months, I not only had to deal with my Dad's death but also the continuing worries over Mandy's health. Our relationship was virtually non-existent as she was at the clinic and any time I got to spend with her, we were always in the company of others. It wasn't going to get any easier with the start of our European tour in May. We rehearsed for about 10 days at the Château de Dangu, near Paris, before we played our first European show in almost eight years. It was in Rotterdam in front of a crowd of 47,000 people.

The band's first Japanese tour – really 10 nights in the same place – was one of their shortest ever and certainly the most lucrative of their career. The shows were seen by 500,000 people and grossed around £20 million from ticket sales and merchandising. The tour was sponsored by a brand which sounded distinctly odd to Western ears – Pocari Sweat, one of Japan's leading soft drinks.

A ticket was 10,000 yen, which was about $70.

'"I run seven miles a day, I lift weights and play team games. I do a lot of boring exercises and lay off the goodies," says Mick. How times change. I remember the days when the closest "Jumpin' Jack Flash" got to off-stage exercise was rolling a joint.' ROSS BENSON, *Daily Express, 23 February, 1990*

The Pacific *February 1990*

14 February Korakuen Dome, Tokyo, Japan
16 February Korakuen Dome, Tokyo, Japan
17 February Korakuen Dome, Tokyo, Japan
19 February Korakuen Dome, Tokyo, Japan
20 February Korakuen Dome, Tokyo, Japan
21 February Korakuen Dome, Tokyo, Japan
23 February Korakuen Dome, Tokyo, Japan
24 February Korakuen Dome, Tokyo, Japan
26 February Korakuen Dome, Tokyo, Japan
27 February Korakuen Dome, Tokyo, Japan

JAPAN
Tokyo

Additional backing musicians were the same as for the US Steel Wheels Tour and the set was retained.

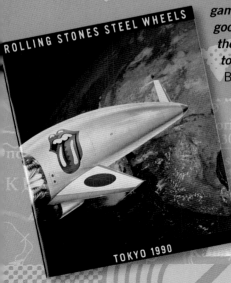

Steel Wheels, Tokyo

A total of 2,429,00 people watched the Stones on their Urban Jungle tour of Europe, paying around £50 million in all. The Stones were accused of short-changing their fans by using a cut-down version of the US Steel Wheels set, but the truth was the European stadiums were generally smaller venues. The full set was used in the Wembley shows.

Urban Chaos?

The $40 million Urban Jungle stage set was based on 'an industrial folly, corroding in a fluorescent jungle of mutant foliage … populated by a band of musicians, Honky Tonk Women and a pack of wild dogs.' Mark Fisher and Jonathan Park designed the 236-foot wide, 82-foot high set. A 300-foot wide wall of flame leapt up as the band kicked off with of 'Start Me Up'.

The lighting rig contained 62 VariLites, six giant light pods and 16 man-operated follow spots. Fireworks costing £30,000 were used in the finale each night. There were 287 in the crew, including 85 drivers, 23 catering staff, 46 stagehands, 14 carpenters, 12 lighting engineers and 15 video camera operators. Each day, 750 meals were eaten. Sixty-four trucks and 10 buses were used, with two stages on the road; one in use and the other under construction. Setting up took four days.

'There's enough cable used to stretch the length of the Amazon and the lighting system, when used to the full capacity, is equal to the power requirement of 300 average Hungarian villages or three or four Midlands suburbs.' MICHAEL AHERN, *production co-ordinator*

Set list

Wembley Stadium, August 25, 1990, Bill's last gig with the Stones:

'Start Me Up'
'Sad Sad Sad'
'Harlem Shuffle'
'Tumbling Dice'
'Miss You'
'Ruby Tuesday'
'Angie'
'Rock And A Hard Place'
'Mixed Emotions'
'Honky Tonk Women'
'Midnight Rambler'
'You Can't Always Get What You Want'
'Before They Make Me Run'
'Happy/Paint It, Black'
'2000 Light Years From Home'
'Sympathy For The Devil'
'Street Fighting Man'
'Gimme Shelter'
'It's Only Rock'n'Roll'
'Brown Sugar'
'Jumpin' Jack Flash'
'Satisfaction'

The United Kingdom/Europe,
May–August 1990

18–19, 21 May Feyenoord Stadium, Rotterdam, Holland

23–24 May Niedersachsenstadion, Hannover, Germany

26 – 27 May Wald Stadium, Frankfurt, Germany

30–31 May Mungersdorfer, Cologne, Germany

2–3 June Olympiastadion, Munich, Germany

6 June Berlin, West Germany

10 June Alvalade Stadium, Lisbon, Portugal

13–14 June Olympic Stadium, Barcelona, Spain

16 – 17 June Calderon, Madrid, Spain

20 June Velodrom, Marseille, France

2 –23, 25 June Parc Des Princes, Paris, France

27 June St Jakob Stadium, Basel, Switzerland

4, 6–7 July Wembley Stadium, London, England

9 July Hampden Park, Glasgow, Scotland

16 July Arms Park, Cardiff, Wales

18 July St James Park, Newcastle upon Tyne, England

20–21 July Maine Road Stadium, Manchester, England

25–27 July Stadio Flaminio, Rome, Italy

28 July Stadio Delle Alpi, Turin, Italy

31 July Praterstadion, Vienna, Austria

3–4 August Eriksberg Sannegarsorton, Gothenburg, Sweden

6–7 August Valle Hovin Stadion, Oslo, Norway

9 August Idretspark, Copenhagen, Denmark

13–14 August Weissensee, East Berlin, Germany

16 August Parkstadion, Gelsenkirchen, Germany

18 August Straiiov, Prague, Czechoslovakia

24–25 August Wembley Stadium, London, England

Support bands

Gun and The Dan Reed Network

Urban Jungle

What the papers said...

Among the hundreds of thousands of words written about the Stones on this tour, there were some gems. The Rolling Stones were generating such vast amounts of money that the financial press took an interest: 'What made all the critics who write off the Stones as boring old tarts look petty, was the enthusiasm which the middle-aged millionaires put into the performance,' said the *Financial Times*.

'Wembley Council banned the Stones' spectacular fireworks display – because of a dead parrot. It died four years ago after the noise from a display gave it a heart attack.' DAILY STAR, *4 July, 1990*

'While you can't always get what you want from a rock band, with the Rolling Stones you just might find you get what you need.' DAILY MIRROR, *6 July, 1990*

'The Rolling Stones are still the best Rolling Stones-type band in the world.' CHARLES SHAAR MURRAY, DAILY TELEGRAPH, *6 July, 1990*

The stage set at Edwin Shirley Trucking's base near West Ham in London

'You can't analyse us too much. At the end of the day, whatever intellectual gloss you put on it, we are still just the Rolling Stones.' MICK, *4 July, 1990*

'Keith Richards is having the time of his life as he celebrates being the first – and most unlikely – rock guitarist to achieve immortality.' THE FINANCIAL TIMES

In the middle of the tour, a gig at Cardiff and two at Wembley had to be postponed because Keith had cut himself and his finger had gone septic. This was the first time Keith had missed a show in his career. The Human Riff proved that, while he may be immortal, he is still human.

'The Rolling Stones will shoot part of their current European tour for super format IMAX, which exhibits in special theaters on screens that run as high as eight stories. The Rolling Stone/IMAX film will include concerts from East Berlin on 13–14 August and the Wembley Stadium dates in London on 24–25 August. The screens measure up to 90 feet by 70 feet, and state-of-the-art, six-channel sound systems are the norm. The 65mm IMAX film yields images 10 times larger than the 35mm images seen in regular theatres.' HOLLYWOOD REPORTER MAGAZINE, *3 August, 1990*

Bouncing Czechs

One newspaper carried a story that Czech President Vaclav Havel had donated £25,000 of his own money towards production costs for the Stones Prague concert. Not true – but a wildly enthusiastic audience of 107,000 attended the gig. It was the first major rock'n'roll event since the country's Communist rule was ousted six months previously. People paid the equivalent of $10 for tickets, about eight per cent of the average monthly wage.

Pavel Prusa, 20, an electrical engineering student, spoke for many: 'The Stones coming to Prague is our revolution. It is a symbolic gesture for young people like myself who, before, had very little to live for.'

'I came prepared to bury them, but what do you do when the corpse kicks off the coffin lid and insists on dancing on the grave?' **EVENING STANDARD,** *5 July, 1990*

Still Rolling

I cannot say that the Steel Wheels and Urban Jungle tours were my favourite periods with the Stones. My dad's death, my relationship with Mandy and my problems took their toll. Everyone, from the band to the road crew, was very supportive throughout and we had some good laughs. During one gig, the road crew got together to hire me a strip-o-gram – she did it in the middle of the show, but under the stage where only I could see her. Everybody said to me afterwards they wanted to see if I'd move to get a better view.

JUST BEFORE OUR LAST Wembley shows, a copy of the £30 cheque we were paid for our 1963 show at the Richmond Jazz and Blues Festival went up for auction at Sothebys. It sold for £3,000.

Nearly 28 years earlier, one of my first gigs with the Stones had been just down the road from Wembley Stadium at the Ealing Club. The synchronicity of it all was plain to see.

With the tour over, it gave me time to try to resolve the impasse with Mandy. Our relationship had reached rock bottom. Throughout the three legs of the tour and in between, I had been working on my autobiography, *Stone Alone*, with Ray Coleman. It came out in October 1990. In the middle of a book signing tour around Britain, I told Mandy that our marriage was over – it had been a disaster from the word go.

A change has come
A week or so later, Woody was involved in an accident. He got out to direct the traffic. He was then hit by another car. He broke both legs. In true Woody fashion, as he lay there in pain, he asked a policeman for a smoke! On a happier note, Mick and Jerry got married in Bali in an Indonesian ceremony.

In January 1991, the Stones were back in the recording studio and I was there too. We worked with Chris Kimsey at the Hit Factory in London for a week on several new songs. Shortly after, rumours began appearing in the press about my leaving the Stones and this time they were correct. At the band's next business meeting we discussed our future plans, but the thought of more recording and touring didn't appeal to me any longer. The events of the last few years had convinced me that there were other things I wanted and needed to do. I had to first get my personal life in order and then I wanted to explore other creative ideas. I know that it may be difficult for many of you to see it the way I do, but playing with the Stones was my job. It was my career and, as with many people, a job is not necessarily for life. I'd been with the Stones for over half

Karen Kearne-Moxey and Bill at a signing

my life and it was time for a change.

Naturally, there was debate about my leaving. I think Keith and Mick thought I would 'come to my senses', whereas Charlie could more easily see my point of view. As there was nothing really happening on the Stones front that required anything to be said, we made no announcement. Everyone kept busy on their solo projects. Charlie recorded with his quintet, Mick was filming the movie *Freejack* and Keith recorded with John Lee Hooker and wrote with Tom Waits. He also starred at the Guitar Legends show in Seville. In November 1991, the other Stones signed a new record deal with Richard Branson's Virgin label, my name was on the contract but I never signed the deal.

Far from alone

On 12 January 1992, Mick and Jerry had their second baby girl, Georgia May. I was recording more solo material and enjoying having a life back. I even got back on stage with Terry Taylor and some other old mates, including Andy Fairweather-Low and Gary Brooker, for a short tour of Sweden as Willie and the Poor Boys. It was

Mick starred in
the sci-fi film *Freejack*.

excellent therapy. In November, Charlie and Mick came over to my flat to give me one last chance to change my mind and stay in the band. I told them I was determined and happy with what I was doing. Throughout the summer I had continued to play cricket and in September I had invited my old girl friend Suzanne Accosta to come and stay. The spark was still there between us.

Three days later I asked her to marry me, but

she wanted time to think it over. She told me a couple of weeks later that she would, as I promised her that I would change my ways. My womanising days were over – I was to be a one-woman man.

Suzanne and I were planning a Christmas at Gedding and I was thinking about when I was going to make a public statement about my retirement from the Stones. I finally chose to do it in early January 1993. I announced it on the TV show *London Tonight* with Matthew Lorenzo. The press carried the story over the next two days and I think the Daily Telegraph said it best: 'Stones To Roll Without Wyman'. Ten days later, Suzanne and I officially got engaged at Gedding and two months after that we went to dinner with writer Ian La Frenais and his wife Doris. Mick and Jerry were there, along with George and Olivia Harrison, Lenny Henry and Dawn French. We didn't talk about the Stones once; it was a great dinner party.

Suzanne and I got married on 21 April, 1993, in Vence and for the first time in a long while I felt really settled. Since then we have had three lovely girls together and my life is complete. And guess what… the Stones are still rolling.

Left, *Suzanne,
Katie, Bill and Jessica at the
launch of* Bill Wyman's Blues Odyssey
*at Sticky Fingers, October 2001, and,
above, Bill with Matilda*

THE REAL ROCK'N'ROLL CIRCUS

'Once I left the Stones, the tours got even longer...'

The view from out front

I saw the Stones at Wembley in July 1995 and went backstage and chatted with the crew, many of whom I knew from previous tours. Mick, Ronnie, Keith and Charlie introduced me to new bassist Darryl Jones and we talked about playing bass with the band. I watched the Stones from the Royal Box, the first time I had ever seen them play... and I really rather liked it. I went backstage again for a while with Suzanne and Katie, my youngest daughter.

Voodoo Lounge

The *Voodoo Lounge* album came out in July 1994. Produced by Don Was and the Glimmer Twins, it attempts to get the Stones back on the rock track, with mixed success. The 15 Mick and Keith originals yielded three singles, 'You Got Me Rocking', 'Out Of Tears' and 'Love Is Strong'.

The new Stones line-up with Darryl Jones, far right, on bass

ROLLING STONES
VOODOO LOUNGE
WORLD TOUR 1994/95

THE ROLLING STONES
STRIPPED

ROLLING STONES
WORLD TOUR 94/95
VOODOO LOUNGE

VIP

7/29

Stripped
Stripped, an 'unplugged' album of live performances, came out in 1995.

ABKCO
and
The Rolling Stones
invite you to
a private screening of

THE
ROLLING STONES
ROCK AND ROLL
CIRCUS

a special event
of the 34th new york film festival

saturday,
october 12, 1996 • 8pm

the walter reade theater
165 west 65th street
plaza level

rsvp: lisa b. cohen
phone: 212-626-2735
fax: 212-626-2799

The tour kicked off on 1 August, 1994, in Washington DC and the US leg continued to 18 December. On 14 January, 1995, the next phase began in Mexico City and after running

through South America they then played South Africa in February, Japan in March, Australia and New Zealand in April. The European leg ran from June to August, starting in Stockholm and finishing in Rotterdam.

Bridges to Babylon Tour

The 108 shows of the 1997/1998 Bridges to Babylon Tour were seen by around 4.6 million people around the world. It visited 25 countries and there were over 60 different songs played during the tour. 'Jumpin' Jack Flash', 'Brown Sugar', 'Honky Tonk Women', 'Tumbling Dice', 'Satisfaction', 'Sympathy For The Devil', 'Little Queenie', 'Gimme Shelter' and 'Start Me Up' were some of those that were played at every show.

Bridges to Babylon

The album came out in September 1997. The 13 tracks again demonstrate the latter day dynamic between Mick and Keith of dance vs guitars.

The Rolling Stones tribute band, The Counterfeit Stones, aped their heroes on a UK tour of small venues, calling it The Flyovers to Basildon Tour.

'Another tour, another live album' is how *All Music Guide* described the *No Security* album. The tour ran through the first three months of 1999, beginning in Oakland in January, to support the live album that came out in November 1998.

Right, *cartoonists are still stimulated by the Stones and, below, a ticket for Bill's Rhythm Kings show in Minnesota in 2001.*

TO Bill Wyman with Best Regards   JEFF STAHLER '97

TWO FOR THE 'STONES'

THE ROLLING STONES BRIDGES TO BABYLON WORLD TOUR 1997/98

NORTHWEST AIRLINES
MUSIC IN THE ZOO
MINNESOTA ZOO AMPHITHEATER
BILL WYMAN
** RAIN OR SHINE **
MON AUG 20, 2001 7:30 P

'Until the next time...'

'By the year 2000, the Rolling Stones will seem to have been as cuddly as teddy bears.'

PETER BLAKE, *artist, in 1963*

MICK AND PETER BOTH RECEIVED KNIGHTHOODS IN HER MAJESTY THE QUEEN'S BIRTHDAY HONOURS LIST OF JUNE 2002.

Index

Picture Credits

All Rolling Stones Records covers appear courtesy of PROMATONE
All Decca/London Records covers appear courtesy of ABKCO Music Inc.
The Rolling Stones tongue logo is a registered trade mark of Musidor
Rolling Stone magazine covers are reproduced by kind permission of Rolling Stone Magazine/Wenner Media LLC

Every effort has been made to trace copyright holders. Dorling Kindersley apologises for any unintentional omissions, and would be pleased, if any such case should arise, to add an appropriate acknowledgement in future editions.

top (t) left (l) right (r) below (b) centre (c) above (a) background (bg) insert (i) montage (m)

The publisher would like to thank the following for their kind permission to reproduce their photographs:
AA: Advertising Archives, **AD:** Alan Davidson, **ADay:** Allan Day, **AH:** Andrew Heritage, **AP:** Associated Press, **ATB:** After the Battle, **AV:** Axel Vandewalle, **BBC:** BBC Picture Archives, **BF:** Barry Feinstein, **BFI:** British Film Institute, **BG:** Courtesy of The Gazette Blackpool, **BO:** Bill Owens, **BON:** Bonhams Photo Library London, **BP:** Barry Plummer, **BS:** Barry Sage, **BT:** Bob Thall, **BWA:** Bill Wyman Archive, **CA:** Curt E Angeledes, **CEA:** Chansley Entertainment Archives, **CG:** Claude Gassian, **CH:** Cheltenham 21 Tram Group/Colin Martin, **CI:** ©Christie's Images Ltd, **CO:** Corbis, **CP:** Camera Press, **DK:** Dorling Kindersley Picture Library, **DK/BWA:** Dorling Kindersley/Trish Gant/Bill Wyman Archive, **DK/CE:** Dorling Kindersley-from the Chris Eborn private collection, **DM:** ©David Montgomery, **DT:** Dominique Tarlé, **EA:** Eugene Aderbari, **ER:** Ethan Russell, **GC:** Gus Coral, **GD:** George Dibble III, **GI:** Getty Images, **GM:** photograph by Gered Mankowitz ©Bowstir Ltd 2002, **GW:** Guy Webster, **HG:** Hulton Archive/Getty Images, **HN:** Historic Newspapers, **IS:** Ian Stewart, **IWM:** Imperial War Museum, **JC:** Jack Crampton, **JH:** John Havers, **JM:** Joe McMichael, **JR:** John Roberts, **KA:** Katz Pictures, **KAL:** Kent Arts & Libraries, **KOB:** Kobal Collection, **LFI:** London Features International, **MB:** Mike Berry, **MC:** Michael Charity, **MCC:** Michael Cooper Collection c/o Adam Coopertsafc@publi.com.a, **MH:** Michael Heeg, **MJ:** ©Michael Joseph from the Raj Prem Collection, **MK:** The Murray the K Archives, **MM:** Mark Makin, **MMD:** Mary McCartney Donald, **MP:** Mike Peters, **MPX:** Mirrorpix.com, **MS:** Mary Synder, **NMM:** National Motor Museum, Beaulieu, **NFA:** Not Fade Away; **PC:** Private Collection/PS, **PH:** Pati Habermann/KoolKatz, **PM:** Peter Moody, **POP:** Popperfoto, **PP:** Pictorial Press Ltd, **PS:** Pauline Smith, **PW:** Peter Whitehead/Hathor Publishing, **RE:** Richard Evans, **RED:** Redferns Music Picture Library, **RET:** Retna Pictures Ltd, **REX:** Rex Features, **RGA:** Ronald Grant Archive, **RH:** Richard Havers, **RR:** Roy Rogers & Dale Evans Museum, **RS:** Richard Sterling, **SC:** The Simpson Collection, **SF:** Stewart Family/Out-Take, **SMA:** Showtime Music Archives (Toronto), **SPL:** Courtesy of Sotheby's Picture Library London, **STAR:** Star File, Inc., **TM:** Trinifold Management, **TON:** Terry O'Neil, **TP:** Topham Picturepoint, **TR:** Tony Rivers, **TT:** Top Topham, **V&A:** Courtesy of the Trustees of the V&A, V&A photo library, **VC:** Victoria Clark, **VM:** Vin Mag Archive

AA: 168tl; **AD:** 487tr; **ADay:** 442tcr, 451c, 451cl, 451cr, 455tl, 471ccr, 499tr, 501clb; **AH:** 423br; **AP:** 354c, 354tl, 354tr, 372b; **ATB:** 15br; **AV:** 63cal, 63car; **BBC:** 22tr; **BF:** 315r; **BFI:** Universal Publishing 265tr; **BG:** 144tl, 45bl, 145clb; **BO:** 350, 351, 352bbg, 352tl, 353bbg, 353bcr, 353cl, 353t, 354-355bg, 354tl; **BON:** 40bc; **BP:** 441bcr; **BS:** 448tr, 449bl, 449cl, 449cla, 449clb, 449tl; **BT:** 128tl; **BWA:** ©David Browne: 63cb, 63cb, 63lbg; ©George Chin: 494cl; ©Pierre Fouriuer: 151tr; Genesis Publications: 491br; ©Jean Louis Rancol: 151cb; ©Klaus Schmalenbach: 202b-all, 207bl; ©Dave Thompson: 158b-all, 191cal, 191cbl, 191tl; ©Philip Townsend: 42-43, 55tl; Town & Country: 239bl; **CA:** 432cb, 498br, 498cr, 499c, 501br; **CEA:** Frank Driggs Collection: 368bl; John Rockwood: 400br; Ray Flerlage: 129trb, 315bl; **CG:** front & back endpapers, 495bl, **CH:** 28cl; ©CI: 31br; **COR:** 13bgm, 492tcl, 492tl, Bettmann: 13bgm; 13bgm, 13bgm, 14tl, 24bg, 26bg, 54tr, 85l, 122b, 134b, 192cra, 195b, 228l, 237tl, 238b, 239tr, 257tr, 268br, 268cr, 269bl, 309bl, 354br, 400bc, 400tr, 402t, 404tr, 432cr, 440b, 487bl; David Reed: 357br; Henry Diltz: 276cr, 276tl, 447b, 455bl, 455br, Hulton-Deutsch Collection: 13bgm,13bgm, 63tl, 157br, 192bbg, 289tr; Lynn Goldsmith: 450-451bg, 450br, 454b, Neil Preston: 401b, 432tl, 488-489bg, 488cb, 489bl, 492c, 492cl, 492bl, 492tr; Roger Wood: 154l; Ted Streshinsky: 277c, 277cl; Terry Cryer: 26l, 37bg, 48tr; Underwood & Underwood: 372tr; **CP:** 384tc; **DK:** 13br, 13cl,13cr, 225bca, 335tr; ©Apple Corps Ltd 235bl; ©Apple Corps Ltd: 231b-far-l, 231blc, 231blr; Derek Hall/Steve Gorton/Neil Fletcher/Ian O'Leary 289 flower drop in; Gered Mankowitz: 1, 9tr, 43tr, 79tr, 121tr, 139tr, 175tr, 215tr, 253tr, 285tr, 321tr, 359tr, 407tr, 457tr; Mathew Ward/owned by Ian Shanks of Northamptonshire: 225bg; **DK/BWA:** 148tr,148br,148c, 154tr, 155cr, 166tr, 170tr, 173br, 173bl, 181bl, 189c, 189tl, 192t, 210br, 218bg, 220cl, 225bc, 225bl, 227tr, 228bc, 230bg, 232bg, 232br, 240cl, 242bl, 244cl, 281c, 288bg, 288bl, 288cl, 293bl (film still from 'How I Won the War' from Rolling Stone, November 9, 1967 © 1967 Rolling Stone LLC All Rights Reserved. Reprinted by Permission), 298bc, 298bcl, 298bcr, 298bl, 298br, 308tr, 332bl, 332c, 332tr, 333cl, 357bc, 365br, 371bl, 375tr, 381tr, 383br, 385t, 389cr, 397bg, 397t, 399bl, 399br, 399cl, 399cr, 399tl, 404tr, 409tr, 410cbl, 410cl, 411tr, 412cl, p412tc (photograph of Mick Jagger © photo Annie Leibovitz © 1973 Rolling Stone LLC All Rights Reserved. Reprinted by Permission), 414br, 415cr, 417tc, 417tr, 418b, 421tr, 424cra, 430c, 430tl, 431bl, 431cl, 436cr, 440tl, 440tr, 441br, 442tr, 443c, 449br, 450tr, 451tl, 451tr, 453t, 459tl, 459tr, 459br (photograph of Mick Jagger and Keith Richards © 1980 Rolling Stone LLC All Rights Reserved. Reprinted by Permission), 464-465b, 470-471bg, 470cb, 471cr, 471tcr, 471tl, 472bg, 472br, 474-475bg, 475cl, 475tl, 476tr, 478c-far-l, 478tr, 479tr, p480t-row (photograph of Mick Jagger © 1968 Rolling Stone LLC All Rights Reserved. Reprinted by Permission), 481blbg, 488cr, 488tr, 489br, 489bri, 489c, 489tc, 490b, 491tl, 493tr, 494tr, 495cr, 495tl, 496cl, 498cr, 499tc, 499tl, 500bl, 500tl, 501cra, 500cl; 459br; Aubrey Powell/Hipgnosis 441c; **DK/CE:** 155tl, 155tr, 164tl, 164tr, 171tl, 224bl, 230tr, 232cb, 232tc, 251bg, 251tl, 258bg, 258tc, 258tl, 287tr, 308br, 314-315bg, 314cl, 314tl, 338bg, 338tr, 344c ,344b, 344tl, 356-357bg, 356tl, 368tr, 379bg, 379br, 379c, 380br, 380cr, 380tl, 394c, 394tl, 395tl, 414-415bg, 414bcr, 414cr, 414tl, 425tl, 434bl, 434cl, 436bg, 436tr, 444bgl, 444t, 446bg, 446br, 448-449bg, 448br, 448cr, 448tl, 455tr, 460bg, 460br, 460tr, 464tr, 465c, 465tl, 467bg, 467tl, 476bca, 478cl, 478cr, 478tl, 480b-row (photograph of Mick Jagger and Keith Richards © 1989 Rolling Stone LLC All Rights Reserved. Reprinted by Permission), 481t-row (photograph of Keith Richards © photo Robert Altman 2002 © 1971 Rolling Stone LLC All Rights Reserved. Reprinted by Permission), 481row-3 (photograph of Keith Richards © photo Annie Leibovitz © 1981 Rolling Stone LLC All Rights Reserved. Reprinted by Permission), 483cl, 483cla, 483clb, 483rbg, 483tc, 490-491bg, 490tr, 498c, 498cl, 498tl, 499cra; **DM:** 381bl, 381ca, 381cl, 381tl; **DT:** 360t, 376-377-all, 378b, 383-all, 385b, 386-387-all, 390b; **EA:** 456-457, 494cr; **ER:** 236bl, 318tl, 318tc, 318tr, 320-321, 322l, 325, 344cra, 344crb, 344tr, 347bcl, 367bl, 373, 393, 396br, 396tr, 402b; **GC:** 82-83-all, 84tr, 86-all; **GD:** 398-399bg, 398tl, 404b, 404bl; **GI:** 122bg; **GM:** 152, 174-175, 209br, 212bl, 216b, 225br, 225c, 246bl, 246cl, 247b, 247tcl, 247tl, 250bl, 251bl, 251cr, 275, 330; **GW:** 213; **HG:** 10tl, 14tr, 15bl, 15tr, 16bg, 16tl, 20bg, 22b, 23t, 24cr, 24tl, 25bl, 25br, 25cl, 26br, 30br, 45tl, 50ct, 54-55bg, 54bc, 55tr, 56, 58b, 59tcl, 59tl, 59tr, 60tr, 61br, 65bl, 66bl, 66br, 66lc, 66lcb, 66lct, 66rc, 66rcb, 66rct, 66tl, 66tr, 67bcl, 67bcr, 67bl, 67lca, 67lc, 67lcb, 67rc, 67rcr, 67tcl, 67tcr, 67tl, 67tr, 69tr, 72bg, 72cr, 74-75, 74br, 76bl, 80-81bg, 88t, 93br, 96bg, 96br, 99c, 108bl, 108br, 108cr, 108tr, 109br, 113br, 120-121, 122-123bg, 123b, 128-129bg, 138-139, 142br, 143bc, 143bl, 143br, 146tc, 147br, 163tr, 166-167bg, 166br, 167tc, 168bl, 186b, 192bcr, 192br, 192crb, 192l, 199b, 206br, 219bl, 227cr, 227tl, 229bc, 229bl, 229br, 229cac, 229cac, 229car, 229cb, 229cl, 229ccr, 229cr, 229tcl, 229tr, 233b, 249tr, 250tl, 256br, 260-261bg, 264tr, 271b, 272-273bg, 272b, 272tr, 273br, 273cra, 278c, 280-281bg, 280l, 281bl, 281br, 283b, 283cl, 283cr, 286cl, 286cr, 286tr, 287bl, 289cr, 292, 304-305t, 306t r, 307t, 311bl, 311cl, 312br, 313bc, 313cl, 313tr, 332-333bg, 334-335bg, 334br, 334c, 335cr, 338bl, 339, 342cb, 342tl, 343b, 345br, 362tr, 369bl, 382br, 412br, 413tl, 419tcr, 429tl, 442bg, 442cl, 445bl, 464b; **HN:** The Daily Express: 249br; The Daily Mirror: 279bl; The News of The World: 260tr; The Times: 392br; **IS:** 161br; **IWM:** 14bg, 15tl; **JC:** 70tc, 70tr; **JH:** 18tl; **JM:** Billboard Magazine: 309bg; **JR:** 50cl; **KA:** 500-501bg; Blackstar: 364-365bg, 364cr, 364tr; Fred Bauman/Gamma Liaison: 126br, 132, 133b, 133tr, 156b; **KAL:** 107bl; **KOB:** 265tl; MGM: 304cr; United Artists: 84cl; 302cr; **LFI:** 126-127bg, 157bl, 157t, 159bl, 159br, 159cl, 159tl, 159tr, 168br, 191bl, 201bl, 217b, 416-417bg, 417bc, 424c, 424cr, 432cl, 498-499bg, 498bl, 499bl, 499cl, 500-501t, 500bl, 500ca, 500cb, 501b, 501tr; **MB:** 101cr; **MC:** 340tl, 341tr; **MCC:** 260br, 261bl, 261br, 261cr, 262-263, 265br, 266bl, 266cl, 266tl, 267b, 274bl, 279cr, 294 –295-all, 305br, 307br, 307cra, 307crb, 331tr, 334tc, 342trb; **MH:** 335br; **MJ:** 284-285, 306bc, 306br, 306bl; **MK:** 137l; **MM:** 235tr; **MMD:** 6; **MP:** 50tr; **MPX:** 2-3, 76t, 80ca, 124br, 124cl, 124t, 125b, 125l, 140t, 145tl, 146b, 150br, 161tl, 198t, 225cl, 225tr, 231c, 246cr, 250br, 255bl, 256tr, 257b, 259b, 260cl, 267tr, 273crb, 278-279bg, 278tl, 278tr, 279t, 281tl, 282br, 304cl, 310cla, 310cr, 310cra, 311bbg, 312bl, 313tl, 326-327t, 334cl, 336-337, 340-341bg, 340b, 341bl, 341br, 364br, 371tr, 374-375bg, 378tr, 390t, 413cr, 433b, 453bl, 480bl; **MS:** 153crb, 153cra; **NMM:** 104cl; **PC:** 92-93b; **NFA:** 59cl, 141bl, 217cl, 217cr, 217tl; **PH:** 103bl, 312t, 206tl; **PM:** 143tcl, 143tcr, 143tl; **POP:** 98b, 119br, 153bg, 374clb, 374tr, 382t; **PP:** 37b, 71b, 73tl, 78-79, 99cr, 102br,191br, 241tr, 244-245bg, 245bl, 245br, 245cb, 248t, 289bl, 293br, 299b, 310cra, 310tr, 324bl, 342tra, 419b; **PS:** 161tr; **PW:** 288br; **RE:** 10bcl, 10tcl, 11bl, 13c, 21c, 24bc, 24cl, 26c, 27tl, 27tr, 30bc, 32l, 35t, 39tl, 41tl, 47bl, 76c, 111bg, 198br, 200bl, 277cr, 388cl, 408cl, 458cb, ©Apple Corps Ltd: 274tr; **RED:** 75bc, Richie Aarons: 461; Bob Baker: 254tr; Bob King: 167bcl, 167cr; Bob Vincent: 27bc; C.Andrews: 149bl; Cummings Archives: 231tr; David Farrell: 91bl; David Redfern: 27br, 30tl, 32bg, 32tl, 75bl, 101br, 103cr, 160br, 244br, 342ca, 388br; Ebet Roberts: 458br; Elliot Landy: 342b; Fin Costello: 419tcl; GEMS: 100tr, 427c-far-r; Gered Mankowitz: 49bl; Glen A Baker: 73tr, 118b, 167bcr, 167br, 176-177bg, 176br, 221c, 276-277bg, 276cl, 277tr, 277b; Harry Goodwin: 94tc, 204crb; Ian Dickson: 419tl; Jeremy Fletcher: 47tr, 85bl, 110br; Jim Wheeler: 370tl; Keith Morris: 427cr, 482; Michael Ochs Archive: 31c, 112cra, 112crb, 112tr, 128cr, 128tr, 158tl, 183bc, 183br, 186tr, 286bl, RB: 66c, 99tr, 200r; Tony Meehan: 101tl; Val Wilmer: 46tr; **RET:** G.Hankeroot/Sunshine: 389t, 408tl; Baron Wolman: 452; John Bellissimo: 426tr; Michael Putland: 413b, 417bcl, 417br, 419tr, 423bl, 424bbg, 424bbg, 426cr, 432tr, 445t, 447tl; The King Collection: 106-107bg, 208-209bg, 504-512bg; **REX:** 19bc, 19tr, 21tr, 23br, 48br, 58t, 64l, 68b, 95b, 102t, 112b, 114b, 119cr, 119tc, 119tl, 119tr, 140bc, 140bl, 140c, 140cl, 140cr, 172tl, 193tl, 211t, 228tr, 316-317bg, 316bl, 316cr, 333bl, 333tr, 334bc, 347bl, 403, 497bl; **RGA:** 21bc, 27tc; **RH:** 24br, 39tr, 41bri, 41tri, 44cl, 45bl, 55bci, 65bri, 66bcr, 66tcl, 66tcr, 67br, 67rcb, 122tr, 28b, 128bc, 30bl, 130br, 141br, 153bl, 230bl; **RR:** 17b; **RS:** 410cbr, 416cr, 441tc; **SC:** 28bl; **SF:** 10r; **SMA:** 165cla, 165tl; Colin Escoll: 164clb; **SPL:** 44tr, 201br; **STAR:** Bob Gruen 1979: 406-407; Gered Mankowitz: 207br, 252-25; Ron Powell: 468tr; **TM:** 93t; **TON:** 349cr; **TP:** 129br, 131b; **TR:** 66bcl; **TT:** 52bl; **V&A:** 282tr; Harry Hammond: 21l; **VC:** 310b; **VM:** 153tl, 164br, 164cr, 171bc, 210bl, 229cac, 229ci, 229tcr, 229tl, 231tri, 234bg, 234bc, 234bl, 270tc, 288c, 299tl, 309br, 309cra, 370b, 394cr, 425bg, 425b

All other images courtesy of the Bill Wyman Archive

Thanks

Where to start? So many people have helped us from all around the world; it truly has been a global undertaking. Many provided information, supplied anecdotes, put us right and kept us straight; some in small ways, others in large.

Thank you Al Kooper, Allan Day, Andrew Oldham, Andria Lisle, Anna Menzies, Axel Vandewalle, Barry Reynolds, Barry Sage, Big Jim Sullivan, Brian Roylance and Oliver Craske at Genesis Publications, Chris Eborn (the largest collection of Stones stuff after Bill!), Colin Hodgkinson, Curt Angeladeś, Cynthia Stewart, Dave Godin, Delia Smith, Dianne Dibble, Domenic Priore, Doug Hinman, Garret Hashimoto, Geary Chansley, George Dibble, Giorgio Gomelsky, Gus Dudgeon (a great record producer, who was sadly killed just as we were going to press), James Hirst, Jeff Peters, Jerry Beckley, Jerry Hall, Jim Dickinson, Jim McCarthy, Joe McMichael, John Carter, John Marshall Carter, John Reed, Julian Ridgway at Redferns, Justin Goult at Mirrorpix, Ken Follett, Lynne Halliday, Mary McCartney, Mary Synder, May Pang, Michael Putland, Michael Raynor, Mike Berry, Mike Crowder, Mike Edwards, Neal Slok, Nigel Pierce, Patti Habermann/KoolKatz, Paul Jones, Pauline Smith, Peter Cole, Richard Stirling, Sam Phillips, Sherman Cooper, Sieb Kroeske, Sjoerd Olrichs, Stefan Gradofielski, Stephen McParland, Terry Blakesley, Terry Rawlins, Tom McGuinness, Tony Glover, Tony Rivers, Tony Visconti, Top Topham, Toru Fujiwara and Virginia Lohle at Starfile. There have been many more over the years who have helped. In particular, the people who have worked with the Rolling Stones organisation deserve special thanks.

Kingsley Abbott did sterling work on researching all sorts of things, either in person or on the Internet. Kingsley is an authority on all things Beach Boys and a writer himself. Check out his excellent book about *Pet Sounds* published by Helter Skelter. Kingsley's friend, Jack 'The Framer' Crampton, put many of Bill's priceless collectables back in their frames.

At Dorling Kindersley many people went far beyond the call of duty. Despite being a Grateful Dead fan, our category publisher

Andrew Heritage showed unfailing commitment and great good humour when things were at their blackest. Andrew has done a great job in pulling the whole thing together and helping to create what will become the standard for music books. The design team, led by Richard Evans and Bryn Walls, has done an amazing job. This book looks so wonderful because both Richard and Bryn brought their creativity to the project. The editorial team under Jake Woodward had an almost impossible task and pulled it off. Jake's not only a fantastic editor and very professional, but he's also a very good person. In the design and editing teams there are some who should get a special mention. Victoria Heyworth-Dunne has done not just brilliant work on editing the book but she has also taken care of all the administration on the project, mostly the stuff that we all hate doing. Thomas Keenes worked alongside Richard Evans in designing the book. They can be proud of what they achieved. Phil Gamble also pulled off some fantastic design work, all in his quiet and efficient way. Victoria Clark, besides doing some great design work, seemed to have almost total recall of the tens of thousands of scans we had on the server. Rachael Smith has done many of the jobs that no one else wanted to do and done them well. Lucian Randall has used his unique editing skills throughout the project. Maria Gibbs, our picture researcher, has done brilliant work in both finding images no one even knew about, and getting the clearances organised for others, from hundreds of different sources around the world.

There were others who pitched in at vital moments. Thanks to Ailsa Heritage, Anne Damerell, Dave Almond and Helen Grainge for all the scanning and retouching, David Lloyd, Eunice Paterson, Gill Pitts, Helena Peacock, Julian Dams, Julian Gray, the *Kiss Guides* team, Lisa Graham, Louise Candlish, Louise Dick, Martyn Page, Nigel Ritchie, Peter Jones, Phil Hunt, Sara Freeman, and Simon Mumford for all the maps.

Many others at DK have worked hard to get this book not just written but marketed and sold. Their commitment has been brilliant and they have always given the impression that we were at the top of their heap, when sometimes we were obviously not. Thank you John Roberts, Deborah Wright, Fiona Allen, Lynne O'Neill, Serena Stent, Hermione Ireland, Vivienne Watton, Catherine Bell and Christopher Davis.

There are many photographers represented in this book and all have done great work. Some should get a special thank you. Adam Cooper, for the access to his father Michael's superb archive of pictures. Ethan Russell, who has taken some of the greatest pictures in rock'n'roll (there is one picture in this book that is possibly the greatest ever). Dominique Tarlé, who has been so kind and generous with his wonderful photographs of the Nellcote period and before. Gered Mankowitz, who is not only a major figure in British photography but also took the cover photograph that will sit among some of his best work.

We should also thank the hundreds and thousands of writers and journalists whose work has added to the story. While many are quoted, many more have unknowingly provided millions of words of background reading and insights into the story of the Stones and the music of the last fifty years.

Bill's lawyer in New York, Howard Siegel, and literary lawyer Bob Stein have been a great help. At Ripple, Bruce Clarke, Mike and Jenny Haugh, Terry Taylor and Penny Thompson have all helped in lots of ways throughout the writing of the book.

Stephen Wyman has been fantastic in getting things together and inputting information into the computer – besides being the inspiration behind the collection of memorabilia in the first place!

Karen Kearne Moxey has run Bill's office so efficiently for a long time and been such great support throughout the book's gestation and beyond. Karen and Suzanne Wyman have also played a very big part in keeping us on track.

In the thanks for *Blues Odyssey* last year, we said: 'Finally, Bill's wife Suzanne and children, Matilda Mae, Jessica Rose and Katherine Noel and Richard's partner Christine Firth have all been long suffering… We love you and we couldn't have done it without you.' Well, this time it's been even harder on them and they have been even more supportive… We love you even more.

BILL WYMAN AND RICHARD HAVERS
London and the Scottish Borders
August 2002

'I'm a silly sod keeping all this stuff.' BILL TO RICHARD, *9.27 pm, 24 March, 2002*